AN INTRODUCTION TO
BEHAVIOR ANALYSIS

AN INTRODUCTION TO
BEHAVIOR ANALYSIS

GREGORY J. MADDEN

DEREK D. REED

FLORENCE D. DIGENNARO REED

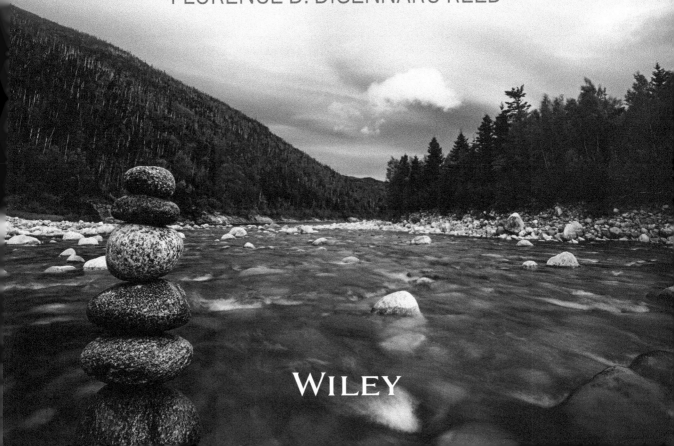

WILEY

Registered Office(s)
John Wiley & Sons, Inc., 111 River Street, Hoboken, NJ 07030, USA
John Wiley & Sons Ltd, The Atrium, Southern Gate, Chichester, West Sussex, PO19 8SQ, UK

Editorial Office
The Atrium, Southern Gate, Chichester, West Sussex, PO19 8SQ, UK

For details of our global editorial offices, customer services, and more information about Wiley products visit us at www.wiley.com.

Wiley also publishes its books in a variety of electronic formats and by print-on-demand. Some content that appears in standard print versions of this book may not be available in other formats.

Library of Congress Cataloging-in-Publication Data
Names: Madden, Gregory J. (Gregory Jude), author. | Reed, Derek D., author.
  | DiGennaro Reed, Florence D., author.
Title: An introduction to behavior analysis / Gregory J. Madden, Derek D.
  Reed, Florence D. DiGennaro Reed.
Description: Hoboken, NJ : John Wiley & Sons, [2021] | Includes
  bibliographical references and index.
Identifiers: LCCN 2020046783 (print) | LCCN 2020046784 (ebook) | ISBN
  9781119126539 (hardback) | ISBN 9781119126553 (pdf) | ISBN 9781119126546 (epub)
Subjects: LCSH: Behavioral assessment.
Classification: LCC BF176.5 .M34 2021 (print) | LCC BF176.5 (ebook) | DDC
  150.28/7--dc23
LC record available at https://lccn.loc.gov/2020046783
LC ebook record available at https://lccn.loc.gov/2020046784

Cover image: © Shaunl / Getty Images
Cover design by Wiley

Set in 10/12pt Minion Pro by Integra Software Services, Pondicherry, India

 M WEP220840 230823

CONTENTS

PREFACE

Why Study Behavior Analysis

The course in which you are currently enrolled will give you substantive training in the behavior-analytic principles that underlie effective behavior-change interventions. For example, the principles covered in this course have proven effective in the treatment of autism spectrum disorders (Bellini & Akullian, 2007; Eldevik et al., 2009), intellectual disabilities (Heyvaert et al., 2012), antisocial behavior (McCart et al., 2006), adult anxiety and depression (Öst, 2008; Powers et al., 2009), and substance-use disorders (Dutra et al., 2008) to name just a few. In this class, you will learn the principles that are foundational to these successes.

Taking a more expansive view, the course will prepare you to pursue further training at one of the more than 250 universities that offer graduate degrees in behavior analysis. Should you choose to pursue this training, you would join more than 51,000 Board Certified Behavior Analysts (BCBA) who are recognized by most US states as the appropriate providers of behavior-analytic services to children and adults with disabilities. These underserved populations depend on students like you to pursue careers in the helping profession of behavior analysis.

For those not drawn to serving those with disabilities, you should know that the principles covered in this book have proven beneficial in the practice of clinical, counseling, and school psychology. For example, in 2012 the *Inter-Organizational Task Force on Cognitive and Behavioral Psychology Doctoral Education* outlined the most important principles that these practice-oriented psychologists must understand to be effective (Klepac et al., 2012). At least 60% of the competencies listed were behavior analytic, and many of these will be covered in this book (e.g., shaping, extinction/exposure).

Perhaps your interests lie elsewhere still. If so, you may be interested to know that the principles covered in this book have been successfully used in business settings. Indeed, some of the most effective managers are those who know how to (1) identify the behaviors of successful employees, (2) measure the occurrence and non-occurrence of those behaviors in all employees, and (3) develop behavior-management plans that encourage those successful behaviors. Managers who can do this are actually managing behavior, rather than acting like authoritarian dictators. Because behavior analysts rely on positive reinforcement in their management practices, employees tend to be happier while being more productive.

Still not interested? Well, consider that most readers of this book will one day be parents, if they are not already. Because the behavior-analytic principles covered in this book have proven so reliable in positively influencing behavior, they constitute the core of most parent-training programs; for example, the *Criando con Amor, Promoviendo Armonía y Superacíon* [*Raising with Love, Promoting Harmony & Improvement*] program (Baumann et al., 2014). So, if you hope to be a loving parent who helps their children to successfully navigate their world, you would do well to learn all you can from this book. Your children will never thank you for it, but you will thank yourself one day, particularly when you see other parents struggling to understand the behavior of their children.

If you are still not interested in the contents of this book, we have only one more plea – consider the words of Socrates who said, "The unexamined life is not worth living." Socrates was encouraging those of his age to use logic, wisdom, and philosophy in pursuit of self-knowledge, better relationships, and a harmonious existence with the natural world. These goals are timeless and universal. This book can open doors of self-discovery. So, use what you are about to learn to examine your life, your actions, your goals, your values. The examined life is even more worth living.

How to Use the Features of This Book

This book is designed to help students identify the important information they should know after taking this class. When important terms are first presented, they appear in bold. When you identify one of these terms you should take the following steps:

1 Write the term on one side of a 3 × 5 inch flashcard. For example, in Chapter 1, the first term defined is "behavior."
2 The definition of the term will always be provided nearby in *italics*. Once you have found the definition, write it on the back of the flashcard. For example, Chapter 1 defines behavior as *an individual living organism's activity, public or private, which may be influenced by external or internal stimulation.*
3 Sometimes the book will pose a question (e.g., what is behavior analysis?). When you identify one of these, write it on a flashcard and then, as you read on, write the answer to this question on the other side of the card.
4 Keep your flashcards with you throughout the day.

Effective Studying

Most college students think reading and rereading the textbook and their lecture notes is a good way to study (Karpicke et al., 2009). It isn't. This method of studying does little to help you remember the materials when you are taking a test or, more importantly, you are trying to apply the concepts in your everyday life. For example, in a study conducted by Roediger and Karpicke (2006), one group of students was asked to study by reading the materials four times (that's probably more than you normally study). Although the students thought this would be effective, when they were tested a week later they could recall only about 40% of the materials – that's a failing grade.

A better way to study is called "repeated retrieval," but most college students don't use it (Karpicke et al., 2009). Repeated retrieval involves reading the information that you are studying and then, without peeking, saying everything you can remember (you can say it out loud or to yourself, both work equally well; Smith et al., 2013). Want to try it right now? If so, without looking, say, write, or think the definition of behavior that was given in the previous section.

If you could not recall all of the important components of the definition, that's not a problem. Compare what you *could* recall with the definition provided above and then (without peeking) try again. When Karpicke and Roediger (2010) asked students to repeat this read-and-retrieve process three times, the students remembered about 80% of the materials one week later. That's twice as much as the students who read the book four times.

Repeated Retrieval Made Easy

The following steps outline a practical way to use repeated retrieval to improve the efficiency and efficacy of your studying (Karpicke et al., 2014):

1. Make the flashcards discussed previously.
2. At least twice a day, go through your flashcards:
   a. Look at the term and say out loud (or to yourself) as much of what's on the back of the card as you can.
   b. Turn the card over and see which parts you missed. If you were not 100% correct, try it one more time before moving on to the next card.
3. If you do this a couple times a day, most every day, you will study less and learn more than ever before.

An Added Benefit

Students who use repeated retrieval, by studying their flashcards 3-4 times a day, don't cram the night before an exam. They sleep anxiety-free. They also have a stack of flashcards to help them study for any comprehensive exams taken later in the semester. So, what are you waiting for? Get some flash cards and start earning better grades. Flash cards too old-school for you? There are several flash card apps you can use on your phone.

The Behavior Analysis Task List

Some readers of this book will be interested in earning the credential of BCBA. This credential is granted by the Behavior Analysis Certification Board (BACB) and it is the gold-standard credential of practicing and applied behavior analysts. The BACB's *Fifth Edition Task List* outlines the *Foundational* principles and concepts that students must master before beginning an internship as a behavior analyst and before earning the BCBA credential. The Appendix of this textbook provides the BACB's list of *Foundations* and indicates the chapter in which each topic is discussed.

Animal Research

As your read this textbook, you will find that many of the foundational principles of behavior analysis were discovered in research conducted with nonhuman animals. It is hard to overstate the importance of this research. What we know today about attention, perception, learning, and decision-making were first discovered by studying the behavior of nonhumans. Current research with nonhuman animals continues to expand our understanding of behavior in important ways. For example, these research findings have proven important in understanding similarities and differences in the behavior of different species. Understanding the unique behavioral abilities of each species is important in guiding conservation efforts around the world (Higham, 2016; O'Brien & Robeck, 2010; Swaisgood et al., 2003; Zimbler-DeLorenzo & Stone, 2011).

Importantly, the findings of research conducted with nonhuman animals have improved the efficacy of the work done by psychologists and behavior analysts tasked with improving the lives of individuals with disabilities, addictions, phobias, anxiety, depression, and so on (Carroll & Overmier, 2001; Madden et al., 2016). For these reasons, the American Psychological Association and the Association for Behavior Analysis International strongly support research and teaching with nonhuman animals. Therefore, this book will draw heavily on research findings from the nonhuman laboratory.

Trigger Warning

This book discusses many different categories of human behavior. Behavior analysts and psychologists are asked to help people who suffer from a myriad of difficulties. This includes anxiety, depression, and posttraumatic stress disorder. So that students will have the opportunity to see the utility of behavior analysis in the treatment of these disorders; this book will discuss them. Examples will be provided. If you believe an unexpected encounter with descriptions or visual depictions of these disorders would be unnecessarily stressful for you, we recommend that you share your concerns with your instructor. They will take care to let you know in advance where these sensitive topics are discussed in the book and in lectures.

References

Baumann, A. A., Domenech Rodríguez, M. M., Amador, N. G., Forgatch, M. S., & Parra-Cardona, J. R. (2014). Parent Management Training-Oregon Model (PMTO™) in Mexico city: Integrating cultural adaptation activities in an implementation model. *Clinical Psychology: Science and Practice*, *21*(1), 32–47. https://doi.org/10.1111/cpsp.12059

Bellini, S., & Akullian, J. (2007). A meta-analysis of video modeling and video self-modeling interventions for children and adolescents with autism spectrum disorders. *Exceptional Children*, 73, 264–287. https://doi.org/10.1177/001440290707300301

Carroll, M. E., & Overmier, J. B. (2001). *Animal research and human health: Advancing human welfare through behavioral science*. Washington, DC: American Psychological Association.

Dutra, L., Stathopoulou, G., Basden, S. L., Leyro, T. M., Powers, M. B., & Otto, M. W. (2008). A meta-analytic review of psychosocial interventions for substance use disorders. *The American Journal of Psychiatry*, *165*(2), 179–187. https://doi.org/10.1176/appi.ajp.2007.06111851

Eldevik, S., Hastings, R. P., Hughes, J. C., Jahr, E., Eikeseth, S., & Cross, S. (2009). Meta-analysis of early intensive behavioral intervention for children with autism. *Journal of Clinical Child and Adolescent Psychology*, 38, 439–450. https://doi.org/10.1080/15374410902851739

Heyvaert, M., Maes, B., Van den Noortgate, W., Kuppens, S., & Onghena, P. (2012). A multilevel meta-analysis of single-case and small-n research on interventions for reducing challenging behavior in persons with intellectual disabilities. *Research in Developmental Disabilities, 33*, 766–780. https://doi.org/10.1016/j.ridd.2011.10.010

Higham, J. P. (2016). Field endocrinology of nonhuman primates: Past, present, and future. *Hormones and Behavior, 84*, 145–155. https://doi.org/10.1016/j.yhbeh.2016.07.001

Karpicke, J. D., Butler, A. C., & Roediger, H. L. (2009). Metacognitive strategies in student learning: Do students practice retrieval when they study on their own? *Memory, 17*, 471–479. https://doi.org/10.1080/09658210802647009

Karpicke, J. D., Lehman, M., & Aue, W. R. (2014). Retrieval-based learning: An episodic context account. In B. H. Ross (Ed.), *Psychology of Learning and Motivation* (Vol. 61, pp. 237–284). Waltham, MA: Academic Press.

Karpicke, J. D., & Roediger, H. L. (2010). Is expanding retrieval a superior method for learning text materials? *Memory & Cognition, 38*, 116–124. https://doi.org/10.3758/MC.38.1.116

Klepac, R. K., Ronan, G. F., Andrasik, F., Arnold, K. D., Belar, C. D., Berry, S. L., Christoff, K. A., Craighead, L. W., Dougher, M. J., Dowd, E. T., Herbert, J. D., McFarr, L. M., Rizvi, S. L., Sauer, E. M., & Strauman, T. J. (2012). Guidelines for cognitive behavioral training within doctoral programs in the United States: Report of the inter-organizational task force on cognitive and behavioral psychology doctoral education. *Behavior Therapy, 43*, 687–697. https://doi.org/10.1016/j.beth.2012.05.002

Madden, G. J., Hanley, G. P., & Dougher, M. J. (2016). Clinical behavior analysis. In J. C. Norcross, G. R. VandenBox, & D. K. Freedheim (Eds.), (Editors-in-Chief). In *APA handbook of clinical psychology: Vol. I. Roots and branches* (pp. 351–368). Washington, DC: APA Books.

McCart, M. R., Priester, P. E., Davies, W. H., & Azen, R. (2006). Differential effectiveness of behavioral parent-training and cognitive-behavioral therapy for antisocial youth: A meta-analysis. *Journal of Abnormal Child Behavior, 34*, 525–541. https://doi.org/10.1007/s10802-006-9031-1

O'Brien, J. K., & Robeck, T. R. (2010). The value of *ex situ* cetacean populations in understanding reproductive physiology and developing assisted reproductive technology for *ex situ* and *in situ* species management and conservation efforts. *International Journal of Comparative Psychology, 23*(3), 227–248. https://escholarship.org/uc/item/1n15q19h

Öst, L. (2008). Efficacy of the third wave of behavioral therapies: A systematic review and meta-analysis. *Behaviour Research and Therapy, 46*, 296–321. https://doi.org/10.1016/j.brat.2007.12.005

Powers, M. B., Zum Vörde Sive Vörding, M. B., & Emmelkamp, P. M. G. (2009). Acceptance and commitment therapy: A meta-analytic review. *Psychotherapy and Psychosomatics, 78*, 73–80. https://doi.org/10.1159/000190790

Roediger, H. L., & Karpicke, J. D. (2006). The power of testing memory: Basic research and implications for educational practice. *Perspectives on Psychological Science, 1*, 181–210. https://doi.org/10.1111/j.1745-6916.2006.00012.x

Smith, M. A., Roediger, H. L., & Karpicke, J. D. (2013). Covert retrieval practice benefits retention as much as overt retrieval practice. *Journal of Experimental Psychology. Learning, Memory, and Cognition, 39*, 1712–1725. https://doi.org/10.1037/a0033569

Swaisgood, R. R., Zhou, X., Zhang, G., Lindburg, D. G., & Zhang, H. (2003). Application of behavioral knowledge to conservation in the giant panda. *International Journal of Comparative Psychology, 16*(2–3), 65–84.

Zimbler-DeLorenzo, H. S., & Stone, A. I. (2011). Integration of field and captive studies for understanding the behavioral ecology of the squirrel monkey (*Saimiri sp.*). *American Journal of Primatology, 73*(7), 607–622. https://doi.org/10.1002/ajp.20946

An Introduction to Behavior Analysis

1

What Is Behavior?

The primary subject matter of this book is *behavior*. Thus, it is important to begin by defining that term. In this book, **behavior** is defined as *an individual living organism's activity, public or private, which may be influenced by external or internal stimulation.*

A fish watches the current, looking for edible materials. When something tasty floats by, the fish strikes. This strike is a **response** – *a single instance of behavior.*

You think about your future and consider what kind of job will make you happy, while simultaneously allowing you to pay the rent on time. Having a thought is also a response – a single instance of a different kind of behavior.

Source: David A Birkbeck / E+ / Getty Images

Let's dissect the definition of behavior provided in italics above. The first word indicates behavior is something *individuals* do – the fish that strikes a bug does so as an *individual*. Likewise, when you think about your job prospects, you think your own thoughts, as an individual. Behavior is something *individuals* do.

Focusing on individual behavior is consistent with the goals of those who seek the expertise of a psychologist, counselor, or behavior analyst. The individual experiencing depression, the parent of a child diagnosed

Source: Mimagephotography/Shutterstock.com

An Introduction to Behavior Analysis, First Edition. Gregory J. Madden, Derek D. Reed, and Florence D. DiGennaro Reed.
© 2021 John Wiley & Sons Ltd. Published 2021 by John Wiley & Sons Ltd.

with autism, the manager of an underperforming employee, they all want the behavior of an individual – self, child, and employee, respectively – to change in an adaptive direction, that is, a reduction in depression, an increase in social interactions, and an increase in productivity. If you were depressed, you would not be satisfied with the services of your therapist if they said, "Sorry you aren't doing any better, but 4 of my other 10 patients are getting better." While that is great for them, this helps you in no way. Your depression is experienced as an *individual,* and an effective therapist who treats individuals will seek to understand *your* behavior and the factors that can effectively reduce *your* depression. This requires a focus on the behavior of the *individual* – you.

The second component of our definition of behavior is that it is something that individual *living organisms* do. Applying an electric current to a dead fish will produce reflexive movement, but it will not produce a fish that strikes when its next meal floats downstream. Likewise, if you were dead, no amount of electrical stimulation to precise brain regions would revitalize your ability to contemplate a future career path. Moreover, while we acknowledge that advancements in the field of artificial intelligence and robotics have created robots that learn and behave in ways remarkably similar to animals, we will restrict our definition of behavior to the actions of biological organisms.

The next part of the definition – *public or private* – simply means that some behavior is *public* (everyone can observe it happening) and some behavior is *private* (you are the only person who can observe it). The bug-striking behavior of our fish is *public* – it can be observed by the fish, other nearby fish, and by anyone who takes the time to set up an underwater camera to watch the fish strike its prey.

By contrast, thinking about your career is a *private* behavior. Only you can observe the entirety of your thoughts as you think them. If you did your career contemplation while lying in a functional magnetic resonance imaging device, we could observe the areas of your brain that are active as you are thinking, but it gives us no access to the content of your thinking. Hence, this behavior remains *private.*

The final component of the definition – *which may be influenced by external or internal stimulation* – means behavior can be affected (changed) by **stimulus events**

Source: Hero Images/Getty Images

(*things you see, hear, smell, taste, or feel*) and these stimulus events can occur outside or inside your body. For example, the bug floating toward the fish is an *external* visual stimulus – the bug is outside the fish's body and when the fish sees it the visual stimulus increases the probability of a striking action. Without the visual stimulus, the probability of striking is very low. Likewise, the *internal stimulation* of hunger increases the probability of searching for food and striking a bug when one is encountered.

Just like the fish, your own private behavior – contemplating career choices – is influenced by *external and internal stimulation.* If your biology instructor is charismatic and speaks convincingly of the joys of being a professor (external stimuli), the probability of contemplating this career path is increased. Simultaneously, a number of internal stimuli can increase (e.g., caffeine's stimulating effects) or decrease (e.g., a headache) the probability of a career contemplation session.

What Is Behavior Analysis?

Behavior analysis may be defined by its goals, its assumptions, and its major activities. We discuss each of these in the sections that follow. But before you read on, you should read the "How to Use the Features of This Book" section of this book's Preface. There you will find important advice about how to read this book and how to study so that you can maximize your learning, enhance your ability to use what you learn to improve your life (and the lives of those around you), *and* to earn a better grade in this class. The advice comes from scientific studies identifying effective ways to study. Interestingly, these studies find very few students use these techniques, opting instead for study methods that are much less effective (e.g., highlighting your textbook and rereading it the night before the exam). You will find the advice provided in the Preface useful not only for this class, but for all of your classes. So, take a few moments to read the "How to Study" section now.

The Goals of Behavior Analysis

The broad goal of any science is to understand the phenomena being studied. Entomologists want to understand insects. Astronomers want to understand the universe. Similarly, behavior analysts seek to understand the behavior of individuals. Whether it's you, me, your pet, or a mountain lion, behavior analysts are interested in the behavior of individual organisms.

There are many different approaches to understanding. Behavior analysts take a pragmatic approach. They want to improve the human condition (and that of the nonhuman animals with whom we share the planet) and this is reflected in the two goals of behavior analysis.

THE FIRST GOAL OF BEHAVIOR ANALYSIS

The first goal of behavior analysis *is to accurately predict behavior*. To understand why behavior analysts want to predict behavior, ask yourself, which would you prefer: a bus that arrives at a *predictable* time or a bus that arrives at an *unpredictable* time? The predictable bus arrives at the hour and the half-hour; it is never late. The unpredictable bus arrives at no particular time, but it arrives at the bus stop twice per hour. So, which bus would you prefer? The answer is obvious. We would all prefer the predictable bus.

Let's make obvious why we prefer the predictable bus. If the bus always arrives on time, then we can plan for its arrival. We can enjoy our conversation with friends a little longer, study a little longer, or finish a meal at a casual pace before we leave to catch the bus. By contrast, if the bus is unpredictable then our behavior will be less efficient as we must spend more time doing what we don't want to do (sitting at the bus stop) and less time doing what we want to do (eating and talking with friends). We prefer the predictable bus because *predictability allows adaptive behavior*.

Source: Wangkun Jia/Shutterstock.com

It's not just buses. We also like to predict the weather and we check our weather apps regularly. Why – because *predictability allows adaptive behavior*. If we know it's going to rain, we can wear a raincoat or grab an umbrella. If we know it's going to be sunny, we can leave both of these at home and save the hassle of carrying them.

Of course, behavior analysts are interested in predicting the behavior of individuals, not of buses or the weather. **What is the utility in predicting the behavior of individuals?** To answer this question, consider your roommate who predictably joins you for breakfast at 8:30 each weekday morning. The utility in accurately predicting when your roommate will arrive, is that *it allows adaptive behavior* – you can make extra coffee, clear a spot at the table, and leave out the box of cereal. Your roommate appreciates this, and these actions increase the probability that your roommate will be nice to you at a later time.

If your roommate's behavior suddenly became unpredictable, sometimes getting up at 3 am, other times at 11 am; your acts of kindness would no longer be *adaptive* – the coffee would go to waste, the spot cleared would not be used, and the cereal box would go unopened.

Predicting behavior is important to all of us because *it allows adaptive behavior*. Have you ever noticed that when you meet someone new (e.g., a new coworker) you ask a lot of questions: What is your name? Where are you from? Are you in school? Which school? What's your major? Do you work? How many brothers and sisters do you have?

We all do this. Why? Because *it allows adaptive behavior*. If you learn, for example, that your new coworker likes street tacos, then you can behave adaptively at lunch time by saying "Hey, want to go to the taco truck for lunch?" There is no guarantee that the answer will be "yes," but the probability is higher than if you had said "Hey, want to go to the vegan restaurant for lunch?"

All of us try to accurately predict long-term patterns of behavior in those around us. We refer to this as a "reputation". If Chauncey has a reputation as a liar, we will not believe it when he tells us that his start-up company is a great investment. If Winter has a reputation for generosity, we will ask her for a ride to work when our car will not start. We keep track of the behavior of others and we use this information adaptively. If we did not track the reputations of others, we would invest in worthless ventures, walk to work, and would, ourselves, get a reputation for being naïve.

Although it is useful to accurately predict behavior, some have argued that it is either impossible or ill-advised to do so. For example, the famous Russian author Fyodor Dostoyevsky commented on the unpredictability of behavior in this way,

Fyodor Dostoyevsky
(1821-1881)

Source: Fine Art Images/
AGE Fotostock

> *If you say one can also calculate all this according to a table, this chaos and darkness, these curses, so that the mere possibility of calculating it all in advance would stop everything and that reason alone would prevail in that case man would go insane deliberately in order not to have reason, but to have his own way![1]*

The ironic thing, of course, is that in arguing against a behavioral science, he made a *prediction* about behavior – the individual would deliberately go insane.

The extent to which we can accurately predict human behavior is a topic that we will return to throughout this textbook. For now, it is enough to remind you that the first goal of behavior analysis is to predict behavior and the reason that predicting behavior is important is that *it allows adaptive behavior*. Table 1.1 shows some predictions about behavior, adaptive behaviors that can occur if the prediction is correct, and the beneficial outcome of this adaptive behavior.

Table 1.1 Predicting behavior is useful.

Prediction about behavior	Adaptive behavior	Beneficial outcome
I will snooze my alarm clock three times tomorrow morning	Set the alarm to go off 45 minutes before I need to get out of bed	Arrive at my appointment on time
Within the next 6 months, I will drop my phone and crack the screen	Buy insurance	Save money when I need a new screen
My roommate will eat my favorite leftovers	Hide the leftovers behind something my roommate dislikes	Leftovers are there when I want them
My boss will be grumpy during the dinner rush	Avoid talking to my boss during the dinner rush	Avoid getting yelled at

* This table shows some predictions about behavior, the adaptive behavior that the prediction allows, and then the beneficial outcome expected because the adaptive behavior occurred.

THE SECOND GOAL OF BEHAVIOR ANALYSIS

The ability to accurately predict behavior is great, and in some sciences, prediction is all you can do. For example, astrophysicists can precisely predict where Mars will be two years from now, but they cannot practically influence the trajectory of the planet. Within a science of behavior, we seek to do more than just predict behavior; we want to influence it. Stated more formally, **the second goal of behavior analysis** *is to discover functional variables that may be used to positively influence behavior.* A **functional variable** is *a variable that, when changed, reliably and systematically influences behavior.*

Throughout this book we will discuss how behavior analysts have discovered functional variables. For now, let's focus on what we mean when we say our goal is to *positively influence behavior.* We mean that the behavior analyst is able to change behavior. Where we predict that a maladaptive behavior will occur (e.g., drunk driving), the behavior analyst can use existing knowledge of functional variables to do something that decreases the probability of this behavior and increases the likelihood that the individual will choose to do something else – something more adaptive (e.g., call an Uber™ when intoxicated).

There are many ways to positively influence the behavior of individuals, and this text-book provides an introduction to these techniques. By carefully studying these techniques, you will acquire insights into how you can improve lives by positively influencing behavior.

DEMAND MORE OF YOUR SCIENCE

We encourage readers to embrace the twin goals of behavior analysis and apply them to all sciences. These goals are practical, useful, and, if realized, will improve our own lives and those of others (Baer et al., 1968). As you evaluate the progress of any science, it is worth asking, does this science make accurate predictions? If not, that is a problem. If astrophysicists cannot predict exactly where Jupiter will be on a specific date four years from today, then they cannot send a probe to the planet to study its atmosphere. That is a problem.

Likewise, it is worth asking if the social and behavioral sciences have identified functional variables that may be used to positively influence behavior. The more functional variables the science has identified, the more it allows us to improve the human condition. Again, by changing those variables (something that behavioral scientists call "therapy" or an "intervention") we change people's behavior and improve their lives. So, whatever social/behavioral science you study, it is worth asking: Can this science accurately predict and positively influence behavior and, in so doing, prove beneficial to society at large?

Reading Quiz 1

Each chapter in this book will include a few reading quizzes embedded within the text. If you can answer all of these questions correctly, then you will know that you are understanding this book. The answers to these quiz questions are provided at the end of the chapter.

1. Behavior is something that _____ living organisms do.
2. _____ is defined as an individual living organism's activity, public or _____, which may be influenced by external or _____ stimulation.
3. A _____ is something you see, hear, smell, taste, or feel. These events can occur outside or inside your body.
4. Stimuli is the plural of _____.
5. One stimulus, two _____.
6. Buying a car is an instance of _____ (public/private) behavior.
7. Changing your clothes is an instance of _____ (public/private) behavior.
8. Thinking that you should not have bought that car because now you don't have enough money for new clothes is an instance of _____(public/private) behavior.
9. The first goal of behavior analysis is to _____ _____ behavior.
10. The second goal of behavior analysis is to discover _____ variables that may be used to _____ _____ behavior.
11. Accurately predicting behavior is important because it allows _____ behavior.

The Assumptions of Behavior Analysis

Recalling from above that behavior analysis may be defined by its goals, its assumptions, and its major activities, we now turn to two assumptions that guide behavior analysis.

Assumption #1: Behavior is determined

Behavior analysts assume that behavior is determined.[2] **What does it mean to say, "behavior is determined?"** It means that *behavior has a cause, or multiple causes*. This is an appropriate assumption for scientists who study behavior. If they assume that behavior is caused by knowable variables, then behavioral scientists will set out to discover those functional variables. If one assumes that behavior is not determined (i.e., behavior occurs without a cause), then one would not bother trying to discover functional variables that are assumed not to exist.

Here is a quick note about the distinction between *functional variables* and *causes*. Behavioral scientists are reluctant to discuss "causes" because it implies that we know everything there is to know about behavior, and that clearly is not the case. In recognition of this incomplete knowledge, we talk about "functional variables." When a functional variable is changed, we can be confident that it will influence behavior. However, to suggest that the functional variable "caused" the behavior change is more than the evidence supports. Perhaps, for example, the functional variable plays no causal role, but is merely correlated with behavior change. We will have more to say about correlations, functional variables, and behavior change in Chapters 2 and 3. For now, we return to the assumption that behavior is determined.

For most members of Western cultures, this assumption of determinism is difficult to accept because we have been taught that some, if not all, of our behavior is self-determined and free from external causal variables. For example, most westerners embrace the concept of *free will*. However, a careful consideration of this issue leads us to reject the idea that behavior is self-determined.

Source: rudall30/Getty Images

Consider your behavior right now. If we accept the concept of free will, then your current behavior (reading this book) is not influenced by any causal variables. If that were true, then it would not be influenced by biological variables; for example, that you have a brain capable of decoding the symbols on this page into meaningful sentences. It would not be influenced by experiences from long ago, such as learning to speak your native language or learning to read through systematic instruction provided by teachers and parents. It would not be influenced by experiences a few months ago; for example, a friend that you trust recommended that you take this class. And your behavior would not be influenced by recent experiences; for example, the instructor assigned this chapter and said that some materials from the book will appear in upcoming exams. Behavior analysis holds that this complex of causal biological and experiential variables combines to determine your behavior.

MENTALISTIC EXPLANATIONS OF BEHAVIOR

When we learn how biological and environmental events combine to influence behavior (like your reading this textbook right now), it makes sense to us. More importantly, understanding how biological and environmental events can change behavior enhances our ability to accurately predict and positively influence behavior. But this scientific way of thinking stands in contrast to how most of us explain why we, or those around us, do the things we do. Consider these examples of everyday explanations of behavior:

- "I ate a sweet potato because I decided I needed more potassium."
- "I went to a movie because I felt like laughing."
- "I hit him because I was angry."

In these sentences, the words before "because" identify the behavior that needs to be explained. The words after "because" provide the sorts of explanations that we all hear and give every day. In the first example, eating a sweet potato (behavior) is said to be caused by "I decided that I needed more potassium." If your brother or sister said this while eating a baked sweet potato you would accept the explanation without a second thought. However, this explanation has a fundamental problem – it explains the first behavior by appealing to a second behavior:

- I ate   because   I decided
- I went   because   I felt
- I hit   because   I was angry

So, now instead of having one behavior to explain (I ate), we have two behaviors to explain (I ate *and* I decided). These everyday explanations of behavior violate Occam's *law of parsimony*, which, when applied to behavior, holds that, all else being equal, the best explanations of behavior are the simplest explanations. Explaining one behavior by appealing to a second behavior lacks parsimony – what was once a simple task (explaining one behavior) is now more complex (explaining two behaviors).

To make matters worse, when we explain one behavior by appealing to a second, the second behavior usually occurs *privately* (mentally) where others cannot observe it. "I decided…" appeals to private decision-making. "I felt…" and "I was angry…" appeal to private sensations. Behavior analysts refer to these as mentalistic explanations of behavior. Behavior analysts reject mentalistic explanations of behavior.[3]

To get a better understanding of the problems with mentalistic explanations, imagine you are a behavior therapist and your patient (a college student identifying as a female) complains that she has no self-control. Her diet is atrocious, she is constantly skipping classes, and when she attends she mostly looks at her social media feed and posts selfies for her friends. In addition, she has occasional anger outbursts, particularly with her partner. Your job, as the therapist, is to help your patient change her behavior.

If you believe one behavior (making the wrong food choice) is caused by a second behavior (I mentally decided to eat…), then the way to change the first behavior is to change the second behavior. Sounds like we have a plan – to change her food choices we need to change a *private behavior* – her mental decision-making. How do we do that? If we follow the logic of our explanation of bad food choices (Behavior 1), that these choices are caused by mental decision-making (Behavior 2), then we would look for a Behavior 3 that caused Behavior 2. Of course, if you found Behavior 3, you would be no closer to improving your client's food choices because to change Behavior 3 you would have to find its cause – Behavior 4. Obviously, this search for mental causes is never ending, and it will not help your patient improve her diet.

To change dietary behavior, we must identify functional variables that can positively influence this behavior. Invariably, these functional variables will be biological and environmental events. A nice thing about this approach is that we can often change biological and environmental events and, when we do, we can evaluate if they change behavior. If they do, then we have found a functional variable that can be used by other behavior therapists to positively influence behavior. For this reason, behavior analysts focus their attention on biological and environmental events that influence behavior. As you will learn throughout this book, this approach has proven effective.

I'M NOT BUYING IT. I DETERMINE MY OWN BEHAVIOR

For many people, the idea that behavior is determined by biological and environmental variables is not easily accepted. Instead, most of us feel that we *will* our own behavior; that is, we feel that we mentally direct our own actions. The main evidence for this feeling is that, occasionally, just before we engage in a behavior we have an internal (private) dialogue in which we actively decide what to do next. For example, when deciding where to eat lunch, we might mentally consider how hungry we are, how we love hamburgers, how much money we have, how far we are from home, and if there is any food at home. All of this private decision-making gives us the feeling that we will our decision – to go home and make a sandwich.

This is an alluring idea because we can hear the internal dialogue that constitutes this mental decision-making process and this dialogue immediately precedes some of our deliberative actions:

Source: AA Film Archive / Alamy Stock Photo

> *Man am I hungry. I sure could go for a hamburger. But I don't have enough money for a hamburger. I guess I could go home and eat. Yeah, I've got that bread that's going to go stale if I don't eat it soon. I think I'll go home and make a sandwich.*

Because we hear this internal dialogue many of us picture this process as a tiny person, or several tiny people inside our head, much like the characters in the Pixar movie, *Inside Out*.

Although *Inside Out* was a great movie, there are at least **three problems** with the theory that a mental decision-maker wills behavior into motion:

1. ***Choice is behavior.*** Engaging in a mental decision-making process (choice) is an activity that meets the definition of behavior – it is an individual living organism's private activity, which may be influenced by external or internal stimulation. As noted earlier, suggesting that one behavior (choice) causes another behavior (making a sandwich) is unsatisfying because it leaves unanswered the question, what causes the choice? Another choice? If so, what causes that choice? You can see the parsimony problem here.

2. ***Choice is determined.*** When one makes a choice, what factors are considered before the choice is made? In the sandwich example, public events (the lack of money, bread at home) combined to influence the decision to eat a sandwich. If any of these factors were different, it would influence the choice *and* what was eaten for lunch. For example, if bread was unavailable at home, the probability of choosing to eat a sandwich would be greatly reduced. If money was more abundant, we would have eaten hamburgers. These *functional variables* influence the choices we make.

3. ***Spurious reason-making.*** One reason we all *feel* like we will our own behavior is because we are good at providing mentalistic reasons for our actions (I'm eating sweet potatoes because I decided...). The problem with this evidence is that Nobel Prize winning research shows that these reasons are spurious (false, fake) – we make these spurious reasons up when asked to do so, even though those "reasons" have nothing to do with our behavior. This was made clear in the 1960s by Roger Sperry and Michael Gazzaniga. They worked with epilepsy patients whose left and right brain hemispheres were surgically disconnected to reduce seizures. After the surgery, the two sides of the brain had no way to communicate. So, when the left ear was told to "get up and go for a walk," only the right part of the brain heard it

(everything on the left side of your body is controlled by your right brain-hemisphere, and vice versa). Spoken language is controlled by the left hemisphere, so when the right hemisphere alone was told to take a walk, the left hemisphere could not explain why the patient was walking. As the patient walked out of the room, the experimenter asked him where he was going. The truthful answer would have been "I have no idea" but the left hemisphere made up a spurious reason on the spot: "I'm going to get a Coke." Perhaps most interesting of all, the patient *believed* the reason he gave was true. That is, he believed he *chose* to get up for a Coke; when in fact, he did not choose this at all.

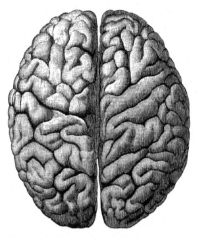

Source: nicoolay/E+/Getty Images

Applied to our own everyday explanations of behavior, we make up spurious explanations for our behavior all the time and, importantly, *we believe them*. This gives us a sincere *feeling* that an internal decision-maker wills our behavior into action. Science disagrees.

If you, the reader, choose to reject these three pieces of evidence (and we expect most of you will), you should be aware of two important implications of your choice. First, if an undetermined will determines behavior, then the first goal of behavior analysis cannot be achieved – accurately predicting behavior. An advanced science will make predictions by considering the biological and environmental variables that influence behavior. If these variables play no role in human behavior, then accurate predictions are impossible. Recalling that the utility in predicting behavior is that it allows us to live more adaptively, we might hope the behavior analysts are right – behavior is determined – as this assumption has the potential to improve our quality of life.

Second, if an undetermined will determines behavior, the second goal of behavior analysis also cannot be achieved – discovering the functional variables that will allow us to positively influence behavior. If will determines what behavior comes next, then the only way to positively influence behavior is to influence will. But if will is not caused by anything, then there is no way to influence will and, therefore, there is no way to influence behavior. This is bad news for all those individuals who hope that an advanced behavioral science can positively influence their behavior, or the behavior of a loved one. Because this leaves us in a hopeless situation, behavior analysts assume that behavior is determined. Thus far, this assumption has proven useful.

Assumption #2: The scientific method is a valid way to reveal the determinants of behavior

A scientific approach to learning about the workings of the natural world originated in the seventeenth century with the work of great scientists like Copernicus, Galileo, and Sir Isaac Newton. Prior to the development of the scientific method humans made very little progress in understanding the workings of the natural world. This is because prescientific explanations were not challenged. For example, during the medieval period physicians explained behavior by referring to the balance of four liquids, called humors, in the human body – black bile, yellow bile, phlegm, and blood. If the physician's patient was depressed it was "explained" by saying the patient possessed a surplus of black bile. The cure? Bloodletting, leaches, and mercury-containing medicines that induced vomiting and diarrhea.

If the medieval physician had been versed in the scientific method, he (they were almost all men) would test his prediction by taking a sample of bodily humors and objectively evaluating the amount of black bile in the sample. If he found high levels of black bile, then an appropriate amount of blood would be

Source: Chronicle / Alamy Stock Photo

extracted, and if the patient's mood improved the physician's prediction would prove correct. Unfortunately, medieval physicians did not do this. They did not empirically test the predictions of the humoral model. Instead, physicians accepted it without questioning the authority of their teachers and elders.

Because the theory of humors was not subjected to empirical tests, the ineffective medical practices informed by it continued for centuries. When the scientific method was eventually applied to medicine, the theory of humors was abandoned.

The widespread use of the scientific method is responsible for discoveries that have improved human lives (life-saving medications, modern forms of transportation, and the cell phone in your pocket; Pinker, 2018). Because the scientific method has proven so useful in revealing the workings of the world, behavior analysts assume that it is a valid method for discovering the determinants of behavior.

Reading Quiz 2

Remember, the answers to these questions are provided at the end of the chapter.

1. The first assumption of behavior analysis is that behavior is _____.
2. When we say, "behavior is determined," we simply mean that behavior has a _____, or multiple _____.
3. In our daily lives, we often explain behavior (I went to the movies) by pointing to private behaviors (I thought going to the movies was a good idea). Behavior analysts refer to these as _____ explanations of behavior.
4. The second assumption of behavior analysis is that the _____ _____ is a valid way to discover the determinants of behavior.

Scientific Method

There is no pure, disinterested, theory-free observation.

~Karl Popper, philosopher of science

The first principle [of science] is that you must not fool yourself – and you are the easiest person to fool.

~Richard Feynman, physicist

The *scientific method* describes the behavior of all scientists as they go about discovering how the natural world works. Here we briefly summarize the characteristics of the scientific method that are of most relevance to behavior analysis. The scientific methods used by behavior analysts will be discussed in Chapters 2 and 3.

Objective: Behavior analysis is an objective, unbiased, scientific approach to discovering how behavior works. Of course, humans are subject to many known biases (Kahneman & Tversky, 2013), so any *individual* behavior analyst cannot be entirely objective. Recognizing that biases can influence the outcome of their work, behavior analysts, like all good scientists, take steps to minimize this possibility. For example, data are recorded by computers or by people who are blinded to the purpose of the study. Where we fail in our objectivity, other behavioral scientists will point out our failings. Indeed, they advance their careers by doing so. Therefore, while individual scientists are fallible and subject to bias, the *scientific enterprise* is self-correcting.

As noted by the great twentieth-century philosopher, Karl Popper, a second meaning of "objective" is that scientists regard no theory as a dogmatic truth. That is, our current understanding of behavior is not finalized. Behavior analysts recognize that we have much still to learn about behavior, and a goal of this textbook is to inspire a next generation of behavior analysts to make clear where we currently have it wrong. This objectivity directed toward the state of current knowledge was embraced by the influential behavior analyst, B. F. Skinner (1979) when he wrote, "Accept no eternal verity. Experiment" (p. 346).

Karl Popper
(1902-1994)

Source: LSE Library/
Flickr, Inc.

Quantitative: Behavior analysts specify the behavior of interest with enough precision that its occurrence can be *counted*. That is, the person(s) measuring behavior has defined that behavior with enough precision that instances and non-instances of the behavior may be discriminated from each other. This discriminability allows behavior analysts to more objectively measure behavior before, during, and after conducting an intervention designed to influence behavior.

Systematic: When behavior analysts conduct an intervention designed to influence behavior, they make sure that it is *implemented exactly as it is supposed to be*. Failure to properly implement the intervention will make it impossible to evaluate if the intervention is effective. If a study is conducted to evaluate an intervention and it proves not to change behavior, a fan of the intervention could say, "Oh, well they didn't implement the intervention correctly." This fan boy might be right, so it is important that behavior analysts document that they implemented the intervention exactly as they were supposed to. If they document this and the intervention does not work, the fan boy has no basis for saying that the intervention is effective.

Empirical: Behavior analysts require empirical evidence to support any claim about behavior. By "empirical" we mean that the *evidence must be observable*. We can do this observing with the naked eye or with the aid of an unbiased measurement device.

Nonempirical evidence, such as appeals to "common sense," to authority figures ("the President of the United States says..."), or to divine revelations ("according to the Bible...") holds no sway among scientists; empirical evidence is what counts.

Falsifiable Predictions: As discussed previously, the first goal of behavior analysis is to accurately predict behavior. Predictions are usually derived from theories (conceptual models of how the world works). Good theories make accurate predictions and incorrect (or incomplete) theories make inaccurate predictions.

Karl Popper went beyond this. He held that good theories make specific predictions about what happens *next*. Popper lived at the same time as Sigmund Freud, and he noticed that Freud's predictions about human behavior were pointing to what happened *before*, not what happens *next*. For example, if Freud's patient was suffering from anxiety, he speculated about past events that caused the anxiety. For example, the patient had a rough time of toilet training; no, really, that was one of his theories. These theories are hard to disprove. If the patient could not remember traumatic toilet training, Freud held that these memories were repressed into the inaccessible subconscious.

Popper thought these kinds of theories were rubbish because they were *unfalsifiable*; there was no way to prove them wrong. Popper said scientists should conduct experiments to prove theories wrong – to falsify them. This practice makes science a destructive force, but so be it. Humans have no shortage of whacky ideas about the world, and especially about human behavior. So, owning a tool like a wrecking ball that can falsify crackpot theories is a good thing. The scientific method is that tool.

Imagine that you came up with one of these half-baked theories and everyone around you loves it. They encourage you to give lectures on your theory and lots of people pay you lots of money to talk about your theory and how it will change the lives of those in the audience. After a few months, you are convinced that your theory is not so whacky after all. It has to be true!

Now, how would you feel about taking out that wrecking ball called the scientific method and trying to disprove your theory? You're probably not going to be a big fan of that idea. After all, you have a lot to lose if your theory is falsified. So, being a good scientist means being brave – you've got to be willing to take out the wrecking ball and apply it to your own theories (even though you love them).

Sciences that make unfalsifiable predictions are, according to Popper, *pseudo-sciences*. Pseudo-sciences contribute nothing to our goals of prediction and influence. By contrast, *natural sciences* make falsifiable predictions about things that happen next. Behavior analysis is one of these natural sciences. As we will see in later chapters, behavior analysts make specific, often quantitatively specific, predictions about behavior. When these predictions are confirmed, they strengthen our confidence in the theories upon which they are based. When the predictions are falsified, the theory is abandoned.

Experimentation: The most powerful scientific method is the experiment and this method is extensively used in behavior analysis. In an experiment, the behavior of an individual is objectively measured long enough that we are confident that if nothing changes the behavior will not change. Next, something is changed. This change is called the **independent variable** – *a publicly observable change, controlled by the experimenter, which is anticipated to influence behavior in a specific way*. In therapeutic settings, the independent variable is the intervention, or the treatment. Everything else that might influence behavior is held constant in an experiment and, therefore, if behavior changes we will conclude that the independent variable is functional; it influenced behavior. If not, the prediction will be falsified.

Peer-Review: When a group of behavioral scientists have discovered something they think is important, they will prepare a written description of the study that led to the discovery. The document will outline how behavior was objectively and quantitatively recorded, how the independent variable was manipulated, and how all other variables that might affect behavior were held constant. If a theory is being tested, a falsifiable prediction will be provided, and the empirical outcomes will be presented.

Before this document can be published in a scientific journal, it will be evaluated by a handful of scientific experts. These reviewers will approach the paper skeptically, looking for problems with the study that might diminish confidence in the discovery. If the paper does not pass this peer-review process, the paper is not published. This peer-review process is designed to ensure that papers published in scientific journals can be trusted. That is, if you were to replicate the methods described in the published paper, you would get the same outcome. Of course, the only way to know for certain that you will get the same outcome is to give it a try. Which takes us to our next topic.

Replication: The most important way to evaluate if scientific discoveries are true is through replication, that is, *repeating the experiment and obtaining the same outcome.*

"*...replication is the essence of believability.*" (Baer et al., 1968, p. 95)

Being able to replicate the results of an experiment is important in any science, but it is particularly important in behavior analysis because many behavior analysts work with individuals with challenging or problem behavior. A behavior analyst who works with a child diagnosed with autism needs to know that the therapeutic methods being used will work. Just like an engineer knows that the laws of physics can be relied upon when designing a building or a bridge, the behavior analyst needs therapeutic methods that produce replicable outcomes.

In 2015, a group of scientists known as the "Open Science Collaboration" published a paper in the prestigious journal, *Science*. The paper described the group's attempts to replicate 100 prominent findings reported in top psychology journals. For example, in one of these studies, college students were randomly assigned to either read about determinism (that behavior is caused by biological and environmental factors) or a neutral topic. The original investigators (Vohs & Schooler, 2008) hypothesized that belief in free will was important in moral action, so they anticipated that reading about determinism would undermine participants' morality. That's what they reported; participants who had just read about determinism were more likely to cheat during the study. This study was widely cited because it made "common sense." But when the Open Science Collaboration group tried, they could not replicate this finding, despite conducting the experiment exactly as described by Vohs and Schooler (2008). Indeed, the Open Science Collaboration (2015) report revealed that more than 60% of the findings published in top psychology journals could not be replicated. This finding has since been replicated (e.g., Klein et al., 2018). Psychologists were stunned by this outcome and some point to the research methods of behavior analysts (those discussed in Chapters 2 and 3) as a pathway out of this "replication crisis."

Replication has been a hallmark of behavior analysis from the beginning. By replicating behavioral outcomes over many sessions, the researcher or behavior therapist becomes increasingly confident in their findings. By replicating behavioral outcomes in several individuals, in several different studies, and in several different labs or settings, confidence is more robustly established. Rest assured that the principles of behavior analysis covered in this book have been replicated many times in many different labs and with many different species; they are believable. Where the evidence has not been replicated, we will point that out, so you may be skeptical.

Reading Quiz 3

1. Within science, there are two meanings of the word _____. The first recognizes that humans are susceptible to biases that cloud how we evaluate evidence that supports and refutes our favorite theories.
2. The second meaning of the word _____ recognizes that our current understanding of behavior is tentative and will be changed in the future as new findings support an alternative viewpoint that better allows us to predict and positively influence behavior.
3. _____ evidence for a scientific finding is either directly observable or observable with the aid of an unbiased measurement device.
4. When a scientist makes a prediction about behavior, the prediction is precise enough that it could be shown to be incorrect. These are referred to as _____ predictions.
5. When scientists discover something, it is important that their research be repeated to see if the finding can be obtained again. This repetition of experiments to evaluate if they produced reliable results is called _____.

What Are the Determinants of Behavior?

Scientists have for the last century or so studied the determinants of behavior and the rest of this book will outline the discoveries that are most important to behavior analysts. Broadly speaking, the determinants of behavior can be organized into two categories: *nature* and *nurture*. Early in the history of behavioral science, researchers asked if behavior was determined by nature (i.e., our genetic inheritance) or nurture (events experienced during one's lifetime). Today we recognize that behavior is determined by a combination of nature *and* nurture.

Nature

The behavioral determinants collectively referred to as "nature" include biological variables such as the evolutionary past of the species and the unique genome of the individual. Innate behaviors are the product of the evolutionary past of the species. Consider two of the innate behaviors of modern human infants – rooting and suckling. When an infant roots, it moves its mouth toward an object that is touching its cheek or lips. Once that object enters the mouth, the infant sucks on it (suckling). In the evolutionary past of the human species, infants who found and sucked on the mother's nipple survived; those who did not died. This survival advantage is the means by which innate behaviors are naturally selected – surviving means you live long enough to get your genes into the next generation. Genetic transmission through mating ensures your children will root and suckle too. The evolutionary past of the species is one determinant of behavior.

Charles Darwin (1809-1882)

Source: Nicku/Shutterstock.com

Another "nature" determinant of behavior is the unique genome of the individual. In sexually reproducing species (like humans), two parent genomes combine to produce a unique genome in the child. Mutations in this genome can produce dramatic effects on the behavior of the child. For example, children born with three copies of chromosome 21 (instead of the usual two) will have Down's syndrome, which profoundly impairs learning.

The genome need not be impacted by mutations to influence behavior. Behavioral tendencies in the parent(s) can be passed genetically to offspring. Consider the tendency to consume alcohol. Extensive studies of human twins (Verhulst et al., 2015), selectively bred nonhuman animals (Murphy et al., 2002), and genetically modified organisms (Roberts et al., 2001) have demonstrated that genes passed from parents to offspring can increase consumption of alcohol.

Nurture

The behavioral determinants collectively referred to as "nurture" include all of the events experienced during an individual's life. Although behavior analysts recognize that nature plays an important role in behavior, most of their efforts are focused on studying how **environmental events** influence behavior. By "environmental" we mean *all of the things you experience through your senses*. For example, you may see a sign that says that your favorite food is available at half-price today. Seeing the sign increases the probability of a specific behavior – going to the store and buying that food. On another day, you might overhear someone say something terrible about you. This environmental event will influence how you behave around that person in the future.

The ways in which individual behavior can be influenced by environmental events is the subject matter of this book. When an individual learns by interacting with its environment, the individual's behavior is changed, often in profound ways. Consider the acquisition of a new skill, like reading. When you learned to read you were embedded in an environment in which reading instruction, reading behavior, and immediate feedback were prominent. After you learned to read, your behavior changed in profoundly adaptive ways. You were no longer dependent on your parents to read your favorite books to you. You could read advice on an online troubleshooting forum when your PlayStation3® stopped working. You could use your reading skills to acquire new behaviors at school (math, science, etc.).

Our interactions with environmental events also influence the frequency of our behavior. If you got your finger caught in the car door, leaving your fingers in harm's way decreased in frequency. If saying, "please, please, please, please, please" was an effective way to get what you wanted, that behavior increased in frequency.

Experiences also influence where and when we behave. If being noisy in the classroom leads to negative consequences but being noisy on the playground leads to positive consequences, then these outcomes will influence where your noisy behaviors are emitted. Likewise, if you attend class on the wrong day or at the wrong time, you will arrive in an empty classroom (or in a different class). This mistake will likely influence when you choose to walk to class. Clearly, environmental events influence our everyday behavior.

Behavioral Epigenetics

Behavioral epigenetics examines how nurture shapes nature. When an environmental event influences gene regulation (specific genes are turned on or off) it influences the growth of brain neurons, the activity of these neurons, and the behavior of the individual. These changes in gene regulation do not change the individual's DNA, but they can be passed on to the offspring.

One of the earliest discoveries in behavioral epigenetics was that a rat's behavior in a stressful environment was influenced by the care provided to the rat when it was a pup. Mother rats that appropriately lick their pups produce pups that grow up to handle stress in adaptive ways. When mother rats lick their pups, it activates a gene that influences a receptor in the rat's brain (the gluco-

Source: ibreakstock/Getty Images

corticoid receptor); maternally neglected pups are left with an inactive gene and they behave less adaptively in stressful situations. When these rats grew up and had pups of their own, the females that had been licked appropriately provided maternal care to their offspring; those that had not tended to neglect their pups (Masterpasqua, 2009). Behavioral epigenetics provides a nice illustration that nature *and* nurture influence individual behavior.

The Activities of Behavior Analysts

Early in this chapter we said that behavior analysis is defined by its goals, its assumptions, and its major activities. We have discussed the goals of behavior analysis (to predict and influence behavior) and the assumptions of behavior analysis (determinism and the scientific method). Chapter 2 discusses the specific scientific methods behavior analysts use to predict and influence behavior. In what remains of this chapter, we examine the activities of behavior analysts.

Before going into specifics, it is important to note that there is strong demand for individuals who provide behavior analytic services. For example, from 2010 to 2017, demand for individuals trained in behavior analysis grew by approximately 800%! So, learning the principles discussed in this book may not only get you a good grade, it may get you a good job.

The Experimental Analysis of Behavior

Although a good deal is known about the determinants of individual behavior, it would be naïve to suggest that our understanding is complete. Thus, many behavior analysts work to expand our ability to predict and influence behavior by conducting research in controlled laboratory settings. Such research is referred to as the "experimental analysis of behavior."

Research conducted in the experimental analysis of behavior is not designed to therapeutically improve behavior or to address socially relevant behavior problems. Pioneers in the experimental analysis of behavior include John B. Watson, Ivan Pavlov, Edward L. Thorndike, and B. F. Skinner. We will study the contributions of each of these scientists in later chapters. The thing that unites these laboratory researchers was their passion for using the scientific method to make important discoveries about environmental events that influence behavior. Contemporary researchers in the experimental analysis of behavior continue to make important discoveries, and these are published in peer-reviewed scientific journals.

Much like Watson and Skinner, most contemporary scientists in the experimental analysis of behavior are employed as university professors. If you are thinking about pursuing such a career, you will need to attend graduate school after earning your bachelor's degree. In graduate school, you will take additional coursework and complete intensive research experiences for four to six years before earning your doctoral degree.

Applied Behavior Analysis

A second category of research in behavior analysis is applied behavior analysis. Applied behavior analysts also conduct rigorous scientific research; however, they focus on socially significant behavior in non-laboratory settings. For example, applied behavior analysts may conduct experiments exploring effective ways to teach reading skills (Daly & Kupzyk, 2013) or to reduce problem behavior in children diagnosed with autism (Hagopian et al., 2013).

Applied behavior analysts are expected to demonstrate a level of effectiveness that is readily apparent to consumers. If the applied behavior analyst is trying to decrease an individual's drug use, the intervention would be deemed effective only if the drug user and their spouse (and perhaps the judge who ordered the user into therapy) agreed that there was a noticeable decrease in drug use. In addition, the intervention must be acceptable to the client and others affected by it. In sum, applied behavior analysis aims to develop practical interventions that produce meaningful improvements in socially significant behavior.

Like those working in the experimental analysis of behavior, applied behavior analysts earn a doctoral degree and are most often employed as university professors. In addition, applied behavior analysts must pass a national certification exam administered by the Behavior Analyst Certification Board (BACB.com).

Behavioral Service Delivery

Those behavior analysts who use the discoveries of laboratory and applied behavior analysts to address the needs of patients are employed in *behavioral service delivery*. Many of these professionals work with children and adults diagnosed with a range of behavioral and intellectual disorders. Others work with individuals in traditional talk therapy settings, addressing issues of anxiety, phobias, depression, obsessive-compulsive disorders, and so on (Madden et al., 2016).

The increase in the prevalence of autism over the last 20 years, combined with the rigorous scientific evidence supporting behavior-analytic therapy in the treatment of autism (National Autism Center, 2015; Reichow, 2012; United States Surgeon General, 1998; Wong et al., 2015), has led to a dramatic increase in the number of professionals employed in behavioral service delivery. At present, more than 30 US states license behavior analysts to provide services. These licensed professionals are certified through the Behavior Analysis Certification Board after classroom training, supervised internships, and upon passing their

Source: Andrii Kondiuk/Shutterstock.com

EXTRA BOX 1: DIMENSIONS OF APPLIED BEHAVIOR ANALYSIS

In a seminal article published in the first issue of the *Journal of Applied Behavior Analysis*, Donald Baer, Montrose Wolf, and Todd Risley defined the seven core dimensions of applied behavior analysis (Baer et al., 1968). Researchers working in the field today aspire to these dimensions, though many important, socially significant applied research domains will not adhere to all seven dimensions (Critchfield & Reed, 2017).

1. *Applied:* The individual, behavior, and/or situation in which the individual behaves is socially important. If the applied behavior analyst can positively influence this behavior, it will improve the life of the individual and other members of society affected by the same behavioral malady (e.g., heroin abuse, pathological gambling, compulsive eating).
2. *Behavioral:* Because applied research is important, it is critical to objectively and accurately measure behavior. Asking people to tell you what they did is an inadequate foundation upon which to base a behavioral science, when the validity of those reports has not been established (e.g., Chermack et al., 2000; Mertz et al., 1991).
3. *Analytic:* An experimental design is employed and adequate replications conducted, thereby allowing the applied behavior analyst to identify which component(s) of the intervention is/are responsible for the behavior change.
4. *Technological:* Scientific reports on intervention efficacy will provide enough technical details that others can replicate the methods and evaluate the intervention's efficacy. The "replication crisis" in psychology underscores the important of this technological requirement.
5. *Conceptual:* The scientific theories and empirically supported principles of behavior that underlie intervention components are identified. Interventions are not pulled out of the air, nor are they a mere "bag of tricks"; they are derived from and contribute to an existing empirical science (Baer et al., 1968, p. 96).
6. *Effective:* Socially (and clinically) significant behavior changes are those that are obvious and meaningful to the stakeholders (client, parents, teacher, etc.). If stakeholders indicate that the behavior change has made no *practical difference*, then the applied intervention lacks efficacy.
7. *Generality:* Applied interventions have generality if they produce a durable (long-lasting) change in behavior that may be observed in a variety of settings where the behavior is adaptive.

certification examination. Demand for licensed and/or board-certified behavior analysts has grown continuously for decades. One level of certification, the BCaBA (Board Certified Assistant Behavior Analyst ®), is available to students after they earn their bachelor's degree and have completed supervised training in service provision. So, if you enjoy this class and want to work in the field without going to graduate school, this is the level of certification for you. More information may be found on the website of the Behavior Analyst Certification Board (BACB.com).

Organizational Behavior Management

The application of behavior analysis to business settings is called "Organizational Behavior Management." The focus of behavior analysis on objective measurement of individual behavior has proven highly compatible with a business focus on employee performance. Identifying environmental events that can be practically changed and that will produce measurable performance improvements translates in corporate settings to improved customer satisfaction, employee satisfaction, and profitability. There are several consulting companies that specialize in Organizational Behavior Management. The minimum educational requirement for employees in these companies is a master's degree in behavior analysis.

Summary

Behavior analysis has been defined by its goals, assumptions, and activities. Like a species, behavior analysis has evolved over time as scientists working in the experimental analysis of behavior, as applied behavior analysts, or as scientists in allied disciplines such as psychology have made new discoveries requiring that the field update its understanding of the determinants of behavior. Each update expands our understanding of behavior and increases the ability of those working in behavioral service delivery to provide an intervention that positively influences behavior and improves human lives. There is little doubt that the evolution of behavior analysis will continue in the decades to come. Perhaps you will be one of the behavior analysts who help to evolve the field and who will make a difference in the well-being of humanity.

Reading Quiz 4

1. Over 100 years of research has demonstrated that individual behavior is influenced by _____ and _____.
2. Those working in the _____ analysis of behavior, most often conduct their research in laboratory settings, where nuisance variables will not get in the way of identifying determinants of behavior.
3. Behavior analysts who conduct scientific research in clinical settings are called _____ behavior analysts.
4. Individuals who deliver behavioral services that are based on the research of laboratory and applied behavior analysts are employed in the field of behavioral _____ _____.

Answers to Reading Quiz Questions

Reading Quiz 1

1. individual
2. behavior; private; internal
3. stimulus

4. stimulus
5. stimuli
6. public
7. public – this one can be tricky. Although we often change clothes in private, changing clothes is a public behavior. It can be observed by anyone who looks in on us. Thinking about changing clothes, however, is a private behavior.
8. private
9. accurately predict
10. functional; positively influence
11. adaptive

Reading Quiz 2

1. determined
2. cause; causes
3. mentalistic
4. scientific method

Reading Quiz 3

1. objective
2. objective
3. empirical
4. falsifiable
5. replication

Reading Quiz 4

1. nature; nurture (the order of these answers does not matter)
2. experimental
3. applied
4. service delivery

Notes

1. Dostoyevsky (1864) *Notes from Underground*.
2. Behavioral scientists recognize the role of randomness (e.g., quantum mechanics) in the causal system that determines behavior. Thus, the state of the universe over time is not lockstep determined and, likewise, random events play a role in human behavior (e.g., random genetic mutations).
3. It is important to note that when behavior analysts reject mentalistic explanations, they are not rejecting the idea that brains (and other parts of the individual) play an important role in behavior. A complete scientific explanation of behavior will include environment and biology (brains, hormones, etc.). Mentalistic explanations do not refer to biology or environment in any meaningful way. Therefore, they are rejected as explanations of behavior.

References

Baer, D. M., Wolf, M. M., & Risley, T. R. (1968). Some current dimensions of applied behavior analysis. *Journal of Applied Behavior Analysis, 1*(1), 91–97.

Chermack, S. T., Roll, J., Reilly, M., Davis, L., Kilaru, U., & Grabowski, J. (2000). Comparison of patient self-reports and urinalysis results obtained under naturalistic methadone treatment conditions. *Drug and Alcohol Dependence, 59*(1), 43–49. doi:10.1016/S0376-8716(99)00106-4

Critchfield, T. S., & Reed, D. D. (2017). The fuzzy concept of applied behavior analysis research. *Behavior Analyst, 40*(1), 123–159. doi:10.1007/s40614-017-0093-x

Daly, E. J. III, & Kupzyk, S. (2013). Teaching reading. In G. J. Madden, W. V. Dube, T. D. Hackenberg, G. P. Hanley, & K. A. Lattal (Eds.), *APA handbook of behavior analysis, Vol. 2. Translating principles into practice* (p. 405–423). American Psychological Association. https://doi.org/10.1037/13938-016

Hagopian, L. P., Dozier, C. L., Rooker, G. W., & Jones, B. A. (2013). Assessment and treatment of severe problem behavior. In G. J. Madden, W. V. Dube, T. D. Hackenberg, G. P. Hanley, & K. A. Lattal (Eds.), *APA handbook of behavior analysis, Vol. 2: Translating principles into practice.* (pp. 353–386). American Psychological Association.

Kahneman, D., & Tversky, A. (2013). Choices, values, and frames. In L. C. MacLean & W. T. Ziemba (Eds.), *Handbook of the fundamentals of financial decision making* (pp. 269–278). Hackensack, NJ: World Scientific. doi:10.1142/9789814417358_0016

Klein, R. A., Vianello, M., Hasselman, F., Adams, B. G., Adams, R. B., Alper, S., … Nosek, B. A. (2018). Many Labs 2: Investigating variation in replicability across samples and settings. *Advances in Methods and Practices in Psychological Science, 1*(4), 443–490. doi:10.1177/2515245918810225

Madden, G. J., Hanley, G. P., & Dougher, M. J. (2016). Clinical behavior analysis. In J. C. Norcross, G. R. VandenBox, & D. K. Freedheim (Editors-in-Chief) *APA Handbook of clinical psychology: Vol. I. roots and branches* (pp. 351–368). Washington, DC: APA Books.

Masterpasqua, F. (2009). Psychology and epigenetics. *Review of General Psychology, 13,* 194–201.

Mertz, W., Tsui, J. C., Judd, J. T., Reiser, S., Hallfrisch, J., Morris, E. R., et al. (1991). What are people really eating? The relation between energy intake derived from estimated diet records and intake determined to maintain body weight. *American Journal of Clinical Nutrition, 54,* 291–295.

Murphy, J. M., Stewart, R. B., Bell, R. L., Badia-Elder, N. E., Carr, L. G., McBride, W. J., … Li, T. (2002). Phenotypic and genotypic characterization of the Indiana University rat lines selectively bred for high and low alcohol preference. *Behavior Genetics, 32,* 363–388.

National Autism Center. (2015). Findings and conclusions: National standards project, phase 2. Randolph, MA: Author.

Open Science Collaboration. (2015). Estimating the reproducibility of psychological science. *Science, 349*(6251). doi:10.1126/science.aac4716

Pinker, S. (2018). *Enlightenment now: The case of reason, science, humanism, and progress.* New York: Viking.

Reichow, B. (2012). Overview of meta-analyses on early intensive behavioral intervention for young children with autism spectrum disorders. *Journal of Autism and Developmental Disorders, 42,* 512–520.

Roberts, A. J., Gold, L. H., Polis, I., McDonald, J. S., Filliol, D., Kieffer, B. L., & Koob, G. F. (2001). Increased ethanol self-administration in delta-opioid receptor knockout mice. *Alcoholism, Clinical, and Experimental Research, 25,* 1249–1256.

Skinner, B. F. (1979). *The shaping of a behaviorist.* New York: Knopf.

United States Surgeon General. (1998). Mental health: A report of the Surgeon General. Washington, DC: Author.

Verhulst, B., Neale, M. C., & Kendler, K. S. (2015). The heritability of alcohol use disorders: A meta-analysis of twin and adoption studies. *Psychological Medicine, 45*(5), 1061–1072. doi: 10.1017/S0033291714002165

Vohs, K. D., & Schooler, J. W. (2008). The value of believing in free will: Encouraging a belief in determinism increases cheating. *Psychological Science, 19,* 45–54.

Wong, C., Odom, S. L., Hume, K. A., Cox, C. W., Fettig, A., Kurcharczyk, S., & Schultz, T. R. (2015). Evidence-based practices for children, youth, and young adults with autism spectrum disorder: A comprehensive review. *Journal of Autism and Developmental Disorders, 45,* 1951–1966.

Understanding Behavioral Research

2

Chapter 1 provided an introduction to the science of behavior known as "behavior analysis." There we learned that behavior analysis has two goals: (1) to accurately predict behavior and (2) to discover functional variables that may be used to positively influence behavior. These are lofty goals. While considerable progress has been made, new discoveries await the efforts of a new generation of behavior analysts.

As noted in Chapter 1, past progress in behavior analysis has been made by using techniques collectively known as the "scientific method." This chapter will take the first steps in summarizing how the scientific method is used by behavior analysts. It begins by honing in on those functional variables used to positively influence behavior. What is a variable and how do we know if it is functional – that is, it affects behavior in a reliable and systematic way? A good place to start is knowing the difference between a cause and a correlation. Identifying functional variables requires going beyond correlations. When a functional variable is discovered, we can predict that turning it "ON" and "OFF" will systematically change behavior. If our goal is to therapeutically increase an adaptive behavior, then an effective intervention will turn ON a functional variable that is known to increase the frequency of this behavior. Likewise, that intervention will try to turn OFF any functional variables known to reduce the desired behavior.

Functional variables are identified in *experiments*. Here the behavior analyst turns variables ON and OFF to see if they systematically and reliably change behavior. Of course, it's a little more complicated than this, and this chapter provides an overview of the essential components of a behavioral experiment. As the chapter continues, we discuss techniques for objectively measuring behavior. These observations yield quantitative data, such as the number of cigarettes smoked per day or the number of hours we procrastinate before beginning work on a homework assignment. Using *numbers* to measure behavior is important. It allows us to evaluate, for example, exactly how much behavior improves when a behavior-change intervention is introduced.

An Introduction to Behavior Analysis, First Edition. Gregory J. Madden, Derek D. Reed, and Florence D. DiGennaro Reed.
© 2021 John Wiley & Sons Ltd. Published 2021 by John Wiley & Sons Ltd.

Variables

The word "variables" is undoubtedly familiar, but what does it mean? When behavioral scientists talk about variables, they are referring to *things that are not the same each time*, that is, things that can be changed. For example, behavior is not the same each time it occurs. Sometimes we drive carefully and sometimes we don't come to a complete stop at the intersection. Because behavior can change, and these changes are often dependent on local conditions (e.g., whether or not we are running late); we refer to behavior as the "dependent variable." More formally, the **dependent variable** in behavior analysis is *the objectively measured target behavior*.

A second category of variables – functional variables – includes all of those things that, if changed, will systematically and reliably influence behavior. As noted in Chapter 1, and as illustrated in the inset figure, functional variables fall into two broad categories: (1) biological variables (e.g., genetics, brain chemistry) and (2) environmental variables (those things we experience through our senses). These categories are shown as overlapping in the figure because of behavioral epigenetics (i.e., environmental variables can influence how genes are regulated, and this is passed on to the individual's offspring, where it influences the behavior of this next generation). Behavior analysts primarily specialize in environmental variables that influence behavior.

To evaluate if a biological or environmental variable can systematically and reliably influence behavior, scientists conduct experiments. In an experiment, a specific variable is manipulated (changed) and the effect of that change on the dependent variable (behavior) is carefully and objectively recorded. When a variable is manipulated within an experiment it is referred to as the "independent variable" because the manipulation of the independent variable does not depend on a change in behavior. We talked about independent variables in Chapter 1 and we will return to them later in this chapter. For now, you should know that if changing the independent variable produces a systematic and replicable change in behavior, then we can conclude that the independent variable is a functional variable.

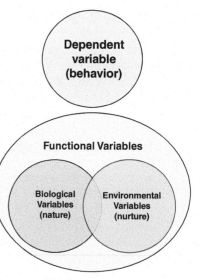

Correlation vs Causation

If two variables are positively correlated, they tend to occur together. For example, a popular study on social media reported that people who have more sex (variable 1) also make more money (variable 2; Drydakis, 2015). Sexual activity and high wages co-occur – they are positively correlated. When this study was published, the Twittersphere was alight with suggestions that increasing our sexual activity would be rewarded with a raise at work. Such useless advice ignores an important scientific maxim:

Correlation does not imply causation.

Just because two things co-occur does not mean that one of those things causes the other. Correlations tell us nothing about causation. Only an experiment can tell us if a functional relation exists.

Consider the case of essential oils, which are very popular in the United States. People who inhale these oils often claim they experience health benefits. According to their proponents, essential oils can clear your skin, improve your mental focus, relieve your stress, and can even cure cancer. If one of our loved ones was diagnosed with cancer, we might find compelling one of the many websites providing testimonial evidence that essential oils can cure cancer. We might even follow the links on these websites, buy the essential oils, and ensure that our loved one inhales them several times a day.

Let's assume, for the sake of argument, that these websites are telling the truth. Yes, these people were diagnosed with cancer. Yes, they used the essential oils. And yes, their cancer went into remission. If all of these things are true, then essential oil use and cancer remission are *correlated*. But the question remains, is there a functional relation between using essential oils and cancer remission? Those who sell essential oils say yes, but there are other possibilities. Sometimes cancer goes into remission for unknown reasons. If these spontaneous remission patients take essential oils, there is a good chance they will attribute the remission to the essential oils. After all, they took them in the hope of a miracle cure.

Another possible explanation for the correlation between essential oil use and cancer remission is that some other variable caused the cancer remission. Like what? Like the surgical removal of the tumor, or the radiation therapy these patients complete while using essential oils (see, e.g., https://www.allisonhuish.com/my-story). Why patients attribute their cancer remission to essential oil use given these other medical treatments is a mystery. What makes it even more mysterious is that when the cancer-curing effects of essential oils have been evaluated in objective scientific *experiments*, they have proven no more effective than a placebo (i.e., a sugar pill; e.g., Bailey et al., 2008).

To summarize, just because behavior (the dependent variable) is correlated with another variable does not mean that a causal relation exists between them. So, don't be fooled by testimonials on web sites, informercials, or miracle cures promised by your friends. Approach these, and all other correlations, with the maxim, *correlation does not imply causation.* Being skeptical can save us from wasting money on the more than 75,000 "miracle cures" that are untested, proven to be ineffective, or don't even contain the active ingredient shown on the label (Paller et al., 2016). Being skeptical can spare us from pursuing a bogus cure instead of one backed by strong scientific evidence (Normand, 2008).

Experiments

While it is true that *correlation does not imply causation*, that does not mean that causally related variables are not correlated. Quite the opposite is true. If the cause of global warming is increased greenhouse gasses, then these variables are correlated – more greenhouse gasses, warmer climate. Therefore, all causal relations are correlated but not all correlations reveal causal relations.

Confused? Don't worry, this is where experiments prove so useful. Experiments separate correlation from causation. Doing so is critical to achieving our goals of predicting and positively influencing behavior. To predict when a behavior will occur, we need to know what variable(s) systematically and reliably influence that behavior. To take a simple example, we know that red traffic lights (a variable that we can turn ON and OFF) cause people to stop their cars. We can *accurately predict* when drivers will stop – whenever the light changes from yellow to red. Cities around the world *positively influence* human behavior every minute of the day by turning ON red traffic lights when stopping one driver would prevent a collision.

Three Components of a Behavioral Experiment

Behavior analysts conduct experiments to identify functional relations between environmental variables and behavior. Therefore, the **first component** of a behavioral experiment is that *the dependent variable is behavior*. If you were a physicist, you might have a different dependent variable (e.g., the motion of a particle), but in behavioral experiments the dependent variable is always behavior.

The **second component** of a behavioral experiment is *a falsifiable hypothesis*. Let's explore this with an example. Imagine that we have a job working for the health department of a large city. During flu season, our office is given the job of positively influencing handwashing in the city's public restrooms. We call a meeting and ask for hypotheses; what variables might cause someone to walk past the sinks without washing their hands? One employee suggests, "Some people are gross." Another says, "And they're lazy!" The problem with these mentalistic hypotheses is that we cannot turn an individual's inner "grossness" or inherent "laziness" ON and OFF to see if doing so positively influences their handwashing. These mentalistic hypotheses are not falsifiable – there is no way to prove them wrong.

Another employee says, "I don't wash my hands in public bathrooms because the paper-towel dispensers are often empty or broken. I don't want to have to walk outside with wet hands." From this, you develop the hypothesis, "paper towel availability plays a functional role in handwashing." This is a falsifiable hypothesis. We can falsify it by turning ON and OFF paper towel availability. If public bathroom users can see that paper towels are available (ON), they should wash their hands more often than when they can't tell if paper towels are available (OFF).

Ford et al. (2014) tested this falsifiable hypothesis in their experiment on handwashing in public bathrooms. In their ON condition, they set the automated paper-towel dispenser so it always had a fresh, clean paper towel hanging from it. In their OFF condition, they set the dispenser so that a paper towel was not visible. If handwashing was no more frequent during the ON condition than the OFF condition, then the hypothesis would be falsified.

The **third component** of a behavioral experiment is *manipulation of the independent variable*. You may recall from Chapter 1 that the formal definition of an **independent variable** is *a publicly observable change, controlled by the experimenter, which is anticipated to influence behavior in a specific way*. In the Ford et al. (2014) experiment, they turned the independent variable ON for a week (the fresh, clean paper towel was displayed) and OFF for the next week (no paper towel visible). They repeated this ON/OFF sequence five times. At the end of their experiment, their hypothesis was supported; handwashing increased by 13% when the paper towel was displayed.

To summarize, an experiment tests a falsifiable hypothesis by seeing if an independent variable reliably and systematically influences behavior. It accomplishes this by turning ON and OFF the independent variable and objectively measuring behavior to see if it changes. If behavior reliably and systematically changes when the independent variable is turned ON and OFF, then it may be identified as a functional variable.

Reading Quiz 1

1. _____ are things that are not the same each time.
2. When a functional variable is changed, it systematically influences _____.
3. _____ does not imply causation.
4. A publicly observable change, controlled by the experimenter, which is anticipated to influence behavior in a specific way is the definition of an _____ _____.
5. The three components of a behavioral experiment are (1) the _____ variable is behavior, (2) the experiment is designed to evaluate a _____ hypothesis, and (3) this hypothesis is evaluated by manipulating the _____ variable.
6. In behavior analysis, the dependent variable is always _____.

Measuring Behavior

Before conducting an experiment, a method of objectively measuring behavior must be selected. A common method in the social sciences is to use **self-reports**. When using a self-report measure, one simply *asks the individual to recall if they have engaged in the behavior.* This is a common technique in health research – participants fill out a survey indicating how much they exercise, what they ate yesterday, or how often they wash their hands after using the bathroom.

Behavior analysts are careful about the use of self-report measures. Caution is warranted because sometimes an individual's self-reports are not as truthful as we would like. For example, society approves of exercising and eating healthy, and frowns on using the bathroom without washing your hands. Therefore, to gain social approval we humans tend to over-report how often we go to the gym (Shuval et al., 2015) and eat healthy foods (Archer et al., 2013), and under-report when we don't wash up after using the toilet (Stanton et al., 1987).

Source: pathdoc/Shutterstock.com

A second reason for caution around self-reports is that they rely upon flawed memory processes. For example, how many times did your mother tell you to stop leaving dirty dishes in the sink? Was it really a million times, as she always claimed, or was it more like 114; you can't say for sure. Likewise, when a manager reviews employee performance it is often biased by recent, memorable events. This is not fair to the employee who had a bad day at the office on the day before quarterly evaluations.

Because self-reports are prone to biases and memory-related inaccuracies, they will not be used unless the self-reports are empirically validated – that is, they have been shown to provide accurate and useful information about the target behavior (e.g., Critchfield & Reed, 2017; MacKillop et al., 2008; Madden et al., 2003).

The alternative to self-reports is **direct observation** of behavior. Here, *behavior is recorded as the behavior occurs, or a lasting product of the behavior is recorded at a later time.* If you own a fitness tracker (like a Fitbit or an Apple watch), then you are using direct observation to measure your exercising. The tracker observes and records each step as you take it. This is more accurate than trying to remember how many steps you took. Furthermore, the device is not interested in social approval, so it is not biased to over-report activity levels.

Sometimes no automated device is available to measure behavior. In these cases, humans must directly observe behavior as it occurs. For example, if we are interested in behaviors that contribute to air pollution, we might decide to count idling vehicles out-side a school. Directly observing this behavior would involve walking through the park-ing lot recording those cars that are idling and those that are not. We might find that 78% of the cars are idling, which might motivate the school to develop a clean-air intervention.

Behavioral Definitions

Counting the number of idling vehicles sounds simple enough, but, in practice, it can be quite difficult. For example, if a motorcycle is idling, does that count? If the car is empty and not idling, does that count as not idling? What if the vehicle is running and is moving very very slowly?

Before behavior analysts conduct direct observations, they spend time developing a **behavioral definition**, which is a *precise specification of the topography of the target behavior, allowing observers to reliably identify instances and non-instances.*[1] Good behavioral defini-tions make data collection objective, that is, not influenced by personal judgments, preju-dice, or bias. How about this behavioral definition:

> *A driver has chosen to idle if the motorized vehicle (occupied or not) is parked (not rolling forward or backward) with the engine running for 5 consecutive seconds. Empty vehicles that are not idling are not counted.*

This definition specifies the topography (physical form) of the choice – a parked vehicle with the engine running for 5+ seconds. The definition is more specific than "idling" or "not idling." It helps the observer differentiate between the two when it is hard to tell. An idling motorcycle counts, slowly moving vehicles do not. A good behavioral definition is specific enough to ensure that the data being collected are not influenced by personal judgments, prejudice, or bias. The next behavioral definition was written by one of our *Introduction to Behavior Analysis* students. The definition is so good at specifying the topography of behavior that we won't bother telling you what response it describes.

> *With hands and toes (and no other body parts) on the floor, arms straight, and the body making a straight line from the head to the toes, the arms are bent and the body lowered until the nose or chest touches the floor. The response is completed when the arms are then fully extended, while keeping the body straight, returning the body to the initial position.*

Observable and Objective

Good behavioral definitions specify the observable topography of the target behavior. Doing so increases our ability to objectively measure the target behavior. When developing a behavioral definition, ask yourself: Could a robot use this definition (and no other information) to make accurate observations? If anything in the definition requires that the robot make a subjective inference about unobserved processes, then the robot will fail. For example, a restaurant manager might wish to evaluate if their

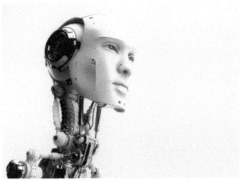

Source: Ociacia/Shutterstock.com

employees "have a good attitude." Unfortunately, a robot cannot observe an attitude, which the manager believes is a mental state responsible for desired employee behaviors. The manager's behavioral definition will need to be refined. It will need to specify the observable behaviors the manager values in their top-performing employees. Behavioral definitions specify observable behaviors that may be objectively recorded, not subjectively inferred.

REFINING THE BEHAVIORAL DEFINITION

When developing a behavioral definition, it is common to test and refine them before starting the experiment. To evaluate the adequacy of a behavioral definition, the behavior analyst "test-drives" it to see if it adequately guides human observers to objectively differentiate instances and non-instances of the behavior. For example, if a vehicle is approached and the driver shuts off their engine, does this count as idling or not idling? If the observers are not sure, then the behavioral definition will need to be refined; it will need to be made more specific.

SOCIAL VALIDITY OF THE BEHAVIORAL DEFINITION

A behavioral definition has **social validity** when *the consumer of the intervention or an expert in the field indicates that the behavioral definition accurately reflects the behavior of interest.* For example, if the consumers of the clean-air intervention are the school board and a group of clean-air researchers at the Environmental Protection Agency, then they will be asked to evaluate the definition of idling. If they approve it, then the definition has social validity. Alternatively, if an intervention is aimed at reducing bullying at school, the behavioral definition of bullying might be evaluated and approved by a group of student advocates and an expert in school bullying. Assessing the social validity of a behavioral definition *before the study begins* is important. If the intervention is successful, then the consumers/experts will be satisfied with the change in this behavior.

FINALIZING THE BEHAVIORAL DEFINITION

The final version of the behavioral definition needs to be saved and used throughout the study. Changing the definition mid-way through the study is not allowed. If the behavioral definition were changed in a way that made it more difficult to count idling as idling (e.g., the car must be idling for 10 seconds instead of 5 seconds), then more drivers would be recorded as "not idling." Changing the behavioral definition would make it appear that idling had decreased, even though behavior had not changed. Once the study begins and direct observations are being collected, the behavioral definition must not be changed (Baer et al., 1968).

Interobserver Agreement (IOA)

To evaluate the objectivity of a behavioral definition, two people will use it while simultaneously making direct observations of the same behavior. If the two observers' recorded data agree, then we will be confident that the behavioral definition is objective. If the two observers' data are divergent (e.g., one observer recorded 13 instances of the behavior and the other recorded only 8), then the observers are not in agreement. When the observers disagree on whether or not an instance of the behavior occurred, the behavioral definition will need to be refined to reduce the subjective judgments being made by the observers.

The agreement between observers is referred to as **interobserver agreement (IOA)** and it is defined as *the extent to which two independent observers' data are the same after having directly observed the same behavior at the same time.* An important word in this definition is "independent." It means that the two observers need to make their observations in a way that insulates them from being influenced by the other observer.

For example, imagine that you are one of two observers asked to count idling and non-idling vehicles. As you turn your attention to the first vehicle, you are not quite sure if the behavioral definition has been met. Should you count this as idling or not? You're not sure. Just then, out of the corner of your eye, you see the other observer recording this car as idling. Your uncertainty is replaced with relief as you do the same. The other observer has influenced your behavior.

If the behavioral definition is not objective enough that two independent observers can almost always agree on instances and non-instances of the behavior, then IOA will be unacceptably low. When IOA is low, the behavioral definition needs to be refined. The formula we will use for calculating IOA is:

$$IOA = \frac{Agreements}{\left(Agreements \ + \ Disagreements\right)} \times 100$$

A simple rule of thumb for acceptable and unacceptable levels of IOA is, if IOA is below 90%, then the behavioral definition should be refined. Why? Because the two observers disagree more than 10% of the time. That is too much subjectivity. When IOA is low, the behavioral definition may need to be refined, or the human observers may need further training.

What IOA Is Not

IOA is not the same as *accuracy*. To know if an observer has accurately recorded behavior requires that we compare it to a perfect record of that behavior (e.g., one collected by our robot friend). Any deviations from this 100% accurate record would reveal inaccuracies of the human observer. When assessing IOA, we are not comparing an observer's data with a perfect record, we are simply comparing it with another human observer, whose accuracy is also unknown. Thus, IOA does not assess accuracy (Johnston & Pennypacker, 2009).

IOA is also not assessing the *reliability* of the observers. Reliability refers to repeatability. For example, if your fitness tracker consistently underestimates the number of steps taken by 3%, then the tracker has high reliability – it makes the same error day after day. Because IOA tells us nothing about repeatability, IOA is not assessing reliability.

If IOA does not assess accuracy or reliability, what good is it? The benefit of IOA is that it increases *believability* (Johnston & Pennypacker, 2009). If the observers collected their data *independently* and their IOA is high, we find their records of behavior just as believable as two eyewitnesses who independently provide descriptions of a crime that are very much the same. If these eyewitness testimonies agree on 98% of the details of the crime, we find the accounts believable. If the testimonies disagree on 30% of the important details, we dismiss both eyewitnesses as unbelievable. In sum, high IOA confers the data collected with believability; it does not ensure the accuracy of the data or the reliability of the observers.

Reading Quiz 2

1. Behavior analysts approach the use of _____-_____ measures with caution.
2. Two potential problems with self-reports are that (i) people do not always tell the _____, particularly when doing so would make them look bad, and (ii) people often cannot _____ their own behavior very well.
3. The alternative to self-reports is _____ _____ of behavior. Here, behavioral is recorded as the behavior occurs, or a lasting product of the behavior is measured at a later time.
4. A behavioral _____ provides a very specific description of the target behavior.
5. The behavior analyst asked the patient's parents and physician to approve the behavioral definition before the experiment began. If both of these stakeholders approve the definition, it has _____ _____. If the intervention positively influences this behavior, the parents and physician will be pleased with the outcome.

6. IOA stands for _____-_____ agreement.

7. Insert the missing information: $\text{IOA} = \dfrac{\rule{3cm}{0.4pt}}{\rule{1cm}{0.4pt} + \rule{2cm}{0.4pt}} \times 100$.

8. IOA is defined as *the extent to which two _____ observers' data are the same after having directly observed the same behavior at the same time.*

9. If IOA is less than _____% , then the observers will need further training, or the behavioral definition will need to be refined.

10. IOA does not assess the _____ of the data collected; nor does it assess its reliability. Instead, high IOA enhances the _____ of the data.

Dimensions of Behavior

When measuring a target behavior, one must decide what dimension of behavior is of interest. Here, we briefly discuss four dimensions of behavior: frequency, latency, duration, and magnitude.

FREQUENCY

When interested in how often the target behavior occurs, the dimension of behavior is *frequency*. **Frequency** is defined as the *response count divided by time or opportunity to respond.* If 20 instances of the target behavior occur during a 20-minute session, then the frequency (or rate) is 20/20 = 1 response per minute. Dividing the response count by time is important. If we only knew the response count (20 responses), we would have no idea how frequently the behavior occurred. Did 20 responses occur in 20 seconds or in 20 years? Dividing by time facilitates comparison across long and short observation sessions.

Alternatively, it may make more sense to divide by the number of opportunities to respond. For example, if the target behavior is washing up after using the bathroom, frequency of behavior would be quantified as the number of times the individual washed up (1 time) divided by the number of times the bathroom was used (3 times). Multiplying the quotient by 100 expresses the frequency as a percentage (1/3 × 100 = 33.3%). Frequency is perhaps the most commonly used dimension of behavior.

LATENCY

When interested in how long it takes for a behavior to begin, we are interested in the dimension of *latency*. **Latency** is defined as *the interval of time between the opportunity to respond and the response itself.* For example, if 1.5 seconds elapses between the traffic light turning green (opportunity to respond) and pressing the accelerator (the response itself), the response latency is 1.5 seconds. The latency to begin a homework assignment is the interval of time between receiving the assignment (Monday at 2:00 pm) and the time the student begins working on the assignment (Tuesday at 2:00 pm; latency = 24 hours). Latency is of interest when we are interested in how long it takes to initiate the target behavior.

DURATION

When interested in how long the behavior lasts, from start to finish, we are interested in the dimension of *duration*. **Duration** is defined as *the interval of time between the start and the end of the behavior.* For example, if you begin working on the homework assignment at 2 pm and complete the assignment at 3:00 pm, then the duration is 1 hour. Duration is an important dimension of behavior when we are interested in how long a target behavior lasts.

MAGNITUDE

When interested in measuring *the force or intensity of a behavior*, we are interested in the dimension of **magnitude**. For example, the magnitude of vocalizations at a football game tends to be louder (greater response magnitude) than vocalizations in bed, when behaving affectionately with a partner. Conversely, a gentle touch (lesser response magnitude) is appropriate to the bedroom, but a more forceful touch is required when lifting weights. When the magnitude of a response is of interest, we might measure the magnitude of each response – 3 grams of force, then 5 grams, and so on. Alternatively, we may be interested in the magnitude of our football fan's cheering, which can be quantified in decibels.

Four Direct-Observation Methods

There are many direct-observation methods used by behavior analysts. This section provides an overview of four commonly used methods. It also helps readers decide which method is best for measuring the target behavior and how to calculate IOA with each method.

Outcome Recording

Let's return to the study of how frequently people wash their hands in public restrooms (Ford et al., 2014). As previously discussed, relying on self-reports is likely to produce biased data – people will over-report their frequency of hand-washing. Thus, we will want to measure this behavior using a direct-observation method. However, two drawbacks are immediately apparent. First, it will be costly to hire two people to sit in the bathroom all day, independently recording whether or not each visitor washes up. Second, the presence of these observers will influence the target behavior. That is, bathroom users are going to wash their hands more often if someone is watching them.

Humans often behave differently when they know they are being watched. When *behavior changes because the individual is aware they are being watched*, we refer to this as **reactivity**. Reactivity, when it occurs, can make the data

Source: t-lorien/iStock/Getty Images

useless. For example, if your observers report that 95% of the bathroom patrons washed their hands, this information is useless if it is inflated by reactivity. The data do not tell us anything about how often these people would wash their hands if no one was watching them.

The first direct-observation method, *outcome recording*, can address these issues of cost *and* reactivity. When using **outcome recording**, observers *record the distinct, observable, and lasting product(s) of behavior, instead of the behavior itself*. To use outcome recording, the target behavior must produce a distinct, observable product each time it occurs. This product needs to last long enough for the observer to record it well after the behavior has occurred.

Ford et al. (2014) used outcome recording in their study of handwashing. The distinct, observable, and lasting product of handwashing was *a bit less soap in the soap dispenser*. To measure this product of handwashing, Ford et al. recorded the amount of soap missing from the dispensers at the end of each week. If more soap was used without an increase in the number of bathroom visitors (recorded by a motion detector), they could conclude that the frequency of washing up had increased. Notice how inexpensive outcome recording was in this study, compared to hiring two people to sit in the restroom all day. Notice also how outcome recording eliminated reactivity – the restroom users had no idea that anyone was measuring soap use, so their handwashing behavior was unaffected by the direct observations.

Outcome recording is commonly used in daily life. For example, your instructor uses outcome recording to measure effective studying behavior. The distinct, observable, and lasting outcome of effective studying is the number of questions answered correctly on the exam. Those with high exam scores studied effectively and those with low exam scores did not. This kind of outcome recording is far more efficient than, for example, stopping by your apartment or the library to see if you are studying. If your professor checked on your studying, in person, several times a day, there is a good chance that a reactivity effect would increase your studying. Therefore, a better measure of your non-reactive studying is provided by the exam score and by using outcome recording.

WHEN TO USE OUTCOME RECORDING

Because outcome recording is efficient and cost effective, and can reduce reactivity when you are interested in the frequency of behavior, outcome recording should be the method given first consideration. Of course, outcome recording can only be used if the target behavior produces a distinct, observable, and lasting product each time the behavior occurs. If nothing is left behind, then behavior will have to be observed in real time, at the moment it occurs. Figure 2.1 provides a flowchart to help decide which direct-observation technique is the right choice. Start in the upper-left, green cell. From there, your answers will determine the path you take to a solution.

A quick warning about outcome recording. Sometimes it is important to observe the target behavior in real time, as it is occurring. For example, if there is reason to anticipate that the individual will cheat, to make their performance look better than it is, then outcome recording may not be right for you. For example, if a student successfully cheats on their exam, they have fooled the instructor into believing that they studied effectively, when in fact they did not.

Similarly, it is important to observe behavior in real time when that behavior is dangerous and needs to be quickly stopped. An individual at risk of suicide must be observed in real time to prevent self-harming behaviors. Waiting to measure the outcomes of such behavior would be reprehensibly unethical.

More optimistically, sometimes behavior analysts will want to positively reinforce adaptive behaviors at the moment they occur. As we will see in later chapters, positive reinforcers will have a greater beneficial impact on behavior when they are delivered immediately, and this is impossible if we are only measuring the outcome of a performance.

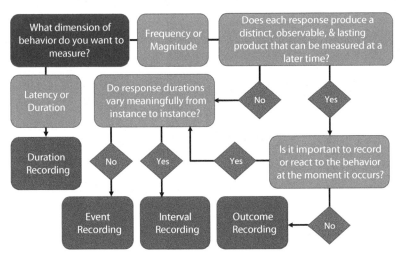

Figure 2.1 A flowchart used to choose the most appropriate direct-observation technique. Start in the upper left (green) cell, and work your way through until reaching one of the orange endpoints.

CALCULATING IOA WHEN USING OUTCOME RECORDING

Once again, the formula for calculating IOA is:

$$IOA = \frac{Agreements}{(Agreements + Disagreements)} \times 100$$

An *agreement* occurs when both of the independent observers agree that the outcome occurred. For example, in Table 2.1, when the exam graders independently scored the student's exam, they agreed that the first question was answered correctly (as indicated by the check mark in the Agreements column). A *disagreement* occurs on item #2, when one observer scores the outcome as having occurred (a correct answer) but the other observer does not. After both observers score the 10-item exam, there are 8 agreements and 2 disagreements. IOA can be easily calculated as follows:

$$IOA = \frac{8}{(8 + 2)} \times 100 = 80\%$$

If you were the student whose exam had been graded by these two observers, would you be satisfied with their objectivity? No. Grader 1 is ready to give you an A (90% correct) whereas Grader 2 wants to give you a C (70% correct). You want more objectivity. The instructor will have to either provide the graders with better behavioral definitions of the correct answers or better train one or more of the graders. Only then will you be satisfied with the objectivity of the grading process.

Table 2.1 Two exam graders' scores (correct or incorrect) for each item on a student's exam.

Item	Grader 1	Grader 2	Agreements	Disagreements
1	Correct	Correct	✓	
2	Correct	Incorrect		✓
3	Incorrect	Incorrect	✓	
4	Correct	Correct	✓	
5	Correct	Correct	✓	
6	Correct	Correct	✓	
7	Correct	Correct	✓	
8	Correct	Correct	✓	
9	Correct	Incorrect		✓
10	Correct	Correct	✓	
		Total	8	2

* The "Agreements" column is checked when the graders agree that the item was answered correctly or they agree that the answer provided was incorrect; otherwise a check is placed in the "Disagreements" column.

Event Recording

When *each instance of behavior is recorded at the moment it occurs*, the observer is using the direct-observativon technique known as **event recording**. Like outcome recording, event recording is useful when we are interested in the frequency or magnitude of the target behavior. For example, when a baseball umpire records the balls and strikes thrown, these recordings are made at the moment the behavior occurs. Similarly, we could use event recording to measure the speed (magnitude) of each pitch, at the moment it occurs. If our fitness tracker increments a counter with each step we take, it too is using event recording to measure behavior in real time.

Source: KeithJJ/Pixabay

WHEN TO USE EVENT RECORDING

Previously, we said that outcome recording should be the default choice when you want to measure how often a behavior is occurring. However, as shown in Figure 2.1, outcome recording cannot be used if the behavior does not produce a distinct, observable, and lasting product. This is the case for the umpire recording balls and strikes in a baseball game. There is no distinct, observable, and lasting product that the umpire can record at a later time. Therefore, the umpire keeps a count of strikes and balls as these pitching behaviors occur.

One limit on event recording is that it can only be used when the duration of each response is about the same each time the behavior occurs. A ball and a strike take about the same amount of time to throw. Similarly, each step counted by your fitness tracker has about the same duration. To understand why this limit on the use of event recording is important, let's measure studying. We will add a number to a counter each time a study session occurs. If these study sessions are about the same duration each time (1 hour), this will provide an accurate record of studying. However, if the duration of study sessions is highly variable (sometimes 2 hours and sometimes only 2 minutes) counting study sessions would tell us very little about how much studying has occurred. For example, 14 two-minute study sessions is less time spent studying than 1 two-hour study session. However, if we are only counting study-session events, we would conclude the opposite – 14 is more than 1. For this reason, event recording is used only when the duration of the target behavior is approximately the same each time it occurs.

CALCULATING IOA WHEN USING EVENT RECORDING

The same formula for calculating IOA is used with event recording. Table 2.2 shows data collected by a baseball umpire on the field and a "sky judge" umpire sitting above the field, behind home plate. The umpire and sky judge agree on the first five pitches but on the last

Table 2.2 Data collected by two observers' – an umpire and a sky judge – using the event-recording method.

Pitch	Umpire	Sky judge	Agreements	Disagreements
1	Strike	Strike	✓	
2	Ball	Ball	✓	
3	Ball	Ball	✓	
4	Strike	Strike	✓	
5	Ball	Ball	✓	
6	Ball	Strike		✓
		Total	5	1

* The "Agreements" column is checked when both observers agree that a strike was thrown, or they agree that a ball was thrown; otherwise the "Disagreements" column is checked.

one they disagree. The umpire called the pitch a ball, whereas the sky judge recorded it as a strike. The IOA between these observers is

$$IOA = \frac{5}{(5+1)} \times 100 = 83.3\%$$

Once again, this IOA is too low. If we were the pitcher or a fan of the baseball team that the pitcher plays for, we would be upset that the umpire behind the plate called a ball, sending the batter to first base, and possibly costing us the game.

A second method for calculating IOA with event recording is used when we need to evaluate if the two observers are counting the same instances of behavior. This is illustrated in Table 2.3. You and a friend counted the number of times Braden said "like" in a 5-minute direct-observation session. You both counted nine total "likes," but this overall agreement hides the fact that you rarely agreed about how many "likes" happened in any 1-minute interval. The two observers got the same count, but they did not record the same instances of behavior.

To more precisely evaluate agreements and disagreements, the right column of Table 2.3 illustrates how to calculate IOA in each of the 1-minute observation intervals. In the first interval, there were no agreements – your friend counted two "likes" but you counted none. Therefore, the IOA for that interval is 0%. In the second minute, you both agree that one "like" occurred, but on the second "like" that you recorded, the two of you disagree. Therefore, the IOA for that 1-minute interval is 50%. The average of the IOAs calculated across all intervals is 41.6%. Calculating IOA in this more exacting way reveals the observations were not as believable as they originally appeared. This minute-by-minute method of calculating IOA is preferred when it is possible that the total response count is hiding disagreements about when/if these behaviors are occurring (Repp et al., 1976).

Table 2.3 Event recording data collected by two observers – you and your friend.

Minute	You	Friend	1-minute IOA
1	0	2	0/(0 + 2) × 100 = 0%
2	2	1	1/(1 + 1) × 100 = 50%
3	4	1	1/(1 + 3) × 100 = 25%
4	1	3	1/(1 + 2) × 100 = 33%
5	2	2	2/(2 + 0) × 100 = 100%
Total "likes"	9	9	**Average IOA = 41.6%**

* Observers are counting the number of times Braden said "like" in each of five 1-minute intervals. The 1-minute IOA column shows the calculation of IOA for each 1-minute interval.

Interval Recording

WHEN TO USE INTERVAL RECORDING

As previously noted, if the duration of the target behavior varies meaningfully from one instance to the next, we cannot use event recording. Likewise, if that behavior produces no distinct, observable, and lasting product, then we cannot use outcome recording. When this happens, and our primary interest is in the frequency of behavior, we will use interval recording (see Figure 2.1).

There are two interval recording techniques. What they have in common is that the target behavior will be observed during back-to-back intervals of time. We will not record the number of times the behavior occurs during the interval; we will simply record whether or not the behavior occurs. The percentage of intervals containing the target behavior provides an estimate of frequency. For example, if the target behavior occurred in 95% of the intervals, we can confidently estimate that the behavior occurs frequently.

Partial-interval recording is *a direct-observation method used to estimate how frequently behavior occurs. Observers record whether or not the behavior occurs <u>during any portion</u> of each in a series of contiguous intervals.* To use partial-interval recording, behavior will be observed over several contiguous (i.e., back-to-back) time intervals. Each of these intervals will be brief and of a fixed duration (e.g., 20 seconds). If the behavior occurs *at any time* during the interval, the observer records this as a positive interval, that is, one in which the behavior occurred. If the behavior occurred three times, it is still scored simply as a positive interval. Remember, we are not counting the behavior, we are just recording whether or not it occurred. If the behavior happens *at no time* during the interval, that one is recorded as a negative interval. When the observations are completed, the frequency of behavior is estimated by the percentage of positive intervals.

For example, a restaurant manager, Emma, wants to see if her new server is checking in with his tables frequently enough. She sits at a table and pretends to be going over sales reports on her tablet. In reality, she is unobtrusively observing the new server's behavior. Emma's tablet prompts her once per minute to record whether or not the waiter checked with any of his tables at any time in the last minute. If he did, even if it was only for a second, she scores this as a positive interval. If the new waiter did not check on any

Source: ESB Professional/Shutterstock.com

of his tables during the entire minute, Emma scores this as a negative interval. At the end of the observation session, Emma sees that the new server checked in with his tables in 6 of the 10 observation intervals (60% of the time). Not bad.

Whole-interval recording is *a direct-observation method used to estimate how frequently behavior occurs. Observers record whether or not the behavior occurs <u>throughout</u> each in a series of contiguous intervals.* Whole-interval recording is the same as partial-interval recording, with one exception – to record a positive interval, the behavior has to occur throughout the entire interval.

Whole-interval recording is used when we want to measure target behaviors that are (or should be) long-lasting. For example, the host who works at the entrance of Emma's restaurant is supposed to remain up front throughout their shift. To see how frequently this is occurring, Emma can unobtrusively observe the host for back-to-back 1-minute intervals. If the host is within 10 feet of their host-stand throughout the entire 1-minute interval, then Emma scores this as a positive interval. If the host leaves that area, for even 1 second, that one is scored as a negative interval.

CALCULATING IOA WHEN USING PARTIAL- OR WHOLE-INTERVAL RECORDING

Table 2.4 shows Emma's record of the host's behavior in each 1-minute observation interval. It also shows the data collected by her assistant manager, Brett, who observed the same host, at the same time, but from a different location in the restaurant. Calculating IOA is straightforward:

$$IOA = \frac{9}{(9+1)} \times 100 = 90\%$$

Their high IOA means that their data are believable. The same technique is used when the data are collected using partial-interval recording.

Table 2.4 Whole-interval recording data collected by two observers, Emma and Brett.

Interval	Emma	Brett	Agreements	Disagreements
1	+	+	✓	
2	–	–	✓	
3	+	–		✓
4	–	–	✓	
5	+	+	✓	
6	+	+	✓	
7	–	–	✓	
8	–	–	✓	
9	+	+	✓	
10	+	+	✓	
	Total		9	1

* In each of the 1-minute intervals, the observers record a "+" if the host is at the front of the restaurant throughout the interval. If the host leaves their post any any time during the 1-minute interval, this is noted with a "–" "sign. "Agreements" and "Disagreements" are scored as before.

Duration Recording

When measuring either the latency or the duration of a target behavior, the behavior analyst is using the direct-observation technique known as **duration recording**. For example, suppose that we are interested in an athlete who is running the 100-meter dash. Duration recording could be used to measure the *latency* to leave the blocks after the starter's gun has fired. For this, we would need a computer to start the timer at the firing of the gun and to stop the timer when the sensors detect that both feet have left the blocks. In addition, we may be interested in the duration of the run; that is, the time it takes from the start of the race until the athlete crosses the finish line.

Source: sirtravelalot/Shutterstock.com

As a second example, Emma, our favorite restaurant manager, is interested in the time it takes her bartender to make drinks for the waitstaff. As before, Emma sits at a table and pretends to be going over sales reports on her tablet. She activates the stopwatch app on her tablet when a waiter's order appears on the bartender's display. To measure *latency*, she notes how long it took the bartender to begin working on the drink order. To measure *duration*, Emma will record how long it took the bartender to complete the order. Emma will start her stopwatch when the bartender begins working on the order and will stop the timer when the last drink in the order has been made.

WHEN TO USE DURATION RECORDING

As shown in Figure 2.1, duration recording is the appropriate choice when the behavioral dimension of interest is related to time – how long it takes to begin (latency) or to complete a behavior (duration).

CALCULATING IOA WHEN USING DURATION RECORDING

Table 2.5 shows Emma and Brett's independent recordings of how long it took the bartender to complete five drink orders. If you look at the first drink order, you can see that Emma's stopwatch said it took the bartender 2 minutes and 32 seconds (152 seconds) to complete the order. Brett's stopwatch provided a very similar reading, 150 seconds. For this drink order, IOA is calculated just as it was before: Emma and Brett agree that it took at least 150 seconds to complete the drink order, what they disagree on is the additional 2 seconds that Emma recorded but Brett did not. The *Duration IOA* column provides the IOA score for each drink order and the average of these IOA values is provided at the bottom of the column. With an average IOA of 98.4%, it is clear that Emma and Brett had excellent IOA on their duration recordings; their observations are believable.

Table 2.5 Duration-recording data collected by two observers, Emma and Brett.

Drink order	Emma	Brett	Duration IOA
1	152	150	$150/(150 + 2) \times 100 = 98.7\%$
2	94	97	$94/(94 + 3) \times 100 = 96.9\%$
3	320	315	$315/(315 + 5) \times 100 = 98.4\%$
4	35	35	$35/(35 + 0) \times 100 = 100\%$
5	113	111	$111/(111 + 2) \times 100 = 98.2\%$
			Average IOA = 98.4%

* For each of the drink orders completed by the bartender, Emma and Brett recorded how long it took for the order to be completed. The Duration IOA column shows the IOA calculation for each observation. The average of these IOAs is shown at the bottom of the table.

Reading Quiz 3

1. _____ occurs when people behave differently because they know they are being observed.
2. When the target behavior leaves behind a distinct, observable, and lasting product, then a cost-efficient way to measure behavior is to use _____ recording.
3. Two observers are independently recording Travis' behavior. Each time the observers observe Travis engage in the target behavior they increment a counter. The observers are using _____ recording to directly observe Travis' behavior.
4. The restaurant manager counted the number of salt shakers that Jamie filled 20 minutes ago, before she went home for the night. The manager is using _____ recording to directly observe Jamie's behavior.
5. Finn wants to record his exercising behavior. He could measure the duration of his exercising sessions, but he knows that sometimes his sessions are longer because he takes a lot of breaks and chats with the employees at the gym. Instead, he decides to simply count the number of times he lifts the weights (i.e., the number of "reps"). Finn has decided to use _____ recording.
6. When interested in the frequency of a behavior that leaves behind no distinct, observable, and lasting product, you will use _____ recording if the behavior takes about the same duration each time (like a weight-lifting rep), and either _____ -interval or _____-interval recording if the duration of the behavior varies from instance to instance.
7. If you are estimating how often behavior occurs by recording whether or not it occurs at any time in each of a series of contiguous intervals, then you are using _____- _____ recording.

Interval	Observer 1	Observer 2
1	+	+
2	+	+
3	–	–
4	+	–
5	–	–
6	–	–
7	+	+
8	+	+
9	+	+
10	–	+

8. For the partial-interval recording data shown in the table above, calculate IOA.
9. Imagine that the target behavior occurs three times during a 30-second observation interval. When using partial-interval recording, how will you record this?
   a. Record three instances of behavior.
   b. Indicate that behavior occurred during the interval.
   c. Indicate that behavior did not occur throughout the interval.
10. If the direct observers agree about 27 of their recorded behaviors, but disagree about 3 of them, what is their IOA?
11. When the direct observers objectively record how long it takes to complete the behavior, they are using _____ recording.

Summary

As noted in Chapter 1, behavior analysis has two goals – to accurately predict behavior and to identify functional variables that may be used to positively influence behavior. The first of these goals – prediction – can be accomplished by studying correlations alone. If sexual activity is positively correlated with income, then yes we can predict that, on average, wealthier people will have a bit more sex. However, because *correlation does not imply causation*, this positive correlation does not mean a causal relation exists between income and sex. To identify functional variables that can be integrated into an intervention or a therapy, we must conduct experiments. That is, putting a falsifiable hypothesis to the test by manipulating the independent variable and seeing if it reliably and systematically affects behavior.

Because behavior is the dependent variable in behavior-analytic experiments, robust methods for objectively measuring behavior are required to conduct valid experiments. While self-reports are widely used in the social and health sciences, behavior analysts recognize that self-reports are often inaccurate, either because we cannot recall past actions or because we are incentivized to stretch the truth ("I *always* wash my hands after going to the bathroom"). Direct observation of behavior is most often a better approach. To accomplish this, a behavioral definition is used to precisely specify what counts and what does not count as an instance of the target behavior. When two independent observers agree that the behavior has or has not occurred, IOA is high and the data collected are believable.

Which of the four direct-observation methods should be used to collect behavioral data depends on the dimension of behavior of interest (frequency, magnitude, latency, or duration). Figure 2.1 can help readers decide which direct-observation method is most appropriate. Precise, socially valid behavioral definitions and direct observations of target behavior are useful tools that help behavior analysts to conduct experiments. Chapter 3 will describe several different approaches to conducting and evaluating the results of those experiments.

Answers to Reading Quiz Questions

Reading Quiz 1

1. Variables
2. behavior
3. Correlation
4. independent variable
5. dependent; falsifiable; independent
6. behavior

Reading Quiz 2

1. self-report
2. truth; recall (remember)
3. direct observation
4. definition
5. social validity
6. interobserver
7. $IOA = \dfrac{Agreements}{\left(Agreements + Disagreements\right)} \times 100$
8. independent
9. 90%
10. accuracy; believability

Reading Quiz 3

1. Reactivity
2. outcome
3. event
4. outcome
5. event
6. event; partial (whole); whole (partial)
7. partial-interval
8. 80% agreement
9. b. indicate that behavior occurred during the interval
10. 90% agreement
11. duration

Note

1. Sometimes behavioral definitions are referred to as "operational definitions." They mean the same thing.

References

Archer, E., Hand, G. A., & Blair, S. N. (2013). Validity of U.S. nutritional surveillance: National healthy and nutrition examination survey caloric energy intake data, 1971–2010. *PLoS One*, *8*(10), e76632. doi: 10.1371/journal.pone.0076632

Baer, D. M., Wolf, M. M., & Risley, T. R. (1968). Some current dimensions of applied behavior analysis. *Journal of Applied Behavior Analysis*, *1*(1), 91–97. doi:10.1901/jaba.1968.1-91

Bailey, H. H., Attia, S., Love, R. R., Fass, T., Chappell, R., Tutsch, K., ... Stewart, J. A. (2008). Phase II trial of daily oral perillyl alcohol (NSC 641066) in treatment-refractory metastatic breast cancer. *Cancer Chemotherapy and Pharmacology*, *62*(1), 149–157. doi:10.1007/s00280-007-0585-6

Critchfield, T. S., & Reed, D. D. (2017). The fuzzy concept of applied behavior analysis research. *Behavior Analyst*, *40*(1), 123–159. doi:10.1007/s40614-017-0093-x

Drydakis, N. (2015). Sexual orientation discrimination in the United Kingdom's labour market: A field experiment, *Human Relations*, *68*(11), 1769–1796. doi:10.1177/0018726715569855

Ford, E. W., Boyer, B. T., Menachemi, N., & Huerta, T. R. (2014). Increasing hand washing compliance with a simple visual cue. *American Journal of Public Health*, *104*(10), 1851–1856. doi:10.2105/AJPH.2013.301477

Johnston, J. M., & Pennypacker, H. S. (2009). *Strategies and tactics of behavioral research* (3rd ed.). New York: Routledge. doi:10.4324/9780203837900

MacKillop, J., Murphy, J. G., Ray, L. A., Eisenberg, D. T. A., Lisman, S. A., Lum, J. K., & Wilson, D. S. (2008). Further validation of a cigarette purchase task for assessing the relative reinforcing efficacy of nicotine in college smokers. *Experimental and Clinical Psychopharmacology*, *16*(1), 57–65. doi:10.1037/1064-1297.16.1.57

Madden, G. J., Begotka, A. M., Raiff, B. R., & Kastern, L. L. (2003). Delay discounting of real and hypothetical rewards. *Experimental and Clinical Psychopharmacology*, *11*(2), 139–145. doi:10.1037/1064-1297.11.2.139

Normand, M. P. (2008). Science, skepticism, and applied behavior analysis. *Behavior Analysis in Practice*, *1*(2), 42–49. doi:10.1007/bf03391727

Paller, C. J., Denmeade, S. R., & Carducci, M. A. (2016). Challenges of conducting clinical trials of natural products to combat cancer. *Clinical Advances in Hematology & Oncology*, *14*(6), 447–455.

Repp, A. C., Deitz, D. E., Boles, S. M., Deitz, S. M., & Repp, C. F. (1976). Differences among common methods for calculating interobserver agreement. *Journal of Applied Behavior Analysis*, *9*(1), 109–113. doi:10.1901/JABA.1976.9-109

Shuval, K., Barlow, C. E., Finley, C. E., Gabriel, K. P., Schmidt, M. D., & DeFina, L. F. (2015). Standing, obesity, and metabolic syndrome: Findings from the cooper center longitudinal study. *Mayo Clinic Proceedings*, *90*(11), 1524–1532. doi:10.1016/J.MAYOCP.2015.07.022

Stanton, B. F., Clemens, J. D., Aziz, K. M., & Rahman, M. (1987). Twenty-four-hour recall, knowledge-attitude-practice questionnaires, and direct observations of sanitary practices: A comparative study. *Bulletin of the World Health Organization*, *65*(2), 217–222.

Experimental Designs in Behavior Analysis

3

Behavior analysis is an incredibly useful science. Its two goals align well with the goals of just about everyone. First, we all would find it useful to accurately predict behavior – our own behavior and that of others. For example, if we could predict with certainty that someone was going to solve the climate crisis, we would all sleep easier at night. Second, it would be even more useful to understand behavior so well that we could positively influence actions contributing to that solution. To accomplish this, we must identify functional variables that influence behavior and, as discussed in Chapter 2, the way to find these behavior-influencing variables is to conduct experiments.

Researchers conduct experiments by manipulating the independent variable. At its simplest, this means, turning the independent variable ON and OFF like a light switch and objectively measuring the effects of this on behavior. Recall that the independent variable is *a publicly observable change, controlled by the experimenter, which is anticipated to influence behavior in a specific way*. Said another way, the independent variable is the thing that the researcher believes will change behavior if it is manipulated. The experiment is a technique allowing the researcher to test this hypothesis. If behavior changes systematically each time the independent variable is turned ON and OFF, the hypothesis is supported; if not, the hypothesis is falsified.

When researchers conduct experiments by turning ON and OFF the independent variable, they are careful to change no other variable. The reason is simple – if a second variable was allowed to change at the same time the independent variable changes, then the researcher would not know whether behavior was positively influenced by the independent variable or the second (uncontrolled) variable. Because behavior analysts want to identify independent variables that influence behavior, they are careful to hold constant (i.e., to control) all other variables when they conduct experiments.

An Introduction to Behavior Analysis, First Edition. Gregory J. Madden, Derek D. Reed, and Florence D. DiGennaro Reed.
© 2021 John Wiley & Sons Ltd. Published 2021 by John Wiley & Sons Ltd.

When evaluating hypotheses about the functional relation between behavior and an independent variable, it is useful to think of the scientist's task as similar to that of a trial attorney who is deciding if the evidence is adequate to convince a jury beyond a reasonable doubt (Baron & Perone, 1998). The "jury" in behavioral science is composed of other scientists who will skeptically evaluate the researcher's claim that the independent variable changed behavior. Because this jury is hard to convince, the behavioral researcher must use experimental

Source: Corbis Corporation / SuperStock

methods that stand up to scrutiny. Chapter 2 discussed methods for objectively measuring behavior, and these are critical in convincing the jury of skeptical scientists.

This chapter focuses on experimental methods used by behavior analysts and other social scientists to reach conclusions about the ability of an independent variable to systematically and reliably influence behavior. When properly used, these experimental methods allow the researcher to rule out many of the common objections raised by the skeptical jury. For example, one juror might not find the scientist's evidence compelling because they are only correlational; "correlation does not imply causation," the juror correctly notes. This chapter discusses several experimental designs that can offer more than correlational evidence.

The experimental designs discussed in this chapter allow the researcher to make a convincing case that the only thing that could possibly explain why behavior changed is the manipulation of the independent variable. For those skeptical jurors who say "I don't believe it," it is often convincing to repeatedly turn ON and OFF the independent variable and show that the individual's behavior changes each time. If the researcher can replicate this systematic behavior change with more than one individual, this provides even more evidence that a functional independent variable has been identified. Such replications will address the "reasonable doubts" of the most skeptical of jurors. If these reasonable doubts are not addressed, the jury will dismiss the scientist's conclusions.

This chapter will discuss two approaches to conducting behavioral experiments – group designs and single-subject designs. While group designs are the norm in the social and behavioral sciences, they are less often used by behavior analysts. The reasons why are discussed later. Unlike group designs, single-subject designs keep the focus on the behavior of the individual (the single subject) and they are transparent about presenting all the data to the jury. Where group designs lump all the data together (i.e., individual data are rarely shown) and ask a computer to decide if behavior changed, single-subject designs transparently show what happened to the behavior of each individual. This allows the jury to decide if they find the behavior change compelling or not.

Next, the chapter provides an overview of four commonly used single-subject experimental designs. The strengths and weaknesses of each are discussed, as are some guidelines about when each design should be used. The chapter discusses how each design provides evidence for or against the independent variable as functional in changing behavior.

The final section of the chapter discusses how to decide if behavior has changed after the independent variable is manipulated. This decision can be difficult when the behavior change is not very large. We offer some guidance for making these decisions, but ultimately the jury decides. That is, if the researcher believes behavior changed but the jury of skeptical scientists disagrees, the jury wins. To convince the jury, the researcher will have to either identify a more effective way of manipulating this independent variable or will have to find a new independent variable that produces a larger behavior change. Either way, science advances if the researcher succeeds.

Group Experimental Designs

Most of the social and behavioral sciences (psychology, sociology, etc.) rely on group experimental designs. Behavior analysts sometimes use these designs, but they more often use single-subject experimental designs; these are discussed later in this chapter. Where single-subject designs focus on the behavior of the *individual*, group designs focus on the behavior of the *group*.

Like all experimental designs, group designs manipulate an independent variable (e.g., by turning it ON and OFF) and objectively measure if this influences behavior in a systematic way. For example, the handwashing study discussed in Chapter 2 (Ford et al., 2014) used a group experimental design. The effect of the independent variable (making the paper towel visible or not) was *not* evaluated by measuring if this increased handwashing by individual patrons. Instead, it was evaluated by comparing handwashing *between* large groups of patrons – those who used the bathroom during the towels-visible phase and those whose bathroom use occurred in the towels-not-visible phase.

Group experimental designs *evaluate if the behavior of a treatment group (independent variable ON) is statistically significantly different from that of a control group (independent variable OFF). If so, then the difference is attributed to the independent variable.* Group designs are frequently used by clinical behavior analysts. For example, Dallery et al. (2017) evaluated the efficacy of an online stop-smoking program by randomly assigning 94 ciga-

Source: Marc Bruxelle/Shutterstock.com

rette smokers to either a treatment group (stop-smoking program ON) or to a control group (program OFF). Cigarette smoking was measured using outcome recording – smokers blew into an internet-connected meter that could detect prior smoking. At the end of the intervention phase, the frequency of smoking in the treatment group was lower than that in the control group; 40% of the treatment group stopped smoking but only 13% of the control group quit. To evaluate if this between-groups difference was *statistically significant*, they conducted an inferential statistical test (one that is beyond the scope of this book). The difference (40% vs 13%) was statistically significant, so the difference was attributed to the independent variable; for this reason, they concluded that the intervention worked.

Group experimental designs are one of the tools in the behavior analyst's toolbox, but they have **four weaknesses** to consider. *First*, when the independent variable is a therapeutic intervention, no one wants to be assigned to the control group. Presumably all of the smokers in the Dallery et al. (2017) study wanted to quit, but only half of them were assigned to the treatment group. If given a choice, they would prefer to receive treatment to help them quit smoking. This weakness of group designs is not insurmountable. Many clinical researchers address this shortcoming by having one of the groups complete a no-intervention control phase first, before the intervention begins (e.g., Horner et al., 2009).

The *second weakness* of group experimental designs is that focusing on the behavior of the group means we are not studying the behavior of the individual. As noted in Chapter 1, behavior is defined as the activity of an *individual*, so understanding behavior requires a thorough consideration of the individual's biology, prior experiences, and current environment.

Other natural sciences also focus on the individual. For example, in high-school chemistry experiments, students mix a handful of chemicals and measure the outcome in the individual beaker. They do not decide if a chemical reaction occurred by measuring the average effect in all the beakers in the classroom. The science of chemistry has advanced enough to allow chemistry instructors to accurately predict and influence *individual* chemical reactions. The science of behavior aims to do the same.

Focusing on individual behavior allows applied behavior analysts to tailor their interventions to the unique needs of the individual and the environment in which their behavior occurs (Iwata et al., 1982). Sometimes, however, this is not practically possible, or desirable. In the Dallery et al. (2017) smoking-cessation experiment, for example, the purpose of the study was not to tailor the stop-smoking program to the needs of the individual. It was to evaluate the efficacy of a standardized online program that might prove to be a low-cost, mostly effective intervention that could be used nationwide. Such a program could save many lives. For this reason, behavior analysts keep group experimental designs in their toolbox of research techniques (Critchfield & Reed, 2017).

The *third weakness* of group designs is that the behavior of the treatment and control groups will differ simply because the people (or nonhuman animals) assigned to the two groups are different. This means the behavior of the two groups is different before the independent variable is ever manipulated. Having different subjects in the groups makes these designs "noisy," making it difficult to detect an effect of the independent variable.

The way that group designs overcome this noise is to randomly assign subjects to the experimental and control groups. The logic, based in probability theory, is that random assignment will equalize the two groups on variables that might affect behavior. Think of it like flipping a coin. From flip to flip there is a lot of noise (sometimes heads, sometimes tails), but the more you flip, the more the percentage of heads approximates 50%. Thus, to conduct a group design, researchers need large groups of subjects (lots of coin flips) to overcome all this between-groups noise. Behavior analysts, particularly those working in clinical settings, may not have access to large groups of individuals needing the same behavior-change intervention.

The *final weakness* of group experimental designs is their reliance on inferential statistics to evaluate if the independent variable changed behavior. The use (and misuse) of inferential statistics in the social and behavioral sciences have been controversial from the beginning. For example, some have speculated that reliance on inferential statistical analyses invites the kinds of errors, subjectivity, and unscrupulous practices that produced the replication crisis in psychology (Munafò et al., 2017); that is, the current situation in which more than half of the experiments published in prestigious psychology journals cannot be replicated (Open Science Collaboration, 2015).

Single-Subject Experimental Designs

The alternative to group designs is the single-subject experimental design. **Single-subject experimental designs** *expose individuals to baseline (independent variable OFF) and experimental (independent variable ON) phases to determine if the independent variable systematically and reliably changes behavior.* Single-subject designs provide behavior analysts with a tool for conducting experiments with *individuals*. That is, when we want to see if an independent variable (a treatment) can positively influence the behavior of an individual, single-subject experimental designs make this possible (Hayes et al., 1999; Sidman, 1960).

To see the utility of single-subject designs, imagine you are a behavior analyst who works with children diagnosed with autism. In your experience, a few of these children behave aggressively and their parents, wracked with worries, don't know what to do. On Tuesday, you get a call from one of these parents. Her son, Josh, engages in aggressive behavior many times a day. Most of his aggression is directed toward others (slapping, yelling, cursing) and sometimes he hits himself. You, as the clinician, will want to positively influence Josh's behavior by decreasing these aggressive acts, but you will also want to know if your intervention is responsible for the improvement. If it is, then you will know that the fee you are charging is justified and, more importantly, you will use the same treatment the next time you face a similar challenge. If it works a second time (i.e., the treatment effect is *replicated* in a new individual), then your confidence in the utility of that intervention will be increased.

If you, as the clinician, only had group experimental designs in your toolkit, then you would not be able to evaluate if your intervention was responsible for Josh's behavior change. To conduct a group experimental design, you need many more participants than Josh. Note also two important disconnects between the goals of Josh's parents – they want to see a large reduction in Josh's aggressive behavior – and what group experimental designs might deliver. First, Josh might be randomly assigned to a no-treatment control group. Clearly, Josh's parents would not be pleased with this; they might even argue that refusing to provide treatment is unethical. Second, group designs are focused on the behavior of a group, not individuals like Josh. His parents will not be pleased if, on average, children receiving the intervention decrease their aggressive behavior but Josh's behavior does not improve. Applied behavior analysts use single-subject experimental designs to tailor the intervention to the unique needs of the patient and to evaluate the efficacy of these interventions.

Internal Validity of Single-Subject Experimental Designs

Successful behavioral experiments allow us (and a jury of skeptical scientists) to evaluate if there is a functional relation between the independent variable and behavior. When the independent variable is a therapeutic intervention, an experiment that improves behavior will allow us to conclude that the intervention (and not something else) positively influenced behavior. In sum, *when an experiment provides clear evidence that a functional relation exists between the independent variable and behavior change, that experiment has* **internal validity**. If an experiment has poor internal validity, it will leave open the possibility that something other than the independent variable is responsible for the behavior change. Experiments that lack internal validity are not convincing to the jury.

An example will help to make this point. If we find that Josh reliably engages in aggressive behavior during the baseline phase (independent variable OFF) and this rate drops to zero after the intervention is introduced (independent variable ON), then Josh's parents will be pleased with the outcome and will thank us for our services. But does our experiment provide clear evidence that the intervention (and not something else) is responsible for the behavior change? Does our experiment have internal validity? No. Several other explanations of the behavior change are possible. Perhaps Josh hurt himself during an aggressive episode at the end of the baseline phase, and he has not behaved aggressively ever since. Perhaps Josh noticed that a new person (the behavior analyst) was in the house during the intervention phase and this distracted him from behaving aggressively. If so, this potentially distracting stimulus is *confounded with* the intervention; that is, it occurred at the same time as the intervention and it could explain why behavior changed. **Confounds** are *variables that influence behavior within an experiment, but are not controlled by the researcher.*

Variables confounded with the independent variable may be responsible for a behavior change that would otherwise be attributed to the independent variable. When confounds cannot be ruled out, the experiment has low internal validity. In an ideal experiment, nothing other than the independent variable could possibly explain the behavior change. When this is true, the experiment has high internal validity. Single-subject experimental designs can help rule out confounds. This will become apparent as we consider four commonly used single-subject experimental designs.

Four Types of Single-Subject Experimental Designs

Single-subject experimental designs evaluate if turning ON and OFF an independent variable produces a reliable and systematic change in the behavior of individuals. If it does and confounds can be ruled out, that independent variable is identified as a functional variable for this individual's behavior. When conducting applied research, the independent variable is an intervention or a treatment designed to positively influence behavior.

COMPARISON (A-B) DESIGN

The simplest single-subject design is the **comparison design**. It *arranges a baseline (A) phase (independent variable OFF) and an experimental (B) phase (independent variable ON).* This simple OFF/ON design is sometimes referred to as an A-B design.

Figure 3.1 shows an example of hypothetical data collected in a comparison design. The prevalence of Josh's aggressive behavior is shown in baseline and experimental phases. The behavior analyst used partial-interval recording with 1-minute observation intervals to measure aggressive behavior during the direct-observation sessions. During the baseline phase, behavior was observed and recorded, but beyond appropriate safety measures, no effort was made to influence Josh's aggressive outbursts. During the experimental phase, the intervention was implemented and behavior was recorded exactly as before. By comparing the prevalence of aggressive acts between phases, we can see if Josh's behavior improved during the experimental phase.

Experiments using a comparison design (and the other single-subject designs) typically start with a baseline phase. The purpose of this phase is to allow for accurate predictions of

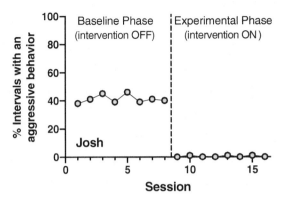

Figure 3.1 A graph showing data collected in a comparison (A-B) design. Behavior in each session is shown in the baseline phase (left of the dashed line) and then the experimental phase (B).

behavior if the independent variable is never turned ON. We feel more confident in making predictions about future behavior when we have observed the behavior for several sessions and it has stabilized across the last several sessions, as it has in Josh's baseline. Behavior is **stable** when, *over repeated observations, there is little "bounce" and no systematic trend* (Perone & Hursh, 2013).

Figure 3.2 explores what is meant by "bounce" and "trend." The top panel shows baseline data containing a lot of "bounce," that is, a lot of variability in behavior from one session to the next. Because of this variability, it is impossible to predict what will happen in the next session. The middle and bottom panels show systematic decreasing and increasing *trends*, respectively. In the absence of an intervention, we would predict these trends would continue in subsequent sessions. In none of these graphs is behavior stable.

Returning to Josh's behavior in Figure 3.1, his prevalence of aggressive behaviors is stable over the last several baseline sessions. There is very little bounce and no upward or downward trend over these sessions. This allows some degree of confidence in predicting that, if nothing changes, he will continue to behave aggressively about 40% of the time. This prediction makes the large reduction in aggression, observed in the experimental phase, surprising.

When behavior improves in this dramatic fashion, Josh's parents and the therapist will be tempted to conclude that the intervention worked. That is, that a functional relation exists between the independent variable and aggressive behavior. As previously discussed, we cannot reach this conclusion based on these data alone. The behavior change is *correlated* with the onset of the intervention, but we cannot say with certainty that the intervention is responsible for this change. Something else happening outside the researcher's control (i.e., a confound) could be responsible for the reduction in aggression. Comparison designs cannot rule out confounds and, therefore, the jury of skeptical scientists can raise reasonable doubts if we argue otherwise. For this reason, the comparison design is often referred to as a *quasi-experimental design*; "quasi" because a well-designed experiment will rule out confounds.

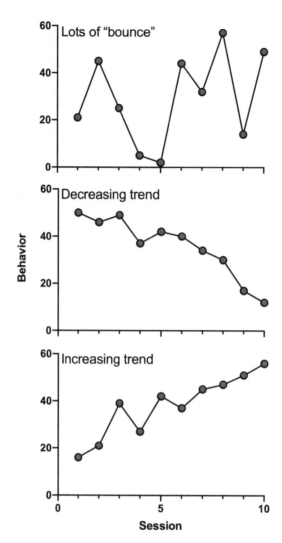

Figure 3.2 Three graphs showing unstable behavior. In the top graph, behavior is highly variable from one session to the next. The middle and bottom panels show systematic trends over time.

REVERSAL (A-B-A) DESIGN

Reversal designs are better equipped to rule out confounds. In a **reversal design** *the individual's behavior is evaluated in repeatedly alternating baseline (A) and experimental (B) phases.* This design is also known as an "A-B-A design."

In the case of Josh, the comparison (A-B) design provided some evidence that the intervention reduced aggressive behavior, but a confound (whether explicitly identified or not) could be responsible for the change. To address this low internal validity, a reversal design adds a third phase in which the independent variable is turned OFF.[1] Turning the independent variable OFF means turning off the intervention and returning to the baseline phase, converting the A-B design to an A-B-A reversal design. If the intervention is responsible for the decreased aggression, then removing it should increase aggressive behavior.

That is what happens in Figure 3.3. This reversal of the therapeutic effect supports the hypothesis that the intervention is responsible for the reduction in aggression during the experimental phase. If this drop was due to a confounded variable, then that confound would have to be turned OFF at the exact same time the independent variable was withdrawn (in the final baseline phase). Although this possibility cannot be ruled out, the return of aggressive behavior in the final phase strengthens the case that a functional relation exists between the intervention and behavior change.

A member of the jury (i.e., the group of skeptical scientists who will evaluate our data) could legitimately look at the data in Figure 3.3 and still not be convinced beyond a reasonable doubt. The lingering doubt is that a confounded variable is *perfectly correlated* with the independent variable. For example, imagine that the intervention was always implemented by a therapist that Josh adores and wants to spend time with. This preferred therapist was not present during the baseline phases, but was present during the intervention (experimental) phase. Perhaps, our skeptical juror argues, it was the therapist and not the intervention that was responsible for the decrease in aggression.

To evaluate the functional role of this confounded variable, we could arrange for the therapist to be in the room during the next several baseline sessions. If the presence of the therapist alone proves to be enough to reduce Josh's aggression, then we must conclude that the intervention was ineffective. However, if the mere presence of the therapist during these sessions has no effect on Josh's aggression, then our skeptical juror may finally be convinced.

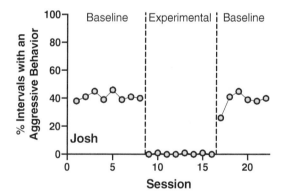

Figure 3.3 An example of data collected in a reversal (A-B-A) design, with problem behavior plotted across sessions in each phase.

ALTERNATING-TREATMENTS DESIGN

The third single-subject experimental design, the **alternating-treatments design**, is a variation on the reversal design. In this design, *the independent variable(s) is turned ON and OFF rapidly to evaluate if this systematically and repeatedly changes behavior* (Sidman, 1960).[2] Behavior analysts use the alternating-treatments design to evaluate functional relations between behavior and one or more independent variables. Because each "phase" is very brief, typically one session, the effects of turning ON and OFF the independent variable (or treatment) must occur quickly. If the treatment is expected to take some time before it is effective, then a reversal design should be used instead.

As an example of an alternating-treatments design, let us assume that Josh's parents and his therapist wish to identify which of three treatments is most effective in reducing Josh's aggression. The details of these fictional treatments are irrelevant for present purposes, so we will refer to them simply as Treatment 1, Treatment 2, and Treatment 3. All three treatments, if they work, are expected to rapidly reduce aggression, and removing the treatments is expected to quickly return aggression to the baseline level. The therapist arranges brief sessions, with a different treatment scheduled for each one. For greater objectivity, the treatment (or no-treatment) arranged in each session will be randomly selected.

The left panel of Figure 3.4 shows the prevalence of Josh's aggressive actions during each of the sessions. Note the different symbols and how they correspond to baseline and the different treatments used in that session. The right panel shows the averages of these data. Where the left panel makes it possible to evaluate trends in the data, the right panel facilitates the detection of changes in level, that is, the prevalence of aggressive behavior in each condition.

A quick glance at the data in Figure 3.4 reveals that aggressive actions occur most frequently in baseline sessions. In the absence of treatment, Josh consistently behaves aggressively; there is no increasing or decreasing trend over time. Next, we can see that Treatment 1 has no clear beneficial effect on Josh's behavior. By contrast, Treatment 2 quickly reduces the prevalence of aggression and Treatment 3 almost eliminates it.

The alternating-treatments design establishes internal validity by repeatedly turning ON and OFF the independent variable and evaluating if this systematically and repeatedly

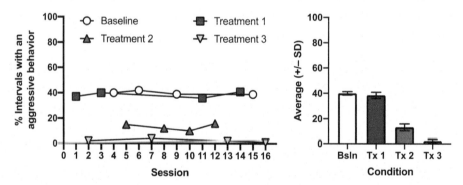

Figure 3.4 An example of hypothetical data collected in an alternating-treatments design. In the left panel, the percentage of intervals with aggressive behavior is shown for each session. Different symbols correspond to the baseline or different treatments arranged in these sessions; these are identified in the figure. The panel to the right shows the average prevalence of aggressive behavior in baseline and each treatment condition. The "error bars" extending above and below the averages correspond to the standard deviation, a measure of "bounce." Standard deviation is the average difference between each data point and the average of all data points in a condition.

changes behavior. When we turn ON Treatment 3, aggressive behavior systematically decreases below baseline levels *and* this effect is replicable – it happens every time Treatment 3 is turned on. As was true of the reversal design, it is possible that a confounded variable is perfectly correlated with the independent variable. If so, this could account for the reduction in Josh's aggression. If no such confound exists, then the stakeholders can select Treatment 3 as the most effective treatment for Josh.

MULTIPLE-BASELINE DESIGNS

Reversal and alternating-treatments designs establish internal validity by (a) showing that behavior is systematically and repeatedly changed when the independent variable is turned ON and OFF, and (b) ruling out confounds that are perfectly correlated with the independent variable. The ON/OFF reversal strategy is impossible to use, however, if the independent variable produces a lasting effect that cannot be reversed when the intervention is turned OFF. For example, if the independent variable is a lesson that teaches an infant the baby sign-language word for "more," the child will acquire this skill and use it often (Hart & Banda, 2010; Thompson et al., 2007). Discontinuing the sign-language lessons (independent variable OFF) will not reduce the use of this word, as long as it keeps producing more tickles, more food, and more hugs. Because this independent variable is anticipated to produce an *irreversible effect* on sign-language use, the behavior analyst cannot evaluate the functional role of the lessons with a reversal or alternating-treatments design.

Source: JGI/Tom Grill/Tetra images/Getty Images

A similar situation arises when it would be unethical to turn OFF the independent variable. For example, if Josh's aggressive behaviors were dangerous to himself or others, then removing the intervention (to find out if it is functionally related to aggressive behaviors) would be unethical. This situation frequently arises when working in therapeutic settings.

If an independent variable is anticipated to produce an *irreversible effect*, or it would be *unethical* to turn OFF the independent variable, then behavior analysts will use a different single-subject experimental design: the multiple-baseline design (Baer et al., 1968). Because behavior analytic interventions often produce irreversible effects and because it is sometimes unethical to discontinue behavior-analytic interventions, the multiple-baseline design is one of the most frequently used single-subject designs (Smith, 2012).

The **multiple-baseline design** *evaluates the functional relation between an independent variable and behavior by conducting a series of time-staggered A-B comparisons either across behaviors, across situations, or across individuals.* Some examples will help to clarify this definition.

The left side of Figure 3.5 shows hypothetical data collected in a multiple-baseline across-behaviors design. The top-left panel shows that signing "more" never occurred during a

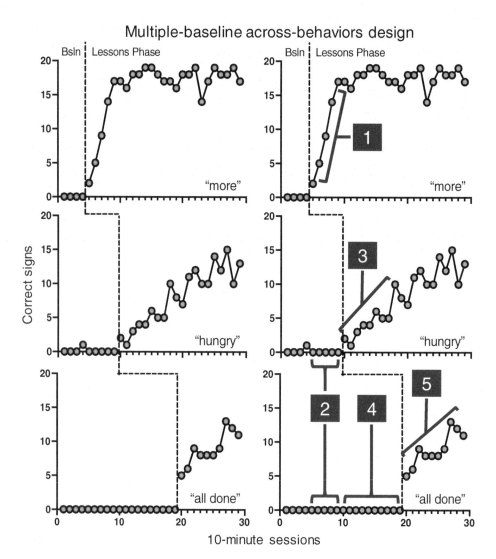

Figure 3.5 The left column of graphs provides an example of data collected in a multiple-baseline across-behaviors design. Each panel shows an A-B comparison, where the introduction of the independent variable (sign-language lessons) is time-staggered. The right column of graphs shows the same data, noting five pieces of evidence that the lessons are responsible for the increase in the frequency of signing.

four-session baseline phase. However, during the phase in which lessons taught the baby to sign "more," the frequency of this behavior increased. Box 1 in the upper-right panel of Figure 3.5 highlights this increase during the first five sessions of the lessons phase. This increase provides one piece of evidence that the lessons are effective. However, this evidence comes from an A-B comparison and, as previously discussed, comparison designs cannot rule out a host of variables that might be confounded with the signing lessons and, importantly, may be responsible for the increase in signing "more."

For example, perhaps the baby learned to imitate the signing behaviors of other babies at the infant-care center and did not learn to sign "more" during our lessons held in the home. If this is the case, then we might expect the baby to begin simultaneously signing other words like "hungry" and "all done." However, as shown in Box 2 (lower-right panel of Figure 3.5), the frequency of signing these other words does not simultaneously increase; the effect is specific to signing "more." This provides a second piece of evidence that the independent variable (lessons) increased signing "more" and not a confounded variable, which should increase signing other words like "hungry" and "all done" as well.

A third piece of evidence supporting the functional role of the independent variable (Box 3) is that the frequency of signing "hungry" increased only after lessons targeted this behavior for training. No confound could easily account for this time-staggered effect. The fourth piece of supporting evidence (Box 4) is that signing "all done" does not increase at the same time the infant is learning to sign "hungry"; the effect of the independent variable is, once again, specific to the behaviors targeted for change. Finally, when the effect of the lessons is replicated a third time (Box 5), the skeptical jury of scientists should be convinced that the lessons are effective in teaching babies to use sign language.

The multiple-baseline design arranges time-staggered introductions of the independent variable. If this produces a systematic and replicable effect, and that effect is specific to the behavior targeted for change, then the evidence is judged convincing, beyond a reasonable doubt, that manipulating the independent variable changed behavior. In Figure 3.5, these replications were conducted across three different behaviors, that is, the signing of three words. When the *time-staggered A-B replications are conducted across behaviors*, the design is called a **multiple-baseline across-behaviors design**.

Figure 3.6 illustrates a different approach – the multiple-baseline across-situations design. This time we evaluate if the effect of the fictional lessons can be replicated across three different situations – when signing "more" produces more food, more access to toys, or more tickles. In evaluating if the lessons or a confounded variable can better account for the increase in signing, we look to the same five pieces of evidence.

First, signing for "more" food increased above the baseline level when lessons began (Box 1). Second, at the same time, signing "more" did not increase in the toys and tickles situations (Box 2). If a confound is responsible for the increase in signing, we might expect it to have affected behavior in more than just the food situation; this did not happen. Lessons, when conducted in the toys situation (Box 3), were effective. Box 4 shows that this effect was specific to the toys situation; signing "more" for tickles did not increase during these sessions. Finally, Box 5 shows a third replication of the effect of lessons. These five pieces of evidence support the efficacy of the lessons and help to argue against a confound. When the *time-staggered A-B replications are demonstrated across situations*, the design is called a **multiple-baseline across-situations design**.

The third multiple-baseline design is the **multiple-baseline across-participants** design. Figure 3.7 provides an example of this design; this time turning ON the independent variable in a time-staggered fashion across three different babies. The same five pieces of evidence are used to evaluate reasonable doubts about the efficacy of the inde-

Multiple-baseline across-situations design

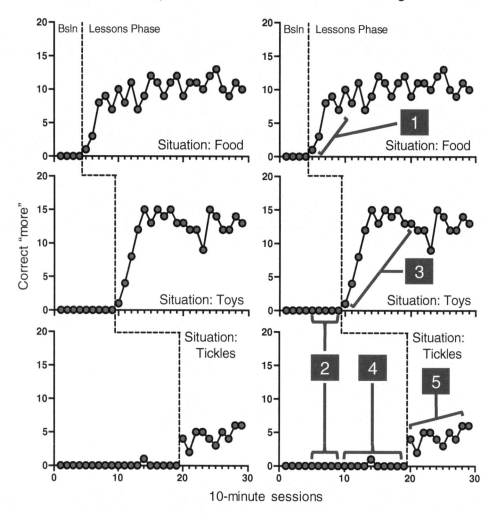

Figure 3.6 An example of data collected in a multiple-baseline across-situations design. Here the independent variable is applied to the same behavior, signing "more," but the introductions of the lessons are time-staggered across three different situations: asking for more food, more toys, and then more tickles. The right panel notes five comparisons used to evaluate (beyond a reasonable doubt) that the independent variable (and not a confound) is responsible for this behavior change.

pendent variable. As before, systematic and replicable effects observed across the time-staggered introductions of the independent variable provide compelling evidence that a confound is not responsible for increased signing. When the *time-staggered A-B replications are demonstrated across participants*, the design is called a **multiple-baseline across-participants design**.

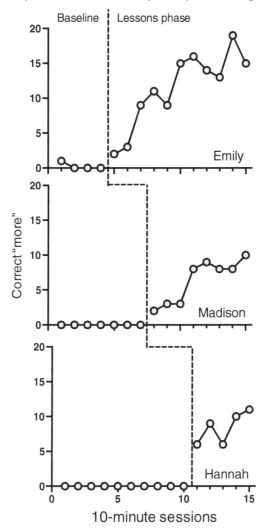

Figure 3.7 An example of data collected in a multiple-baseline across-participants design.

Defining Features of Single-Subject Designs

Table 3.1 shows four defining features of single-subject experimental designs. First, as the name implies, the focus is on the behavior of the individual – the single subject. Second, every individual receives the intervention. These first two features make single-subject designs particularly useful for clinical behavior analysts who work with one patient at a time. Third, behavior is repeatedly measured in each phase until we can confidently predict what will happen if nothing changes. Although the alternating-treatments design arranges brief exposures to each of the independent variables, enough sessions are conducted until we can confidently predict what will happen the next time we turn ON and OFF the independent variable(s).

Table 3.1   Four defining features of single-subject experimental designs.

1. The focus is on the behavior of individuals, not groups.
2. Each subject experiences the baseline and experimental (intervention) phases.
3. Behavior is measured repeatedly in each phase until confident predictions about behavior may be made.
4. Internal validity is assessed through replication and evaluating the functional role of confounded variables.

Finally, single-subject experimental designs evaluate internal validity by investigating if the independent variable produces systematic and replicable effects on behavior. Because psychologists are increasingly concerned about the replicability of their research findings, there are merits in using one of the single-subject research designs that establishes internal validity through replication.

Three Kinds of Replication

This chapter has discussed the importance of replication in behavior analysis and the social/behavioral sciences. Replication builds confidence that an independent variable can reliably influence behavior. Without scientific replication, there can be no technology. If the laws of physics, for example, were not highly replicable, technologies such as building construction, aerospace engineering, and quantum computing could not exist. Analogously, highly replicable principles of behavior allow behavior analysts to positively influence behavior. The remaining chapters of this textbook discuss these replicable principles of behavior.

For now, however, it is important to point out the **three kinds of replications built into single-subject experimental designs**. The first of these replications is *within-individual replication*. In each of the four single-subject designs, the behavior of the individual is repeatedly observed after the independent variable is turned ON. If behavior is changed by that intervention, each new session conducted within the intervention phase is a test for replication – will behavior remain changed or will it revert to the pre-intervention baseline level? Many independent variables produce temporary effects on behavior, so it is important to evaluate if the intervention effect can be sustained. Single-subject experiments allow us to evaluate this within-individual replication.

The second kind of replication is *across-individual replication*. Here we will evaluate if the effects of an independent variable can systematically and reliably influence the behavior of more than one individual. When an intervention effect proves to have good within-individual replication, we will want to see if it can benefit others as well. An intervention with a 10% across-individual replication rate (i.e., the behavior of only 1 individual out of 10 is changed) is not nearly as impressive as one that benefits 90% of those receiving it. Replication *across individuals* is a necessity for a technology of behavior change.

The final important category of replication is *replication across labs or clinics*. If the behavior analysts at university A have demonstrated that an independent variable produces *within-* and *across-individual* behavior change but researchers at universities B, C, and D cannot replicate the effect, then there is a cause for concern. Perhaps the behavior changes demonstrated at university A are due to an unrecognized confound rather than the independent variable.

Effective interventions are built from independent variable manipulations that have proven replicable within individuals, across individuals, and across labs/clinics. This is a bottom-up approach to scientific discovery. Start small, by studying the effects of an independent variable on individual behavior. Success leads to an evaluation of replication across individuals, and success there leads to an evaluation of replication across labs/clinics. Stacking one replication upon another builds a firm foundation for a technology of behavior.

Reading Quiz 1

1. In _____ experimental designs, not the individual.
2. In group experimental designs, inferential ___ behavior changed when the independent varia
3. In a _____-_____ experim of the individual, not the group.
4. When an experiment demonstrates that beh variable was turned ON and OFF, that ex _____.
5. If another variable changed when the indepen variable could explain why behavior change _____.
6. Good experiments are those that can rule out _____ _____.
7. When confounds cannot be ruled out, the experiment has _____ internal validity.
8. In the _____ design, behavior is compared between a baseline and a single intervention phase.
9. Comparison designs are often referred to as *quasi-experimental designs* because they do not rule out _____ by repeatedly demonstrating that the independent variable has a systematic effect on behavior.
10. In the graph to the right, there is a systematic increasing _____ in behavior during the baseline phase.
11. In the same graph, if the independent variable is not manipulated, our best prediction is that this _____ trend will continue into the intervention phase.

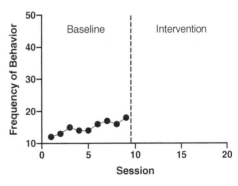

12. In a single-subject experimental design, it is always true that every individual will experience the _____ and experimental (intervention) phases.
13. In a single-subject experimental design, internal validity is assessed through _____. For example, if the independent variable systematically influences behavior every time it is turned ON and OFF, then the experiment has high internal validity.
14. The _____-_____ design is used either when it would be unethical to turn OFF the independent variable or when the independent variable is anticipated to produce a lasting (irreversible) effect.

Handwritten answer key:

1. group
2. statistics
3. single-subject
4. internal validity
5. confound
6. internal validity
7. low
8. comparison or A-B
9. confounds
10. trend
11. increasing
12. baseline
13. replication
14. multiple-baseline
15. reversal; alternating-treatments
16. multiple-baseline

15. Two of the single-subject experimental designs establish internal validity by turning ON and then OFF the independent variable. The first of these is the _____ design. The other is the _____-_____ design.

16. In a _____-_____ design, the effects of the independent variable may be replicated across behaviors, across situations, or across individuals.

Did Behavior Change?

Experiments are conducted to evaluate if an independent variable influences behavior. The evidence for this is (1) a systematic and replicable change in behavior each time the independent variable is turned ON or OFF and (2) no confounded variable can explain this change. Thus far we have provided examples of behavior change that are very clear – changing the independent variable always produced big changes in behavior. In the real world, the data don't always look like that. Therefore, the behavior analyst will need to use some judgment in evaluating whether behavior changed after the independent variable was turned ON. This, of course, has the potential to introduce subjectivity, prejudice, and bias into the scientific process. Not good.

A seemingly appropriate way to avoid subjectivity is to use a set of objective decision-rules when answering the question, *did behavior change?* In most of the social and behavioral sciences, *inferential statistics* are used to answer this question; these were briefly discussed in the section on group experimental designs. In the abstract, the use of inferential statistics plays out like this: scientist conducts experiment, scientist enters data into computer, computer uses inferential statistics to decide whether or not behavior changed, scientist reports the results, and scientific community (the jury) is satisfied with this objectivity. In practice the process is much more subjective.

The subjectivity and errors in how social scientists use and interpret the results of inferential statistics have been well documented (Branch, 1999; Rosenthal, 1979; Tversky & Kahneman, 1971; Young, 2019) and have undoubtedly played a role in psychology's replication crisis (Colling & Szűcs, 2018; Open Science Collaboration, 2015). One approach to addressing this crisis is greater transparency (Peng, 2015), to prevent scientists from using "objective decision-rules" in a way that gives them the result they want (e.g., their intervention changed behavior). One form of transparency asks researchers to publish in advance exactly how they will conduct the experiment and how they will analyze their data. By publishing the plan for all to see, researchers commit themselves to the plan and this precludes changing the plan later, when doing so would produce a more favorable outcome. Such transparency can reduce subjectivity and inadvertent bias from affecting the conclusions reached.

A different approach, the *visual analysis of behavior*, has a long history in behavior analysis (Skinner, 1938) and the psychological sciences (Ebbinghaus, 1885; Pavlov, 1927). As the name suggests, **visual analysis** *involves looking at a graph of time-series single-subject behavior to evaluate if a convincing change occurred when the independent variable was introduced/removed.* This approach is far from perfect, but it has two key advantages over the use of inferential statistics. First, it requires that the behavior analyst develop methods for producing large changes in behavior, that is, changes that are apparent to the naked eye (Perone, 1999). This goal – to produce big changes in behavior – is consistent with the goals of those who seek the services of applied behavior analysts. They don't want a statistical test to tell them their lives are improved; they want to be able to see it themselves, with the naked eye.

A second advantage of visual analysis is that it recognizes the inherent subjectivity of the scientific enterprise; it does not attempt to hide this behind a set of "objective decision-rules" that, in reality, are used by humans who are prone to errors, biases, and prejudices. Visual analysis recognizes that it is humans who are analyzing data (not computers) and attempts to reduce biases by putting the behavior analyst's reputation on the line (Perone, 1999). For example, if a behavior analyst claims that their intervention is improving behavior but the evidence for this is weak, then the jury of skeptical scientists will not only disagree, they will downgrade the reputation of the behavior analyst who makes this claim. Conversely, if the behavior analyst claims efficacy only when the intervention has clearly made a difference, then they will develop a reputation as a careful scientist, someone who can be trusted. Science has always been a subjective, social enterprise; visual analysis embraces this by holding the scientist responsible for their subjectivity. In so doing, they encourage scientists to produce large intervention effects and to carefully evaluate their own data.

Two Patterns of Behavior Change

The central question to answer when conducting a visual analysis is, *did behavior change when the independent variable changed*? There are two ways in which behavior can change from a no-intervention baseline: it can change in *trend* and *level*. **Trend** refers to *a systematic change in behavior over time*. **Level** refers to *the prevalence of the behavior during the stable portion of a phase/condition*.

The left panels in Figure 3.8 illustrate changes in trend, while the right panels show changes in level. In panel A we have drawn a "trend arrow" through the baseline data. The trend arrow is drawn with the aid of a *least-squares linear regression*, which software such as Microsoft Excel can conduct for you (if you are interested). The trend arrow predicts what will happen to behavior, in the immediate future, if nothing is changed. This prediction is provided by extending the arrow to the right, beyond baseline, into future sessions. If, during the intervention phase, in which the independent variable is turned ON, the trend in behavior clearly changes, as it does in panel A, this suggests that a functional relation between behavior and the independent variable *might* exist.[3] In panel B, the trend arrow reveals a clear downward trend during baseline; one that reverses during the intervention phase. In panel C, the trend arrow reveals no upward or downward trend during the baseline phase (behavior is stable), but this changes after the intervention begins.

In panel D of Figure 3.8, the level of behavior (shown by the green lines) changed quickly after the independent variable was introduced. In panels E and F, there was a more gradual change in level, which stabilized in the final five or six sessions. Notice how the green lines are drawn only through the stable sessions, rather than through all of the data. The stable data best reflect the magnitude of the level change and they represent a prediction about the level of behavior anticipated if additional sessions are conducted in the intervention phase. If the researcher, or the jury of skeptical scientists, is not convinced that the new level is predictive of future behavior, there is nothing preventing us from scheduling additional sessions until either we are all convinced or we realize that behavior was not stable after all.

What Makes a Change Convincing?

Changes in trend and level are convincing when the change is big relative to the amount of bounce in the data. When the change is small, relative to the bounce, the change is not convincing. This is illustrated in Figure 3.9. In panels A and B, the changes in trend and level are large

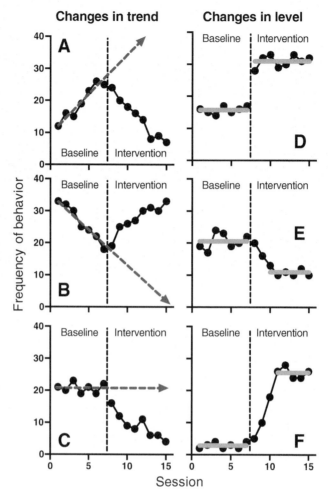

Figure 3.8 The left column of graphs (A-C) illustrates changes in trend following the introduction of the intervention (independent variable ON). The red "trend arrows" are drawn through the baseline data and extended into the intervention phase. This extension of the trend arrow illustrates our best prediction of what will happen to behavior in the immediate future if the intervention had never begun. The right column of graphs (D-E) illustrates changes in level of behavior across the baseline and intervention phases. The green horizontal lines show these levels; they are based on the averages of the stable data.

relative to the small amount of bounce in the data. Minimal bounce makes obvious the changes in trend and level. These changes will be convincing to the jury of skeptical scientists.

The bottom panels of Figure 3.9 show data that have considerably more bounce from session to session. When we asked Microsoft Excel to draw trend arrows through the baseline and intervention data in panel C, the placements of those arrows were exactly the same as the ones in panel A. Although the changes in trend are the same, the change in panel C is less convincing because of all the bounce. The same is true of the level change in panel D. Although the size of the level change is the same as in panel B, it is less convincing because of all the bounce.

Because changes in trend and level are less convincing when the data are bouncy, behavior analysts will take steps to minimize session-to-session variability. Anything that changes

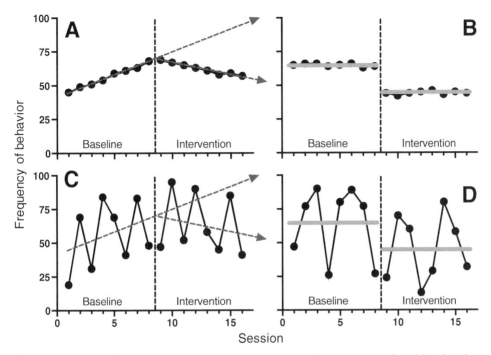

Figure 3.9 Examples of convincing and unconvincing changes in trend and level. What makes the changes in panels A and B convincing is that the changes are large *relative to* the bounce. The trends and levels in panels C and D are exactly the same as in the panels above but they are unconvincing because of all the bounce in the data. The size of the trend or level change alone does not determine whether or not the change is convincing. It is the size of the change *relative to* the bounce.

between sessions can increase bounce in the behavioral data. To minimize bounce, the behavior analyst will look for opportunities to minimize between-session changes. This might mean scheduling the session at the same time every day. It might mean ensuring that the participant has gotten a good night's sleep before every session. It might mean preventing changes in the physical environment, such as changing rooms, people, or potential distractions between sessions. Such bounce-minimizing steps will help to detect a behavior change after the independent variable is turned ON.

Guidelines for Conducting the Visual Analysis

Now that we have identified two ways in which behavior can change – in trend and level – and have discussed what makes a change convincing (the change is large *relative to* the bounce), we can practice conducting visual analyses. Remember, not only do *we* need to find the change convincing, the jury of skeptical scientists needs to find it convincing as well. If we stand up in front of this jury and claim that behavior has changed when they overwhelmingly believe it has not, our reputation will suffer.

We will suggest three simple steps to guide the visual analysis. These should be viewed as *guidelines*, not as rules that must be rigidly followed.

Step 1: Draw a trend arrow through the baseline data to predict what will happen if the independent variable is never turned ON.

This step is illustrated in the baselines of panels A through C in Figure 3.10. In each panel, the trend arrow was drawn through the middle of the baseline data and extended into the next phase. Again, the trend arrow illustrates our best prediction about what will happen to behavior in the near future if the independent variable is never turned ON.

Step 2: Evaluate if behavior in baseline is too variable (bouncy) to have confidence in the prediction of the trend arrow.

In panel A of Figure 3.10 there is minimal variability around the baseline trend arrow, so we can confidently predict that, if the independent variable is never turned ON, the upward trend will continue. In panel B, there is a visually apparent downward trend, but there is also more bounce, which reduces our confidence in predicting what will happen next, if the

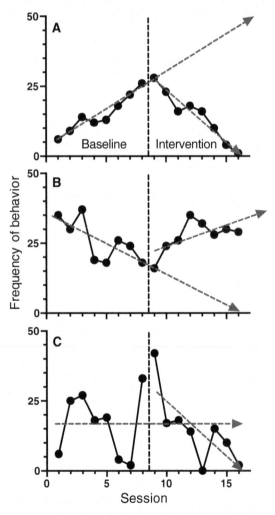

Figure 3.10 Changes in trend that are less convincing moving from panels A to C. The increase in variability makes the changes less and less convincing.

independent variable remains OFF. In panel C, the bouncy baseline data give us no confidence in predicting the level of behavior in future sessions.

Step 3: Draw trend or level lines through the intervention data. Evaluate if there is a convincing change in trend or level (whichever change is of interest).

We will focus on changes in trend first. Figure 3.10 shows three changes in trend that become less convincing as we move down from panel A to panel C. What makes the trend change in panel A so convincing is that the size of the change is large *relative to* the variability (bounce) around the trend arrows. In panel B the trend change is visually apparent, but the increased variability around the trend arrows slightly reduces our confidence that the trend has changed. In panel C the trend arrows change direction, but there is so much bounce that we are not at all confident in saying the trend in behavior has changed.

The same points can be made about the level changes in Figure 3.11. The change in panel A is most convincing; during the stable portions of the baseline and intervention phases,

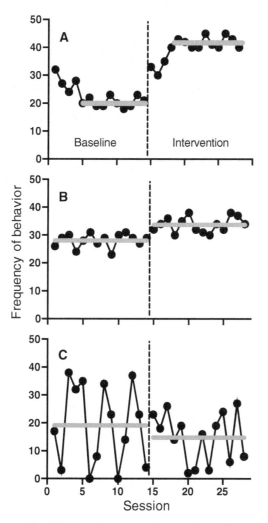

Figure 3.11 Changes in level that are less convincing moving from panels A to C.

there is little bounce around the green level lines. Thus, the change in level is large relative to the amount of bounce. In panel B the change is a bit less convincing. The change in level is modest relative to the amount of bounce. This makes it hard to decide if behavior has changed or not. Some jurors might find this change convincing, others may not. In panel C the small change in level is overwhelmed by the large amount of variability in the baseline and intervention data. No one will find this change in behavior convincing.

Figure 3.12 provides a final opportunity for us to evaluate if behavior changed in trend or level during the intervention phase. This one is a little trickier than the last examples, so the three steps are completed in separate panels.

At Step 1, a trend arrow is drawn through the baseline data and extended into the future. At Step 2, we note there is very little bounce around this baseline trend. Therefore, we predict

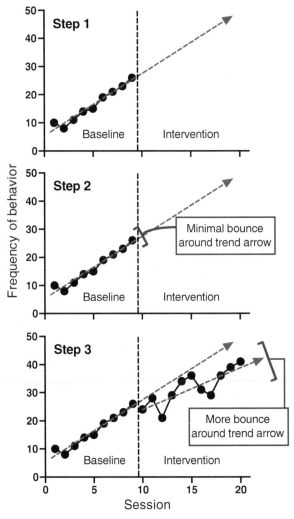

Figure 3.12 The three steps of the visual analysis are used to evaluate if a convincing change in trend occurred after the independent variable was turned ON, during the intervention phase.

that behavior will continue to increase in frequency, even without the intervention. At Step 3, we draw a trend arrow through the data in the intervention phase and evaluate whether the change in trend is convincing. The upward trend observed in baseline continues into the intervention phase. There is a small decrease in the slope of the trend arrow during the intervention phase, but the increased bounce during this phase makes the change unconvincing.

If we are interested in changes in level, at Step 3, we would usually draw level lines through the baseline and intervention data, but it would be inappropriate to do so with the data shown in Figure 3.12. Level lines are supposed to summarize the stable level of behavior at the end of the phase, but there is no stable level – the behavior is increasing throughout both phases.

A second problem with drawing level lines through these data is illustrated in Figure 3.13. This "bar graph" shows the same data in Figure 3.12, but it does so in a way that lacks transparency. Where Figure 3.12 showed all of the data collected in every session and showed the trends in the data over time, Figure 3.13 shows the average frequency of behavior across all of the sessions conducted in each phase (the height of the bars). The "error bars" extending above each of these averages represent the variability in the data, but they do not capture the systematic trends that are occurring in behavior over time. Those can only be seen in Figure 3.12. If the jury was only shown Figure 3.13, they might be impressed with how much behavior changed during the intervention phase. They might even entertain the idea that the intervention produced this behavior change. However, this would be a mistake. The baseline trend was already heading in an upward direction. Our best prediction about this behavior was that it would increase in frequency, even if the independent variable was never turned ON. Therefore, there is no reason to entertain the idea that the intervention is responsible for the increase.

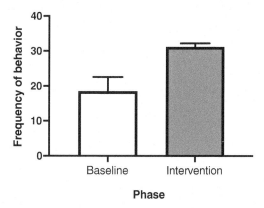

Figure 3.13 The data in Figure 3.12 are regraphed here showing only the average frequency of behavior in the baseline and intervention phases. This graphing method is inappropriate to single-subject data. It prevents others from evaluating if the baseline trend could explain the change in level.

What Is Responsible for the Change

If the visual analysis reveals a convincing change in trend or level, the behavior analyst will ask if the independent variable is responsible for this change. This is a different question than *did behavior change*? This is a question about the internal validity of the experiment.

This question was addressed earlier in the chapter, when discussing how single-subject experimental designs are used to evaluate whether the independent variable is responsible for the behavior change.

Reading Quiz 2

Questions 1–4 refer to the data graphed at right.

1. Draw a trend arrow through the baseline data and extend it into the future.
2. Are the baseline data trending upward or downward, or is the trend arrow flat over time?
3. Is there a lot of "bounce" around the trend line in these baseline data?
4. How confident are you that if the independent variable is left OFF, behavior will fall pretty close to the trend arrow (pretty confident, not confident)?

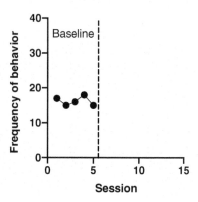

Questions 5–8 refer to the data graphed at right.

5. Draw a trend arrow through the baseline data and extend it into the intervention phase.
6. Are the baseline data trending upward or downward, or is the trend arrow flat over time?
7. Is there a lot of "bounce" in these baseline data?
8. How confident are you that if the independent variable is left OFF, behavior will fall pretty close to the trend arrow (pretty confident, not confident)?

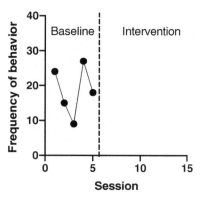

Questions 9–13 refer to the data graphed at right.

9. We have drawn the baseline trend arrow for you. How much variability is there around this arrow?
10. Draw a trend arrow through the intervention-phase data. How much variability is there around *this* trend arrow?
11. When the intervention was introduced, did behavior convincingly deviate from the baseline trend?
12. If this intervention was designed to decrease the frequency of a problem behavior, then we might be tempted to conclude that it worked. However, something else might be responsible for this change in trend *and* level. These "something else" variables are referred to as _____.
13. These data come from a comparison (A-B) design. This design does not allow us to rule out confounds. Therefore, we must conclude that the experiment has low _____ _____.

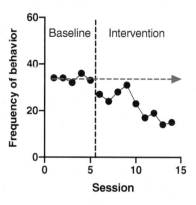

Questions 14 and 15 refer to the data graphed at right.

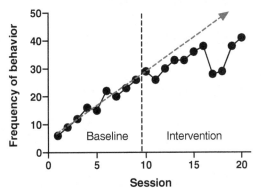

14. When the intervention was introduced, did the trend convincingly change?
15. Is it appropriate to entertain the possibility that the intervention produced a level change?

Questions 16–23 refer to the data graphed at right.

16. Which single-subject experimental design was used?
17. Draw a trend arrow through the data collected in the first baseline phase. How much variability is there around *this* trend arrow?
18. When the intervention was introduced, did the trend convincingly change?
19. Is there a convincing change in level by the end of the intervention phase?
20. Draw a trend arrow through the entire intervention phase.

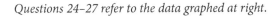

21. Did the trend change from the intervention phase to the final baseline phase?
22. By the end of the final phase of this experiment, is there a convincing change in level when compared with the data collected in the stable portion of the intervention phase?
23. Behavior increased when the independent variable was turned _____ and decreased when it was turned _____. This provides evidence that a *functional relation* exists between the independent variable and behavior.

Questions 24–27 refer to the data graphed at right.

24. Draw a trend arrow through the baseline data and extend it into the future, that is, into the intervention phase.
25. Based on the baseline data alone, how confident are you that if the intervention were never turned ON, behavior would continue to decrease in frequency?
26. When the intervention was introduced, did the trend convincingly change?
27. You are attending a student paper session and these data are shown while

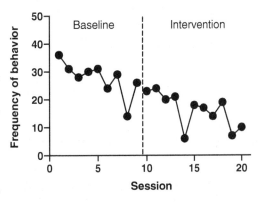

the student who collected them says, "As you can see, the intervention was clearly effective. It decreased the frequency of this behavior." Do you agree? Why or why not?

Questions 28 and 29 refer to the data graphed at right.

28. Now imagine that you are at the same student paper session and the presenter shows the same data graphed in a different way (as the bar graph shown at right). When the student says, "As you can see, the intervention was clearly effective," would you have any way of knowing that there was a decreasing trend in the baseline data?

29. Being a connoisseur of experimental designs, you ask the student, "Was there any trend, upward or downward in the baseline data?" The presenter replies, "I don't know, I didn't look." When the presenter gives this answer, the jury of skeptical scientists in the audience will _____ (upgrade, downgrade) the presenter's reputation as a competent scientist.

Questions 30–34 refer to the data graphed at right.

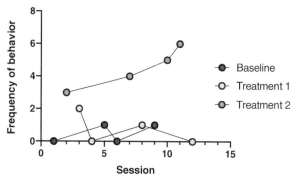

30. In the graph to the right, which single-subject experimental design was employed?

31. Across the four baseline sessions, is there an upward trend, downward trend, or are the data stable?

32. If the independent variable was never changed, we would predict behavior would
    a. never occur again
    b. occur infrequently
    c. occur with increasing frequency over time
    d. occur frequently

33. Is there a convincing level change in the Treatment 1 sessions?

34. Is there a convincing level change in the Treatment 2 sessions?

35. Which single-subject experimental design was used?

36. The baselines of Behaviors A, B, and C are all a little different. Behavior A is stable, B has no upward or downward trend but has a lot of _____, and C has a downward trend.

37. The intervention was applied to Behavior A from sessions 5 through 15. Behavior B started receiving the intervention from session 8 and beyond. Behavior C entered the intervention phase at session 11. The _____-staggered introductions of the independent variable help in evaluating the internal validity of the experiment.

38. Because three behaviors were reliably and _____ influenced by the intervention (i.e., behavior always increased when the intervention began), we can conclude that the experiment has high internal validity *and* that a functional relation exists between the intervention and these behaviors.

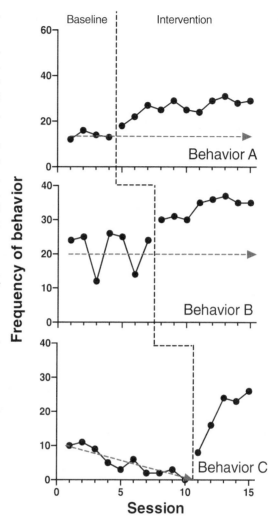

Supplementing the Visual Analysis with Inferential Statistics

Many behavior analysts use inferential statistics to supplement their visual analyses. One reason for doing this is that social and behavioral scientists outside of behavior analysis regard inferential statistics as a "gold-standard" method for evaluating behavior change. If one of these social scientists is on the jury evaluating a behavior analyst's data, they will reject the data as "unconvincing" or "too subjective." Because visually convincing behavior-changes will almost always pass an inferential statistical test, many behavior analysts use these tests, not to convince themselves, but to encourage other social and behavioral scientists to take their findings seriously.

As previously noted, one problem with using inferential statistics in behavior analysis is that statistics require large numbers of participants. This is true of some statistics, but not all of them. Davison (1999) argued that one category of inferential statistics – nonparametric statistics – could detect behavior changes with as few as five participants, and many behavior analysts have used those statistics ever since (e.g., Donlin et al., 2008; Lionello-DeNolf et al., 2010; Madden et al., 2007; Williams et al., 2006). In these researchers' hands, inferential statistics are not a replacement for visual analysis; they are a supplement.

A second problem with the traditional inferential statistics used by social scientists is that they were not designed for use with time-series data like those graphed throughout this chapter. Modern advances in statistics, however, have yielded a number of tests that are appropriate to these data (Borckardt et al., 2013; Young, 2019). One of these modern inferential statistics is the simulation modeling analysis (SMA; Borckardt et al., 2008; Crosbie, 1993). The SMA was designed for use with single-subject time-series data and can be conducted with freely available software.[4] The SMA tests for changes in trend *and* level, making it an ideal supplement for visual analysis. Best of all, when behavior analysts supplement their visual analysis with results of the SMA, or another inferential statistical analysis, social scientists outside of behavior analysis will take the findings more seriously.

As an illustration of the utility of the SMA, we asked it to tell us if the trend changes in Figure 3.10 were convincing. The SMA indicated the change in panel A (Figure 3.10) was very convincing, the change in panel B was not as convincing (but still statistically significant), and panel C was unconvincing. The SMA produced similar conclusions about the level changes in Figure 3.11. As we move down from panels A through C, the SMA found the differences less and less convincing.

Summary

Behavior analysis has two goals: to accurately predict behavior and to identify functional variables that may be used to positively influence behavior. Science can achieve the first of these goals by simply looking for correlations. Because behavior analysts also want to positively influence behavior, they must conduct experiments designed to identify functional variables. Moreover, because behavior analysts are focused on behavior, and behavior is something that *individuals* do, single-subject experimental designs are used more often than group designs. Single-subject experimental designs evaluate if an independent variable is functional by turning it ON and OFF and looking for systematic and replicable changes in behavior (reversal and alternating-treatments designs) or by replicating the intervention effect across behaviors, settings, or individuals (multiple-baseline designs). While inferential statistical analyses are the norm in other social/behavioral sciences, behavior analysts will primarily visually analyze their data, looking for convincing changes in trend and level. This technique is admittedly subjective, leading scientists to sometimes disagree about whether an independent variable has changed behavior. While some view this potential for disagreements as a weakness, we view it as a strength. Disagreements are good for science. If the jury is not entirely convinced that a therapeutic intervention improved behavior, this will encourage behavior analysts to keep working to improve the therapy. Is there a way to enhance the therapy, make it more effective, and thereby convince the remaining jurors? If so, then this is good for science and good for those who rely on behavior analysts to positively influence their behavior, and that of their loved ones.

Answers to Reading Quiz Questions

Reading Quiz 1

1. group
2. statistics
3. single-subject
4. internal validity
5. confound
6. internal validity
7. low
8. comparison or A-B
9. confounds
10. trend
11. increasing
12. baseline
13. replication
14. multiple-baseline
15. reversal; alternating-treatments
16. multiple-baseline

Reading Quiz 2

1. Your trend arrow should look approximately like this:
2. Flat; because the trend arrow is flat and the bounce is minimal, we can describe these data as "stable."
3. No, not much bounce
4. Pretty confident

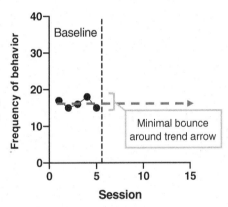

5. Your trend arrow should look approximately like this:
6. Flat; there is too much bounce to describe these data as "stable."
7. Lots of bounce

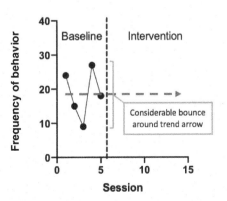

8. Not very confident

9. There is very little variability around the baseline trend arrow. Therefore, we can be pretty confident that behavior will remain at this level in subsequent sessions.

10. The green trend arrow at right shows what you should have drawn. There is a bit of bounce around the arrow, but the trend is visually apparent.

11. Yes. There is a convincing decreasing trend in behavior after the intervention is introduced.

12. confounds or confounded variables

13. internal validity

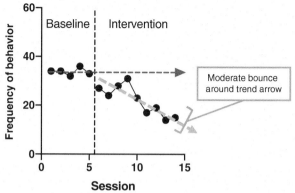

14. No. There was an upward trend in baseline and that trend continued in the intervention phase.

15. No. The baseline trend predicted the level change that was observed. Therefore, there is no reason to attribute that level change to the intervention.

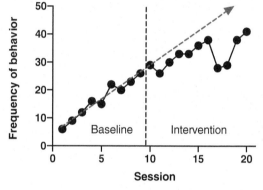

16. Reversal (A-B-A) design

17. Your baseline trend arrow should look like the red arrow shown at right. There is not much variability around that trend arrow, so we feel confident that the frequency of behavior will remain low if the independent variable is never turned ON.

18. Yes, there is a clear shift in trend. After the intervention is introduced, there is a steep upward trend (purple arrow at right).

19. Yes, there is a large increase in the frequency of behavior by the end of the intervention phase.

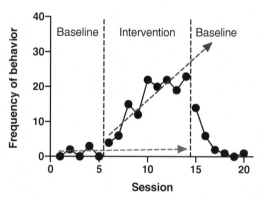

20. Your trend arrow in the intervention phase should look like the purple arrow.

21. Yes. The upward trend in the intervention phase reverses in the final baseline phase.

22. Yes, there is a convincing decrease in the level of behavior from the end of the intervention phase to the end of the final baseline phase.

23. ON; OFF

24. Your trend arrow should look like the red one shown at right.
25. Based on this baseline data, we can be pretty confident that if the independent variable was never turned ON, the decreasing trend would continue.
26. No. The trend does not change in the intervention phase.
27. You should disagree with this statement. The decreasing trend in baseline may be used to predict that behavior would decrease in frequency even if the independent variable was never turned ON. Therefore, there is no reason to attribute the reduction in behavior to the intervention.

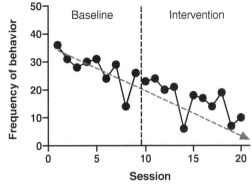

28. No, the bar graph is inappropriate for presenting single-subject, time-series data. They provide no information about trends in either phase.
29. downgrade

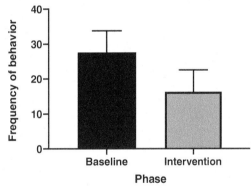

30. Alternating-treatments design
31. As shown by the trend arrow at right, the data are stable over time in the baseline phase.
32. b. occur infrequently
33. No. The level of behavior in the Baseline and Treatment 1 phases are similar.
34. Yes, the level of behavior in the Treatment 2 sessions is much higher than in the Baseline sessions.

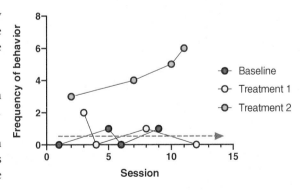

35. Multiple-baseline (across behaviors) design
36. bounce
37. time
38. systematically

Notes

1. Note that if Josh's aggression was dangerous to himself or others, we would not turn OFF the intervention; doing so would be unethical if it increases aggressive actions. In such cases, a multiple-baseline design (discussed later in the chapter) would be used.
2. This design is sometimes called a *multi-element design*.
3. "Might" because this is a comparison design, which cannot rule out a confound that could be responsible for the change in trend.
4. For readers interested in using the SMA to supplement their visual analysis of time-series data, the free software may be downloaded at https://www.clinicalresearcher.org/software.htm.

References

Baer, D. M., Wolf, M. M., & Risley, T. R. (1968). Some current dimensions of applied behavior analysis. *Journal of Applied Behavior Analysis, 1*(1), 91–97.

Baron, A., & Perone, M. (1998). Experimental design and analysis in the laboratory study of human operant behavior. In K. A. Lattal & M. Perone (Eds.), *Applied clinical psychology. Handbook of research methods in human operant behavior* (p. 45–91). Plenum Press. https://doi.org/10.1007/978-1-4899-1947-2_3

Borckardt, J. J., Nash, M. R., Balliet, W., Galloway, S., & Madan, A. (2013). Time-series statistical analysis of single-case data. In J. J. Madden, W. V. Dube, T. D. Hackenberg, G. P. Hanley, & K. A. Lattal (Eds.), *APA handbook of behavior analysis, Vol. 1: Methods and principles.* (pp. 251–266). Washington: American Psychological Association. doi:10.1037/13937-011

Borckardt, J. J., Nash, M. R., Murphy, M. D., Moore, M., Shaw, D., & O'Neil, P. (2008). Clinical practice as natural laboratory for psychotherapy research a guide to case-based time-series analysis. *American Psychologist, 63*(2), 77–95. doi:10.1037/0003-066X.63.2.77

Branch, M. N. (1999). Statistical inference in behavior analysis: Some things significance testing does and does not do. *The Behavior Analyst, 22*(2), 87–92. doi:10.1007/BF03391984

Colling, L. J., & Szűcs, D. (2018). Statistical inference and the replication crisis. *Review of Philosophy and Psychology*, 1–27. doi:10.1007/s13164-018-0421-4

Critchfield, T. S., & Reed, D. D. (2017). The Fuzzy concept of applied behavior analysis research. *The Behavior Analyst, 40*(1), 123–159. doi:10.1007/s40614-017-0093-x

Crosbie, J. (1993). Interrupted time-series analysis with brief single-subject data. *Journal of Consulting and Clinical Psychology, 61*, 966–974.

Dallery, J., Raiff, B. R., Kim, S. J., Marsch, L. A., Stitzer, M., & Grabinski, M. J. (2017). Nationwide access to an internet-based contingency management intervention to promote smoking cessation: A randomized controlled trial. *Addiction, 112*, 875–883. doi:10.1111/add.13715

Davison, M. (1999). Statistical inference in behavior analysis: Having my cake and eating it? *The Behavior Analyst, 22*, 90–103. doi: 10.1007/BF03391986

Donlin, W. D., Knealing, T. W., Needham, M., Wong, C. J., & Silverman, K. (2008). Attendance rates in a workplace predict subsequent outcome of employment-based reinforcement of cocaine abstinence in methadone patients. *Journal of Applied Behavior Analysis, 41*(4), 499–516. doi:10.1901/jaba.2008.41-499

Ebbinghaus, H. (1885). *Memory: A contribution to experimental psychology.* Dover: New York.

Ford, E. W., Boyer, B. T., Menachemi, N., & Huerta, T. R. (2014). Increasing hand washing compliance with a simple visual cue. *American Journal of Public Health, 104*(10), 1851–1856. doi:10.2105/AJPH.2013.301477

Hart, S. L., & Banda, D. R. (2010). Picture exchange communication system with individuals with developmental disabilities: A meta-analysis of single subject studies. *Remedial and Special Education, 31*(6), 476–488. doi: 10.1177/0741932509338354

Hayes, S. C., Barlow, D. H., & Nelson-Gray, R. O. (1999). *The scientist practitioner: Research and accountability in the age of managed care* (2nd ed.). Needham Heights, MA: Allyn & Bacon.

Horner, R. H., Sugai, G., Smolkowski, K., Eber, L., Nakasato, J., Todd, A. W., & Esperanza, J. (2009). A randomized, wait-list controlled effectiveness trial assessing school-wide positive behavior support in elementary schools. *Journal of Positive Behavior Interventions, 11*(3), 133–144. doi:10.1177/1098300709332067

Iwata, B. A., Dorsey, M. F., Slifer, K. J., Bauman, K. E., & Richman, G. S. (1982). Toward a functional analysis of self-injury. *Analysis and Intervention in Developmental Disablities, 2*(1), 3–20. doi:10.1016/0270-4684(82)90003-9

Lionello-DeNolf, K. M., Dube, W. V., & McIlvane, W. J. (2010). Evaluation of resistance to change under different disrupter conditions in children with autism and severe intellectual disability. *Journal of the Experimental Analysis of Behavior, 93*(3), 369–383. doi:10.1901/jeab.2010.93-369

Madden, G. J., Smethells, J. R., Ewan, E. E., & Hursh, S. R. (2007). Tests of behavioral-economic assessments of relative reinforcer efficacy II: Economic complements. *Journal of the Experimental Analysis of Behavior, 88*(3), 355–367. doi:10.1901/jeab.2007.88-355

Munafò, M. R., Nosek, B. A., Bishop, D. V. M., Button, K. S., Chambers, C. D., Percie Du Sert, N., … Ioannidis, J. P. A. (2017). A manifesto for reproducible science. *Nature Human Behaviour, 1*(1), 1–9. doi:10.1038/s41562-016-0021

Open Science Collaboration. (2015). Estimating the reproducibility of psychological science. *Science, 349*(6251), aac4716. doi:10.1126/science.aac4716

Pavlov, I. P. (1927). *Conditional reflexes: An investigation of the physiological activity of the cerebral cortex.* Oxford, England: Oxford University Press.

Peng, R. (2015). The reproducibility crisis in science: A statistical counterattack. *Significance, 12*(3), 30–32. doi:10.1111/j.1740-9713.2015.00827.x

Perone, M. (1999). Statistical inference in behavior analysis: Experimental control is better. *The Behavior Analyst, 22*(2), 109–116. doi: 10.1007/BF03391988

Perone, M., & Hursh, D. E. (2013). Single-case experimental designs. In G. J. Madden (Ed.), *APA handbook of behavior analysis: Volume 1* (pp. 107–126). Washington, DC: APA Books.

Rosenthal, R. (1979). The "file drawer problem" and tolerance for null results. *Psychological Bulletin, 86*, 638–641.

Sidman, M. (1960). *Tactics of scientific research.* New York: Basic Books.

Skinner, B. F. (1938). *The behavior of organisms: An experimental analysis.* Oxford, England: Appleton-Century.

Smith, J. D. (2012). Single-case experimental designs: A systematic review of published research and current standards. *Psychological Methods, 17*(4), 510–550. doi:10.1037/a0029312

Thompson, R. H., Cotnoir-Bichelman, N. M., McKerchar, P. M., Tate, T. L., & Dancho, K. A. (2007). Enhancing early communication through infant sign training. *Journal of Applied Behavior Analysis, 40*(1), 15–23. doi:10.1901/jaba.2007.23-06

Tversky, A., & Kahneman, D. (1971). Belief in the law of small numbers. *Psychological Bulletin, 76*(2), 105–110. doi:10.1037/h0031322

Williams, D. C., Johnston, M. D., & Saunders, K. J. (2006). Intertrial sources of stimulus control and delayed matching-to-sample performance in humans. *Journal of the Experimental Analysis of Behavior, 86*(2), 253–267. doi:10.1901/jeab.2006.67-01

Young, M. E. (2019). Modern statistical practices in the experimental analysis of behavior: An introduction to the special issue. *Journal of the Experimental Analysis of Behavior, 111*(2), 149–154.

Phylogenetic Behavior and Pavlovian Learning

4

Why do you behave? Let's turn the question on its head: Why don't you just sit in one place, without movement throughout your life? Sure, it would be boring, but so is breathing, drinking water, sleeping, and going to the bathroom. You do all of those things every day, so avoiding boredom can't explain why you behave.

To answer the "why behave" question, let's conduct a thought experiment. You go into the wilderness, far away from other behaving humans, and randomly select a spot to sit throughout the remainder of your life, never moving, never making a sound, never attending to the world around you. If you adopt this no-behavior strategy, how long will you be alive? Well, if your randomly selected spot is one in which drops of liquid protein and nutrients consistently flow into your mouth, and ambient temperatures are neither too hot nor too cold, then you'll be fine. But that is not very likely, and it is also unlikely that a carnivore, who has not sworn off behaving, notices that you aren't moving. For that creature you will make a lovely meal. So, why do you behave? Because behavior is important for survival, from the moment you are born until the time you die.

But just behaving is not enough. If you were to behave randomly, you would be just as likely to take a drink of water as to jump off a cliff. Behavior helps the individual survive only if the action suits the local environment. Cliff-dwelling goats born with a strong tendency to jump do not survive long enough to pass to their offspring the genes responsible for this maladaptive behavior. Meanwhile, goats who step carefully possess behavior well suited to their environment. These careful goats survive, and their offspring, genetically predisposed to step carefully, populate the cliff walls for generations to come.

An Introduction to Behavior Analysis, First Edition. Gregory J. Madden, Derek D. Reed, and Florence D. DiGennaro Reed.
© 2021 John Wiley & Sons Ltd. Published 2021 by John Wiley & Sons Ltd.

So, behavior helps individuals survive as long as their behavior is a good match with the local conditions. What if those conditions change? For example, what if a family of eagles takes up residence at the top of the cliffs and begins feeding on baby goats. If the goats' behavior is fixed, then they are doomed. The eagles will consume all of their babies. But if the goats' behavior can adaptively change, then they have a chance. The goats might learn to avoid the area near the eagles' nest. They might learn to protect their babies when they hear an approaching eagle. But all of this requires *learning*. Individuals

Source: Annora L. Madden

capable of learning are able to adapt to a changing environment in ways that their genes do not prepare them for. Simply put, learning helps individuals survive in an ever-changing environment.

In this chapter, we outline some of the phylogenetically selected behaviors of humans – a fancy word for behaviors we inherit them from our parents, who inherited them from their parents, and so on. These phylogenetically selected behaviors are well suited to stable environmental conditions, those that have not changed for eons in the history of the species. For example, two stable environmental conditions are that (1) human infants are born to mothers who provide nutrition by breast-feeding, and (2) these mothers carry the infant from place to place. These conditions have been stable for hundreds of thousands of years. As you will see, phylogenetically selected behaviors prepare the human infant to survive in these stable conditions.

But as noted earlier, environmental conditions change; for example, at some point your parents refused to put diapers on you and became upset when you soiled the carpeting. To adapt to these changes, the individual must learn new behaviors that match the local conditions. Chapter 5 (and beyond) will discuss how we learn these new behaviors. Before we get to that, this chapter outlines the learning that occurs when we adjust our inherited (phylogenetic) behaviors to new environments. We will discuss two types of learning – habituation and Pavlovian learning. As you will see, both of these types of learning are important in the everyday behavior of animals and humans alike.

Phylogenetically Selected Behavior

Humans and animals enter the world genetically "programmed" to engage in a handful of reflexive behaviors in response to specific stimulus events. For example, when a human infant experiences a sudden loss of head support (a stimulus event), it reacts with the *Moro reflex* – it extends its head and widely spreads the arms with palms in front, fingers extended, and thumbs flexed. This reflex can save the life of a falling child, for example, if the mother grabs the extended arm and saves the child from the fall.

A second reflex, the *Palmar grasp reflex*, is also important in this life-saving maneuver. If you place your pinky fingers into the palms of an infant and lift, you will see that it is strong enough to hold much of its weight. If the infant is falling and its Moro reflex puts the infant's palm in contact with something, it will grab it with enough strength to break the fall, saving its life. If individuals displaying these two reflexes are more likely to survive than those who do not, then those with these reflexes will be more likely to survive long enough to procreate and pass the genes responsible for these behavior on to their offspring. This natural selection process is phylogenetically selecting behaviors that provide a survival advantage.

When a specific stimulus occasions a specific reflex response, we say that the stimulus **elicits** the response. Other life-saving reflexes include the *swimming reflex* (elicited by being sur-

rounded by water – don't try this at home; the reflex is far from perfect and infants can swallow large amounts of water and die), the *rooting reflex* (moving the mouth toward an eliciting object touching the cheek – only occurs when the infant is hungry), the *suckling reflex* (elicited by an object – typically the mother's nipple – that passes the lips), the *parachute reflex* (elicited by the sensation of falling forward, the infant extends its arms in front, thereby breaking the fall), and the *respira-*

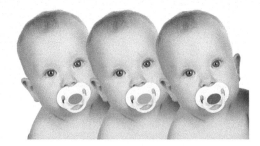

Source: kurhan/Shutterstock.com

tory occlusion reflex (elicited by a lack of oxygen, the infant pulls the head backward, brushes the face with the hands, and cries, all of which may remove the breathing obstruction).

These, and other, phylogenetically selected behaviors fade as the infant ages, but some reflexes occur throughout human life. For example, if an object or a puff of air enters the eye, this stimulus elicits the *corneal reflex* (a rapid eye-blink). Likewise, if you touch a hot stove, the *withdrawal reflex* will quickly remove your arm from danger. Loud noises cause a *startle reflex*, tastes in the mouth elicit the *salivary reflex*, and when an infant suckles at the nipple, the mother's *milk let-down reflex* releases milk into the infant's mouth.

What makes these responses so adaptive is that they occur only at the moment they will increase the individual's likelihood of survival. If they occurred willy-nilly, they would get in the way of other adaptive responding, thereby reducing the individual's chances of survival.

Reflex
Learning – Habituation

Although these reflexive responses to stimuli are phylogenetically selected, they also change as the individual interacts with its environment. That is, they can change with *learning*. For example, a small squirt of lemon juice on the tongue elicits the *salivary reflex*. Squirting lemon juice on the tongue once every 2 minutes (with a water rinse in between) will cause a grad-

Source: André Karwath aka/Wikipedia/CC BY-SA 2.5

ual reduction in saliva production (Epstein et al., 1992). This *gradual reduction in responding following repeated presentations of the eliciting stimulus* is referred to as **habituation**.

Habituation is a form of learning. It is not due to fatigue or, in this case, a lack of saliva. If a new flavor is squirted on the tongue following habituation, the new stimulus will elicit a much larger amount of saliva (Epstein et al., 2003).

Habituation learning has been replicated many times, in many species (rats, monkeys, humans, octopuses, etc.) and in many response modalities (salivation, eye-blink, startle, exploration, etc.). Humans habituate to stimuli all the time. If we enter a room containing a really foul smell, at first we can barely stand it. However, a minute later we have habituated to the smell and can no longer detect it. We might think the smell is gone until someone new walks in and says, "Oh my, that's quite a smell!"

The "Nature and Nurture" Answer to the "Nature vs Nurture" Debate

In the early history of psychology, there was considerable debate about the relative impact on behavior of nature (phylogenetic influences) and nurture (learning). As noted in Chapter 1, the debate was initially framed as "nature vs nurture," but we now know that the answer to this question is "nature *and* nurture."

If behavior was entirely determined by nature, our actions would be completely reflexive; that is, all behavior would be elicited lockstep by environmental stimuli. In this "nature only" world, individuals would not learn from their experiences. Clearly this is not the case, as even the most nature-influenced reflexes habituate to the repeated presentation of the eliciting stimulus.

More generally, in a "nature only" world, individuals would be at a horrible disadvantage relative to other individuals who learn from their experiences. The more you learn, the more adaptive your behavior is to a changing world. For example, if an employee's only skill is driving a taxi, then the individual will be unemployed when a fleet of autonomous taxis replaces the human driver. To adapt to the new economic situation requires learning new skills.

The remainder of this chapter introduces the reader to Pavlovian conditioning – a type of learning that influences our behavior every day. Later chapters will describe a second type of learning – operant learning. Understanding these two types of learning can help us move toward the two-pronged goal of behavior analysis: to predict behavior and to identify functional variables that may be used to positively influence behavior.

Elicited or Evoked?

Behavior analysts use two words to describe how stimuli occasion responses. When a stimulus causes a reflexive response, we say that the stimulus **elicits** the response. For example, extreme heat applied to a finger *elicits* a reflexive withdrawal from the heat source. For all other instances of behavior influenced by a stimulus, we say that the stimulus **evokes** the response. It will not matter if the stimulus became evocative because of Pavlovian learning (see below) or operant learning (see Chapter 5), we will use the word "evoke" (see Domjan, 2016 for an empirical defense of this verbal practice).

Reading Quiz 1

1. When behavior systematically changes as a result of past experiences, we call this _____.

2. Natural selection "programs" individuals with innate _____ behaviors that help them survive in environments resembling those of their evolutionary ancestors.

3. These innate reflexive behaviors are _____ (elicited/evoked) by specific stimuli, such as loss of support under an infant's head.

4. _____ is the term used to describe the gradual reduction in responding following repeated presentations of the evocative stimulus.

Elicited or evoked:

5. Johan walked into the room and noticed the lights were off. The darkness _____ the behavior of flipping the light switch on.

6. Dr. Smith tapped the patella tendon just below Ashley's kneecap. This _____ a reflexive kneejerk response (Ashley's leg kicked forward).

7. The baby pictured on the cover of Nirvana's *Nevermind* album was placed in a swimming pool. This aquatic stimulus _____ the swimming reflex.

Pavlovian Learning

Pavlovian conditioning (sometimes called "classical conditioning" or "respondent conditioning") is named after Ivan Pavlov (1849–1936), the Russian physiologist who won a Nobel prize for his study of the digestive system. The word "conditioning," as in "Pavlovian conditioning," is synonymous with "learning." Behavior analysts will interchangeably talk about "Pavlovian learning" and "Pavlovian conditioning."

Ivan Pavlov
1849-1936

Source: Ivan Petrovitch Pavlov/Wellcome collection/CC BY 4.0

As part of his research, Pavlov measured the salivary reflex; saliva plays an important role in digesting food. For many of his studies, Pavlov squirted a bit of meat powder into a dog's mouth and then measured the amount of saliva produced. After a few sessions, Pavlov noticed that the dog was salivating *before* the meat powder was squirted into the mouth. All of Pavlov's dogs did this. As you might imagine, Pavlov was puzzled by this. Why would the dog salivate if there was nothing in the mouth to elicit this response? Pavlov realized that he had stumbled upon an orderly form of animal learning, so he dropped everything else and studied it.

Source: Jaromir Chalabala/Shutterstock.com

Pavlov found that many different stimuli, when they reliably preceded food delivery, evoked salivation. For example, when Pavlov started a ticking metronome a few seconds before squirting meat powder into the dog's mouth, the dog gradually learned that "tick, tick, tick" preceded the presentation of food. As a result, the ticking sound itself came to evoke salivation, even if the meat powder was withheld. Salivating after the ticking sound is just one example of how learning allows phylogenetic behavior to adjust to new environments – environments in which ticking precedes food.

A Simple Pavlovian Conditioning Procedure

You can replicate Pavlov's experiment at home if you have a dog and a box of dog biscuits. Whether you plan to try this or not, read the rest of this section. It outlines important steps in Pavlovian conditioning.

Source: Mike Mozart/Flickr/CC BY 2.0

Step 1 is a baseline phase (see Figure 4.1). The question asked here is, does the stimulus evoke the response? With your dog sitting in front of you, shake the box of biscuits for a few seconds. Does this sound evoke salivation? If not, then we can classify it as a *neutral stimulus*. It is neutral because it does not evoke the behavior of interest – salivating. If your dog is salivating, then you cannot proceed with the experiment. The shaking noise already evokes salivating, so it is not a neutral stimulus. If this happens, choose a different stimulus. For example, make a "click-click" sound with your tongue.

During Step 2 we will evaluate the ability of the dog biscuit itself to elicit the salivary reflex. Place the biscuit in your dog's mouth and observe the increase in salivating. Pavlov collected saliva from the dog's mouth and measured it – you can do a visual inspection if you like. Because a biscuit will elicit salivation with no prior learning, the biscuit is classified as an **Unconditioned Stimulus (US)** and salivating is classified as an **Unconditioned Response (UR)**. Definitions of these terms appear at the bottom of Figure 4.1.

Now that we know the US elicits salivation and the neutral stimulus does not evoke this response, it is time to move on to Step 3 – the Pavlovian conditioning procedure itself. Here you will shake the box for a few seconds (or make the "click-click" sound with your tongue) before placing a biscuit in your dog's mouth. Be sure to shake the box before delivering the biscuit. If you shake the box at any other time, the dog will not learn that the shaking sound is a reliable predictor of the biscuit. Repeat Step 3 several times, waiting 2–3 minutes between each "shake → biscuit" event. This waiting period, or the time between US events, is important in Pavlovian conditioning. After 6–7 biscuits, each separated by a couple minutes, end the training by walking away. Over the next few days, repeat Step 3 several times.

After a few training sessions, it is time to see if Pavlovian learning has occurred (see Step 4 in Figure 4.1). Call your dog and shake the box for a few seconds, just like you did before. For this test of Pavlovian learning, however, don't toss the dog a biscuit. After making the shaking sound a few times, see if your dog is salivating. If so, then the behavioral *function* of the sound has changed. Before Pavlovian conditioning the shaking sound had no *function* – it did not influence behavior – it was a *neutral stimulus*. After Pavlovian conditioning the same sound functions as a **Conditioned Stimulus (CS)** that evokes the **Conditioned Response (CR)** – salivating (see Figure 4.1 for definitions of these terms).

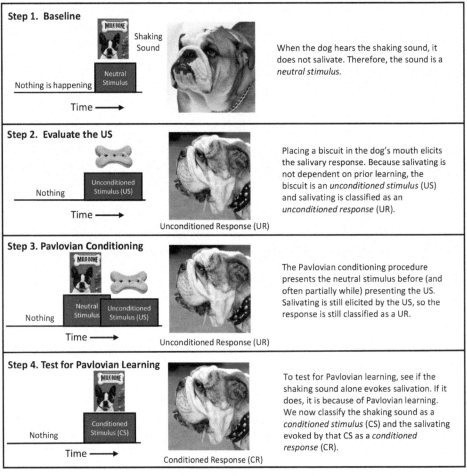

Figure 4.1 An overview of Pavlovian conditioning. Definitions of key terms are as follows:

Neutral Stimulus: A stimulus that does not occasion the response of interest, in this case, salivating.

Unconditioned Stimulus (US): A stimulus that elicits a response without any prior learning (e.g., a biscuit in the dog's mouth elicits salivation).

Unconditioned Response (UR): The response (in this case, salivating) reliably elicited by the US.

Conditioned Stimulus (CS): A formerly neutral stimulus that now evokes a conditioned response. Referred to as "conditioned" because the ability of the stimulus to evoke the response requires new learning (or "conditioning").

Conditioned Response (CR): The response evoked by the CS. This may not be the same as the UR.

Source: Mike Mozart/Flickr/CC BY 2.0; Buckandsons/Wikipedia/CC BY-SA 3.0; State Farm Insurance/Flickr/CC BY 2.0

Pavlovian Conditioning of Emotions

If you conduct the experiment shown in Figure 4.1, you will see that not only does your dog salivate when you shake the box, but this sound also evokes emotional responding. When you shake the box, the dog gets excited. Its tail wags, it has a hard time keeping still, it might whimper, all while intently watching you and the box. The shaking sound has acquired an emotion-evoking function – it increases the dog's excitement.

Source: Christian Bertrand/Shutterstock.com

Human emotions are also strongly influenced by Pavlovian conditioning. When a neutral stimulus reliably precedes the onset of a US that elicits a pleasant emotion (the UR), that stimulus can come to function as a CS evoking a CR. For example, children at birthday parties get very excited when the birthday candles are lit. They jump up and down, rub their hands together, and yell things like "I LOVE cake!" Cake in the child's mouth is a US that elicits salivation and positive emotions (URs). Because lit candles reliably precede the serving of cake at birthday parties, the lit candles come to function as a CS that evokes positive emotional responding (CR).

You can probably think of other CS events from your life that evoke positive emotions. If you enjoyed playing video games as a child, then the distinct sound that your PlayStation or X-Box made as it booted up evoked a feeling of excitement. That sound (CS) reliably preceded the exciting stimuli embedded in the games (US). Therefore, the function of the boot-up sound changed from a neutral stimulus to a CS that evoked a positive emotion (CR). Indeed, if you heard that sound today, after many years of not playing on the gaming platform, it would probably still evoke a pleasant emotion.

Source: GlobalStock/Getty Images

Sexual stimulation can also function as a US eliciting a complex of sexual-preparatory responses and positive emotions. Neutral stimuli that reliably precede pleasant sexual stimulation can come to function as a CS, evoking positive emotions on their own. For example, a song (CS) played prior to a couple's first pleasurable sexual encounter (US) may become "our song," evoking pleasant feelings when heard many years later. Similarly, a perfume/cologne worn only when a partner is sexually receptive can come to function as a CS evoking pleasant emotions and sexual-preparatory responses (CRs) even when sexual stimulation (the US) is not forthcoming (Hoffmann et al., 2004, 2012).

Pavlovian Fear Conditioning

Of course, the world is not filled entirely with birthday cakes, video games, and consensual sexual encounters. The life of every individual is also peppered with unpleasant (aversive) events and Pavlovian conditioning is just as relevant to learning about stimulus events that reliably precede aversive US events.

Consider a rat's reaction to a cat. Laboratory studies have shown that the smell of a cat is a US that elicits an unconditioned freezing response (McGregor et al., 2002). This phylogenetically selected behavior can save the life of the rat; a perfectly still rat is less likely to be noticed by the cat than a rat that moves. Pavlovian fear conditioning can occur if another stimulus (e.g., the sound of a door opening) reliably precedes the smell of the cat. This sound→odor sequence follows the same shake→dog-biscuit sequence seen in Figure 4.1. Pavlovian fear conditioning occurs if the rat becomes fearful and freezes (the CR) as soon as it hears the door opening (the CS).

The Little Albert Experiment

In one of the most influential experiments conducted in the early history of psychology, John B. Watson and Rosalie Rayner used Pavlovian fear conditioning to produce a phobia of white rats in a human infant named Albert. By today's standards, the Watson and Rayner (1920) experiment was unethical. At the time, however, scientists believed that experiences in infancy played little or no role in later development. Ironically, Watson and Rayner's research proved these ideas wrong, thereby revealing the unethical nature of their own research. Unfortunately, another 50 years would pass before ethical standards for the protection of human subjects would become mandatory in psychological research.

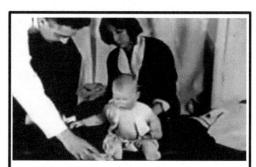

John B. Watson (left), Rosalie Rayner (right), and "Little Albert," who may be seen here looking at a white rat. Albert was selected for this study of Pavlovian fear conditioning because of his fearlessness.

Source: Image(s) provided courtesy of www.all-about-psychology.com/

The 9-month-old infant, "Little Albert," was probably the son of a nurse who worked at the Johns Hopkins University hospital, where Watson and Rayner's experiment was conducted (Powell et al., 2014). As shown in Figure 4.2, Watson and Rayner began their experiment by showing Albert a white rat and recording his emotional reaction. Albert was not afraid of the rat, so they classified it as a *neutral stimulus*.

At Step 2, the researchers looked for a US that would reliably elicit a fear response. Albert proved to be afraid of almost nothing (dogs, rabbits, monkeys, rats, even a burning newspaper). Eventually, they found that Albert was afraid of loud noises. Loud noises elicited a fear response in which Albert hid his face in the mattress and whimpered. The loud noise was classified as a US because it elicited this cluster of fear responses (the UR).

Pavlovian fear conditioning in the Watson and Rayner (1920) experiment consisted of presenting the neutral **stimulus** – the white rat – prior to the onset of the US – the loud noise. After just five encounters with the rat→noise sequence, Albert became fearful of the rat.

When the rat was presented without the loud noise (Step 4 in Figure 4.2), Albert made a pouting face, whimpered, and fell over on the mattress. When Albert was retested five days later, his fear of the white rat was as strong as ever.

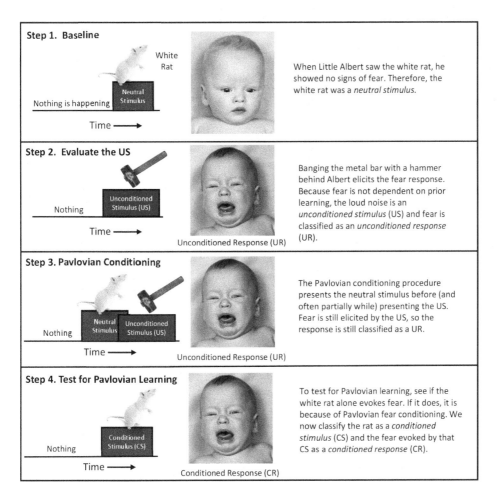

Step 1. Baseline

White Rat

Neutral Stimulus

Nothing is happening

Time ⟶

When Little Albert saw the white rat, he showed no signs of fear. Therefore, the white rat was a *neutral stimulus*.

Step 2. Evaluate the US

Unconditioned Stimulus (US)

Nothing

Time ⟶

Unconditioned Response (UR)

Banging the metal bar with a hammer behind Albert elicits the fear response. Because fear is not dependent on prior learning, the loud noise is an *unconditioned stimulus* (US) and fear is classified as an *unconditioned response* (UR).

Step 3. Pavlovian Conditioning

Neutral Stimulus

Unconditioned Stimulus (US)

Nothing

Time ⟶

Unconditioned Response (UR)

The Pavlovian conditioning procedure presents the neutral stimulus before (and often partially while) presenting the US. Fear is still elicited by the US, so the response is still classified as a UR.

Step 4. Test for Pavlovian Learning

Conditioned Stimulus (CS)

Nothing

Time ⟶

Conditioned Response (CR)

To test for Pavlovian learning, see if the white rat alone evokes fear. If it does, it is because of Pavlovian fear conditioning. We now classify the rat as a *conditioned stimulus* (CS) and the fear evoked by that CS as a *conditioned response* (CR).

Figure 4.2 An overview of Pavlovian conditioning within Watson and Rayner's "Little Albert" experiment. Key terms are as in Figure 4.1.

Source: cleanpng.com; Irina Rogova/Shutterstock.com; Aleksandr Pobedimskiy/Shutterstock.com

Watson and Rayner (1920) used Pavlovian conditioning to establish a rat phobia in Little Albert. Next, they showed Albert some other objects, to see if his phobia was specific to the white rat, or if it would generalize to other creatures or other furry things. Albert proved to be frightened by a white rabbit, a dog, a fur coat, a bag of cotton wool, and even a Santa Claus mask.

WHAT BECAME OF LITTLE ALBERT?

Watson and Rayner (1920) chose Albert for their experiment because of his fearlessness at baseline. After their experiment, however, Albert was phobic of white furry objects, living or not. Watson and Rayner planned to therapeutically reverse this Pavlovian learning, but Albert was withdrawn from the hospital before the therapy phase could begin. Although Powell et al. (2014) reported that Albert lived a normal life (never knowing he was the famous "Little Albert") he was not fond of dogs or other animals. Whether this mild dislike was a product of his early experience with Pavlovian fear conditioning cannot be known, but Watson and Rayner foresaw the possibility: "Our own view…is that these responses in the home environment are likely to persist indefinitely, unless an accidental method for removing them is hit upon" (Watson & Rayner, 1920, p. 12).

Fear Conditioning and Posttraumatic Stress Disorder

The treatment of phobias and other acquired negative emotional responses are as important today as they were in the days of Little Albert. Soldiers returning from battle, refugees escaping civil wars, and sexually/physically abused individuals can suffer from debilitating posttraumatic stress disorder (PTSD) in which previously neutral stimuli evoke unwanted emotions. Those diagnosed with PTSD are at increased risk of substance abuse and suicide (Bremner et al., 1996; Jakupcak et al., 2009), and their suffering increases emotional distress in their spouses (Dekel & Solomon, 2007).

Recalling the twin goals of behavior analysis – to predict and positively influence behavior – those wishing to help individuals recover from PTSD will be more effective if they thoroughly understand Pavlovian conditioning. In addition, some of the behavior-change principles and techniques discussed in the rest of this book are built on Pavlovian learning. Thus, it is important that behavior analysts understand Pavlovian learning. The sections that follow provide that understanding by answering three questions: (1) what is learned during Pavlovian conditioning; (2) what are the principles of effective Pavlovian conditioning, and (3) what principles should guide Pavlovian-based therapies? But first, let's take a reading quiz.

Source: Photographee.eu/Shutterstock.com

Reading Quiz 2

1. You will recall from Chapter 1 that the word "*stimulus*" refers to an environmental event that can be observed (seen, heard, smelled, etc.) by an individual. Thus, the color red is a _____.

2. More than one stimulus is referred to as *stimuli*. The plural of stimulus is _____.

3. When food is placed into the dog's mouth, the dog salivates. Food is the _____ _____ and salivating is the _____.

4. Before Pavlovian conditioning, the sound produced by shaking the box of dog biscuits was a _____ _____ because it did not increase salivation.

5. During Pavlovian conditioning, the function of the box-shaking sound changed from a _____ _____ to a _____ _____.

6. When the US elicits salivation, salivating is classified as a(n)_____ _____.

7. When the CS evokes salivation, salivating is classified as a(n)_____ _____.

8. Before Pavlovian conditioning, the neutral stimulus has no function – it does not influence behavior. After Pavlovian conditioning, the _____ of the neutral stimulus changes; it is now a CS that evokes the CR.

What Is Learned During Pavlovian Conditioning?

Most people have never experienced what a combat veteran has been through. One moment, while walking on patrol through the city, everything is fine. Then there is a commotion in the crowd. People begin to shout in the local dialect. There is pushing and shoving, and then there is an explosion. People are running in all directions. There are bodies on the ground, covered in blood. Just like everyone else at the scene, the soldier's autonomic nervous system is aroused into a fight-or-flight state: rapid heart rate, pupil dilation, a feeling of panic. Calm is slow in coming as the chaos and bloodshed are everywhere.

Let's examine this experience from a Pavlovian learning perspective. First, we identify the US – the explosion. Like all US events, it is a phylogenetically important event, that is, a stimulus event important in the survival of the individual (Baum, 2005). The UR elicited by the US is the autonomic fight-or-flight response. This response is elicited by the US because, in the phylogenetic history of the human species, a highly aroused individual is better equipped than a calm one to either attack or run away from danger.

Pavlovian learning is adaptive because it allows the individual to predict when the US will occur. The soldier in a combat zone may know that life-threatening events happen about once a month, but they don't know exactly when the next one will happen. For obvious reasons, knowing when the next explosion will occur would be a useful thing to learn.

Pavlovian conditioning is the way in which individuals learn when US events will occur. A neutral stimulus, like the commotion in the crowd that preceded the explosion, can come to function as a CS that evokes the fight-or-flight response (the CR). After Pavlovian learning has occurred, the CS provides information about when the next explosion will happen – soon! You might think of the CS as a Paul Revere[1] stimulus – "The US is coming! The US is coming!"

Source: dcroswhite/Getty Images

Three Things Learned During Pavlovian Conditioning

The **first thing learned in Pavlovian conditioning** is that *the CS signals a delay reduction to the US*. By "delay reduction" we mean that the time (delay) to the next US event is less than it was before the CS occurred (Fantino, 1977; Shahan & Cunningham, 2015). For example, for the soldier, the time between life-threatening events is about 1 month. When the CS occurs, it signals a *delay reduction* to the next dangerous event – from a delay of about 1 month to a delay of about 2 seconds. "The US is coming! The US is coming!"

Learning about informative CS events can save the solder's life. When a commotion in a crowd is subsequently encountered (CS), activating fight-or-flight responding (CR) in preparation for the impending explosion (US) can remove the soldier, and perhaps others, from harm.

The **second thing learned in Pavlovian conditioning** is that *the CS signals when the US is coming*. If the US reliably occurs 10 seconds after the CS onset, the CS will not immediately evoke the CR. Instead, as shown in Figure 4.3, the CR will increase in probability as the scheduled US event draws nearer (e.g., Balsam, et al., 2002; Drew et al., 2005). "The US is coming (in 10 sec)! The US is coming (in 10 sec)!" Because CRs are timed to the delivery of the US, there is good reason to conclude that Pavlovian learning involves learning *when* the US will occur.

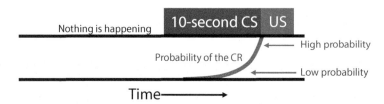

Figure 4.3 When the US does not quickly follow the onset of the CS, the CR will increase in probability as the time of the US event approaches. This provides evidence that individuals learn that the CS signals precisely when the US is coming.

The **third thing learned in Pavlovian conditioning** is that *the CS signals which US is coming*. This was demonstrated by Jenkins and Moore (1973) and is shown in Figure 4.4. Pigeons were shown, at different times, two different CS stimuli. One stimulus signaled a delay reduction to a water US, the CS_W. The other signaled a delay reduction to a food US, the CS_F. When the CS_W was lit, the pigeons pecked it. The pigeons also pecked when the CS_F signaled a delay reduction to a food US. However, the form of the pecks directed at these stimuli were different. When the CS_W was lit, the pigeons pecked with a closed beak, which is the way pigeons drink water. When the CS_F was lit, they pecked with an open beak, which is how they eat food.[2] The form of these pecks provides evidence that the pigeons learned that the CS signals *which* US is coming – water or food (see Colwill & Motzkin, 1994 for additional evidence).

It is important to note that Pavlovian learning is not conscious learning. Soldiers experiencing traumatic events do not consciously ask themselves, "what stimulus preceded the explosion" nor do they sit down and calculate the delay reduction to the US signaled by the CS. Pavlovian learning happens automatically – it is what brains do; soldiers' brains and pigeons' brains. All brains do it, whether we like it or not.

Figure 4.4 During Pavlovian conditioning, individuals learn that the CS signals a delay reduction to a *specific US*. When Pigeon 204 saw the CS_W, which always signaled a delay reduction to the water US, it pecked the light with a closed beak, the topography of sipping water. When the CS_F was lit (signaling a delay reduction to the food US), the same pigeon pecked with an open beak – the topography of eating a piece of food.
Source: Photos from Jenkins, H. M., & Moore, B. R. (1973). The form of the auto-shaped response with food or water reinforcers. *Journal of the Experimental Analysis of Behavior, 20*(2), 163–181. https://doi.org/10.1901/jeab.1973.20-163

If it were up to individuals diagnosed with PTSD, they would not experience the CR when they encounter a CS event. Fight-or-flight responding is not pleasant and it can impair a soldier's behavior while discharging duties. Furthermore, when they return home, encountering a CS event during daily life, or even during a dream, can evoke debilitating and stigmatizing conditioned fear responses. Unfortunately, experiencing these CRs is not something that one can choose to stop by "force of will." Pavlovian learning occurs because it served our evolutionary ancestors well; it kept them alive long enough to procreate and pass the genes responsible for Pavlovian learning to their offspring.

If Pavlovian conditioning is responsible for phobias and PTSD, then a science of behavior should be useful in treating these disorders. Before providing an overview of Pavlovian interventions for treating phobias and PTSD, it is important to identify effective procedures for establishing Pavlovian learning in the first place. Knowing how to establish an effective CS may point to effective ways of rendering the CS inert.

Principles of Effective Pavlovian Conditioning

Nearly a century of research on Pavlovian conditioning has produced many theories about how this learning process works. Prominent theories include the Rescorla–Wagner model (Rescorla & Wagner, 1972), information-theoretic models (Gallistel & Gibbon, 2002), attentional models (Mackintosh, 1975), and the comparator hypothesis (Miller & Matzel, 1988). Rather than outlining the pros and cons of these theories, this section takes a practical approach by briefly describing **four empirically supported principles that increase the efficacy of Pavlovian conditioning**.

1. *Use an important US:* The more phylogenetically important the US, the more effective is Pavlovian conditioning. For example, Pavlovian conditioning with a food US will go more smoothly if the individual is hungry (Sparber et al., 1991). If we are thirsty or

really craving a pizza, our own Pavlovian learning about liquid or pizza US events will proceed more quickly. An explosion is always a phylogenetically important US event, and Pavlovian learning is facilitated by the phylogenetic importance of such life-threatening US events.

2. *Use a salient CS*: Pavlovian conditioning will proceed more quickly if the CS (which starts out as a neutral stimulus) is *salient*, that is, something noticeable (Hall et al., 1977). If the neutral stimulus reliably precedes the US but the individual never sees it, smells it, hears it, and so on, then it will never come to function as a CS.

One way to ensure the CS is salient is to use a novel stimulus as the CS, that is, something new and unexpected. For example, if a person wearing a chicken suit sat down in the front row of your biology class, this would be novel – it has never happened before. Because of this novelty, everyone in the class would notice it – "Look at that person in the chicken suit!" If the arrival of the chicken suit signals a delay reduction to an important US event (e.g., when the person in the chicken suit shows up, the professor always arrives a few minutes later with coffee and doughnuts), then the chicken suit should come to function as a CS. It would evoke the CR; that is, the coffee and doughnut lovers in the class would feel a positive emotional state when they see the chicken suit enter the room.

3. *Use a CS that signals a large delay reduction to the US*: Pavlovian learning proceeds quickly and generates a CS that reliably evokes the CR when the CS signals a large delay reduction to the US. Said another way, Pavlovian conditioning works better when the CS→US interval is much briefer than the time separating successive US events. To practically use this third principle, we need a way to measure the amount of delay reduction signaled by the CS. The *delay–reduction ratio* is useful for this purpose. It can be calculated using math that you learned in elementary school. Simply follow these three-steps:

- **Step 1: Determine the average time between US events.** Below we refer to the average time, usually expressed in seconds, between US events as the US→US interval. If the average time between food deliveries is 60 seconds, then the US→US interval = 60 seconds.

- **Step 2: Measure the CS→US interval.** The CS→US interval is the time between the onset of the CS and the delivery of the US. For example, if a light in the pigeon's chamber illuminates (CS) and, 1 second later, food is delivered (US), then the CS→US interval is 1 second.

- **Step 3: Enter these two values into the delay–reduction ratio.** The delay–reduction ratio (Fantino et al. 1993; Gibbon et al., 1977) provides an objective measure of the amount of delay reduction signaled by the CS:

$$\text{delay-reduction ratio} = \frac{\text{US} \to \text{US interval}}{\text{CS} \to \text{US interval}}$$

For the pigeon, the US→US interval was 60 seconds, so insert this value in the numerator:

$$\text{delay-reduction ratio} = \frac{60}{\text{CS} \to \text{US interval}}$$

The CS→US interval was 1 second, so place this in the denominator:

$$\text{delay-reduction ratio} = \frac{60}{1} = 60$$

A delay–reduction ratio of 60 means that the CS signals that the individual is now 60 times closer (in time) to the US, compared to the average US→US interval. A CS that signals the US is 60 times more imminent will function as an effective CS; it will reliably evoke conditioned responding (e.g., pecking at the food-signaling CS).

In general, the larger the delay–reduction ratio, the more effective is the CS in evoking behavior (Gibbon et al., 1977).[3] With a large delay–reduction ratio, the neutral stimulus will acquire CS function rapidly and the CS will reliably evoke the CR (Gallistel & Gibbon, 2002).

This relation between the delay–reduction ratio and the efficacy of Pavlovian conditioning is illustrated in Figure 4.5. The y-axis shows the number of learning trials required before the CS evokes the CR; that is, how long does it take for Pavlovian learning to occur. The x-axis shows the delay–reduction ratio. The different colored data points in the graph come from the different experiments summarized by Gibbon and Balsam (1981). The red line drawn through the data summarizes the relation between the independent variable (the delay–reduction ratio) and the dependent variable (trials to acquisition). What is apparent from the figure is that when the CS

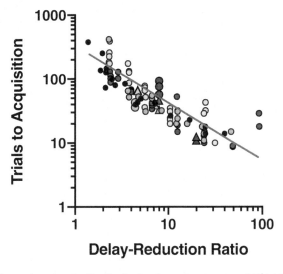

Figure 4.5 How long does it take for Pavlovian learning to occur? That is, how many times does the CS→US event have to be experienced before the CS evokes the CR? This graph shows data collected in several experiments conducted in different labs. What is clear from these data is that when the delay–reduction ratio is low (the CS signals the delay to the US has been reduced only a little), it takes lots of experience with the CS→US event before the CR occurs. However, when the CS signals a large delay reduction (right end of the x-axis), Pavlovian learning happens quickly. Note the logarithmic scaling of the axes.

Source: Gibbon, J., & Balsam, P. D. (1981). Spreading associations in time. In C. M. Locurto, H. S. Terrace, & J. Gibbon (Eds.), *Autoshaping and conditioning theory* (pp. 219–253). New York: Academic Press.

signals a small delay reduction, it takes many more trials before Pavlovian learning is acquired. As the delay–reduction ratio increases, fewer trials are required, that is, learning happens faster.

To get a sense of why Pavlovian learning is slow when the delay–reduction ratio is small, consider a thirsty pigeon placed in a chamber in which the CS signals that water will be delivered in 55 seconds. The extent to which that is good news depends on how often water is usually delivered. If the average time between US events is 60 seconds, then the CS signals a very small delay reduction to the US – who cares? This is reflected in a low delay–reduction ratio:

$$\text{delay-reduction ratio} = \frac{\text{US} \to \text{US interval}}{\text{CS} \to \text{US interval}}$$

As before, insert the US→US interval in the numerator:

$$\text{delay-reduction ratio} = \frac{60}{\text{CS} \to \text{US interval}}$$

And the CS→US interval in the denominator:

$$\text{delay-reduction ratio} = \frac{60}{55} = 1.09$$

When the delay–reduction ratio equals 1, it means the CS signals no delay reduction to the US, none whatsoever. The ratio just calculated, 1.09, is very close to 1, so the CS signals a small, meaningless delay reduction.

It is important to note that the problem with this 55-second CS is not that it is too long. The problem is that this CS signals a small delay reduction to the US. To prove this, we can make this same 55-second stimulus into a very effective CS. Simply increase the time between US events to 3,600 seconds (1 hour). By doing so, the 55-second CS now signals that the US will occur 65.45 times faster than before the CS onset:

$$\text{delay-reduction ratio} = \frac{3,600}{55} = 65.45$$

Looking at Figure 4.5, you should be able to see that moving from 1.09 to 65.45 on the x-axis should decrease the trials to acquisition (faster conditioning; see Rescorla, 1988).

So, don't be fooled into thinking that a brief CS→US interval guarantees the CS will effectively evoke the CR – it doesn't. The CS→US interval can only be interpreted in the context of the usual wait between US events. To know in advance how effective the CS will be, calculate the delay–reduction ratio.

4. *Make sure the CS is not redundant*: The final principle of effective Pavlovian conditioning concerns the informativeness of the CS. A stimulus will acquire CS function more quickly and will evoke the CR more reliably if it *uniquely* signals the delay reduction to the US. If another CS already signals this delay reduction, then the new stimulus is redundant and is unlikely to acquire CS function (Rescorla, 1988).

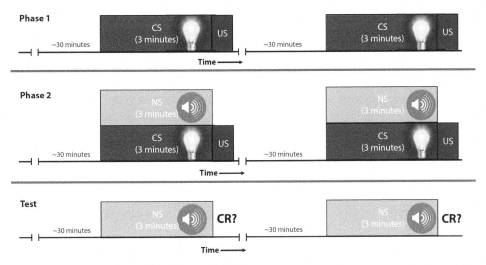

Figure 4.6 Diagram of Kamin's (1969) blocking experiment. Sessions were 2-hours long with four CS→US events programmed in Phases 1 and 2. These CS→US events were separated by an average US→US interval of 30 minutes. In Phase 2, a neutral stimulus (NS) was presented at the same time as the CS that had been well established in Phase 1. Although the NS signaled a delay reduction to the US, it was redundant with the CS. Therefore, when the NS was presented alone in the Test phase, it did not evoke the CR.
Source: kisspng.com

This redundancy principle of effective Pavlovian conditioning was first demonstrated with rats by Kamin (1969) and has since been replicated many times in humans and nonhuman animals (Yamada, 2010).[4] In the Kamin experiment, the time between US events averaged 30 minutes (US→US interval = 30 minutes) and a CS (the illumination of a light) was presented for 3 minutes prior to the US (3-minute CS→US interval; see Phase 1 in Figure 4.6). The delay–reduction ratio was 30/3 = 10. That is a big delay reduction; the CS signaled that the US would occur 10 times faster than normal. Because of this large delay reduction, Pavlovian learning happened quickly – the CS, when presented without the US (not shown in the figure), reliably evoked the CR.

In Phase 2, a redundant stimulus (the auditory neutral stimulus – "NS" in Figure 4.6) was presented at the same time as the well-established CS. Note how the NS signals the same delay reduction to the US as the CS. Based on this alone, we might expect the NS to quickly acquire CS function. The problem with the NS, however, is that it is entirely redundant with the CS – the NS doesn't tell the rat anything it didn't already know. Therefore, according to the final principle of effective Pavlovian conditioning, the NS should not acquire CS function.

This prediction was evaluated in the Test phase of Kamin's (1969) experiment. In that phase, when the NS was presented by itself, it failed to evoke the CR. Because the previously established CS blocked the redundant NS from acquiring CS function, this is often referred to as the "blocking effect."

Applying these principles to PTSD

These four principles of effective Pavlovian conditioning can be applied to PTSD. First, near-death experiences in a combat zone or physical/sexual abuse at the hands of a perpetrator are phylogenetically important US events (Principle 1). These stimuli reliably elicit debilitating emotions and fight-or-flight responses. Second, for the individual diagnosed with PTSD, the conditioned stimuli (CSs) evoking these conditioned emotional responses are often highly salient (Principle 2). A commotion in a public space is uncommon, so this attention-drawing stimulus is likely to acquire CS properties if it precedes an explosion. Similarly, the abuse perpetrator is a highly salient stimulus; one that cannot be missed.

Third, these salient stimuli will come to evoke debilitating emotions and fight-or-flight responding if they signal a large delay reduction to the US, that is, the next life-threatening event. To quantify how large this delay reduction is, we use the delay–reduction ratio.

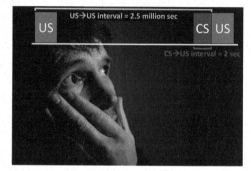

Source: John Gomez/Shutterstock.com

- **Step 1: Determine the average time between US events.** The average time between life-threatening US events in the combat zone was 1 month. That's about 2.5 million seconds.
- **Step 2: Determine the CS→US interval.** For our soldier, the commotion in the crowd (CS) happened about 2 seconds before the explosion (US); thus, the CS→US interval is 2 seconds.
- **Step 3: Calculate the delay reduction ratio** using the values obtained in Steps 1 and 2:

$$\text{delay reduction ratio} = \frac{2,500,000}{2} = 1,250,000$$

The commotion in the crowd is a highly effective CS in evoking the soldier's fight-or-flight response because it signals a massive delay reduction to the explosion.

Finally, the commotion in the crowd becomes an effective CS because it is not redundant – no other stimulus signals the delay reduction to the explosion (Principle 4). If another warning stimulus had already signaled the impending explosion – imagine a countdown clock in a James Bond movie – then the commotion in the crowd would be entirely redundant and would not acquire CS properties.

Reading Quiz 3

1. Through Pavlovian conditioning, individuals learn three things: (1) the CS signals a _____ reduction to the US; (2) the CS signals _____ the US is coming; and (3) the CS signals _____ US is coming.
2. The first principle of effective Pavlovian conditioning is to use a phylogenetically important _____.

3. The second principle of effective Pavlovian conditioning is that the CS should be _____, that is, noticeable.
4. The third principle of effective Pavlovian conditioning is, the CS should signal a large _____ _____ to the US.
5. The fourth and final principle of effective Pavlovian condition is to be sure that no other _____ signals a delay reduction to the US.
6. If the CS always precedes the US by 2 seconds, and the average time between US events (US→US interval) is 200 seconds, what is the delay–reduction ratio?

    delay-reduction ratio = ————— = _____

    Will this stimulus function as an effective CS? _____ (yes/no)

7. If the average time between US events is 60 seconds and the CS always precedes the US by 55 seconds, what is the delay–reduction ratio?

    delay-reduction ratio = ————— = _____

    Will this stimulus function as an effective CS? _____ (yes/no)

Generalization

After Watson and Rayner (1920) established Little Albert's fear of white rats, they tested to see if this fear would generalize to other objects: toy blocks, a rabbit, a dog, a fur coat, cotton wool, and a Santa Claus mask. Prior to Pavlovian fear conditioning, Albert was afraid of none of these objects, but after conditioning, he was afraid of all of them, except the blocks. This occurred despite the fact that the fear-eliciting loud noise followed the presentation of none of these test objects.

Pavlovian generalization may be defined as *conditioned responding to a novel stimulus that resembles the CS*. The Santa Claus mask was a novel stimulus – one not used during Pavlovian conditioning. Because the mask's furry white beard resembled the furry white rat (the CS), Albert's conditioned fear response generalized to this stimulus.

The amount of generalization depends on how closely the novel stimulus resembles the CS. For example, toy blocks do not at all resemble a white furry rat. When these toys were placed in front of Albert, he played with them without any fear. But anything white and furry evoked fear.

In laboratory studies of generalization, the CS and the novel stimuli that more or less resemble the CS are presented without the US. Of interest is how effective each stimulus is in evoking the CR. Typically the CS is the most effective in evoking the CR, and the novel stimuli are less effective as they resemble the CS less and less.

This is illustrated by the *generalization gradient* shown in Figure 4.7. In this study of human Pavlovian conditioning (Hovland, 1937), an auditory CS (beeeeeeep) signaled an upcoming electric shock (US) that reliably elicited a galvanic skin response (the participant's palms began to sweat; the UR). After Pavlovian conditioning, presenting the CS tone by itself was enough to evoke sweaty palms (CR). But notice how less sweating occurred as lower or higher pitched tones were presented. The shape of the *generalization gradient* shown in Figure 4.7 is a very reliable finding, which has been replicated in a wide range of species (Ghirlanda & Enquist, 2003).

Generalization can be thought of as occurring along a continuum spanning from *discrimination* to *overgeneralization*. The black data points in Figure 4.8 show an idealized gen-

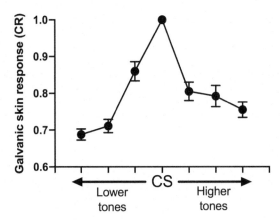

Figure 4.7 Generalization gradient composed of conditioned responses (CRs) evoked by the CS and by test tones that had either higher or lower pitches than the CS. As the test tones more closely resembled the CS, more CRs occurred. Data expressed as proportion responding evoked by the CS.

Source: Hovland, C. I. (1937). The generalization of conditioned responses: I. The sensory generalization of conditioned responses with varying frequencies of tone. *The Journal of General Psychology, 17*(1), 125–148. https://doi.org/10.1080/0

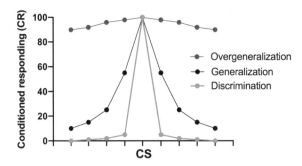

Figure 4.8 Idealized gradients illustrating overgeneralization (red), generalization (black), and discrimination (green). The CS in the center of the x-axis reliably evokes the CR. As we move away from the CS, either to the left or the right on the x-axis, the test stimulus less and less resembles the CS. As the test stimulus less closely resembles the CS, it is less effective in evoking the CR.

eralization gradient. As in the Hovland (1937) study, the CS is the most effective stimulus in evoking the CR. Novel stimuli that less closely resemble the CS are less effective in evoking the CR.

The green data points in Figure 4.8 illustrate *discrimination*. Here the CS is the only stimulus that evokes the CR. Stimuli that closely resemble the CS are largely ineffective. Such a pattern of responding illustrates that the individual discriminates the CS from all other stimuli. While this illustrates very precise learning, too much discrimination is a bad thing. If our soldier's fight-or-flight response was evoked only by the exact CS event that preceded the explosion, then adaptive fight-or-flight responding would not be evoked by similar stimuli; for example, if a commotion occurred in another market, in a restaurant, or inside a shop.

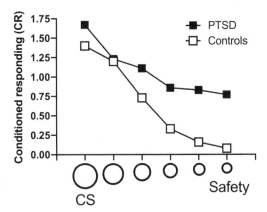

Figure 4.9 Conditioned responses (CRs) to CS and test stimuli in two groups of participants – those diagnosed with PTSD and Controls (never experienced PTSD symptoms). Test stimuli evoked more CRs in the PTSD group. That is, their conditioned responding showed greater generalization to novel stimuli that resembled the CS.

Source: Lissek, S., & van Meurs, B. (2015). Learning models of PTSD: Theoretical accounts and psychobiological evidence. *International Journal of Psychophysiology, 98*(3), 594–605. https://doi.org/10.1016/J.IJPSYCHO.2014.11.006

The red data points in Figure 4.8 illustrate the other end of the continuum – overgeneralization. Here the CS evokes the CR, but so does just about any other stimulus that even remotely resembles the CS. This too can be maladaptive. A soldier will be at a great disadvantage if stimuli that barely resemble the CS (e.g., a group of children playing in a park) evoke the fight-or-flight response.

Some evidence suggests soldiers diagnosed with PTSD display overgeneralization of Pavlovian fear conditioning. This is illustrated in Figure 4.9, which shows just one side of a generalization gradient. In this study (Lissek & van Meurs, 2015), the CS (a large circle) appeared on a computer screen just before a shock was administered (the US). At other times, when a tiny circle appeared on the screen, it served as a safety signal correlated with a shock-free period. For PTSD patients and Controls (individuals never experiencing PTSD), peak conditioned responding occurred when the CS alone was presented. The two groups differed in their responding to the safety signal and to the novel stimuli that looked less and less like the CS. Where the Control group's conditioned responding conformed to a typical generalization gradient, the gradient was flatter (overgeneralization) in the PTSD sufferers. Translated to daily life, their fight-or-flight emotional reactions are more likely to be evoked by stimuli that even remotely resemble the CS. You can see how this poses a challenge to the treatment of PTSD (see Extra Box 1).

Pavlovian Extinction-Based Therapy

In the case of Little Albert, Watson and Rayner (1920) never had the opportunity to provide therapy. They planned to use *Pavlovian extinction*. That is, they planned to repeatedly present the CS (the white rat) without subsequently presenting the US (the loud noise). In this way, the CS would no longer signal a delay reduction to the US. This Pavlovian extinction procedure would cause the CS to gradually lose its ability to evoke Little Albert's fear response. Unfortunately for Albert, he and his mother moved before extinction could begin.

Pavlovian extinction: *The procedure of repeatedly presenting the CS without the US, the effect of which is a reduction or elimination of the CS's ability to evoke the CR.*

A few years after the Little Albert experiment, Mary Cover Jones (1924) demonstrated that Pavlovian extinction could be used therapeutically to reduce a fear of furry animals in a preschooler named Peter. By repeatedly presenting the CS (a rabbit) without the US (i.e., without anything bad happening), Peter's phobia was gradually reduced. By the end of the therapy, Peter was holding the rabbit, playing with it in his bed, and letting the rabbit nibble at his fingers.

Mary Cover Jones
(1897-1987)

Source: Psychology's Feminist Voices Multimedia Internet Archive, 2010

Graduated Exposure Therapy

Mary Cover Jones' phobia-reducing therapy was not viewed as revolutionary at the time. Cover Jones herself did not further develop the therapy during her long and productive career in psychology. The technique was rediscovered in the 1960s by Joseph Wolpe and has been studied and expanded upon ever since. Today this Pavlovian-extinction-based therapy is known as *graduated exposure therapy*, and it remains the most effective intervention for reducing human phobias (Wolitzky-Taylor et al., 2008).

One of Cover Jones' (1924) innovations was to begin therapy by presenting an approximation of the CS – one that evoked little or no fear. In the case of Peter, this was a caged rabbit placed 12 feet away. When Peter showed no fear of this CS-approximation, the cage was gradually brought closer. During **graduated exposure therapy**, *the client is gradually exposed to successively stronger approximations of the CS. Before each new CS-approximation is presented, steps are taken to reduce/eliminate any fear evoked by the prior CS-approximation.*

Phobic clients find graduated exposure therapy much more acceptable than Pavlovian extinction alone. Take the case of Annora, a 7-year-old girl with an extreme fear of dogs.[5] When she was a preschooler, a dog chased her (US) and frightened her (UR). Subsequently, whenever she heard a dog barking nearby (CS), she displayed panic (CR) and immediately climbed into the arms of her parents. This phobia negatively impacted her life. She was unable to visit friends' houses or attend social events with her parents if it meant an encounter with a dog.

To understand why we find graduated exposure therapy so much more acceptable than Pavlovian extinction, it helps to imagine what extinction alone would look like for Annora. Pavlovian extinction would involve extended exposure to dogs without the US happening (i.e., nothing bad would happen). Understandably, Annora would not have agreed to this, so graduated exposure therapy was offered as a gentler approach. Therapy began by arranging a CS-approximation anticipated to evoke little or no fear: sitting with her father in the safety of the family car, in the parking lot of the pet shelter.

Therapists using graduated exposure therapy help their clients to relax when the CS-approximation is presented (this is the technique that Joseph Wolpe added to Mary Cover Jones' therapy). So, while in the car, Annora was encouraged to breath normally, listen to the dogs barking, and notice that nothing bad was happening (no US event). Her father made light of the situation, as humor can also be an effective component of graduated exposure therapy (Ventis et al., 2001).

On the second visit to the shelter's parking lot, a closer approximation of the CS was presented – Annora lowered her car window. At subsequent visits she got out of the car and set the pace as she and her father walked to the shelter entrance, but they did not go in. Later, they entered the shelter and Annora gradually made her way to the kennels where she looked at the dogs from a distance. Eventually, they picked out their new dog, Sir Edwin, who spent his nights sleeping with Annora for the rest of his life. A few sessions of graduated exposure therapy cured Annora of a years-long debilitating phobia and it helped little Edwin find a loving home.

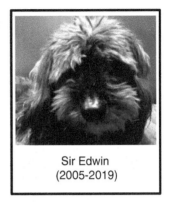

Sir Edwin
(2005-2019)

Source: Photograph (with permission) by Gregory Madden.

Spontaneous Recovery

In Pavlov's (1927) extinction experiments, he noted that after the CS no longer evoked the CR in session 1, it spontaneously recovered its salivation-evoking function in session 2. This is illustrated in Figure 4.10. Session 1 was composed of six extinction trials. In each, the CS was presented without the US (meat powder in the mouth). By the fifth extinction trial, the CS had lost its ability to evoke the CR (salivation). However, 2 hours later, at the beginning of session 2, the CS spontaneously recovered its ability to evoke salivation. This *increase in conditioned responding following the passage of time since Pavlovian extinction* is

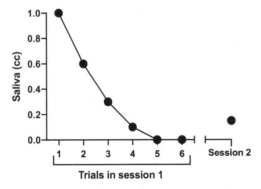

Figure 4.10 Over the course of six extinction trials in session 1, the CS gradually lost its ability to evoke the CR (salivating). Later, in Session 2, the CS "spontaneously recovered" its evocative function.

Source: Pavlov, I. P. (1927). Conditional reflexes: an investigation of the physiological activity of the cerebral cortex. Oxford, England: Oxford University Press. Retrieved from https://psycnet.apa.org/record/1927-10319-000

referred to as **spontaneous recovery**. Spontaneous recovery is a reliable finding that has been replicated in many laboratory settings and in many species, including humans (Lattal, 2013; Rescorla, 2004).

Applying this finding to Pavlovian fear conditioning, when Annora returned to the shelter a week later for a second round of graduated exposure therapy, we would expect spontaneous recovery of fear. This is exactly what happened. However, after just a minute or two of relaxing in the car, Annora was ready to slowly walk toward the shelter's entrance.

In treating phobias, behavior therapists should expect some spontaneous recovery at the start of each session (Rachman & Lopatka, 1988). How much depends on three factors. First, the more time that passes between Pavlovian extinction/exposure sessions, the more spontaneous recovery will occur (Quirk, 2002). So, it's better to schedule therapeutic sessions frequently.

Second, spontaneous recovery decreases as more Pavlovian extinction sessions are conducted (Rescorla, 2004). This is shown in Figure 4.11. As the rats had more opportunities to learn that the CS no longer signaled a delay reduction to the US, spontaneous recovery gradually declined.

Third, less spontaneous recovery will occur if each Pavlovian extinction session is continued until the CS no longer evokes the CR (Rescorla, 2004). In the study shown in Figure 4.11, the sessions were brief, and the CS was still evoking the CR at session's end. As a result, the amount of spontaneous recovery occurring day-after-day was larger than in Pavlov's original study shown in Figure 4.10.

In sum, Pavlovian extinction (and extinction-based therapies) will be more effective when (1) several sessions are conducted, (2) sessions are conducted often, and (3) sessions are continued until the CS no longer evokes the CR (Wolitzky-Taylor et al., 2008). Extra Box 1 explores how Pavlovian extinction has been used to aid in the treatment of military PTSD.

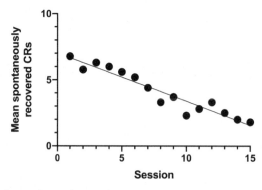

Figure 4.11 Number of conditioned responses (CRs) occurring on the first two presentations of the CS within each extinction session (data from the rest of each session are not shown).

Source: Rescorla, R. A. (2004). Spontaneous recovery. *Learning & Memory, 11*(5), 501–509. https://doi.org/10.1101/lm.77504

EXTRA BOX 1: POSTTRAUMATIC STRESS DISORDER IN MILITARY VETERANS

Individuals with military combat experience or who have been sexually assaulted are at risk of posttraumatic stress disorder (PTSD; Rizzo, Hartholt, Grimani, Leeds, & Liewer, 2014). Risk of PTSD increases as soldiers are exposed to larger numbers of traumatic events (Kok, Herrell, Thomas, & Hoge, 2012).

From a Pavlovian perspective, the traumatic event is the US and the negative emotion elicited is the UR. Any salient and informative stimulus that signals a delay reduction to the US will, through Pavlovian conditioning, function as a CS that can later evoke a similar form of the negative emotion (the CR). This process can help to explain how a triggering event (CS) can evoke a swarm of negative feelings in those suffering from PTSD.

Most soldiers who experience trauma will temporarily experience PTSD-like symptoms of anxiety, fear, and a desire to avoid situations in which the trauma occurred. For many trauma victims these symptoms fade over a few months (Rothbaum & Foa, 1993), perhaps as they are repeatedly exposed to the CS without the US (Pavlovian extinction). For others (11–42% of trauma survivors), the PTSD symptoms will persist and require a systematic intervention, such as graduated exposure therapy.

PTSD, however, has proven difficult to treat. For those suffering from PTSD, the entire environment in which the US was experienced may function as a complex CS evoking fear (Grillon et al., 2009). Consistent with this, the fear-evoking effects of the CS overgeneralize to stimuli that merely resemble the CS (Lissek et al., 2005). Thus, a cardboard box on the side of the road (resembling a road-side bomb) or a crowd of noisy people can trigger the fight-or-flight feeling of panic. In addition, PTSD victims show more spontaneous recovery following Pavlovian extinction therapy (Milad et al., 2008) and find it difficult to learn to inhibit fear responding when presented with CS events (Milad et al., 2009).

Given this tendency for a wide range of stimuli to function as CSs triggering PTSD symptoms and enhanced spontaneous recovery, effective interventions will involve repeated exposure sessions in which clients may be safely exposed to a wide range of triggering stimuli (Lissek & van Meurs, 2015). Virtual reality may prove beneficial on both counts. PTSD sufferers are given a headset and a series of therapeutic programs designed to gradually expose the veteran to a wide range of stimuli that might function as a CS. This allows the veteran to

Source: U.S. Air Force photo/Airman 1st Class Jordan Castelan

complete an exposure session every day at a convenient time, without the expense of an office visit to a therapist. Few well-controlled studies have been conducted on this therapy so far, but there are some encouraging findings (Rizzo et al., 2014).

Nonhuman studies suggest that Pavlovian extinction "therapy" needs to continue for a long time to prevent spontaneous recovery of fear (Denniston et al., 2003); the convenience and engaging qualities of the virtual-reality experience may prove beneficial in achieving this long-term compliance with graduated exposure therapy. Spontaneous recovery of fear is also decreased when nonhumans undergo extended Pavlovian extinction in a wide variety of situations (Thomas et al., 2009). Once again, the virtual-reality environment is well suited to arranging these wide varieties of environments in which the CS is encountered without the US. In the coming years, clinical researchers will continue to explore effective methods for helping individuals diagnosed with PTSD. Such research holds promise for positively influencing human behavior.

Reading Quiz 4

1. In a procedure known as Pavlovian _____, the _____ is presented repeatedly without the US.
2. The effect of Pavlovian extinction on behavior is a reduction or elimination of the CS's ability to evoke the _____.
3. The therapy technique used to help Annora overcome her fear of dogs is called _____ _____ therapy.
4. An early form of graduated exposure therapy was used by Mary _____ _____ to help Peter overcome his fear of rabbits and other furry animals.
5. When graduated exposure therapy is used to treat phobias, the first CS _____ (e.g., a caged rabbit placed at a 12-feet distance) should be a stimulus anticipated to evoke little or no fear.
6. The most effective treatment for human phobias is known as _____ _____ therapy.
7. Following an extinction session, it is common for the CS to _____ _____ its ability to evoke the CR.
8. When using Pavlovian extinction to treat human phobias, _____ _____ is a bad thing because, after the extinction session, the client experiences fear when the CS is presented.
9. If more time passes between Pavlovian extinction sessions, _____ (more/less) spontaneous recovery will occur.
10. Spontaneous recovery decreases as _____ (more/less) Pavlovian extinction sessions are conducted.
11. Spontaneous recovery can be minimized by continuing each extinction session until the _____ is completely extinguished.

Pavlovian Conditioning in Everyday Life

You may never have developed a debilitating phobia, but you probably learned, through Pavlovian conditioning, to fear other stimuli. If a bully tormented you as a child, or a boss berates you on a regular basis (both US events), then the sight/sound/smell of the bully or boss (the CS) signals a delay reduction to the US. When these CSs are encountered, a negative emotion is evoked. Similarly, parents who compulsively criticize, hit, or yell at their children should not be surprised when their children fear them more than they love them. Something to consider if you have or plan to have children of your own.

Consider the emotions evoked by the approach of a close friend. If the sight/sound/smell of the friend signals a delay reduction to a positive experience (the US), then this CS alone will evoke positive emotions. These positive emotions are tangible in children who jump up and down with joy when they see their best friend approaching, and in teenagers who display their positive emotions with hugs, fist-bumps, and verbal displays (e.g., "Oh yea!").

The remainder of this chapter examines two final examples of Pavlovian conditioning that commonly influence human behavior: taste-aversion learning and advertising.

Taste-Aversion Learning

Is there a food or drink that you used to enjoy, but then there was that time you got really sick after eating/drinking it? Ever since, you have not been able to touch it. If this sounds familiar, then you have first-hand experience with a form of Pavlovian conditioning known as *taste-aversion learning*.

For example, let's say that you occasionally eat guacamole. It's not your favorite food, but it's also not something you dislike – it is a neutral stimulus. You go out to a new pub with friends on a Friday night, and the waiter gives you some free chips and guacamole. You eat a healthy amount of the guacamole and, 5 hours later, you get really sick – vomiting, extreme pain in your gut, and diarrhea. Not fun. The next time you go to the pub, the mere sight of the guacamole turns your stomach.

One of the amazing things about taste-aversion learning is that it is *one-trial learning* (Garcia et al., 1974). That is, the CS (taste) acquires its ability to evoke the CR (revulsion) after a single encounter with the CS→US (illness) relation. Pavlovian learning with other stimuli typically requires several such encounters.

Also amazing is the long interval between the CS (tasting the guacamole) and the US (getting violently ill) – 5 hours. But if we calculate the delay reduction ratio, the finding is not unexpected. The time between food poisonings is, let's say, 3 years (i.e., 94,609,095 seconds). This value goes in the numerator:

$$\text{delay-reduction ratio} = \frac{94,609,095}{\text{CS} \rightarrow \text{US interval}}$$

Next, we specify the interval of time that elapses between the CS and the US; in this case 5 hours (i.e, 18,000 seconds).

$$\text{delay-reduction ratio} = \frac{94,609,095}{18,000} = 525.6$$

Thus, the guacamole CS signaled a very large delay reduction to a violent illness (US) – the CS signals an illness will happen 525 times faster than normal. As noted earlier, the larger the delay reduction, the more quickly Pavlovian learning occurs, and the more reliably the CS will evoke the CR (Gallistel & Gibbon, 2002; Gibbon et al., 1977).

Advertising

John B. Watson's academic career came to an end in 1920 when his extra-marital relationship with his research associate, Rosalie Rayner, was discovered and he was forced to resign his appointment. Watson and Rayner were later married, and they remained so until her untimely death in 1936.

John B. Watson
(1878 – 1958)

Source: Prakruthi Prasad/
Wikipedia/CC BY-SA 4.0

After leaving Johns Hopkins University, Watson was hired by the largest advertising firm in the United States. They hired him to improve the efficacy of their advertisements. Prior to Watson's time, advertisements mostly appealed to consumers' intellect (our product is better for the following reasons ...), not to their emotions. A problem arises for such advertisements when all of the products on the shelf are of equivalent quality. For example, in blind taste-tests most consumers cannot tell the difference between Coke, Pepsi, or any other cola on the market. Likewise, consumers can't tell if their clothes were cleaned with a cheap or an expensive laundry detergent. If all of the products are similar, companies will struggle to convince anyone to buy *their* product.

Advertisers needed a different strategy, one based in human emotions. Who better than the behaviorist who studied Pavlovian learning and human emotions? Watson encouraged the development of print advertisements designed to evoke emotional responses. For example, Watson played a role in redesigning Johnson's baby powder advertisements, so they would evoke feelings of love and tenderness. Presenting the baby powder (CS) with a tender image of a mother with her child (US) increased positive feelings toward the product (CR). When consumers exposed to Watson's advertisements saw *Johnson's* baby powder packaging on the store shelves, its ability to evoke positive feelings influenced choice. As Winkler and Bromberg (1939, p. 306) wrote, "Dr. Watson was proving one thing that no amount of debate could refute – Behaviorism could make money."

Today, advertisers present their products with emotion-evoking stimuli all the time. Television beer commercials, repeatedly aired (as though Pavlov himself had arranged the experiment), display people having good times. Rationally, we watch and know that drinking their beer will not make us any happier than drinking another beer. But natural selection has preprogrammed us to learn through Pavlovian conditioning. Therefore, when faced with a beer choice, we are the unwitting victims of these emotions evoked by the distinctive logo (CS) on the bottle of beer.

Source: Rawpixel.com/Shutterstock.com

Summary

Natural selection has prepared individuals to behave in adaptive ways when phylogenetically important events occur. These phylogenetically selected behaviors, however, cannot help us survive when the environment changes. Adapting to a changing world requires learning. A simple form of learning, habituation, occurs when reflex responses gradually decrease after the eliciting stimulus is presented repeatedly.

Pavlovian learning describes how individuals learn to use the CS to make *predictions* about the US. That is, after Pavlovian conditioning, the individual's behavior changes in a way that reveals the CS is useful in predicting (1) the CS is coming (i.e., the CS signals a delay reduction to the US), (2) *when* the US will occur (e.g., 10 seconds after the CS), and (3) *what* the US will be (e.g., food, water, or a good time with friends). These three predictions allow the individual to survive, procreate, and live more adaptively.

These CS-US predictions are not conscious predictions. No one sees the waiter bringing their favorite pizza to the table and thinks, "Oh boy, it's almost here! Time to start salivating." Instead, natural selection has programmed your body to engage in this Pavlovian response without your conscious involvement. Thank goodness. Who wants to have to consciously manage all our Pavlovian responses each day?

Although Pavlovian learning is adaptive, it is not without its drawbacks. Individuals exposed to traumatic events can develop phobias or PTSD that negatively impacts their ability to thrive. Behavior therapists have developed successful Pavlovian-based therapies for phobias (e.g., graduated-exposure therapy) but additional research and therapy development is needed for the treatment of PTSD.

If Pavlovian learning describes how individuals come to make *predictions* about the US, this learning does not allow the individual to *influence* the US. Salivating does not produce food, it is merely evoked by the food-signaling CS. Little Albert's fear response did not stop the loud noise from occurring, it was merely evoked by the noise-signaling CS (the white rat). Behavior that *influences* the environment in which it occurs is called *operant behavior*, and it is the topic of Chapter 5.

Answers to Reading Quiz Questions

Reading Quiz 1

1. learning
2. reflexive
3. elicited
4. habituation
5. evoked
6. elicited
7. elicited

Reading Quiz 2

1. stimulus
2. stimuli
3. unconditioned stimulus (US); unconditioned response (UR)
4. neutral stimulus
5. neutral stimulus; conditioned stimulus (CS)
6. unconditioned response (UR)
7. conditioned response (CR)
8. function

Reading Quiz 3

1. delay; when; what (or which)
2. unconditioned stimulus (US)
3. salient
4. delay reduction
5. stimulus (or CS)
6. delay–reduction ratio = (200/2) = 100; yes this will function as an effective CS
7. delay–reduction ratio = (60/55) = 1.09; no this will not function as an effective CS

Reading Quiz 4

1. extinction; CS
2. CR
3. graduated exposure
4. Cover Jones
5. approximation
6. graduated exposure
7. spontaneously recover
8. spontaneous recovery
9. more
10. more
11. CR

Notes

1. Paul Revere is a famous figure in the American war for independence. He is remembered for alerting the American militia of the approaching British armies prior to a key battle in the war. His warning call, yelled through the streets of Concord Massachusetts, was "The Regulars are coming! The Regulars are coming!" The "Regulars" referred to the British army.
2. You might wonder why pigeons peck these lights in the first place. They don't have to peck them to earn food or water, but they do it anyways. The reason is that, outside the lab, in the natural environment in which pigeons live, the stimuli that signal a delay reduction to food or water are not different kinds of lights, they are the sight

of food and water. Therefore, in the wild, approaching and touching the beak to the CS is an adaptive response. One sees similar CS-approach behaviors in other species when the US is food. This behavior continues even when the CR cancels the delivery of the food (Killeen, 2003; Timberlake et al., 1982).

3. The limiting condition to this principle is that when the CS is presented at the exact same time as the US the ratio is undefined, for a reason. If the CS is presented simultaneous with the US, it is redundant, it provides no useful information about when the US will occur. It's already occurring! It would be like Paul Revere riding with the British army while screaming, "The Regulars are coming! The Regulars are coming!" The American militia will find this warning to be completely useless, something to be ignored. This is the fourth principle of effective Pavlovian conditioning (the CS cannot be redundant).

4. Maes et al. (2016) reported a series of experiments with mice that failed to replicate Kamin's blocking effect. In a follow-up paper, Soto (2018) explained how modern theories of Pavlovian learning, theories beyond the scope of this book, provide an account of why Maes et al. failed to replicate the blocking effect. Soto also pointed to several studies that have obtained blocking in mice, the species used by Maes et al. (e.g., Sanderson, Jones, & Austen, 2016).

5. Annora is the daughter of one of the authors of this book. She consented to having her story told here.

References

Balsam, P. D., Drew, M. R., & Yang, C. (2002). Timing at the start of associative learning. *Learning and Motivation*, *33*(1), 141–155. doi:10.1006/LMOT.2001.1104

Baum, W. M. (2005). *Understanding behaviorism: Behavior, culture, and evolution* (2nd ed.). Malden, MA: Blackwell.

Bremner, J. D., Southwick, S. M., Darnell, A., & Charney, D. S. (1996). Chronic PTSD in Vietnam combat veterans: Course of illness and substance abuse. *American Journal of Psychiatry*, *153*(3), 369–375. doi: 10.1176/ajp.153.3.369

Colwill, R. M., & Motzkin, D. K. (1994). Encoding of the unconditioned stimulus in Pavlovian conditioning. *Animal Learning & Behavior*, *22*(4), 384–394. doi:10.3758/BF03209158

Cover Jones, M. (1924). A laboratory study of fear: The case of Peter. *Pedagogical Seminary*, *31*, 308–315. Retrieved from https://search.proquest.com/openview/b5f757043a0be46aba934466c9ed4bcf/1?cbl=1818970&pq-origsite=gscholar

Dekel, R., & Solomon, Z. (2007). Secondary traumatization among wives of war veterans with PTSD. In C. R. Figley & W. P. Nash (Eds.), *Routledge psychosocial stress series. Combat stress injuury: Theory, research, and management* (p. 137–157). New York: Routledge. Retrieved from https://psycnet.apa.org/record/2007-00766-007

Denniston, J. C., Chang, R. C., & Miller, R. R. (2003). Massive extinction treatment attenuates the renewal effect. *Learning and Motivation*, *34*(1), 68–86. doi:10.1016/S0023-9690(02)00508-8

Domjan, M. (2016). Elicited versus emitted behavior: Time to abandon the distinction. *Journal of the Experimental Analysis of Behavior*, *105*(2), 231–245. doi:10.1002/jeab.197

Drew, M. R., Zupan, B., Cooke, A., Couvillon, P. A., & Balsam, P. D. (2005). Temporal control of conditioned responding in Goldfish. *Journal of Experimental Psychology: Animal Behavior Processes*, *31*(1), 31–39. doi:10.1037/0097-7403.31.1.31

Epstein, L. H., Rodefer, J. S., Wisniewski, L., & Caggiula, A. R. (1992). Habituation and dishabituation of human salivary response. *Physiology & Behavior*, *51*(5), 945–950. doi:10.1016/0031-9384(92)90075-D

Epstein, L. H., Saad, F. G., Handley, E. A., Roemmich, J. N., Hawk, L. W., & McSweeney, F. K. (2003). Habituation of salivation and motivated responding for food in children. *Appetite*, *41*(3), 283–289. doi:10.1016/S0195-6663(03)00106-5

Fantino, E. (1977). Conditioned reinforcement: Choice and information. In W. K. Honig & J. E. Staddon (Eds.), *Handbook of operant behavior* (pp. 313–339). Engelwood Cliffs, NJ: Prentice-Hall.

Fantino, E., Preston, R. A., & Dunn, R. (1993). Delay reduction: Current status. *Journal of the Experimental Analysis of Behavior*, *60*(1), 159–169. doi:10.1901/jeab.1993.60-159

Gallistel, C. R., & Gibbon, J. (2002). *The symbolic foundations of conditioned behavior*. Mawwah, NJ: Lawrence Erlbaum Associates.

Garcia, J., Hankins, W. G., & Rusiniak, K. W. (1974). Behavioral regulation of the milieu interne in man and rat. *Science, 185*, 824–831. doi: 10.1126/science.185.4154.824

Ghirlanda, S., & Enquist, M. (2003). A century of generalization. *Animal Behaviour, 66*(1), 15–36. doi:10.1006/ANBE.2003.2174

Gibbon, J., Baldock, M. D., Locurto, C., Gold, L., & Terrace, H. S. (1977). Trial and intertrial durations in autoshaping. *Journal of Experimental Psychology: Animal Behavior Processes, 3*(3), 264–284. doi: 10.1037/0097-7403.3.3.264

Gibbon, J., & Balsam, P. D. (1981). Spreading associations in time. In C. M. Locurto, H. S. Terrace, & J. Gibbon (Eds.), *Autoshaping and conditioning theory* (pp. 219–253). New York: Academic Press.

Grillon, C., Pine, D. S., Lissek, S., Rabin, S., Bonne, O., & Vythilingam, M. (2009). Increased anxiety during anticipation of unpredictable aversive stimuli in posttraumatic stress disorder but not in generalized anxiety disorder. *Biological Psychiatry, 66*(1), 47–53. doi:10.1016/J.BIOPSYCH.2008.12.028

Hall, G., Mackintosh, N. J., Goodall, G., & Martello, M. D. (1977). Loss of control by a less valid or by a less salient stimulus compounded with a better predictor of reinforcement. *Learning and Motivation, 8*(2), 145–158. doi:10.1016/0023-9690(77)90001-7

Hoffmann, H., Janssen, E., & Turner, S. L. (2004). Classical conditioning of sexual arousal in women and men: Effects of varying awareness and biological relevance of the conditioned stimulus. *Archives of Sexual Behavior, 33*(1), 43–53. doi:10.1023/B:ASEB.0000007461.59019.d3

Hoffmann, H., Peterson, K., & Garner, H. (2012). Field conditioning of sexual arousal in humans. *Socioaffective Neuroscience & Psychology, 2*(1), 17336. doi:10.3402/snp.v2i0.17336

Hovland, C. I. (1937). The generalization of conditioned responses: I. The sensory generalization of conditioned responses with varying frequencies of tone. *The Journal of General Psychology, 17*(1), 125–148. doi:10.1080/00221309.1937.9917977

Jakupcak, M., Cook, J., Imel, Z., Fontana, A., Rosenheck, R., & McFall, M. (2009). Posttraumatic stress disorder as a risk factor for suicidal ideation in Iraq and Afghanistan War veterans. *Journal of Traumatic Stress, 22*(4), 303–306. doi:10.1002/jts.20423

Jenkins, H. M., & Moore, B. R. (1973). The form of the auto-shaped response with food or water reinforcers1. *Journal of the Experimental Analysis of Behavior, 20*(2), 163–181. doi:10.1901/jeab.1973.20-163

Kamin, L. J. (1969). Predictability, surprise, attention, and conditioning. In B. A. Cambell & R. M. Church (Eds.), *Punishment and aversive behavior* (pp. 279–296). New York: Meredith Corporation.

Killeen, P. R. (2003). Complex dynamic processes in sign tracking with an omission contingency (negative automaintenance). *Journal of Experimental Psychology: Animal Behavior Processes, 29*(1), 49–61. doi:10.1037/0097-7403.29.1.49

Kok, B. C., Herrell, R. K., Thomas, J. L., & Hoge, C. W. (2012). Posttraumatic stress disorder associated with combat service in Iraq or Afghanistan. *The Journal of Nervous and Mental Disease, 200*(5), 444–450. doi:10.1097/NMD.0b013e3182532312

Lattal, K. M. (2013). Pavlovian conditioning. In G. J. Madden (Ed.), *APA handbook of behavior analysis: Vol. 1 methods and principles* (pp. 283–306). Washington, DC: American Psychological Association.

Lissek, S., Powers, A. S., McClure, E. B., Phelps, E. A., Woldehawariat, G., Grillon, C., & Pine, D. S. (2005). Classical fear conditioning in the anxiety disorders: A meta-analysis. *Behaviour Research and Therapy, 43*(11), 1391–1424. doi:10.1016/J.BRAT.2004.10.007

Lissek, S., & van Meurs, B. (2015). Learning models of PTSD: Theoretical accounts and psychobiological evidence. *International Journal of Psychophysiology, 98*(3), 594–605. doi:10.1016/J.IJPSYCHO.2014.11.006

Mackintosh, N. J. (1975). A theory of attention: Variations in the associability of stimuli with reinforcement. *Psychological Review, 82*. doi:10.1037/h0076778

Maes, E., Boddez, Y., Alfei, J. M., Krypotos, A.-M., D'Hooge, R., De Houwer, J., & Beckers, T. (2016). The elusive nature of the blocking effect: 15 failures to replicate. *Journal of Experimental Psychology: General, 145*(9), e49–e71. doi:10.1037/xge0000200

McGregor, I. S., Schrama, L., Ambermoon, P., & Dielenberg, R. A. (2002). Not all 'predator odours' are equal: Cat odour but not 2,4,5 trimethylthiazoline (TMT; fox odour) elicits specific defensive behaviours in rats. *Behavioural Brain Research, 129*(1–2), 1–16. doi:10.1016/S0166-4328(01)00324-2

Milad, M. R., Orr, S. P., Lasko, N. B., Chang, Y., Rauch, S. L., & Pitman, R. K. (2008). Presence and acquired origin of reduced recall for fear extinction in PTSD: Results of a twin study. *Journal of Psychiatric Research, 42*(7), 515–520. doi:10.1016/J.JPSYCHIRES.2008.01.017

Milad, M. R., Pitman, R. K., Ellis, C. B., Gold, A. L., Shin, L. M., Lasko, N. B., ... Rauch, S. L. (2009). Neurobiological basis of failure to recall extinction memory in posttraumatic stress disorder. *Biological Psychiatry, 66*(12), 1075–1082. doi:10.1016/J.BIOPSYCH.2009.06.026

Miller, R. R., & Matzel, L. D. (1988). The comparator hypothesis: A response rule for the expression of associations. *Psychology of Learning and Motivation, 22*, 51–92. doi:10.1016/S0079-7421(08)60038-9

Pavlov, I. P. (1927). *Conditional reflexes: An investigation of the physiological activity of the cerebral cortex.* Oxford, England: Oxford University Press.

Powell, R. A., Digdon, N., Harris, B., & Smithson, C. (2014). Correcting the record on Watson, Rayner, and Little Albert: Albert Barger as "Psychology's lost boy". *American Psychologist, 69*(6), 600–611. doi:10.1037/a0036854

Quirk, G. J. (2002). Memory for extinction of conditioned fear is long-lasting and persists following spontaneous recovery. *Learning & Memory, 9*(6), 402–407. doi:10.1101/lm.49602

Rachman, S., & Lopatka, C. (1988). Return of fear: Underlearning and overlearning. *Behaviour Research and Therapy, 26*(2), 99–104. doi:10.1016/0005-7967(88)90108-8

Rescorla, R. A. (1988). Behavioral studies of Pavlovian conditioning. *Annual Review of Neuroscience, 11*(1), 329–352. Retrieved from www.annualreviews.org

Rescorla, R. A. (2004). Spontaneous recovery. *Learning & Memory, 11*(5), 501–509. doi:10.1101/lm.77504

Rescorla, R. A., & Wagner, A. R. (1972). A theory of Pavlovian conditioning: Variations in the effectiveness of reinforcement and nonreinforcement. *Classical Conditioning II: Current Research and Theory, 2*, 64–99. Retrieved from https://pdfs.semanticscholar.org/afaf/65883ff75cc19926f61f181a687927789ad1.pdf

Rizzo, A., Hartholt, A., Grimani, M., Leeds, A., & Liewer, M. (2014). Virtual reality exposure therapy for combat-related posttraumatic stress disorder. *Computer, 47*(7), 31–37. doi:10.1109/MC.2014.199

Rothbaum, B. A., & Foa, E. B. (1993). Subtypes of posttraumatic stress disorder and duration of symptoms. In J. R. Davidson & E. B. Foa (Eds.), *Posttraumatic stress disorder: DSM-IV and beyond* (pp. 23–35). Washington, DC: American Psychiatric Press.

Sanderson, D. J., Jones, W. S., & Austen, J. M. (2016). The effect of the amount of blocking cue training on blocking of appetitive conditioning in mice. *Behavioural Processes, 122*, 36–42. doi:10.1016/J.BEPROC.2015.11.007

Shahan, T. A., & Cunningham, P. (2015). Conditioned reinforcement and information theory reconsidered. *Journal of the Experimental Analysis of Behavior, 103*(2), 405–418. doi:10.1002/jeab.142

Soto, F. A. (2018). Contemporary associative learning theory predicts failures to obtain blocking: Comment on Maes et al. (2016). *Journal of Experimental Psychology: General, 147*(4), 597–602. doi:10.1037/xge0000341

Sparber, S. B., Bollweg, G. L., & Messing, R. B. (1991). Food deprivation enhances both autoshaping and autoshaping impairment by a latent inhibition procedure. *Behavioural Processes, 23*(1), 59–74. doi:10.1016/0376-6357(91)90106-A

Thomas, B. L., Vurbic, D., & Novak, C. (2009). Extensive extinction in multiple contexts eliminates the renewal of conditioned fear in rats. *Learning and Motivation, 40*(2), 147–159. doi:10.1016/J.LMOT.2008.10.002

Timberlake, W., Wahl, G., & King, D. A. (1982). Stimulus and response contingencies in the misbehavior of rats. *Journal of Experimental Psychology: Animal Behavior Processes, 8*(1), 62–85. doi:10.1037/0097-7403.8.1.62

Ventis, W. L., Higbee, G., & Murdock, S. A. (2001). Using humor in systematic desensitization to reduce fear. *The Journal of General Psychology, 128*(2), 241–253. doi:10.1080/00221300109598911

Watson, J. B., & Rayner, R. (1920). Conditioned emotional reactions. *Journal of Experimental Psychology, 3*(1), 1–14. doi:10.1037/h0069608

Winkler, J. R., & Bromberg, W. (1939). *The mind explorers*. New York: Reynald and Hitchcock, Advertising Publications, Inc.

Wolitzky-Taylor, K. B., Horowitz, J. D., Powers, M. B., & Telch, M. J. (2008). Psychological approaches in the treatment of specific phobias: A meta-analysis. *Clinical Psychology Review, 28*(6), 1021–1037. doi:10.1016/J.CPR.2008.02.007

Yamada, K. (2010). Strain differences of selective attention in mice: Effect of Kamin blocking on classical fear conditioning. *Behavioural Brain Research, 213*(1), 126–129. doi:10.1016/J.BBR.2010.04.037

Operant Learning I: Reinforcement

5

Operant Behavior

Imagine that you have a class on the 14th floor of a building on campus. To get there, you walk into an open elevator and press the button with the number 14 on it. This simple button-pressing response is an instance of operant behavior. **Operant behavior** may be defined as *behavior influenced by antecedent and consequence events.*[1] An **antecedent** is an *observable stimulus that is present before the behavior occurs*. The elevator button is an antecedent stimulus. You saw the 14-button before the button-pressing behavior occurred *and* it influenced this behavior – the clearly visible number 14 increased the probability of pressing that particular button. We will have much to say about antecedent events in future chapters. But for now, we will focus on consequences and how they influence operant behavior.

A **consequence** is an *observable stimulus change that happens after behavior occurs*. The consequence of pressing the elevator button is the activation of the elevator (the doors close and the elevator lifts you to the 14th floor). Many of our everyday behaviors have consequences. The consequence of lifting a glass of water to your lips is that water flows into your mouth. The consequence of scratching your nose is the removal of an itch. The consequence of pressing the home button

Source: Toshe Ognjanov/ Shutterstock.com

An Introduction to Behavior Analysis, First Edition. Gregory J. Madden, Derek D. Reed and Florence D. DiGennaro Reed.
© 2021 John Wiley & Sons Ltd. Published 2021 by John Wiley & Sons Ltd.

on your phone is that it exits the currently active app. The consequence of saying "can you help me lift this couch" is that someone nearby provides assistance. The consequence of changing direction too quickly when running is a sprained ankle. The consequence of coughing in someone's face is that person saying, "Dude! Totally uncool."

Operant behavior changes the environment and, in turn, is influenced by that consequence. If pressing the 14-button changes our environment by activating the elevator and subsequently arriving on the 14th floor, how does this consequence influence the button-pressing operant behavior? To find out, we need to measure the effects of this consequence on behavior. As discussed in Chapter 3, we need to turn ON and OFF the consequence (the independent variable) and see if it affects behavior. If we turn off the consequence (the button is pressed, but the elevator fails to operate), then, as shown in Figure 5.1, this behavior would rarely occur (you would take the stairs instead). If we turn the consequence back on, the number of times you press the button each day would increase. Clearly, the consequence *influences* button-pressing behavior. Pressing the button is operant behavior because it is influenced by antecedents (the button itself) and consequences (the doors close and the elevator begins to move).

Table 5.1 explores how consequences influence the four instances of operant behavior that we have discussed already. In each case, the operant behavior occurs in two situations – once when the consequence is on (the consequence follows the behavior) and once when the consequence is off (the behavior occurs but the consequence does not). In the last column of the table, we speculate on how this consequence or lack of consequence would *influence* the behavior.

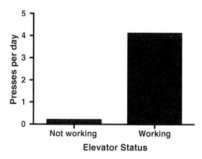

Figure 5.1 The number of times per day that the elevator button is pressed when the elevator is not working (left) and when it is working as normal (right).

Reading Quiz 1

1. Operant behavior is behavior influenced by antecedent and _____ events.
2. An antecedent is an observable stimulus that is present _____the behavior occurs.
3. A _____ is an observable stimulus change that happens after behavior occurs.

   For the next four items, indicate if the *italicized text* is an antecedent or a consequence of behavior (which is shown in bold text).

4. Cloe **takes a bite of her burrito**. It *tastes so good!*

5. Liam has *an itchy ear*. He **sticks his finger in and gives it a good scratch**.
6. Madeleine **gets up** when *her alarm goes off*.
7. Jasmine **presses the play button** on her podcast app. *The podcast begins to play.*

Response–Consequence Contingencies

When you press the elevator button (response), the elevator begins to operate (consequence). If you don't press the elevator button, then the elevator will not operate, and you will not arrive on the 14th floor. In this way, there is a *contingent relation* between response and consequence.

In Table 5.1, when the consequence was on, there was a contingent relation between response and consequence. *IF* the behavior occurred → *THEN* the consequence followed. When the consequence was off, there was no response–consequence contingent relation.

There are many other examples of response–consequence contingencies in our everyday lives. For example, your house or apartment is filled with response–consequence contingencies:

Table 5.1 Four operant behaviors, two possible consequences of each, and their effects on the future probability of this behavior.

Operant behavior	Independent variable	Influence on operant behavior
Lift glass to your lips	Consequence on: Water flows into your mouth	Each time thirst returns, this behavior will occur
	Consequence off: Glass is empty so nothing flows into your mouth	Behavior eventually stops occurring
Scratch your nose	Consequence on: Itch is relieved	Each time the itch returns, this behavior will occur
	Consequence off: Itch is not relieved in any way	Behavior eventually stops occurring
Changing direction quickly while running	Consequence on: Pain of a sprained ankle	Next time you turn a corner you don't do it so quickly
	Consequence off: No injury	No reduction in the probability of making dangerously fast turns
Coughing in someone's face	Consequence on: That person says "Dude! Totally uncool!"	Next time you direct your cough away from others
	Consequence off: That person does not react in any way	Next time a cough comes on, you are just as likely as before to cough in someone's face

- *IF* you put your key in the lock, turn it, and push the door (response) → *THEN* the front door opens (consequence).
- *IF* you turn on the heater (response) → *THEN* warm air is blown into the room (consequence).
- *IF* you open the refrigerator → *THEN* you can see all of the food and drinks available (consequence).
- *IF* you operate the microwave → *THEN* your food is heated.
- *IF* you add soap to the water → *THEN* the water is bubbly and helps you to clean your dishes.
- *IF* you set your alarm for 7:00 am → *THEN* the alarm goes off the next day at 7:00 am.

In each of these contingencies there are two terms – response and consequence. For this reason, this basic operant contingency is referred to as a **two-term contingency**. When behavior is influenced by a response–consequence (two-term) contingency, the individual has learned how to *operate* some aspect of their environment. Operant behavior operates the environment by producing consequences.

Let's provide a formal definition:

> A **response–consequence contingency** *describes the causal (IF → THEN) relation between an operant behavior and its consequence.*

Putting the key in the lock and turning it caused the door to open. The door did not open magically, and it would not have opened unless this operant response occurred. Because the response caused the consequence, we say a response–consequence contingency exists.

Learning Response–Consequence Contingencies

If an individual can learn the contingent relation between a response and its consequence, it is more likely to survive. If an animal is hungry and it has previously learned the contingent relation between searching for food (response) and finding food (consequence), then it can address its hunger by searching for food now. Likewise, if wandering away from the herd (response) leads to a dangerous encounter with a predator (consequence), then the animal increases its chance of survival if it learns the contingent relation between wandering and this life-threatening consequence.

This all might seem obviously true to you, but sometimes "common sense" knowledge is wrong. Is there good scientific evidence that individuals learn response–consequence contingencies? The most widely used method to test for this learning is the *reward-devaluation test*. An example of this is provided by a study conducted by Hogarth and Chase in 2011. In Phase 1 of their experiment, they let cigarette smokers choose between pressing two buttons. When the smoker pressed the left button, they occasionally earned a cigarette; when they pressed the right button, they occasionally earned a chocolate. The researchers wanted to know if the participants learned the following two contingencies:

1. *IF* left button press → *THEN* cigarette
2. *IF* right button press → *THEN* chocolate

To find out if participants learned these response–consequence contingencies, the value of the cigarette reward was devalued – the participants were allowed to smoke all they wanted.

With no remaining motivation for cigarettes, chocolate was the only thing that would function as a reinforcer. Did they know how to get chocolate, or would they press both buttons equally, only moving to the right after earning non-reinforcing cigarettes on the left? During their cleverly designed test session, button pressing produced no rewards. So the only thing that could guide responding was prior learning of the response-consequence contingencies. Consistent with the hypothesis that participants had learned these contingencies, they pressed the right button (chocolates) more often than the left one (cigarettes).

Similar studies have been conducted with nonhuman animals and the results are very similar. For example, in an experiment conducted by Colwill and Rescorla (1985), rats learned to press a lever for a grain-based food pellet and to pull a chain hanging from the ceiling for a sip of sweet liquid. The two response–consequence contingencies that could be learned were:

1. *IF* lever-press → *THEN* grain
2. *IF* chain-pull → *THEN* sweet liquid

To devalue the grain reward, some rats were fed grain and then injected with a medication that made them ill. We'll call them the "gross grain" (or GG) rats. The other rats were made sick after drinking the sweet liquid – the "gross sweet" (or GS) rats.

Just like in the cigarette and chocolate study, during the test session, no rewards were given. Nonetheless, GG rats demonstrated their contingency learning by mostly chain pulling (previously produced the sweet liquid; see top panel of Figure 5.2). Conversely, GS rats mostly pressed the lever. These results reveal that humans and nonhumans both learn the contingent relations between responses and their consequences.

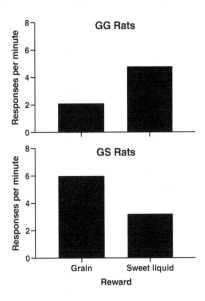

Figure 5.2 Test-session response rates of rats that had previously learned response–consequences contingencies for obtaining grain and liquid. GG rats no longer wanted food because they got sick the last time they ate it. GS rats got sick the last time they drank the sweet liquid. That GG rats responded more for liquid, and GS rats responded more for grain demonstrates that rats had learned the response–consequence contingencies.

Source: Colwill, R. M., & Rescorla, R. A. (1985). Postconditioning devaluation of a reinforcer affects instrumental responding. *Journal of Experimental Psychology: Animal Behavior Processes, 11*, 120–132.

Noncontingent Consequences

Contingent consequences occur when an *IF → THEN* relation exists between response and consequence. Sometimes, however, there is a *noncontingent* relation between response and consequence. For example, I raised my hand and then, coincidentally, a bird flew overhead. I bought lunch and then received a text that my grandmother had fallen and hurt herself. A **noncontingent consequence** *occurs after a response, but not because the response caused it to occur.*

Raising my hand did not cause the bird to fly overhead. If I raise my hand again, it will not cause another bird to fly overhead. My grandmother does not fall if I buy lunch; it was merely a coincidence that she fell after I bought lunch. When there is no causal relation between response and consequence, the relation between them is noncontingent.

Table 5.2 provides more examples of contingent and noncontingent consequences. Some of the examples provide blank spaces to give you some practice identifying responses and consequences. The answers appear at the end of the chapter.

Table 5.2 Several examples of contingent and noncontingent consequences. The blank spaces offer an opportunity for you to identify the response and the consequence.

Contingent relation (*IF → THEN*) between response and consequence:

1. You move a pen horizontally across a page (response) and a horizontal line appears on the page (consequence).
2. The alarm stops (consequence) when you press the snooze button (response).
3. You study the flashcards that you made for this class (_____) and you get a better grade on the exam (_____).
4. The cucumber is halved (_____) when you apply pressure to the knife (_____).
5. You receive a paycheck (_____) because you worked last month (_____).

Noncontingent relation between response and consequence:

6. You are sitting outside talking to a friend (response) and a fly lands on your chair (consequence).
7. While visiting the Washington Monument, you point up (_____) and your phone starts to ring (_____).
8. Just as you look out the window (_____), it starts to rain (_____).
9. A booger falls out of your nose and onto your shirt (_____) just after you begin studying (_____).
10. You hear a plane flying overhead (_____) after you turn on the TV (_____).

Superstitious Behavior

You probably know someone who you would describe as *superstitious*; you might have a few superstitions of your own. Superstitious behaviors frequently occur around sports. You might have a lucky shirt, eat the same food before every game, or leave the room because "every time I watch, they lose."

Players also engage in superstitious behaviors. Early in his professional career, Michael Jordan, one of the greatest basketball players of all time, wore a pair of blue and white shorts from his college basketball team (the University of North Carolina Tar Heels) under his Chicago Bulls shorts. Jordan won a national championship in college and thought the shorts might bring him good luck. Because he played well as a professional player, he behaved as though there was a response–consequence contingent relation between wearing the shorts (response) and winning games (consequence). Because the relation was noncontingent (i.e., there was no causal, *IF →THEN*, relation between response and consequence), the behavior would be classified as superstitious behavior.

Michael Jordan
(1963 –present)

Source: El Gráfico/Wikipedia/ CC0

Superstitious behavior *occurs when the individual behaves as though a response–consequence contingency exists when, in fact, the relation between response and consequence is noncontingent.*

The research on superstitious behavior is inconsistent. Skinner (1948) reported that several of his pigeons engaged in superstitious movements when he delivered food every 15 seconds, regardless of what the pigeon was doing. But later research suggested these movements were phylogenetic behavior patterns induced by the occasional delivery of food (Falk, 1971; Killeen, 1975; Staddon & Simmelhag, 1971; Timberlake & Lucas, 1985).

Koichi Ono (1987) evaluated superstitious behavior in college students. He found that only 1 of 20 participants developed a superstitious behavior when noncontingent points (worth money at the end of the session) were presented to a computer screen. Several participants engaged briefly in superstitious behaviors, such as jumping to touch the ceiling, but these behaviors didn't last very long.

When superstitious behavior occurs in humans outside the lab, it appears to be related to language. That is, we humans often verbally describe response–consequence contingencies ("*IF* I study my flash-cards → *THEN* I'll get a good grade on the next exam") but we sometimes get them wrong ("*IF* I wear my Red Sox cap inside-out → *THEN* my favorite baseball team will win the game"). If we ignore all those times that wearing the cap inside-out did not work, and remember all the times that it "worked," then superstitious behavior can persist. We will have more to say about language in Chapter 14.

Reading Quiz 2

1. You post a picture of your trip to the museum on your favorite social media platform _____ (response or consequence). Later that day you see that the picture was "liked" _____ (response or consequence).
    The relation between response and consequence is _____ (contingent/noncontingent).

2. Your mouth feels cleaner _____(response or consequence) after you brush your teeth _____ (response or consequence).
   The relation between response and consequence is _____ (contingent/noncontingent).
3. After you sit down in the movie theater _____ (response or consequence) the movie starts _____ (response or consequence).
   The relation between response and consequence is _____ (contingent/noncontingent).

Changing Behavior with Contingent Consequences

You will recall that the two goals of behavior analysis are to accurately predict behavior and to identify functional variables that may be used to positively influence behavior. Because operant behavior is influenced by antecedents and consequences, these are two categories of functional variables that may be used therapeutically to change behavior. Identifying functional *antecedent* variables and functional *consequence* variables is the core of behavior analysis. Changing these variables is what behavior analysts do to positively influence behavior. Again, we will discuss antecedents of operant behavior later in the book, for now we will keep things simple and discuss consequence-based interventions.

If our goal is to positively influence behavior, and the plan for accomplishing this is to introduce new consequences (e.g., a reward or a penalty), then we will be far more successful if we keep in mind the response–consequence contingency. Imagine that you are enrolled in two college classes: one is taught by Dr. Contingent and the other by Dr. Noncontingent. In Dr. Contingent's class, you have to study effectively to earn a good grade – *IF* you study effectively → *THEN* you are awarded a good grade. By contrast, Dr. Noncontingent is philosophically opposed to awarding grades contingent on effective studying. Instead, Dr. Noncontingent believes students learn best when they are given the freedom to do what they want, even if it means never coming to class. For which class are you more likely to study? The answer is obvious: Dr. Contingent's class.

Research has shown that teachers can positively influence children's classroom behavior by establishing a response–consequence contingency between good behavior and praise from the teacher (Baer & Wolf, 1968). That is, if the teacher praises children who are studying, playing appropriately, sharing, and so on, these pro-social behaviors will increase above baseline levels. But if praise is provided noncontingently (regardless of how the children are behaving), good behavior will occur less often (Hart et al., 1968).

Another example of skillfully using contingent consequences is a treatment for drug abuse called "Contingency Management." Individuals diagnosed with a substance-use disorder and who participate in Contingency Management treatment are informed of a new causal relation between drug abstinence (behavior) and a reward (consequence): *IF* you abstain from using drugs for the next two days → *THEN* you will earn a modest reward (something worth about $8). This simple response–

Source: © Evgeny Atamanenko/Shutterstock.com

consequence contingency can substantially increase drug abstinence (for a review of the efficacy of this treatment, see Benishek et al., 2014).

The importance of the contingency in Contingency Management may be illustrated by providing the rewards noncontingently. For these patients, rewards are received regardless of their drug use. If the patient uses drugs, he gets the reward. If he doesn't use drugs he still gets the reward. These patients do not increase their drug abstinence (Higgins et al., 2000). Clearly response–consequence contingencies are important when your goal is to positively influence behavior. This distinction between contingent and noncontingent consequences is discussed further in Extra Box 1.

EXTRA BOX 1:   NONCONTINGENT CONSEQUENCES IN NORTH KOREA

North Korea is a communist nation that has been ruled since the mid 1940s by a family of dictators known as the Kims. A guiding principle of communism is equality. In the abstract this sounds like a great idea – why should one person inherit wealth, and another person work very hard for very little income? In North Korea, this equality is played out in every way – everyone wears the same kinds of clothes; everyone lives in the same kind of apartment; everyone gets the same food in the same amounts. No matter how well (or how poorly) you do your job, you get the same clothes, the same apartment, and the same food. One might conceptualize this as a set of noncontingent consequences.

When beneficial consequences are provided noncontingently, performance suffers. If you get the same clothes, apartment, and food even when you don't work hard, don't innovate, and don't think creatively, then this noncontingent relation between behavior and consequences will reduce productivity, innovation, and creativity (Tidmarsh, 1993).

Such was the situation in the North Korean film industry in the 1970s. Their movies were terrible – bad acting, bad writing, bad everything. This didn't sit well with North Korea's supreme leader at the time, Kim Jong-il, who was a movie lover. To address this, Kim ordered the kidnapping of two filmmakers from their homes in nearby South Korea (a capitalist democracy). After their kidnap, Kim met with the filmmakers and explained that he wanted them to make North Korean films that would be good enough to be shown in Western nations; films that would win awards and bring glory to North Korea (Gourevitch, 2003).

Kim Jong-il
(1941-2011)

Source: Jesse Charlie/ Wikipedia, CC0

In the meeting, which was secretly recorded by the filmmakers, Kim admitted that the problem with North Korean movies was the communist system. To paraphrase Kim, "In our country there is no incentive to do any better. My screen writers write something dreadful, they get their rations. My filmmakers make an awful film, they get their rations. They get paid no matter what." The lesson is simple: If you want to positively influence behavior, you will wisely arrange contingent relations between behavior and consequences.

Reinforcers, Reinforcement, and Rewards

Many of our everyday behaviors are operant behaviors influenced by contingent consequences such as grades, paychecks, soothed infants, smiles, frowns, speeding tickets, and so on. Behavior analysts categorize consequences based on how they influence behavior. If the consequence *increases* behavior above its baseline level, then it is categorized as a **reinforcer**.

> A **reinforcer** *is a consequence that increases operant behavior above its baseline level.*

Source: Spotify, Inc.

For example, when you press the Spotify icon on your phone, the consequence of this behavior is that the app launches; the behavior caused the consequence. Is this consequence a reinforcer? To answer this question, we need to imagine the rate of pressing the Spotify icon if it produces no consequence. Take a second to imagine this. You download the Spotify app, you press the icon, and nothing happens. Press…nothing. Press…nothing. You might try rebooting your phone, but if pressing the app still doesn't launch the program, then you would stop pressing it.

If you use Spotify, you press the app icon because it produces a consequence – the app launches and you can listen to your music. If we were to draw a graph of the number of times you press the Spotify icon when it works and when it doesn't work, it would look a lot like the elevator graph in Figure 5.1. Because the consequence increases the frequency of pressing the Spotify icon above a no-reinforcer baseline level, we can classify this consequence as a reinforcer.

Before we consider another example, here is a note about vocabulary. The term *reinforcer* refers to the consequence itself – the consequence of behavior. **Reinforcement** refers to *the process or procedure whereby a reinforcer increases operant behavior above its baseline level.* Thus, in the prior example, the launch of the app was the "reinforcer," whereas the whole process (i.e., a consequence increased the behavior above its baseline level) is described as "reinforcement."

Source: Meryll/Shutterstock.com

Here is another example. The consequence of using an ATM is that the machine dispenses money from your bank account. The operant behavior involves inserting your card, entering your PIN, and pressing the withdrawal button. Does the dispensed money function as a reinforcer? As discussed before, to answer this question we need to know if the rate of using the ATM is higher when the reinforcer is delivered than when it is not; the latter is the baseline (no-reinforcer) rate of using the ATM machine. Because no one uses ATM machines that are out of order (machines that do not dispense money), we can be pretty sure that the dispensed money is a reinforcer for this behavior. Reinforce*ment* describes the process by which the dispensed money increases the probability of ATM-behavior above its baseline level.

Finally, it is important to make a distinction between reinforcers and rewards. **Rewards** are *beneficial consequences that we think will function as reinforcers, but we don't know yet if they will.* One of the authors of this book *thought* that a rawhide dog treat would reinforce his new dog's behavior. From the author's perspective, the rawhide was a *reward* because he thought that it would function as a reinforcer. To find out, the author arranged a contingent relation between sitting on command and delivery of the reward. The first time the dog sat, the rawhide was placed in the dog's mouth. Immediately after, the dog opened its mouth and the rawhide fell to the floor. This was repeated several times but sitting on command did not increase above the baseline level. Because the consequence did not increase the operant behavior, we conclude the reward does not function as a reinforcer. Just because you think the reward *should* function as a reinforcer does not mean that it will.

Reading Quiz 3

1. James established a contingent relation between sitting on command and dog treats. James thinks that the dog treats will function as a _____, but until he can demonstrate that they increase the probability of sitting on command, James can only describe them as _____.
2. A consequence that increases operant behavior above its baseline level is a _____.
3. The process by which a reinforcer increases operant behavior above its baseline level is referred to as _____.
4. If a consequence occurs independent of behavior, there is no response–consequence contingency. We refer to such events as _____ consequences.

The Discovery of Reinforcement

The first scientist to demonstrate that reinforcers increase the probability of behavior was **Edward L. Thorndike**. To conduct his groundbreaking research, Thorndike (1911) built the puzzle box shown in Figure 5.3. The box arranged a response–consequence contingency: *IF* the cat placed in the box pulled a string, connected through a series of pulleys to the door latch → *THEN* the door would open. Of course, the cat did not know how the box worked, so it tried many unsuccessful behaviors (e.g., trying to squeeze through the bars) before chancing upon an escape route. Eventually, the cat pulled the string and opened the door. Thorndike wanted to know if this consequence would increase the probability of pulling the string the next time the cat was placed in the box.

Edward L. Thorndike
(1874-1949)

Source: THE INTERNET ARCHIVE

Figure 5.4 shows how quickly Cat 12 pulled the string each time it was placed in the box. The red data point in the lower-left of the graph shows that the baseline speed of pulling the string was very low. On this first time in the box, Cat 12 spent nearly 3 minutes before it pulled the string and opened the door. After that, the cat pulled the string increasingly quickly when placed back into the puzzle box.

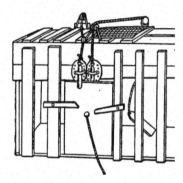

Figure 5.3 Drawing of puzzle Box A, used by Edward L. Thorndike in the early twentieth century to discover reinforcement.
Source: Modified from Google image search (labeled for reuse with modification): Thorndike puzzlebox. (Source: Flickr).

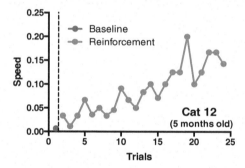

Figure 5.4 Cat 12's speed of escaping from Thorndike's Box A. Speed is calculated as 1 divided by the time required to escape from the box.
Source: Based on Thorndike, E. L. (1911). Animal intelligence. New York: MacMillan.

How to Tell If a Consequence Functions as a Reinforcer

Did the door-opening consequence function as a reinforcer? That is, did it increase string-pulling behavior above baseline (no-reinforcer) levels. To find out, we will use the flowchart shown in Figure 5.5. We will use this flowchart several times in this chapter, and later we will ask you to use it on your own, so you should follow along closely.

When using the flowchart, start at the top by identifying the behavior of interest – in this case, pulling the string inside the puzzle box – and the stimulus change that might (or might not) function as a reinforcer – the door of the puzzle box opens.

Next, we answer the question posed in the bubble at the top of the flowchart – does the stimulus change happen after the behavior of interest? Yes, the puzzle box door opened after the string was pulled, so the stimulus change is a consequence of behavior. Reinforcers are always consequences of behavior. If the stimulus change had happened before the string pull, then we would conclude that the stimulus change was not a reinforcer.

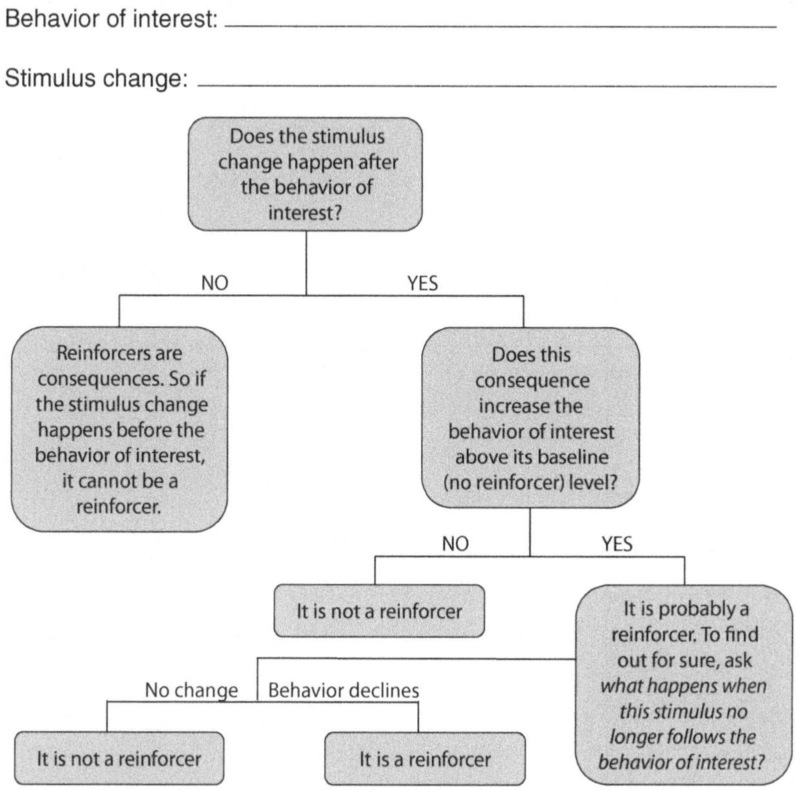

Behavior of interest: _____

Stimulus change: _____

Figure 5.5 Use this flowchart to evaluate if a stimulus change functions as a reinforcer.

Following the "YES" branch we next ask – Does this consequence increase the behavior above its baseline (no-reinforcer) level? The green data points in Figure 5.4 show how quickly Cat 12 pulled the string after this response produced the door-opening consequence. The clear effect of this consequence was that the speed of pulling the string increased across trials. Thus, for Cat 12 we can say "YES," this consequence increased the behavior of interest above the no-reinforcer baseline level.

The next bubble in Figure 5.5 notes that the door-opening consequence was *probably* a reinforcer. To be certain about this, we would want to turn OFF the consequence. That is, Cat 12 would pull the string but the door would never open – a Reversal design. Thorndike did not do this. Instead, he replicated the Cat 12 experiment with four new cats. Figure 5.6 shows the average speed at which these cats pulled the string once they were placed inside the puzzle box. The results were the same as before – the no-reinforcer baseline speed of string-pulling was very low on the first trial. However, with successive reinforcers (escapes from the box) the speed at which the cats pulled the string increased dramatically. These replications convinced Thorndike that the door-opening consequence reinforced the cats' string-pulling behavior.

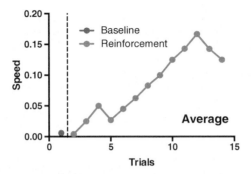

Figure 5.6 The average speed of four cats that escaped from Thorndike's Box A.
Source: Based on Thorndike, E. L. (1911). Animal intelligence. New York: MacMillan.

From Puzzle Boxes to Skinner Boxes

In the late 1920s, B. F. Skinner, a young graduate student attending Harvard University, was studying how consequences influenced animal behavior. Unlike Thorndike, Skinner was studying rats as they navigated mazes in search of food rewards. Just as Thorndike found that an open puzzle-box door reinforced string-pulling behavior, Skinner found that when food was delivered contingent upon arriving at a location in the maze (*IF* rat travels to the location → *THEN* food is delivered), the rats ran to that location more quickly when compared to their baseline (no-reinforcer) rates of travel.

B.F. Skinner (1904-1990)

Source: Silly rabbit/Wikipedia/CC BY 3.0

In subsequent experiments, Skinner built what he called a "problem box" (a homage to Thorndike's puzzle box). The behavior of interest was pressing a lever (labeled A in Figure 5.7), such that it operated a food dispenser (B) and dropped a piece of food down a tube (C) and into a cup (not shown). Because the rat operated the food dispenser by pressing the lever, Skinner called the behavior *operant behavior*. Many researchers refer to this as *instrumental behavior* because the behavior is instrumental in acquiring the reinforcer; the two terms mean the same thing.

Eventually, Skinner automated his experiments by connecting the box to a device that recorded each of the rat's lever-pressing responses. This allowed Skinner to leave the rat undisturbed while it acquired food reinforcers, and it allowed Skinner to get a cup of coffee or study for an exam while he was conducting the experiment.

The ease of conducting experiments in Skinner's problem box motivated Skinner and his students to build lots of them. These would eventually come to be called "Skinner boxes" and thousands of researchers would install them in their labs. Skinner was never fond of this name, preferring to call them "operant-conditioning chambers."

The operant-conditioning chamber proved to be an efficient and effective way to study animal behavior. It is hard to overestimate the impact that these operant chambers had on behavior analysis. Modern versions of these chambers continue to be used today in labs all over the world.

Figure 5.7 An apparatus that B. F. Skinner invented to study operant behavior. The operant response was to press down the lever (labeled A). This caused the food dispenser (B) to turn, and to drop of piece of food down a tube (C) and into a food cup (not shown).
Source: Reproduced with permission from Aubrey Daniels International, Inc. and the Aubrey Daniels Institute. https://www.aubreydaniels.com/behavioral-apparatus-museum-environments.

Reading Quiz 4

1. The first scientist to demonstrate that reinforcers influence behavior was _____.
2. If a stimulus change happens after behavior, it is called a(n) _____.
3. If a stimulus change happens before behavior, it is called a(n) _____.
4. Antecedents cannot be classified as reinforcers because reinforcers happen _____ behavior.
5. If a consequence increases behavior above its baseline level, we call it a _____.

Response Variability: Exploring and Exploiting

An essential ingredient in operant learning is response variability. If Thorndike's cat had engaged in only one behavior when placed in the puzzle box – trying to squeeze its body through the bars – it would never have escaped from the box. The reinforcement contingency required that the cat pull the string to open the door. Had the cat never done this, it would never have obtained the reinforcer. If a reinforcer never occurs, it cannot increase behavior. Behaving variably is critical to solving the puzzle of a new reinforcement contingency.

We might think of response variability as *exploration*. When individuals are exposed to new contingencies of reinforcement, they tend to respond more variably – they explore in a trial-and-error way. Consider the Japanese puzzle box shown to the right. There are no handles, latches, hinges, or anything else that provides a clue about how to open it. If you were told that there was a $20 bill

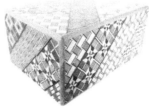

Source: Nipaylah/Wikipedia/CC BY 3.0

inside the box and that it was yours if you could open it, you would engage in trial-and-error exploration – pushing and pulling on every part of the box. Eventually, you would chance upon the solution to the box – your behavior would be reinforced by the opening of the box and the receipt of $20. If the cash-loaded box was given to you a second time, response variability would greatly decrease as your behavior transitions from exploration to *exploitation*. That is, you would efficiently emit the reinforced behavior, opening the puzzle box quickly and easily pocketing your $20 each time.

The importance of response variability in mastering a reinforcement contingency was illustrated by the renowned actor, Phillip Seymour Hoffman. Hoffman was famous for *exploration* when given a new acting role. One of his directors reported that as rehearsals began, Hoffman explored many different ways of playing his character. He was a model of response variability. Some days he would speak loudly when delivering his lines; other days he could barely be heard. Some days he would stand in locations specified by the director; other days he stood elsewhere. All of this drove his director crazy, but Hoffman insisted upon exploring many variations on a role before finding the performance that worked – one that was reinforced by positive comments, applause, and admiration from the director and his fellow actors. These successful response variations would then be exploited, as Hoffman played the role in this way over many stage performances, to

Phillip Seymour Hoffman
(1967-2014)

Source: Georges Biard/
Wikipedia/CC BY-SA 3.0

standing ovations and several acting awards. You might know Hoffman for his Academy Award winning portrayal of Truman Capote, or as Plutarch Heavensbee in the *Hunger Games* films. Extra Box 2 encourages you to consider the benefits of adding variability into your own life.

EXTRA BOX 2:   ADD SOME VARIABILITY TO YOUR LIFE

When individuals learn how a reinforcement contingency works, they shift from exploration to exploitation – behaving efficiently and rarely trying something new. Consider the subway riders in the London Underground (the Tube). Most commuters who take the subway to work, to school, or to go shopping use the same series of trains every time they travel to these destinations. They do this for years, for a lifetime. If asked, they would say, "Well, that's the fastest way to get there" and many of them would be right. But in 2014 much of the London Underground staff went on strike, closing down most of the Tube stations. In doing so, they forced subway riders to behave variably – to try something new. Some took the bus. Some walked. Some took the Underground lines that remained open.

An interesting thing happened after the strike ended. About 1 in 20 commuters discovered from their trial-and-error commuting that there was a more efficient way to get to work, to school, or to the shops. The variability forced upon them by the strike allowed them to find a better solution to their commuting problem.

A similar thing happened to the jazz pianist Keith Jarrett. When he walked onto the stage at the Cologne Opera House in 1975, he found the piano to be completely inadequate.

The pedals didn't work, the black keys were sticking, and the rest were out of tune. Rather than walk away, he behaved variably. He tried something new. He avoided the keys that didn't work, he pounded the keys that did work, and found internal echoes of the piano that could be used to enhance the piano's sound. The result is today referred to as the Köln Concert; it is considered one of the greatest performances in the history of jazz. Take a break from studying and go listen to a portion of it now.

Source: dpa picture alliance / Alamy Stock Photo

If you just Googled the Köln Concert, then you just interacted with an artificial intelligence (AI) – the Google search engine. Did you know that AI uses trial-and-error learning *and* forced variability to solve complex problems? It's true. Much like living beings, AI programs explore solutions in a trial-and-error way and they learn from the consequences of their actions. When they find an action that works, the program does more of that. Sounds a bit like reinforcement, doesn't it?

The problem is that if the AI exploited the first successful action (by exclusively engaging in that action) then it would settle upon a satisfactory solution, but not an optimal one. The thing that makes AI so effective in finding optimal solutions is that it is willing to continuously try something new. Every AI program is written with a forced-variability component. No matter how successful the AI is in solving the problem, its programming forces it to do something different some of the time. You might think of it as the AI taking a different London Underground train just to see what would happen. Most of the time, the trial ends in error – the instance of forced variability is not as good as the current solution. But sometimes, a better solution is found and the AI will redirect its efforts in that direction.

So, think about your own life. Is there something that you do the same way every time? If so, consider if you need to introduce a bit of variability into your life. Before you do, remember that most of these variability trials will end in error. So be careful.

The Generic Nature of Operant Behavior

As these examples illustrate, response variability is important when learning a new operant behavior. What about after a response has been acquired; when behavior has shifted from exploration to exploitation? Is variability still important then?

To answer this question, consider, once again, your behavior of pressing the Spotify icon on your phone. Is the behavior identical every time it occurs? Almost definitely not. Sometimes you press the app with your thumb, sometimes with your index finger; we've even seen someone press the app with their nose! Even when you press the app icon with your thumb, the movement is not exactly the same each time. Despite all of these topographical differences, each response has the same function – they all launch the Spotify app.

Recognizing that not every operant response is an identical copy of the last one that was reinforced, we will revise our prior definition of **operant behavior** to note that it is *a generic class of responses influenced by antecedents, with each response in the class producing the same consequence.*[2] The Spotify-pressing operant is composed of a generic class of many varieties of app-pressing responses, all of which are influenced by antecedents (the feel of the phone in your hand, the location of the Spotify app on your screen) and all of which produce the same consequence (Spotify loads when the icon is pressed).

Just as variability is adaptive when learning a new operant behavior, variability can be adaptive after the behavior is acquired. For example, sometimes you can't make the most efficient response topography – your right hand is full and, therefore, you can't press the Spotify app with your right thumb. At other times, a specific response topography does not produce the reinforcer – a light press on the Spotify icon does not launch the app. In either of these cases, an adaptive response is to engage in one or more of the other response topographies in the generic operant class. If pressing the icon with the right index finger is impossible, then pressing with the left index finger may do the trick. If pressing lightly does not launch the app, then pressing hard or pressing for a longer duration may produce the outcome. Reinforcing all of the various responses within the generic operant class increases the probability of reinforcement when a specific response is no longer possible or when the most efficient response no longer produces the reinforcer.

Not Every Consequence Functions as a Reinforcer

Behavior often produces consequences that do not function as reinforcers. That is, the response produces a consequence but that outcome does not increase the future probability of behavior above a no-reinforcer baseline level. Some consequences have no effect on behavior. You cannot classify a consequence as a reinforcer unless it increases behavior above a no-reinforcer baseline level.

Other consequences *decrease* the probability of your behavior and these are not reinforcers either; they are "punishers" and we will discuss them later in the book. As an example of a punisher, the consequence of arriving late to the airport is that the check-in computer informs you that you have missed your flight and the next flight to your destination does not leave for 7 hours. After you experience this consequence once, the probability of showing up late again is reduced. Thus, just because the stimulus is a consequence does not mean that it functions as a reinforcer. Any consequence that increases the future probability of operant behavior above its no-reinforcer baseline level is a reinforcer. Anything that does not have this effect is not a reinforcer.

Reading Quiz 5

You will understand the reinforcement process better if you are able to tell the difference between reinforcers and other types of stimulus events. Use the flowchart in Figure 5.5 to consider if the stimulus change (*underlined and italicized*) in the scenarios below is a reinforcer or not. If you find that the stimulus change is not a reinforcer, you can skip the rest of the questions in each item. To help you identify the behavior of interest, it is set in **bold** in each scenario. If you get stuck, remember the answers are provided at the end of the chapter.

1. The manager of the appliance store noticed that Karl was **selling** only about $20,000 worth of appliances per month. To improve Karl's sales, the manager told Karl that she would give him a bonus: 0.3% of all monthly sales exceeding $30,000. Where Karl had been selling $20,000 worth of appliances per month before the bonus, Karl now sells $50,000 worth of appliances each month (earning *a $60 bonus* for himself). The manager did such a good job that she was promoted to a larger store. The new manager thought the bonus was a waste of company resources, so he discontinued them. Karl's sales went back down to about $20,000 per month.
   a. What is the stimulus change: _____
   b. When did the stimulus change happen: _____ (before/after behavior)
   c. Does this consequence increase the behavior of interest above its baseline level: _____ (yes/no)
   d. What happens when this consequence is turned OFF?
   e. Is it a reinforcer: _____ (yes/no)

2. Alex **followed the recipe when baking a birthday cake**. *The cake came out of the oven looking and smelling great!* Alex kept the recipe and used it every time he needed a cake. When Alex moved to New Zealand, he found that the recipe no longer worked – the cake did not taste very good. He never understood why, but he stopped following the recipe after he moved to New Zealand.
   a. What is the stimulus change: _____
   b. When did the stimulus change happen: _____ (before/after behavior)
   c. Does this consequence increase the behavior of interest above its baseline level: _____ (yes/no)
   d. What happens when this consequence is turned OFF?
   e. Is it a reinforcer: _____ (yes/no)

3. Terry **creates a new Twitter hashtag** but no one posts anything to it. Terry keeps creating hashtags. Still, no one ever reacts to his posts.
   a. What is the stimulus change: _____
   b. When did the stimulus change happen: _____ (before/after behavior)
   c. Does this consequence increase the behavior of interest above its baseline level: _____ (yes/no)
   d. What happens when this consequence is turned OFF?
   e. Is it a reinforcer: _____ (yes/no)

4. On a whim, Ashley **bought a lottery ticket** and *won $250*. She took all of her friends out for a big meal at a nice restaurant. She really had a great time. Ashley never bought another lottery ticket.
   a. What is the stimulus change: _____
   b. When did the stimulus change: _____ (before/after behavior)
   c. Does this consequence increase the behavior of interest above its baseline level: _____ (yes/no)
   d. What happens when this consequence is turned OFF?
   e. Is it a reinforcer: _____ (yes/no)

5. This next story is a little tricky because the no-reinforcer baseline happens second, instead of first. We've added a graph to help you visualize what the scenario describes. Jack **turned the faucet handle to the left** and *water came out*. On an average day, Jack used the faucet about 6 times. In January, Jack forgot to pay his water bill and the city turned off his water. He stopped using his faucet until he remembered to pay his bill and his water was turned back on. After that, he turned the faucet about 6 times per day.

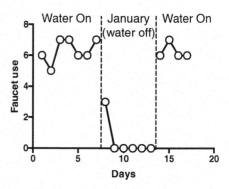

a. What is the stimulus change: _____
b. When did the stimulus change happen _____ (before/after behavior)
c. Does this consequence increase the behavior of interest above its baseline level: _____ (yes/no)
d. What happens when this consequence is turned OFF?
e. Is it a reinforcer: _____ (yes/no)

For the rest of the quiz questions, use the flowchart in Figure 5.5 *to evaluate if the stimulus change is a reinforcer or not. Try to do this without looking at the aforementioned prompt questions (a–e).*

6. Carla **presses the button on the pedometer** that her partner bought for her. When she presses the button, she can see *lots of information about how much she is exercising and how many calories she is burning.* Carla presses the button at least 10 times a day. Last weekend, Carla forgot to charge the battery in her pedometer, so when she pressed the button, she got no information about her exercise. She didn't press the button again until she got back to work and recharged the battery. After the battery was charged, she pressed the button on the pedometer about 10 times a day.

7. The instructor says, *"The assignment is due on Monday."* On Monday, **Britney turned in her assignment**.

8. Dave **ordered the massive "Big Bill" hamburger** sold by his local pub. *The waitress brought the burger and it was delicious!* Every bite was a real treat – the perfect char on the burger, the ripe tomatoes and lettuce, the melted cheese, the fresh-baked bun – wow! Dave returned the next week and ordered another Big Bill but the waitress told him they took it off the menu. Dave was a little upset but then ordered the nachos. They were good too. Dave returns to the pub once a week but doesn't order the Big Bill burger for 3 weeks, until he sees another customer eating a Big Bill. When his waitress arrives he says, "Yee Ha! I'll have a Big Bill!" The waitress thinks Dave is a little strange, but she serves him his burger. Dave continues to order the burger each time he visits the pub.

9. About 2 years ago, Jennifer went **hiking** outside her home town but found it incredibly boring – she did not see a single animal; walking and looking at a boring trail was not a lot of fun. Then Jennifer moved to Alaska and tried hiking again. In Alaska, *she saw a lot of wildlife she had never seen before* (two eagles, a moose, and even a bear). Jennifer became an avid hiker after moving to Alaska. Two months ago, Jennifer moved back to her home town. She has not been hiking since.

Nearly everyone uses social media or plays video games. Most of us check our social media accounts or play in these virtual worlds every day, often for several hours per day. That's a lot of behavior. Is it operant behavior maintained by reinforcement? If so, what are the reinforcers that maintain all of this behavior?

To answer this question, we have to be specific about the behavior and the reinforcer. What is the reinforcer for posting something to Twitter, Instagram, or Facebook? In each case, the reinforcer is probably some form of social approval – someone follows your Twitter feed, likes the picture you posted on Instagram, or comments on your Facebook post. All of these consequences are provided contingent upon your behavior of posting something. If these consequences were no longer obtained, your behavior would probably decrease to a no-reinforcer baseline level.

Of course, to be certain that these social consequences function as reinforcers we would need to turn them ON and OFF and evaluate the effects of these changes on the probability of posting things to social media. When these consequences are turned ON in our thought experiment, you would post as much as you usually do. When they are turned OFF, you would probably see that your posting behavior becomes more variable as you *explore* other ways of obtaining the usual consequences. For example, you might start posting more compelling content. But if none of these other responses produced any social consequences, then you would probably stop posting; you might feel a little depressed too. If the rate of posting was higher when the social consequences were ON than when they were OFF, then we would classify these consequences as reinforcers.

The same is true of video games. Executing a specific sequence of button presses and joystick movements moves a virtual avatar over a pit of fire. This consequence is contingent upon the correct sequence of movements – one small mistake and your avatar is incinerated. If pressing the buttons and moving the joystick had no effect on the movement of the avatar, you would soon stop engaging in these behaviors.

One of the things that makes video games so engaging is that just as quickly as one reinforcer is obtained, another one is needed. For example, when you've landed safely just past the pit of fire, now you need to execute another skillful sequence of button presses and joystick movements to avoid an incoming projectile. In this way, the game influences your behavior through a series of reinforcement contingencies.

Video game design requires an understanding of how to arrange many varieties of contingent reinforcers to keep the player engaged. For example, not only has your avatar defeated a foe (a reinforcer for skillful player behaviors), but she has also earned experience points (more reinforcers) that can be used to level-up to a higher status (even more reinforcers) within the virtual world.

Games for Good

If the reinforcers obtained from social media and within the virtual world of a video game can influence so much human behavior, one might wonder if these reinforcers could be used to address some of the public health or environmental crises that we face in contemporary society. For example, could a video game or a smartphone app help people lose weight, and keep it off?

Consolvo and her colleagues (2008) wondered if the information provided by personal activity monitors functions as a reinforcer for physical activity. Participants whose monitors displayed the number of steps taken were 30% more active than participants whose smartphone recorded steps but would not display this information. It would appear that people were more active because of the contingent relation between activity and having larger numbers appear on the display (a reinforcer).

A game-based approach to positively influencing behavior need not involve computers or smartphones. Could something as simple as a game narrative be used to positively influence public health? This was the approach taken in a behavioral intervention called the *FIT Game* (Jones et al., 2014a, 2014b; Joyner et al., 2017). Participants were elementary school children who, during a no-reinforcer baseline phase, rarely ate vegetables in the school cafeteria. To encourage healthy eating, the FIT Game created a response-reinforcer contingency between eating more vegetables and positive outcomes in a good vs. evil narrative. This simple *IF you eat vegetables → THEN something good happens in the story* contingency doubled the amount of vegetables that children ate each day (Joyner et al., 2017). In another school, the virtual rewards were used to increase physical activity at school (Joyner et al., 2019). Love video games? Want to positively influence behavior? An understanding of reinforcement contingencies may prove instrumental in marrying these passions.

Summary

Operant behavior is behavior influenced by antecedents and consequences. In this chapter, we focused on consequences and discussed how contingent consequences can influence behavior. Contingent consequences are *caused* by the operant response; that is, there is an *IF response → THEN consequence* relation between them. As you will see in later chapters, there isn't always a one-response–one-consequence relation. Sometimes, the contingency requires that many responses occur before the consequence occurs (e.g., all of the studying that goes into earning a good grade on an exam).

An important type of consequence is called a "reinforcer." Reinforcers increase behavior relative to a no-reinforcer baseline. When we turn ON and OFF the consequence and behavior increases and decreases, respectively, that consequence functions as a reinforcer. Much of our everyday behavior is maintained by reinforcers. See how many you can identify in your own life.

Understanding the reinforcers that influence your behavior can help you live a better life. Are there some reinforcers that lead to adaptive behavior? Can you arrange more of those? What about reinforcers that maintain maladaptive behavior? Can you minimize those? Are you repeating the same behaviors and getting lackluster results? Should you introduce some variability into your life? One of the joys of studying principles of behavior analysis is using them to improve your own life and the lives of those around you.

Answers to Reading Quiz Questions and Questions Posed in Table 5.2

Reading Quiz 1

1. consequence
2. before
3. consequence
4. consequence
5. antecedent
6. antecedent
7. consequence

Table 5.2

3. response/consequence
4. consequence/response
5. consequence/response
7. response/consequence
8. response/consequence
9. consequence/response
10. consequence/response

Reading Quiz 2

1. response/consequence; contingent
2. consequence/response; contingent
3. response/consequence; noncontingent

Reading Quiz 3

1. reinforcer; rewards
2. reinforcer
3. reinforcement
4. noncontingent

Reading Quiz 4

1. Thorndike
2. consequence

3. antecedent
4. after
5. reinforcer

Reading Quiz 5

1. Selling appliances
   a. The bonus
   b. Karl gets the bonus at the end of the month, **after** he sells more than $30,000 in appliances.
   c. Yes
   d. Selling goes back down to the baseline (no-reinforcer) level.
   e. Yes
2. Baking a cake
   a. A nice looking (and smelling) cake.
   b. The pleasant cake happed **after** the recipe was used.
   c. Yes
   d. Following the recipe goes back down to the baseline (no-reinforcer) level.
   e. Yes
3. Twitter hashtag
   a. No stimulus change is mentioned.
   b. NA
   c. NA
   d. NA
   e. No
4. Lottery ticket
   a. Winning $250
   b. After behavior
   c. No
   d. NA – there is no mention of turning the consequence OFF.
   e. No
5. Turning the faucet
   a. Water comes out of the faucet
   b. After behavior
   c. Yes
   d. The frequency of turning the faucet goes down to a baseline (no-reinforcer) level.
   e. Yes
6. Yes – the information on the pedometer functions as a reinforcer. If you did not get this answer right, we provide the answers to the a–e questions here.
   a. Information provided by the pedometer
   b. After behavior
   c. Yes
   d. When the stimulus change was turned OFF (dead battery), behavior decreased.
   e. Yes
7. No – the instructor's description of the due date happened *before* the behavior of interest.

8. Yes – the burger functions as a reinforcer. If you did not get this answer right, we provide the answers to the a–e questions here.
   a. The waitress brought the delicious burger
   b. After behavior
   c. Yes
   d. The no-reinforcer baseline level occurred when they took the Big Bill burger off the menu and Dave stopped ordering it – the no-reinforcer baseline level of ordering is zero.
   e. Yes
9. Yes – Seeing wildlife functions as a reinforcer. If you did not get this answer right, we provide the answers to the a–e questions here.
   a. Seeing wildlife
   b. After behavior
   c. Yes
   d. When the availability of wildlife was turned OFF (hiking outside her home town), her behavior decreased.
   e. Yes

Notes

1. Later in the chapter we will expand this definition. You may want to wait until then before making the flash card that you will use to study.
2. This is the final definition of operant behavior. You can make your flash card using this definition.

References

Baer, D. M., & Wolf, M. M. (1968). The reinforcement contingency in preschool and remedial education. In R. D. Hess & R. M. Bear (Eds.), *Early education: Current theory, research, and practice*. Chicago: Aldine.

Benishek, L. A., Dugosh, K. L., Kirby, K. C., Matejkowski, J., Clements, N. T., Symour, B. L., & Festinger, D. S. (2014). Prize-based contingency management for the treatment of substance abusers: A meta-analysis. *Addiction, 109*, 1426–1436. doi:10.1111/add.12589

Colwill, R. M., & Rescorla, R. A. (1985). Postconditioning devaluation of a reinforcer affects instrumental responding. *Journal of Experimental Psychology: Animal Behavior Processes, 11*, 120–132. doi:10.1037/0097-7403.11.1.120

Consolvo, S., Klasnja, P., McDonald, D. W., Avrahami, D., Froehlich, J., LeGrand, L., Libby, R., Mosher, K., & Landay, J. A. (2008). Flowers or a robot army? Encouraging awareness and activity with personal mobile displays. In: *Proceedings of the 10th international conference on ubiquitous computing* (UbiComp 2008). ACM, New York, pp. 54–63.

Falk, J. L. (1971). The nature and determinants of adjunctive behavior. *Physiology and Behavior, 6*, 577–588. doi:10.1016/0031-9384(71)90209-5

Gourevitch, P. (2003, November, 2). The madness of Kim Jong-il. *The Guardian*. Retrieved from https://www.theguardian.com/theobserver/2003/nov/02/features.magazine37

Hart, B. M., Reynolds, N. J., Baer, D. M., Brawley, E. R., & Harris, F. R. (1968). Effect of contingent and noncontingent social reinforcement on the cooperative play of a preschool child. *Journal of Applied Behavior Analysis, 1*, 73–76. doi:10.1901/jaba.1968.1-73

Higgins, S. T., Wong, C. J., Badger, G. J., Ogden, D. E., & Dantona, R. A. (2000). Contingent reinforcement increases cocaine abstinence during outpatient treatment and 1 year of follow-up. *Journal of Consulting and Clinical Psychology, 68*, 1051–1061. doi:10.1037//0022-006x.68.1.64

Hogarth, L., & Chase, H. W. (2011). Parallel goal-directed and habitual control of human drug-seeking: Implications for dependence vulnerability. *Journal of Experimental Psychology: Animal Behavior Processes, 37*(3), 261–276. doi:10.1037/a0022913

Jones, B. A., Madden, G. J., & Wengreen, H. J. (2014a). The FIT Game: Preliminary evaluation of a gamification approach to increasing fruit and vegetable consumption in school. *Preventive Medicine, 68*, 76–79. doi:10.1016/j.ypmed.2014.04.015

Jones, B. A., Madden, G. J., Wengreen, H. J., Aguilar, S. S., & Desjardins, E. A. (2014b). Gamification of dietary decision-making in an elementary-school cafeteria. *PLoS One, 9*(4), e93872. doi:10.1371/journal.pone.0093872

Joyner, D., Wengreen, H., Aguilar, S., & Madden, G. (2019). Effects of the FIT game on physical activity in sixth graders: A pilot reversal design intervention study. *JMIR Serious Games, 7*(2), e13051. doi:10.2196/13051

Joyner, D., Wengreen, H. J., Aguilar, S. S., Spruance, L. A., Morrill, B. A., & Madden, G. J. (2017). The FIT game III: Reducing the operating expenses of a game-based approach to increasing healthy eating in elementary schools. *Games for Health Journal, 6*(2), 111–118. doi:10.2196/13051

Killeen, P. R. (1975). On the temporal control of behavior. *Psychological Review, 82*, 89–115. doi:10.1037/h0076820

Ono, K. (1987). Superstitious behavior in humans. *Journal of the Experimental Analysis of Behavior, 47*, 261–271. doi:10.1901/jeab.1987.47-261

Skinner, B. F. (1948). Superstition in the pigeon. *Journal of Experimental Psychology, 38*, 168–172. doi:10.1037/h0055873

Staddon, J. E., & Simmelhag, V. L. (1971). The "superstition" experiment: A reexamination of its implications for the principles of adaptive behavior. *Psychological Review, 78*, 3–43. doi:10.1037/h0030305

Thorndike, E. L. (1911). *Animal intelligence*. New York: MacMillan.

Tidmarsh, K. (1993). Russia's work ethic. *Foreign Affairs, 72*, 67–77.

Timberlake, W., & Lucas, G. A. (1985). The basis of superstitious behavior: Chance contingency, stimulus substitution, or appetitive behavior? *Journal of the Experimental Analysis of Behavior, 44*, 279–299. doi:10.1901/jeab.1985.44-279

Operant Learning II: Positive and Negative Reinforcement

6

In Chapter 5 you learned how reinforcing events increase operant behaviors above their no-reinforcer baseline level. In this chapter, we will distinguish between positive and negative reinforcers. This is one of the most frequently confused distinctions in the study of operant behavior, so we will provide clear definitions and plenty of examples and non-examples. One thing to keep in mind as you read on: positive and negative reinforcers have the same directional effect on operant behavior – they both increase it. Don't let the word "negative" fool you. If it is a reinforcer, it increases operant behavior above its baseline level.

The second section of the chapter advances beyond the basics of positive and negative reinforcement. Once you understand these different ways in which to deliver reinforcers, the chapter addresses some real-world issues, such as how to productively use reinforcement to address the behaviors that underlie public health deficits (e.g., inactivity and overeating) and workplace behaviors impacting productivity and safety. The final section of the chapter addresses two contemporary theories of how reinforcement works.

Positive Reinforcement

Reinforcers, whether positive or negative, increase operant behavior above its no-reinforcer baseline level. It doesn't matter whether the reinforcer is positive or negative, its effect on behavior is to increase it above baseline.

An Introduction to Behavior Analysis, First Edition. Gregory J. Madden, Derek D. Reed, and Florence D. DiGennaro Reed.
© 2021 John Wiley & Sons Ltd. Published 2021 by John Wiley & Sons Ltd.

In Chapter 5 we said that reinforcers are consequences; they are observable stimulus changes that happen after behavior. What is a stimulus change? Think of a blank piece of paper. If a pencil drops onto the paper, it will leave a small black mark on the paper. This is an example of a stimulus change. The paper went from all white to white with a small black mark on it. Simple enough.

What if an eraser is applied to the small black mark, removing the mark from the page? Is this a stimulus change? Yes, because we go from white

Source: Devanath/Shutterstock.com

with a black mark to all white – that is a stimulus change. Thus, either the presentation or removal of a stimulus is classified as a stimulus change. Lights turn on or lights turn off, they are both stimulus changes. Pain presented or pain removed, they are both stimulus changes. Paycheck deposited or funds removed from your account, they are both stimulus changes.

Any of these stimulus presentations or removals can be a consequence of operant behavior. If you release the pencil you were holding over the paper, this is an operant response that produces the black mark on the page. If you rub the pencil's eraser on the black mark, this is an operant response that has mark removal as its consequence. Can either of these types of consequences function as reinforcers? That is, can a stimulus presentation or a stimulus removal increase the operant response above its no-reinforcer baseline level? The simple answer is yes, and this leads us to some important definitions. Let's start with the simplest definition:

> **Positive Reinforcement (SR+):** *The presentation of a consequence, the effect of which is to increase operant behavior above its no-reinforcer baseline level.*

This definition of positive reinforcement (symbolized as SR+) should look familiar. It is very similar to the general definition of reinforcement given in Chapter 5. This definition, however, specifies the consequence – a stimulus *presentation*. For example, if you buy a lottery ticket (operant response) and you win $20 (*presentation* of a stimulus) and thereafter you buy more lottery tickets (an increase above the no-reinforcer baseline level), then we would say the win positively reinforced the operant behavior of buying a lottery ticket. Any time that reinforcement involves the *presentation* of a stimulus, we will classify it as a positive reinforcer.

Just as "reinforcement" describes the process and "reinforcer" describes the consequence, "positive reinforcement" is the term used to describe the process by which positive reinforcers increase behavior above a no-reinforcer baseline level.

Positive Reinforcement in the Lab

In an early study of positive reinforcement, Olds and Milner (1954) placed electrodes in the so-called pleasure centers in brains of rats. Subsequently, each rat was placed in an operant-conditioning chamber in which it could press a lever to send a brief electrical pulse to its own brain. The consequence of pressing the lever was a stimulus *presentation*: the electric pulse to the brain. If the pulse increases behavior above its baseline (no-reinforcer level), then we can conclude that it functions as a positive reinforcer.

Figure 6.1 shows the behavior of one of Olds and Milner's rats – rat A5. When pressing the lever produced a pulse in the brain (Pulse ON), the rat pressed about once every 2 seconds.

When pressing the lever never produced a pulse, the behavior returned to its baseline (no-reinforcer) level.

Did electric brain stimulation function as a reinforcer? To find out, we can use the flowchart that was introduced in Chapter 5. We've reproduced it in Figure 6.2 for your convenience.

Lever pressing is the behavior of interest and electric brain stimulation is the stimulus change. In the top bubble, we note that brain stimulation occurred after behavior – it was a consequence of pressing the lever. In the next bubble down, we are asked if this consequence increases lever pressing above the baseline

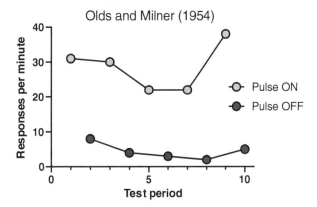

Figure 6.1 The rate at which rat A5 pressed a lever when it produced an electric pulse to the pleasure center of his brain (Pulse ON) and when it produced nothing (Pulse OFF).

Source: Olds, J., & Milner, P. (1954). Positive reinforcement produced by electrical stimulation of septal area and other regions of rat brain. *Journal of Comparative and Physiological Psychology*, *47*(6), 419–427.

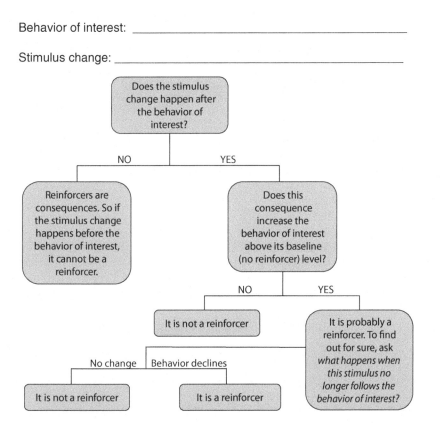

Figure 6.2 Use this flowchart to evaluate if a stimulus change functions as a reinforcer.

(no-reinforcer level). In Figure 6.1, it is clear that lever pressing was much more frequent when the consequence was ON. So, it's probably a positive reinforcer, but to find out for sure we turn the reinforcer OFF. This happens five times in Figure 6.1 and behavior declines all five times. This highly replicable effect definitively demonstrates that response-contingent electrical brain stimulation functioned as a positive reinforcer for rat A5's lever pressing.

Negative Reinforcement

The other reinforcement process is negative reinforcement, and there are two categories of negative reinforcement.

Negative Reinforcement – Escape (SR$_E$-)

Negative reinforcement – escape (symbolized SR$_E$-) is defined as *a consequent removal or reduction of a stimulus, the effect of which is to increase operant behavior above its no-reinforcer baseline level*. What makes SR$_E$- unique is the consequence of behavior is the *removal or reduction of a stimulus*. When you erased the black pencil mark on the page, the consequence was *removal* of a stimulus. If your erasing only partially removed the black mark, the consequence would be a stimulus *reduction*. If either of these consequences increases erasing above its no-reinforcement baseline level, then we would classify it as a negative reinforcer of the SR$_E$- variety.

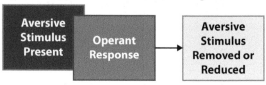

Negative Reinforcement - Escape (SR$_E$-)

There are many examples of SR$_E$-. What they all have in common is that a stimulus is present when the operant response occurs, and that stimulus is *removed or reduced* after the response. In most instances of SR$_E$-, the stimulus present is an aversive stimulus; that is, a stimulus that the individual will take action to remove or reduce.

Consider an operant behavior as mundane as getting a haircut. When this response occurs, there is an aversive stimulus present – hair judged to be too long. If Amelia gets her hair cut (i.e., she goes to the stylist and asks for a haircut), the consequence is the removal or reduction of unwanted hair. This removal or reduction of the aversive stimulus is the consequence of the operant behavior.

Does this consequence negatively reinforce Amelia's haircut-seeking behavior? To find out, use the flowchart in Figure 6.2. Starting at the top, we begin by identifying the behavior of interest: getting a haircut; and the stimulus change: unwanted hair removal/reduction. Next, we ask,

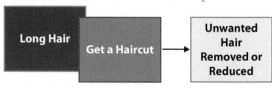

Negative Reinforcement - Escape (SR$_E$-)

Does the stimulus change happen after this behavior? Hair removal is a consequence of going to the stylist and asking for a haircut, so we can move down the flowchart along the "YES" path.

In the next two bubbles of Figure 6.2, we will conduct a thought experiment to evaluate if the haircut functions as an SR_E^-. What would happen if we turned OFF this consequence? In this thought experiment, Amelia will go to the same stylist as always – the one who has always done a great job of cutting her hair. This time, however, something weird happens: The stylist makes a lot of hair-cutting sounds with scissors, engages in

Source: JackF/Adobe Stock Photo

small talk for 20 minutes, charges Amelia $35, but doesn't actually cut her hair. If we turn OFF this hair-removal consequence, does Amelia's haircut-seeking behavior decrease? Yes. She is very unlikely to visit that stylist again. Instead, she will take her business elsewhere.

Getting a haircut with this stylist continued as long as the consequence – removal of unwanted hair – occurred. When that consequence was turned OFF, the behavior decreases to the baseline (no-reinforcer) level. Thus, hair removal is a consequence that negatively reinforces (SR_E^-) Amelia's behavior.

Table 6.1 lists several examples of everyday behaviors that are maintained by stimulus removal/reductions that function as negative reinforcers of the escape variety (SR_E^-).

To summarize, the *escape* category of negative reinforcement always involves complete or partial escape from a stimulus. The aspirin taker escapes from the pain of the headache. The nose picker escapes from an annoying booger. Nearly every behavior that you think of when you hear the word "escape" (e.g., escaping from a problem relationship, escaping from a terrible professor by dropping their class, escaping unwanted thoughts by drinking alcohol) is operant behavior maintained by SR_E^-.

Table 6.1 Many of our everyday actions are operant behaviors that are maintained by the removal or reduction of a stimulus. Such consequences function as SR_E^-.

Behavior of interest	Stimulus removal/reduction
Deleting an email	Email removed from inbox
Taking an aspirin	Headache goes away
Picking your nose	Booger is removed
Soothing an infant	Baby stops crying
Taking out the trash	Garbage removed from apartment
Putting out a fire	Fire stops burning
Agreeing to go to the bar	Peer pressure ends
Seeing a behavior therapist	Depression is reduced
Leaving a room	Ending an unwanted conversation

NEGATIVE REINFORCEMENT – ESCAPE (SR_E⁻) IN THE LAB

In a simple illustration of the effects of SR_E^- on behavior, Solomon and Wynne (1953) placed a dog in one compartment of a two-compartment cage called a shuttle-box (see Figure 6.3). The compartments were separated by a barrier that the dog could jump over. Periodically, the experimenters sent an electric current to the floor grid in one compartment and, if the dog jumped the barrier, it escaped from shock to the no-shock compartment.

The inset graph in Figure 6.3 shows how quickly a typical dog jumped the barrier. The dog never jumped the barrier in a baseline session in which no shocks were presented (data not shown in the graph). However, when shocks were encountered, the dog jumped the barrier and did so more quickly each time upon encountering the shock. The dog's operant jumping response was negatively reinforced (SR_E^-) with shock removal.

The effects of SR_E^- on operant behavior have been replicated in hundreds of experiments with a variety of species, including humans. For example, an SR_E^- that contributes to human cigarette smoking is the removal/reduction of the aversive properties of nicotine withdrawal (George & Koob, 2017).

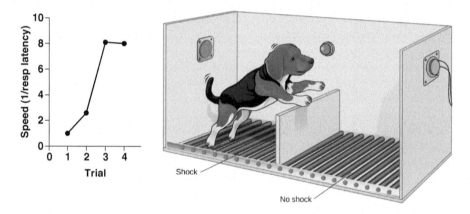

Figure 6.3 Shuttle-box similar to the one used by Solomon and Wynne (1953) to study SR_E^- in dogs. The graph shows the speed at which a dog jumped a mid-chamber barrier the first four times it was placed in the box and experienced a shock. Speed is calculated as 1 divided by the latency to jump over the barrier; the quotient is then multiplied by 100. Based on Solomon and Wynne's Figure 4.

Source: Psychology (OpenStax) by Rose M. Spielman, Kathryn Dumper, William Jenkins, Arlene Lacombe, et al. is licensed under a Creative Commons Attribution 4.0 International License.

Negative Reinforcement – Avoidance (SR_A⁻)

The other kind of negative reinforcement is **negative reinforcement – avoidance (SR_A^-)**, defined as *a consequent prevention of a stimulus change, the effect of which is to increase operant behavior above its no-reinforcer baseline level.*

Comparing the definitions of SR_A^- and SR_E^-, there are two differences. First, in the case of SR_A^-, the aversive stimulus is not present when the operant behavior occurs. Instead, a warning stimulus typically (but not always) precedes the operant response. The warning stimulus signals the aversive stimulus is imminent. Second, the operant response prevents the aversive stimulus change from happening.

As an example of SR_A^-, imagine that you are driving and you see a large pothole in your lane. The sight of the pothole is a warning stimulus; it signals that an aversive event is about to occur – a loud thud as your tire hits the pothole. You swerve to the left and avoid hitting the pot-

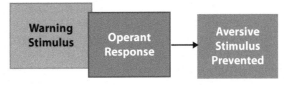

Negative Reinforcement - Avoidance (SR_A^-)

Warning Stimulus → Operant Response → Aversive Stimulus Prevented

hole. Swerving (operant response) *prevents a stimulus change* – the loud thud. Assuming that the prevention of this stimulus change functions as a reinforcer, it would be classified as a negative reinforcer of the avoidance variety (SR_A^-).

As a second example, imagine you went to a party a few weeks ago and you just didn't fit in. The other people there had different interests than yours, so you were bored with them and they seemed uninterested in you. Furthermore, there was a real jerk at the party who belittled you. On the whole, it was not a fun evening.

Now a friend is giving you a ride home and he says he's going to stop in on another party being held by the belittling jerk. What your friend just said is a warning stimulus. If you do nothing, then you'll find yourself at another boring party with the belittler. But if you say "No way! Take me home," then your action prevents a stimulus change – an encounter with the belittling jerk. If avoiding this encounter functions as a reinforcer, it would be classified as a negative reinforcer of the avoidance variety (SR_A^-).

Nearly every behavior that you think of when you hear the word "avoid" (e.g., avoiding an argument by walking away before it begins, avoiding a hangover by refusing additional drinks) takes the form of operant behavior maintained by SR_A^-. To find out for sure, we would turn ON and OFF the negative reinforcer and see how it influences behavior. If avoidance behavior occurs when the aversive event can be avoided (SR_A^- ON) and decreases when the avoidance response no longer works (SR_A^- OFF), then we can be certain that this consequence functions as a negative reinforcer. Table 6.2 lists several other everyday behaviors maintained by SR_A^-.

Table 6.2 Many of our everyday behaviors are instances of operant behavior maintained by the prevention of an aversive stimulus. Such consequences function as SR_A^-.

Behavior	Aversive event prevented
Turning in an assignment on time	Avoid a late penalty
Putting on sunblock	Avoid getting a sunburn
Paying your electricity bill	Avoid a service interruption
Ordering medium-heat wings	Avoid burning mouth
Saying "yes, that shirt looks good on you"	Avoid your friend getting upset
Withdrawing your hand from a growling dog	Avoid getting bit
Using a condom	Avoid an unplanned pregnancy

NEGATIVE REINFORCEMENT – AVOIDANCE (SR$_A$-) IN THE LAB

In the previously described shuttle-box experiment of Solomon and Wynne (1953), each shock was preceded by a warning stimulus. At the beginning of a trial, the light in the dog's compartment was turned off (warning stimulus) and 10 seconds later, a shock was given through the floor. Figure 6.4 shows that in the first four trials, the dog did not jump the barrier fast enough to avoid the shock (these are the escape data that were shown in Figure 6.3). On the fifth trial, the dog jumped the barrier fast enough to avoid the shock. Thereafter, and with the exception of two trials, the dog's behavior transitioned from escaping shocks to avoiding shocks.

The effects of SR$_A$- on nonhuman and human behavior have been replicated in hundreds of experiments. The aversive events avoided range from electric shocks (Brogden et al., 1938) to monetary losses (avoided by pressing buttons while humans lay in an fMRI scanner; Schlund & Cataldo, 2010).

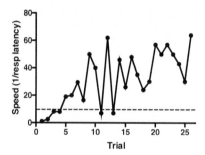

Figure 6.4 Speed at which the dog jumped the barrier after the warning stimulus onset. When the response speed was > 10 seconds (dashed line), the dog avoided the shock by jumping the barrier before the shock was delivered. The data are from the same dog as shown in Figure 6.3.

EXTRA BOX 1: WHAT IS THE CONSEQUENCE IN SR$_A$-?

Perhaps you noticed that avoidance responses produce no obvious consequence. When you swerved to avoid a pothole, it was the *absence* of a thud that functioned as the SR$_A$-. When you asked your friend to take you home before going to the party, it was the *absence* of belittling that functions as the SR$_A$-. But the absence of a stimulus change is not a consequence. So, what is the SR$_A$- that maintains these behaviors? This question has stumped behavioral scientists for generations, and we still do not have a definitive answer. Here we briefly survey two theories of SR$_A$-.

Two-Factor Theory. According to two-factor theory, avoidance responses *do* produce a consequence: fear reduction. The warning stimulus (the sight of the pothole in your lane) evokes fear (pupil dilation, momentary increase in heart rate, etc.) and the avoidance response has the consequence of terminating the fear. Similarly, when the shuttle-box dog saw the warning stimulus, shock was imminent, and it must have occasioned fear. According to two-factor theory, the dog's avoidance response (jumping the barrier) is negatively reinforced with fear reduction. Fear reduction is the consequence that serves as the SR_A-.

Two-factor theory relies on two learning processes (two factors): Pavlovian and operant conditioning. Pavlovian conditioning explains why fear arises (the warning stimulus is a CS that evokes fear) and operant conditioning explains why avoidance behavior occurs (fear reduction is the consequence that functions as an SR_A-).

While this is an appealing theory, there are several problems with it. For example, when fear is physiologically measured in SR_A- experiments, the CS evokes fear for a while, but after the aversive event (US) is reliably avoided, the CS no longer evokes fear (Mineka, 1979). If by trial 20 in Figure 6.4 our shuttle-box dog is no longer terminating fear by jumping the barrier, then what is the consequence that maintains its continued avoidance responding?

One-Factor Theory. One-factor theory holds that operant conditioning alone can explain SR_A-. The other factor – Pavlovian conditioning – is not necessary. Herrnstein and Hineline (1966) designed an experiment to falsify two-factor theory. Rats were placed in operant chambers where shocks were scheduled to occur at unpredictable times without warning. Without a warning stimulus (CS), the rat should not experience momentary fear that occasions an avoidance response. Instead, when the rat pressed the avoidance lever, it temporarily reduced the frequency of shocks from 9 per minute to 3 per minute. This consequence alone was enough to maintain avoidance responding in all but one rat.

Source: U3144362/Wikipedia/CC BY-SA 4.0

Subsequent research revealed that shock-delay was the SR_A- that maintained responding under unsignaled avoidance contingencies. In these experiments, rats reliably pressed the lever to delay shocks, even though doing so either did not decrease or actually increased the number of shocks received per session (Gardner & Lewis, 1976; Hineline, 1970). Thus, according to one-factor theory, momentarily *preventing* the aversive event is the consequence that maintains SR_A- behavior. There is no need for fear reduction.

The Controversy Continues. Although one-factor theorists have shown that CS termination is not required, two-factor theorists have countered, suggesting that Pavlovian conditioning is still important. Specifically, two-factor theorists hold that the avoidance response (pressing the lever) produces a CS that one-factor theorists are ignoring: a safety-stimulus consequence that immediately precedes the prevention of shock. What is that safety stimulus? The tactile feeling of making the avoidance response. That is, when the avoidance lever is pressed down, the rat feels the lever move down and this functions as a safety-stimulus consequence that maintains avoidance behavior.

Although one-factor theorists hold that speculating about unobserved CS events is unnecessary, at present there is no agreement that one side or the other has won the theoretical debate. Perhaps someone reading this chapter will solve this mystery. After all, great researchers like Herrnstein, Hineline, and Mineka were all undergraduate students reading books just like this one at one point in their lives.

Reading Quiz 1

For each of the questions here, indicate if the consequence is a stimulus presentation, a stimulus removal/reduction, or involves the prevention of a stimulus change. The consequence is italicized in each item.

Next, assuming that the consequence functions as a reinforcer, indicate if it is a positive reinforcer (SR+), a negative reinforcer – escape (SR$_E$-), or a negative reinforcer – avoidance (SR$_A$-).

1. Armand turned off his car and *the engine stopped running*. Assuming that this stimulus _____ (presentation, removal/reduction, or prevention) functions as a reinforcer, it would be classified as a _____ (SR+, SR$_E$-, or SR$_A$-).

2. The last time Jenna went skiing on a sunny day, she got terrible sunburn on her face. Today she is skiing and sees that the sun is shining brightly. Jenna applies sunscreen so that she will *not get a sunburn*. Assuming this stimulus _____ (presentation, removal/reduction, or prevention) functions as a reinforcer, it would be classified as a _____ (SR+, SR$_E$-, or SR$_A$-).

3. Catherine takes a drive through a scenic park. She is delighted with *the sights of trees, a lake, and an elk*. Assuming this stimulus _____ (presentation, removal/reduction, or prevention) functions as a reinforcer, it would be classified as a _____ (SR+, SR$_E$-, or SR$_A$-).

4. Terrence notices that his stomach is upset, so he takes an antacid. About 10 minutes later, he notices that *his stomach pain is almost gone*. Assuming this stimulus _____ (presentation, removal/reduction, or prevention) functions as a reinforcer, it would be classified as a _____ (SR+, SR$_E$-, or SR$_A$-).

5. Jonathan's boss yells at him every time he sees him. It doesn't matter what Jonathan is doing, his boss will find something to yell at him about. Jonathan has gotten good at identifying the sound of his boss' footsteps. Now when he hears his boss approaching, he hides under his desk. Jonathan can still hear the footsteps under there, but hiding allows him to *avoid getting yelled at*. Assuming this stimulus _____ (presentation, removal/reduction, or prevention) functions as a reinforcer, it would be classified as a _____ (SR+, SR$_E$-, or SR$_A$-).

6. Greg's dad cut his hair when he was upset with Greg. When Greg looks at himself in the mirror, he is crushed. When Greg puts on a hat *the awful haircut is hidden*. Assuming this stimulus _____ (presentation, removal/reduction, or prevention) functions as a reinforcer, it would be classified as a _____ (SR+, SR$_E$-, or SR$_A$-).

7. Alyssa's husband is snoring again. She rolls him over and *he stops*. Assuming this stimulus _____ (presentation, removal/reduction, or prevention) functions as a reinforcer, it would be classified as a _____ (SR+, SR$_E$-, or SR$_A$-).

8. Nevada was waiting at the bus stop on a rainy day. A large puddle of water had accumulated in the gutter in front of the bench. Nevada elected to stand to the side of the bench so that *she would not get splashed when the bus arrived*. Assuming this stimulus _____ (presentation, removal/reduction, or prevention) functions as a reinforcer, it would be classified as a _____ (SR+, SR$_E$-, or SR$_A$-).

9. Becky sent a picture of her dog to @dog_rates and got *a score of 12 out of 10*. Assuming this stimulus _____ (presentation, removal/reduction, or prevention) functions as a reinforcer, it would be classified as a _____ (SR+, SR$_E$-, or SR$_A$-).

Source: ARTSILENSE/ Shutterstock.com

10. The Los Angeles Dodgers baseball team got its name in 1913 because pedestrians in Brooklyn (where the team was located back then) were good at dodging streetcars as they sped through the urban streets. Assuming that *not being hit by a streetcar* (presentation, removal/reduction, or prevention) functions as a reinforcer, it would be classified as a _____ (SR+, SR_E^-, or SR_A^-).

Positive or Negative Reinforcement: Is There Really a Difference?

In Reading Quiz 1, the scenarios are described in a way that makes it fairly easy to tell whether the consequence is a stimulus presentation, removal/ reduction, or the prevention of a stimulus change. In the real world it can be difficult to tell the difference.

Source: Osman Rana/Unsplash

Imagine that you are outside, waiting for the bus on the coldest day of the year. Your coat is not keeping you warm enough so you walk to a nearby building and step inside to warm up. One could say that the contingent consequence of stepping inside is the *presentation* of heat (SR+). But one could just as easily say it is the *removal/reduction* of the freezing temperatures (SR_E^-) or the *prevention* of frostbite (SR_A^-).

Because of the difficulty in telling the difference between SR+, SR_E^-, and SR_A^-, some behavioral scientists have recommended that the distinction between these concepts be abandoned (Baron & Galizio, 2005; Michael, 1975). Next, we present three reasons for distinguishing between positive and negative reinforcement.

Reason 1: Heuristics

When considering ways in which to positively influence behavior through reinforcement, it is important to *remember all your options* (Hackenberg & Defulio, 2007). The concepts of SR+, SR_E^-, and SR_A^- provide a heuristic for remembering three different ways in which you can arrange reinforcement contingencies: consequences can be presented (SR+), removed/reduced (SR_E^-), or prevented (SR_A^-). When designing a behavior-change plan, the skilled behavior analyst will evaluate the pros and cons of all three methods. If the intervention is effective in positively influencing behavior, it will not matter if someone says it's SR+ and someone else says it's SR_E^-; all that will matter is that the behavior analyst who designed the intervention knew every way in which reinforcement contingencies could positively influence behavior, and that this know-how improved the life of an individual.

Reason 2: Loss Aversion

A second reason to distinguish between positive and negative reinforcement is what behavioral economists call *loss aversion* (Kahneman & Tversky, 1979).

> **Loss Aversion:** *The tendency for loss prevention (SR_A-) to influence behavior more than presentation of the same stimulus (SR+).*

In a classic experiment conducted by Kahneman et al. (1990), college students were asked how much they would pay for a coffee cup. The amount paid – about $2.25 – put a value on this stimulus presentation (SR+). A second group of students operated under a negative-reinforcement contingency. They were given the same mug for free and asked to put a price on avoiding the loss of the mug (SR_A-). That is, they were asked how much they would sell it for. The selling price – about $5.25 – put a higher

Source: Fotofermer/Shutterstock.com

value on preventing the loss of the mug than the value of obtaining the same mug.

Many studies have evaluated the effects of loss prevention vs. an equivalent gain. Halpern et al. (2015) found that avoiding monetary losses (SR_A-) was a more effective consequence for motivating smokers to quit than was earning monetary rewards (SR+). In a laboratory experiment in which steady-state behavior was measured, Rasmussen and Newland (2008) estimated that loss prevention was three times as effective as gains.

In the "real world" outside the lab, credit-card customers who were informed they could avoid monetary losses (check processing fees) by using their credit card went on to use their cards twice as much as customers whose check-processing savings were described as "gains" (Ganzach & Karsahi, 1995). In 2014, when the Affordable Care Act ("Obamacare") was framed as a health-insurance gain, only 37% of Americans approved of the law. However, in 2018, when federal lawmakers debated its repeal (a warning signal threatening a loss of healthcare), a majority of Americans approved of the program.

At the same time, several studies have shown that negative reinforcers are *not* more effective in influencing behavior than equivalent positive reinforcers (e.g., Asgarova, 2019; Magoon & Critchfield, 2008; Magoon et al., 2017). These studies have provided participants with extended exposure to both consequences, where most prior studies asked participants to make one-off choices between hypothetical outcomes. Recognizing this discrepancy in outcomes, we will simply note that many of the most important choices we make in life (e.g., to get married or not) are between prospective outcomes we are yet to experience. In these situations, we make our choices by drawing on our past experience with positive and negative reinforcers. Because loss aversion is prevalent in our prospective choices, an argument can be made for distinguishing between positive and negative reinforcers.

Reason 3: Preference for Positive Reinforcement

Imagine that you have decided to give up a bad habit (pick your favorite) and are going to use reinforcement to get the job done. For this reinforcement-based intervention, would you rather use a positive-reinforcement contingency (loosely speaking, getting something you want when you succeed) or a negative reinforcement contingency (avoiding something aversive when you succeed)?

When Halpern et al. (2015) asked treatment-seeking cigarette smokers this question, about 95% were happy with an intervention in which they could earn money for quitting (SR+). However, less than 15% were happy with an intervention in which they could avoid losing money by quitting (SR_A^-). If individuals object to negative reinforcement contingencies but not positive reinforcement, then it is important to distinguish between these two types of reinforcement.

Source: rakimm/Shutterstock.com

Using Reinforcement to Positively Influence Behavior

Positive and negative reinforcement are two behavior-analytic principles that can be used to positively influence behavior. This is an important technology of behavior change and it has already been used to make a better world.

As an early example, in the 1950s, behavior analysts began teaching independent-living skills to adults and children with intellectual and developmental disabilities (Ellis et al., 1960) and developed interventions to reduce severe problem behaviors such as self-injury and aggression directed toward others (Hagopian et al., 2013). These interventions proved highly effective (Kurtz & Lind, 2013) and, when they were disseminated across the US over several decades, people of the 1970s

Source: olesiabilkei/Getty Images

began to rethink how individuals with intellectual and developmental disabilities were being treated. Where prior to behavior analysis many of these individuals were housed in large institutions, outside of cities; today they live with their families or in supported living arrangements. They play, care for themselves, learn, work, and contribute to society because of the technology of reinforcement.

More recently, reinforcement has revolutionized the treatment of children with autism. Systematic behavior-change programs based in large part on positive reinforcement have helped thousands of children to acquire social and daily living skills that allow them to live with dignity (Ahearn & Tiger, 2013; Cohen et al., 2006; Eldevik et al., 2009).

Today, behavior analysts are using reinforcement to develop more effective ways to positively influence behaviors that are at the heart of public health deficits. These include increasing exercise and adherence to a healthy diet (Zerger et al., 2016, 2017), practicing safe sexual behaviors (Björkman-Nyqvist et al., 2013), and reducing cigarette smoking and prescription drug abuse (Morean et al., 2015). Behavior analysts have even used positive reinforcement to teach critical helping behaviors to family pets (Protopopova et al., 2016) and therapy animals who provide support and guidance to individuals with disabilities (Bennett, 2016; Pryor & Ramirez, 2014). These applications are just the tip of the iceberg.

Source: cglade/iStock/Getty Images

Reinforcement in the Workplace

Much of our behavior at work is operant behavior. Some of the consequences of operant work-behavior are positive reinforcers and some are negative reinforcers. What percentage would you estimate are positive reinforcers (e.g., your paycheck, praise from your boss)? It depends on where you work, and who is your boss. Some managers use a lot of positive reinforcement – when they see their employees doing excellent work, they let them know that it is appreciated, and they occasionally provide bonuses for doing extraordinary work. Other managers use a lot of negative reinforcement; their employees work to avoid getting in trouble or fired.

Like the smokers in the Halpern et al. (2015) study, most of us would rather work for the manager who uses positive reinforcement. If your boss uses negative reinforcement, you might choose the ultimate negative reinforcer – you quit so that you can avoid any further badgering from your boss. When this happens, the company loses a valuable employee (you) and that is expensive because now they have to search for and train a new employee. Good companies retain good employees and positive reinforcement can help.

The systematic application of positive reinforcement (and other behavioral principles covered in this book) in workplace settings is called "Organizational Behavior Management" (OBM). Behavior analysts trained in OBM consult with companies to integrate positive reinforcement into the workplace. For example, if a manufacturing company is not meeting its quality-control goals, a restaurant has poor customer service, or a utility company has low compliance with safety protocols, an OBM specialist can help. Often these specialists find that, other than a paycheck, positive reinforcers are absent from the workplace. In other cases, they find that managers are positively reinforcing the wrong behaviors, or exclusively using negative reinforcement to create a fear-driven workplace.

The use of behavior-analytic principles in OBM improves employee performance by an average of 69% (Duncan, 1989). Think about that for a moment. If a man-

Source: Jetta Productions Inc/Getty Images

ufacturing company could increase output by 69%, this would allow it to ship orders on time and improve customer satisfaction. If the wait staff at a restaurant improved customer service by 69%, their customers would return often, *and* the wait staff would earn better tips. If employees at the utility company increased adherence to the safety protocols, fewer accidents would occur and more employees would return safely to their family at night.

Three Objections to Reinforcement

Within behavior analysis, reinforcement has always been viewed as a good thing – something that could help in meeting the twin goals of predicting and positively influencing behavior. As already noted, reinforcement has proven useful on both counts. Knowing that consequences can influence behavior and developing a technology that puts this prediction to good use has improved human lives. Nonetheless, some scientists have raised concerns about using reinforcement to influence human behavior. These are not misguided dullards; they are smart people who are concerned about possible side effects of reinforcement, and we should carefully evaluate their arguments. Here, we consider three common objections and evaluate how data relevant to these concerns should influence our use of reinforcement contingencies.

Objection 1: Intrinsic Motivation

The first objection is that reinforcement permanently decreases intrinsic motivation for a behavior. To understand and evaluate this objection, you have to understand what "intrinsic motivation" means. Psychologists define **intrinsic motivation** as *the natural drive to engage in a behavior because it fosters a sense of competence.* Consider a child coloring with crayons. A psychologist might say coloring occurs because the child is intrinsically motivated to color; this behavior yields automatic reinforcers that foster self-competence (e.g., a pleasing picture, Ryan & Deci, 2002). **Extrinsic reinforcers**, by contrast, are *those reinforcers that are not automatically obtained by engaging in the behavior; instead, they are artificially arranged* (e.g., giving the child a small toy for coloring a pleasing picture). Psychologists often object to using extrinsic reinforcers because such consequences are thought to undermine, or crowd out, intrinsic motivation. That is, when the extrinsic reinforcer is introduced, the child might start coloring for toys, rather than for the satisfaction of producing a pleasing picture.

Source: Arthur Tilley/Getty Images

How do we test this theory that extrinsic reinforcers crowd out intrinsic motivation? Most studies randomly assign participants to groups who either earn an extrinsic reinforcer for doing something like solving a puzzle (the extrinsic-reinforcement group) or who solve puzzles for the intrinsic enjoyment of doing so (the intrinsic-motivation group). In the next phase, extrinsic reinforcers are suspended, and time spent doing puzzles is compared across groups. If the extrinsic-reinforcement group spends less time with the puzzles than the intrinsic-motivation group, this suggests that the extrinsic reinforcers have crowded out intrinsic motivation for puzzling.

More than 100 studies have evaluated this hypothesis. The overall finding is that *extrinsic reinforcers do not decrease intrinsic motivation to engage in behavior* (Cameron et al., 2001; Cerasoli et al., 2014). When the probability of a behavior is very low (e.g., children eating vegetables), extrinsic reinforcers can increase this behavior both while reinforcers are earned and afterwards (Deci et al., 2001; Madden et al., 2017). One of the authors of this book gave his children small monetary (extrinsic) reinforcers contingent on tasting several different vegetables they thought they would hate. Both children increased their tasting of these foods (a positive reinforcement effect), and both discov-

Source: Hero Images/Getty Images

ered a couple vegetables that they were surprised to find they liked (the rest they really did hate). Extrinsic reinforcers helped them find automatic reinforcers (the few good tastes) that they would otherwise have never experienced. Both children continued to eat these and many other vegetables for years to come, despite never again being paid to do so.

So, we can reject the hypothesis that extrinsic reinforcers always have a negative effect on intrinsic motivation. What about high-probability behaviors (e.g., writing music lyrics, playing video games, helping others)? Do extrinsic reinforcers do more harm than good with these behaviors? It depends on the extrinsic reinforcer. *Verbal* extrinsic reinforcers (e.g., telling the individual they've done a good job) seems to enhance intrinsic motivation, that is, increase these behaviors even more (Deci, 1975). This is easy to imagine. If you like to write song lyrics and then a friend whose opinion you value says, "You know, you've got a real talent for writing lyrics," you are probably going to spend more time doing so. Likewise, if you enjoy serving meals at the homeless shelter and the director says, "Your compassion is admirable," you are more likely to continue serving meals even when months go by without anyone recognizing your service.

So, are the psychologists who object to using reinforcement crazy? No. Extrinsic reinforcers can have a temporary negative impact, but only when they are tangible (e.g., money) and only when they are used to reinforce "high-interest" behaviors. For example, if you enjoy writing song lyrics and I contract you to write three new songs for $850, then after the contract is fulfilled, your motivation to write additional lyrics (for no money) may be temporarily reduced (Cameron et al., 2001). Importantly, these negative effects of tangible rewards are temporary and can be avoided if the reinforcer comes as a surprise.

That's a lot to keep track of. After considering two more objections to reinforcement, we will provide some guidelines on the right way to use positive reinforcers.

Objection 2: Performance-Inhibiting Properties of Reinforcement

A second concern about using positive reinforcement is that reinforcement contingencies can actually *inhibit* performances. This performance decline takes two forms – reinforcers reduce creativity and reinforcers can lead to "choking under pressure." Let's briefly look at each of these concerns.

CREATIVITY

In a famous study, Amabile (1996) asked professional artists to submit several of their paintings that were either commissioned (i.e., the buyer told the artist what to paint) or noncommissioned (the artist was unpaid and they painted whatever they wanted). When these paintings were judged by a panel of art experts who did not know if the paintings were commissioned or not, the noncommissioned paintings were usually rated as more creative. While this evidence has been viewed as convincing by critics of reinforcement (Pink, 2009), it is not a surprising outcome when one considers the contingencies of reinforcement. When the person commissioning the painting prescribes what is to be painted the oppor-

Source: shotsstudio/Getty Images

tunity to express the artist's creativity is constrained. Indeed, if the artist is too creative, the patron may not pay for the commissioned work.

If creativity is an important component of the performance (as it is in any artistic endeavor, and in many problem-solving contexts), a contingent relation should be established between creativity and obtaining the reinforcer. Glover and Gary (1976), for example, included creativity in a positive reinforcement contingency applied to young writers. When social reinforcers could be obtained for writing non-repetitive, elaborate, and original words, these components of creative writing increased. Similar beneficial effects of creativity-inducing reinforcement contingencies have been reported across the lifespan and for many creative acts (Eisenberger et al., 1998; Goetz, 1989). Indeed, even Amabile (1996) found that when the artists' commission allowed them to express their creativity, the art experts rated those commissioned paintings as just as creative as their noncommissioned paintings.

There are many examples of positive reinforcement contingencies that facilitate creativity. If you write a boring restaurant review for Yelp, will your fellow Yelpers press the Useful, Funny, or Cool buttons? Probably not. Those positive reinforcers are contingent upon excellent, funny, or trendy reviews. If you want to be a top Yelper, you'd do well to get creative. Likewise, the MacArthur genius award provides very large cash rewards (over a half-million dollars) in recognition of great artistic or intellectual behaviors. The reward comes with no strings attached – the genius is recognized for their past actions and encouraged to be as creative as they want in the future. Now that's genius!

CHOKING UNDER PRESSURE

In a classic study of chocking under pressure, researchers visited a poor village in India and asked residents to complete a range of skillful tasks such as rolling a ball through a maze or reproducing a sequence of lights and tones by pressing buttons on a Simon toy (Ariely et al., 2009). Some of the villagers were promised a huge monetary reward (as much as they usually spend in an entire month) for performing very well. Others were offered more modest rewards. Not surprisingly, participants offered huge rewards choked under pressure, scoring worse on the tasks than those offered more modest rewards. Similar outcomes have been reported in tasks that require creative thinking (Glucksberg, 1962). Contingencies arranging very large rewards would appear to increase the probability of choking under pressure.

On the one hand, the solution to this problem is obvious – don't arrange huge rewards. On the other hand, maybe these researchers came to the wrong conclusion. Let's go back to that Indian village and instead of promising a massive reward for a top score on Simon *today*, let's inform the villagers that we will return in two months and, if they can earn a high score

Source: Hempdiddy/Wikipedia

on Simon at that time, we will give them the huge reward. What do you think would happen? Villagers given this opportunity would undoubtedly spend many hours each night playing Simon, developing effective strategies for improving their working memory. How would they score relative to villagers given two months to prepare, but promised much smaller or no rewards? At this point, this will have to be a thought experiment. No one has conducted a real version of it. If the Indian villagers are like adolescents who aspire to earn huge salaries by playing professional sports, there is a good chance that those given the opportunity to earn huge rewards would spend more time preparing and would score better than their less incentivized counterparts.

Objection 3: Cheating

If cheating can produce the positive reinforcer more easily than engaging in the desired behavior, some people will succumb to the temptation. Consider the Wells Fargo Banking scandals. In 2016, Wells Fargo paid a $185 million fine for fraudulently opening bank accounts and issuing credit cards to customers who never asked for them (Corkery, 2016). How did this happen? Managers at Wells Fargo offered financial incentives (positive reinforcers) to employees for landing new accounts and issuing new credit cards. Operating under this contingency, many employees cheated by opening new accounts for about 1.5 million people who didn't ask for them and didn't want them. Managers were so focused on the profits from these new accounts, they failed to monitor employee behavior to ensure cheating was not occurring. What's to be done about this? You will find the answer at the bottom of Table 6.3.

Table 6.3 Three objections to using reinforcement were summarized in the preceding sections. The practices listed here can help readers to skillfully use reinforcement, so as to avoid (SR_A-) negative side effects.

- The primary reason to arrange a reinforcer is to improve behavior. If the individual is already behaving at an acceptable level, then occasional competence-building reinforcers is all you need (e.g., "You really put your best effort into that, and I appreciate it").
- If you want to tangibly recognize a brilliant achievement, surprise the individual with an unexpected reward.
- If the individual must engage in a low-probability behavior (e.g., strictly adhering to a safety protocol), then reinforcers can be very useful.

(Continued)

- If reinforcing a low-probability behavior allows the individual to sample automatic reinforcers (e.g., the child who tastes curried carrots finds that she loves them), then these intrinsic reinforcers can maintain the behavior once your extrinsic reinforcers are withdrawn.
- Be careful with large rewards. They can induce cheating and increase the probability of choking under pressure.
- If you need to encourage highly skillful performances that take a lot of time and dedication to accomplish (e.g., playing sports at a professional level, completing a doctoral degree) large reinforcers may be needed.
- If creativity is important, either include it in the reinforcement contingency or make sure the contingency does not constrain creative performances.
- Anticipate cheating. Let everyone know that cheating will be monitored and those proven guilty will be punished.

Reading Quiz 2

1. Three reasons were provided for distinguishing between positive and negative reinforcement. The first reason, *heuristics*, was that it is useful to remember there are three ways in which reinforcement can be arranged: _____, _____, and _____.
2. The second reason for distinguishing between positive and negative reinforcement is that the value of avoiding a loss (SR_A-) appears to be greater than the value of acquiring a gain ($SR+$). Behavioral economists call this _____ _____.
3. The third reason for distinguishing between positive and negative reinforcement is that individuals tend to prefer _____ reinforcement contingencies over _____ reinforcement contingencies.
4. Organizational Behavior Management (OBM) uses _____ reinforcement to increase workplace performances by an average of 69%.
5. Positively reinforcing low-probability behaviors, like exercise, does not reduce _____ motivation. Instead, it often allows individuals to contact automatic reinforcers (e.g., I feel and look better now that I have been exercising) that they would otherwise not experience.
6. If creativity is important, include this dimension of behavior in your *IF → THEN* reinforcement _____.
7. If you want to avoid choking under pressure, the easiest solution is to avoid arranging _____ reinforcers for the skillful behavior.
8. Anytime you arrange a reinforcement contingency, there is a chance that individuals will _____. Monitoring unethical behavior can reduce the chances that it will occur.

Theories of Reinforcement

Reinforcement is, on the one hand, a very simple process by which consequences increase the future probability of behavior. You can do a lot to improve the lives of others with this level of understanding. But underlying this simple description is an important question that we don't yet have a good answer to: How does reinforcement work?

There are at least two ways to approach answering this question. Both approaches have merit and complement each other (i.e., the strengths of one approach compensate for the weaknesses of the other, and vice versa). The first approach is to investigate the neurological events that occur when reinforcers are obtained. How do these events change the organism in a way that influences the future probability of operant behavior? If reinforcers influence future behavior, they must do this by changing the biology of the individual (e.g., synaptic patterns in the brain). This is an active area of research within behavioral neuroscience (Salamone et al., 2012), but it is beyond the scope of this text. Students who master the behavioral principles presented in this introductory course and who have an interest in the biology underlying these principles should pursue further study in behavioral neuroscience.

The second approach to answering the *how does reinforcement work* question investigates this process at the level of the whole organism and how it interacts with its environment (without going into the neurological specifics that underlie the reinforcement process). Obviously, this will not further our understanding of the biological mechanisms underlying the process, but it will reveal in further detail how present behavior is influenced by past events. Behavioral neuroscientists will need these details when evaluating their hypotheses. For example, if their hypothesis does not correspond to the replicable behavioral data, then it is wrong. In addition, remaining at the level of the whole organism is, at present, the most practical approach to positively influencing human behavior. For example, knowing the genetics responsible for Down syndrome is important, but it does not point to practical interventions that will help these individuals to acquire skills allowing them to live more meaningful lives with their families.

Embracing this practical approach, while recognizing the importance of biology, this book provides an analysis of behavior at the level of the whole organism. The next sections of this chapter outline two contemporary whole-organism theories of reinforcement. We will revisit these theories in subsequent chapters, evaluating the strengths and weaknesses of each theory as new information is revealed about ways in which reinforcers influence behavior.

The Response Strengthening Theory of Reinforcement

When Thorndike and Skinner discussed reinforcement they often referred to it metaphorically as a process through which reinforcing consequences "stamp in" or "strengthen" behavior (Skinner, 1938; Thorndike, 1911). Each obtained reinforcer is hypothesized to strengthen the behavior it follows. The more frequently an operant behavior is followed by a reinforcer, the theory goes, the more firmly it is established, and the more difficult it will be to disrupt (Nevin & Grace, 2000). A metaphor for this hypothesis is a bucket of water – the heavier the bucket, the more response strength; the more response strength, the more probable is the response. Obtained reinforcers give the bucket its weight. Each reinforcer adds a bit more water to the bucket. Frequent or big reinforcers create a heavier bucket than infrequent or small reinforcers.

Source: Jon Pallbo/Wikipedia

The Response-Strengthening Theory of Reinforcement is consistent with the examples discussed in this chapter. When reinforcers are obtained following behaviors such as buying a lottery ticket, escaping from a problem relationship, or avoiding a pothole, weight is added to the metaphorical buckets representing the strength of these operant behaviors. The more reinforcers obtained, the more firmly established is the behavior. When these response-strengthening consequences are withheld, the bucket is gradually drained of response strength and behavior decreases in probability.

Evidence supporting the Response-Strengthening Theory of Reinforcement comes from many experiments. One of the more important of these is a laboratory study in which pigeons could emit two different operant behaviors to earn food reinforcers – they could peck a *left* button in the chamber or they could peck a *right* button (Herrnstein, 1961). Traditionally these buttons are referred to as "keys." If a response on the left key produces a reinforcer, then the Response-Strengthening Theory predicts a bit of water is added to the left-key bucket. Doing so increases its weight, that is, its response strength. Likewise, when a right-key peck produces a reinforcer, the strength of that operant behavior is increased.

The Herrnstein (1961) experiment allowed pigeons to freely choose between the two keys. According to the Response-Strengthening Theory, the pigeons should allocate their behavior in a way that reflects the relative strength of the behaviors. Said another way, if the left-key bucket is three times as heavy as the right-key bucket, then three times as many pecks should be allocated to that key. This is exactly what Herrnstein found. When, in a later phase, three times as many reinforcers were obtained on the right key, the pigeons stopped preferring the left key and reallocated their pecking to the right key. The results of Herrnstein's experiment have been replicated many times with several species (Davison & McCarthy, 1988; Herrnstein, 2000) including humans (Madden & Perone, 1999; Magoon et al., 2017).

The Information Theory of Reinforcement

An alternative to the Response-Strengthening Theory of Reinforcement is the *Information Theory*. The Information Theory agrees that reinforcers increase operant behavior above a baseline level, but it disagrees about how this happens. The Information Theory holds that reinforcers provide information that allows the individual to predict when or where subsequent reinforcers may be obtained. In much the same way that a road sign can direct you to Albuquerque, the delivery of a reinforcer provides information directing individuals to more reinforcers. In the words of Cowie and Davison (2016), "Behavior is… controlled by the likely future, as exemplified in the past" (p. 249; see also Dragoi & Staddon, 1999).

Consider an African wolf searching for food. It sees a rodent as it enters its hole in the ground. The wolf digs and attacks (operant behavior) and receives a tasty bit of food for its effort (reinforcer). According to

Source: oliver.dodd/Flickr/CC BY 2.0

the Information Theory, the wolf's foraging behavior should be *controlled by the likely future as exemplified in the past*. In the past (just before eating), a rodent was found in the hole. This provides informative about the likely future: the most likely place to find another rodent is in the hole. Thus, the next time the wolf is hungry, it should return to this rodent hole to find its next meal.

Evaluating the Theories

So, how does one differentiate between these theories? After all, the Response-Strengthening Theory also predicts the coyote will return to the hole because the strength of this response was increased by the reinforcer. In Chapter 7 we will evaluate how these theories perform in explaining complex environment–behavior interactions. For now, we will simply note that theories are important. Theories require scientists to specify their assumptions in a way that allows them and other scientists to put the theory to an empirical test. When assumptions are made explicit (in theories), they may be found to be at odds with existing data. When assumptions lurk under our explanations of behavior, their validity is never evaluated. Specifying our assumptions in a theory also allows us to evaluate if the theory is falsifiable. You will recall from Chapter 1 that theories that cannot be falsified are not scientific theories.

Reading Quiz 3

1. According to the _____ theory of reinforcement, each obtained reinforcer increases the strength of the operant behavior.
2. According to the _____ theory of reinforcement, reinforcers do not strengthen behavior, they provide information about where and when reinforcers may be obtained.

Summary

Operant behavior increases when followed by positive or negative reinforcers. Positive reinforcers (SR+) are stimulus presentations that follow a response, whereas negative reinforcers either remove/reduce a stimulus (SR_E-) or prevent a stimulus from occurring (SR_A-). Reasons for distinguishing between positive and negative reinforcement are (1) it helps us remember there is more than one way to influence behavior, (2) negative reinforcers might have a greater influence on behavior than positive reinforcers, and (3) humans and animals tend to prefer positive reinforcement contingencies. There are many ways in which reinforcement has been used to improve human behavior in therapeutic, educational, and workplace settings. Despite these advances, some social and behavioral scientists are concerned that reinforcement contingencies can have negative side effects such as a reduction in intrinsic motivation or creativity. These side effects, where there is evidence for them, can be avoided by following the guidelines in Table 6.3. Finally, two theories of reinforcement were discussed – the *Response-Strengthening Theory* and the *Information Theory* – and we provided some reasons why theories are important in a behavioral science.

Answers to Reading Quiz Questions

Reading Quiz 1

1. removal/reduction; SR_E^-
2. prevention; SR_A^-
3. presentation; SR+
4. removal/reduction; SR_E^-
5. prevention; SR_A^-
6. removal/reduction; SR_E^-
7. removal/reduction; SR_E^-
8. prevention; SR_A^-
9. presentation; SR+
10. prevention; SR_A^-

Reading Quiz 2

1. SR+, SR_E^-, and SR_A^- (the order doesn't matter)
2. loss aversion
3. positive; negative
4. positive
5. intrinsic
6. contingency
7. huge, large (anything like that is correct)
8. cheat

Reading Quiz 3

1. response-strengthening
2. information

References

Ahearn, W. H., & Tiger, J. (2013). Behavioral approaches to the treatment of autism. In G. J. Madden, W. Dube, T. D. Hackenberg, G. P. Hanley, & K. A. Lattal (Eds.), *APA handbook of behavior analysis, Vol. 2: Translating principles into practice* (pp. 301–327). Washington, DC: APA Books.

Amabile, T. M. (1996). *Creativity in context: Update to the social psychology of creativity.* Boulder, CO: Westview Press.

Ariely, D., Gneezy, U., Loewenstein, G., & Mazar, N. (2009). Large stakes and big mistakes. *Review of Economic Studies, 76*, 451–469. doi:10.1111/j.1467-937X.2009.00534.x

Asgarova, R. (2019). *Gain-loss asymmetry in human experiential tasks* [Unpublished master's thesis]. Victoria University of Wellington.

Baron, A., & Galizio, M. (2005). Positive and negative reinforcement: Should the distinction be preserved? *The Behavior Analyst, 28*, 85–98. doi:10.1007/BF03392107

Bennett, P. E. (2016). Reviewing assistance animal effectiveness. *Final report to the National Disability Insurance Agency*. Bendigo Victoria, Australia: Latrobe University.

Björkman-Nyqvist, M., Corno, L., De Walque, D., & Svensson, J. (2013). P4. 120 evaluating the impact of short term financial incentives on HIV and STI incidence among youth in Lesotho: A randomised trial. *Sexually Transmitted Infections, 89*(Suppl 1), A325-A325. doi:10.1136/sextrans-2013-051184.1017

Brogden, W. J., Lipman, E. A., & Culler, E. (1938). The role of incentive in conditioning and extinction. *American Journal of Psychology, 51*, 109–117. doi:10.2307/1416419

Cameron, J., Banko, K. M., & Pierce, W. D. (2001). Pervasive negative effects of rewards on intrinsic motivation: The myth continues. *The Behavior Analyst, 24*, 1–44. doi:10.1007/BF03392017

Cerasoli, C. P., Nicklin, J. M., & Ford, M. T. (2014). Intrinsic motivation and extrinsic incentives jointly predict performance: A 40-year meta-analysis. *Psychological Bulletin, 140*(4), 1–29. doi:10.1037/a0035661

Cohen, H., Amerine-Dickens, M. T., & Smith, T. (2006). Early intensive behavioral treatment: Replication of the UCLA model in a community setting. *Journal of Developmental Behavioral Pediatrics, 27*, 143–155.

Corkery, M. (2016, September). Wells Fargo fined $185 million for fraudulently opening accounts. The New York Times. https://www.nytimes.com/2016/09/09/business/dealbook/wells-fargo-fined-for-years-of-harm-to-customers.html

Cowie, S., & Davison, M. (2016). Control by reinforcers across time and space: A review of recent choice research. *Journal of the Experimental Analysis of Behavior, 105*(2), 246–269. doi:10.1002/jeab.200

Davison, M., & McCarthy, D. (1988). *The matching law: A research review*. New York: Lawrence Erlbaum Associates.

Deci, E. L. (1975). *Intrinsic motivation*. New York: Plenum.

Deci, E. L., Koestner, R., & Ryan, R. M. (2001). Extrinsic rewards and intrinsic motivation in education: Reconsidered once again. *Review of Educational Research, 71*(1), 1–27. doi:10.3102/00346543071001001

Dragoi, V., & Staddon, J. E. R. (1999). The dynamics of operant conditioning. *Psychological Review, 106*(1), 20–61. doi:10.1037/0033-295X.106.1.20

Duncan, P. (1989). OBM and success: What's the PIP? *Journal of Organizational Behavior Management, 10*(1), 258–266. doi:10.1300/J075v10n01_14

Eisenberger, R., Armeli, S., & Pretz, J. (1998). Can the promise of reward increase creativity? *Journal of Personality and Social Psychology, 74*(3), 704–714. doi:10.1037/0022-3514.74.3.704

Eldevik, S., Hastings, R. P., Hughes, J. C., Jahr, E., Eikeseth, S., & Cross, S. (2009). Meta-analysis of early intensive behavioral intervention for children with autism. *Journal of Clinical Child and Adolescent Psychology, 38*, 439–450. doi:10.1080/15374410902851739

Ellis, N. R., Barnettt, C. D., & Pryer, M. W. (1960). Operant behavior in mental defectives: Exploratory studies. *Journal of the Experimental Analysis of Behavior, 3*, 63–69. doi:10.1901/jeab.1960.3-63

Ganzach, Y., & Karsahi, N. (1995). Message framing and buying behavior: A field experiment. *Journal of Business Research, 32*(1), 11–17. doi:10.1016/0148-2963(93)00038-3

Gardner, E. T., & Lewis, P. (1976). Negative reinforcement with shock-frequency increase. *Journal of the Experimental Analysis of Behavior, 25*, 3–14. doi:10.1901/jeab.1976.25-3

George, O., & Koob, G. F. (2017). Overview of nicotine withdrawal and negative reinforcement (Preclinical). In *Negative affective states and cognitive impairments in nicotine dependence* (pp. 1–20). London: Academic Press.

Glover, J., & Gary, A. L. (1976). Procedures to increase some aspects of creativity. *Journal of Applied Behavior Analysis, 9*(1), 79–84. doi:10.1901/jaba.1976.9-79

Glucksberg, S. (1962). The influence of strength of drive on functional fixedness and perceptual recognition. *Journal of Experimental Psychology, 63*(1), 36-41. doi:10.1037/h0044683

Goetz, E. M. (1989). The teaching of creativity to preschool children. In *Handbook of creativity* (pp. 411–428). Boston, MA: Springer US.

Hackenberg, T. D., & Defulio, A. (2007). Timeout from reinforcement: Restoring a balance between analysis and application. *Mexican Journal of Behavior Analysis, 33*, 37–44. Retrieved from https://www.redalyc.org/pdf/593/59309905.pdf

Hagopian, L. P., Dozier, C. L., Rooker, G. W., & Jones, B. A. (2013). Assessment and treatment of severe problem behavior. In G. J. Madden, W. Dube, T. D. Hackenberg, G. P. Hanley, & K. A. Lattal (Eds.), *APA handbook of behavior analysis, Vol. 2: Translating principles into practice* (pp. 353–386). Washington, DC: APA Books.

Halpern, S. D., French, B., Small, D. S., Saulsgiver, K., Harhay, M. O., Audrain-McGovern, J., … Volpp, K. G. (2015). Randomized trial of four financial-incentive programs for smoking cessation. *New England Journal of Medicine, 372*(22), 2108–2117. doi:10.1056/NEJMoa1414293

Herrnstein, R. J. (1961). Relative and absolute strength of response as a function of frequency of reinforcement. *Journal of the Experimental Analysis of Behavior, 4*(3), 267–272. doi:10.1901/jeab.1961.4-267

Herrnstein, R. J. (2000). *The matching law: Papers in psychology and economics.* Cambridge, MA: Harvard University Press.

Herrnstein, R. J., & Hineline, P. N. (1966). Negative reinforcement as shock frequency reduction. *Journal of the Experimental Analysis of Behavior, 9*, 421–430. doi:10.1901/jeab.1966.9-421

Hineline, P. N. (1970). Negative reinforcement without shock reduction. *Journal of the Experimental Analysis of Behavior, 14*, 259–268. doi:10.1901/jeab.1970.14-259

Kahneman, D., Knetsch, J. L., & Thaler, R. H. (1990). Experimental tests of the endowment effect and the Coase theorem. *Journal of Political Economy, 98*(6), 1325–1348. doi:10.1086/261737

Kahneman, D., & Tversky, A. (1979). Prospect theory: An analysis of decision under risk. *Econometrica, 47*, 263–291. doi:10.1142/9789814417358_0006

Kurtz, P. F., & Lind, M. A. (2013). Behavioral approaches to treatment of intellectual and developmental disabilities. In G. J. Madden, W. Dube, T. D. Hackenberg, G. P. Hanley, & K. A. Lattal (Eds.), *APA handbook of behavior analysis, Vol. 2: Translating principles into practice* (pp. 279–299). Washington, DC: APA Books.

Madden, G. J., & Perone, M. (1999). Human sensitivity to concurrent schedules of reinforcement: Effects of observing schedule-correlated stimuli. *Journal of the Experimental Analysis of Behavior, 71*(3), 303–318. doi:10.1901/jeab.1999.71-303

Madden, G. J., Price, J., & Sosa, F. A. (2017). Behavioral economic approaches to influencing children's dietary decision making at school. *Policy Insights from the Behavioral and Brain Sciences, 4*(1), 41–48. doi:10.1177/2372732216683517

Magoon, M. A., & Critchfield, T. S. (2008). Concurrent schedules of positive and negative reinforcement: differential-impact and differential-outcomes hypotheses. *Journal of the Experimental Analysis of Behavior, 90*(1), 1–22. doi:10.1901/jeab.2008.90-1

Magoon, M. A., Critchfield, T. S., Merrill, D., Newland, M. C., & Schneider, W. J. (2017). Are positive and negative reinforcement "different"? Insights from a free-operant differential outcomes effect. *Journal of the Experimental Analysis of Behavior, 107*(1), 39–64. doi:10.1002/jeab.243

Michael, J. (1975). Positive and negative reinforcement: A distinction that is no longer necessary; or a better way to talk about bad things. *Behaviorism, 3*, 33–44. Available at https://www.jstor.org/stable/27758829

Mineka, S. (1979). The role of fear in theories of avoidance learning, flooding, and extinction. *Psychological Bulletin, 86*, 985–1010. doi:10.1037/0033-2909.86.5.985

Morean, M. E., Kong, G., Camenga, D. R., Cavallo, D. A., Carroll, K. M., Pittman, B., & Krishnan-Sarin, S. (2015). Contingency management improves smoking cessation treatment outcomes among highly impulsive adolescent smokers relative to cognitive behavioral therapy. *Addictive Behaviors, 42*, 86–90. doi:10.1016/j.addbeh.2014.11.009

Nevin, J. A., & Grace, R. C. (2000). Behavioral momentum: Empirical, theoretical, and metaphorical issues. *Behavioral and Brain Sciences, 23*(1), 117–125. doi:10.1017/S0140525X00502404

Olds, J., & Milner, P. (1954). Positive reinforcement produced by electrical stimulation of septal area and other regions of rat brain. *Journal of Comparative and Physiological Psychology, 47*(6), 419–427. doi:10.1037/h0058775

Pink, D. H. (2009). *Drive: The surprising truth about what motivates us.* New York: Riverhead Books.

Protopopova, A., Kisten, D., & Wynne, C. (2016). Evaluating a humane alternative to the bark collar: Automated differential reinforcement of not barking in a home-alone setting. *Journal of Applied Behavior Analysis, 49*(4), 735–744. doi:10.1002/jaba.334

Pryor, K., & Ramirez, K. (2014). Modern animal training. In F. K. McSweeney & E. S. Murphy (Eds.), *The Wiley Blackwell handbook of operant and classical conditioning* (pp. 453–482). Chichester, UK: John Wiley & Sons, Ltd.

Rasmussen, E. B., & Newland, M. C. (2008). Asymmetry of reinforcement and punishment in human choice. *Journal of the Experimental Analysis of Behavior, 89,* 157–167. doi:10.1901/jeab.2008.89-157

Ryan, R. M., & Deci, E. L. (2002). Self-determination theory and the facilitation of intrinsic motivation, social development, and well-being. *American Psychologist, 55,* 68–78. doi:10.1037/0003-066X.55.1.68

Salamone, J. D., Correa, M., Nunes, E. J., Randall, P. A., & Pardo, M. (2012). The behavioral pharmacology of effort-related choice behavior: Dopamine, adenosine and beyond. *Journal of the Experimental Analysis of Behavior, 97*(1), 125–146. doi:10.1901/jeab.2012.97-125

Schlund, M. W., & Cataldo, M. F. (2010). Amygdala involvement in human avoidance, escape and approach behavior. *NeuroImage, 53*(2), 769–776. doi:10.1016/j.neuroimage.2010.06.058

Skinner, B. F. (1938). *The behavior of organisms: An experimental analysis.* Engelwood Cliffs, NJ: Prentice Hall.

Solomon, R. L., & Wynne, L. C. (1953). Traumatic avoidance learning: Acquisition in normal dogs. *Psychological Monographs: General and Applied, 67*(4), 1–19. https://doi.org/10.1037/h0093649

Zerger, H. M., Miller, B. G., Valbuena, D., & Miltenberger, R. G. (2017). Effects of student pairing and public review on physical activity during school recess. *Journal of Applied Behavior Analysis, 50,* 529–537. doi:10.1002/jaba.389

Zerger, H. M., Normand, M. P., Boga, V., & Patel, R. R. (2016). Adult attention and interaction can increase moderate-to-vigorous physical activity in young children. *Journal of Applied Behavior Analysis, 49*(3), 449–459. doi:10.1002/jaba.317

Extinction and Differential Reinforcement

7

Chapters 5 and 6 described reinforcement, a process through which consequences increase and maintain behavior above a baseline (no-reinforcer) level. This chapter explores what happens when a normally reinforced behavior no longer works, that is, when it no longer produces a reinforcer. This process is called *operant extinction*.

Consider a common behavior in humans – reading. You are doing it right now. What are the reinforcers that maintain reading? To have insight on this, please read the following text:

Rwekle queldrem embtack jhabbstle krepppto bahhlenwavvder opyxim

Were the usual reinforcers obtained when you read this? No. If the rest of the chapter were filled with this sort of text, would you read it? No. If you went to a new book store and found all of their books were written like this, would you buy any of them? No.

When you read these "words," you did what you were supposed to do to get the reinforcer, but there was no reinforcer. Said more technically, you met the *IF behavior* part of the response-reinforcer contingency, but the *THEN reinforcer* part didn't happen.

When a normally reinforced response occurs (like reading), but the reinforcer is not provided, this is called "operant extinction."

Operant Extinction: *Responding that meets the reinforcement contingency no longer produces the reinforcer and, as a result, it falls to baseline (no-reinforcer) levels.*

Note that there are two components of this definition. One is procedural: A response that would normally be reinforced is no longer working – it no longer produces the reinforcer.

An Introduction to Behavior Analysis, First Edition. Gregory J. Madden, Derek D. Reed, and Florence D. DiGennaro Reed.
© 2021 John Wiley & Sons Ltd. Published 2021 by John Wiley & Sons Ltd.

The second component describes an effect of this procedure on behavior: The behavior returns to its baseline level, when that response never produced a reinforcer. When reading the nonsense words goes unreinforced, our reading of such words decreases – perhaps you did not even finish reading the last word "opyxim." This is operant extinction.

Consider another example of operant extinction. Imagine you are talking to a friend one evening. The behavior of interest is your *talking*. What is the reinforcer? For most readers, it will be the reaction of your friend. When you say, "I saw this great film last night," your friend reinforces this statement by saying something like, "Oh yea? What was it about?" In a good conversation, the listener (your friend) reinforces the behavior of the speaker (you) by asking questions, nodding, and looking interested. People who deliver a lot of these reinforcers at just the right times are called "good listeners"; we might think of them as good at providing positive reinforcers.

So, normally your speaking is maintained by reinforcers provided by a listener. Now imagine that your listener falls asleep without you noticing it. You talk, but the usual reinforcers aren't happening. Your friend is not nodding, asking questions, or looking interested. You might keep talking for a few seconds, but after the flow of reinforcers stops, you will stop talking to your snoozing friend.

Operant extinction is the process by which responding decreases to baseline levels after the reinforcer is no longer delivered. That being said, this response-eliminating effect is just one of the effects that operant extinction has on behavior. Extinction can increase emotional responding (e.g., frustration and anger) and also increase the probability of behaviors other than the previously reinforced response. We will discuss these other effects later, but first, let's see how the response-eliminating effect of extinction has been studied in controlled laboratory conditions using positive and negative reinforcers.

Operant Extinction Following Positive Reinforcement

In his 1938 book, *The Behavior of Organisms*, B. F. Skinner described the extinction of rats' lever-pressing behavior. Skinner had already taught his rats to press the lever for a food reinforcer using a simple positive-reinforcement contingency:

IF lever press → *THEN* food

After each of the rats had pressed the lever and earned food about 100 times, Skinner disconnected the feeder so lever pressing no longer produced this reinforcer. By doing so, Skinner (1938) introduced an extinction contingency:

IF lever press → *THEN* no food

Figure 7.1 shows the rate at which a typical rat in Skinner's experiment pressed the lever over one hour of extinction. Once the operant extinction contingency was introduced, the rate of lever pressing gradually decreased until pressing returned to its baseline (no-reinforcer) level. This effect of extinction has been replicated many times, with species ranging from pigeons to humans (Bruzek et al., 2009; Holz et al., 1963).

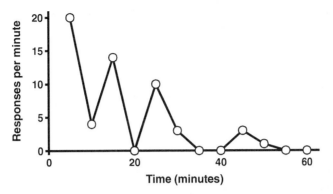

Figure 7.1 After a rat had earned many reinforcers, B. F. Skinner changed the contingency to extinction. The graph shows the number of lever presses that occurred over 60 minutes of extinction. Based on Skinner (1938), Figure 9.

Source: Skinner, B. F. (1938). The behavior of organisms: An experimental analysis. Oxford, England: Appleton-Century.

One of the reasons that behavior analysts are interested in operant extinction is that it can be used to eliminate problem behavior. If you were a teacher and the graph shown in Figure 7.1 was the rate of disruptive outbursts in your classroom, then you would be pleased that operant extinction substantially reduced this problem behavior. As we will see later, operant extinction can't fix every problem behavior, and when it works, it doesn't always work this quickly.

Operant Extinction Following Negative Reinforcement (Escape Extinction)

Recall that negatively reinforced behaviors either remove/reduce (escape, SR_E^-) or prevent (avoidance, SR_A^-) an aversive stimulus. For example, a rat presses a lever and terminates an aversive noise:

IF lever press → *THEN* aversive noise ends *(SR_E^-)*

To introduce an operant extinction contingency, we would ensure that the lever press no longer turns off the noise:

IF lever press → *THEN* no noise termination

Davenport and Olson (1968) conducted this experiment with rats. In the SR_E^- phase, pressing the lever turned off the aversive noise. As shown in Figure 7.2, this negative reinforcement contingency maintained a lot of noise-removing lever presses. However, in the extinction phase, pressing the lever no longer worked; no matter how many times the lever was pressed, the noise persisted. When this contingency change occurred, lever pressing decreased to the baseline level (shown by the dotted line in Figure 7.2).

Operant extinction of negatively reinforced behavior is called "escape extinction."

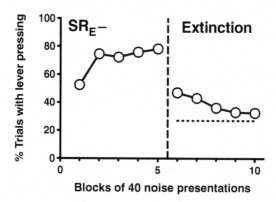

Figure 7.2 In the first phase of the Davenport and Olsen (1968) study, rats learned to press a lever to terminate an aversive noise (SR$_E$-). Rats pressed the lever most of the times the noise was presented. In the extinction phase, pressing the lever no longer turned off the noise. Pressing rapidly decreased.

Source: Davenport, D. G., & Olson, R. D. (1968). A reinterpretation of extinction in discriminated avoidance. *Psychonomic Science, 13*(1), 5–6. https://doi.org/10.3758/bf03342380.

> **Escape Extinction:** *Responding that meets the negative reinforcement contingency no longer removes or reduces the aversive event. As a result, responding decreases to baseline (no-reinforcer) levels.*

Escape extinction can be an effective way to decrease problem behaviors maintained by negative reinforcement. For example, children often refuse to eat certain foods at dinner time and may throw a tantrum when their parents ask them to eat these foods. If the consequence of food refusal or tantruming is the removal of the disliked food such that:

IF food refusal (tantrum) → *THEN* parent removes the disliked food

then the parents are inadvertently arranging a negative reinforcement – escape (SR$_E$-) contingency. Refusing to eat healthy foods can have a negative effect on child health and development. In extreme cases, food refusers are at risk of malnourishment and starvation.

How could escape extinction be used to decrease childhood food refusal? In theory, it is simple:

IF food refusal (tantrum) → *THEN* disliked food is not removed

If the child throws a tantrum and hurls the broccoli at the wall, the vegetable would be returned to the plate and the child would not be allowed to leave the table until it was consumed. As you might imagine, many parents will not be willing to implement this intervention. They can anticipate that extinction will increase their child's tantruming and, when this happens, they will reluctantly remove the broccoli from the plate. When they do, they will have returned to the original SR$_E$- contingency, thereby further reinforcing food refusal.

When children are at risk of malnourishment, escape extinction can be an effective intervention method, when administered by Board Certified Behavior Analysts® (see Kodak & Piazza, 2008; Piazza, 2008 for reviews). Take, for example, the case of an 8-year-old boy with cerebral palsy whose long-lasting food refusals left him extremely undernourished. The behavior analysts (Voulgarakis & Forte, 2015) introduced two contingency changes. The first, escape extinction, was designed to reduce food refusals:

IF food refusal (tantrum) → *THEN* food is not removed

The second contingency change, negative reinforcement escape (SR_E-), was designed to increase eating:

IF food consumed → *THEN* child can choose to end the meal

Figure 7.3 shows the efficacy of this intervention. During baseline, before the contingency change, the boy consumed only about two bites per meal. In the next phase, refusing to eat did not end the meal. Instead, the boy could choose to end the meal only after consuming at least 5 bites. As shown in Figure 7.3, when the boy was required to eat 5, 7, and then 10 bites to end the meal, he did so. At some meals, he even ate a few more bites than was required.

You will notice that after the boy was eating 10 or more bites, the behavior analysts reduced the number of bites required to end the meal. Why? They wanted to find out if the combined escape-extinction SR_E- contingency was responsible for the increases in eating. Perhaps a confound variable could explain the increase in eating. Maybe the child increasingly enjoyed eating. If either of these were true, then reducing the contingency to 7 bites should have no effect on this increasing trend. But because eating decreased, Voulgarakis and Forte could conclude that their contingencies were responsible for the behavior change. In the final phase, increasing the contingency to 12 bites provided further evidence of the efficacy of the intervention.

This simple intervention helped the boy increase his self-feeding. By the end of the intervention, he was eating enough to meet his daily nutritional needs (see Ahearn et al., 2001; Piazza et al., 2015; Taylor et al., 2017 for systematic replications of this effect of escape extinction).

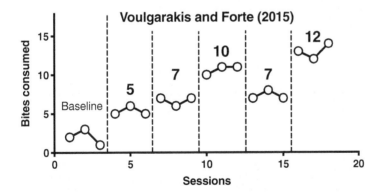

Figure 7.3 Number of bites of food consumed per session during baseline and across five phases in which a combined negative reinforcement + escape contingency – was in place. The number in each phase corresponds to the number of bites that was required to leave the table.

Source: Voulgarakis, H., & Forte, S. (2015). Escape extinction and negative reinforcement in the treatment of pediatric feeding disorders: A single case analysis. *Behavior Analysis in Practice*, 8(2), 212–214. https://doi.org/10.1007/s40617-015-0086-8 © 2015, Springer Nature.

How Quickly Will Operant Extinction Work?

In clinical settings, operant extinction is used to decrease problem behaviors such as food refusal, aggression, or self-injury. Because problem behavior can be harmful to the patient, family members, and those who care for them, it would be useful to predict how long it will take for extinction to decrease the problem behavior. If extinction will take a long time to work, we may want to choose a different intervention.

There are two factors that influence how quickly behavior decreases to baseline levels under an operant-extinction contingency. The first factor is the rate of reinforcement prior to extinction – the higher the rate of reinforcement, the faster extinction will work. The second is the individual's motivation to acquire the reinforcer – the more the reinforcer is needed, the more persistent behavior will be during extinction. Let's look at each of these factors in more detail.

Rate of Reinforcement Prior to Extinction

If behavior has been reinforced every time it occurs (high rate of reinforcement), then after extinction starts, behavior will quickly decrease to baseline levels. Conversely, if behavior was infrequently reinforced (low rate of reinforcement), then following the contingency change to extinction it will take longer for behavior to decrease to baseline levels. This *direct relation between prior reinforcement rate and how quickly behavior undergoes extinction* is called the **partial reinforcement extinction effect (PREE)**. The PREE has proven replicable across rats, pigeons, and humans (Horsley et al., 2012; Jenkins & Stanley, 1950; Zarcone et al., 1997).

We can get an intuitive sense of the PREE by thinking of behaviors that are reinforced either very often or very rarely. For example, starting a car is reinforced very often – just about every time we press the start button (or turn the key) the car starts. According to the PREE, this frequently reinforced behavior will quickly return to baseline levels after extinction begins. So, imagine for a moment that you try to start your car, the engine makes the usual sounds, but it never actually starts. How long will you continue to press the button? You might press it a dozen or so times before giving up in frustration. Extinction has worked very quickly.

Now consider another button-pressing behavior, but this one rarely produces a reinforcer – playing a slot machine. When the reinforcement contingency is operating as normal on a slot machine, money (the reinforcer) is dispensed infrequently. If the slot machine stops paying out altogether – operant extinction – the PREE predicts play will continue for a long time before this button-pressing behavior returns to its baseline level. Slot machine players don't give up in frustration after about a dozen unreinforced plays, they keep pumping the money in hoping that the next button press will be a winner. The PREE works to the advantage of casinos, as players persist for long periods of time during operant extinction. For an interesting extension of how the PREE can help inform theories of reinforcement, see Extra Box 1.

Source: Virrage Images/Shutterstock.com

Returning to the morning when your car would not start, imagine what would happen if you *had* to get to campus because of a final exam starting in an hour. No doubt, we would describe you as "highly motivated" to get the car started. Would this impending deadline increase how many times you tried to start your car before finally giving up?

Perin (1942) asked this question about motivation with rats that had previously pressed a lever for food reinforcers. Prior to the operant extinction session, Perin manipulated motivation by controlling the rats' level of hunger. As you can see in Figure 7.4, the hungriest rats (those deprived of food for 23 hours) pressed the lever during extinction far more often than rats that had eaten 1–3 hours ago. This motivational effect of hunger on persistence during extinction has been replicated in several experiments with nonhumans (Cautela, 1956; Horenstein, 1951) but to our knowledge has not been studied in humans. Such an experiment need not deprive humans of their next meal. There are many ways to increase motivation. These are discussed in Chapter 9, so stay tuned.

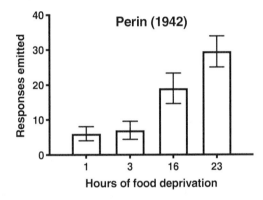

Figure 7.4 Number of responses emitted in extinction by rats under different levels of food deprivation. Hungrier rats (23 hours of food deprivation) responded more in extinction than rats at lower levels of food restriction.

Source: Perin, C. T. (1942). Behavior potentiality as a joint function of the amount of training and the degree of hunger at the time of extinction. *Journal of Experimental Psychology, 30*(2), 93–113.

Spontaneous Recovery of Operant Behavior

When an operant response has undergone extinction, it returns to its no-reinforcer baseline level. Figure 7.5 shows two sessions of operant extinction from Skinner (1938). Data in the first session are the same as those shown in Figure 7.1. By the end of the first session, lever pressing had completely stopped; the behavior had undergone extinction. It is, therefore, surprising that 48 hours later (Session 2), when the rat was returned to the chamber for a second extinction session, the rat briefly resumed responding at the beginning of the session. It did this despite never obtaining a reinforcer for lever pressing in the 48 hours separating these sessions.

This *temporary resumption in operant responding following time away from the extinction setting* is called **spontaneous recovery of operant behavior**. Spontaneous recovery has been reported in studies of operant extinction in rats, pigeons, and humans (e.g., Graham & Gagne, 1940; Rescorla, 2004; Thomas & Sherman, 1986; Thrailkill et al., 2018). As you can

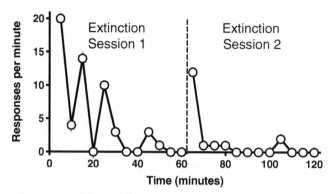

Figure 7.5 An individual rat's response rate across two 60-minute extinction sessions. Note the spontaneous recovery of lever pressing at the beginning of Session 2.

Source: Skinner, B. F. (1938). The behavior of organisms: An experimental analysis. Oxford, England: Appleton-Century.

see in the rest of the rat's Session 2, responding quickly decreased to baseline levels as the behavior interacts with the operant extinction contingency. If a third extinction session were conducted, we would anticipate a smaller amount of spontaneous recovery of lever pressing, followed, once again, by rapid extinction.

Reading Quiz 1

1. Operant extinction is defined as _____
   _____.

2. When a previously reinforced response no longer produces the reinforcer, we call this
   _____ _____.

3. In Skinner's (1938) experiment, when lever pressing no longer produced a food reinforcer, the rate of lever pressing gradually _____.

4. Imagine that you broke your leg and are in the hospital recovering. You are in a lot of pain. Your nurse gives you a pain-killing drug called oxycodone. It takes the pain away wonderfully. Later in the night, the pain returns and you ask the nurse for another dose of oxycodone. If asking for oxycodone is the behavior of interest, this is an example of _____ reinforcement (SR__).

5. If you asked for the oxycodone before the pain returned, this would be an example of _____ reinforcement (SR__).

6. Now imagine that, after your fifth dose of oxycodone, it no longer works. The pain is vivid and taking a sixth dose does not help either. You stop asking for oxycodone. What accounts for the decrease in asking for oxycodone? _____

7. According to the PREE, the decrease in asking for oxycodone should happen _____ (slowly/quickly) because prior to extinction, this behavior was reinforced at a high rate.

8. But that pain is really awful, so you are highly motivated to escape from the pain. This should make the decrease happen more _____ (slowly/quickly).

9. In Figure 7.5, the rat's behavior underwent extinction in session 1. Despite this response decrement, at the beginning of session 2, responding resumed at a fairly high rate. This temporary increase in operant responding at the beginning of session 2 is called
   _____ _____.

EXTRA BOX 1: HOW EXTINCTION INFORMS THEORIES OF REINFORCEMENT

You may recall from Chapter 6 that we introduced two theories that try to explain how reinforcement works. The first was the Response-Strengthening Theory of Reinforcement, and it suggested that each time a reinforcer is obtained, the strength of the response it follows is increased. You remember the bucket of water metaphor – every reinforcer adds a bit more water to the bucket and the weight of the bucket corresponds to response strength. Operant responses with a lot of response strength, the theory holds, are the most likely to occur.

How might we think of extinction using the bucket of water metaphor? We might say that each operant response that goes unreinforced after extinction removes a ladle of water from the bucket. As more unreinforced responses are emitted, and ladles of water are removed, the strength of the operant response declines. Eventually, when the bucket is empty, the behavior is completely extinguished. From this metaphor of response strength, we would predict that full buckets would take longer to empty in extinction than half-full buckets. That is, frequently reinforced behaviors should take longer to extinguish than infrequently reinforced behaviors.

Of course, the prior sentence is inconsistent with the PREE. Reinforcing every response should fill the bucket quickly, generating high response strength relative to reinforcing behavior intermittently. But the PREE shows the opposite: Intermittently reinforced behaviors (with their partially filled buckets) take longer to extinguish than behaviors that were reinforced every time. Several other findings, including spontaneous recovery of operant behavior, are inconsistent with the Response-Strengthening Theory of Reinforcement. If the response strength of the lever-pressing operant in Figure 7.5 is zero at the end of Session 1, it is difficult to explain why behavior temporarily resumes at the beginning of Session 2. In sum, several extinction effects are at odds with the Response Strengthening Theory of Reinforcement.

How about the other theory introduced in Chapter 6 – the Information Theory of Reinforcement? It holds that "behavior is…controlled by the likely future, as exemplified in the past" (Cowie & Davison, 2016). Said another way, past reinforcement experiences provide information about what's likely to happen next. To explain the PREE, Information Theory holds that the estimate of the likely future is updated only when the individual detects a change in the reinforcement rate (Baum, 2012). When every response (R) is reinforced (SR+):

$$R \rightarrow SR+ \ldots R \rightarrow SR+ \ldots R \rightarrow SR+ \ldots R \rightarrow SR+ \ldots R \rightarrow SR+ \ldots$$

it's easy to detect the change in reinforcement rate during extinction:

$$R \ldots R \ldots R \ldots R \ldots R \ldots$$

Think of yourself taking a drink from a water bottle. Every time you lift the bottle to your lips (R), you get the liquid reinforcer (SR+). When the bottle is empty (extinction), lifting the bottle to your lips is not reinforced and you immediately detect the reduction in reinforcement rate (from 1 sip per lift to 0 sips per lift). When the reduction in reinforcement rate is as easily detected as this, the estimate of the "likely future" changes rapidly. Because behavior is controlled by the likely future (as exemplified in the past) responding undergoes extinction quickly.

However, when responding is intermittently reinforced...

R ... R ... R ... R ... R ... R ... R ... R ... R ... R → SR+ ... R ... R ... R ... R ... R ... R ... R...R...R...R...R → SR+

it is more difficult to tell that the reinforcement rate has declined during extinction:

R...R...R...R...R...R...R...R...R...R...R...R...R...R...R...R...R...R...R... R...R...R...R...

Think of yourself playing a game on your phone (e.g., solitaire). You don't win every time so if the game's contingency switches to extinction it would take a long time before you notice the change. If it's difficult to detect the change in reinforcement rate following extinction, then the estimate of the likely future is unchanged for a much longer period of time (Baum, 2012). That is, the "likely future" is still *intermittent reinforcement*. All the while, you keep playing solitaire, exactly in accord with the PREE.

Several behavioral researchers provide theories describing how new information is incorporated into estimates of the likely future (Devenport & Devenport, 1994; Gallistel & Gibbon, 2002; Mazur, 1996). The mathematical specifics of these theories are beyond the scope of this book, but their general approach can be summarized in an intuitive way. Imagine you are Skinner's rat, pressing the lever in the operant chamber, earning food for the last 10 days. The estimate of the likely future is pretty well established: food will reliably follow lever pressing. Now, on day 11, you press the lever as normal, but no food is dispensed (extinction). This is pretty quickly detected and by the end of the session, you are no longer pressing the lever (as in Figure 7.5). After the session, Skinner takes you back to your home cage where you get a meal, some nice bedding, and a good night's sleep. Life if good.

On day 12, Skinner takes you back to the operant chamber, puts you inside, and closes the door. What is your estimate of the likely future, as exemplified in the past? One simple accounting notes that the lever has produced food for 10 of the last 11 days, so there is a 10:1 chance that it will work today. Not bad, so you begin pressing, just like Skinner's rat did in Session 2 of Figure 7.5 – spontaneous recovery. A more complex estimate will assign less weight to older experiences and more weight to newer ones. So, on day 12 the exemplified past is closer to a 5:1 chance of getting food – still worth a try.

In sum, the effects of extinction on operant behavior are more easily explained by the Information Theory of Reinforcement than the Response Strengthening Theory.

Other Effects of Extinction

The *primary* effect of operant extinction is that it returns behavior to its baseline (no-reinforcer) level. However, there are four other predictable effects of extinction on behavior: (1) extinction-induced emotional behavior, (2) extinction burst, (3) extinction-induced variability, and (4) extinction-induced resurgence. Being able to predict these effects when using extinction allows behavior analysts to compassionately and purposefully design treatment to prevent them or safely address them when they do occur.

Extinction-Induced Emotional Behavior

The first predictable "other effect" of extinction is that it induces emotional behavior. In one demonstration of this effect, researchers taught infants to pull a string (operant response) to produce an audio-visual display in their crib (a positive reinforcer; Sullivan et al., 1992). Subsequently, the researchers changed the contingency to extinction and objectively measured the infants' reactions. The infants were engaged, interested, and enjoying themselves during the positive reinforcement phase. However, during extinction their emotions shifted to anger. Later in life, emotional responses induced by extinction can lead to frustration and even physical aggression against others (Azrin et al., 1966; Huston et al., 2012). Consider how angry, frustrated, and potentially violent you might feel if your employer informed you that you would not be paid for two weeks of work just completed. These are extinction-induced emotional behaviors.

Source: Aurelie and Morgan David de Lossy/Cultura/Getty Images

Long-term extinction contingencies placed on behaviors that previously produced important reinforcers can lead to debilitating emotions such as depression (Hammen, 2005). Consider someone who loses their job and, despite their best efforts, cannot find employment. Work and job-searching behaviors are no longer reinforced with important financial reinforcers. Under such long-term extinction contingencies, depression is common. Consider the increased use of antidepressant medications during the great recession of 2008–2009 (Modrek et al., 2015). Reversals from extinction to employment (positive reinforcement of work) reduced the use of these medications (Kaspersen et al., 2016). The longest economic decline in modern times (1929–1939) was aptly named "the great depression."

Extinction Burst

The second of the "other effects" of operant extinction is the extinction burst. Terminating the reinforcement contingency sometimes, but not always, produces *a temporary increase in the rate, magnitude, or duration of the previously reinforced response*; this is called an **extinction burst** (Lerman & Iwata, 1995; Lerman et al., 1999). For example, when a vending machine fails to deliver the selected item, it has imposed an extinction contingency – a previously reinforced response (pressing the button) is no longer reinforced. When this has happened to you, what has been your reaction? If your rate of button-pressing temporarily increases (pressing rapidly), the magnitude of your presses increases (pressing really hard), or the duration of your presses increases (holding the button down longer than normal), then this was an extinction burst. Chances are good that extinction also induced a negative emotion and perhaps you even behaved aggressively toward the machine.

Extinction bursts do not always happen and the variables influencing them are not well understood. There are only a few laboratory studies that have examined extinction bursts. Some provide evidence that they occur (Harris et al., 2007; Yokel & Wise, 1975), others do not (Salamone et al., 1995), and no systematic patterns allow us to predict when they will and will not occur. Similarly, in clinical settings, extinction bursts happen in about half the cases in which extinction is the only therapy employed (Lerman & Iwata, 1995; Lerman et al., 1999). Because extinction bursts can be stressful and can lead to accidental lapses in extinction-based therapy, it is important to continue studying the variables influencing extinction bursts.

Extinction-Induced Variability

The third predictable "other effect" of operant extinction is extinction-induced variability. Consider the behavior of the rat in Figure 7.6 (Iversen, 2002). In the top row of photos, each time the rat moved the rod suspended from the ceiling two things happened: (1) it obtained a positive reinforcer (a piece of food) and (2) Dr. Iversen's camera took a picture of the rat. As you can see, the rat's rod-deflecting behavior was almost identical each time.

After response 140 (the final picture in the top row), Iversen changed the contingency to operant extinction, that is, moving the pole did not produce a food reinforcer. Responses 141 and 142 were unchanged, but after that the topography of the pole-movement behaviors was more variable. This is an example of extinction-induced variability. **Extinction-induced variability** is *an increase in the variety of operant response topographies following extinction.*

To evaluate if extinction was responsible for the increase in response variability, Iversen used a reversal design, returning the contingency back to positive reinforcement. For responses 161–165, every movement of the pole produced a food reinforcer. As you can see in the bottom row of Figure 7.6, as soon as a reinforcer was obtained, response variability fell to pre-extinction levels.

It's easy to think of examples of extinction-induced variability in your daily life. Have you ever said, "Hey Siri" or "Ok Google" and not had your electronic personal assistant make the beeping noise that indicates it is awaiting your request? If so, then you can probably recall how your vocal response-variability increased upon extinction. You may have repeated the request with a different tone of voice, said it slower, or said it more assertively. This mirrors

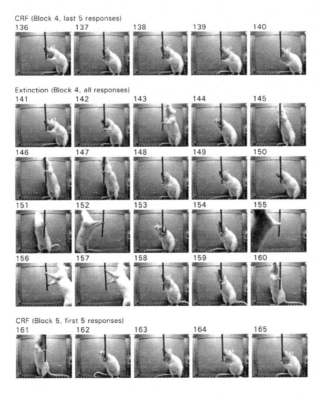

CRF (Block 4, last 5 responses)
136   137   138   139   140

Extinction (Block 4, all responses)
141   142   143   144   145
146   147   148   149   150
151   152   153   154   155
156   157   158   159   160

CRF (Block 5, first 5 responses)
161   162   163   164   165

Figure 7.6 An individual rat deflecting a ceiling rod and a camera takes a picture at the time the rod is deflected. In this way, Iversen (2002) could record exactly what the rat was doing when food reinforcers were delivered following every rod deflection (denoted as "CRF", pictures 136–140), during extinction (141–160), and during the reversal to reinforcement (161–165). During extinction, there is a clear increase in response variability. This variability quickly declines when reinforcement is resumed.

Source: Iversen, I. H. (2002). Response-initiated imaging of operant behavior using a digital camera. *Journal of the Experimental Analysis of Behavior*, *77*(3), 283–300. https://doi.org/10.1901/jeab.2002.77-283

the extinction-induced variability that Iversen (2002) observed in rats. In published experiments, extinction-induced variability has been observed in several species (Neuringer et al., 2001), including humans (Grow et al., 2008; Morgan & Lee, 1996).

Extinction-Induced Resurgence

The fourth predictable "other effect" of operant extinction is called **extinction-induced resurgence**. Here is the definition: *When one operant behavior is extinguished, other (different) behaviors that were previously reinforced are emitted again*; that is, they become "resurgent." For example, when the pioneering animal trainer, Karen Pryor, stopped reinforcing swimming near the bottom of the tank, the porpoise, Hou, began to emit behaviors that used to be

Source: Rene/Wikipedia

reinforced (some time ago) with fish treats (Pryor et al., 1969). Hou began corkscrewing, tail-slapping, and jumping in and out of the water during extinction. None of these previously reinforced behaviors were being reinforced now; they simply resurged when swimming near the bottom of the tank was no longer reinforced. Extinction-induced resurgence has been observed in well-controlled laboratory studies in a variety of species (Kuroda et al., 2017; Lieving & Lattal, 2003; Reed & Morgan, 2006), including humans (Doughty et al., 2010; Smith et al., 2017).

The real-world relevance of extinction-induced resurgence has been shown in several experiments (Fuhrman et al., 2016). In one of these studies, Bruzek et al. (2009) found that when one infant-caregiving behavior (e.g., rocking the baby) no longer soothed the crying child (escape extinction), old caregiving behaviors that used to be negatively reinforced (e.g., feeding or playing with the baby) resurged. In this study of infant care, resurgence of previously successful behaviors was a good thing – it helped the caretakers sooth a crying infant.

Extinction-induced resurgence may also help to understand maladaptive behaviors, like relapse to drug-taking behavior. In the first phase of a study conducted by Podlesnik et al. (2006), rats learned to press a lever to obtain a small alcoholic beverage (see Table 7.1). In Phase 2, pressing the lever no longer produced alcohol (operant extinction). Instead, if the rat pulled a chain suspended from the ceiling, it obtained food pellets. By the end of Phase 2, the rats learned to stop pressing the lever and to pull the chain instead. The test for extinction-induced resurgence came in Phase 3. When chain-pulling no longer produced a food reinforcer, not only did chain-pulling return to its low baseline (no-reinforcer) level, but the rats went back to lever pressing – resurgence of alcohol-seeking behavior.

The behavior of these rats is similar to the behavior of humans. Individuals who have recovered from a substance-use disorder can often relapse to drug use when they lose a significant source of positive reinforcement (Vuchinich & Tucker, 1988). For example, an abstinent person with alcohol-use disorder is at risk of resurgent drinking if they lose their job or their spouse – both are sources of significant positive reinforcers. Providing therapeutic, positive reinforcement-based supports when extinction is inevitably encountered may reduce resurgence of problem drug-taking.

Table 7.1 Conditions arranged in Podlesnik et al. (2006).

Phase	Lever pressing	Chain pulling
1	Reinforced with alcohol	Not applicable
2	Extinction	Reinforced with food
3	Extinction	Extinction

We Tried It at Home

Finn is a 4-year-old Portuguese Water Dog/Standard Poodle mix. He and one of the authors of this book walk to work every day, where Finn's job is sleeping, licking lunchtime dishes "clean," and making student-visitors happy. Finn knows a handful of tricks, including sitting, standing up on his hind legs, and giving a high-five.

We recently asked Finn to sit, which is usually reinforced with a treat or a scratch on the head, but this time we changed the contingency to operant extinction. As you can see in panel A of Figure 7.7, when asked to do so, Finn sat as he normally does but this was not reinforced in any way – no treat, no scratches, not even a "good boy." It was hard; he was such a good boy!

When Finn got up, we kindly asked him to sit again and he was happy to comply. Still, no reinforcers. Like a human trying to start a malfunctioning car, Finn sat several times on command. As we continued to extinguish each sit, he started to whine and bark (panel B). These were *extinction-induced emotional responses*.

In panel C you can see that, after a few minutes, Finn slightly changed the topography of his sit – *extinction-induced variability*. He also got up and sat down, got up and sat down several times in a row without being asked to do so – perhaps an *extinction burst*. Finally, in panels D and E, you can see instances of *extinction-induced resurgence*. Finn began doing other tricks that had been reinforced before.

In the end, sitting on command decreased to its baseline (no-reinforcer) level – Finn walked away and ignored our request to "sit." Of course, the next day, when we asked Finn to sit, he did so – *spontaneous recovery* – and we gave him the reinforcer he deserved. He's such a good boy.

Figure 7.7 A backyard example of the "other effects" of operant extinction. When Finn's sitting on command (A) goes unreinforced, he displays negative emotions (B), varies the topography of his sit (C), and displays two other of his previously reinforced tricks (D and E).

Source: Photographs courtesy of Annora L. Madden.

Reading Quiz 2

1. The primary effect of operant extinction is that it _____ the rate of a previously reinforced behavior to its baseline (no-reinforcer) level.
2. Operant extinction can induce negative _____, such as frustration, anger, and depression.

3. Such an increase in emotion following extinction is called extinction-_____ emotional behavior.

4. You are discussing politics with your parents. You want them to vote for your favorite candidate but they are not providing this reinforcer (i.e., they are not swayed by your arguments). As they extinguish your efforts, you change your tactics and say, "If you really love me, you will vote for my candidate." This variation in strategy is an example of extinction-induced _____.

5. Sometimes, after extinction begins, a temporary, often emotion-filled burst of the previously reinforced response occurs. This is called an extinction _____.

6. When Tyson was in high school, he used flash cards to study and got good grades. When he got to college he found that he could get good grades just by reading the book and studying his lecture notes. Then Tyson took a class in which this study method was not working. He got really bad grades on the first two exams. Tyson went back to the flash-card method of studying. This return to a previously successful study method is an example of extinction-induced _____.

Using Extinction to Positively Influence Behavior

Extinction decreases behavior, so if it would be adaptive to *reduce* a behavior, then extinction may prove therapeutic. For example, most of us would like to reduce how often we eat junk food, drink more alcohol than we planned, and think cruel things about ourselves (e.g., "What's wrong with me that I keep eating junk food and getting drunk?").

Before we can use extinction to positively influence behavior, we need to do two things. First, we have to determine if the problem behavior is operant behavior. This first step is critical because not all behavior is operant behavior. If the problem behavior of interest is not an operant behavior, then extinction is not the right therapeutic tool.

Second, if the problem behavior is indeed an operant, then we need to identify the reinforcer that maintains it. To implement extinction, we need to turn OFF the reinforcer that maintains the problem behavior. We can't do that if we don't know what the reinforcer is. Therefore, behavior analysts have developed a technique for identifying the reinforcer(s) that maintain a problem behavior. This technique, known as the *functional analysis of behavior*, is most often used in clinical settings, but the logic may be used in your daily life.

Functional Analysis of Behavior

The scientific method used to (1) determine if a problem behavior is an operant and (2) identify the reinforcer that maintains that operant is called a **functional analysis of behavior** (Carr & Durand, 1985; Iwata, Dorsey, Slifer, Bauman, & Richman, 1982, 1994). The functional analysis is a brief experiment in which consequences that might be reinforcers are turned ON and OFF, while the effects of these manipulations on problem behavior are recorded. If the problem behavior occurs at a higher rate when one of these consequences is arranged, then we may conclude that the consequence functions as a reinforcer. If no experimenter-controlled consequences function as reinforcers, then either the behavior is maintained by an automatic reinforcer (described later in the chapter) or the problem behavior is not an operant behavior.

Consider a child who throws temper tantrums each night at bedtime. Is this operant behavior? It might be a fear response evoked by conditioned stimuli (CS) signaling a delay reduction to being left alone in the dark (US). But it might instead be operant behavior maintained by a positive reinforcer (getting to hear another story) or a negative reinforcer (avoiding tooth brushing). To find out, a functional analysis would turn ON and OFF these contingencies and record what happens to tantruming at bedtime.

For example, on the first night of the functional analysis displayed in Figure 7.8, one of the hypothesized positive reinforcement contingencies was ON: Each time the child threw a tantrum, the parent read another story. That night, the child threw 6 tantrums before falling asleep; a typical rate, according to the parents. On nights 4, 7, and 10, when the same *IF tantrum → THEN story* contingency was in place, the rate of tantruming was always high.

Lower rates of tantruming occurred on nights when different contingencies were arranged. The avoidance of tooth-brushing did not maintain much tantruming, so it must not be the reinforcer that normally maintains this behavior. Likewise, in the control condition, when additional stories were read non-contingently (i.e., the parents read stories regardless of whether or not the child threw a tantrum), the rate of tantruming was low. The differentiated rates of tantruming across these conditions reveal that (1) tantruming is operant behavior and (2) the contingent reinforcer that maintains this behavior is getting to hear another story at bedtime.

The results of a functional analysis of behavior are useful. If the problem behavior is not an operant, then an operant-based intervention may not be the right approach (perhaps a Pavlovian intervention, like graduated-exposure therapy, would work better). But if the

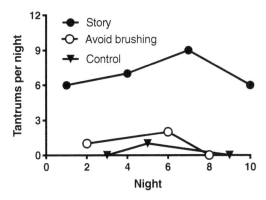

Figure 7.8 Hypothetical data illustrating the results of a functional analysis of behavior. Each night, a different consequence of tantruming behavior is arranged. On the first night, if the child tantrums, the parent says, "It's ok sweetie, let's read one more story." On avoid-brushing nights, throwing a tantrum allows the child to skip the usual tooth-brushing routine. And on Control nights, stories are read to the child regardless of tantruming. The results provide strong evidence that gaining access to another story is the reinforcer that maintains tantruming.

problem behavior *is* an operant, then a consequence-based intervention can help to reduce the behavior. For example, the parents of the tantruming child might choose to use operant extinction to reduce this problem behavior. Specifically, the child would get one story at bedtime and no amount of tantruming would ever cause the parents to read another story. Because tantruming had been reinforced every time prior to extinction, the PREE predicts tantruming will decrease quickly (though probably not as quickly as the parents would like).

Studies have shown that conducting a functional analysis improves the efficacy of behavioral interventions (Hurl et al., 2016; Lane et al., 2009; Piazza et al., 1997; Scotti et al., 1991; Vollmer & Iwata, 1992; Wacker et al., 2017). Functional analysis has proven so useful, it is commonly used in treatment settings ranging from public schools to zoos (Beavers et al., 2013; Dorey et al., 2009). If you are interested in learning more about functional analysis of behavior, we recommend episodes 1 or 45 of the Behavioral Observations podcast, with Matt Cicoria.

Source: With permission from Matthew Cicoria

Functional Analysis of Self-Injurious Behavior

Individuals diagnosed with intellectual and developmental disabilities, including autism, sometimes display persistent patterns of self-injurious behavior. These take a variety of forms, including face slapping, skin picking, and self-biting. These behaviors often prevent the individual from attending school or holding a job and, in extreme cases, are life-threatening and require hospitalization (Hagopian et al., 2013).

Conducting a functional analysis of behavior is critical in the treatment of self-injurious behavior. Is this behavior an operant? If so, what reinforcer could possibly maintain behavior that is so clearly harmful to the individual? Answers to these questions will influence the treatment prescribed. Therefore, it is good news that a functional analysis of behavior identifies the reinforcer maintaining problem behavior most of the time (Beavers et al., 2013; Hanley et al., 2003).

Prior to conducting a functional analysis, the behavior analyst works with caregivers to develop hypotheses about the reinforcers that *might* maintain the problem behavior. In the case of self-injurious behavior, the physical stimulation produced by slapping, picking, biting, and so on could be a reinforcer. This will be a counterintuitive hypothesis to most readers. Although long-distance runners may understand how pain can function as a reinforcer, the rest of us may find it difficult to empathize. Because the physical stimulation of self-injurious behavior is an automatic consequence of the response, if it functions as a reinforcer, it will be identified as an *automatic reinforcer* (Vollmer, 1994).

> **Automatic Reinforcer:** *A consequence that is directly produced by the response – it is not provided by someone else – and which increases the behavior above a no-reinforcer baseline.*

To find out if self-injury is maintained by automatic reinforcement, the individual would, safety permitting, be given some time alone while the behavior analyst discretely records the frequency of self-injury. If self-injury occurs at the usual rate while alone, then the only consequence that might maintain this behavior is the automatic outcome of that response, that is, the "painful" stimulation. If automatic reinforcers maintain a problem behavior, then extinction is impossible – the therapist cannot turn OFF the automatic stimulation experienced each time face slapping occurs (Vollmer et al., 2015). Preventing self-injury by restraining the client is not extinction – during extinction, the response occurs but the reinforcer does not.

Let's assume that automatic reinforcement is not responsible for the self-injurious behavior. During a functional analysis of behavior, several other hypothesized reinforcers will be evaluated. Does problem behavior occur primarily when attention is the consequence of self-injurious behavior? If so, then extinction will involve no longer delivering this positive reinforcer contingent upon self-injury (Lovaas et al., 1965). However, it is often ethically impossible to extinguish attention-maintained self-injurious behavior. One cannot ignore self-injury if serious physical harm to the client is the outcome (Vollmer et al., 2015).

Alternatively a functional analysis may reveal that self-injurious behavior occurs because it allows the individual to escape from everyday tasks (Fisher et al., 2014). For example, if self-injury occurs when the individual is asked to change clothes or transition to a new activity, then negative reinforcement (escape from the activity) is responsible for the problem behavior. In such cases, escape extinction can be effective in reducing self-injury (Iwata et al., 1990); that is, clothes will be changed and transitions between activities will occur regardless of self-injurious behavior. But, as mentioned earlier, the behavior analyst should be prepared for extinction-induced emotions, physical aggression, and topographical variability in the self-injurious behavior, including an increase in the magnitude of the self-injurious response. Such reactions may make it impossible to use extinction alone.

Because a functional analysis of behavior improves the efficacy of behavior-change interventions, it has become a standard practice in the treatment of self-injurious behavior (Hagopian et al., 2013), particularly when extinction is combined with reinforcement – the topic of the next section. Federal law requires that some form of functional analysis of behavior inform the treatment of self-injurious behavior among individuals with intellectual and developmental disabilities (the US *Individuals with Disabilities Education Act* of 1997). Behavior analysts continue to investigate ways to make functional analyses more effective, or easier to conduct while retaining efficacy (Jessel et al., 2016). If these efforts are successful, more individuals in need of behavior-analytic services can receive these sometimes lifesaving interventions.

Differential Reinforcement

Differential reinforcement is *a procedure in which a previously reinforced behavior is placed on extinction while a second behavior is reinforced.* The effect of differential reinforcement is a decrease in the first behavior and an increase in the sec-

Differential Reinforcement	
Behavior 1	Extinction
Behavior 2	Reinforcement

ond. For example, when your watch battery died, suppose you didn't replace it because you own a cell phone that shows you the time. Subsequently, when needing to check the time, you looked at your nonfunctioning watch. When this response was not reinforced (operant extinction), you reach for your cell phone and obtain the desired reinforcer.

Seeing how this contingency change influences your behavior can be humorous. You may continue to look at your wrist for weeks, rolling your eyes at how persistent this behavior is

Source: Syda Productions/Shutterstock.com

in the face of extinction. Eventually, looking at your dead watch returns to its baseline (no-reinforcer) level, whereas reaching for the cell phone completely replaces it. In this way, differential reinforcement replaces an extinguished behavior with one that is reinforced.

Returning to our former example of the individual recovering from a substance-use disorder, and who just lost their job, the extinction of work-behaviors may produce a resurgence of drug-seeking behaviors (e.g., going to the liquor store) and drug-taking behaviors (drinking a vodka and cranberry juice). If drinking alcohol is negatively reinforced with escape from difficult thoughts and emotions, and positively reinforced with a feeling of intoxication, then the environment has imposed a differential reinforcement contingency that is not in the individual's best interests. As long as this differential reinforcement contingency is unchanged, treating this resurgent addiction will be difficult.

Differential Reinforcement	
Behavior 1: Working	Extinction
Behavior 2: Drinking	Reinforcement

Differential Reinforcement of Problem Behavior

Throughout human history, the most prevalent means of decreasing problem behavior has been punishment. For example, in the nineteenth century, spanking, slapping, and hitting misbehaving children were standard practice in US schools (Gershoff & Font, 2016). In the twentieth century, nearly all US parents physically "punished" their children (Sears et al., 1957). Evidence that parental use of physical punishment is ineffective and harmful (Gershoff & Grogan-Kaylor, 2016) and doctor's advice to stop using it have only modestly decreased these rates, particularly in low-income populations (Zolotor et al., 2011). And it is not just children who are punished. It goes without saying that punishment is the dominant approach to criminal justice, and even some religions threaten their followers with promises of horrific punishment in the afterlife (Skinner, 1971). Chapter 10 will address the issue of punishment in a way that is informed by scientific evidence.

Differential reinforcement offers parents, teachers, therapists, and the larger culture an alternative method for reducing problem behavior. This nonpunitive, differential reinforcement approach is consistent with Skinner's (1948) goal of developing a world without punishment.[1] Differential reinforcement also (1) provides the opportunity to teach an adaptive behavior that will replace the problem behavior and (2) decreases the frequency of extinction bursts and extinction-induced aggression (Lerman et al., 1999). These outcomes make differential reinforcement popular with parents, teachers, clients, and caregivers (Kazdin, 1980; Kazdin et al., 1981; Singh et al., 1987).

Differential reinforcement has proven effective in reducing a wide variety of problem behaviors in children, adults, and animals. For example, children's disruptive behaviors that interfere with classroom learning can be reduced with differential reinforcement (LeGray et al., 2013). More difficult to treat behaviors such as chronic food refusal, aggression, and destructive behaviors may be reduced with differential reinforcement (Chowdhury & Benson, 2011; Petscher et al., 2009). Differential reinforcement is also effective in reducing problem behavior among children diagnosed with autism (Wong et al., 2015) or those with intellectual and developmental disabilities (Bonner & Borrero, 2018). You can use the same technique to stop your pet from begging for treats. To do this, simply put begging on extinction and provide treats only when a more desirable behavior occurs, for example, coming to you when you call.

Source: RoyBuri/Pixabay

A surprising use of differential reinforcement is in treating substance-use disorders. Recalling that differential reinforcement involves extinction, applying it to substance use requires that drug-taking behavior no longer produces the reinforcer. That is, *IF* the drug is consumed, *THEN* there are no reinforcing effects (no intoxication and no escape from unwanted thoughts and feelings). Although this sounds impossible, behavioral pharmacologists are investigating medications designed to extinguish drug-taking.

For example, Nasser et al. (2016) reported that providing a slow-release medication called buprenorphine significantly blocked the reinforcing effects of an opiate drug (see also Sigmon et al., 2004). Subsequently, to implement differential reinforcement, Nasser et al. combined buprenorphine's extinction effects with reinforcement of drug-refusal behaviors. The results were striking, the opiate-dependent participants greatly reduced their use of opiate drugs during differential reinforcement. Interventions such as these can help to address the US epidemic of heroin abuse and the misuse of prescription opiates.

Differential Reinforcement	
Behavior 1: Opiate Use	Extinction
Behavior 2: Opiate Refusal	Reinforcement

How to Effectively Use Differential Reinforcement

Differential reinforcement is frequently used to reduce problem behavior while simultaneously increasing more adaptive behaviors. Many studies have evaluated how to increase the efficacy of differential-reinforcement interventions, and we have discussed a couple of these methods already. Figure 7.9 provides a flowchart to guide the use of differential reinforcement when treating problem behavior.

Let's work through this flowchart by considering a problem behavior encountered in a zoo (Martin et al., 2011). The "patient" was a 27-year-old male chimpanzee whose problem behaviors included feces throwing and cage shaking. Step 1 was to conduct a functional analysis to identify the reinforcer(s) that maintained these problem behaviors. The functional analysis revealed that problem behavior was maintained by contingent attention and sips of juice. It seems that prior to the functional analysis the zookeepers were "distracting" the chimp with juice and "scolding" him with verbal reprimands (contingent attention). The functional analysis revealed that these well-meaning consequences were functioning as reinforcers that maintained the problem behaviors.

Next, Martin et al. (2011) asked if they could prevent the problem behaviors from producing these reinforcers. That is, could

Source: oculo/Shutterstock.com

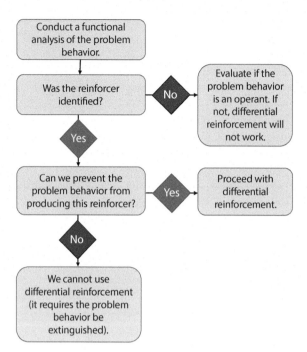

Figure 7.9 A flowchart used when evaluating if differential reinforcement can be used in the treatment of a problem behavior.

they implement the extinction component of differential reinforcement? Extinction was practical, so they implemented differential reinforcement by extinguishing problem behavior (no more sips of juice or verbal reprimands) and reinforcing an alternative response: holding onto a ring outside the cage. This alternative response was selected because holding onto the ring was incompatible with feces throwing and cage shaking. By extinguishing problem behavior and reinforcing ring holding (with juice and positive attention), Martin et al. reported that problem behavior decreased by 90%.

Differentially Reinforcing Response Topography

Differential reinforcement procedures will often extinguish the problem behavior while reinforcing a more adaptive response topography. Said a bit less technically, they will provide reinforcers for doing something else. Here, we discuss some commonly used procedures that differ in what that "something else" is.

In **differential reinforcement of incompatible behavior (DRI)** the "something else" is a response that is topographically incompatible with the problem behavior. This was the technique used in the zoo study – holding the ring outside the cage was topographically incompatible with throwing feces and shaking the cage. Had the researchers instead chosen a behavior such as "maintaining eye contact with the zookeeper," the monkey could have simultaneously maintained eye contact while hurling feces, not an optimal treatment outcome.

A similar procedure is **differential reinforcement of alternative behavior (DRA)**; the only difference is that the reinforced response can be any adaptive behavior (it need not be topographically incompatible with the problem behavior). A teacher who calls on children when they raise their hand appropriately, and ignores children when they yell out the answer, is using DRA to encourage appropriate classroom behavior.

Source: Hero Images/Getty Images

The common strategy of DRI and DRA is providing reinforcers for an adaptive response that can take the place of the problem behavior. This often allows the individual the freedom to choose when to obtain reinforcers and how many to obtain (Hagopian et al., 2013). For example, in **Functional Communication Training**, problematic demands for attention (e.g., tantruming) are extinguished while appropriate requests (e.g., "will you play with me please") are established and reinforced. When a child has learned the latter response, they can appropriately request attention when they want it. Functional Communication Training has proven effective in reducing inappropriate requests for social reinforcers in a variety of populations and settings (Grow et al., 2008; Gutierrez et al., 2007; Tiger et al., 2008).

The final differential reinforcement technique commonly used in the treatment of problem behavior is **differential reinforcement of other behavior (DRO)**. When this procedure is used, reinforcement is provided contingent upon abstaining from the problem behavior for a specified interval of time; presumably while "other behavior" is occurring. By setting a short time interval (e.g., *IF* the individual abstains from the problem behavior for 5 seconds → *THEN* the reinforcer will be delivered), the DRO procedure can arrange a high rate of therapeutic reinforcement, which can effectively compete with the reinforcement contingency maintaining problem behavior. As the patient succeeds in abstaining from the problem behavior, the contingency can be modified to require gradually longer intervals before the therapeutic reinforcer is delivered again. This strategy can be effective (Whitaker, 1996), although it does not teach a specific activity to replace the problem behavior (Hagopian et al., 2013), and increasing intervals between reinforcers can produce resurgence of problem behavior (Briggs et al., 2018).

Differential reinforcement of variability is a unique contingency in which responses, or patterns of responses, that have either never been emitted before or have not been emitted in quite some time are reinforced, and repetition or recent response topographies are extinguished. Researchers in applied settings have begun to explore the utility of differentially reinforcing variability in children with autism, a diagnosis often characterized by rigid patterns of activity or speech (Esch et al., 2009; Galizio et al., 2020; Rodriguez & Thompson, 2015; Sellers et al., 2016).

You may recall how variability — behaving and thinking differently — is important in problem-solving, improving performance efficiency, and adapting to a changing world. Steve Jobs recognized the importance of variability and positively reinforced it in his workforce at Apple.

Source: Matthew Yohe/Wikipedia/ CC BY-SA 3.0

In laboratory studies of differential reinforcement of variability, human and nonhuman participants obtain reinforcers by emitting novel topographies; repetitions are extinguished. For example, Ross and Neuringer (2002) asked college students to draw squares and rectangles on a computer screen. In one group, reinforcers were obtained only if the images drawn were novel in size. For another group, reinforcers were contingent on drawing the image in a novel location on the screen. None of the students were informed of these differential reinforcement contingencies, but both groups increased their variability along the appropriate dimension (size or location of the drawing). Interestingly, many of the students whose behavior was influenced by this differential reinforcement contingency had no idea that behaving variably was how to earn more reinforcers. We need not be consciously aware of reinforcement contingencies in order for them to influence our behavior.

Differentially Reinforcing Rate of Operant Behavior

Sometimes the problem with a behavior is not its topography, but the rate at which it occurs. Rates of responding may be increased or decreased with differential reinforcement. If the rate of a behavior is too slow, then **differential reinforcement of high-rate behavior (DRH)** can help. Here, low-rate responding is put on extinction and high-rate responding is reinforced. For example, in the game *5-Second Rule,* players have just 5 seconds to name three things that fit the category, for example, professional hockey teams. If the player responds quickly, they get the reinforcer (points). If not, no points are awarded (extinction).

Differential reinforcement of low-rate behavior (DRL) is just the opposite – responding quickly is extinguished and responding slowly is reinforced. This happens naturally if you

Source: Andrew/Flickr/CC BY-SA 2.0

visit a foreign country with only a basic comprehension of their language. If the person giving you directions to the bus terminal speaks too quickly, you cannot understand them, so you look at them quizzically and withhold the usual reinforcers such as "merci." When the person repeats the directions slowly, you understand and then say, "merci beaucoup."

Of course, it is possible to differentially reinforce response dimensions other than rate. For example, sometimes vocal responses are too soft to be heard or too loud to be tolerated – a problem of response magnitude. When the vocalization is too soft, we extinguish the behavior (after all, we didn't hear it) but will reinforce the vocal response when it is loud enough to be heard. In this way, we differentially reinforce a higher-magnitude response. Similarly, we could differentially reinforce responses with short latencies or longer durations. The principles of differential reinforcement are the same.

Reading Quiz 3

1. There are two reasons to conduct a _____ analysis of behavior. First, to determine if the problem behavior is an operant behavior.

2. The second reason to conduct a functional analysis of behavior is to identify the _____ that maintains the problem behavior.

3. Scratching an itch produces automatic consequences – skin stimulation and escape from the itchy feeling. These consequences are called _____ reinforcers.

4. _____ reinforcement is a procedure in which one response is reinforced and the other is extinguished.

5. If it is impossible to prevent the reinforcer from occurring after an operant response, then it will be impossible to implement _____. Because this is an important component of differential reinforcement, if you can't withhold the reinforcer, then you can't implement differential reinforcement.

6. The difference between DRA and DRI is that in DRI you reinforce a response that is _____ with the problem behavior.

7. If the goal is to decrease the rate of an operant response, the _____ procedure can be very effective. If the goal is to increase the response rate, then you will want to use _____.

Summary

Operant extinction occurs when the reinforcer that previously maintained the behavior no longer happens. Following this contingency change, the behavior returns to its baseline (no-reinforcer) level. The time course of extinction depends primarily on how frequently the response was reinforced prior to extinction. If the behavior was reinforced every time, extinction proceeds quickly. If behavior was infrequently reinforced, the behavior will prove more persistent. Other effects of operant extinction include increased negative emotions (frustration, aggression, depression, etc.), increased variability of the operant response, and a resurgence of old behaviors that used to be reinforced.

To use extinction therapeutically requires the therapist identify the reinforcer maintaining problem behavior. The method used to identify that reinforcer is called a *functional analysis of behavior*. Functional analyses are used in a wide variety of clinical settings because they increase the efficacy of the interventions that follow. For example, the results of a functional analysis may tell us what consequence is reinforcing problem behavior. With this knowledge we can arrange one of the many differential reinforcement procedures. These procedures have in common the reinforcement of one behavior and the extinction of another one – the problem behavior. Differential reinforcement is a nonpunitive approach to decreasing one behavior, while replacing it with something more adaptive. For this reason, the procedure is popular with parents, teachers, and other stakeholders (Kazdin et al., 1981).

Answers to Reading Quiz Questions

Reading Quiz 1

1. responding that meets the reinforcement contingency no longer produces the reinforcer and, as a result, falls to baseline (no-reinforcer) levels
2. operant extinction
3. decreased (or extinguished)
4. negative; SR_E-
5. negative; SR_A-
6. operant extinction (or extinction)
7. quickly
8. slowly
9. spontaneous recovery

Reading Quiz 2

1. decreases
2. emotions
3. induced
4. variability
5. burst
6. resurgence

Reading Quiz 3

1. functional
2. reinforcer
3. automatic
4. Differential
5. extinction
6. incompatible
7. DRL; DRH

Note

1. Skinner's vision of a punishment-free society is, as we will learn in Chapter 10, probably not realistic. Punishment plays an important role in holding societies together, and some problem behaviors are so dangerous to oneself or others that punishment may be a necessary component of an effective intervention.

References

Ahearn, W. H., Kerwin, M. E., Eicher, P. S., & Lukens, C. T. (2001). An ABAC comparison of two intensive interventions for food refusal. *Behavior Modification*, *25*(3), 385–405. doi:10.1177/0145445501253002

Azrin, N. H., Hutchinson, R. R., & Hake, D. F. (1966). Extinction-induced aggression. *Journal of the Experimental Analysis of Behavior*, *9*(3), 191–204. doi:10.1901/jeab.1966.9-191

Baum, W. M. (2012). Extinction as discrimination: The molar view. *Behavioural Processes*, *90*(1), 101–110. doi:10.1016/j.beproc.2012.02.011

Beavers, G. A., Iwata, B. A., & Lerman, D. C. (2013). Thirty years of research on the functional analysis of problem behavior. *Journal of Applied Behavior Analysis*, *46*(1), 1–21. doi:10.1002/jaba.30

Bonner, A. C., & Borrero, J. C. (2018). Differential reinforcement of low rate schedules reduce severe problem behavior. *Behavior Modification*, *42*(5), 747–764. doi:10.1177/0145445517731723

Briggs, A. M., Fisher, W. W., Greer, B. D., & Kimball, R. T. (2018). Prevalence of resurgence of destructive behavior when thinning reinforcement schedules during functional communication training. *Journal of Applied Behavior Analysis*, *51*(3), 620–633. doi:10.1002/jaba.472

Bruzek, J. L., Thompson, R. H., & Peters, L. C. (2009). Resurgence of infant caregiving responses. *Journal of the Experimental Analysis of Behavior*, *92*(3), 327–343. doi:10.1901/jeab.2009-92-327

Carr, E. G., & Durand, V. M. (1985). Reducing behavior problems through functional communication training. *Journal of Applied Behavior Analysis*, *18*(2), 111–126. doi:10.1901/jaba.1985.18-111

Cautela, J. R. (1956). Experimental extinction and drive during extinction in a discrimination habit. *Journal of Experimental Psychology*, *51*(5), 299–302. https://doi.org/10.1037/h0043813

Chowdhury, M., & Benson, B. A. (2011). Use of differential reinforcement to reduce behavior problems in adults with intellectual disabilities: A methodological review. *Research in Developmental Disabilities*, *32*(2), 383–394. doi:10.1016/j.ridd.2010.11.015

Cowie, S., & Davison, M. (2016). Control by reinforcers across time and space: A review of recent choice research. *Journal of the Experimental Analysis of Behavior, 105*(2), 246–269. doi:10.1002/jeab.200

Davenport, D. G., & Olson, R. D. (1968). A reinterpretation of extinction in discriminated avoidance. *Psychonomic Science*, *13*(1), 5–6. doi:10.3758/bf03342380

Devenport, L. D., & Devenport, J. A. (1994). Time-dependent averaging of foraging information in least chipmunks and golden-mantled ground squirrels. *Animal Behaviour*, *47*(4), 787–802. doi:10.1006/anbe.1994.1111

Dorey, N. R., Rosales-Ruiz, J., Smith, R., Lovelace, B., & Roane, H. (2009). Functional analysis and treatment of self-injury in a captive olive baboon. *Journal of Applied Behavior Analysis*, *42*(4), 785–794. doi:10.1901/jaba.2009.42-785

Doughty, A. H., Cash, J. D., Finch, E. A., Holloway, C., & Wallington, L. K. (2010). Effects of training history on resurgence in humans. *Behavioural Processes*, *83*(3), 340–343. doi:10.1016/j.beproc.2009.12.001

Esch, J. W., Esch, B. E., & Love, J. R. (2009). Increasing vocal variability in children with autism using a lag schedule of reinforcement. *The Analysis of Verbal Behavior*, *25*(1), 73–78. doi:10.1007/bf03393071

Fisher, W. W., Greer, B. D., Querim, A. C., & DeRosa, N. (2014). Decreasing excessive functional communication responses while treating destructive behavior using response restriction. *Research in Developmental Disabilities*, *35*(11), 2614–2623. doi:10.1016/j.ridd.2014.06.024

Fuhrman, A. M., Fisher, W. W., & Greer, B. D. (2016). A preliminary investigation on improving functional communication training by mitigating resurgence of destructive behavior. *Journal of Applied Behavior Analysis*, *49*(4), 884–899. doi:10.1002/jaba.338

Galizio, A., Higbee, T. S., & Odum, A. L. (2020). Choice for reinforced behavioral variability in children with autism spectrum disorder. *Journal of the Experimental Analysis of Behavior*, *113*(3), 495–514. doi:10.1002/jeab.591

Gallistel, C. R., & Gibbon, J. (2002). *The symbolic foundations of conditioned behavior*. Mawwah, NJ: Lawrence Erlbaum Associates.

Gershoff, E. T., & Font, S. A. (2016). Corporal punishment in U.S. Public Schools: Prevalence, disparities in use, and status in state and federal policy. *Social Policy Report*, *30*(1), 1–26. doi:10.1002/j.2379-3988.2016.tb00086.x

Gershoff, E. T., & Grogan-Kaylor, A. (2016). Spanking and child outcomes: Old controversies and new meta-analyses. *Journal of Family Psychology*, *30*(4), 453–469. doi:10.1037/fam0000191

Graham, C. H., & Gagne, R. M. (1940). The acquisition, extinction, and spontaneous recovery of a conditioned operant response. *Journal of Experimental Psychology*, *26*(3), 251–280. https://doi.org/10.1037/h0060674

Grow, L. L., Kelley, M. E., Roane, H. S., & Shillingsburg, M. A. (2008). Utility of extinction-induced response variability for the selection of mands. *Journal of Applied Behavior Analysis*, *41*(1), 15–24. doi:10.1901/jaba.2008.41-15

Gutierrez, A., Vollmer, T. R., Dozier, C. L., Borrero, J. C., Rapp, J. T., Bourret, J. C., & Gadaire, D. (2007). Manipulating establishing operations to verify and establish stimulus control during mand training. *Journal of Applied Behavior Analysis*, *40*(4), 645–658. doi:10.1901/jaba.2007.645-658

Hagopian, L. P., Dozier, C. L., Rooker, G. W., & Jones, B. A. (2013). Assessment and treatment of severe problem behavior. In G. J. Madden (Ed.), *APA handbook of behavior analysis: Volume 2* (pp. 353–386). Washington, DC: American Psychological Association.

Hammen, C. (2005). Stress and depression. *Annual Review of Clinical Psychology*, *1*(1), 293–319. doi:10.1146/annurev.clinpsy.1.102803.143938

Hanley, G. P., Iwata, B. A., & McCord, B. E. (2003). Functional analysis of problem behavior: A review. *Journal of Applied Behavior Analysis*, *36*(2), 147–185. doi:10.1901/jaba.2003.36-147

Harris, A. C., Pentel, P. R., & LeSage, M. G. (2007). Prevalence, magnitude, and correlates of an extinction burst in drug-seeking behavior in rats trained to self-administer nicotine during unlimited access (23 h/day) sessions. *Psychopharmacology*, *194*(3), 395–402. doi:10.1007/s00213-007-0848-2

Holz, W. C., Azrin, N. H., & Ayllon, T. (1963). Elimination of behavior of mental patients by response-produced extinction1. *Journal of the Experimental Analysis of Behavior*, *6*(3), 407–412. doi:10.1901/jeab.1963.6-407

Horenstein, B. (1951). Performance of conditioned responses as a function of strength of their hunger drive. *Journal of Comparative and Physiological Psychology*, *44*(2), 210–224. https://doi.org/10.1037/h0059362

Horsley, R. R., Osborne, M., Norman, C., & Wells, T. (2012). High-frequency gamblers show increased resistance to extinction following partial reinforcement. *Behavioural Brain Research*, *229*(2), 438–442. doi:10.1016/j.bbr.2012.01.024

Hurl, K., Wightman, J., Haynes, S. N., & Virues-Ortega, J. (2016). Does a pre-intervention functional assessment increase intervention effectiveness? A meta-analysis of within-subject interrupted time-series studies. *Clinical Psychology Review, 47,* 71–84. doi:10.1016/j.cpr.2016.05.003

Huston, J. P., van den Brink, J., Komorowski, M., Huq, Y., & Topic, B. (2012). Antidepressants reduce extinction-induced withdrawal and biting behaviors: A model for depressive-like behavior. *Neuroscience*, *210*, 249–257. doi:10.1016/j.neuroscience.2012.02.024

Iversen, I. H. (2002). Response-initiated imaging of operant behavior using a digital camera. *Journal of the Experimental Analysis of Behavior*, *77*(3), 283–300. doi:10.1901/jeab.2002.77-283

Iwata, B. A., Dorsey, M. F., Slifer, K. J., Bauman, K. E., & Richman, G. S. (1982). Toward a functional analysis of self-injury. *Analysis and Intervention in Developmental Disabilities*, *2*(1), 3–20. doi:10.1016/0270-4684(82)90003-9

Iwata, B. A., Dorsey, M. F., Slifer, K. J., Bauman, K. E., & Richman, G. S. (1994). Toward a functional analysis of self-injury. *Journal of Applied Behavior Analysis*, *27*(2), 197–209. doi:10.1901/jaba.1994.27-197

Iwata, B. A., Pace, G. M., Kalsher, M. J., Cowdery, G. E., & Cataldo, M. F. (1990). Experimental analysis and extinction of self-injurious escape behavior. *Journal of Applied Behavior Analysis*, *23*(1), 11–27. doi:10.1901/jaba.1990.23-11

Jenkins, W. O., & Stanley, J. C. (1950). Partial reinforcement: A review and critique. *Psychological Bulletin*, *47*(3), 193–234. https://doi.org/10.1037/h0060772

Jessel, J., Hanley, G. P., & Ghaemmaghami, M. (2016). Interview-informed synthesized contingency analyses: Thirty replications and reanalysis. *Journal of Applied Behavior Analysis*, *49*(3), 576–595. doi:10.1002/jaba.316

Kaspersen, S. L., Pape, K., Ose, S. O., Gunnell, D., & Bjørngaard, J. H. (2016). Unemployment and initiation of psychotropic medication: A case-crossover study of 2 348 552 Norwegian employees. *Occupational and Environmental Medicine*, *73*(11), 719–726. doi:10.1136/oemed-2016-103578

Kazdin, A. E. (1980). Acceptability of alternative treatments for deviant child behavior. *Journal of Applied Behavior Analysis*, *13*(2), 259–273. https://doi.org/10.1901/jaba.1980.13-259

Kazdin, A. E., French, N. H., & Sherick, R. B. (1981). Acceptability of alternative treatments for children: Evaluations by inpatient children, parents, and staff. *Journal of Consulting and Clinical Psychology*, *49*(6), 900–907. doi:10.1037/0022-006X.49.6.900

Kodak, T., & Piazza, C. C. (2008). Assessment and behavioral treatment of feeding and sleeping disorders in children with autism spectrum disorders. *Child and Adolescent Psychiatric Clinics of North America*, *17*(4), 887–905. doi:10.1016/j.chc.2008.06.005

Kuroda, T., Mizutani, Y., Cançado, C. R. X., & Podlesnik, C. A. (2017). Reversal learning and resurgence of operant behavior in zebrafish (Danio rerio). *Behavioural Processes*, *142*, 79–83. doi:10.1016/j.beproc.2017.06.004

Lane, K. L., Kalberg, J. R., & Shepcaro, J. C. (2009). An examination of the evidence base for function-based interventions for students with emotional and/or behavioral disorders attending middle and high schools. *Exceptional Children*, *75*(3), 321–340. doi:10.1177/001440290907500304

LeGray, M. W., Dufrene, B. A., Mercer, S., Olmi, D. J., & Sterling, H. (2013). Differential reinforcement of alternative behavior in center-based classrooms: Evaluation of pre-teaching the alternative behavior. *Journal of Behavioral Education*, *22*(2), 85–102. doi:10.1007/s10864-013-9170-8

Lerman, D. C., & Iwata, B. A. (1995). Prevalence of the extinction burst and its attenuation during treatment. *Journal of Applied Behavior Analysis*, *28*(1), 93–94. doi:10.1901/jaba.1995.28-93

Lerman, D. C., Iwata, B. A., & Wallace, M. D. (1999). Side effects of extinction: Prevalence of bursting and aggression during the treatment of self-injurious behavior. *Journal of Applied Behavior Analysis*, *32*(1), 1–8. doi:10.1901/jaba.1999.32-1

Lieving, G. A., & Lattal, K. A. (2003). Recency, repeatability, and reinforcer retrenchment: An experimental analysis of resurgence. *Journal of the Experimental Analysis of Behavior*, *80*(2), 217–233. doi:10.1901/jeab.2003.80-217

Lovaas, O. I., Freitag, G., Gold, V. J., & Kassorla, I. C. (1965). Experimental studies in childhood schizophrenia: Analysis of self-destructive behavior. *Journal of Experimental Child Psychology*, *2*(1), 67–84. doi:10.1016/0022-0965(65)90016-0

Martin, A. L., Bloomsmith, M. A., Kelley, M. E., Marr, M. J., & Maple, T. L. (2011). Functional analysis and treatment of human-directed undesirable behavior exhibited by a captive chimpanzee. *Journal of Applied Behavior Analysis*, *44*(1), 139–143. doi:10.1901/jaba.2011.44-139

Mazur, J. E. (1996). Past experience, recency, and spontaneous recovery in choice behavior. *Animal Learning & Behavior*, *24*(1), 1–10. doi:10.3758/BF03198948

Modrek, S., Hamad, R., & Cullen, M. R. (2015). Psychological well-being during the great recession: Changes in mental health care utilization in an occupational cohort. *American Journal of Public Health*, *105*(2), 304–310. doi:10.2105/AJPH.2014.302219

Morgan, D. L., & Lee, K. (1996). Extinction-induced response: Variability in humans. *Psychological Record*, *46*(1), 145–159. doi:10.1007/BF03395168

Nasser, A. F., Greenwald, M. K., Vince, B., Fudala, P. J., Twumasi-Ankrah, P., Liu, Y., … Heidbreder, C. (2016). Sustained-release buprenorphine (RBP-6000) blocks the effects of opioid challenge with hydromorphone in subjects with opioid use disorder. *Journal of Clinical Psychopharmacology*, *36*(1), 18–26. doi:10.1097/JCP.0000000000000434

Neuringer, A., Kornell, N., & Olufs, M. (2001). Stability and variability in extinction. *Journal of Experimental Psychology: Animal Behavior Processes*, *27*(1), 79–94. https://doi.org/10.1037/0097-7403.27.1.79

Perin, C. T. (1942). Behavior potentiality as a joint function of the amount of training and the degree of hunger at the time of extinction. *Journal of Experimental Psychology*, *30*(2), 93–113. https://doi.org/10.1037/h0058987

Petscher, E. S., Rey, C., & Bailey, J. S. (2009). A review of empirical support for differential reinforcement of alternative behavior. *Research in Developmental Disabilities, 30*(3), 409–425. doi:10.1016/j.ridd.2008.08.008

Piazza, C. C. (2008). Feeding disorders and behavior: What have we learned? *Developmental Disabilities Research Reviews, 14*(2), 174–181. doi:10.1002/ddrr.22

Piazza, C. C., Fisher, W. W., Hanley, G. P., Remick, M. L., Contrucci, S. A., & Aitken, T. L. (1997). The use of positive and negative reinforcement in the treatment of escape-maintained destructive behavior. *Journal of Applied Behavior Analysis, 30*(2), 279–298. doi:10.1901/jaba.1997.30-279

Piazza, C. C., Milnes, S. M., & Shalev, R. A. (2015). A behavior-analytic approach to the assessment and treatment of pediatric feeding disorders. In H. S. Roane, J. L. Ringdahl, & T. S. Falcomata (Eds.) *Clinical and organizational applications of applied behavior analysis* (pp. 69–94). Amsterdam: Elsevier. doi:10.1016/b978-0-12-420249-8.00004-6

Podlesnik, C. A., Jimenez-Gomez, C., & Shahan, T. A. (2006). Resurgence of alcohol seeking produced by discontinuing non-drug reinforcement as an animal model of drug relapse. *Behavioural Pharmacology, 17*(4), 369–374. doi:10.1097/01.fbp.0000224385.09486.ba

Pryor, K. W., Haag, R., & O'Reilly, J. (1969). The creative porpoise: Training for novel behavior. *Journal of the Experimental Analysis of Behavior, 12*(4), 653–661. doi:10.1901/jeab.1969.12-653

Reed, P., & Morgan, T. A. (2006). Resurgence of response sequences during extinction in rats shows a primacy effect. *Journal of the Experimental Analysis of Behavior, 86*(3), 307–315. doi:10.1901/jeab.2006.20-05

Rescorla, R. A. (2004). Spontaneous recovery varies inversely with the training-extinction interval. *Animal Learning & Behavior, 32*(4), 401–408. doi:10.3758/BF03196037

Rodriguez, N. M., & Thompson, R. H. (2015). Behavioral variability and autism spectrum disorder. *Journal of Applied Behavior Analysis, 48*(1), 167–187. doi:10.1002/jaba.164

Ross, C., & Neuringer, A. (2002). Reinforcement of variations and repetitions along three independent response dimensions. *Behavioural Processes, 57*(2–3), 199–209. doi:10.1016/S0376-6357(02)00014-1

Salamone, J. D., Kurth, P., McCullough, L. D., & Sokolowski, J. D. (1995). The effects of nucleus accumbens dopamine depletions on continuously reinforced operant responding: Contrasts with the effects of extinction. *Pharmacology Biochemistry and Behavior, 50*(3), 437–443. doi:10.1016/0091-3057(94)00294-S

Scotti, J. R., Evans, I. M., Meyer, L. H., & Walker, P. (1991). A meta-analysis of intervention research with problem behavior: Treatment validity and standards of practice. *American Journal of Mental Retardation, 96*, 233–256.

Sears, R. R., Maccoby, E. E., & Levin, H. (1957). *Patterns of child rearing*. Evanston, IL: Row, Peterson and Co.

Sellers, T. P., Kelley, K., Higbee, T. S., & Wolfe, K. (2016). Effects of simultaneous script training on use of varied mand frames by preschoolers with autism. *The Analysis of Verbal Behavior, 32*(1), 15–26. doi:10.1007/s40616-015-0049-8

Sigmon, S. C., Wong, C. J., Chausmer, A. L., Liebson, I. A., & Bigelow, G. E. (2004). Evaluation of an injection depot formulation of buprenorphine: Placebo comparison. *Addiction, 99*(11), 1439–1449. doi:10.1111/j.1360-0443.2004.00834.x

Singh, N. N., Watson, J. E., & Winton, A. S. W. (1987). Parents' acceptability ratings of alternative treatments for use with mentally retarded children. *Behavior Modification, 11*(1), 17–26. doi:10.1177/01454455870111002

Skinner, B. F. (1938). *The behavior of organisms: An experimental analysis*. Oxford, UK: Appleton-Century.

Skinner, B. F. (1948). *Walden two*. Indianapolis, IN: Hackett.

Skinner, B. F. (1971). *Beyond freedom and dignity*. New York: Alfred A. Knopf.

Smith, B. M., Smith, G. S., Shahan, T. A., Madden, G. J., & Twohig, M. P. (2017). Effects of differential rates of alternative reinforcement on resurgence of human behavior. *Journal of the Experimental Analysis of Behavior, 107*, 1. doi:10.1002/jeab.241

Sullivan, M. W., Lewis, M., & Alessandri, S. M. (1992). Cross-age stability in emotional expressions during learning and extinction. *Developmental Psychology*, *28*(1), 58–63. doi:10.1037/0012-1649.28.1.58

Taylor, T., Kozlowski, A. M., & Girolami, P. A. (2017). Comparing behavioral treatment of feeding difficulties and tube dependence in children with cerebral palsy and autism spectrum disorder. *NeuroRehabilitation*, *41*(2), 395–402. doi:10.3233/NRE-162071

Thomas, D. R., & Sherman, L. (1986). An assessment of the role of handling cues in "spontaneous recovery" after extinction. *Journal of the Experimental Analysis of Behavior*, *46*(3), 305–314. doi:10.1901/jeab.1986.46-305

Thrailkill, E. A., Kimball, R. T., Kelley, M. E., Craig, A. R., & Podlesnik, C. A. (2018). Greater reinforcement rate during training increases spontaneous recovery. *Journal of the Experimental Analysis of Behavior*, *109*(1), 238–252. doi:10.1002/jeab.307

Tiger, J. H., Hanley, G. P., & Bruzek, J. (2008). Functional communication training: A review and practical guide. *Behavior Analysis in Practice*, *1*(1), 16–23. doi:10.1007/bf03391716

Vollmer, T. R. (1994). The concept of automatic reinforcement: Implications for behavioral research in developmental disabilities. *Research in Developmental Disabilities*, *15*(3), 187–207. doi: 10.1016/0891-4222(94)90011-6

Vollmer, T. R., & Iwata, B. A. (1992). Differential reinforcement as treatment for behavior disorders: Procedural and functional variations. *Research in Developmental Disabilities*, *13*(4), 393–417. doi:10.1016/0891-4222(92)90013-V

Vollmer, T. R., Peters, K. P., & Slocum, S. K. (2015). Treatment of severe behavior disorders. In H. S. Roane, J. L. Ringdahl, & T. S. Falcomata (Eds.), *Clinical and organizational applications of applied behavior analysis* (pp. 47–67). Amsterdam: Elsevier. doi:10.1016/b978-0-12-420249-8.00003-4

Voulgarakis, H., & Forte, S. (2015). Escape extinction and negative reinforcement in the treatment of pediatric feeding disorders: A single case analysis. *Behavior Analysis in Practice*, *8*(2), 212–214. doi:10.1007/s40617-015-0086-8

Vuchinich, R. E., & Tucker, J. A. (1988). Contributions from behavioral theories of choice to an analysis of alcohol abuse. *Journal of Abnormal Psychology*, *97*(2), 181–195. doi:10.1037//0021-843x.97.2.181

Wacker, D. P., Schieltz, K. M., Berg, W. K., Harding, J. W., Padilla Dalmau, Y. C., & Lee, J. F. (2017). The long-term effects of functional communication training conducted in young children's home settings. *Education and Treatment of Children*, *40*(1), 43–56. doi:10.1353/etc.2017.0003

Whitaker, S. (1996). A review of DRO: The influence of the degree of intellectual disability and the frequency of the target behaviour. *Journal of Applied Research in Intellectual Disabilities*, *9*(1), 61–79. doi:10.1111/j.1468-3148.1996.tb00098.x

Wong, C., Odom, S. L., Hume, K. A., Cox, A. W., Fettig, A., Kucharczyk, S., … Schultz, T. R. (2015). Evidence-based practices for children, youth, and young adults with autism spectrum disorder: A comprehensive review. *Journal of Autism and Developmental Disorders*, *45*(7), 1951–1966. doi:10.1007/s10803-014-2351-z

Yokel, R. A., & Wise, R. A. (1975). Increased lever pressing for amphetmaine after pimozide in rats: Implications for a dopamine theory of reward. *Science*, *187*(4), 547–549.

Zarcone, T. J., Branch, M. N., Hughes, C. E., & Pennypacker, H. S. (1997). Key pecking during extinction after intermittent or continuous reinforcement as a function of the number of reinforcers delivered during training. *Journal of the Experimental Analysis of Behavior*, *67*(1), 91–108. doi:10.1901/jeab.1997.67-91

Zolotor, A. J., Theodore, A. D., Runyan, D. K., Chang, J. J., & Laskey, A. L. (2011). Corporal punishment and physical abuse: Population-based trends for three-to-11-year-old children in the United States. *Child Abuse Review*, *20*(1), 57–66. doi:10.1002/car.1128

Primary and Conditioned Reinforcement and Shaping

8

Thus far you have learned a lot about the reinforcement of operant behavior. Reinforcers, skillfully applied, can be used to direct behavior toward actions that benefit the individual, those they interact with, and society at large. Suspending the reinforcement contingency (extinction) can decrease problem behaviors, and reinforcing an alternative action (differential reinforcement) can produce even better outcomes.

All of this behavior-change technology is built on reinforcement, and we have talked about positive and negative contingencies and how to use them. This chapter makes yet another distinction, this time between primary reinforcers and conditioned reinforcers. Primary reinforcers are those that work because of our genetic inheritance – these reinforcers help us survive. Human and nonhuman animals don't have to learn anything for primary reinforcers to work – we are phylogenetically prepared for these consequences to reinforce our behavior. Conditioned reinforcers are different. We have to learn something before these consequences will function as reinforcers. This chapter describes that learning. Don't worry, it's not a new kind of learning; it's Pavlovian conditioning.

The chapter concludes by describing a technique for establishing new behaviors or gradually moving existing behaviors in an adaptive direction – shaping. Shaping is a particularly useful way to teach an individual a new behavior when that individual is nonverbal, that is, when they cannot understand instructions. Shaping can be used to establish new behaviors in nonhuman animals such as the family pet, zoo animals, or animals in the wild. As you will see, shaping is a positive reinforcement-based technique that improves human–nonhuman interactions; it holds considerable potential for improving the way in which humans interact with and influence the lives of those with whom we share this Earth.

An Introduction to Behavior Analysis, First Edition. Gregory J. Madden, Derek D. Reed, and Florence D. DiGennaro Reed.
© 2021 John Wiley & Sons Ltd. Published 2021 by John Wiley & Sons Ltd.

Of course, shaping can also be used to help verbal humans acquire new behaviors, new skills, or move existing behaviors in a desired direction. The video-gaming industry understands shaping and uses it to teach players skills that enhance the engagement and fun of their games. We will get to that later, but first let's focus on primary reinforcers.

Primary Reinforcers

In 1987, B. F. Skinner, the father of behavior analysis, and E. O. Wilson, the father of evolutionary psychology, met to discuss the intersection of their two sciences. One topic on which they found considerable agreement was that, when it comes to reinforcers, "…everything goes back to genes" (Naour, 2009, p. 70). Said another way, our genes have prepared us, and all other creatures on this planet, to find certain consequences reinforcing. How so? By ensuring that consequences needed for survival – food, water, air, and so on – function as reinforcers.

Natural selection favors those who repeat behaviors that produce life-sustaining consequences. As an illustrative thought experiment, consider two infants living in Paleolithic (cave-person) times. One infant finds its mother's milk highly reinforcing – suckling behaviors that produce this milk are repeated again and again (Kron, 1967). The second infant's behavior is not reinforced by milk – the milk was sampled once and suckling was not repeated. The genes of the first infant have prepared it for survival. It did not need to learn anything new for mother's milk to reinforce its behavior; the first sip was enough to increase the future probability of successful suckling behaviors. The second infant's genes are, sadly, a death sentence in an age without modern medical technologies. An early death prevents these genes from reaching the next generation. The result of this natural selection process is that mother's milk functions as a reinforcer for virtually all human infants and other mammals.

Individuals are more likely to survive if their genes establish life-sustaining consequences as reinforcers. Behavior analysts refer to these life-sustaining consequences as **primary reinforcers**.[1]

> **Primary Reinforcer**: *A consequence that functions as a reinforcer because it is important in sustaining the life of the individual or the continuation of the species.*

Table 8.1 lists many of the life-sustaining consequences that function as primary reinforcers for human behavior. The logic is the same across all these primary reinforcers: If this consequence did not function as a reinforcer, the individual would be less likely to survive. Without oxygen, we die; therefore, oxygen-seeking behaviors (swimming to the water's surface) are reinforced with access to this primary reinforcer. Operant behaviors such as fanning ourselves or starting a fire are reinforced with temperature-changing consequences that can save our lives in extreme heat or cold. Similarly, if a young child did not find contact with its mother reinforcing, it would be more likely to wander away from the safety of its mother's watchful eye. And finally, if we did not find sexual contact reinforcing, we would be less likely to have sex. If we didn't have sex, our genes would be stranded in this generation. Yes, "everything goes back to genes."

Table 8.1 Primary reinforcers for humans

Food	Stimulus changes allowing temperature regulation
Water	Termination of pain
Oxygen	Infant contact with mother
Sleep	Infant control over stimulus changes
Sexual contact (onset in adolescence)	

Conditioned Reinforcers

A second category of reinforcers, **conditioned reinforcers**, are those *consequences that function as reinforcers only after learning occurs.* Infants will suckle for mother's milk (primary reinforcer), but they won't suckle if the only consequence of suckling is a $50 bill. Later in life, after the child has learned about money, the $50 bill will function as a powerful conditioned reinforcer. Learning changes the function of the $50 bill – from a useless piece of paper to a valuable consequence of operant behavior.

As you will see later in this chapter, conditioned reinforcement is incredibly useful when teaching an individual to engage in new and complex behaviors. Therefore, those wishing to positively influence behavior will be more successful if they know precisely how to turn a neutral stimulus (e.g., a useless piece of paper) into an effective conditioned reinforcer (a $50 bill).

What learning is necessary to affect this change? To answer this question, basic researchers have for decades studied conditioned reinforcement in nonhuman animals and humans. Their findings are clear and replicable: Pavlovian learning is responsible for the transformation of a neutral consequence into a conditioned reinforcer (for reviews of this evidence, see Fantino, 1977; Shahan & Cunningham, 2015; Williams, 1994).

Pavlovian Learning and Conditioned Reinforcers

A reinforcing consequence, whether it is a primary or conditioned reinforcer, increases behavior above a baseline level. But conditioned reinforcers acquire their reinforcing function during the lifetime of the individual. Said another way, the individual has to learn something before the conditioned reinforcer works. The individual must learn that the conditioned reinforcer signals a delay reduction to an already established reinforcer. This is Pavlovian learning, so this will already be familiar to you.

To illustrate, consider a simple procedure that B. F. Skinner (1938) used to study conditioned reinforcement. A rat was placed in an empty chamber with a cup attached to a wall. Periodically a mechanical dispenser made an audible noise – "ka-chunk" – and then, about a half-second later, a small piece of food fell into the cup. Figure 8.1 illustrates the temporal sequence of this procedure. Note how the "ka-chunk" (shown as a red bar) occurs just before each food delivery (the green bar).

Figure 8.1 should look familiar to you. It is similar to the event records used in Chapter 4 to explain Pavlovian conditioning. Like all examples of Pavlovian conditioning, the neutral

Figure 8.1 Record of events occurring during an experiment conducted by Skinner (1938). The red bars indicate when the food-dispenser makes an audible "Ka-chunk," followed 0.5 seconds later by a food delivery. The time between food deliveries is variable but averages out to 30 seconds.

stimulus (ka-chunk) signals a reduction in the delay to the unconditioned stimulus (US). In this experiment, the US was food – a primary reinforcer. Because of this signaled delay reduction, ka-chunk comes to function as a conditioned stimulus (CS). In Figure 8.1, food is delivered once, on average, every 30 seconds. When the ka-chunk happens, the delay is reduced to a half-second; that's quite a delay reduction. Because of this large delay reduction, ka-chunk acquires a CS function – it evokes conditioned responding such as salivation and physiologically detectable excitation.

If Pavlovian learning is necessary for a neutral consequence to become a conditioned reinforcer, then when the ka-chunk functions as a CS it should also function as a conditioned reinforcer. To test this, Skinner arranged an operant contingency between pressing a lever (newly introduced to the chamber) and the ka-chunk:

IF lever press → *THEN* ka-chunk

Note that the only consequence of pressing the lever was a ka-chunk; no food was provided. If Skinner's rats learned to press the lever (which they had never seen before), then he could conclude that ka-chunk functions as a reinforcer – a conditioned reinforcer.

Indeed, Skinner's rats learned to press the lever when the only consequence was the ka-chunk. However, as they continued to earn ka-chunks, they gradually decreased their rate of lever pressing. Why? Because of *Pavlovian extinction*. When the CS (ka-chunk) was repeatedly presented without the US (food), the CS no longer signaled a delay reduction to the US. Eventually ka-chunk stopped functioning as a CS or as a conditioned reinforcer.

A good deal of research evidence supports the position that Pavlovian learning underlies conditioned reinforcement (Fantino, 1977; Shahan & Cunningham, 2015; Williams, 1994). For one thing, all of the principles of effective Pavlovian conditioning apply to conditioned reinforcement. We briefly review these principles later in the chapter. For now, note that it would be odd for these principles to prove so useful if Pavlovian learning did not underlie conditioned reinforcement.

To summarize, the learning necessary to transform a neutral consequence into a conditioned reinforcer is Pavlovian learning. That is, salient, nonredundant CS events that signal delay reductions to food, water, or other phylogenetically important reinforcing US events will also function as conditioned reinforcers.

Verbal Learning and Conditioned Reinforcers

It is impossible to remember how you learned the conditioned-reinforcing function of money. Perhaps you repeatedly saw your parents hand money to the clerk just moments before they gave you a chocolate shake, a new toy, or that Pokemon t-shirt that you so desperately wanted. If so, then you saw how money predicted a delay reduction to the acquisition of these rewards. However, we learn about money at such an early age, and in so many situations, that it is hard to know exactly how it acquired conditioned-reinforcing properties.

Perhaps it is easier to remember how you learned that prize tickets at the pizza-gaming center were valuable conditioned reinforcers. The first

Source: Stephen Barnes / Alamy Stock Photo.

time you earned the tickets they were neutral consequences – you may not have even noticed the machine was spitting them out. However, when your parents showed you the many toys and candies the tickets could be exchanged for, you acquired a strong interest in earning more tickets. In showing you what tickets could buy, your parents verbally explained that tickets were delay-reduction stimuli. Said less technically, if you had a bucket full of tickets, then you could get some toys and candy *now*! After your parents imparted this wisdom upon you, the tickets functioned as conditioned reinforcers for skillfully playing games.

Therefore, a second way in which a consequence can come to function as a conditioned reinforcer is through verbal learning (Shull & Lawrence, 1998). During verbal learning, information is provided indicating that the conditioned reinforcer signals a delay reduction to another reinforcer. That is, the Pavlovian CS→US contingency is verbally described.

Laboratory studies reveal that humans are capable of verbally learning Pavlovian contingencies. For example, if humans are instructed that a red light will precede the delivery of an electric shock (US), when that instructed CS is encountered, an involuntary physiological fear response occurs (the conditioned response [CR]), even when the shock does not (Phelps et al., 2001). Similarly, in your everyday life, if a friend tells you their dog bites in a vicious and unpredictable way (an event that would function as a highly aversive US), then when you see the dog approaching (CS), you will experience fear (CR), despite having never seen the dog bite anyone.

When children are instructed that game tickets signal that prizes are on the way, they show excitement (CR) when the gaming machine spits out those tickets (CS). Importantly, they also spend more of their time playing games that provide tickets. Such ticket-seeking operant behavior is maintained by conditioned reinforcers. In sum, when an individual learns, either through direct experience or through instructions, that a neutral consequence signals a reduction in the delay to a backup reinforcer, that consequence becomes a CS and a conditioned reinforcer.[2]

The Token Economy

While ticket-dispensing arcade games became popular only recently, the use of conditioned reinforcers has been around much longer (Hackenberg, 2018). For example, when early humans abandoned hunter-gatherer living and began to farm the land, they used clay coins as conditioned reinforcers. Today, we take for granted money and electronic currency exchanges – Amazon sends the shoes I want (behavior), and I give them a conditioned reinforcer ($39.99).

In the 1960s applied behavior analysts developed a conditioned-reinforcement system known as the "token economy" (Ayllon & Azrin, 1965). In this therapeutic system, tokens were used to reinforce prosocial and life-skill behaviors among hospitalized psychiatric patients, individuals with developmental disabilities, and delinquent youth (Kazdin, 1981).

A **token economy** is *a set of rules governing the delivery of response-contingent conditioned reinforcers (tokens, points, etc.) that may be later exchanged for one or more backup reinforcers.* A **backup reinforcer** is *the reinforcer provided after the conditioned reinforcer signals the delay reduction to its delivery.* In a token economy, earning a

Token reinforcer used in the Ayllon and Azrin (1965) studies.

Source: Photograph (with permission) by Derek Reed.

token signals that the individual is nearer in time to a desired product or service (the backup reinforcer) than they were before the token was given to them. For example, in the studies conducted with hospitalized psychiatric patients (Ayllon & Azrin, 1965), tokens could be used to purchase candy, coffee, new clothes, books, and so on, or they could be used to gain access to preferred activities, like watching a movie, listening to the radio, or watching TV.

To earn these tokens, patients could complete a variety of different "*IF* response → *THEN* conditioned reinforcer" contingencies. For example, patients could earn tokens by bathing or dressing, working in the laundry, the kitchen, or the hospital's offices. Each task completed was awarded a different number of tokens, depending on its difficulty. For example, helping to prepare the dining area was worth 1 token, whereas working in the dishwashing areas was reinforced with 6 tokens. Where prior to the token economy these patients were written off as incapable of learning, and doomed to a life in the mental hospital, this enormously successful program demonstrated that patients could learn skills that would allow their reintegration into society.

Token economies have also proven effective in schools. Perhaps, when you were growing up, your elementary-school teacher used a version of the "Good Behavior Game" (Barrish et al., 1969). In this game, students are assigned to teams and points, later exchangeable for goods and privileges, are given (and taken away) contingent upon appropriate and inappropriate behavior. This token economy approach was immortalized in J. K. Rowling's *Harry Potter* books – "5 points for Gryffindor!" In the fictional game played at Hogwarts, the house with the most points at the end of the school year is awarded the backup reinforcer – the House Cup.

Source: Suzelfe, Wikipedia, CC BY-SA 4.0.

The Good Behavior Game is intuitive, inexpensive, and effective (Flower et al., 2014). It has even been used to increase physical activity in schools (Galbraith & Normand, 2017). Recent meta-analyses (i.e., quantitative analyses of a large number of peer-reviewed studies) reveal that token economies reliably produce large improvements in academic performance (Soares et al., 2016) and prosocial behavior (Bowman-Perrott et al., 2016).

Token economies have several attractive features (Russell et al., 2018):

- **Motivationally robust:** Because tokens can be exchanged for many different backup reinforcers, motivation to earn them remains fairly constant. For example, when a psychiatric patient uses his tokens to buy a shirt, he is still motivated to earn more tokens because they can be exchanged for candy, movies, and so on.
- **Nondisruptive:** Reinforcing an ongoing behavior with a token is easier than with a backup reinforcer that disrupts the performance. For example, providing a token when a patient buttons his shirt is less disruptive than taking him to the hospital's theater to watch a movie.
- **Fair compensation:** In a token economy, it is easy to assign larger reinforcers to motivate challenging or less-preferred behaviors – simply assign a larger number of tokens to that behavior. This ensures fair compensation is provided for each activity.
- **Portability.** Tokens are easy to keep on hand at all times and this allows reinforcement of appropriate behavior whenever it is observed. Likewise, points can be added to a team's score with nothing more than a whiteboard marker. This portability increases the probability that appropriate behavior will be reinforced.
- **Delay-bridging.** If professor Dumbledore told the Hogwarts students that the best-behaved students would win the House Cup at the end of the year, they would soon forget about this delayed reward. However, by providing points immediately after a desirable response, the delay is bridged between good behavior and the awarding of the House Cup. Nonfictional evidence for the importance of delay-bridging comes from animal experiments in which responding stops when backup reinforcers are delayed by just a few minutes. When the same animals' responding produces an immediate conditioned reinforcer, their behavior continues even when the backup reinforcer is delayed by an hour or more (see Hackenberg, 2018 for review).

Because of these attractive features, the token economy has also proven effective in reducing criminal activities in adolescents (see Larzelere et al., 2004 for review) and reducing drug use in cigarette smokers, alcoholics, and those diagnosed with other substance-use disorders (see Davis et al., 2016 for review). In short, the use of conditioned reinforcement within the token economy has proven to be one of the most effective and widely used methods of positively influencing human behavior.

Reading Quiz 1

1. Natural selection has prepared us to find some consequences reinforcing. We refer to such consequences as _____ reinforcers.
2. _____ reinforcers are those that will not reinforce behavior until the individual has learned that the consequence signals a delay reduction to a backup reinforcer.
3. The learning that must occur before a conditioned reinforcer will function as a reinforcer was thoroughly discussed in Chapter 4. That learning is _____ conditioning.
4. When it comes to conditioned reinforcers, verbally capable humans have an advantage over nonverbal organisms. Instead of learning the Pavlovian CS (conditioned reinforcer) → US (_____ reinforcer) relation, someone can simply verbally describe this contingency.
5. The _____ _____ is one of the most widely used conditioned-reinforcement technologies in applied behavior analysis. Points, tokens, tickets,

and so on are provided immediately upon the desired behavior and are later exchanged for backup reinforcers.

6. Real and fictional schools use a version of the token economy known as the _____ _____ Game to encourage desirable student behavior.

Arranging Effective Conditioned Reinforcers

The overview provided thus far may make it seem easy to effectively use conditioned reinforcers – just award some points to Gryffindor and the rest will fall into place. In reality, there is a science to arranging effective conditioned reinforcers, and that science is built on Pavlovian conditioning (Shahan & Cunningham, 2015; Williams, 1994). If we want to effectively use conditioned reinforcers, we will need to recall the principles of effective Pavlovian conditioning introduced in Chapter 4. Let's review those principles and translate them to conditioned reinforcement.

Principle 1: Use an effective backup reinforcer. The first principle of Pavlovian conditioning was "Use an important US." The more important the US, the better the Pavlovian conditioning. Translated to conditioned reinforcement, this becomes, *Use an effective backup reinforcer*. The better the backup reinforcer, the more effective the conditioned reinforcer will be.

For example, a token exchangeable for a scoop of ice cream is fine, but a token exchangeable for admission to your favorite concert is a whole lot better. The concert is a more effective backup reinforcer and a concert ticket is likely to maintain more behavior than a coupon for a scoop of ice cream. Simply put, the more effective the backup reinforcer, the more effective the conditioned reinforcer (see Hackenberg, 2018 for review).

One strategy for arranging an effective conditioned reinforcer is to use a token that can be exchanged for a lot of different backup reinforcers (Skinner, 1953). For example, a $100 bill is a highly effective conditioned reinforcer because its receipt signals a delay reduction to many different backup reinforcers (ice cream, concert tickets, a new pair of shoes, etc.). When *a conditioned reinforcer signals a delay reduction to more than one backup reinforcer*, it is referred to as a **generalized conditioned reinforcer**.

Perhaps because it seemed so obviously true, researchers have only recently begun to evaluate the hypothesis that generalized conditioned reinforcers are more effective than simple conditioned reinforcers (i.e., those signaling a delay reduction to just one backup reinforcer). Most studies support the hypothesis (Andrade & Hackenberg, 2017; Becraft & Rolider, 2015; DeFulio et al., 2014; Moher et al., 2008; Sran & Borrero, 2010), but one pigeon study has failed to replicate this finding (Tan & Hackenberg, 2015). Perhaps readers of this chapter will be inspired to further explore this important, but understudied topic.

Principle 2: Use a salient conditioned reinforcer. The second principle of Pavlovian conditioning was "Use a salient CS." Translated to conditioned reinforcement, this becomes, *Use a salient conditioned reinforcer*. Simply put, a noticeable conditioned reinforcer will work better than one that is easily overlooked. For example, giving a child a token and having her place it in her token bank is more salient than dropping the token into the bank for her. If you are going to deliver a conditioned reinforcer, you want to be certain the individual observes it. If they don't observe the conditioned reinforcer, it will never positively influence behavior.

To increase the salience of conditioned reinforcers, animal trainers often use clickers instead of saying something like, "good boy" (after all, animals don't speak English). Clickers, which are inexpensive and may be purchased at most pet supply stores, present a salient auditory stimulus "click-click." This sound is established as a conditioned reinforcer by ensuring that it signals a delay reduction to an effective backup reinforcer, like a favorite treat. The sound of the clicker is unique. Pets, farm animals, and captive animals in zoos have never heard a sound like this before. This novelty makes the sound salient, that is, something that's difficult to miss.

A second advantage of the clicker is that its "click-click" sound is brief, much briefer than the time it would take to say, "good boy." This brevity is important because an effective conditioned reinforcer *marks* the desired response (and no other behavior) as it occurs (Urcuioli & Kasprow, 1988; Williams, 1999). When we say **marking**, we mean that *the conditioned reinforcer immediately follows the response, and this helps the individual learn which response produced the backup reinforcer.*

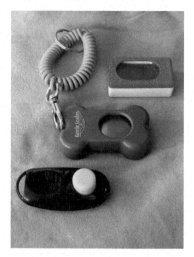

Source: Elf/Wikipedia/CC BY-SA 3.0

For example, when teaching a dog to sit, the trainer presents the "click-click" at the exact moment that the dog's backside touches the ground. This clearly marks the response that produced the "click-click" and helps the dog learn the "*IF* sit → *THEN* treat" contingency. Had the trainer only tossed the treat to the dog, 3–4 seconds may elapse between the sitting response and the treat. During that 3–4 second delay, the dog will do other things – looking at the trainer, standing up, tilting the head. From the dog's perspective, it is difficult to tell which one of these produced the food. By presenting the "click-click" right after the sit, this response is marked, and this greatly facilitates learning (Williams, 1999). So, when skillfully used, a conditioned reinforcer marks the desired response and nothing else.

Source: Elf/Wikipedia/CC BY-SA 3.0

Principle 3: Use a conditioned reinforcer that signals a large delay reduction to the backup reinforcer. The third principle of Pavlovian conditioning was, "Use a CS that signals a large delay reduction to the US." Translation: *Use a conditioned reinforcer that signals a large delay reduction to the backup reinforcer.* The bigger the delay reduction to the backup reinforcer, the more effective the conditioned reinforcer will be (Fantino, 1969; Fantino & Silberberg, 2010; Shahan & Cunningham, 2015). As in Chapter 4, the amount of delay reduction signaled by the conditioned reinforcer is easily calculated using the delay-reduction ratio:

$$\text{Delay-reduction ratio} = \frac{\text{US} \rightarrow \text{US interval}}{\text{CS} \rightarrow \text{US interval}}$$

In this equation, the US→US interval refers to the average time between backup reinforcers. The CS→US interval is the time separating the conditioned reinforcer and the delivery of the backup reinforcer.

Let's fill in this equation using numbers from an experiment conducted by Williams and Fantino (1978). In their experiment, pigeons could obtain food once, on average, every 52 seconds by pecking a response key. Therefore, we insert this value in the numerator of the delay-reduction ratio:

$$\text{delay-reduction ratio} = \frac{52 \text{ seconds}}{\text{CS} \rightarrow \text{US interval}}$$

In one arrangement, pecking the key periodically changed the key blue. When this happened, it signaled a delay reduction to food – from 52 to 20 seconds. Thus, the CS→US interval was 20 seconds:

$$\text{delay-reduction ratio} \left(\text{blue}\right) = \frac{52 \text{ seconds}}{20 \text{ seconds}} = 2.6$$

So, when the blue light was illuminated, it signaled that food would be delivered 2.6 times faster than normal. Not bad.

In a second arrangement, Williams and Fantino (1978) arranged a different conditioned reinforcer, one that signaled a larger delay reduction to food. This time the key color changed to white. When this happened, the delay to food was reduced from 52 to 10 seconds. To evaluate the efficacy of this conditioned reinforcer, we use the delay-reduction ratio:

$$\text{delay-reduction ratio} \left(\text{white}\right) = \frac{52 \text{ seconds}}{10 \text{ seconds}} = 5.2$$

The white key signaled a larger delay reduction to food than the blue key. Therefore, it should function as a more effective conditioned reinforcer.

The graph shown on the right side of Figure 8.2 shows what happened when Williams and Fantino (1978) let pigeons choose between pecking the blue and the white keys. As you can see and as predicted by the delay-reduction ratio, the white key was preferred – it was a better conditioned reinforcer than the blue key.

A large number of studies have replicated this core finding – a conditioned reinforcer's efficacy is strongly influenced by the delay reduction it signals until the delivery of the backup reinforcer (see Fantino et al., 1993 for review). Therefore, those wishing to effectively use conditioned reinforcers should ensure that these consequences signal large delay reductions to the backup reinforcer.

Principle 4: Make sure the conditioned reinforcer is not redundant. The final principle of Pavlovian conditioning was, "Make sure the CS is not redundant." Translated to conditioned reinforcement, we want our conditioned reinforcer to be the only stimulus signaling a delay reduction to the backup reinforcer. For example, imagine that you want to start using a clicker as a conditioned reinforcer when training your dog. Establishing "click-click" as a conditioned reinforcer will be easier if you avoid simultaneously presenting a stimulus that already functions as a conditioned reinforcer. So, if

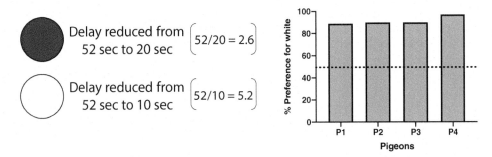

Figure 8.2 Results of an experiment conducted by Williams and Fantino (1978). All four pigeons strongly preferred the conditioned reinforcer that signaled the larger delay reduction to food delivery. The dotted line indicates where choice would be if the pigeons did not prefer one conditioned reinforcer over the other.
Source: Williams and Fantino (1978).

you normally praise your dog just before giving her a treat, then praise probably already functions as a conditioned reinforcer. If you click at the same time that you praise the dog, then the click is a redundant stimulus – the praise already signals a delay reduction to the treat. Because the "click-click" is redundant with praise, it is unlikely to acquire conditioned reinforcing properties. Instead, when establishing "click-click" as a conditioned reinforcer, you should withhold the praise throughout. This ensures that "click-click" is the only stimulus signaling a delay reduction to the treat.

EXTRA BOX 1: CONDITIONED REINFORCERS IN ZOOS

Thanks to advances in behavior analysis, animal trainers understand how conditioned reinforcers can improve the efficacy of their teaching methods (Pryor, 1973). In the inset picture, a trainer at the San Diego Zoo is teaching an elephant that the sound of a whistle is a conditioned reinforcer. For this training, she uses apple slices as an effective backup reinforcer (Principle 1). The whistle in her mouth makes a unique and salient noise (Principle 2), which signals a delay reduction to the next apple slice (Principle 3). The trainer is careful not to present any other stimulus change that could signal a delay reduction to food (Principle 4); for example, she does not reach into the bucket for an apple slice until the sound of the whistle is finished. After just a few of these training sessions, the sound of the whistle functions as a conditioned reinforcer.

Notice the long stick with the blue and white ball at the end (between the trainer's feet). This "target stick" will be used in teaching the elephant one of its first helpful behaviors – touching the target. At first, the target (the ball) is placed very close to the trunk and when the elephant touches the target, the trainer blows the whistle, *marking* the desired response at the exact moment it occurs. Each touch earns a whistle and, a few seconds later, a tasty slice of apple.

Throughout these sessions, the trainer uses differential reinforcement. That is, only the desired behavior is reinforced with a whistle. All other apple-seeking behaviors are extinguished. For example, if the elephant moves its trunk toward the bucket of apples, the trainer will turn her back to the elephant and hold the bucket out of reach. In this way, she extinguishes inappropriate apple-seeking behaviors. The only behavior that will produce a whistle, and then an apple slice, is touching the target with the trunk.

After just a few of these training sessions, the elephant will quickly touch the target each time it is presented. If the target is moved out of reach, the elephant

Source: Gregory Madden.

will walk to it. Once this target-touching behavior is well established, the trainer can use the target stick to gracefully move this 10,000-pound creature to a different area of the display. The trainer simply moves the target to wherever she wants the elephant to go. This entirely positive interaction stands in stark contrast to the way circus trainers have historically moved their elephants. They coerce movement from their elephants by jabbing them with a bull hook (negative reinforcement – escape, SR_E^-). Conditioned reinforcement has greatly improved human–elephant interactions.

Clicker Training with Humans

Dr. Martin Levy is the director of the medical-residency program at Mountefiore Medical Center in the Bronx. In his spare time, he teaches people how to throw a Frisbee, so their dogs can catch them in mid-air, or so they can improve their skills in ultimate Frisbee. He finds that his Frisbee students learn better when he uses a clicker – yes, the same one used by animal trainers.

When Dr. Levy trains Frisbee throwing, he shows the individual how to hold the Frisbee correctly, waits for them to do it, and then delivers a "click-click" at the exact second they do it right. This *marks* the correct response, which, when combined with repetition, helps them to learn the desired response. Later he uses the clicker to mark when they position their arm correctly, flick their wrist correctly, and so on. The clicker marks each component skill needed to reliably make good throws. Over the years, Dr. Levy found this technique worked better than any other method.

When the American Board of Orthopedic Surgeons encouraged medical schools, like Dr. Levy's, to improve how they taught students to execute complex surgical techniques (e.g., tying sutures inside a human body), Dr. Levy thought of clicker training. He sought the help of Karen Pryor, the behavior analyst who, in the 1960s, made groundbreaking advances in conditioned reinforcement while training porpoises. Together, they developed a clicker-training program that proved more effective in establishing expert performances than the usual methods of teaching (Levy et al., 2016).

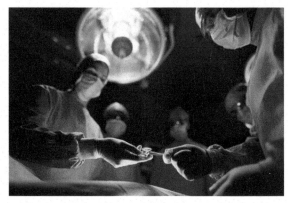

Source: Shannon Fagan/Getty Images.

Levy, when interviewed in 2018 by the *Hidden Brain* podcast, noted that clicker training has another, less easily quantified, advantage – using a clicker keeps the learner focused on the performance. Using verbal praise and criticism, the traditional teaching method, continuously draws the medical student's attention away from the surgical technique and places it on the teacher's evaluation of the student's competency as a person. Clickers, Levy noted, are "language free...baggage free...I'm quiet, you're quiet; we're just learning a skill." Learners find clicker feedback less disruptive and more fair than verbal feedback (Herron et al., 2018). A simple click keeps things objective, and better surgeons are the result.

Using clickers to teach humans to execute complex behaviors has only begun to be studied, but the results are encouraging. Clicking *marks* correct responses at the moment they occur. This improves the skilled performances of athletes (Stokes et al., 2010), dancers (Quinn et al., 2015), and individuals with autism as they learn important life skills (Wertalik & Kubina, 2018). They might also prove effective with patients in physical therapy, when learning to do the exercise their physical therapist is teaching. Here it is important that the exercise be done exactly correctly, lest the patient further injure themselves, or not benefit from the exercise as they should. Perhaps you too will think of an application of clicker training to positively influence human behavior.

Reading Quiz 2

1. The four principles of effective conditioned reinforcement very closely parallel the four principles of effective _____ conditioning.
2. The first of these principles of effective conditioned reinforcement is that the _____ reinforcer needs to be effective, that is, something that will readily reinforce behavior.
3. One strategy for arranging an effective conditioned reinforcer is to arrange lots of different backup reinforcers and let the individual decide which one they want. When a conditioned reinforcer (like a token) is exchangeable for more than one backup reinforcer, we refer to it as a _____ conditioned reinforcer.
4. According to the second principle of effective conditioned reinforcement, we will ensure that our conditioned reinforcer is highly _____, that is, it stands out and will be easily noticed when it occurs.

5. The conditioned reinforcer, when delivered immediately after the desired behavior, _____ the response that produced the reinforcer. This helps the individual learn which response fulfilled the response→ backup reinforcer contingency, especially when the backup reinforcer is delayed.

6. Effective conditioned reinforcers signal a large _____ _____ to the delivery of a backup reinforcer. This is the third principle of effective conditioned reinforcement.

7. The final principle of effective conditioned reinforcement is that the conditioned reinforcer should be the only stimulus signaling the delay reduction to the backup reinforcer. If another stimulus already signals this, then the token, points, click-click, and so on will be _____. The individual already knows the delay has been reduced. As a result, the stimulus we want to function as a conditioned reinforcer will not acquire this function.

Shaping

In Extra Box 1, conditioned reinforcers were used to make a small change in an elephant's behavior. When the elephant's trunk made a small movement toward, and then touched the target, the conditioned reinforcer was delivered; that is, the trainer blew the whistle and then gave the elephant a slice of apple. Once this target-touching behavior was mastered, the target was moved further away. Now the elephant had to do a little bit more to earn the conditioned reinforcer (and the apple slice). Because the trainer asked for only a little more than before, the elephant succeeded in touching the target. This general strategy of asking for just a little bit more and gradually moving behavior toward a desired behavior is called "shaping." Here is a more technical definition:

Shaping: *Differential reinforcement of successive approximations to a terminal behavior.*

Let's dissect this definition so readers will fully understand shaping. First, you will recall from Chapter 7 that *differential reinforcement* involves reinforcing the desired behavior and extinguishing previously reinforced behaviors. For the elephant, the desired behavior is touching the trunk to the target stick. All other apple-seeking behaviors (e.g., trying to take apples from the trainer's bucket) are extinguished.

Second, the *terminal behavior* is the performance you ultimately want. The trainer ultimately wants the elephant to walk to the target whenever and wherever it is presented. However, the trainer knows that if she asks for this performance at the beginning of training, the elephant will not be able to do it. If this happens, training fails, and the behavior of both the trainer and elephant is extinguished. Recalling that operant extinction can induce negative emotional behavior (Chapter 7), shaping can help to keep a 5-ton pachyderm calm and contented throughout the training session.

Finally, shaping involves differentially reinforcing *successive approximations* to the terminal behavior. That is, we begin by reinforcing a first approximation of the terminal behavior; something simple, something we anticipate the elephant can already do. If the target is placed just an inch away from the trunk, the elephant will probably touch it. When the target is touched, the conditioned reinforcer is delivered and then the backup reinforcer is provided.

The conditioned reinforcer marks the correct response and signals a delay reduction to the apple. All other apple-seeking behaviors are extinguished.

Once the first approximation is mastered, shaping continues through a series of successive approximations of the terminal behavior. The next approximation is taking a step to reach the target. When the step is taken and the target is touched, the conditioned reinforcer marks the response and the backup reinforcer follows. The previous approximation, reaching for the target without taking a step, is extinguished, as are all other apple-seeking behaviors. Once the second approximation is mastered, the trainer moves on to the third (two steps must be taken to reach the target) and so on, until the terminal behavior is mastered. See Extra Box 2 for an interesting example of using shaping with another nonhuman animal species.

EXTRA BOX 2:   SHAPING ANIMAL BEHAVIOR ON THE FARM

Shaping has great potential in farm settings, but to date it is infrequently used. An exception to this rule is a delightful study reported by Ferguson and Rosales-Ruiz (2001). They worked with quarter horses who were afraid to enter a horse-trailer used for transportation. Prior to the study, when the horses refused to enter the trailer their handlers used ropes and whips, sometimes for more than an hour, to force the horses in.

Ferguson and Rosales-Ruiz knew there was a better way – shaping. First, they established the sound of a clicker as a conditioned reinforcer. A variety of treats (Principle 1) were delivered a few seconds after the salient sound of a clicker (Principle 2). Clicks signaled a delay reduction to the backup reinforcers (Principle 3) and clicks were the only stimulus that signaled when treats would be given (Principle 4).

The terminal behavior was voluntarily walking into the trailer, and the first approximation of this was touching a target (a red potholder) placed close to the horse's nose. Touching the potholder earned a click and then a treat. Each "click-click" *marked* the correct response at the moment it occurred. All other behaviors were extinguished.

The second approximation was to touch the target regardless of its location, for example, on the ground, on a fencepost, and in a tree. Walking to and touching the potholder produced a click-click and, a few seconds later, a treat. All other treat-seeking behaviors were extinguished.

By gradually placing the potholder further inside the trailer, differential reinforcement of successive approximations was used to teach the horses the terminal behavior – voluntarily entering the trailer without incident. This outcome illustrates the potential of shaping to improve the way we interact with farm animals.

Source: Jupiterimages/Getty Images

Shaping Human Behavior

Shaping is an effective way to help humans learn complex terminal behaviors, that is, those requiring skills that make it impossible for the novice to obtain a reinforcer. For example, if the terminal behavior is winning on the final level of Plants vs. Zombies, there is no chance that a novice can emit the complex responses necessary to kill all the zombies encountered in that final level. They simply come too fast and the novice lacks the skills to build an adequate defense. This is where shaping proves so useful. Shaping can transform the novice player into a zombie-killing machine.

Source: Electronic Arts Inc.

Before dissecting how Plants vs. Zombies was designed using shaping, imagine what would happen if the novice player's first experience with the game was the extreme challenge of the final level. The outcome would be disastrous. The brain-hungry zombies would quickly overrun the house and the reinforcer (defeating the level) would not be obtained. No matter how many times the novice tried to beat the final level, his game-playing behavior would be extinguished.

The designers of Plants vs. Zombies understood that extinction induces negative emotions (frustration, sadness, anger), so they designed the game to reinforce successive approximations of the terminal behavior. That is, they arranged lots of conditioned reinforcers for behaviors that were mere approximations of the skills needed to win when playing the final level.

If you've played the game, you may remember that the first approximation taught to novice players is clicking on a seed packet (they appear in the upper left corner of the screen). This response produces a conditioned reinforcer – the sound of the packet being torn open. This sound *marks* the correct response and signals a small delay reduction to the backup reinforcer – killing all the zombies and winning the first level.

The next approximation is to click suns as they fall from the sky. The first time this is done, another auditory conditioned reinforcer marks the response and points are added to a counter. In this token economy, points (generalized reinforcers) may be exchanged for many different backup reinforcers – zombie-killing plants, zombie-blocking obstacles, and sunflowers that produce more suns/points. All told, the game differentially reinforces thousands of successive approximations before the terminal behavior is acquired. When framed as a protracted learning task in which thousands of new skills must be acquired, it sounds tedious. But because the game designers so effectively used shaping, we use other words to describe the game – "fun," "engaging," and "a place where I lose all track of time."

Shaping and Flow

When people play a video game like Plants vs. Zombies, they sometimes say they feel a sense of "flow." **Flow** is defined as *a state in which one feels immersed in a rewarding activity and in* *which we lose track of time and self* (Nakamura & Csikszentmihalyi, 2014). While flow is commonly experienced when playing an immersive video game, it can also be achieved in nongaming situations. For example, musicians report being in flow while playing a song. Rock climbers describe the flow state achieved when on the wall. Reading a page-turning novel can also produce a feeling of flow.

Because feeling in flow is a pleasant state in which we are engrossed in the task at hand, we might ask when this state is most likely to the experienced. This question is consistent with the first goal of behavior analysis – predicting behavior. Some of the best research on flow was conducted by Dr. Mihaly Csikszentmihalyi (pronounced "Me-high Cheek-sent-me-high"). In one of his studies, participants wore pagers that interrupted them at unpredictable times during the day. At each interruption, participants recorded what they were doing and how they felt. Csikszentmihalyi found that flow was related to response-reinforcer contingencies.

To get a sense of this, consider a rock climber engaged in an afternoon ascent. Will she experience flow? Csikszentmihalyi's research suggests she will if the response-reinforcer contingencies naturally imposed by the rock face have three characteristics. *First,* flow will occur if the climb is neither too easy nor too difficult for the skills of our climber. If she has chosen a climb that is too easy, she will be bored. Conversely, if the climb is too difficult, she will feel frustrated, angry, and so on as her climbing fails to produce reinforcers (extinction). Flow will be achieved only in the "Goldilocks zone," where the challenge is neither too difficult nor too easy. It needs to be "just right" for her skill level. The responses required to meet the reinforcement contingency will require her complete attention.

Source: zhukovvvlad/Shutterstock.com

Second, our climber is more likely to experience flow if the rock wall naturally arranges what Csikszentmihalyi called "proximal goals." A proximal goal on the wall might be making it past a difficult set of holds and crossing over to the next section of the climb. This consequence signals a delay reduction to the ultimate reinforcer – getting to the top of the wall. Therefore, a "proximal goal" can be thought of as a contingency arranging a conditioned reinforcer along the way.

Third, the flow state will be achieved if the wall provides immediate task-relevant consequences for the climber's behavior. Said another way, when a skillful or unskillful response occurs, she needs to know that right away. This immediate feedback is provided when the climber either loses a toehold (the immediate, contingent consequence of an unskillful response) or makes it to the next hold (contingent on a skillful response). These consequences are immediate; they *mark* the exact response that produced the outcome.

What does flow have to do with shaping? Although the climber is not a novice, she is constantly improving her skills. If she chooses to climb on a Goldilocks-zone rock wall, the contingencies inherent to the wall will differentially reinforce skillful responses that she finds challenging, but not impossible. Less skillful responses are not reinforced with progress up the wall. These skillful responses are approximations of the terminal skillset she desires – a skillset that would allow her to climb a wall that today she would find nothing but frustrating. Effective shaping, whether imposed naturally by a good rock wall or arranged artificially by a skilled video game designer or behavior analyst, will meet the learner where they are — offering challenges, immediately reinforcing skillful responses, and arranging conditioned reinforcers along the way. When achieved, the learner improves or acquires new skills, while achieving a state of flow in which all sense of time and self is lost.

Principles of Effective Shaping

Whether you are a video game designer or a behavior analyst working with an individual with an intellectual disability, shaping is a useful tool for teaching new skills. When done right, shaping can produce an engaging sense of flow. It's a win-win – the teacher succeeds and the learner enjoys the learning experience. In service of achieving this ideal outcome, Table 8.2 lists **six principles of effective shaping**. Let's walk through the table by seeing how the designers of Plants vs. Zombies used these principles while developing their game. Later, we'll show you how to use shaping on your own.

Shaping **Principle 1** asks us to provide an objective definition of the terminal behavior. That is, describe the terminal behavior in enough detail that it can be objectively measured. The terminal behavior in Plants vs. Zombies – beating the final level of the game – involves a lot of skills that the game shapes up over time. Let's simplify things by focusing on just one of these skills – the expert player clicks things *quickly*. For example, when suns fall from the sky, the expert clicks them immediately after they appear. Likewise, when a desired seed packet is available, the expert player clicks it right away. When playing at the highest levels of the game, clicking slowly is disastrous – brains!

Shaping **Principle 2** asks us to evaluate what the novice player can currently do and how that falls short of the terminal behavior. The designers of Plants vs. Zombies knew that novice players could click things – after all, they clicked the app that loaded the game. However, novices do not normally click apps the millisecond they become available.

Figure 8.3 shows a hypothetical frequency distribution of clicking speeds of a novice player. The x-axis shows the range of speeds, from very slow on the left to very fast on the right. The y-axis shows how often the novice player clicks at each of these speeds. Most of the player's clicks are in the slower range, with only an occasional click happening very quickly.

The dotted line shows how quickly the player will have to click things in order to win at the highest level of the game. This is the speed of the terminal behavior. Clearly, the current

Table 8.2 Principles of effective shaping

1. Objectively define the terminal behavior.

2. Along what dimension does the learner's current behavior fall short of the terminal behavior?

3. When mapping out the sequence of successive approximations, ensure that each one is neither too easy nor too difficult.

4. Differential reinforcement: Reinforce the current response approximation and extinguish everything else, including old response approximations.

5. Be sure the learner has mastered each response approximation before advancing to the next one.

6. If the next approximation proves too difficult (extinction), lower the reinforcement criterion until responding is earning reinforcers again.

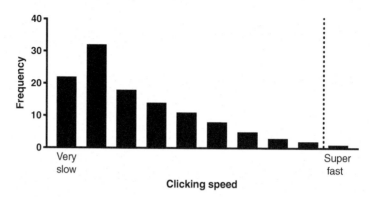

Figure 8.3 A frequency distribution shows how frequently (how often) different speeds of button-clicking responses are happening. On the far left of the x-axis, button pressing is very slow and as we move to the right, the clicking speeds are faster. The height of each bar shows how often that clicking speed is happening. At present the player mostly clicks buttons slowly. The dotted line shows the terminal behavior – the speed needed to win on the final level of Plants vs. Zombies.

speed falls short. Identifying this gap between current and terminal performance helps the designers identify a dimension along which behavior needs to change – it needs to get faster (reduced latency between stimulus and response). Once this dimension is identified, the game designer can set the reinforcement contingency for the first response approximation.

Shaping **Principle 3** provides advice for setting the reinforcement contingencies – the response approximations should challenge the player, but not so much that reinforcers cannot be obtained. Throughout shaping we need to hit that Goldilocks zone in which reinforcers can be earned, but only if the performance is a little better than before. If we set the reinforcement contingency at the superfast level shown in Figure 8.3, the player would never beat the level; that is, they would never obtain critical reinforcers in the game. Operant extinction would leave these players feeling frustrated and angry, and they would, in turn, leave negative reviews in the app store. Not a good thing if you are trying to make a living in video game design.

The red dashed line in Figure 8.4 shows a reinforcement contingency that is neither too easy nor too difficult. If the player clicks things at least this quickly (anywhere in the reinforcement zone), the reinforcer will be obtained; that is, the player will defeat the zombies and win the level. Clicking slower than that (the extinction zone) is not reinforced. Reinforcing one response and extinguishing other, previously reinforced responses is, of course, *differential reinforcement* – **Principle 4**.

Shaping **Principle 5** suggests we ensure the learner has mastered the current response approximation before moving on to the next one. This is achieved in Plants vs. Zombies by not letting players advance to the next level (where suns will have to be clicked a little faster) until they beat the current level. Beating a level demonstrates the player has mastered the current response approximation.

When mastery is achieved, the red dotted line in Figure 8.4 will be shifted a little further to the right. Clicking at this slightly faster rate will be reinforced, but slower clicking will not. If the individual struggles to obtain reinforcers at this next level, **Principle 6** instructs us to lower the criterion for reinforcement. The new criterion has asked for too much from this learner; the sequence of successive approximations will need to proceed more gradually.

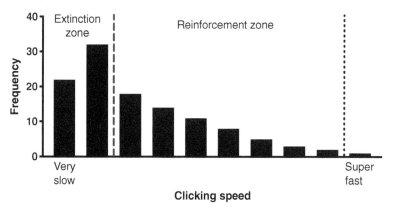

Figure 8.4 The new contingency (red dashed line) will reinforce button clicking if it is faster than those click speeds in the extinction zone.

Plants vs. Zombies follows Principle 6 by constantly monitoring the player's performance during the initial levels. If the player is clicking things too slowly, the game lowers the reinforcement contingency a little. Zombies appear a bit slower, and the level is extended in duration to give the player more practice with the new contingency. By lowering the requirement for reinforcement, the game keeps the reinforcers flowing and prevents the player from encountering extinction. It also gives the player more practice, so they can continue to advance toward the terminal behavior. Keeping the game just a little bit challenging keeps players in flow.

By applying these six principles to the acquisition of skills within their game, the designers of Plants vs. Zombies created one of the most popular video games ever. If you dissect any enormously popular video game, you will find these six principles are closely

followed. Take, for example, Guitar Hero – one of the most widely played games in the 2000s. Its designers identified the terminal behavior (rapidly pressing fret buttons and the strum bar at precise times, as indicated by scrolling notes on the screen) and began by verbally reinforcing simple response approximations such as pressing the strum bar ("That's right!" says the game's narrator) while pressing each of the fret buttons ("Sounding good!").

Source: The 5th Ape/Flickr/CC BY 2.0

After the novice player mastered these first approximations, the game presented a meticulously designed series of songs, each slightly more difficult than the last one. These successive approximations of the terminal guitar-playing performance allowed players to earn thousands of reinforcers along the way. These reinforcers included clean-sounding musical chords, audience excitement (the Rock meter going into the green zone), points (another token economy), and access to new songs; the latter provided only after the prior response approximation (song) is mastered. Like Plants vs. Zombies, Guitar Hero players lost themselves in the game – flow – and the game's designers were rewarded handsomely for following the six principles of effective shaping.

Try It at Home: The Shaping Game

For decades, students have honed their shaping skills by playing the "shaping game." The object of the game is to shape a novel terminal behavior (something the player doesn't normally do), but without telling the player what they're supposed to do. For example, the teacher might choose "stand on a chair" as the terminal behavior. Then, using the six principles of shaping, the teacher reinforces successive approximations (e.g., walking toward the chair) until the player emits the terminal behavior.

If you want to play, identify a player and ask them to leave the room. The remaining people are the teachers, but only one of them will deliver the conditioned reinforcer – a "click-click" from a clicker works well, as it saliently marks the correct response approximation when it occurs. Each click-click signals a reduction in the delay to the backup reinforcer – the player wins the game by emitting the terminal behavior.

While the player is out of the room, the teachers decide what terminal behavior they want the player to do. Think of something fun, but not anything insensitive, dangerous, or so complex that the player will never get it – you want the game to be fun, safe, and brief. Principle 1 invites the teachers to objectively define the terminal behavior. Objectivity is important – the teachers should all agree when the behavior has happened (the player is standing upright with both feet on the seat of the chair) and when it has not (anything short of this).

While the player is still out of the room, consider shaping Principle 2: What does the player normally do in this room, and how does that fall short of the terminal behavior? The player normally doesn't stand on the chair, so normal behavior falls short in several ways: they don't usually approach this chair without sitting in it, they never lift a leg onto the seat of the chair, and they never climb up on it.

The next step is to map out the sequence of successive approximations of the terminal behavior. In doing so, remember shaping Principle 3 – the response approximations should be neither too easy, nor too difficult. You want the learner to have fun. If they are not earning conditioned reinforcers (extinction) they will become frustrated, embarrassed, and so on. Here are some approximations that usually prove neither too easy nor too difficult:

Approximation 1:	Reinforce (click-click) as soon as the player orients toward the chair.
Approximation 2:	Reinforce taking one step toward the chair.
Approximation 3:	Reinforce taking two steps toward the chair.
Approximation 4:	Reinforce arriving at the chair.
Approximation 5:	While the learner is close to the chair, reinforce any upward movement of a leg or foot.
Approximation 6:	While the learner is close to the chair, reinforce lifting a foot completely off the ground.
Approximation 7:	Reinforce placing a foot on the seat of the chair.
Terminal behavior:	Reinforce standing on the seat of the chair.

Now invite the player back into the room and begin by telling them that the "click-click" sound is the reinforcer and that they should try to get as many of these as they can. Also instruct them that when they earn a reinforcer, they need to walk to the teacher and touch the clicker. This resets the behavior after each reinforcer and allows the player to do something *active* each time the response approximation is emitted. The teacher wants to reinforce an action – *arriving* at the chair (Approximation 4) instead of inaction – standing by the chair.

With these instructions given, the game begins. The player has no idea what they are supposed to do, and the teachers are forbidden from giving any hints – verbal or otherwise. Wait for the first response approximation to occur and provide the "click-click" immediately. All other behaviors, no matter how funny, are not reinforced. Differential reinforcement (Principle 4) provides the immediate task-relevant consequences recommended by Csikszentmihalyi to promote the feeling of flow.

Once the player masters the first response approximation (Principle 5), move on to the next one. As always, differentially reinforce this new approximation and nothing else, including prior approximations. If, at any point during the game, the learner is not earning reinforcers, then shaping Principle 6 is invoked: This new approximation is too difficult – start giving reinforcers when the learner emits some of the old approximations. Remember, you don't want the learner's behavior to undergo extinction. When this happens, the game loses its fun and its flow.

Reading Quiz 3

1. Shaping involves the _____ reinforcement of successive approximations to a terminal behavior.
2. Recalling from Chapter 7, when we differentially reinforce behavior, we will _____ a desired behavior and _____ another, previously reinforced behavior.
3. Within this definition of shaping, the _____ behavior refers to the ultimate goal – where we ultimately want the behavior to stabilize, at an adaptive level, for example, zero cigarettes smoked per day.
4. When shaping is done right, the individual who is acquiring new skills, or perfecting old ones, can experience a state of _____. In this state, the individual is so into the task that they lose all sense of time, and all sense of self.
5. The third principle of effective shaping is very important in achieving that sense of flow. The reinforcement contingency should require a response that is neither too _____, nor too _____. It should fall in the so-called Goldilocks zone.
6. According to shaping principle 5, a well-designed video game will not let the player advance to a higher level until they have _____ the skill being taught at the lower level. Letting the player advance too quickly sets them up for failure – operant extinction.

Automating Shaping: Percentile Schedules of Reinforcement

Effective video game designers build the six principles of effective shaping into their programs. These automated shaping routines are highly complex, and they require thousands of hours of programming and testing. Behavior analysts working in applied settings don't have the resources to build such complex systems. Fortunately, the **percentile schedule of reinforcement** offers *a simple automated training technique incorporating the six principles of* *effective shaping.* Behavior analysts have used percentile schedules of reinforcement to improve academic performance (Athens et al., 2007; Freeland & Noell, 2002) and social interactions among children with disabilities (Hall et al., 2009) and to reduce cigarette smoking (Lamb et al., 2010).

Let's illustrate how you could use a percentile schedule to increase your daily activity levels. If you are like most people, you've tried to increase your activity level. You know that being active is important for your health, and you may have gone so far as making a new-year's resolution, and "committed" to it by buying a gym membership or a fitness-tracking watch. Alas, after a few weeks of over exerting yourself, you are sore, exhausted, and dreading the thought of going back to the gym. Feeling like a failure, you are not a bit healthier.

Perhaps the problem is not with you, but with the method used to encourage more activity. Rather than trying to drastically increase your exercise, what if you took a shaping approach to becoming more active. It took you a long time to get *out* of shape, so what if you accepted the fact that it will take you a long time to develop better habits to get back into shape. Shaping takes time, but it has the benefit of avoiding soreness, injury, and exhaustion.

To illustrate how a percentile schedule of reinforcement works we will walk through a fictional case: Roan wants to increase her fitness level, so she bought a fitness tracker and objectively defined her terminal behavior (Principle 1): 12,500 steps per day.

Next, Roan collects baseline data by wearing the tracker for 10 days. These data are plotted in the top panel of Figure 8.5; ignore the dashed red line for now. The dimension along which Roan's baseline activity falls short of her goal is frequency – she's not getting enough steps per day (Principle 2).

Source: StockSnap/Pixabay

Roan's supportive partner wants to provide a small reinforcer (e.g., "I'm proud of you") each day that Roan makes progress. To determine when these reinforcers should, and should not, be provided, Roan will let the percentile schedule set the reinforcement contingency. The contingency should be set so it is neither too easy nor too difficult to earn a reinforcer (Principle 3). Roan chooses the 60th percentile of her current performance as the level separating the reinforcement zone from the extinction zone.[3] The red line in the top panel of Figure 8.5 illustrates this 60th percentile. If tomorrow's daily step count is at or above the red line, Roan's partner will provide the reinforcer. If it's below the line, then the reinforcer will be withheld (Principle 4).

You probably have some experience with percentiles. Your ACT and SAT scores were interpreted using percentiles. If you scored at the 50th percentile, then you scored right in the middle of those who took the test – half the people did better than you and half did worse. If you scored at the 60th percentile, then 40% of the people did better than you and 60% did worse. Applying this to Roan's baseline data, at the 60th percentile, 4 of the 10 data points are above the 60th percentile and the remaining 6 are below the line.

With his modest goal in mind, Roan resolves tomorrow to take a few more steps than normal, but she's not going to over exert herself. As shown in the middle panel of Figure 8.5, Roan's first day goes well; she met her goal (and earns the reinforcer). Not only does her partner offer words of praise, Roan feels good about herself for having met her goal.

Tomorrow's goal is selected automatically by the percentile schedule of reinforcement. As before, it takes the 60th percentile of Roan's last 10 days. That means it includes today's data (the filled data point) and it tosses out the oldest data point, recorded on the first day of

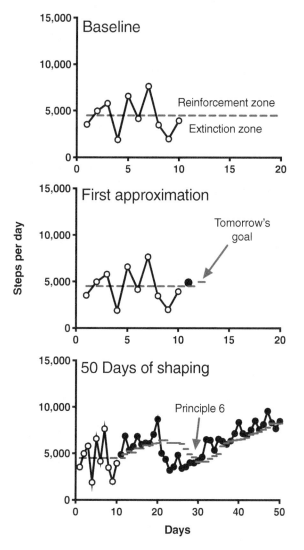

Figure 8.5 Hypothetical step-count data collected during 10 day of baseline (top panel), on the first day of the intervention (center panel), and on the remaining days of the intervention (bottom panel).

baseline. Note how tomorrow's goal is only slightly higher than todays. The percentile schedule automates Principle 5 – it "decides" when the learner has mastered the response approximation and when it's time to advance to the next one.

The bottom panel of Figure 8.5 shows how Roan did over the first 50 days of the shaping-based intervention. There are two things to notice. First, the percentile schedule continues to very gradually increase the reinforcement contingency as Roan masters each response approximation. Second, consistent with Principle 6, when Roan is struggling to earn reinforcers, the percentile schedule automatically lowers the reinforcement criterion. That is, it lowers the level separating the reinforcement zone from the extinction zone.

After 50 days, Roan has made some progress, but she is still a long way from her ultimate goal – 12,500 steps per day. This could be discouraging, but Roan has been earning reinforcers during most of this time. These bits of praise from her partner and her own improved self-esteem keep her upbeat about her chances of continued success. It may take Roan another 4–5 months before she is reliably meeting her exercise goal. Over those months, she will devise new ways to change her daily routine, so she can get the steps she needs (e.g., she may decide to sell her car and walk to work).

Percentile schedules show great potential in therapeutic settings. Several studies suggest they can help patients smoke less (Lamb et al., 2004, 2010), exercise more (Adams et al., 2013, 2017; Joyner et al., 2019; Kurti & Dallery, 2013; Valbuena et al., 2015), and eat a healthier diet (Jones et al., 2014; Joyner et al., 2017). One of the larger of these studies reported that percentile schedules helped obese individuals increase their daily activity levels over a 4-month period (Adams et al., 2017). If you would like to gradually change some dimension of your behavior, you might give the percentile schedule of reinforcement a try.

Summary

This chapter discussed the differences between primary and conditioned reinforcers. Primary reinforcers will work without the individual learning that these consequences are reinforcing; that is not true of conditioned reinforcers. Through Pavlovian conditioning, the individual has to learn that a conditioned reinforcer signals a delay reduction to a backup reinforcer. For humans, everyday conditioned reinforcers include money, movie tickets, and messages on your phone that say "Your order has been placed. Your new shoes will arrive in 2 days." Each of these consequences of operant behavior signal a reduction in the delay until you get the backup reinforcer (e.g., a movie or a pair of shoes).

Conditioned reinforcers have proven effective in promoting adaptive behavior in a wide variety of therapeutic settings. For example, the token economy has been used to help psychiatric patients, juvenile delinquents, and substance-dependent individuals to change their behavior in life-altering directions. Because conditioned reinforcers are such an effective tool of behavior change, it is important to understand how best to arrange them effectively. This chapter provided four principles for arranging effective conditioned reinforcers, and they parallel the principles of effective Pavlovian conditioning.

Conditioned reinforcers have also been used to change the way humans interact with animals. Where the prior generation thought that prodding a circus elephant into motion was an acceptable practice, today we revile such treatment because we know how operant conditioning and conditioned reinforcement can promote a cooperative, voluntary relation between, for example, zookeepers and the animals they care for.

Sometimes we need to teach a new behavior or move an existing behavior in a desired direction. Reinforcing a series of successive approximations of the terminal behavior – shaping – can promote such learning and engagement. Indeed, video game programmers use principles of shaping to give their players a feeling of "flow" while they play the game. The programmers build their game so that it continuously reinforces performing a little better than normal, while being careful to not ask for so much that operant extinction is the result. Whether you want to program your own video game or enrich your pet's life by teaching it a new trick, you will find this chapter's principles of effective shaping to be useful in those endeavors.

These principles of shaping are automated by the percentile schedule of reinforcement (Galbicka, 1994). If you want to gradually change an important dimension of your own behavior (e.g., eating a little better, studying a little more), then you might consider using the percentile schedule of reinforcement in service of those goals. Taking a shaping approach to these difficult to change behaviors may be the difference between long-term success (shaping) and short-term failure (trying to change everything at once). But don't take our word for it. Give it a try!

Answers to Reading Quiz Questions

Reading Quiz 1

1. primary
2. conditioned
3. Pavlovian
4. backup
5. token economy
6. good behavior

Reading Quiz 2

1. Pavlovian
2. backup
3. generalized
4. salient
5. marks
6. delay reduction
7. redundant

Reading Quiz 3

1. differential
2. reinforce; extinguish
3. terminal
4. flow
5. easy; difficult
6. mastered

Notes

1. Primary reinforcers are sometimes referred to as "unconditioned reinforcers"; the two terms mean the same thing.
2. If you have already read Chapter 12, then you will know that a bucket full of tickets at the pizza gaming center also functions as a discriminative stimulus (S^D). The bucket of tickets not only signals a delay reduction to candy and toys, it also increases the probability of an operant behavior (ticket exchanging behavior) because it is reinforced with access to candy and toys. Because discriminative stimuli signal delay reductions to the backup reinforcer, they can also function as conditioned reinforcers if one arranges the *IF* behavior → *THEN* S^D contingency. For example, if you had a magic button that turned the traffic light green (an S^D for driving forward), then you would press that button (operant behavior) often. In sum, nonhuman animals and humans will engage in operant behavior to produce an S^D because it functions as a conditioned reinforcer.
3. Spreadsheets like Microsoft Excel will calculate percentiles for you. You can also search online for a free percentile calculator.

References

Adams, M. A., Hurley, J. C., Todd, M., Bhuiyan, N., Jarrett, C. L., Tucker, W. J., … Angadi, S. S. (2017). Adaptive goal setting and financial incentives: A 2 × 2 factorial randomized controlled trial to increase adults' physical activity. *BMC Public Health*, *17*(1), 1–16. doi:10.1186/s12889-017-4197-8

Adams, M. A., Sallis, J. F., Norman, G. J., Hovell, M. F., Hekler, E. B., & Perata, E. (2013). An adaptive physical activity intervention for overweight adults: A randomized controlled trial. *PLoS ONE*, *8*, 12. doi:10.1371/journal.pone.0082901

Andrade, L. F., & Hackenberg, T. D. (2017). Substitution effects in a generalized token economy with pigeons. *Journal of the Experimental Analysis of Behavior*, *107*(1), 123–135. doi:10.1002/jeab.231

Athens, E. S., Vollmer, T. R., & St. Peter Pipkin, C. C. (2007). Shaping academic task engagement with percentile schedules. *Journal of Applied Behavior Analysis*, *40*(3), 475–488. doi:10.1901/jaba.2007.40-475

Ayllon, T., & Azrin, N. H. (1965). The measurement and reinforcement of behavior of psychotics. *Journal of the Experimental Analysis of Behavior*, *8*(6), 357–383. doi:10.1901/jeab.1965.8-357

Barrish, H. H., Saunders, M., & Wolf, M. M. (1969). Good behavior game: Effects of individual contingencies for group consequences on disruptive behavior in a classroom. *Journal of Applied Behavior Analysis*, *2*(2), 119–124. doi:10.1901/jaba.1969.2-119

Becraft, J. L., & Rolider, N. U. (2015). Reinforcer variation in a token economy. *Behavioral Interventions*, *30*(2), 157–165. doi:10.1002/bin.1401

Bowman-Perrott, L., Burke, M. D., Zaini, S., Zhang, N., & Vannest, K. (2016). Promoting positive behavior using the good behavior game. *Journal of Positive Behavior Interventions*, *18*(3), 180–190. doi:10.1177/1098300715592355

Davis, D. R., Kurti, A. N., Skelly, J. M., Redner, R., White, T. J., & Higgins, S. T. (2016). A review of the literature on contingency management in the treatment of substance use disorders, 2009–2014. *Preventive Medicine*, *92*, 36–46. doi:10.1016/j.ypmed.2016.08.008

DeFulio, A., Yankelevitz, R., Bullock, C., & Hackenberg, T. D. (2014). Generalized conditioned reinforcement with pigeons in a token economy. *Journal of the Experimental Analysis of Behavior*, *102*(1), 26–46. doi:10.1002/jeab.94

Fantino, E. (1969). Choice and rate of reinforcement. *Journal of the Experimental Analysis of Behavior*, *12*(5), 723–730. doi:10.1901/jeab.1969.12-723

Fantino, E. (1977). Conditioned reinforcement: Choice and information. In W. K. Honig & J. E. Staddon (Eds.), *Handbook of operant behavior* (pp. 313–339). Engelwood Cliffs, NJ: Prentice-Hall.

Fantino, E., Preston, R. A., & Dunn, R. (1993). Delay reduction: Current status. *Journal of the Experimental Analysis of Behavior, 60*(1), 159–169. https://doi.org/10.1901/jeab.1993.60-159

Fantino, E., & Silberberg, A. (2010). Revisiting the role of bad news in maintaining human observing behavior. *Journal of the Experimental Analysis of Behavior, 93*(2), 157–170. doi:10.1901/jeab.2010.93-157

Ferguson, D. L., & Rosales-Ruiz, J. (2001). Loading the problem loader: The effects of target training and shaping on trailer-loading behavior of horses. *Journal of Applied Behavior Analysis, 34*(4), 409–423. doi:10.1901/jaba.2001.34-409

Flower, A., McKenna, J. W., Bunuan, R. L., Muething, C. S., & Vega, R. (2014). Effects of the good behavior game on challenging behaviors in school settings. *Review of Educational Research, 84*(4), 546–571. doi:10.3102/0034654314536781

Freeland, J. T., & Noell, G. H. (2002). Programming for maintenance: An investigation of delayed intermittent reinforcement and common stimuli to create indiscriminate contingencies. *Journal of Behavioral Education, 11*(1), 5–18. doi:10.1023/A:1014329104102

Galbicka, G. (1994). Shaping in the twenty-first century: Moving percentile schedules into applied settings. *Journal of Applied Behavior Analysis, 27*(4), 739–760. doi:10.1901/jaba.1994.27-739

Galbraith, L. A., & Normand, M. P. (2017). Step it up! Using the good behavior game to increase physical activity with elementary school students at recess. *Journal of Applied Behavior Analysis, 50*(4), 856–860. doi:10.1002/jaba.402

Hackenberg, T. D. (2018). Token reinforcement: Translational research and application. *Journal of Applied Behavior Analysis, 51*(2), 393–435. doi:10.1002/jaba.439

Hall, S. S., Maynes, N. P., & Reiss, A. L. (2009). Using percentile schedules to increase eye contact in children with fragile X syndrome. *Journal of Applied Behavior Analysis, 42*(1), 171–176. doi:10.1901/jaba.2009.42-171

Herron, M. A., Lotfizadeh, A. D., & Poling, A. (2018). Using conditioned reinforcers to improve behavior-change skills: Clicker training for practitioners. *Journal of Organizational Behavior Management, 38*(2–3), 172–190. doi:10.1080/01608061.2018.1454874

Jones, B. A., Madden, G. J., Wengreen, H. J., Aguilar, S. S., & Desjardins, E. A. (2014). Gamification of dietary decision-making in an elementary-school cafeteria. *PLoS ONE, 9*(4), e93872. doi:10.1371/journal.pone.0093872

Joyner, D., Wengreen, H., Aguilar, S., & Madden, G. J. (2019). Effects of the FIT game on physical activity in sixth graders: A pilot reversal design intervention study. *JMIR Serious Games, 7*(2), e13051. doi:10.2196/13051

Joyner, D., Wengreen, H. J., Aguilar, S. S., Spruance, L. A., Morrill, B. A., & Madden, G. J. (2017). The FIT game III: Reducing the operating expenses of a game-based approach to increasing healthy eating in elementary schools. *Games for Health Journal, 6*(2), 111–118. doi:10.1089/g4h.2016.0096

Kazdin, A. E. (1981). The token economy. In G. Davies (Ed.), *Psychology in progress* (pp. 59–80). London: Methuen & Co. Ltd.

Kron, R. E. (1967). Instrumental conditioning of nutritive sucking behavior in the newborn. In J. Wortis (Ed.), *Recent advances in biological psychiatry* (pp. 295–300). Boston, MA: Springer New York. doi:10.1007/978-1-4684-8228-7_22

Kurti, A. N., & Dallery, J. (2013). Internet-based contingency management increases walking in sedentary adults. *Journal of Applied Behavior Analysis, 46*(3), 568–581. doi:10.1002/jaba.58

Lamb, R. J., Kirby, K. C., Morral, A. R., Galbicka, G., & Iguchi, M. Y. (2010). Shaping smoking cessation in hard-to-treat smokers. *Journal of Consulting and Clinical Psychology, 78*(1), 62–71. doi:10.1037/a0018323

Lamb, R. J., Morral, A. R., Kirby, K. C., Iguchi, M. Y., & Galbicka, G. (2004). Shaping smoking cessation using percentile schedules. *Drug and Alcohol Dependence, 76*(3), 247–259. doi:10.1016/j.drugalcdep.2004.05.008

Larzelere, R. E., Daly, D. L., Davis, J. L., Chmelka, M. B., Handwerk, M. L., & Town, G. (2004). Outcome evaluation of Girls and Boys Town's family home program. *Education and Treatment of Children, 27*(2), 130–149.

Levy, I. M., Pryor, K. W., & McKeon, T. R. (2016). Is teaching simple surgical skills using an operant learning program more effective than teaching by demonstration? *Clinical Orthopaedics and Related Research*, *474*(4), 945–955. doi:10.1007/s11999-015-4555-8

Moher, C. A., Gould, D. D., Hegg, E., & Mahoney, A. M. (2008). Non-generalized and generalized conditioned reinforcers: Establishment and validation. *Behavioral Interventions*, *23*(1), 13–38. doi:10.1002/bin.253

Nakamura, J., & Csikszentmihalyi, M. (2014). The concept of flow. In M. Csikszentmihalyi (Ed.), *Flow and the foundations of positive psychology* (pp. 239–263). Dordrecht: Springer.

Naour, P. (2009). *E. O Wilson and B. F. Skinner: A dialogue between sociobiology and radical behaviorism.* New York: Springer.

Phelps, E. A., O'Connor, K. J., Gatenby, J. C., Gore, J. C., Grillon, C., & Davis, M. (2001). Activation of the left amygdala to a cognitive representation of fear. *Nature Neuroscience*, *4*(4), 437–441. doi:10.1038/86110

Pryor, K. W. (1973). Behavior and learning in porpoises and whales. *Naturwissenschaften, 60*(9), 412–420. https://doi.org/10.1007/BF00623553

Quinn, M. J., Miltenberger, R. G., & Fogel, V. A. (2015). Using TAGteach to improve the proficiency of dance movements. *Journal of Applied Behavior Analysis*, *48*(1), 11–24. doi:10.1002/jaba.191

Russell, D., Ingvarsson, E. T., Haggar, J. L., & Jessel, J. (2018). Using progressive ratio schedules to evaluate tokens as generalized conditioned reinforcers. *Journal of Applied Behavior Analysis*, *51*(1), 40–52. doi:10.1002/jaba.424

Shahan, T. A., & Cunningham, P. (2015). Conditioned reinforcement and information theory reconsidered. *Journal of the Experimental Analysis of Behavior*, *103*(2), 405–418. doi:10.1002/jeab.142

Shull, R. L., & Lawrence, P. S. (1998). Reinforcement: Schedule performance. In K. M. Lattal & M. Perone (Eds.), *Handbook of research methods in human operant behavior* (pp. 95–129). New York: Plenum.

Skinner, B. F. (1938). *The behavior of organisms: An experimental analysis.* Oxford, UK: Appleton-Century.

Skinner, B. F. (1953). *Science and human behavior.* New York: Macmillan.

Soares, D. A., Harrison, J. R., Vannest, K. J., & McClelland, S. S. (2016). Effect size for token economy use in contemporary classroom settings: A meta-analysis of single-case research. *School Psychology Review*, *45*(4), 379–399. doi:10.17105/SPR45-4.379-399

Sran, S. K., & Borrero, J. C. (2010). Assessing the value of choice in a token system. *Journal of Applied Behavior Analysis*, *43*(3), 553–557. doi:10.1901/jaba.2010.43-553

Stokes, J. V., Luiselli, J. K., Reed, D. D., & Fleming, R. K. (2010). Behavioral coaching to improve offensive line pass-blocking skills of high-school football athletes. *Journal of Applied Behavior Analysis*, *43*(3), 463–472. doi:10.1901/jaba.2010.43-463

Tan, L., & Hackenberg, T. D. (2015). Pigeons' demand and preference for specific and generalized conditioned reinforcers in a token economy. *Journal of the Experimental Analysis of Behavior*, *104*(3), 296–314. doi:10.1002/jeab.181

Urcuioli, P. J., & Kasprow, W. J. (1988). Long-delay learning in the T-maze: Effects of marking and delay-interval location. *Learning and Motivation*, *19*(1), 66–86. doi:10.1016/0023-9690(88)90026-4

Valbuena, D., Miltenberger, R., & Solley, E. (2015). Evaluating an Internet-based program and a behavioral coach for increasing physical activity. *Behavior Analysis: Research and Practice*, *15*(2), 122–138. doi:10.1037/bar0000013

Wertalik, J. L., & Kubina, R. M. (2018). Comparison of TAGteach and video modeling to teach daily living skills to adolescents with autism. *Journal of Behavioral Education, 27*(2), 279–300.

Williams, B. A. (1994). Conditioned reinforcement: Experimental and theoretical issues. *The Behavior Analyst*, *17*(2), 261–285. doi:10.1007/BF03392675

Williams, B. A. (1999). Associative competition in operant conditioning: Blocking the response-reinforcer association. *Psychonomic Bulletin and Review*, *6*(4), 618–623. doi:10.3758/BF03212970

Williams, B. A., & Fantino, E. (1978). Effects on choice of reinforcement delay and conditioned reinforcement. *Journal of the Experimental Analysis of Behavior, 29*(1), 77–86. https://doi.org/10.1901/jeab.1978.29-77

Motivation, Reinforcer Efficacy, and Habit Formation

9

With eight chapters under our collective belts, it is time to take stock of what we know, and what we might do with that knowledge. Chapters 1–3 outlined the philosophical foundations of behavior analysis and the experimental methods most commonly used to advance that science. Chapter 4 discussed Pavlovian learning and emphasized the role this learning plays in our emotions (recall the Little Albert experiment). Chapters 5–8 provided an introduction to operant learning – how reinforcing consequences impact our everyday behaviors, and how behavior analysts have arranged those consequences to positively influence human and animal behavior. For example, we discussed how operant extinction can help to reduce problem behavior, and how combining extinction with reinforcement (differential reinforcement) is useful in replacing problem behavior with prosocial behavior.

These methods and principles are foundational to the behavior analytic approach to behavior change. In this and the next three chapters, we build upon that foundation by discussing additional principles that can further enhance the efficacy of an intervention. One concept critical to this behavior-change agenda is motivation. In this chapter, we begin by questioning the utility of everyday understandings of motivation, replacing them with a more practical approach that looks for motivational variables; that is, environmental and biological variables that can increase or decrease the momentary efficacy of a reinforcer. Examples of these motivation-enhancing and motivation-diminishing variables are provided, as is a discussion of how these variables have been used in clinical settings.

Intertwined with motivation is the motive – the reinforcer. Behavior change is greatly facilitated by identifying an effective reinforcer; a consequence the individual prefers and is "willing" to work for. Two methods for identifying reinforcers – *reinforcer surveys* and *stimulus preference assessments* – are discussed.

An Introduction to Behavior Analysis, First Edition. Gregory J. Madden, Derek D. Reed, and Florence D. DiGennaro Reed.
© 2021 John Wiley & Sons Ltd. Published 2021 by John Wiley & Sons Ltd.

But identifying a potential reinforcer is only half the battle, the other half is optimizing the reinforcer itself, so it has maximum impact. To that end, we discuss four dimensions of a reinforcer that affect its efficacy (contingency, size, quality, and immediacy). When the individual is properly "motivated" and dimensions of the reinforcer are optimized, we are in a better position to have a positive impact on behavior.

Finally, this chapter introduces you to habits – what are they and how are they formed? Habits are behaviors that occur in specific settings, even when our motivation to obtain the reinforcer is low. Those with good habits will exercise, study, and brush their teeth, even if they don't feel like it. Those with bad habits will continue to snack, drink, or smoke, even when they are not hungry, thirsty, or in need of a nicotine hit. Habits are operant behaviors that have shifted from consequence/motivational control to antecedent-stimulus control. That will make more sense later in the chapter. For now, know that behavior-analytic principles, when skillfully deployed, can increase the probability of forming good habits that enhance our physical and mental health.

Everyday Concepts of Motivation

We all have an intuitive sense of what we mean when we hear words like "motivated" or "motivation." For example, we know that motivated students are those who study long hours; they make flashcards while reading textbook chapters, and they earn good grades on their exams. Employees with "high motivation" arrive to work early, they leave after their shift ends, and their productivity is better than other employees with "low motivation." Motivated parents provide their children with love and support, as best they can, within the constraints of their social and economic situation.

Source: Hero Images/Getty images

In each of these examples, there are two ways to interpret "motivation." The first interpretation is that "motivation" is nothing more than a concise (one-word) description of a long-term pattern of behavior. That is, a *motivated* student, employee, or parent is someone who has performed well for weeks, months, or years. This concise description of behavior has utility – it allows us to make *predictions* about human behavior. If Sherri's last employer describes her as "highly motivated," we can be pretty sure that if we hire Sherri, she will work hard for our company too. Thus, if our goal is to predict behavior, this interpretation of "motivation" is pretty useful. It can help us decide whether or not to hire Sherri.

But the other interpretation is more common and, we will argue, less useful. According to this second interpretation, "motivation" is inherent to the individual. It's as if "motivation" is a mental essence existing inside the individual, explaining why they behave the way they do. For example, our job applicant, Sherri, might be described as *having* high motivation. Whatever motivation is, she has a lot of it *and* it's responsible for her vocational success. If we could bottle her motivation and pass it out to our other employees, our company would prosper.

As discussed in Chapter 1 (we know that was a long time ago), behavior analysts reject **mentalistic explanations of behavior.** *Such "explanations" put the cause of behavior in the* *individual's vaguely defined "mind."* Accordingly, high-performing employees like Sherri are assumed to have minds full of motivation, while poor-performing employees have motivational deficits.

One reason to reject mentalistic accounts of behavior is illustrated in Figure 9.1. Here Sherri's exemplary performance at work is explained mentalistically by pointing to her high level of motivation. But a behavior analyst will ask, how do we know that Sherri possesses high motivation? Unfortunately, the only evidence for this is her exemplary performance at work. That's a problem – Sherri's performance is what motivation is supposed to explain. If the only evidence for the cause (motivation) is the effect (performance), then the explanation is circular. Behavior analysts reject circular explanations of behavior.

Another reason to reject mentalistic explanations is revealed when Sherri reports to work for our company but she keeps coming to work late, she isn't completing assignments on time, and she keeps dozing off during important meetings. In a word, she seems to have lost her "motivation." Where did it go? How can she get it back? As long as motivation is conceptualized as a mental essence that causes her actions, these questions cannot be answered. The mentalistic account leaves us powerless to improve Sherri's performance.

Recalling the second goal of behavior analysis – to identify functional variables that may be used to positively influence behavior – we can positively influence Sherri's performance only if we focus on variables that can be turned ON or OFF. Can we turn ON motivation? Not if it is conceptualized as a mental essence. Therefore, behavior analysts focus their efforts primarily on environmental variables that can be turned ON or OFF to positively influence behavior. But they also recognize that biological variables can profoundly affect behavior, and these too may sometimes be turned ON and OFF. Because a mentalistic concept of motivation cannot be turned ON or OFF, behavior analysts reject this everyday conceptualization of motivation.

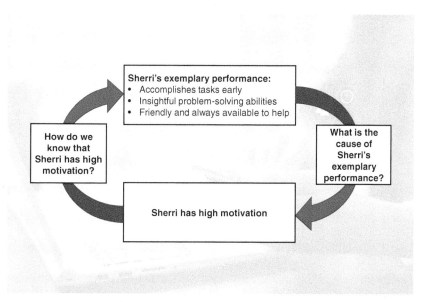

Figure 9.1 An illustration of the circular logic of explaining behavior with a motivation intrinsic to the individual.
Source: Busakorn Pongparnit/Getty Images

From Motivation to Motivating Operations

Conceptualizing motivation as a characteristic of the individual is deeply ingrained in Western culture. But it is at odds with modern behavioral science. Rather than viewing motivation as a mysterious essence existing inside the individual, behavior analysts point to environmental and/or biological factors that, when turned ON or OFF, change how much the individual "wants" the reinforcer and is "willing" to emit operant behavior to get it (Berridge & Robinson, 2003). We refer to those environmental and/or biological factors as "motivating operations" (MOs) (Laraway et al., 2003).

A **motivating operation (MO)** is *an environmental and/or biological event that (1) temporarily alters the value of a specific reinforcer and (2) increases/decreases the probability of behaviors yielding that reinforcer.*[1] Let's walk through this definition systematically. First, an MO is an observable event. It can be objectively measured by behavioral or biological scientists (it is not a mental essence).

Next, the MO temporarily alters the value of a reinforcer. It might *increase* reinforcer value, and it might *decrease* it. To illustrate a temporary increase in reinforcer value, consider a simple MO – food deprivation. Each day we engage in operant food-procuring and eating behaviors. We buy food, we prepare it, we employ utensils to move it into our mouth, we chew it, and we swallow it. These behaviors don't occur all day long. Instead, they occur mostly when our stomach has been deprived of food – an MO. Food deprivation is both an environmental event (no food has passed our lips for 4 hours) and a biological event (our digestive system sends ghrelin [a hormone] to the brain, which makes us feel hungry). When this MO occurs, the reinforcing value of food temporarily increases.

This takes us to the final component of our definition – the MO increases or decreases behaviors yielding that reinforcer. In the case of food deprivation, this MO increases the probability of food-seeking, food-preparing, and food-eating behaviors, as each of these actions are ultimately reinforced when food passes the lips.

Two Kinds of Motivating Operations

Figure 9.2 illustrates that there are two kinds of MOs. Food deprivation is an example of the first kind of MO, the establishing operation. An **establishing operation (EO)** *is an environmental and/or biological event that (1) temporarily increases the value of a specific reinforcer and (2) increases the probability of behaviors yielding that reinforcer.* There are

Motivating operations (MOs)	
Establishing operation (EO)	**Abolishing operation (AO)**
• Temporarily increases the value of a specific reinforcer. • Increases behaviors that yield that reinforcer.	• Temporarily decreases the value of a specific reinforcer. • Decreases behaviors that yield that reinforcer.

Figure 9.2 Two kinds of motivating operations.

many examples of EOs, and we will explore some of them here. For now, just recognize that EOs temporarily (1) increase reinforcer efficacy and (2) increase the behaviors that produce that reinforcer.

The other MO shown in Figure 9.2 is the abolishing operation (AO). An **abolishing operation (AO)** *is an environmental and/or biological event that (1) temporarily decreases the value of a specific reinforcer and (2) decreases the probability of behaviors yielding that reinforcer.* A stomach full of food is an AO that temporarily *decreases* the reinforcing value of food. For example, after eating a whole pizza, a full digestive system sends a different hormone (leptin) to the brain, producing a feeling of satiation that we might describe as "I'm so stuffed." These environmental/biological events temporarily decrease the reinforcing value of pizza. Thus, operant behaviors reinforced with pizza (ordering pizza, making pizza, eating pizza) are, for the moment, less likely to occur.

EXAMPLES OF EOS

Our everyday lives are filled with EOs. Depriving an individual of any primary reinforcer is an EO. For example, when swimming underwater we are deprived of oxygen – a primary reinforcer. This (1) greatly increases the reinforcing efficacy of oxygen and (2) increases the probability of swimming to the surface. Depriving us of water, heat, and so on all have the effects of (1) temporarily increasing the efficacy of the primary reinforcer and (2) increasing behaviors that produce these reinforcers.

Depriving an individual of an operant behavior (and the reinforcer that maintains it) is also an EO. Such *response deprivation* (1) increases the efficacy of access to that behavior/reinforcer and (2) increases the behaviors that will allow access to that behavior/reinforcer. For example, if we normally exercise for 40 minutes each day, then depriving us of exercise will (1) increase the reinforcing efficacy of the freedom to exercise when we want and (2) increase behaviors that will give us that freedom (Premack et al., 1964; Timberlake & Allison, 1974). Indeed, "freedom" might be conceptualized as the removal of restrictions on doing what we want (Skinner, 1971). Such restrictions are EOs that increase the reinforcing efficacy of "freedom" and increase freedom-seeking behaviors.

But not all EOs involve restriction and deprivation. Consider what happens if we eat a tub of salty popcorn. Consuming all that salt does not deprive us of a drink of water, but this EO has the effect of (1) temporarily increasing the reinforcing value of a drink and (2) increasing the probability that we will go to the refrigerator to get a drink. Similarly, getting a sunburn does not deprive us of a bottle of aloe vera, but this EO (1) temporarily increases the reinforcing value of this pain-reducing lotion and (2) increases the probability that we will go to the drug store to buy some. Similarly, a headache is an EO that increases the reinforcing value of pain-reducing medications.

Source: Leon Rafael/Shutterstock.com

A final point that can be made through examples is that not all EOs involve primary reinforcers. The services of a mechanic are not a primary reinforcer, but if your car breaks down on the side of the road, this EO will (1) temporarily increase the reinforcing value of the services of a mechanic and (2) increase the probability that you will call a mechanic for help. Similarly, when the waiter brings the plate of spaghetti that you ordered, this is an EO that (1) temporarily increases the reinforcing value of a fork and napkin and (2) increases the probability that you will ask the waiter for these items.

EXAMPLES OF AOS

As was true of EOs, our everyday lives are littered with AOs. For example, sexual climax functions as an AO because it (1) temporarily decreases the value of sexual stimulation as a reinforcer and (2) decreases sex-seeking behaviors. Similarly, as we sleep at night, a biological AO is occurring that, in the morning, has the effect of (1) temporarily decreasing the value of sleep as a reinforcer (relative to how much we wanted to go to bed last night) and (2) decreases the probability that we will engage in sleep-seeking operant behaviors (going to the bedroom, getting under to covers, finding our teddy bear).

Many prescription and recreational drugs have well-established AO effects. For example, the weight-loss drug *phentermine* is a stimulant (like amphetamine or cocaine) that (1) decreases the reinforcing efficacy of food and (2) decreases food-seeking behaviors (Stafford et al., 1999). Antianxiety medications such as Xanax and Valium also have AO effects. They (1) decrease the value of sex as a reinforcer and (2) decrease sex-seeking behaviors.

Marijuana is widely thought to have an AO effect, reducing smokers' "motivation" to work, study, and so on. Despite this widespread belief, well-controlled human laboratory experiments do not robustly support this assumption (see Hirst et al., 2017 for review). Although we cannot conclude that smoked marijuana has an AO effect, it does function as an EO, increasing (1) the reinforcing value of snack foods and (2) trips to the nearest convenience store to procure them.

Motivating Operations Require Response-Reinforcer Contingency Learning

So, MOs (EOs and AOs) have two effects on behavior: (1) they temporarily alter the efficacy of a reinforcer and (2) they change the probability of behaviors that lead to that reinforcer. The second of these effects is possible only if the individual has learned the response-reinforcer contingency. Let's spell this out with a concrete example.

After a marathon study session, you notice you are starving. A food-deprivation EO has increased the efficacy of food reinforcers. With your stomach gurgling away, you know what you want – food – but how do you get it? The second effect of the food-deprivation EO is an increased probability of food-seeking behaviors (hitting the drive-thru, boiling up some pasta, etc.). But note that these behaviors are highly unlikely to occur if you have not learned the *IF food-seeking behavior* → *THEN food reinforcement* contingency. Food may be a powerful reinforcer, but if you don't know which of the thousands of behaviors you are capable of will actually produce it, you will be stuck in a motivated state – I know what I want, but I don't know how to get it.

As you have no-doubt deduced, an inability to learn response-reinforcer contingencies would be highly maladaptive (Balleine & Dickinson, 1998). If we were incapable of learning which of our many behaviors will address our critical biological needs (nutrition, water, heat, sex), those needs are likely to go unaddressed. When famished we are just as likely to pick our noses as we are to order a pizza. When thirsty we are just as likely to dig a hole and jump in as we are to get a drink of water. An individual who cannot learn response-reinforcer contingencies is unlikely to survive very long.

As reviewed in Chapter 5 (see the section titled "Learning Response-Reinforcer Contingencies"), considerable experimental evidence reveals that humans and nonhuman animals learn response-reinforcer contingencies. For example, if a rat learns to move a metal pole to the left for a food pellet and to move it to the right for a sip of a starchy liquid, does it actually learn these two response-reinforcer contingencies:

IF left → THEN food pellet
IF right → THEN starchy liquid

To find out, we will give the rat a big meal of food pellets before a session in which it will not receive reinforcers for moving the pole. The presession meal is an AO that decreases the reinforcing efficacy of food pellets and should also decrease the probability of moving the pole to the left. But for this decrease to happen, the rat will have to have learned the *IF left → THEN food-pellet* contingency. So, how do rats do? Very well. Following AOs like this, rats will move the pole to the left far less often than they move it to the right (Dickinson et al., 1996). This finding has been replicated many times with different responses, reinforcers, and species, including humans (Balleine & Dickinson, 1998; Colwill & Rescorla, 1985; Hogarth & Chase, 2011).

The Therapeutic Utility of Motivating Operations

Earlier we argued against conceptualizing "motivation" as a mental essence that is responsible for our behavior. This way of thinking does not help those suffering from "motivational deficits" because it fails to identify a functional variable that can be turned ON or OFF in an effort to improve performance. If Sherri is underperforming in her new job, we can *describe* this by saying she "lost her motivation," but this does not tell us how she can get it back.

By contrast, viewing "motivation" as the product of MOs suggests Sherri's motivational decline may be due to an AO – an environmental or a biological factor that has (1) reduced the value of vocational reinforcers (e.g., money, positive feedback from her manager) and (2) reduced Sherri's on-the-job behaviors that normally produce these reinforcers. For example, if Sherri inherited a large sum of money, then her paycheck may no longer have the same value, and her performance at work would reflect this. Alternatively, positive feedback from her new manager may not be as valuable as the feedback she received from her old manager, at the other company. This reduction in reinforcer efficacy could be responsible for her lackluster performance. Improving Sherri's performance may be as simple as assigning her a new manager.

In clinical settings, applied behavior analysts have found EOs and AOs to be especially helpful. For example, when teaching children with autism how to ask for items such as blocks or crayons, researchers have found it useful to constrain the child's access to these items. A child who has not played with blocks for a while will find them much more valuable than if a block-playing session just ended. Block deprivation is an EO because it (1) increases the reinforcing value of blocks and (2) increases the probability that the child with autism will be "motivated" to practice saying, "Can I have the blocks" (O'Reilly et al., 2012).

AOs are also used to improve clinical practice. For example, repeatedly reinforcing the verbal operant "Can I have the blocks" with access to blocks will have a gradual AO effect. That is, each block-playing session decreases the child's "motivation" for another round with the blocks. For this reason, behavior analysts working in clinical settings will often vary the reinforcers presented, thereby reducing the probability that an AO will occur with any single reinforcer (Bowman et al., 1997; Egel, 1981; Milo et al., 2010). This reinforcer-variation strategy works well, as long as the reinforcers used are all highly preferred items. A related strategy for maintaining motivation is to allow the individual to choose which of several highly preferred reinforcers they would like to have now. Because the client is best positioned to know what reinforcer they want right now, this EO/AO-based strategy not only enhances motivation but is also preferred by the client (Thompson et al., 1998; Tiger & Reed, 2015).

EXTRA BOX 1:   THE COST OF MENTALISTIC REASONING

Vaguely conceptualizing motivation as an inherent characteristic of the individual has hidden costs when it is applied to real-world problems. Perhaps the most salient example of this is the climate crisis. The problem is well understood, but the solution is most often described in mentalistic, motivational terms. Consider this quote from former vice president Al Gore, who in his Nobel lecture said (emphasis added):

"We have everything we need to get started, save perhaps, **political will.** *But* **political will** *is a renewable resource."*

While we applaud Mr. Gore's mission and congratulate him on his Nobel prize, we are concerned about the vaguely defined solution, which lies in the mentalistic construct, "political will." This construct is a favorite among politicians and columnists in the opinion pages, but is typically defined metaphorically, for example, as a "renewable resource." This leaves us at a loss to know what to do when political will is "weak." The only solution, it would appear, is to give a motivational speech. Indeed, at the conclusion of his Nobel address, Mr. Gore reveals his solution:

Source: Kjetil Bjørnsrud/Wikipedia/CC BY-SA 3.0

"So, let us renew it [political will], and say together: 'We have a purpose. We are many. For this purpose we will rise, and we will act.'"

This may inspire us in the moment, but does it positively influence day-to-day decisions about recycling, setting our thermostat, using public transportation, or calling our legislators to demand that they do something about the climate crisis? Given that more than 10 years have passed since the speech and the crisis has only worsened, we fear the answer is no.

If we knew how to generate political will, we would have done it long ago. Because a lack of political will is thought to exist in the minds of, for example, greedy, out-of-touch politicians, one solution is for the voters to "have a purpose" and vote them out of office. Sounds good in the abstract, but one wonders about the strategy when the new political office holder loses their "political will" shortly after taking their oath of office. Perhaps the problem is not inside the mind, but in the MOs and the contingencies of reinforcement and punishment operating inside the halls of government.

If the causes of behavior are to be found in the interactions between behavior, biology, and environmental events, then our reform efforts should be directed toward understanding those interactions as they play out in government and political systems. What are the relevant MOs (e.g., the need to raise huge amounts of money from special interest groups to afford running for re-election)? What contingencies are currently operating (e.g., *IF you vote for the bill that benefits my company but trashes the environment → THEN I will write a big check for your re-election campaign*) and how can they be modified to generate the behavior needed to effectively tackle the climate crisis? We cannot answer these questions now (the research has yet to be conducted); we can only point in a direction which may prove more effective than our current, mentalistic approach.

Reading Quiz 1

1. Behavior analysts reject _____ explanations of behavior. Such "explanations" put the cause of behavior in the individual's vaguely defined "mind."
2. If the only evidence for the cause (motivation) is the effect (performance), then the explanation is _____.
3. There are two kinds of _____ operations. These environmental and/or biological events temporarily alter the efficacy of a reinforcer, and change the probability of behaviors that produce that reinforcer.
4. The first kind of MO is the _____ operation. When these environmental and/or biological events occur, they temporarily *increase* the efficacy of a specific reinforcer, and they *increase* the probability of behaviors that produce that reinforcer.
5. The second kind of MO is the _____ operation. When these environmental and/or biological events occur, they temporarily *decrease* the efficacy of a specific reinforcer, and they *decrease* the probability of behaviors that produce that reinforcer.
6. Having a garden full of corn is an _____ (establishing or abolishing) operation because it temporarily decreases the reinforcing value of a store-bought ear of corn, and it decreases the probability of purchasing one at the grocery store.
7. Spilling sriracha sauce on your shirt is an _____ (establishing or abolishing) operation because it temporarily increases the reinforcing value of a clean shirt, and it increases the probability of going home to get one.
8. Having an itchy back is an _____ (establishing or abolishing) operation because it temporarily increases the reinforcing value of the stimulation produced by a good scratching, and it increases the probability that you will ask your partner to scratch your back.

Identifying Effective Reinforcers: The "Liking" Strategy

MOs take "motivation" out of the sphere of mind and direct our attention to biological and environmental events that alter a reinforcer's value (and the probability of behavior that yields that reinforcer). When MOs happen, they change how much we "want" the reinforcer, and the effort we will exert to get it. Thus, an EO will make reinforcers more effective and, therefore, are important when using reinforcers to positively influence behavior.

A second strategy when arranging effective reinforcers is to identify things that the individual "likes." The logic is simple – things that we like should function as effective positive reinforcers. Let's apply this "liking" strategy to Sherri, the new employee hired because of her "high motivation," but who has struggled to perform well in her new position. As her manager, we might arrange a reinforcement contingency designed to help her succeed. For example, we might take a shaping approach – setting

Source: Rasulov/Shutterstock.com

approachable goals, reinforcing her successes, and gradually increasing the goals to keep things challenging but supportive. For this to work, we need to identify an effective incentive that will reinforce Sherri's performance. To accomplish this, behavior analysts have a couple tools to choose from – reinforcer surveys and stimulus preference assessments.

Reinforcer Surveys

To identify things that individuals like and that might function as reinforcers, behavior analysts can ask the individual, or those who spend a lot of time with them, to complete a reinforcer survey. A **reinforcer survey** is *a structured interview or written survey that asks the individual to identify highly preferred activities* (Daniels, 1989; Mintz et al., 2007). Table 9.1 provides an example of a reinforcer survey that we might ask Sherri to fill out in her spare time. In filling it out, Sherri might say that she enjoys cooking for her family on weekends (Item 2). If so, then an effective (and thoughtful) reinforcer might be a gift certificate to a local cooking-supply store, a cookbook, or a subscription to a home-chef service.

Table 9.1 Example of a written reinforcer survey.

Instructions: Please complete the following sentences.
Take time to think about what you really enjoy. There are no right or wrong answers.

1. When I get home after work, the thing I most like to do is…
2. On weekends I really enjoy…
3. When I get together with friends, we usually…
4. The thing I most enjoy doing at work is…
5. When I get a break at work, I like to…
6. Do you like to play a sport? If so, which one?
7. Do you like to watch a sport? If so, which one?
8. Do you like to go shopping? If so, what do you like to shop for?
9. Do you enjoy live performances? If so, what is your favorite kind?
10. Do you like to listen to music? If so, who are your favorite artists?
11. If I had a little more money, next weekend I would…
12. The perfect gift for me would be…
13. I wish I knew how to…
14. At work, I would really like to learn how to…
15. True or false: I like it when my boss praises me for doing a task particularly well.

When completing reinforcer surveys, people sometimes struggle to think of things they enjoy doing. To aid in this, the survey will often include items designed to jog the person's memory. Questions 6–10, for example, ask Sherri if she enjoys specific activities. such as watching sports. Each item should include follow-up questions. For example, if Sherri says she enjoys watching football, the follow-up question might ask which team is her favorite (the Kansas City Chiefs), and which player she likes best (Patrick Mahomes). Now we know that anything related to the Chiefs and Patrick Mahomes is likely to function as an effective reinforcer, if provided contingent upon Sherri's improved performance.

Beyond identifying behaviors that the individual *currently* likes to do, the reinforcer surveys will ask about wish-list activities. That is, something Sherri cannot afford to do (question 11) or doesn't know how to do (questions 13 and 14). Arranging lessons, training, and/or access to these activities may also function as an effective reinforcer.

Reinforcer surveys are a simple, practical way to identify *potential* reinforcers. However, they are not foolproof. The individual may list things that are impractical (a new car), not in their own best interests (drugs), or things that do not actually function as reinforcers. Fortunately, the available research suggests that, in workplace settings, most employees are able to identify things that function as reinforcers (Waldvogel & Dixon, 2008; Wine et al., 2014). So, they are a useful tool in the behavior-analytic toolbox.

Stimulus Preference Assessments

The other method used to identify potentially effective reinforcers is the stimulus preference assessment. This technique is used when working with nonhuman animals or individuals with limited or no expressive language capabilities (Cote et al., 2007; Green et al., 1988). During a **stimulus preference assessment**, *a rank-ordered list of preferred stimuli is obtained by observing choices between those stimuli.* That is, the potential reinforcers (referred to as "stimuli") are presented concurrently (at the same time) and the individual chooses the one they like the most. The stimuli might be an array of different snack foods (cheese puffs, pretzels, peanut-butter cups) or pictures of preferred activities (riding a bike, playing a game, doing an art project). Individuals with severe developmental disabilities can usually reach for or point to their preferred stimulus (Hagopian et al., 2004; Pace et al., 1985) particularly if they are allowed to eat the item or engage in the activity right away.

Prior to conducting the stimulus preference assessment, the behavior analyst will identify several stimuli that might function as reinforcers. To narrow the list, parents and caregivers might be asked to complete a reinforcer survey (Fisher et al., 1996). For example, the parents might be asked to identify half a dozen candies that the child really likes. The left column in Table 9.2 shows several edible stimuli that might be used in a stimulus preference assessment. The table also shows the **preference hierarchy** – a *list of stimuli rank ordered from most to least preferred.*

To conduct the stimulus preference assessment described in Table 9.2, all six candies would be arranged on a table and the child would be asked to choose one (and then allowed to eat it). If the first stimulus selected is the salted caramel, that one is placed at the top of the preference hierarchy; it is the most preferred of

Source: WilleeCole/Getty Images

Table 9.2 Stimuli that might be used in a preference assessment conducted with a child.

Stimuli	Preference hierarchy
Gummy worm	1. Salted caramel (most preferred item)
Chocolate bar	2. Sour chew
Jelly beans	3. Chocolate bar
Salted caramel	4. Jelly beans
Sour chew	5. Gummy worm
Hard candy	6. Hard candy (least preferred item)

* The Preference Hierarchy column shows the results of the stimulus preference assessment – a list of the stimuli rank-ordered from most to least preferred.

the stimuli available. Next, the individual gets to choose from the remaining stimuli, with each item chosen placed sequentially in the preference hierarchy. This continues until all of the stimuli are consumed. The assumption underlying this technique is that the stimuli at or near the top of the preference hierarchy will function as the most effective reinforcers.[2]

The stimulus preference assessment can also be used to identify effective reinforcers in nonhuman animals. For example, you could conduct one with your pet by placing several treats (cheese, kibble, pepperoni, etc.) on the floor in a big circle. Then, place your pet in the center and wait for one of the treats to be chosen. If you conducted the test for several days and cheese was always chosen first, this would go to the top of the preference hierarchy. If pepperoni is usually chosen second, that would go next in the preference hierarchy, and so on. Importantly, we will now be pretty confident that cheese and pepperoni can be effectively used as reinforcers for this pet.

Pet food companies frequently use stimulus preference assessments to improve the likeability of their product. They know that if our dogs prefer a competitor's dog food more than theirs, sales will decline. Therefore, in pet food research labs they are constantly trying to improve the taste of their foods. New versions of the food are developed and placed before their canine preference assessors. By recording the dogs' preference hierarchies, the researchers learn what dogs like. As it turns out, an ingredient pretty high on dogs' list is freeze-dried swine liver (Baskot, 2008). Who knew?

To summarize, to identify potential reinforcers, behavior analysts often ask individuals what they like. This can be done by having the individual complete a reinforcer survey or by letting them choose between several, concurrently available stimuli in a stimulus preference assessment. Letting the individual select their own reinforcers is a more sensitive, humane, and effective method relative to having the therapist, manager, or pet owner decide what they like and imposing it on others (Bannerman et al., 1990; Hanley, 2010). That said, this "liking" strategy for identifying effective reinforcers is not foolproof. The most preferred stimulus – a salted caramel – may be adequate to increase low-effort selections of that item, but it may prove inadequate to reinforce a high-effort performance. The ultimate test of a reinforcer's efficacy is its ability to increase the behavior targeted for change.

EXTRA BOX 2: AVOIDING CIRCULARITY – THE PREMACK PRINCIPLE

Earlier we critiqued the everyday practice of conceptualizing "motivation" as an inherent characteristic of the mental state of the individual. Specifically, we said that explaining Sherri's poor performance at work by pointing to her "low motivation" was a circular explanation. The only evidence for the cause (low motivation) is the very thing it is supposed to explain (underachievement at work). Said another way, there is no *independent* evidence for the existence of motivation.

A similar issue arises when explaining performance improvements with reinforcement. As shown in Figure 9.3, we have arranged a reinforcement contingency for Sherri – *IF she completes a major assignment on time at work → THEN she is awarded two tickets to a professional football game.* When her performance improves, we conclude that the tickets functioned as a reinforcer. But how do we know the tickets are a reinforcer? The only evidence for this – the performance improvement – is the very thing reinforcement is asked to explain (Postman, 1947). Said another way, there is no *independent* evidence that the tickets are reinforcers.

There are two ways to approach this circularity problem. The first is to ignore it as something that bothers philosophers, not those of us who are trying to positively influence human behavior. From this perspective, stimuli are given a try as contingent consequences, and if they increase behavior above the no-reinforcer baseline level, then they are declared to be reinforcers. This can work and many of those who are making *real improvements* in human behavior adopt this strategy.

The other approach seeks to predict what will function as a reinforcer *independent* of evaluating if it works. That is, we need to be able to say "that stimulus change will function

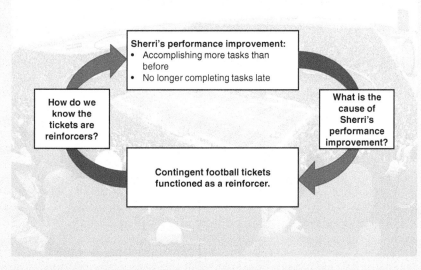

Figure 9.3 An illustration of the circularity issue inherent to reinforcement. Avoiding circularity requires a way of independently identifying a reinforcer.
Source: U.S. Air Force photo by Senior Airman Carlin Leslie

as a reinforcer" *before* we give it a try. This second approach has the practical advantage that, if we could accurately predict what would function as a reinforcer, we would spend less time trying out stimuli that do not work (Timberlake & Farmer-Dougan, 1991).

To address the circularity problem, David Premack conducted a series of experiments in which rats were given free access to water and an exercise wheel for an hour. Premack found that rats spent more time running than drinking, so he classified running as the *high-probability behavior* and drinking as the *low-probability behavior*. Next, Premack made a prediction about what would function as a reinforcer – *access to a high-probability behavior will function as a reinforcer when made contingent upon a low-probability behavior*; this has come to be known as the **Premack principle** (Premack, 1959). Note how Premack made this prediction *before* he tested whether or not access to running (the high-probability behavior) would actually reinforce the low-probability behavior – drinking.

In Premack's experiment, he next arranged this contingency: *IF drink → THEN unlock the running wheel.* That is, access to the high-probability behavior (running) was made contingent on emitting the low-probability behavior (drinking). As predicted, the rats increased their drinking – access to the running wheel had indeed functioned as a reinforcer.

Returning to the circularity problem in Figure 9.3, we cannot predict if the football tickets will function as a reinforcer *independent* of their effect on Sherri's performance at work. Premack addressed this problem by predicting what will function as a reinforcer *before* the consequence is tried out. According to the Premack principle, the football tickets will function as a reinforcer if they are a higher-probability behavior than Sherri's performance at work.

Let's apply the Premack principle to your behavior at home. If we were to log the time you spend doing different things at home, we might find that playing video games and streaming movies are high-probability behaviors, whereas doing the dishes and studying are low-probability behaviors. You might say you "like" playing or watching more than scrubbing or studying, but what is more important from Premack's perspective are the relative probabilities of these behaviors. The Premack principle predicts that strictly enforcing the following contingency:

IF I do all the dishes → THEN I can play my video game

Source: Fuse/Getty Images

will increase dishwashing behavior. That is, the Premack principle predicts the high-probability behavior (video game access) will function as a reinforcer, and importantly, it predicts this *before* we implement the contingency. If you are like most readers, your intuition tells you that Premack is right, but this has a "duh, of course it works" quality to it.

Going beyond "duh," the Premack principle predicts that access to *any* high-probability behavior will reinforce a lower probability behavior. Really? What about clipping our fingernails (a low-probability behavior – about 90 seconds per week) and studying (a higher-probability behavior – about 5 hours per week). Could we increase fingernail clipping by strictly enforcing this contingency:

IF I clip my nails for 90 seconds → THEN I can study for an hour

Your intuition might be, no way! Access to a 1 hour study session would never function as a reinforcer. But think about it a little longer. If you don't increase your nail clipping under this contingency, you will not be allowed to get in your usual 5 hours of studying, and your grades will suffer. To avoid this, you would probably clip your nails five times a week, just to earn your usual 5 hours of study time. Five clippings per week is 90×5=450 seconds, which is a big increase, thereby revealing a reinforcement effect. So, yes, even access to studying can function as a reinforcer, if studying is the higher probability behavior.

There is considerable laboratory research support for the Premack principle and its variants (Timberlake & Allison, 1974) and it has been used effectively in applied and clinical settings (Amari et al., 1995; Charlop et al., 1990; Hanley et al., 2003). For example, the Premack principle informs the way that behavior analysts conduct reinforcer surveys. The reinforcer survey in Table 9.1 asked Sherri to tell us about activities she likes to do when she has free time (e.g., When I get together with friends, we usually…). If Sherri is a good observer of her own behavior, then she will tell us about her *high-probability* behaviors. Access to these behaviors will, according to the Premack principle, serve as effective reinforcers for her *low-probability* work behaviors.

Reading Quiz 2

1. A _____ _____ is a structured interview or written survey that asks the individual to identify highly preferred activities.
2. The reason for asking someone to complete a reinforcer survey is to identify something that might function as a _____, if provided contingent upon a desired behavior.
3. For individuals with limited or no language ability, or for nonhuman animals, a useful way of identifying potential reinforcers is the stimulus _____ _____.
4. The final product of a stimulus preference assessment is a list of stimuli rank ordered from most to least preferred. This list is known as a preference _____. Stimuli at the top of this list are most likely to function as reinforcers.
5. The Premack principle states that access to a _____-probability behavior can function as a reinforcer if made contingent upon emitting a _____-probability behavior.
6. A benefit of the Premack principle is that it allows us to predict what will function as a reinforcer _____ we try it out. This allows us to avoid the circularity problem.

Measuring Reinforcer Efficacy

Let's assume that we have asked Sherri to complete a reinforcer survey and she has identified those football tickets as something she would really like to have. Will the tickets function as a reinforcer? Well, it depends on what she has to do to earn them. If we give her two tickets to the game each time she says "football," Sherri is likely to say "football" 40 or 50 times a day, much more than her baseline (pre-reinforcer) level. But will the tickets reinforce a high-effort behavior like completing projects on time at work? That's a different matter – a matter of reinforcer efficacy.

We know that reinforcers are effective if they increase behavior above a baseline level, but we also know that some reinforcers (1 billion dollars) are more effective than others (1 cent). One way to measure reinforcer efficacy is to let the individual choose between them. No doubt, everyone reading this chapter will select 1 billion dollars, so we may conclude that it is the relatively more effective reinforcer. The stimulus preference assessment uses choice as its measure of reinforcer efficacy. Stimuli at the top of the preference hierarchy are judged to be the most effective of the available reinforcers.

Using choice to measure reinforcer efficacy is easy. Asking Sherri to choose between professional and college football tickets takes seconds of our time. However, choice does not tell us how much more reinforcing the preferred stimulus might be. Are professional football tickets 10% more reinforcing? 100% more reinforcing? We don't know.

Another approach to measuring reinforcer efficacy is to evaluate *the maximum amount of behavior the reinforcer will maintain*, that is, the **breakpoint**. Figure 9.4 shows the results of an experiment that compared the breakpoints of two stimulant drugs: chlorphentermine and cocaine (Griffiths et al., 1978). Cocaine's breakpoint was about four times higher than chlorphentermine's; that is, the baboons participating in this study worked four times as hard for a cocaine reinforcer than for chlorphentermine. Therefore, we may conclude that cocaine is four times as reinforcing – it maintained four times as much behavior.

This is useful information; it helped the US Food and Drug Administration conclude that chlorphentermine was safe to use as an appetite-suppressant medication, whereas cocaine was not. Cocaine was simply too reinforcing. If doctors prescribed it, their patients might develop a substance-use disorder. Breakpoint tells us what choice cannot – it tells us *how much more* reinforcing one stimulus is than another.

Because it is often impractical to actually measure breakpoints in clinical or workplace settings (Poling, 2010), researchers developed the *purchase task* (Jacobs & Bickel, 1999; MacKillop et al., 2008). In this task, participants indicate how many reinforcers they would hypothetically purchase if they were available at a range of prices. For example, how many professional football tickets would you buy if they cost $10, $20, $30, …, $1,000 each. Under this task, the breakpoint is the highest price at which the individual continues to purchase the reinforcer. When Sherri tells us that the maximum she would pay for a professional football ticket is $100, but the maximum for a college football ticket is $20, then we may conclude that the former is about five times as reinforcing as the latter.

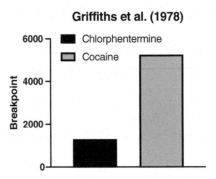

Figure 9.4 Breakpoints of two drugs with appetite-suppressant effects. In the experiment, baboons pressed a lever to obtain infusions of the drugs. The response requirement increased between sessions until the breakpoint was reached. Data shown are from subject CL, whose relative breakpoints were comparable to the other baboons.
Source: Griffiths, R. R., Brady, J. V, & Snell, J. D. (1978). Progressive-ratio performance maintained by drug infusions: Comparison of cocaine, diethylpropion, chlorphentermine, and fenfluramine. *Psychopharmacology*, 56, 5–13.

Dimensions of Effective Reinforcers

Prior sections of this chapter have considered what kinds of contingent stimuli function as reinforcers. That is, what kinds of candies, football tickets, or drugs are reinforcers, and how reinforcing they are. In this section we will address the efficacy-impacting dimensions of a reinforcer. Said another way, what are the generic characteristics of highly effective reinforcers? Knowing those characteristics will help us to arrange effective reinforcers, no matter what the reinforcer is. There are four of these dimensions of effective reinforcers, and they are discussed in the following sections.

Contingency

The first dimension of a reinforcer that can influence its efficacy is the contingency according to which it may be obtained. As we have said many times before, reinforcers are more effective when delivered contingently and ineffective when provided noncontingently (Thompson et al., 2003). Few will work for a reinforcer that may be obtained for free. For example, this contingency

If I do the dishes → THEN I can play my video game

will work a lot better if noncontingent (free) video game sessions are completely unavailable. If the only way to play video games is to do the dishes first, then dishes it is. However, if you cheat on this self-imposed contingency, allowing yourself to play video games despite a sink full of dirty dishes, then video game access will fail to function as a reinforcer. Your reinforcer has faltered on the dimension of *contingency*.

Applying this to our performance-improvement project at work, football tickets are likely to be an effective reinforcer if they are provided contingent upon Sherri completing projects on time. We should not give the tickets away for free.

Reinforcer Size

The second dimension of a reinforcer that can influence its efficacy is its size. Imagine that your middle-aged, perfectly healthy neighbor offers to pay you $0.25 for every garbage bag that you fill with leaves from his 5-acre property. If you are like most readers, the size of this reward is insufficient to maintain (or even initiate) your raking and bagging behaviors. If the neighbor instead offered $25 per bag, most of us would pick up a rake and begin working. Indeed, with a reinforcer of that size, we will probably work until the 5-acre lot is devoid of further leaves. This thought experiment illustrates the simple point that larger reinforcers are more effective than smaller reinforcers, and a large empirical literature supports this (Catania, 1963; Herrnstein, 1970).

The caveat to this rule is that the larger the reinforcer, the sooner satiation will occur. For example, if the neighbor was Jeff Bezos (the CEO of Amazon) and he was offering to pay us 1 billion dollars per bag of raked leaves, we would all immediately stop what we are doing and run for the nearest rake. However, this massive reinforcer would not maintain behavior for very long. After stuffing a half-dozen bags, we would charter a jet to the Bahamas, where we would retire with our friends drinking piña coladas on the beach. The larger the reinforcer, the sooner satiation (an AO) will occur and, when it does, the behavior will come to an end. Thus, the behavior analyst hoping to initiate and maintain behavior will want to use a reinforcer of adequate size to get the behavior going, but not so large that the accumulated reinforcers have an AO effect.

Source: stokpic/pixabay

Reinforcer Quality

The third dimension of a reinforcer that can influence its efficacy is its quality. **Quality** refers to *the subjective value of a reinforcer, which can vary from one individual to the next* (Hollard & Davison, 1971; Neef & Shade, 1993). For Sherri, tickets to a professional football game are more valuable (higher quality) than tickets to a college football game. Hence, her performance at work is more likely to be improved if we offer to reinforce it with pro football tickets, not college football tickets. For other employees, the relative quality of these reinforcers might be the opposite, and for others still, tickets to a football game will not reinforce behavior at all – they have a subjective value of zero.

Reinforcer Immediacy

The fourth dimension of a reinforcer that can influence its efficacy is immediacy. Considerable empirical evidence (and our intuition) tell us that reinforcers are more effective when they are obtained immediately (Chung & Herrnstein, 1967; Reed & Martens, 2011). Figure 9.5 illustrates this effect of immediacy on the behavior of a typical pigeon (Reilly & Lattal, 2004). Immediate food reinforcers (a zero-second delay on the x-axis)

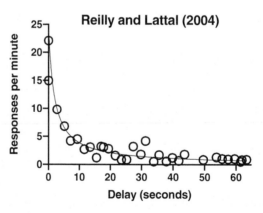

Figure 9.5 Response rates of pigeon 1326 when food reinforcers were delivered immediately (0-second delay) or following the delays shown on the x-axis. The curved line illustrates reduced reinforcer efficacy with increased reinforcer delays.

Source: Reilly, M. P., & Lattal, K. A. (2004). Within-session delay-of-reinforcement gradients. *Journal of the Experimental Analysis of Behavior*, 82(1), 21–35. https://doi.org/10.1901/jeab.2004.82-21

maintained the highest rate of key-pecking. Imposing a delay between the key-peck and the reinforcer decreased responding.

One reason that delayed reinforcers are less effective than immediate reinforcers likely has to do with the stable environment of our evolutionary ancestors. In that environment, a lot of bad things could happen while waiting for a delayed reinforcer. The individual could be killed by a predator while waiting and, if that happens, the delayed reinforcer would be lost. Less dramatically, a bigger, stronger competitor could come along during the delay and steal the upcoming reinforcer. The reinforcers these ancients were waiting for were not football tickets or salted caramels, they were critical reinforcers needed for survival, for example, food, water, and mating opportunities (important in the survival of genes; Dawkins, 1976). If waiting for *these* reinforcers translates to sometimes not getting them, then organisms would be at a survival advantage if their behavior was highly sensitive to reinforcer delays (as in Figure 9.5; Stevens & Stephens, 2010). Modern creatures, like you and I, have inherited the genes of these delay-sensitive survivors; hence, our aversion to waiting.

A second reason why delayed reinforcers might lose their efficacy is that they make it more difficult to learn response-reinforcer contingencies. This is illustrated in Figure 9.6. In panel A, a pigeon pecks the key and immediately gets a food reinforcer. Because no time separates the peck from the reinforcer, it is easy to learn the contingency: *IF peck → THEN food*.

However, panel B illustrates why delaying the reinforcer by 20 seconds makes it difficult to learn this contingency. Between the peck and the eventual delivery of food, several other behaviors occur. The pigeon walks away from the key, flaps its wings, and then scratches its belly. After the belly-scratching, food is delivered. These intervening responses, all of which occur closer in time to the reinforcer, make it difficult to learn that it was the peck that actually caused the food reinforcer (Catania, 1971; Killeen, 2011).

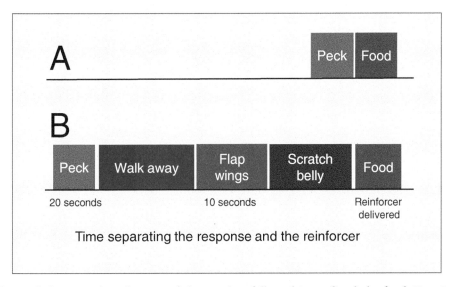

Figure 9.6 In panel A, the pigeon's key-peck is followed immediately by food. Here it is easy for the pigeon to learn the contingent relation between the peck and the reinforcer. However, in Panel B, the reinforcer is delayed by 20 seconds and several other responses intervene between the peck and the food that it produced. Here it will be much more difficult to learn the contingent relation between pecking and food delivery.

Among humans and nonhumans alike, immediate reinforcers are more effective than delayed reinforcers. So, if we are going to give Sherri those football tickets after she completes a major project on time, we would do well to award them as quickly as possible.

Summary

The four dimensions of effective reinforcers are (1) contingency, (2) size, (3) quality, and (4) immediacy. Behavior analysts will use their knowledge of these dimensions to arrange effective reinforcers. Thus, if a reinforcer is not increasing behavior as much as is desired, then we will examine if our reinforcer is *only* available contingent upon the desired behavior. By getting rid of any noncontingent sources of the reinforcer, we will increase its ability to positively influence behavior. Likewise, we will evaluate if the size of the reinforcer is adequate, or if the quality of the reinforcer might be improved. Finally, we will see if it is possible to provide the reinforcer more immediately after the desired behavior has occurred. Improving one or more of these reinforcer dimensions can improve the efficacy of a behavior-change program.

Habit Formation

In this final section of the chapter we will explore habit formation and how habitual behavior can continue even when an AO has greatly diminished the reinforcer's efficacy. A good place to start is to define what we mean by a habit. The dictionary definition of a habit is, a pattern of behavior that is repeated so often that it becomes almost involuntary. Perhaps cigarette smoking springs to mind. Lighting a cigarette, drawing on it, exhaling, and so on. This pattern of behavior has been repeated so many times that it seems to happen automatically in predictable situations – smoking after a meal, smoking after completing a task, smoking after sex. Other, nonaddictive habits abound. Our morning routines are often habitual. We get up, go to the bathroom, make breakfast, check social media; all of this executed in an unchanging sequence, without much conscious thought. When researchers study our daily GPS locations, travel routes, and so on, they see habitual patterns repeated day after day (Song et al., 2010). We habitually engage in these behaviors without explicitly considering their consequences and some of those consequences are not in our long-term best interests. Because we all want to break our bad habits (eating junk food) and replace them with good habits (eating more fruits and vegetables), behavioral scientists have studied what habits are and how they are formed.

Habits – What Are They and How Are They Formed

When behavioral scientists study habitual behavior, they define a **habit** as *operant behavior that (1) is evoked by antecedent stimuli and (2) persists despite the imposition of an AO*. When behavior becomes habitual, AOs no longer decrease the probability of the behavior that produces those reinforcers. Said another way, habits are less influenced by motivation to acquire the reinforcer and more influenced by the antecedent stimuli that were reliably present when the response was reinforced. These stimuli evoke habitual responding, even though the "reinforcer" is no longer reinforcing.

As an everyday example of this, consider how many times we all open the refrigerator and peruse our options, even though we are not hungry. The refrigerator is an antecedent stimulus that was present when operant food-gathering behaviors were emitted and reliably reinforced. Now the sight of the refrigerator evokes habitual perusing, even when we are not hungry. Similarly, cigarette smokers light up after a meal regardless of their momentary need for another hit of nicotine. The behavior is reliably evoked by an antecedent stimulus – the end of the meal – rather than being influenced by the smoker's motivation for a hit of nicotine.

Source: Iakov Filimonov/123RF

Bad habits, like drinking alcohol even when we are neither thirsty nor motivated by intoxication, can be studied in the laboratory with rats pressing levers in operant conditioning chambers. For example, in an experiment conducted by Corbit et al. (2012), rats learned to press a lever to produce an alcohol reinforcer (a tiny rat cocktail, if you will). After 1 week of these alcohol-reinforcement sessions, lever pressing was not yet habitual. You can see this in the left-hand side of Figure 9.7. When an AO was imposed (rats were allowed to freely drink alcohol before a test session), it had its twin effects – it decreased the reinforcing value of another cocktail and it decreased lever pressing by 40%. However, after 8 weeks of training, the same AO no longer decreased the rats' alcohol seeking – the behavior had become habitual. **Habits are formed when** *an operant response has been repeatedly reinforced, hundreds, if not thousands, of times in the presence of the same antecedent stimulus.*

Applied to the behavior of humans, repeatedly drinking at 5 pm can shift an operant behavior from consequence/motivational control ("I could really go for a drink") to antecedent stimulus control ("It's 5 o'clock – time for a cocktail"). This shift from consequence to

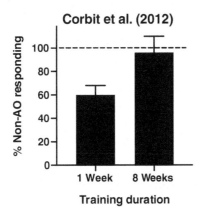

Figure 9.7 Rats' rate of pressing a lever for an alcohol reinforcer is represented by the dashed line. After 1 week of training under this operant contingency, an AO (free access to alcohol before a test session) decreased responding (left filled bar). However, after 8 weeks of training under this contingency, behavior was unaffected by the AO; pressing the lever had become habitual.

Source: Corbit, L. H., Nie, H., & Janak, P. H. (2012). Habitual alcohol seeking: Time course and the contribution of subregions of the dorsal striatum. *Biological Psychiatry, 72*(5), 389–395. https://doi.org/10.1016/j.biopsych.2012.02.024

antecedent control of habitual behavior has been replicated with several different drug reinforcers, non-drug reinforcers, and in different species, including humans (see Everitt & Robbins, 2016 for review).

Our Everyday Habits

Now that you know what a habit is, and how habits are formed, can you think of any behaviors that you do habitually? As we contemplate this question, it is instructive to focus on the strong antecedent stimulus control of the behavior. Habits occur nearly every time we find ourselves in specific stimulus situations. The habitual behavior occurs even when our motivation to acquire the reinforcer is minimal.

Consider the good habit of brushing your teeth in the morning. This behavior is reliably evoked by an antecedent stimulus – standing at the bathroom sink after we wake up. Long ago, we explicitly learned the sequence of individual operant responses – grabbing the toothbrush, apply toothpaste, moving the brush back and forth. They were all reinforced with predictable consequences (a loving parent praising our skillful brushing, fresh breath after brushing, etc.). But today, after the behavior has been reinforced thousands of times, the antecedent stimulus-situation reliably evokes habitual brushing behaviors regardless of our momentary motivation for the reinforcers. The ability of these antecedent stimuli to control our habitual tooth brushing is more evident when the stimuli are removed. For example, when we go camping, all of the antecedent stimuli in our bathroom are gone. Without these stimuli, we often "forget" to brush until, much later in the day, when we are motivated by a negative reinforcer of the escape variety – ugh, my breath is horrible.

You can also probably think of some bad habits that are mindlessly evoked by antecedent stimuli. For example, many of us habitually sit on the couch and turn on the TV, not because we want to watch a program, but because it feels like the thing to do in the living room. The couch and remote are antecedent stimuli that were present when relaxing and watching were reinforced thousands of times. Now these stimuli evoke habitual, slothful behaviors most every time we walk into the room.

Whether good or bad, a habit is like a path cut through an overgrown field. The more we walk the path, the more distinct it becomes. The more distinct the path, the more it evokes sticking to the path, and the more difficult it becomes to deviate from the path.

Source: don cload/geograph.org.uk/CC BY-SA 2.0

Replacing Bad Habits with Good Ones

Bad habits are, at their core, operant behaviors that have been reinforced hundreds, if not thousands, of times. What makes a habit bad is that it feels good now, but the more we do it, the worse things get for us. For example, smoking one cigarette per year is not a bad habit. But the more often you smoke, the more likely it is to become habitual, and the worse it is for your health.

Conversely, what makes a good habit good is, very often, that it does not feel that good now, but the more we do it, the better it is for us. Consider exercising. Going out for a run once a year is not a habit – we've only done it once. However, if the behavior becomes habitual, it will be reliably evoked by antecedent stimuli, regardless of how we feel about the consequences of running. When running happens habitually, we gradually experience the physical and mental-health benefits of running. When a good habit is acquired, we take on a desired identity – we think of ourselves as *runners.*

So, how do we replace bad habits with good habits? The scientific literature offers considerable guidance about how to cut a new, more adaptive path through the overgrown field of our lives (Clear, 2018). We will outline five strategies here.

First, identify the antecedent stimuli that reliably evoke our bad habits. To do this, simply notice when and where you are when you find yourself engaged in the bad habit. After directly observing your behavior for a few days, consider if there are a set of antecedent stimuli that reliably set the occasion for the bad habit. If so, consider if these stimuli can be hidden from view (or hearing, smell, etc.). For example, if you have a bad habit of snacking when you see the bag of chips on the couch, get rid of the chips. Throwing them away will work, but a less drastic strategy is to put them in a cabinet, well behind other foods that are better for your health. If you are less likely to run across the chips, you are less likely to mindlessly eat them.

Second, replace those stimuli that evoke bad habits with stimuli that will evoke good ones. These stimuli will not work at first, but carefully selecting these stimuli now will pay dividends later. Let's assume that we want to replace snacking on the couch with walking on the treadmill. What antecedent stimuli could we arrange that would, in the short run, remind us to walk and, in the long run, would reliably evoke habitual walking behavior? Well, we could move the couch to where the treadmill is now, and move the treadmill into the prime real-estate that the couch currently holds. Now the first thing you see as you enter the living room is the treadmill, not the couch. If our good habit is to be reliably evoked by an antecedent stimulus, then we must ensure we notice that stimulus every day.

Source: mediaphotos/Getty images

Third, we must reinforce the desired behavior hundreds, if not thousands of times. To accomplish this, the behavior needs to occur hundreds, if not thousands, of times. Uh…how do we do that? We set the bar low. That is, we arrange a reinforcement contingency that asks very little of us. That's right, we reinforce successive approximations of the target behavior – we use *shaping.*

Applied to treadmill walking, when we head to the living room to watch a bit of TV, we see the treadmill in its new, central location and we hop onto it and walk for 30 seconds. That's the first approximation, and when we do it (and this is the fourth strategy – make sure the behavior is reinforced), we feel good about ourselves – today we met our goal to becoming *an exerciser* (our new identity). We did not overdo it, leaving us sore tomorrow (and less likely to want to get on the treadmill). Instead, we began the long process of getting into the habit of seeing the treadmill and exercising. In addition, now that the treadmill holds that prime real-estate in the living room, we notice how much easier it is to see the TV from up there (another reinforcer for exercising).

The fifth strategy will follow the advice of Chapter 8, the next in the sequence of successive approximations will arrange the self-esteem building reinforcer for walking just a little more – 45 seconds. The idea is not to get into shape right now; it is to get into the *habit* of exercising. Each time we see the treadmill, we get on it and we walk. We don't dread getting on it because it is a painless, positive-identity building activity. Each day we are forming a good habit with physical and mental-health benefits that will compound over the lifetime.

So, if you are ready to form a good habit, (1) find the antecedents that evoke bad habits and (2) replace them with stimuli that will, one day, evoke a good habit. Then, (3) set the bar very low and (4) experience the self-esteem-building intrinsic reinforcers that can only be sampled when we, even briefly, engage in the desired behavior. Finally, (5) gradually increase the daily goal, remembering to keep it easy – the goal is to keep doing the behavior in the presence of the antecedent stimuli until, one day, it becomes habitual. It's just something we do, whether we feel like it or not.

Reading Quiz 3

1. When measuring reinforcer efficacy, an individual's _____ can tell us which of the available stimuli is most likely to be the most effective reinforcer.
2. A second measure of reinforcer efficacy is _____. This measure quantifies how much behavior can be maintained by a specific reinforcer.
3. List the four dimensions of reinforcer efficacy.
4. The second graders will complete more math problems when working for a gold star than a silver star. Which of the four dimensions of reinforcer efficacy is most relevant in this example?
5. The second graders were less enthusiastic about working for gold stars after the gym teacher gave the children a sheet of gold stars for free. Which of the four dimensions of reinforcer efficacy is most relevant in this example?
6. Research has shown that infants will babble more when a social reinforcer is provided contingent on this vocal response (Ramey & Ourth, 1971). However, if this reinforcer is delayed by as little as 3 seconds, it will lose its ability to reinforce this response (presumably because the delay makes it difficult for the baby to learn the *IF* babble → *THEN* social-reinforcer contingency). Which of the four dimensions of reinforcer efficacy is most relevant in this example?
7. When a behavior becomes habitual, an AO no longer has its twin effects. The AO no longer _____ the efficacy of a specific reinforcer and it no longer decreases the _____ that yields that reinforcer.
8. When a behavior becomes habitual, it is evoked by _____ stimuli, even when the individual is not motivated to acquire the consequence.
9. Habits are formed when an operant behavior is _____ hundreds, if not thousands, of times in the presence of an antecedent stimulus.

Summary

This chapter argued that our common, everyday understanding of motivation as a kind of internal, mental force lacks practical utility. It does not help us to positively influence behavior because this "force" cannot be dialed up when performance is poor, nor dialed down when behavior exceeds a desirable level. A more practical approach is to focus on MOs; that is, environmental and biological variables that increase (establishing operations) or decrease (abolishing operations) the efficacy of a reinforcer, thereby impacting the behaviors that produce these outcomes.

When the goal of an intervention is to increase a desired performance, it is important not only to focus on motivation but also to explicitly arrange effective reinforcers. A first step in this process is to identify a consequence that will function as a reinforcer. Two useful tools here are the *reinforcer survey* and the *stimulus preference assessment*. A second step is to optimize the four dimensions of effective reinforcers. That is, (1) the consequence should be provided *contingent* on the desired performance, (2) the *size* and (3) the *quality* of the consequence should be optimized, and (4) the consequence should be delivered *immediately* after the desired behavior. Effective reinforcers are preferred (chosen) and will maintain more behavior than less effective reinforcers.

When an operant behavior is reinforced many times in a particular setting, it can become habitual. Habits are evoked by the antecedent stimuli that were present when the behavior was reinforced over and over again. When a behavior becomes habitual, it will occur in the presence of these stimuli, even if we are not "motivated" by the reinforcer (recall those mindless, habitual trips to the refrigerator). Bad habits can significantly decrease our health and quality of life. Good habits can be difficult to establish, but the advice provided in the "Replacing Bad Habits with Good Ones" section can help. If you skipped that section, it's not too late to go back and read it. Who knows? Maybe it could "motivate" a change that the future-you would thank the present-you for. Other than 5 minutes of your time, what else have you got to lose?

Answers to Reading Quiz Questions

Reading Quiz 1

1. mentalistic
2. circular
3. motivating
4. establishing
5. abolishing
6. abolishing
7. establishing
8. establishing

Reading Quiz 2

1. reinforcer survey
2. reinforcer
3. preference assessment
4. hierarchy
5. high; low
6. before

Reading Quiz 3

1. choice, preference, or something along those lines
2. breakpoint
3. contingency, size, quality, and immediacy
4. quality
5. contingency
6. immediacy
7. decreases; behavior, response, or something similar
8. antecedent
9. reinforced

Notes

1. Motivating operations also apply to punishment, but because this is an introductory textbook, we will confine our coverage to motivating operations applicable to reinforcement.
2. There are several other techniques that may be used to conduct stimulus preference assessments. Interested students are referred to two reviews of the published literature (Kang et al., 2013; Virués-Ortega et al., 2014).

References

Amari, A., Grace, N. C., & Fisher, W. W. (1995). Achieving and maintaining compliance with the ketogenic diet. *Journal of Applied Behavior Analysis, 28*(3), 341–342. doi:10.1901/jaba.1995.28-341

Balleine, B. W., & Dickinson, A. (1998). Goal-directed instrumental action: Contingency and incentive learning and their cortical substrates. *Neuropharmacology, 37*(4–5), 407–419. doi:10.1016/S0028-3908(98)00033-1

Bannerman, D. J., Sheldon, J. B., Sherman, J. A., & Harchik, A. E. (1990). Balancing the right to habilitation with the right of personal liberties: The rights of people with developmental disabilities to eat too many doughnuts and take a nap. *Journal of Applied Behavior Analysis, 23*(1), 79–89. doi:10.1901/jaba.1990.23-79

Baskot, S. (2008). Palatability test shows dog's preference. *Feed Mix, 16*(1), 10–11.

Berridge, K. C., & Robinson, T. E. (2003). Parsing reward. *Trends in Neuroscience, 26*(9), 507–513. doi:10.1016/S0166-2236(03)00233-9

Bowman, L. G., Piazza, C. C., Fisher, W. W., Hagopian, L. P., & Kogan, J. S. (1997). Assessment of preference for varied versus constant reinforcers. *Journal of Applied Behavior Analysis, 30*(3), 451–458. doi:10.1901/jaba.1997.30-451

Catania, A. C. (1963). Concurrent performances: A baseline for the study of reinforcement magnitude. *Journal of the Experimental Analysis of Behavior, 6*(2), 299–300. doi:10.1901/jeab.1963.6-299

Catania, A. C. (1971). Reinforcement schedules: The role of responses preceding the one that produces the reinforcer. *Journal of the Experimental Analysis of Behavior, 15*(3), 271–287. doi:10.1901/jeab.1971.15-271

Charlop, M. H., Kurtz, P. F., & Casey, F. G. (1990). Using aberrant behaviors as reinforcers for autistic children. *Journal of Applied Behavior Analysis, 23*(2), 163–181. doi:10.1901/jaba.1990.23-163

Chung, S., & Herrnstein, R. J. (1967). Choice and delay of reinforcement. *Journal of the Experimental Analysis of Behavior, 10*(1), 67–74. doi:10.1901/jeab.1967.10-67

Clear, J. (2018). *Atomic habits: An easy and proven way to build good habits and break bad ones*. New York: Penguin Random House.

Colwill, R. M., & Rescorla, R. A. (1985). Postconditioning devaluation of a reinforcer affects instrumental responding. *Journal of Experimental Psychology: Animal Behavior Processes, 11*(1), 120–132. doi:10.1037/0097-7403.11.1.120

Corbit, L. H., Nie, H., & Janak, P. H. (2012). Habitual alcohol seeking: Time course and the contribution of subregions of the dorsal striatum. *Biological Psychiatry, 72*(5), 389–395. doi:10.1016/j.biopsych.2012.02.024

Cote, C. A., Thompson, R. H., Hanley, G. P., & McKerchar, P. M. (2007). Teacher report and direct assessment of preferences for identifying reinforcers for your children. *Journal of Applied Behavior Analysis, 40*(1), 157–166. doi:10.1901/jaba.2007.177-05

Daniels, A. C. (1989). *Performance management: Improving quality productivity through positive reinforcement* (3rd ed.). Tucker, GA: Performance Management Publications.

Dawkins, R. (1976). *The selfish gene*. Oxford University Press.

Dickinson, A., Campos, J., Varga, Z. I., & Balleine, B. (1996). Bidirectional instrumental conditioning. *Quarterly Journal of Experimental Psychology Section B: Comparative and Physiological Psychology, 49*(4), 289–306. doi:10.1080/713932637

Egel, A. L. (1981). Reinforcer variation: Implications for motivating developmentally disabled children. *Journal of Applied Behavior Analysis, 14*, 345–350. doi: 10.1901/jaba.1981.14-345

Everitt, B. J., & Robbins, T. W. (2016). Drug addiction: Updating actions to habits to compulsions ten years on. *Annual Review of Psychology, 67*(1), 23–50. doi:10.1146/annurev-psych-122414-033457

Fisher, W. W., Piazza, C. C., Bowman, L. G., & Adrianna, A. (1996). Integrating caregiver report with a systematic choice assessment to enhance reinforcer identification. *American Journal on Mental Retardation, 10*(1), 15–25.

Green, C. W., Reid, D. H., White, L. K., Halford, R. C., Brittain, D. P., & Gardner, S. M. (1988). Identifying reinforcers for persons with profound handicaps: Staff opinion versus systematic assessment of preferences. *Journal of Applied Behavior Analysis, 21*(1), 31–43. doi:10.1901/jaba.1988.21-31

Griffiths, R. R., Brady, J. V., & Snell, J. D. (1978). Progressive-ratio performance maintained by drug infusions: Comparison of cocaine, diethylpropion, chlorphentermine, and fenfluramine. *Psychopharmacology, 56*, 5–13. doi: 10.1007/BF00571401

Hagopian, L. P., Long, E. S., & Rush, K. S. (2004). Preference assessment procedures for individuals with developmental disabilities. *Behavior Modification, 28*(5), 668–677. doi:10.1177/0145445503259836

Hanley, G. P. (2010). Toward effective and preferred programming: A case for the objective measurement of social validity with recipients of behavior-change programs. *Behavior Analysis in Practice, 3*(1), 13–21. doi:10.1007/bf03391754

Hanley, G. P., Iwata, B. A., Roscoe, E. M., Thompson, R. H., & Lindberg, J. S. (2003). Response restriction analysis: II. Alteration of activity preferences. *Journal of Applied Behavior Analysis, 36*(1), 59–76. doi:10.1901/jaba.2003.36-59

Herrnstein, R. J. (1970). On the law of effect. *Journal of the Experimental Analysis of Behavior, 13*(2), 243–266. doi:10.1901/jeab.1970.13-243

Hirst, R., Sodos, L., Gade, S., & Rathke, L. (2017). Motivation in chronic cannabis use. In *Handbook of cannabis and related pathologies: Biology, pharmacology, diagnosis, and treatment* (pp. 288–297). Elsevier Inc. doi:10.1016/B978-0-12-800756-3.00034-X

Hogarth, L., & Chase, H. W. (2011). Parallel goal-directed and habitual control of human drug-seeking: Implications for dependence vulnerability. *Journal of Experimental Psychology: Animal Behavior Processes, 37*(3), 261–276. doi:10.1037/a0022913

Hollard, V., & Davison, M. C. (1971). Preference for qualitatively different reinforcers. *Journal of the Experimental Analysis of Behavior, 16*, 375–380. doi: 10.1901/jeab.1971.16-375

Jacobs, E. A., & Bickel, W. K. (1999). Modeling drug consumption in the clinic using simulation procedures: Demand for heroin and cigarettes in opioid-dependent outpatients. *Experimental and Clinical Psychopharmacology*, 7(4), 412–426. doi:10.1037/1064-1297.7.4.412

Kang, S., O'Reilly, M., Lancioni, G., Falcomata, T. S., Sigafoos, J., & Xu, Z. (2013, April 1). Comparison of the predictive validity and consistency among preference assessment procedures: A review of the literature. *Research in Developmental Disabilities*, 34(4), 1125–1133. doi: 10.1016/j.ridd.2012.12.021

Killeen, P. R. (2011). Models of trace decay, eligibility for reinforcement, and delay of reinforcement gradients, from exponential to hyperboloid. *Behavioural Processes*, 87(1), 57–63. doi:10.1016/j.beproc.2010.12.016

Laraway, S., Snycerski, S., Michael, J., & Poling, A. (2003). Motivating operations and terms to describe them: Some further refinements. *Journal of Applied Behavior Analysis*, 36(3), 407–414. doi:10.1901/jaba.2003.36-407

MacKillop, J., Murphy, J. G., Ray, L. A., Eisenberg, D. T. A., Lisman, S. A., Lum, J. K., & Wilson, D. S. (2008). Further validation of a cigarette purchase task for assessing the relative reinforcing efficacy of nicotine in college smokers. *Experimental and Clinical Psychopharmacology*, 16(1), 57–65. doi:10.1037/1064-1297.16.1.57

Milo, J.-S., Mace, F. C., & Nevin, J. A. (2010). The effects of constant versus varied reinforcers on preference and resistance to change. *Journal of the Experimental Analysis of Behavior*, 93(3), 385–394. doi:10.1901/jeab.2010.93-385

Mintz, C., Wallace, M. D., Najdowski, A. C., Atcheson, K., & Bosch, A. (2007). Reinforcer identification and evaluation of choice within an educational setting. *Journal of Behavioral Education*, 16(4), 333–341. doi:10.1007/s10864-007-9045-y

Neef, N. A., & Shade, D. (1993). Impulsivity in students with serious emotional disturbance: The interactive effects of reinforcer rate, delay, and quality. *Journal of Applied Behavior Analysis*, 26, 37–52. doi: 10.1901/jaba.1993.26-37

O'Reilly, M., Aguilar, J., Fragale, C., Lang, R., Edrisinha, C., Sigafoos, J., … Didden, R. (2012). Effects of a motivating operation on the maintenance of mands. *Journal of Applied Behavior Analysis*, 45(2), 443–447. doi:10.1901/jaba.2012.45-443

Pace, G. M., Ivancic, M. T., Edwards, G. L., Iwata, B. A., & Page, T. J. (1985). Assessment of stimulus preference and reinforcer value with profoundly retarded individuals. *Journal of Applied Behavior Analysis*, 18(3), 1308015. doi:10.1901/jaba.1985.18-249

Poling, A. (2010). Looking to the future: Will behavior analysis survive and prosper? *The Behavior Analyst*, 33(1), 7–17. doi:10.1007/BF03392200

Postman, L. (1947). The history and present status of the law of effect. *Psychological Bulletin*, 44(6), 489–563. doi: 10.1037/h0057716

Premack, D. (1959). Toward empirical behavior laws: I. Positive reinforcement. *Psychological Review*, 66(4), 219–233. doi:10.1037/h0040891

Premack, D., Schaeffer, R. W., & Hundt, A. (1964). Reinforcement of drinking by running: Effect of fixed ratio and reinforcement time. *Journal of the Experimental Analysis of Behavior*, 7(1), 91–96. doi:10.1901/jeab.1964.7-91

Ramey, C. T., & Ourth, L. L. (1971). Delayed reinforcement and vocalization rates of infants. *Child Development*, 42(1), 297. doi:10.2307/1127083

Reed, D. D., & Martens, B. K. (2011). Temporal discounting predicts student responsiveness to exchange delays in a classroom token system. *Journal of Applied Behavior Analysis*, 44(1), 1–18. doi:10.1901/jaba.2011.44-1

Reilly, M. P., & Lattal, K. A. (2004). Within-session delay-of-reinforcement gradients. *Journal of the Experimental Analysis of Behavior*, 82(1), 21–35. doi:10.1901/jeab.2004.82-21

Skinner, B. F. (1971). *Beyond freedom and dignity*. New York: Alfred A. Knopf.

Song, C., Qu, Z., Blumm, N., & Barabási, A. L. (2010). Limits of predictability in human mobility. *Science*, 327(5968), 1018–1021. doi:10.1126/science.1177170

Stafford, D., LeSage, M. G., & Glowa, J. R. (1999). Effects of phentermine on responding maintained by progressive-ratio schedules of cocaine and food delivery in rhesus monkeys. *Behavioural Pharmacology, 10*(8), 775–784. doi:10.1097/00008877-199912000-00009

Stevens, J. R., & Stephens, D. W. (2010). The adaptive nature of impulsivity. In G. J. Madden & W. K. Bickel (Eds.), *Impulsivity: The behavioral and neurological science of discounting* (pp. 361–387). Washington, DC: American Psychological Association. doi:10.1037/12069-013

Thompson, R. H., Iwata, B. A., Hanley, G. P., Dozier, C. L., & Samaha, A. L. (2003). The effects of extinction, noncontingent reinforcement, and differential reinforcement of other behavior as control procedures. *Journal of Applied Behavior Analysis, 36*(2), 221–238. doi:10.1901/jaba.2003.36-221

Thompson, R. H., Fisher, W. W., & Contrucci, S. A. (1998). Evaluating the reinforcing effects of choice in comparison to reinforcement rate. *Research in Developmental Disabilities, 19*(2), 181–187. doi:10.1016/s0891-4222(97)00050-4

Tiger, J. H., & Reed, D. D. (2015). Translational and applied choice research. In *Autism service delivery: Bridging the gap between science and practice* (pp. 193–208). New York: Springer. doi:10.1007/978-1-4939-2656-5_7

Timberlake, W., & Allison, J. (1974). Response deprivation: An empirical approach to instrumental performance. *Psychological Review, 81*(2), 146–164. doi: 10.1037/h0036101

Timberlake, W., & Farmer-Dougan, V. A. (1991). Reinforcement in applied settings: Figuring out ahead of time what will work. *Psychological Bulletin, 110*(3), 379–391. doi:10.1037/0033-2909.110.3.379

Virués-Ortega, J., Pritchard, K., Grant, R. L., North, S., Hurtado-Parrado, C., Lee, M. S. H., … Yu, C. T. (2014). Clinical decision making and preference assessment for individuals with intellectual and developmental disabilities. *American Journal on Intellectual and Developmental Disabilities, 119*(2), 151–170. doi:10.1352/1944-7558-119.2.151

Waldvogel, J. M., & Dixon, M. R. (2008). Exploring the utility of preference assessments in organizational behavior management. *Journal of Organizational Behavior Management, 28*(1), 76–87. doi:10.1080/01608060802006831

Wine, B., Reis, M., & Hantula, D. A. (2014). An evaluation of stimulus preference assessment methodology in organizational behavior management. *Journal of Organizational Behavior Management, 34*(1), 7–15. doi:10.1080/01608061.2013.873379

Punishment

10

Before we begin, let us recognize that many readers will already have an opinion about punishment, and chances are it's a negative one. No one wants to have their behavior punished, and when considering the best versions of ourselves, we like to think we never punish the behavior of others. This chapter seeks to go beyond a simple "punishment bad, reinforcement good" stance, evaluating instead what punishment is, its prevalence in nature, and why it has been used by humans from the beginning.

To that end, we invite you to imagine for a moment that you are a hunter-gatherer human, living in the Holocene period (about 12,000 years ago), before the development of agriculture and the domestication of farm animals. Your family and those two dozen or so others in your tightly knit community depend on each other for survival. Working cooperatively, your group keeps predators at bay; cares for your young, injured, and sick; and ensures that no one dies of starvation. Striking out on your own is not a viable option; it is a dangerous world out there.

Source: alexerich/Getty Images

As your small foraging party leaves the camp one morning, pangs of hunger increase the efficacy of food as a reinforcer. Searching in a remote location, you stumble upon a bush with just enough ripe berries to satisfy your hunger. What do you do? At one extreme of your options you will call the others, strip the bush of its ripe fruit, and share the berries with all community members. At the opposite extreme, you will eat the berries and do your best to

An Introduction to Behavior Analysis, First Edition. Gregory J. Madden, Derek D. Reed, and Florence D. DiGennaro Reed.

keep their location a secret, so you can return tomorrow for another meal. Behaving selfishly increases your *own* chances of survival, but it does not help the group. Behaving altruistically (sharing) is good for others, but, in the immediate term, it is less good for you.

As noted in Chapter 9, immediate reinforcement is a powerful behavior-influencing force. If it were the only factor that could impact your behavior, then your choice would be clear – eat the berries. Sharing will reduce the size of your reinforcer and it will introduce a delay until the berries can be distributed and consumed. Reinforcement, it appears, is pushing you toward greed. But this is not apparently how our Holocene ancestors behaved.

What we know of early human behavior comes from studying the few remaining hunter-gatherer groups with no prior contact with outsiders. Systematic observations of these groups reveal that they are cooperative and egalitarian; that is, they work together for the common good, and they share. How can this be so when immediate reinforcement is pushing their behavior toward greed? One answer to this question is *punishment*. When greedy behavior is detected, like hoarding the berries, it is punished by other members of the community. Studies of the bushman of Botswana and the pygmies of the Congo, for example, reveal that greedy behaviors are punished immediately with ridicule and shaming. Later, if the infraction is serious enough, the group may collectively impose harsher punishers – confiscating the cheater's possessions, banishing the cheater from the group, and possibly even killing the cheater (Boehm, 2012; Turnbull, 1961; Wiessner, 2005).

Punishment, when combined with reinforcement of altruistic acts, plays an important role in decreasing greed and, instead, promoting cooperation, sharing, and group cohesion (Critchfield, 2014; Dai & Fishbach, 2013; Fehr & Gächter, 2002; Gächter & Herrmann, 2009; Norenzayan, 2013). Punishment bad, reinforcement good? It's more complicated than that. But we are getting ahead of ourselves. Let's begin with some definitions.

Punishers and Punishment

Behavior analysts define a **punisher** as *a contingent consequence that decreases the future probability of behavior below its pre-punishment level.* Thus, like reinforcers, punishers are consequences; it's just that they have the opposite effect on behavior. Instead of increasing behavior (reinforcers), punishers decrease behavior.

For example, if the contingent consequence of running a red light is a costly ticket issued by a police officer, the ticket is classified as a punisher if, and only if, the future probability of running red lights decreases. If the ticket does not decrease the individual's red-light running behavior, then it is not classified as a punisher.

Given the way it is used in our daily lives, students will often think that a "punisher" is *something I would not want to happen to me.* This is not the way behavior analysts use this term. Behavior analysts define punishers based on their function – they decrease the future probability of the behavior that produced the punisher.

The definition of a punisher specifies that it is the *future probability* of behavior that the punisher must affect. Many consequences that are not punishers can decrease the probability of behavior *while the consequence is occurring.* For example, a child's violent temper tantrum may momentarily decrease if the child is restrained in a parent's loving arms. This therapeutic restraint makes it impossible to tantrum but does it function as a punisher? To find out, we must measure the *future probability* of tantruming, after the child is released. If tantruming decreases when the *IF tantrum → THEN therapeutic restraint* contingency is in place, then this consequence is a punisher. If the frequency of tantruming *increases* after the contingency is imposed, then loving restraint functions as a reinforcer. Punishers do more than prevent the behavior from occurring; they decrease the behavior when the individual is free to choose whether to make the punished response or not.

Figure 10.1 provides a flowchart to help tell the difference between reinforcers, punishers, and consequences that have no behavioral function. For example, take the hoarding of berries. The consequence of this behavior is that the hoarder is caught and brought before the council of elders. There the cheater is shamed with insults and laughter. The flowchart in Figure 10.1 asks us first to identify the effect of these consequences on hoarding – if they decrease the future probability of hoarding, then they probably function as punishers. To find out for sure, we would have to turn ON and OFF these consequences in an experiment. In that experiment, if hoarding was no longer shamed and it subsequently increased in frequency, then we could conclude that shaming was, in fact, a punisher. When the punisher is turned ON, the future probability of the behavior decreases; when the punisher is turned OFF, the behavior returns to its pre-punishment level.

Just as *reinforcement* is the process or procedure whereby a reinforcer increases operant behavior, **punishment** *is the process or procedure whereby a punisher decreases the future probability of an operant response.* Thus, the hunter-gatherer community harnessed the power of punishment by arranging an *IF hoarding → THEN shaming* contingency.

Note again that this functional use of the terms "punisher" and "punishment" is different from how we use them in daily life. When parents talk of punishing their child, they rarely

Behavior of interest: _____

Consequence: _____

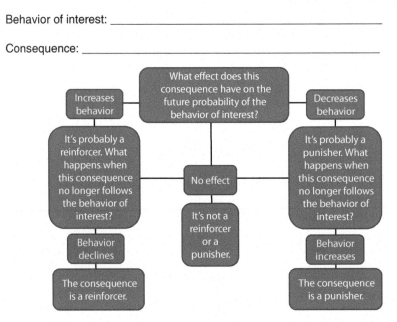

Figure 10.1 Use this flowchart to evaluate if a consequence functions as a reinforcer or a punisher.

consider whether the consequence decreases problem behavior. Instead, the parent is angry and arranges a negative consequence that seems "just." This is not a behavior-analytic approach.

Behavior analysts argue that putting the emphasis on the *function* of the consequence is more humane. The job of a punisher is to decrease the future probability of the problem behavior, not to exact retribution. Defining punishment functionally keeps us connected to one of the core goals of behavior analysis – to discover functional variables that may be used to positively influence behavior.

Two Kinds of Punishment – Both Decrease Behavior

Figure 10.2 illustrates that just as there are two kinds of reinforcement (positive reinforcement and negative reinforcement), there are two kinds of punishment (positive punishment and negative punishment). Said another way, there are two ways to deliver reinforcers and two ways to deliver punishers (Hackenberg & Defulio, 2007).

The horizontal rows in Figure 10.2 describe the behavioral consequence and the columns describe how that consequence influences behavior. If the consequence is the presentation of a stimulus and it systematically influences behavior, then it is either a *positive reinforcer* (increases the future probability of behavior) or a *positive punisher* (decreases the future probability of behavior).

When the behavior-influencing consequence is that a stimulus is removed, reduced, or prevented (bottom row in Figure 10.2), then it is either a negative reinforcer (increases the behavior) or a negative punisher (decreases the behavior). The following sections present more specific information about the two methods of delivering punishers. They also describe some of the research that has informed our understanding of punishment.

Consequence	Future probability of behavior	
	Increases	Decreases
Stimulus presented	Positive reinforcement	Positive punishment
Stimulus removed, reduced, or prevented	Negative reinforcement	Negative punishment (penalty)

Figure 10.2 The two kinds of reinforcement and punishment are distinguished from one another based on the type of consequences (rows) and how this consequence influences the future probability of behavior (columns).

Positive Punishment

The first method of delivering a punisher is positive punishment. **Positive punishment** is *the contingent presentation of a consequence that decreases the future probability of the behavior below its no-punishment level.* When a positive-punishing consequence occurs, it adds something to the environment; something that was not there before the punished behavior occurred. For example, the taste of spoiled milk is an added consequence; it was not there before the milk-drinking behavior occurred. If this consequence decreases the future probability of thoughtlessly drinking milk from the carton, without checking the expiration date, then we would classify it as a positive punisher.

Positive punishers are common in nature and need not be arranged by humans attempting to influence behavior. For example, stepping on a thorn is positively punished (presentation of a painful stimulus) if the future probability of walking barefoot decreases. Animals in nature frequently punish the behavior of other animals. For example, a lion attacks a water buffalo from behind and receives a stiff kick in the head. If, after the kick, the lion is less likely to attack buffalos from the rear, the kick functioned as a positive punisher.

Positive punishment has been extensively studied in the lab. A common procedure is to establish a baseline rate of operant behavior by arranging a contingent reinforcer. After a stable no-punishment baseline is established, the positive-punishment contingency is introduced. For example, in the experiment conducted by Herman and Azrin (1964), humans pulled two knobs on a vending machine to obtain cigarette reinforcers. As shown in Figure 10.3, during the pre-punishment baseline participants pulled the knobs somewhere between 30 and 120 times per minute, depending on the participant. However, in the punishment phase, all three participants quickly learned to stop pulling the knob that produced a loud noise (the punisher), in addition to cigarettes. Instead, they pulled the other, punishment-free knob to obtain their cigarette reinforcers (those data are not shown). The finding that positive punishers decrease behavior has been replicated with many species (for a review, see Azrin & Holz, 1966). That said, because of the aversive-consequence nature of this research, much less research has been conducted on punishment than on reinforcement.

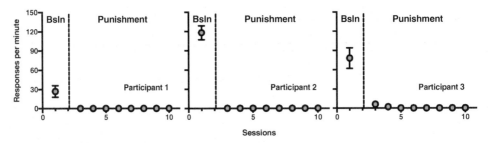

Figure 10.3 The effects of a positive punisher on the behavior of three human participants.
Source: Herman, R. L., & Azrin, N. H. (1964). Punishment by noise in an alternative response situation. *Journal of the Experimental Analysis of Behavior, 7*(2), 185–188. Retrieved from https://www.ncbi.nlm.nih.gov/pmc/articles/PMC1404315/pdf/jeabehav00182- 0059.pdf

Negative Punishment

The other way to deliver a punisher is negative punishment. **Negative punishment** is *the contingent removal, reduction, or prevention of a reinforcer; the effect of which decreases the future probability of the behavior below its no-punishment level.* Negative punishers might be thought of as effective penalties (Becirevic et al., 2016). For example, if *removing* a toy from a child who just hit his little brother decreases the future probability of such violent acts, then the toy-removal *penalty* is a negative punisher. Likewise, if the child is *prevented* from watching his favorite anime show and this *penalty* decreases the future probability of hitting his little brother, then this too is classified as a negative punisher.

In hockey, when a referee *penalizes* a player for violating a player-safety rule, the size of the player's team is reduced for some period of time (a negative punisher), leaving them at a disadvantage. If these penalties decrease rule violations below the level of mayhem that would presumably occur if there were no such rules, then these penalties function as negative punishers.

Nature is filled with negative punishers. Contingent *removal* of a reinforcer can punish carelessly dropping food into a rushing river (away goes the food) or behaving too aggressively during play (away goes the play partner). Contingent reinforcer *reduction* can punish inattention while eating if another member of the monkey troop is trying to steal food. Contingent *prevention* may punish the decision of a frog to climb a stem that easily bends, thereby *preventing* it from reaching the top of the plant, where the best mating opportunities may be found.

Source: Berndt Fischer/AGE Fotostock

Like positive punishers, there are many laboratory experiments investigating negative punishers. For example, during a baseline phase, Raiff et al. (2008) taught pigeons to peck a response

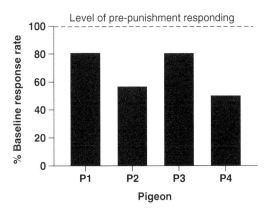

Figure 10.4 The effects of a negative punisher on the behavior of four pigeons. The dashed line shows their baseline rate of pecking, and the filled bars show the percentage decline in pecking after the negative-punishment contingency (the penalty) was introduced.
Source: Raiff, B. R., Bullock, C. E., & Hackenberg, T. D. (2008). Response-cost punishment with pigeons: Further evidence of response suppression via token loss. *Learning and Behavior*, *36*(11), 29–41. https://doi.org/10.3758/LB.36

key. In the pre-punishment phase, pecking the key was occasionally reinforced with token-reinforcers displayed on a computer screen; these could be later exchanged for food. The pigeons frequently pecked the key and filled their visually displayed bank accounts with tokens. During the negative-punishment phase, pecking the key had two consequences – it continued to produce tokens as it had before, but some of the pecks also subtracted tokens from the pigeon's account. The effect of these penalties is shown in Figure 10.4. Each of the four pigeons' rate of pecking is expressed as a percentage of their baseline rate, before the negative-punishment contingency was introduced. Because the filled bars are below the dashed line, a punishment effect is evident – the rate of pecking fell below the baseline, pre-punishment, level. Because all of the pigeons pecked less during the punishment phase, token loss was classified as a negative punisher.

Reading Quiz 1

1. Behavior analysts define a _____ as *a contingent consequence that decreases the future probability of behavior below its pre-punishment level.*
2. Punishers are contingent consequences, so they happen _____ (before/after) behavior.
3. The effect of a reinforcer is that it _____ the future probability of behavior, whereas the effect of a punisher is that it _____ the future probability of behavior.
4. The process or procedure whereby a punisher decreases the future probability of an operant response is called _____.
5. When a car thief is convicted and put in prison, they are unable to steal cars for the duration of their sentence. Based on this information alone, can we classify the prison sentence as a punisher?
6. Positive reinforcers _____ the future probability of behavior, and negative reinforcers _____ the future probability of behavior.
7. Positive punishers _____ the future probability of behavior, and negative punishers _____ the future probability of behavior.
8. When a positive punisher is delivered, a stimulus is _____. When a _____ punisher occurs, a stimulus is removed, reduced, or prevented.

When Should We Punish?

Which of these behaviors would you be more likely to punish: pushing someone out of line at the grocery store or pushing someone out of an airplane without a parachute? Clearly, the second behavior is more problematic than the first, despite the first being inappropriate to a civil society. What makes the second behavior so in need of punishment is how dangerous it is. Punishment decreases the future probability of behavior, so we are inclined to use it when it is imperative to decrease behavior *now*, before someone is hurt.

Punishment is used in applied (clinical) settings when the behavior is dangerous to oneself or others. In addition, punishment is most often used only after other interventions have failed. For example, sometimes a reinforcement-based intervention, like differential reinforcement (Chapter 7), will reduce problem behavior without punishment, but sometimes it will not. When these interventions do not reduce a behavior that is dangerous to oneself or others, effective punishment is needed (Hagopian et al., 1998; Lydon et al., 2015). Indeed, it is the position of the Association for Behavior Analysis International (ABAI, 2010) that clients have a right to effective behavioral treatment, and sometimes that treatment will include punishment.

Behavior analysts working in applied/clinical settings adhere to a set of ethical guidelines when using punishment. These guidelines require that the client freely consent to the use of punishment. Although one might think that consenting to have your own behavior punished would never happen, it actually does. Consider a study in which children displaying severe forms of problem behavior (aggression and self-injury) were allowed to choose the intervention that would be used to positively influence their behavior. After sampling the available interventions – one of which included a brief-restraint punisher – the children were allowed to choose the intervention that would be used thereafter in each therapy session. All of the children preferred the intervention that worked, and that was the intervention that included punishment (Hanley et al., 2005; see Donaldson et al., 2014; Layer et al., 2008 for replications). If a well-meaning individual who strictly held a "reinforcement good, punishment bad" opinion had prohibited the use of punishment, it would have deprived these children of an effective treatment that they clearly preferred. This issue is further explored in Extra Box 1.

EXTRA BOX 1:   PUNISHMENT IS THE NORM – USING IT EFFECTIVELY IS HUMANE

Despite our professed distaste for punishment, humans have always used it to reduce behavior they consider problematic or dangerous. As discussed at the beginning of this chapter, early hunter-gatherer humans used a variety of punishers to decrease selfish behavior. Later, when humans settled into agricultural communities and cities, they developed new consequences designed to function as punishers. Those accused of a range of crimes were, for example, confined in the stocks, which were placed prominently in public squares. Not only was the ability to move reduced by this negative punisher, but the individual's reputation was also tarnished by hurling trash at them (positive punisher) or by "fiendish boys [who] improved the occasion by deliberately pulling off their shoes and tickling the soles of their defenseless feet" (Ker, 1887).

Source: Cultural Archive / Alamy Stock Photo

In modern times, the use of negative consequences remains the norm. Teachers scold their misbehaving students. Bosses threaten to fire employees. Twitter users dox those whose behavior they find vile. Nations develop laws and impose consequences designed to function as punishers (e.g., economic sanctions). Although contingencies like *IF you do the crime → THEN you do the time* are designed to punish inappropriate behavior, we might wonder if they work. Do our governments use punishment effectively? If they do, then the future probability of the problem behavior will decline. If they do not, then problem behavior will continue. When the consequence does not work, society feels compelled to "punish" again and again (Curtis et al., 2018). Such practices cost a lot of taxpayer money, reduce public safety, and might be thought of as "cruel and unusual punishment."

Let's bring this discussion closer to home. Consider that if you are not one already, you will probably be a parent one day. Virtually all parents use some combination of positive and negative punishment to decrease the future probability of problem behavior. For example, despite pediatrician opposition to the practice, two-thirds of US parents report spanking their children (Caron, 2018). Short of this, parents yell at, threaten, and ground their children, all in the name of punishment. Negative consequences are used by virtually every parent, even those who hoped they would be the perfect, most loving parent.

If you plan to be a loving parent, you will want to use punishment as infrequently as possible. Likewise, if a government has an obligation to care for the life, liberty, and pursuit of happiness of its people, then it too should aim to use punishment as little as possible. Punishment can be used infrequently if it is used *effectively*. That is, if a single punisher produces a rapid and long-lasting reduction in the future probability of problem behavior, then this is more humane than using ineffective negative consequences three times a day, every day, 365. If the latter is your parental practice, then what your children will learn from your "punishment" is not that they should stop engaging in problem behavior, but that you are a reliable source of negative consequences. In short, your children will learn that you are cruel.

Think about this as you read the following section in this chapter ("Six Characteristics of Effective Punishment Interventions"). Punishment is not going away, so if our governments, schools, employers, and parents are going to use it (as they always have), then they should strive to use it humanely by ensuring that it actually reduces problem behavior.

Six Characteristics of Effective Punishment Interventions

You will recall from Chapter 9 that there are four characteristics of effective reinforcement. For example, a high-quality reinforcer obtained immediately will maintain more behavior than a lower-quality reinforcer obtained after a delay. Behavioral scientists conducting laboratory and applied research have also studied the characteristics of effective interventions that use punishment (Azrin & Holz, 1966; Hineline & Rosales-Ruiz, 2013; Lerman & Vorndran, 2002). The following sections outline six characteristics of effective punishment. The list represents current best practices in the use of punishment. That said, like so many aspects of an ever-improving science, there is much still to be learned about how to most effectively and humanely use punishment.

1. FOCUS ON REINFORCEMENT FIRST

To effectively reduce a problem behavior, it is helpful to first identify the reinforcer(s) maintaining that behavior. Identifying the reinforcer is important because the efficacy of a punisher is partially determined by the efficacy of the reinforcer maintaining the problem behavior (Hineline & Rosales-Ruiz, 2013). Think about this as a tug of war, with the reinforcer pulling behavior in one direction and the punisher pulling it the other way. Which of these forces will win? It depends. If the reinforcer is the King Kong of reinforcers (contingent, large, high-quality, and immediate), then it will win unless a highly effective punisher (the Godzilla of punishers) pulls in the opposite direction (see Critchfield et al., 2003 for a more technical, quantitative discussion).

Reinforcer   Punisher

Source: wiredforlego/Flickr/CC BY-SA 2.0

A humane approach to punishing behavior will seek to weaken King Kong rather than unleashing Godzilla. For example, an abolishing operation (AO) can reduce the efficacy of the reinforcer, which will decrease motivation to engage in the punishable response. In nonhuman experiments, punishing a food-reinforced response (like lever pressing) is more effective when the animal is less food deprived (Azrin & Holz, 1966). When the rat's King Kong hunger was reduced (AO), the punisher more effectively decreased the future probability of behavior.

To know if you are up against King Kong, you must identify the reinforcer. Chapter 7 discussed how to do this using the technique known as the *functional analysis of behavior*. As a quick reminder, a functional analysis individually turns ON and OFF several consequences to see if problem behavior is more frequent when each one is ON. If turning ON and OFF the consequence turns the problem behavior on and off, then that consequence functions as a reinforcer.

Once the reinforcer is identified, the behavior analyst will evaluate its efficacy – is it immediate, contingent, and so on? If it is, the *"focus on reinforcement first"* strategy will look for ways to reduce King Kong to a baby chimp. Can we delay the reinforcer? Can we deliver it noncontingently, over and over again (an AO)? These interventions can increase the efficacy of punishment (Carr et al., 2002).

2. COMBINE PUNISHMENT WITH EXTINCTION AND/OR DIFFERENTIAL REINFORCEMENT

When a functional analysis of behavior identifies the reinforcer maintaining problem behavior, that behavior can sometimes be reduced through extinction alone (ensure that the problem behavior is no longer reinforced) or differential reinforcement of an alternative response (extinction of problem behavior+reinforcement of alternative behavior). However, some instances of problem behavior cannot be reduced to a safe level using extinction or differential reinforcement alone (Hagopian et al., 1998). When that is true and the problem behavior puts the client or others at risk of injury or death, then punishment should be used in combination with extinction and/or differential reinforcement (Lerman & Toole, 2011).

Laboratory experiments reveal that the efficacy of punishment is enhanced by adding extinction or differential reinforcement (Azrin & Holz, 1966; Deluty, 1976; Fantino, 1973). Likewise, differential reinforcement procedures are more effective in reducing problem behavior when punishment is added (Pelloux et al., 2015).

When possible, it is the ethical stance of applied and practicing behavior analysts that punishment should be combined with reinforcement-based interventions designed to teach an appropriate behavior that can either access the functional reinforcer or a substitute reinforcer (ABAI, 2010). This practice is widely adhered to, for example, when differential reinforcement is combined with punishment (Lydon et al., 2015). However, it is often impractical or unethical to use differential reinforcement. If, for example, the problem behavior is maintained by a socially unacceptable reinforcer – aggressive behavior reinforced by seeing others suffer – then it would be inappropriate to teach the client an alternative way to access *this* reinforcer. Instead, it will be necessary to identify a substitute reinforcer.

3. DELIVER PUNISHERS IMMEDIATELY

Just as immediate reinforcers are more effective than delayed reinforcers, immediate punishers are more effective than delayed punishers. For example, Camp et al. (1967) found that positive punishers were much more effective in reducing rats' lever-pressing behavior when delivered immediately. As the delay to the punisher increased (from 0 to 30 seconds), its efficacy systematically decreased (see Baron, 1965; Byrne & Poling, 2017; Kamin, 1959 for replications).

The same effect of punishment immediacy has been observed in humans as well. Figure 10.5 shows the results of an experiment conducted by Banks and Vogel-Sprott (1965). They gave participants the opportunity to press a button to earn money. Their baseline (pre-punishment) level of pressing is represented by the dashed line at the top of the graph. Next, they introduced a positive-punishment contingency: *IF press → THEN electric shock* delivered to the fingers. As you can see, when shocks were immediate (0-second delay) button pressing decreased by 80%. However, delaying the shock by as little as 30 seconds greatly reduced the efficacy of the punisher; when delayed by a minute or more, the punisher was

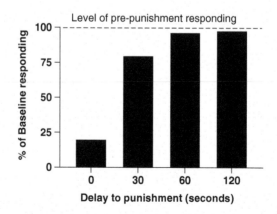

Figure 10.5 The effects of delaying the delivery of a positive punisher on human behavior.
Source: Banks, R. K., & Vogel-Sprott, M. (1965). Effect of delayed punishment on an immediately rewarded response in humans. *Journal of Experimental Psychology, 70*(4), 357–359. https://doi.org/10.1037/h0022233

ineffective – it produced virtually no reduction in behavior. Similar effects are observed when immediate and delayed negative-punishment contingencies are used (Trenholme & Baron, 1975) and when punishers are delayed in applied/clinical settings (Abramowitz & O'Leary, 1990).

Practical issues often make it impossible to deliver immediate punishment. For example, we might discover that a child has stolen candy from a store several hours after the behavior occurred. Although the most effective punisher would be imposed right after the theft occurred, delayed punishers can still decrease behavior if the contingent relation between the problem behavior (stealing) and the punisher is clarified (Meindl & Casey, 2012). This may be accomplished (1) verbally ("because you did ____, your punishment is ____"), (2) by playing an audio or video recording of the inappropriate behavior before it is punished, or (3) by having the individual re-enact the problem behavior just prior to delivering the punisher (Rolider & Van Houten, 1985; Van Houten & Rolider, 1988; Verna, 1977).

While these contingency-clarifying procedures can help, some delays to punishment are undoubtedly too long to deter much problem behavior. For example, how many believers languish in guilt at their lack of "willpower," when a contributing factor to their problem behavior is that the punishment for their sins is too delayed – occurring (as their beliefs suggest) decades later, after they die. In sum, punishers are more effective when delivered immediately.

4. DELIVER PUNISHMENT CONTINGENTLY

Punishers are, by definition, effective when delivered contingent upon a problem behavior. Noncontingent punishment – that is, presentation of a punisher regardless of whether problem behavior occurs – does not decrease the future probability of problem behavior (Huppert & Iversen, 1975).

Figure 10.6 shows the results of an illustrative experiment conducted in an applied setting by Oliver et al. (1974). Two boys (S1 and S2) were referred to treatment because of excessive aggressive behavior. During baseline (leftmost bars), both children engaged in aggressive acts (hitting, biting, etc.) when no punishing consequences were administered. These behaviors decreased considerably in the next phase, when the consequence of aggression was a negative punisher (a 3-minute time-out from positive reinforcement; a procedure that is defined and explained later). During the final phase of the experiment, time-outs were given noncontingently. That is, the teacher occasionally escorted the child to time-out regardless of his behavior. Not only did noncontingent time-out not decrease aggressive behaviors, it substantially *increased* it above baseline levels. This finding – that noncontingent punishers can elicit aggression – has been reported in laboratory studies as well (Hutchinson, 1977; Oliver et al., 1974; Ulrich & Azrin, 1962).

The practical implication of this finding is clear: Parents and managers who noncontingently "punish" their children or employees are not going to reduce problem behavior. Instead, their actions may elicit negative emotions and aggression. Good parents and good managers are those who understand and adhere to good contingencies of reinforcement and punishment (Tremblay et al., 2013).

5. PUNISH EVERY TIME

Punishers are more effective when delivered following every instance of the problem behavior (Deluty, 1976). If a bully's aggressive behaviors are infrequently punished, it should not be surprising that bullying continues. Similarly, most people steal music

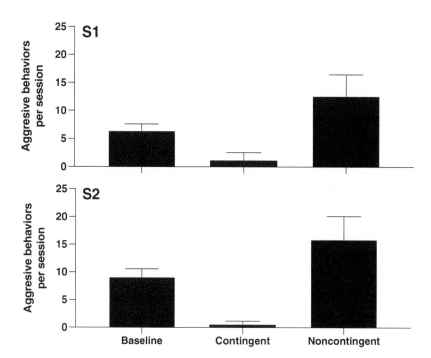

Figure 10.6 The effects of contingent and noncontingent time-out on the aggressive behavior of two boys (S1 and S2). Contingent time-out decreased aggressive behavior below the pre-punishment baseline level. However, delivering the same time-out consequence noncontingently *increased* aggression in both boys.
Source: Oliver, S. D., West, R. C., & Sloane, H. N. (1974). Some effects on human behavior of aversive events. *Behavior Therapy*, 5(4), 481–493. https://doi.org/10.1016/S0005-7894(74)80038-9

and movies online because, if their behavior has been punished at all, it has been punished infrequently. At a societal level, when a government collapses and the police go unpaid, criminal acts are infrequently punished and criminal behavior spikes. For example, after the collapse of the Libyan government in 2011, the rates of murder and theft increased by approximately 500% (Libya Herald, 2013). Simply put, intermittent punishment is not as effective as punishing every time (Lerman & Vorndran, 2002).

Of course, punishing every instance of problem behavior can be impractical. Even the most diligent parent will be distracted by a riveting show on Netflix now and again, thereby missing instances of dangerous behavior that could be reduced, if punished. If an unpunished problem behavior leaves behind a permanent product – such as a crying little brother with a bloody nose – an effective punisher can still be delivered by clarifying the contingency between the problem behavior and the punisher.

6. USE A PUNISHER IN THE GOLDILOCKS ZONE

This final characteristic of effective punishment is concerned with the intensity/size of the punishing stimulus. The humane use of punishment seeks to find the least restrictive punisher that reduces the future probability of behavior. That punisher exists in the so-called Goldilocks zone: Not too aversive and not so benign that it does not decrease behavior.

One intuitive, but ineffective, strategy for finding that Goldilocks-zone punisher is to start with a low-intensity punisher and gradually increase its aversiveness until it works. Unfortunately, habituation learning (discussed in Chapter 4) renders this strategy ineffective. As a refresher, habituation occurs when an eliciting stimulus (e.g., lemon juice in the mouth) gradually elicits less phylogenetic behavior (salivation) when that stimulus is presented repeatedly. Applied to punishment, repeatedly presenting an aversive stimulus reduces negative reactions to that stimulus (Bradley et al., 1993) and decreases its efficacy as a punisher (Capaldi et al., 1985; Deur & Parke, 1970).

In applied/clinical settings, behavior analysts have developed techniques for finding the Goldilocks-zone punisher. In one technique, potential punishers are presented briefly (to avoid habituation) and the client's response is recorded. Potentially effective punishers are those that elicit the beginnings of a negative emotional response and/or evoke escape behaviors such as turning away or holding up a hand to stop (Fisher et al., 1993; Zarcone et al., 1999). Conducting these brief punisher assessments can increase the efficacy of punishment-based interventions (Lydon et al., 2015). After all, one person's punisher might be another person's reinforcer.

Reading Quiz 2

1. Punishment is used in applied (clinical) settings when the behavior is _____ to oneself or others.
2. When designing an effective intervention that will include punishment, it is important to identify the _____ that maintains the problem behavior.
3. When the reinforcer maintaining problem behavior has been identified, the behavior analyst designing the punishment-based intervention will explore procedures that can _____ the efficacy of those reinforcers. If the reinforcer can be weakened, the punisher will be more effective.
4. An effective punishment-based intervention will combine punishment with _____ or _____ _____.
5. Punishers are more effective when delivered _____ after the problem behavior occurs.
6. If it is impossible to deliver the punisher immediately, then the next best practice is to clarify the _____ (IF→THEN) relation between the past behavior and the present punisher.
7. Punishers are effective only when they are delivered _____ on the problem behavior. Administering noncontingent punishers will not work.
8. In the Oliver et al. (1974) study (see Figure 10.6), noncontingent punishment actually _____ the future probability of aggressive behavior.
9. Punishing a problem behavior every once in a while is not an effective way to use punishment. Instead, punishers should follow _____ instance of problem behavior.
10. Arranging the least-restrictive punishment contingency means finding a punisher in the Goldilocks zone. That is, the punisher should not be too _____, nor should it be so benign that it does not decrease problem behavior.

Primary and Conditioned Punishment

Just as reinforcers may be classified as primary and conditioned reinforcers, so too can punishers be categorized as primary and conditioned punishers. A **primary punisher** is *a contingent consequence that functions as a punisher because, in the evolutionary past of the species, this consequence decreased the chances of survival.* Primary punishers are pain-inflicting stimuli (e.g., extreme heat or cold) or the removal/reduction of a primary reinforcer such as food, water, a sexual partner, and so on. Each of these consequences decreases the individual's (or the individual's genes) chances of survival; therefore, natural selection has prepared us to find these consequences punishing. No new learning is required.

By contrast, the punishing function of a conditioned punisher must be learned. The learning process is Pavlovian. A **conditioned punisher** is *a contingent consequence that signals a delay reduction to a backup punisher.* In the lab, we can establish a new conditioned punisher through Pavlovian conditioning. For example, if a mild electric shock (an unconditioned stimulus [US]) is delivered to the participant's leg once, on average, every 2 minutes, and a blue light precedes each shock by 2 seconds, the blue light will quickly acquire a conditioned-stimulus (CS) function (top panel of Figure 10.7; Hake & Azrin, 1965). This happens because the blue light signals a very large reduction in the delay to the next shock. Said another way, the CS functions as a Paul Revere stimulus signaling that "The shock is coming! The shock is coming!"

Once this Pavlovian learning is established, we can arrange the blue light as a conditioned punisher. This is accomplished by establishing a contingent relation between an operant response and the conditioned punisher. For example, we can turn on the blue light each time the participant turns his head to the left. If the baseline (pre-punishment) rate of left turns decreases after this contingency is imposed (as it does in the graph in Figure 10.7), then we may conclude that the blue light functions as a conditioned punisher (Dorsey et al., 1980).

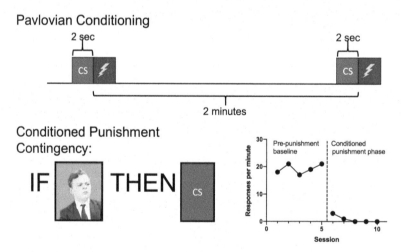

Figure 10.7 In the upper panel, a blue light acquires conditioned stimulus (CS) properties because it signals a delay reduction to an electric shock, the unconditioned stimulus (US). The left side of the lower panel illustrates the conditioned punishment contingency – IF the participant turns his head to the left, *THEN* the blue light is turned on. The inset graph shows hypothetical data illustrating a conditioned punishment effect. During the conditioned punishment phase, the rate of turning to the left decreases.
Source: Stockbyte/Getty Images

Primary and conditioned punishers are built into the popular underground fencing technologies that keep the family dog in the yard. These fences work by arranging primary and conditioned punishers. The primary punisher is an electric shock delivered by a special collar worn by the dog. The shock is delivered contingent on crossing over the underground fence installed at the perimeter of the yard. The conditioned punisher is a salient tone provided by the collar. The tone signals a delay reduction to shock.

For the underground fencing to work, a skilled animal behaviorist will put the dog on a leash so the dog can learn the tone→shock sequence. The trainer will also positively reinforce turning away each time the dog hears the tone. By doing so, the dog avoids the shock (a negative reinforcer). All told, the dog learns that (1) the tone signals that "The shock is coming! The shock is coming!" and (2) turning around is an effective shock-avoidance response. When properly trained, the dog will rarely come close enough to the perimeter to activate the conditioned punisher and will almost never contact the primary punisher.

Source: Ammit Jack/Shutterstock.com

Conditioned punishers are common in our everyday human lives as well. What they all have in common is that they signal a delay reduction to a backup punisher. For example, parents often call their children by their full name – "Robert Joseph Terrel, you get over here right now!" – just before a backup punisher is delivered. If the consequence of a mischievous act is hearing your full name shouted in this way, that consequence functions as a conditioned punisher if, and only if, it decreases the future probability of this mischievous action. Other conditioned punishers are more subtle. For example, a subtle facial expression, such as a raised eyebrow, can function as a conditioned punisher (decreasing the future probability of texting in class) if the individual has learned that it signals a delay reduction to a backup punisher (e.g., being shamed in front of the class).

Like conditioned reinforcers, conditioned punishers will gradually lose their ability to influence behavior if they are presented repeatedly without the US – the backup punisher. The reason for this loss of function is Pavlovian extinction. That is, when the CS is repeatedly presented without the US, the individual learns that it no longer signals a delay reduction to the US. In the case of conditioned punishment, a threat is only effective if it actually signals a delay reduction to the backup punisher. Empty threats to punish, whether they come from parents or employers, are soon ignored by children and employees.

Finally, like conditioned reinforcers, conditioned punishers may be established through verbal learning (Hayes et al., 1991). That is, explaining that the onset of a stimulus signals a delay reduction to a backup punisher will, in principle, establish that stimulus as a conditioned punisher. To ensure that this happens, it is good to know a thing or two about how to arrange effective conditioned punishers.

Arranging Effective Conditioned Punishers

The principles of effective Pavlovian conditioning outlined in Chapter 4 apply to conditioned punishment as well. That is, the conditioned punisher will more effectively suppress behavior when (1) the backup punisher (US) is a phylogenetically important event, (2) the conditioned punisher (CS) is highly salient (noticeable), (3) the conditioned punisher signals a large delay reduction to the US, and (4) the conditioned punisher is not redundant with another stimulus that already signals the US is coming (Evans, 1962; Mowrer & Aiken, 1954).

The delay-reduction ratio used in Chapters 4 and 8 may also be used to calculate how big the delay reduction (to the US) signaled by the onset of the CS is:

$$\text{delay reduction ratio} = \frac{\text{US} \rightarrow \text{US interval}}{\text{CS} \rightarrow \text{US interval}}$$

In our hypothetical laboratory experiment illustrated in Figure 10.7, the average time between mild electric shocks was 2 minutes (US → US interval=120 seconds) and the blue light was turned on 2 seconds before each shock (CS → CS interval=2). Thus, the delay-reduction ratio is

$$\frac{120}{2} = 60$$

This means that the CS signals the shock will be delivered 60 times sooner than normal. Such a large delay reduction is conducive to rapidly learning the function of the CS, necessary in establishing a conditioned punisher.

Some Commonly Used Punishers

Most readers of this text will not pursue careers in behavior analysis. Almost all readers, however, will use punishment throughout their life. Many readers will become parents who, for example, must decrease their child's aggressive behaviors before they are expelled from their preschool classroom. Other readers will be employed as managers who need to decrease any number of problematic employee behaviors – being rude to customers, stealing from the company, habitually arriving late to work, and so on.

The following sections describe two commonly used punishment contingencies: (1) time-out from positive reinforcement and (2) response-cost punishment. Both of these are negative-punishment contingencies. Because stakeholders find the removal of a positive reinforcer to be more acceptable than the presentation of a punishing stimulus (Kazdin, 1980), these punishment contingencies are widely used by applied behavior analysts and parents. With a little creativity, they can also be used by managers who need to reduce behaviors that put a company at risk.

Time-Out from Positive Reinforcement

If you grew up in the United States in the last 50 years, there is a good chance you are personally familiar with a negative-punishment procedure known as *time-out from positive reinforcement*. Although it is often referred to as "time-out," we use the longer term "time-out from positive reinforcement" because it is important to keep in mind that time-outs work only if they are time-outs from positive reinforcement. By way of formal definition, a **time-out from positive reinforcement** is *a signaled response-contingent suspension of a positive-reinforcement contingency, the effect of which decreases the future probability of problem behavior.*

Source: Daniel Grill/Tetra images/Getty Images.

The time-out from positive reinforcement procedure was discovered, like so many procedures in behavior analysis, in the animal research laboratory (Herrnstein, 1955). In an illustrative experiment, Ferster (1958) found that the future probability of food-reinforced behavior of pigeons and chimpanzees was greatly reduced by a signaled (lights out) 10-minute time-out from the opportunity to earn food reinforcers. Subsequent applied research revealed that time-out could be effective in reducing a range of inappropriate behaviors in children, from thumbsucking to aggression (Baer, 1962; Donaldson & Vollmer, 2012; Wolf et al., 1963).

Although time-out is widely used and is endorsed as an effective behavior-change technique by pediatricians (American Academy of Pediatrics, 2018), it is often implemented in ways that reduce its efficacy. Well-meaning parenting books, magazines, and websites often provide advice that is not supported by scientific research (Corralejo et al., 2018). Below are **four guidelines for effectively using time-out from positive reinforcement**; they are based on decades of applied research conducted with human children (Corralejo et al., 2018).

1. *Provide no more than one verbal warning:* Time-out from positive reinforcement is more effective when it is implemented following either one or no verbal warnings, such as "You need to stop or you will go to time-out" (Roberts, 1983). Providing a second or third warning makes time-out ineffective (Jones et al., 1992; Twyman et al., 1994; Velasquez et al., 2016). The reason for this is straightforward from a Pavlovian learning perspective. An effective warning is a conditioned punisher (CS) that signals a delay reduction to a punishing US. Providing multiple verbal warnings without the US is Pavlovian extinction – a procedure that decreases the ability of the conditioned punisher to decrease the future probability of behavior.

2. Time-outs from positive reinforcement are effective when they *significantly reduce access to reinforcers* (Shriver & Allen, 1996; Solnick et al., 1977). If the child in time-out can play with a toy, self-stimulate, or joke with a friend, then the consequence

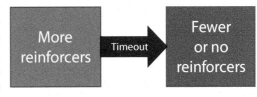

is not a time-out from positive reinforcement, and it is unlikely to reduce problem behavior. Worse, if the "time-out" removes the child from something aversive – for example, providing a time-out from an aversive math assignment – it can function as a negative reinforcer of the escape variety (SR_E-), thereby *increasing* problem behavior (Perone & Galizio, 1987; Plummer et al., 1977). To be effective, time-outs must be a time-out from positive reinforcement.

3. Time-out from positive reinforcement should *end after no more than 5 minutes, even if the child is not sitting quietly.* Again, intuition tells us that older children should get longer time-outs and that the child should have to calm down before they are allowed to return to the reinforcing activity, but the scientific evidence does not support these

practices (Corralejo et al., 2018; Donaldson & Vollmer, 2011; Mace et al., 1986). So, set a timer for no more than 5 minutes and let the child return to positive reinforcement after it goes off.

4. Time-out from positive reinforcement works best when *every instance of the problem behavior produces a time-out* (Lerman et al., 1997). Don't wait for the child to misbehave several times before implementing a time-out. An exception to this rule is that, after time-out is used consistently and it has significantly reduced the problem behavior, intermittent time-outs can be effective in maintaining these improvements (Donaldson & Vollmer, 2012; Lerman et al., 1997; Northup et al., 1997).

When these four guidelines are followed, time-out from positive reinforcement can be an effective way to negatively punish problem behavior. It is a more humane approach to punishment than the corporal punishment techniques (spanking, whipping, etc.) that were common prior to the 1960s, when time-out was first introduced as an alternative to these aversive consequences.

Of course, if you are managing behavior in a workplace setting, you will not even think about spanking your employees when they are rude to customers. Instead, a time-out from positive reinforcement may do the trick. First, to arrange a time-out from positive reinforcement, we must identify a positive reinforcer in the workplace. For employees who are paid by the hour, being on the clock is presumably a positive reinforcer; if it was not, the employee would not come to work. To impose a time-out on rude employee behavior, we would simply instruct the employee to clock-out. By doing so, we shift the employee from more monetary reinforcers to no monetary reinforcers. If this procedure reduces the employee's frequency of making rude comments to customers, then this time-out from positive reinforcement functions as a negative punisher.

Response-Cost Punishment

In applied settings, *negative punishers that involve the removal or reduction of a reinforcer* are often referred to as **response-cost punishers**. We have already considered several examples of response-cost punishers. When a parent takes a toy away from a misbehaving child, that stimulus removal functions as a response-cost punisher if, and only if, the future probability of misbehavior decreases. In a previous chapter we discussed the Good-Behavior Game, which was immortalized in the Harry Potter books and movies – "Five points for Gryffindor!" Fans of Harry Potter will recall that not only were points earned for heroic behaviors, but points were lost for misdeeds. For example, when Harry, Hermione, and Neville Longbottom are found wandering the halls at night, they were each penalized 50 points. This consequence decreased the future probability of nighttime hall-wandering, so yes, it functioned as a response-cost punisher.

Figure 10.8 illustrates that contingent point losses can decrease problem behavior in real schools attended by nonfictional children (Conyers et al., 2004). In this study, conducted in an unruly classroom, children were engaged in disruptive behaviors most of the time during the pre-punishment baseline sessions. During the response-cost phase, individual children lost points (exchangeable for candy) when they engaged in inappropriate behavior. As is clear from Figure 10.8, this response-cost punishment contingency quickly decreased problem behavior. When this contingency was turned OFF during the second baseline phase, problem behavior resumed and continued until response-cost was reintroduced in the final phase. Such effects have been replicated in

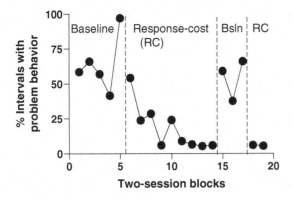

Figure 10.8 High levels of problem behavior in baseline are decreased by response-cost punishment in this A-B-A-B reversal design.
Source: Conyers, C., Miltenberger, R., Maki, A., Barenz, R., Jurgens, M., Sailer, A., … Kopp, B. (2004). A comparison of response cost and differential reinforcement of other behavior to reduce disruptive behavior in a preschool classroom. *Journal of Applied Behavior Analysis*, *37*(3), 411–415. https://doi.org/10.1901/jaba.2004.37-411

controlled laboratory conditions with human and nonhuman subjects (Pietras et al., 2010; see Hackenberg, 2009 for review).

Response-cost punishment has also been used to reduce problem behavior in workplace settings. Bateman and Ludwig (2004), for example, reduced the number of food orders sent to the wrong restaurant by subtracting money from warehouse employees' bonus accounts that otherwise accumulated as they met weekly goals. The response-cost intervention reduced errors and saved the company thousands of dollars in lost food.

The Watchful Eye of the Punisher

When you were a teenager living at home, when would you schedule a house-party attended by all your boisterous friends? Would you schedule it when your parents were home, sitting in the living room watching network TV? Or would you wait until they went on vacation? The answer is obvious, as is the reason why – if your parents catch you holding the party, punishment will follow. We all know that the best time to engage in a punishable act is when no one is looking. J. K. Rowling knew this too – that's why she gave Harry Potter the cloak of invisibility, so he could wander the halls at night without fear of punishment.

Considerable research supports our intuition that when punishing agents (parents, police, or Hogwarts professors) are watching, problem behavior is less likely to occur. For example, a number of applied studies have reported that problem behaviors displayed by individuals with intellectual disabilities or autism are less likely to occur when a "you're being watched by a punishing agent" stimulus is on display (Doughty et al., 2007; Piazza et al., 1996; Tiger et al., 2017). Figure 10.9 shows, for individual clients in the Doughty et al. (2007) study, the percentage of observation intervals in which a problem behavior occurred. When the *you're being watched* stimulus was presented, problem behavior was infrequent. When the *you're not being watched* stimulus was presented, the frequency of problem behavior

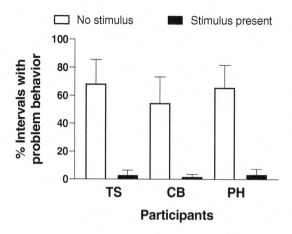

Figure 10.9 Three human participants were rarely engaged in a problem behavior when a stimulus signaled that a punishing agent was watching (filled bars). When that stimulus was removed (open bars), problem behavior increased considerably.

Source: Doughty, S. S., Anderson, C. M., Doughty, A. H., Williams, D. C., & Saunders, K. J. (2007). Discriminative Control of Punished Stereotyped Behavior in Humans. *Journal of the Experimental Analysis of Behavior, 87*(3), 325–336. https://doi.org/10.1901/jeab.2007.39-05

skyrocketed. In sum, when the watchful eye of the punisher is trained on us, we refrain from engaging in punishable behaviors.

The connectivity of the cellphone in our pockets increases the number of watchful eyes. If we begin to behave very badly and someone pulls out their cellphone to record our misdeeds, we quickly cease the inappropriate action, lest it be posted all over social media, leading to a wide variety of negative punishers (loss of friends, followers, and possibly even our job; Gstalter, 2020). Similarly, when police-monitored surveillance cameras are installed, criminal activities like shootings and car theft decrease within the camera's viewing range (Caplan et al., 2011). The cameras function as a "you're being watched by a punishing agent" stimulus because the chances of getting caught and punished are higher when the crime is committed within the camera's range (Piza et al., 2014).

Social scientists have speculated that the evolution of gods into beings who punished the immoral acts of humans corresponded with the transition from hunter-gatherer life to living in cities (Laurin et al., 2012; Norenzayan, 2013). Where the gods of hunter-gatherers cared only about their own godly activities (creating storms, fires, and floods), the gods of city dwellers were constantly monitoring human behavior and, at times, angrily punishing those who sinned. Consider Zeus, who was so angered by Sisyphus' self-pride, that he condemned him to an eternity of pointless toil.

In Roman mythology, Zeus punished Sisyphus' wickedness by forcing him to push a boulder up a hill, and then to forever repeat the task when it rolled back down.

Source: Abraham Jansz/The Warburg Institute Library/Wikipedia

Why were watchful, punishing gods needed in the cities but not among hunter-gatherers? One hypothesis is that city dwellers, like most readers of this book, are surrounded by strangers who mostly turn a blind eye to bad behavior ("I don't know that belligerent drunk guy, so I'm not getting involved"). By contrast, hunter-gatherers had to live with "that guy" day after day, so punishing his inappropriate behavior now paid off immediately (the belligerence ceases) and later (the future probability of belligerence decreases). By convincing city dwellers that they are always being monitored by gods who will punish their transgressions, everyone enjoys the benefits of punishment (a more civil society, more sharing, less belligerence) without having to do any punishing themselves. Did it work? The data suggest it did. In modern times, when people encounter stimuli that suggest they are being watched by the predominant god in their culture (e.g., seeing a church or a religious symbol), they are less likely to engage in antisocial behavior, even *if they are not religious* (Ahmed & Salas, 2013; Malhotra, 2008; Xygalatas, 2013). Punishment bad, reinforcement good? Again, it is more complicated than that.

The Role of Reinforcement in the Act of Punishing

This chapter has summarized how punishment decreases the future probability of problem behavior. This effect on behavior happens among those receiving the punisher (the fine, the slap on the wrist, etc.). In this final section, we shift our focus to the behavior of the individual delivering the punisher.

Delivering a punisher contingent upon problem behavior is, itself, an operant response – one that is maintained by reinforcers (Seymour et al., 2007). One reinforcing consequence is that the problem behavior stops. Consider a teacher who observes a bully tormenting another child in class. When she informs the bully that his actions will land him in after-school detention, the bullying stops. This immediate cessation of bullying undoubtedly functions as a negative reinforcer of the escape variety (SR_E-); that is, it increases the future probability that the teacher will use this punisher again.

Laboratory studies of human cooperation reveal that negative attitudes about punishment (punishment bad, reinforcement good) soon give way to strong preferences for punishment when cheating is encountered. That is, when delivering punishers is reinforced with reductions in cheating and increases in cooperation, people warm up to punishment. A good example of this occurred in a cooperation/competition game arranged by Gurek et al. (2006). In the game, participants repeatedly decided to either altruistically cooperate (more money for everyone) or to cheat (more money for me, less for everyone else). After each round of play, participants could choose between two versions of the game – one in which they could punish cheaters, and another in which they could not.[1] Figure 10.10 shows that most participants initially preferred the no-punishment version of the game. However, as they continued to play the game, their preference for punishment substantially increased. Choosing to punish was reinforced with two consequences: (1) cheating decreased (a negative reinforcer) and (2) income increased (a positive reinforcer).

Neuroeconomists have studied the activity of the human brain when we punish unfair behavior. When unfair or greedy actions are detected, brain regions that are active during

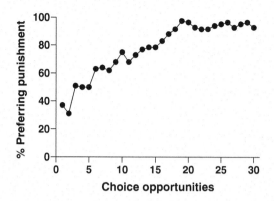

Figure 10.10 The percentage of human participants who preferred to play a cooperation/ competition game that allowed them to punish cheaters. As participants played the game and saw how punishment decreased cheating (and increased cooperative behavior), they far preferred to play the game in which punishment was an option.
Source: Gurek, O., Irlenbusch, B., & Rockenbach, B. (2006). The competitive advantage of sanctioning institutions. *Science, 312*, 108–111. https://doi.org/10.1126/science.1123633

negative emotional experiences are activated. Norm violations elicit such neural activity and may function as an establishing operation that increases punishment as a reinforcer (Montague & Lohrenz, 2007). Said less technically, when we see someone cheating, bullying, pulling into our parking space, and so on, it makes us angry and we really want to see them get what they deserve. Seeing their behavior get punished functions as a reinforcer. Indeed, when we punish such unfair behaviors, reward-processing regions of our brain are activated (de Quervain et al., 2004; Strobel et al., 2011). These reinforcement processes increase our inclination to punish cheating, when we detect it. This appears to have been critical in the evolutionary history of our species, when living in small hunter-gatherer communities required cooperation to survive.

Reading Quiz 3

1. A _____ punisher is a contingent consequence that functions as a punisher because, in the evolutionary past of the species, this consequence decreased the chances of survival.
2. _____ punishers signal a delay reduction to a backup punisher.
3. A conditioned punisher will be more effective in decreasing problem behavior when (1) the backup punisher (US) is a phylogenetically important event, (2) the conditioned punisher (CS) is highly salient, (3) the conditioned punisher signals a large _____ _____ to the US, and (4) the conditioned punisher is not redundant with another stimulus that already signals the US is coming.
4. A time-out from _____ _____ is a signaled response-contingent suspension of a positive-reinforcement contingency, the effect of which is to decrease the future probability of problem behavior.
5. The data suggest one should never provide more than _____ verbal warning(s) before administering a time-out from positive reinforcement.

6. Time-out from positive reinforcement will not reduce problem behavior if, during the time-out, the availability of _____ is not reduced.

7. In applied settings, behavior analysts refer to negative punishers as _____ _____ punishers. These involve a response-contingent reduction or removal of a stimulus that functions as a positive reinforcer; the effect of which is to decrease the future probability of problem behavior.

8. When a stimulus signals that a behavior is very likely to be punished, the frequency of that behavior _____.

9. When humans observe a stimulus that suggests the dominant god(s) of their culture is(are) watching, anti-social behavior _____.

10. Using punishment to reduce problem behavior is itself an operant behavior. That is, this behavior is _____ when the problem behavior decreases.

11. In cooperation/competition games, humans increasingly prefer the version of the game that allows them to use _____. The reason why is that they experience the benefits of this behavior-influencing consequence.

Summary

Punishment is a process or procedure in which contingent consequences decrease the future probability of behavior. This is a functional definition – which is to say it points to the effects of the punisher on behavior; it does not define a punisher as something we dislike. Punishment procedures can be used in applied/clinical settings to reduce behaviors that put the individual, or those around them, at risk of injury or death; the more serious the problem behavior, the more open we are to using punishment (Kazdin, 1980).

There are two kinds of punishment – positive and negative punishment. Don't be confused by the names, they both decrease the future probability of behavior. Positive punishment adds a new stimulus to the environment, whereas negative punishment removes, reduces, or prevents a stimulus from occurring. Any salient stimulus that signals a large delay reduction to the delivery of a punisher comes to function as a conditioned punisher, at least for a while. If the conditioned punisher is presented repeatedly without the backup punisher, Pavlovian extinction will occur, and the punishing function of the stimulus will be lost.

Although we often have negative feelings about punishment, it is important to underscore a few points about punishment. First, it occurs in nature – any time a naturally occurring consequence decreases the behavior that produced it, that consequence is a punisher. Second, some behaviors are dangerous to oneself and others, and when a reinforcement-based intervention is unable to decrease these behaviors, punishment is necessary (e.g., if a humane form of punishment could decrease dangerously aggressive acts in your child's preschool classroom, you would probably be willing to give it a try). Third, some behaviors are maintained by such powerful reinforcers (e.g., cheating the elderly of their retirement funds) that punishment may be necessary to promote the greater good. And finally, the principles of effective punishment discussed in this chapter can help you to use punishment humanely. Arranging humane punishers means punishment is infrequent and so is problem behavior. Two of those humane forms of punishment are time-out from positive reinforcement and response-cost punishment. Both involve the removal or reduction of a positive reinforcer and, when implemented according to the guidelines outlined in this chapter, can effectively reduce problem behavior.

So, how do you feel about punishment now? "Punishment bad, reinforcement good?" If you still feel that way, may we suggest you spend more time trying to cooperate with cheaters. That might change your mind.

Answers to Reading Quiz Questions

Reading Quiz 1

1. punisher
2. after
3. increases; decreases
4. punishment
5. No. To classify a consequence as a punisher, we need to know if the *future probability* of the punished behavior decreases. That is, after the consequence is over, does the problem behavior decline? In the case of the car thief, we need to know if stealing cars decreases after the individual is released from prison. If they continue stealing cars, then the time in prison did not function as a punisher. If car stealing decreases, then the prison sentence was a punisher.
6. increase; increase
7. decrease; decrease
8. presented; negative

Reading Quiz 2

1. dangerous
2. reinforcer
3. weaken
4. extinction; differential reinforcement
5. immediately
6. contingent
7. contingent
8. increased
9. every
10. aversive

Reading Quiz 3

1. primary
2. conditioned
3. delay reduction

4. positive reinforcement
5. one
6. reinforcement, "reinforcers" is also a correct answer
7. response-cost
8. decreases
9. decreases
10. reinforced
11. punishment, "punishers" is also a correct answer

Note

1. In the punishment version of the game, participants could also reward cooperative behaviors. However, participants used punishment more often than rewards, so here we highlight how punishing cheaters is reinforced.

References

ABAI. (2010). *Statement on restraint and seclusion.* https://www.abainternational.org/about-us/policies-and-positions/restraint-and-seclusion,-2010.aspx

Abramowitz, A. J., & O'Leary, S. G. (1990). Effectiveness of delayed punishment in an applied setting. *Behavior Therapy, 21*(2), 231–239. https://doi.org/10.1016/S0005-7894(05)80279-5

Ahmed, A., & Salas, O. (2013). Religious context and prosociality: An experimental study from valparaíso, Chile. *Journal for the Scientific Study of Religion, 52*(3), 627–637. https://doi.org/10.1111/jssr.12045

Azrin, N. H., & Holz, W. C. (1966). Punishment. In W. K. Honig (Ed.), *Operant behavior: Areas of research and application* (pp. 380–447). Englewood Cliffs, NJ: Prentice-Hall.

Baer, D. M. (1962). Laboratory control of thumbsucking by withdrawal and re-presentation of reinforcement. *Journal of the Experimental Analysis of Behavior, 5*(4), 525–528. https://doi.org/10.1901/jeab.1962.5-525

Banks, R. K., & Vogel-Sprott, M. (1965). Effect of delayed punishment on an immediately rewarded response in humans. *Journal of Experimental Psychology, 70*(4), 357–359. https://doi.org/10.1037/h0022233

Baron, A. (1965). Delayed punishment of a runway response. *Journal of Comparative and Physiological Psychology, 60*(1), 131–134. https://doi.org/10.1037/h0022326

Bateman, M. J., & Ludwig, T. D. (2004). Managing distribution quality through an adapted incentive program with tiered goals and feedback. *Journal of Organizational Behavior Management, 23*(1), 33–55. https://doi.org/10.1300/J075v23n01_03

Becirevic, A., Critchfield, T. S., & Reed, D. D. (2016). On the social acceptability of behavior-analytic terms: Crowdsourced comparisons of lay and technical language. *The Behavior Analyst, 39*(2), 305–317. https://doi.org/10.1007/s40614-016-0067-4

Boehm, C. (2012). Costs and benefits in hunter-gatherer punishment. *Behavioral and Brain Sciences, 35*, 19–20. https://doi.org/10.1017/S0140525X11001403

Bradley, M. M., Lang, P. J., & Cuthbert, B. N. (1993). Emotion, novelty, and the startle reflex: Habituation in humans. *Behavioral Neuroscience, 107*(6), 970–980. https://doi.org/10.1037/0735-7044.107.6.970

Byrne, T., & Poling, A. (2017). Behavioral effects of delayed timeouts from reinforcement. *Journal of the Experimental Analysis of Behavior*, *107*(2), 208–217. https://doi.org/10.1002/jeab.246

Camp, D. S., Raymond, G. A., & Church, R. M. (1967). Temporal relationship between response and punishment. *Journal of Experimental Psychology*, *74*(1), 114–123. https://doi.org/10.1037/h0024518

Capaldi, E. D., Sheffer, J. D., Viveiros, D. M., Davidson, T., & Campbell, D. H. (1985). Shock preexposure and the reduced effectiveness of shock. *Learning and Motivation*, *16*(4), 357–380. https://doi.org/10.1016/0023-9690(85)90021-9

Caplan, J. M., Kennedy, L. W., & Petrossian, G. (2011). Police-monitored CCTV cameras in Newark, NJ: A quasi-experimental test of crime deterrence. *Journal of Experimental Criminology*, *7*(3), 255–274. https://doi.org/10.1007/s11292-011-9125-9

Caron, C. (2018, November 5). Spanking is ineffective and harmful to children, pediatricians' group says. *New York Times*. https://www.nytimes.com/2018/11/05/health/spanking-harmful-study-pediatricians.html

Carr, J. E., Dozier, C. L., Patel, M. R., Adams, A. N., & Martin, N. (2002). Treatment of automatically reinforced object mouthing with noncontingent reinforcement and response blocking: Experimental analysis and social validation. *Research in Developmental Disabilities*, *23*(1), 37–44. https://doi.org/10.1016/S0891-4222(01)00090-7

Conyers, C., Miltenberger, R., Maki, A., Barenz, R., Jurgens, M., Sailer, A., … Kopp, B. (2004). A comparison of response cost and differential reinforcement of other behavior to reduce disruptive behavior in a preschool classroom. *Journal of Applied Behavior Analysis*, *37*(3), 411–415. https://doi.org/10.1901/jaba.2004.37-411

Corralejo, S. M., Jensen, S. A., Greathouse, A. D., & Ward, L. E. (2018). Parameters of time-out: Research update and comparison to parenting programs, books, and online recommendations. *Behavior Therapy*, *49*(1), 99–112. https://doi.org/10.1016/J.BETH.2017.09.005

Critchfield, T. S. (2014). Skeptic's corner: Punishment - destructive force or valuable social "adhesive"? *Behavior Analysis in Practice*, *7*(1), 36–44. https://doi.org/10.1007/s40617-014-0005-4

Critchfield, T. S., Paletz, E. M., MacAleese, K. R., & Newland, M. C. (2003). Punishment in human choice: Direct or competitive suppression? *Journal of the Experimental Analysis of Behavior*, *80*(1), 1–27. https://doi.org/10.1901/jeab.2003.80-1

Curtis, A., Youssef, G., Guadagno, B., Manning, V., Enticott, P. G., Lubman, D. I., & Miller, P. (2018). Swift, certain and fair justice: Insights from behavioural learning and neurocognitive research. *Drug and Alcohol Review*, *37*, S240–S245. https://doi.org/10.1111/dar.12628

Dai, X., & Fishbach, A. (2013). When waiting to choose increases patience. *Organizational Behavior and Human Decision Processes*, *121*(2), 256–266. https://doi.org/10.1016/J.OBHDP.2013.01.007

de Quervain, D. J. F., Fischbacher, U., Treyer, V., Schellhammer, M., Schnyder, U., Buck, A., & Fehr, E. (2004). The neural basis of altruistic punishment. *Science*, *305*(5688), 1254–1258. https://doi.org/10.1126/science.1100735

Deluty, M. Z. (1976). Choice and the rate of punishment in concurrent schedules1. *Journal of the Experimental Analysis of Behavior*, *25*(1), 75–80. https://doi.org/10.1901/jeab.1976.25-75

Deur, J. L., & Parke, R. D. (1970). Effects of inconsistent punishment on aggression in children. *Developmental Psychology*, *2*(3), 403–411. https://doi.org/10.1037/h0029170

Donaldson, J. M., DeLeon, I. G., Fisher, A. B., & Kahng, S. (2014). Effects of and preference for conditions of token earn versus token loss. *Journal of Applied Behavior Analysis*, *47*(3), 537–548. https://doi.org/10.1002/jaba.135

Donaldson, J. M., & Vollmer, T. R. (2011). An evaluation and comparison of time-out procedures with and without release contingencies. *Journal of Applied Behavior Analysis*, *44*(4), 693–705. https://doi.org/10.1901/jaba.2011.44-693

Donaldson, J. M., & Vollmer, T. R. (2012). A procedure for thinning the schedule of time-out. *Journal of Applied Behavior Analysis*, *45*(3), 625–630. https://doi.org/10.1901/jaba.2012.45-625

Dorsey, M. F., Iwata, B. A., Ong, P., & McSween, T. E. (1980). Treatment of self-injurious behavior using a water mist: Initial response suppression and generalization. *Journal of Applied Behavior Analysis*, *13*(2), 343–353. https://doi.org/10.1901/jaba.1980.13-343

Doughty, S. S., Anderson, C. M., Doughty, A. H., Williams, D. C., & Saunders, K. J. (2007). Discriminative control of punished stereotyped behavior in humans. *Journal of the Experimental Analysis of Behavior, 87*(3), 325–336. https://doi.org/10.1901/jeab.2007.39-05

Evans, W. O. (1962). Producing either positive or negative tendencies to a stimulus associated with shock. *Journal of the Experimental Analysis of Behavior, 5*(3), 335–337. https://doi.org/10.1901/jeab.1962.5-335

Fantino, E. (1973). Aversive control. In J. A. Nevin & G. S. Reynolds (Eds.), *The study of behavior: Learning, motivation, emotion, and instinct* (pp. 239–279). Glenview, IL: Scott, Foresman.

Fehr, E., & Gächter, S. (2002). Altruistic punishment in humans. *Nature, 415*(6868), 137–140. https://doi.org/10.1038/415137a

Ferster, C. B. (1958). Control of behavior in chimpanzees and pigeons by time out from positive reinforcement. *Psychological Monographs: General and Applied, 72*(8), 1–38. https://doi.org/10.1037/h0093787

Fisher, W., Piazza, C., Cataldo, M., Harrell, R., Jefferson, G., & Conner, R. (1993). Functional communication training with and without extinction and punishment. *Journal of Applied Behavior Analysis, 26*(1), 23–36. https://doi.org/10.1901/jaba.1993.26-23

Gächter, S., & Herrmann, B. (2009). Reciprocity, culture and human cooperation: Previous insights and a new cross-cultural experiment. *Philosophical Transactions of the Royal Society B: Biological Sciences, 364*(1518), 791–806. https://doi.org/10.1098/rstb.2008.0275

Gstalter, M. (2020, May 25). Woman loses her job after viral video shows her calling police on black birdwatcher in Central Park. *The Hill*. Retrieved from https://thehill.com/blogs/blog-briefing-room/news/499570-woman-loses-her-job-after-viral-video-shows-her-calling-police

Gurek, O., Irlenbusch, B., & Rockenbach, B. (2006). The competitive advantage of sanctioning institutions. *Science, 312*, 108–111. https://doi.org/10.1126/science.1123633

Hackenberg, T. D. (2009). Token reinforcement: A review and analysis. *Journal of the Experimental Analysis of Behavior, 91*(2), 257–286. https://doi.org/10.1901/jeab.2009.91-257

Hackenberg, T. D., & Defulio, A. (2007). Timeout from reinforcement: Restoring a balance between analysis and application. *Mexican Journal of Behavior Analysis, 33*, 37–44. Retrieved from https://www.redalyc.org/pdf/593/59309905.pdf

Hagopian, L. P., Fisher, W. W., Sullivan, M. T., Acquisto, J., & LeBlanc, L. A. (1998). Effectiveness of functional communication training with and without extinction and punishment: A summary of 21 inpatient cases. *Journal of Applied Behavior Analysis, 31*(2), 211–235. https://doi.org/10.1901/jaba.1998.31-211

Hake, D. F., & Azrin, N. H. (1965). Conditioned punishment1. *Journal of the Experimental Analysis of Behavior, 8*(5), 279–293. https://doi.org/10.1901/jeab.1965.8-279

Hanley, G. P., Piazza, C. C., Fisher, W. W., & Maglieri, K. A. (2005). On the effectiveness of and preference for punishment and extinction components of function-based interventions. *Journal of Applied Behavior Analysis, 38*(1), 51–65. https://doi.org/10.1901/jaba.2005.6-04

Hayes, S. C., Kohlenberg, B. S., & Hayes, L. J. (1991). The transfer of specific and general consequential functions through simple and conditional equivalence relations. *Journal of the Experimental Analysis of Behavior, 56*, 119–137. https://doi.org/10.1901/jeab.1991.56-119

Herman, R. L., & Azrin, N. H. (1964). Punishment by noise in an alternative response situation. *Journal of the Experimental Analysis of Behavior, 7*(2), 185–188. https://doi.org/10.1901/jeab.1964.7-185

Herrnstein, R. J. (1955). *Behavioral consequences of the removal of a discriminative stimulus associated with variable-interval reinforcement.* [Unpublished doctoral dissertation]. Harvard University.

Hineline, P. N., & Rosales-Ruiz, J. (2013). Behavior in relation to aversive events: Punishment and negative reinforcement. In G. J. Madden (Ed.), *APA handbook of behavior analysis, Vol. 1: Methods and principles.* Washington, DC: American Psychological Association.

Huppert, F. A., & Iversen, S. D. (1975). Response suppression in rats: A comparison of response-contingent and noncontingent punishment and the effect of the minor tranquilizer, chlordiazepoxide. *Psychopharmacologia, 44*(1), 67–75. https://doi.org/10.1007/BF00421186

Hutchinson, R. R. (1977). By-products of aversive control. In W. K. Honig & J. E. R. Staddon (Eds.), *Handbook of operant behavior1* (pp. 415–431). Engelwood Cliffs, NJ: Prentice-Hall.

Jones, R. N., Sloane, H. N., & Roberts, M. W. (1992). Limitations of "don't" instructional control. *Behavior Therapy*, 23(1), 131–140. https://doi.org/10.1016/S0005-7894(05)80313-2

Kamin, L. J. (1959). The delay-of-punishment gradient. *Journal of Comparative and Physiological Psychology*, 52(4), 434–437. https://doi.org/10.1037/h0045089

Kazdin, A. E. (1980). Acceptability of alternative treatments for deviant child behavior. *Journal of Applied Behavior Analysis*, 13, 259–273. https://doi.org/10.1901/jaba.1980.13-259

Ker, D. (1887, November 13). England in old times. *New York Times*, p. 11.

Laurin, K., Shariff, A. F., Henrich, J., & Kay, A. C. (2012). Outsourcing punishment to god: Beliefs in divine control reduce earthly punishment. *Proceedings of the Royal Society B: Biological Sciences*, 279(1741), 3272–3281. https://doi.org/10.1098/rspb.2012.0615

Layer, S. A., Hanley, G. P., Heal, N. A., & Tiger, J. H. (2008). Determining individual preschoolers' preferences in a group arrangement. *Journal of Applied Behavior Analysis*, 41(1), 25–37. https://doi.org/10.1901/jaba.2008.41-25

Lerman, D. C., Iwata, B. A., Shore, B. A., & DeLeon, I. G. (1997). Effects of intermittent punishment on self-injurious behavior: An evaluation of schedule thinning. *Journal of Applied Behavior Analysis*, 30(2), 187–201. https://doi.org/10.1901/jaba.1997.30-187

Lerman, D. C., & Toole, L. M. (2011). Developing function-based punishment procedures for problem behavior. In W. W. Fisher, C. C. Piazza, & H. S. Roane (Eds.), *Handbook of applied behavior analysis* (pp. 348–369). New York: Guilford.

Lerman, D. C., & Vorndran, C. M. (2002). On the status of knowledge for using punishment: Implications for treating behavior disorders. *Journal of Applied Behavior Analysis*, 35(4), 431–464. https://doi.org/10.1901/jaba.2002.35-431

Libya Herald (2013, January 9). Murder rate up 500% in two years. https://www.libyaherald.com/2013/01/09/murder-rate-up-500-in-two-years/

Lydon, S., Healy, O., Moran, L., & Foody, C. (2015). A quantitative examination of punishment research. *Research in Developmental Disabilities*, 36, 470–484. https://doi.org/10.1016/J.RIDD.2014.10.036

Mace, F. C., Page, T. J., Ivancic, M. T., & O'Brien, S. (1986). Effectiveness of brief time-out with and without contingent delay: A comparative analysis. *Journal of Applied Behavior Analysis*, 19(1), 79–86. https://doi.org/10.1901/jaba.1986.19-79

Malhotra, D. (2008). (When) are religious people nicer? Religious salience and the "Sunday Effect" on pro-social behavior. *Harvard Business School NOM Working Paper*, (09-066). https://doi.org/10.2139/ssrn.1297275

Meindl, J. N., & Casey, L. B. (2012). Increasing the suppressive effect of delayed punishers: A review of basic and applied literature. *Behavioral Interventions*, 27, 129–150. https://doi.org/10.1002/bin.1341

Montague, P. R., & Lohrenz, T. (2007). To detect and correct: Norm violations and their enforcement. *Neuron*, 56(1), 14–18. https://doi.org/10.1016/J.NEURON.2007.09.020

Mowrer, D. H. & Aiken, E. G. (1954). Contiguity vs. drive reduction in conditioned fear: Temporal variations in conditioned and unconditioned stimulus. *American Journal of Psychology*, 67, 26–38.

Norenzayan, A. (2013). *Big gods: How religion transformed cooperation and conflict*. Princeton, NJ: Princeton University Press.

Northup, J., Fisher, W., Kahng, S. W., Harrell, R., & Kurtz, P. (1997). An assessment of the necessary strength of behavioral treatments for severe behavior problems. *Journal of Developmental and Physical Disabilities*, 9(1), 1–16. https://doi.org/10.1023/A:1024984526008

Oliver, S. D., West, R. C., & Sloane, H. N. (1974). Some effects on human behavior of aversive events. *Behavior Therapy*, 5(4), 481–493. https://doi.org/10.1016/S0005-7894(74)80038-9

Pelloux, Y., Murray, J. E., & Everitt, B. J. (2015). Differential vulnerability to the punishment of cocaine related behaviours: Effects of locus of punishment, cocaine taking history and alternative reinforcer availability. *Psychopharmacology*, 232(1), 125–134. https://doi.org/10.1007/s00213-014-3648-5

Perone, M., & Galizio, M. (1987). Variable-interval schedules of timeout from avoidance. *Journal of the Experimental Analysis of Behavior*, 47(1), 97–113. https://doi.org/10.1901/jeab.1987.47-97

Piazza, C. C., Hanley, G. P., & Fisher, W. W. (1996). Functional analysis and treatment of cigarette pica. *Journal of Applied Behavior Analysis*, 29(4), 437–450. https://doi.org/10.1901/jaba.1996.29-437

Pietras, C. J., Brandt, A. E., & Searcy, G. D. (2010). Human responding on random-interval schedules of response-cost punishment: Role of reduced reinforcement density. *Journal of the Experimental Analysis of Behavior*, 93(1), 5–26. https://doi.org/10.1901/jeab.2010.93-5

Piza, E. L., Caplan, J. M., & Kennedy, L. W. (2014). Is the punishment more certain? An analysis of CCTV detections and enforcement. *Justice Quarterly*, 31(6), 1015–1043. https://doi.org/10.1080/07418825.2012.723034

Plummer, S., Baer, D. M., & LeBlanc, J. M. (1977). Functional considerations in the use of procedural timeout and in effective alternative. *Journal of Applied Behavior Analysis*, 10(4), 689–705. https://doi.org/10.1901/jaba.1977.10-689

Raiff, B. R., Bullock, C. E., & Hackenberg, T. D. (2008). Response-cost punishment with pigeons: Further evidence of response suppression via token loss. *Learning and Behavior*, 36(11), 29–41. https://doi.org/10.3758/LB.36.1.29

Roberts, M. W. (1983). The effects of warned versus unwarned time-out procedures on child noncompliance. *Child & Family Behavior Therapy*, 4(1), 37–53. https://doi.org/10.1300/J019v04n01_04

Rolider, A., & Van Houten, R. (1985). Suppressing tantrum behavior in public places through the use of delayed punishment mediated by audio recordings. *Behavior Therapy*, 16(2), 181–194. https://doi.org/10.1016/S0005-7894(85)80044-7

Seymour, B., Singer, T., & Dolan, R. (2007). The neurobiology of punishment. *Nature Reviews Neuroscience*, 8, 300–311. https://doi.org/10.1038/nrn2119

Shriver, M. D., & Allen, K. D. (1996). The time-out grid: A guide to effective discipline. *School Psychology Quarterly*, 11(1), 67–75. https://doi.org/10.1037/h0088921

Solnick, J. V., Rincover, A., & Peterson, C. R. (1977). Some determinants of the reinforcing and punishing effects of timeout. *Journal of Applied Behavior Analysis*, 10(3), 415–424. https://doi.org/10.1901/jaba.1977.10-415

Strobel, A., Zimmermann, J., Schmitz, A., Reuter, M., Lis, S., Windmann, S., & Kirsch, P. (2011). Beyond revenge: Neural and genetic bases of altruistic punishment. *NeuroImage*, 54(1), 671–680. https://doi.org/10.1016/J.NEUROIMAGE.2010.07.051

Tiger, J. H., Wierzba, B. C., Fisher, W. W., & Benitez, B. B. (2017). Developing and demonstrating inhibitory stimulus control over repetitive behavior. *Behavioral Interventions*, 32(2), 160–174. https://doi.org/10.1002/bin.1472

Tremblay, M., Vandenberghe, C., & Doucet, O. (2013). Relationships between leader-contingent and non-contingent reward and punishment behaviors and subordinates' perceptions of justice and satisfaction, and evaluation of the moderating influence of trust propensity, pay level, and role ambiguity. *Journal of Business and Psychology*, 28(2), 233–249. https://doi.org/10.1007/s10869-012-9275-4

Trenholme, I. A., & Baron, A. (1975). Immediate and delayed punishment of human behavior by loss of reinforcement. *Learning and Motivation*, 6(1), 62–79. https://doi.org/10.1016/0023-9690(75)90035-1

Turnbull, C. M. (1961). *The forest people*. London: Jonathan Cape.

Twyman, J. S., Johnson, H., Buie, J. D., & Nelson, C. M. (1994). The use of a warning procedure to signal a more intrusive timeout contingency. *Behavioral Disorders*, 19(4), 243–253. https://doi.org/10.1177/019874299401900407

Ulrich, R. E., & Azrin, N. H. (1962). Reflexive fighting in response to aversive stimulation. *Journal of the Experimental Analysis of Behavior*, 5(4), 511–520. https://doi.org/10.1901/jeab.1962.5-511

Van Houten, R., & Rolider, A. (1988). Recreating the scene: An effective way to provide delayed punishment for inappropriate motor behavior. *Journal of Applied Behavior Analysis*, 21(2), 187–192. https://doi.org/10.1901/jaba.1988.21-187

Vaziri Flais, S. & American Academy of Pediatrics. (Ed.). (2018). *Caring for your school-age child: Ages 5 to 12*. New York: Bantam Books.

Velasquez, L. D., Cathcart, A., Kennedy, A., & Allen, K. D. (2016). The effect of warnings to timeout on child compliance to parental instructions. *Child & Family Behavior Therapy*, *38*(3), 225–244. https://doi.org/10.1080/07317107.2016.1203148

Verna, G. B. (1977). The effects of four-hour delay of punishment under two conditions of verbal instruction. *Child Development*, *48*(2), 621–624. Retrieved from https://www.jstor.org/stable/pdf/1128662.pdf

Wiessner, P. (2005). Norm enforcement among the Ju/'hoansi bushmen: A case for strong reciprocity? *Human Nature*, *16*(2), 115–145. https://doi.org/10.1007/s12110-005-1000-9

Wolf, M., Risley, T., & Mees, H. (1963). Application of operant conditioning procedures to the behaviour problems of an autistic child. *Behaviour Research and Therapy*, *1*(2–4), 305–312. https://doi.org/10.1016/0005-7967(63)90045-7

Xygalatas, D. (2013). Effects of religious setting on cooperative behavior: A case study from Mauritius. *Religion, Brain and Behavior*, *3*(2), 91–102. https://doi.org/10.1080/2153599X.2012.724547

Zarcone, J. R., Crosland, K., Fisher, W. W., Worsdell, A. S., & Herman, K. (1999). A brief method for conducting a negative-reinforcement assessment. *Research in Developmental Disabilities*, *20*(2), 107–124. https://doi.org/10.1016/S0891-4222(98)00036-5

Complex Contingencies of Reinforcement

11

Until now, most of the operant learning examples in this book were all-or-nothing, simple contingencies. That is, behavior was reinforced every time it occurred. For example, *IF we press the app icon → THEN the app loads. IF the rat presses the lever → THEN a food reinforcer is provided.* Such examples clearly illustrate the contingent relation between a response and a reinforcer, but our experiences in the real world tell us that reinforcement contingencies are often much more complex.

This chapter explores some of the complex contingencies of reinforcement that operate in our everyday lives. A common type of complexity is that not every response is reinforced. For example, most applications on our computers will open only if we double-click them (*IF two clicks → THEN app access*). Similarly, a dirty pan requires a dozen or so scrubbing responses before it is clean (*IF a dozen scrubs → THEN clean pan*). And most employers pay their contracted employee only after making many more responses still (*IF ~ 1,000 raking and leaf-bagging responses → THEN $75 payment*).

Another common type of complexity is that reinforcers are often unavailable until some interval of time has passed. For example, if our friend is away from their phone for 48 minutes, then trying to video chat with them will not be reinforced until 48 minutes have passed, no matter how many times we send them a chat request. As soon as they return, they will accept the request and then

Source: lekoh/Pixaby

An Introduction to Behavior Analysis, First Edition. Gregory J. Madden, Derek D. Reed, and Florence D. DiGennaro Reed.
© 2021 John Wiley & Sons Ltd. Published 2021 by John Wiley & Sons Ltd.

our behavior will be reinforced (*IF 48 minutes pass and one chat request → THEN social reinforcers are obtained during the chat*).

This chapter discusses these two types of complex contingencies in greater detail – that is, contingencies that require more than just one response and contingencies that involve the passage of time. These complex contingencies are often referred to as *schedules of reinforcement*, and so the chapter starts there. As we go through these contingencies, we will discuss the unique and systematic patterns of behavior that often occur under each schedule of reinforcement. Perhaps you have already noticed systematic patterns of behavior in your own life. For example, you have probably noticed that when people finish one task (reading this chapter), they usually take a break before beginning the next task (reading a chapter for another class). During that break they may experience a feeling of dread about the upcoming task and may succumb to peer pressure to do something fun instead. Such a pattern of working, taking a break and perhaps escaping from the next thing on our to-do list, is just one of the patterns of behavior we will discuss.

Later in the chapter we discuss how behavior analysts have arranged complex contingencies of reinforcement to better understand socially important human behaviors. But for now, let's start simple.

Schedules of Reinforcement

Contingencies of reinforcement can range from simple to complex. As a starting place for this discussion, look at Figure 11.1. On the left side of this continuum, the reinforcement contingency is very simple – **continuous reinforcement**, wherein *every instance of the response is reinforced*. The right side of this continuum is also very simple – extinction, wherein the response is never reinforced. Between these extremes is the zone of **intermittent reinforcement**, wherein *the response is sometimes but not always reinforced*. In this intermittent reinforcement zone, the contingent relation between response and reinforcer is more complex.

Recognizing that a good deal of our everyday behavior does not produce a reinforcer every time, it is important to study intermittent reinforcement contingencies. B. F. Skinner began researching intermittent reinforcement in the early 1930s, and he quickly

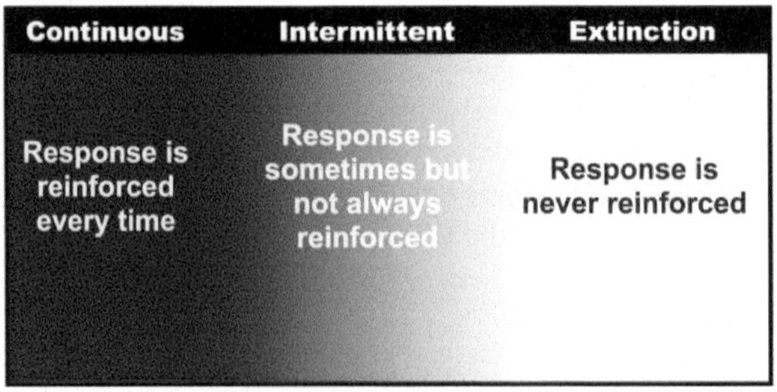

Figure 11.1 A continuum of contingencies.

found that different contingencies produced very different response rates and patterns of behavior. For example, when behavior is reinforced every time it occurs, Skinner's nonhuman subjects responded quickly, when given the opportunity to do so. By contrast, when Skinner reinforced the first response that occurred after a 1-minute timer elapsed, the subjects learned not to waste effort by responding early in the 1-minute interval. Instead, they waited for time to pass and then began responding, only when the available reinforcer got nearer in time. Skinner, fascinated by these orderly and replicable patterns of behavior, stud-

Charles B. Ferster (left) and B. F. Skinner (right), the authors of *Schedules of Reinforcement*.

Source: Jff119/Wikipedia/ CC BY-SA 3.0 us

Source: Msanders nti/Wikipedia/CC BY-SA 4.0

ied complex contingencies of reinforcement for two decades with his collaborator, Charles Ferster. They eventually published a >700-page summary of their findings in a book titled, *Schedules of Reinforcement* (Ferster & Skinner, 1957).

A **schedule of reinforcement** *precisely specifies the nature of the contingent relation between a response and its reinforcer.*[1] Said another way, the schedule of reinforcement tells us exactly how the response-reinforcer contingency works. The simplest schedule of reinforcement is the continuous schedule shown on the left side of Figure 11.1. According to this schedule, *IF one response → THEN one reinforcer.* Undoubtedly you can think of other schedules of reinforcement. How about *IF two responses → THEN one reinforcer*, or perhaps *IF one response → THEN two reinforcers.* The possibilities are endless. For our purposes, we will discuss just two of the broad categories of schedules studied by Ferster and Skinner (1957) – ratio and interval schedules of reinforcement.

Ratio Schedules of Reinforcement

A **ratio schedule of reinforcement** *specifies the number of responses that must be made in order for the reinforcer to be delivered.* The term "ratio" refers to the ratio of responses to reinforcers. For example, the ratio might be 3:1; that is, *IF 3 responses → THEN 1 reinforcer.* When a ratio schedule of reinforcement is in operation, there is a direct relation between the number of responses and the number of reinforcers. The more responses we make, the more reinforcers we get. The faster we respond, the faster we get the reinforcer.

Another way to think about ratio schedules is that they specify the *price* of the reinforcer. Instead of saying that the ratio of reinforcers to responses is 3:1, we could say that the price of the reinforcer is three responses. Will the individual pay this price (will they respond three times and "buy" a reinforcer) and if so, how many reinforcers will they buy – how much will they spend? By conceptualizing ratio schedules as the *price* of the reinforcer, behavior analysts have been able to explore topics of interest to economists, which launched important areas of behavioral-economic research (Kagel et al., 1995). We will have more to say about price, spending, and ratio schedules later. For now, let's look at the two most important kinds of ratio schedules – fixed-ratio and variable-ratio schedules of reinforcement.

Fixed-Ratio Schedules

Under a **fixed-ratio (FR) schedule** *the number of responses required per reinforcer is the same every time.* For example, under a fixed-ratio 3 schedule (abbreviated FR 3), three responses are required to satisfy the reinforcement contingency. Under an FR 10 schedule, the reinforcer will not be delivered until the 10th response is made.

Figure 11.2 depicts an FR 3 schedule of reinforcement. Each black circle represents a response and the green arrows indicate when reinforcers are delivered. Because this is an FR schedule, the reinforcer is provided after the third response, every time. It does not matter how much time passes between responses; reinforcers are delivered only after the third response is made. Said another way, the *ratio requirement* is three responses, every time.

Any time that a fixed amount of work is required to obtain a reinforcer, an FR schedule is in operation. For example, if we are earning extra money by completing online surveys, then a survey that offers to pay us to answer 30 questions has arranged an FR 30 schedule of reinforcement. Similarly, in 2019, the Tennessee Titans (a National Football League team) put an FR 23 schedule in the contract of their quarterback Ryan Tannehill. The contract specified that *IF he threw 23 touchdown passes → THEN he was awarded a $1,000,000 bonus* (Corry, 2019). Unfortunately for him, he threw only 22, so he did not get his bonus.

A little closer to home, if a college student gives herself a break contingent upon answering six questions in her textbook, then she has arranged an FR 6 schedule of reinforcement. Speaking of which, Table 11.1 provides six examples of FR schedules. Blank spaces are provided to give you some practice identifying the type of schedule and/or the ratio requirement (i.e., the number of responses required per reinforcer). If you like, you could take a break after correctly answering these questions. The answers are provided at the end of the chapter.

Source: Chipermc/Wikipedia/CC BY-SA 4.0

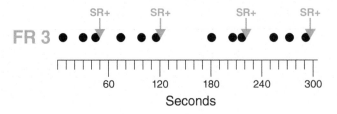

Figure 11.2 A visual representation of an FR 3 schedule of reinforcement.

Table 11.1 Examples of FR schedules. The blank spaces offer an opportunity to practice identifying the <u>type of schedule</u> and/or the <u>ratio requirement</u> for reinforcement.

1. A telemarketer is paid a $10 bonus after making 5 calls that result in sales. (FR ____)
2. A child receives a coupon for 1 free pizza after reading her 20th book. (FR ____)
3. A pigeon earns grain after pecking the key 100 times. (__R ____)
4. The coach screams "Nice work!" only if the athlete lifts the weight 20 times. (_____)
5. The link opens after it is double-clicked. (_____)
6. A dog earns a treat every other time he rolls over when instructed. (_____)

To see the unique patterns of behavior that each schedule of reinforcement maintains, we need a way to visually display the data. The method that Skinner developed is called a "cumulative record." A **cumulative record** is *a graphical display of responding as it unfolds over time*. The three panels of Figure 11.3 show examples of cumulative records. In each panel, time unfolds from left to right along the x-axis and cumulative responses increase as we move up the y-axis. The blue line in each panel is the record of responding over time.

In the top panel (panel A), the subject is not making the target response and the result is a horizontal line – the cumulative number of responses shown is zero. In panel B, the subject makes a single response. This is displayed as an upward deflection of the blue line. Right after that, a downward green line records the delivery of a reinforcer. Apparently this hypothetical subject was operating under an FR 1 (continuous) schedule of reinforcement.

Panel C contains two cumulative records. The one on the left shows that the subject did not respond at first (horizontal line) and then eventually made three responses, each separated by a pause. Because this hypothetical subject was responding under an FR 3 schedule, the reinforcer was delivered immediately after the third response. The cumulative record on the right side of panel C shows another subject responding under an FR 3 schedule, but this cumulative record is steeper – the subject is responding faster. The three responses are made

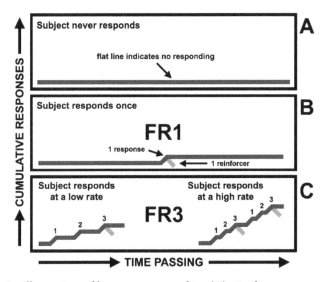

Figure 11.3 An illustration of how non-responding (A), single responses and reinforcers (B), and multiple responses and reinforcers are displayed on a cumulative record.

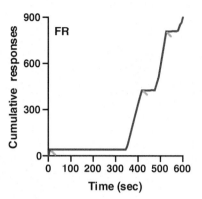

Figure 11.4 A cumulative record of a pigeon's stable key pecking on an FR 360 schedule of reinforcement.
Source: Ferster, C. B., & Skinner, B. F. (1957). Schedules of reinforcement. New York: Appleton-Century-Crofts.

quickly and response pausing is confined to the period right after the reinforcer. The steepness of the cumulative records makes it visually obvious which subject is responding at a higher rate and earning more reinforcers in the same amount of time.

Now that we know how to read a cumulative record, take a look at Figure 11.4; it shows the **typical pattern of responding under an FR schedule of reinforcement** – a *post-reinforcement pause followed by a high-constant rate of responding that ends with a reinforcer.* That is, following each reinforcer, the pigeon whose record is shown takes a break. Some of these breaks are brief, others are longer. When the pigeon resumes working, pecking occurs at a high rate, with no interruptions. This response pattern is called a "break-and-run" pattern because the subject takes a break before the response "run" to the reinforcer. Perhaps you can empathize with a rat, pigeon, or monkey that decides to take a break before starting into the next FR run.

Although FR schedules produce reliable patterns of "break-and-run" responding in nonhuman species, the effect has not been consistently demonstrated in human laboratory studies (see reviews by Schlinger et al., 2008; Williams et al., 2011). Humans typically do not pause after the delivery of the reinforcer. "Why" is uncertain, but it may be due to differences in the way human and animal experiments are conducted. For example, pecking a key to obtain a food reward is probably the most exciting thing that happens in the daily life of a laboratory pigeon, but for a human it is incredibly boring to repeatedly press a button to earn points on a computer screen – worst computer game ever! If the task and contingencies arranged are so mind-numbingly boring that humans do not attend to the consequences of their behavior, that behavior cannot be systematically influenced by those consequences (Galizio, 1979; Madden & Perone, 1999). In our everyday lives, however, taking a break between large tasks, like a large FR requirement for a pigeon, is normal.

Understanding what causes the FR schedule's characteristic post-reinforcement pause may be helpful in understanding our tendency to procrastinate, or a child's tendency to become emotional or aggressive when asked to transition from one activity to the next (Jessel et al., 2016b; Schlinger et al., 2008). One theory of the post-reinforcement pause is that the individual has learned how the contingency of reinforcement operates – they have learned that after a reinforcer, the FR response counter is reset to zero. Therefore, the next reinforcer has never been further away, both in terms of the amount of work and time to the next reinforcer. This distance to the next reinforcer is aversive and it can evoke negative emotions, aggression, and escape (Azrin, 1961; Gentry, 1968; Huston & Desisto, 1971). It is not surprising, then, that when children are asked to transition from a reinforcing activity (playing with a friend) to an activity that requires more work and more time to reach the next reinforcer, emotional outbursts may occur (Castillo et al., 2018; Jessel et al., 2016a; Williams et al., 2011).

For adults who no longer have to do what their parents tells them to do, post-reinforce-ment "procrastination" is of greater interest. For example, when we finish writing a term paper and have the freedom to decide what to do next, most of us will take a break – we grab lunch with friends, watch a movie, or take the dog for a walk – we don't immediately begin working on the next term paper. Such instances of "procrastination" may occur because, once again, the FR response-counter has been reset to zero – the next reinforcer for task completion has never been further away. Undertaking the next big project is an aversive prospect and we avoid it by engaging in other behaviors that will produce a more immediate, less-effortful reinforcer, like lunch. Thus, procrastination is natural – we all do it, including our nonhuman friends.

One strategy for reducing the harm of procrastination is to plan for it. That is, make con-crete plans to take a break after completing a big task, but commit to making it a healthy break; an hour for lunch with a friend, a 20-minute walk outside to clear the head, a "nap-puccino" – drink a cup of coffee, take a 25-minute nap, and then undertake the next task (Pink, 2018). This strategy sets an end-time on the break, so we are less likely to move con-tinuously from one break to the next, endlessly procrastinating from the next task.

Variable-Ratio Schedules

The second type of ratio schedule of reinforcement is the variable-ratio schedule. Under a **variable-ratio (VR) schedule**, *the number of responses required per reinforcer is not the same every time*. Under a VR schedule, the numerical value corresponds to the *average* number of responses required per reinforcer. For example, under a VR 3, reinforcers are delivered after an average of 3 responses. This is depicted in Figure 11.5. The first reinforcer is delivered after the very first response, but after that, reinforcers are delivered after 6 responses, then 2 responses, and then 3 responses. The average number of responses per reinforcer is 3 (that is, $[1 + 6 + 2 + 3]/4 = 3$). Under a VR schedule, one cannot predict which response will be reinforced.

VR schedules are common in nature. For example, the average number of cheetah attacks per meal (the reinforcer) is about 2; that is, when they see a prey and initiate an attack, they will succeed about half the time (Lee, 2013). Thus, their hunting behavior operates under a

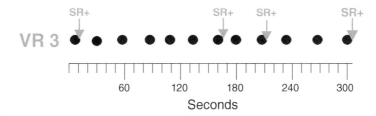

Figure 11.5 A visual representation of a VR 3 schedule of reinforcement.

VR 2 schedule of reinforcement. Lions have a rougher time of it, they operate under a VR 4 (an average of 4 attacks before they get a kill) and tigers have it harder still – VR 20 (Elliott et al., 1977; Schaller, 1967).

Among humans, a VR schedule operates when reinforcers are probabilistic.[2] For example, if a wizard in a game of Dungeons and Dragons will cast a successful spell against a powerful opponent only if she rolls a 10 on a 10-sided die, then her probability of success is just 10%. That is,

Source: Demetrius John Kessy/Flickr/CC BY 2.0

on average, her spellcasting will succeed 1 time in 10 attempts – a VR 10 schedule of reinforcement. Likewise, if a baseball batter gets on base an average of 1 time in 5 at bats, then they are operating under a VR 5 schedule of reinforcement (in baseball parlance, we'd say their batting average is "200," because 1/5 = 0.200).

Probabilistic reinforcers are the rule in games of chance. If a slot machine is programmed to pay out, on average, 1 time in 50, then that machine is operating according to a VR 50 schedule of reinforcement. As is true of all VR schedules, it is impossible for the player to predict whether the next slot-machine play will be reinforced or not. Most players have no idea what schedule of reinforcement they are operating under. All they know is that the very next play may be the one that pays off – so let's play!

Table 11.2 provides more examples of VR schedules. As before, spaces are left for you to practice identifying the type of schedule and/or the ratio requirement. The answers appear at the end of the chapter.

Table 11.2 Examples of VR schedules. The blanks spaces offer an opportunity for you to identify the <u>type of schedule</u> and/or the <u>ratio requirement</u> for reinforcement.

1. On average, Geoffrey asks 4 people to go on a date before 1 of them says yes. (VR ____)
2. A novice basketball player makes a basket, on average, 1 time in 9 attempts. (__R ____)
3. The chance of throwing a Yahtzee (five dice, all with the same number showing) is about 1 in 100. Said another way, if you throw the dice all day, you will throw an average of 100 times before getting a Yahtzee. Of course, it is unpredictable when the next Yahtzee will be thrown. (____ ____)
4. At the grocery store, each time customers make a purchase they have a 1 in 75 chance of getting a $10 off coupon. (____ ____)
5. A casino Blackjack player wins on the 1st hand. Then he wins again after 4 hands, then again after 2 hands, and finally after playing 5 hands. (____ ____)
6. Chuck shucks oysters at the pub. He's done it all his life. On average, 1 time out of 12,000, when he opens an oyster, he finds a pearl. (____ ____)

Figure 11.6 shows **the typical pattern of responding under a VR schedule** – *a high-rate of responding with little or no post-reinforcement pause.* There are three things to notice in the figure. First, note how the reinforcers (green lines) are irregularly spaced. This occurs because under a VR schedule the number of responses per reinforcer is *variable*; it is not the same

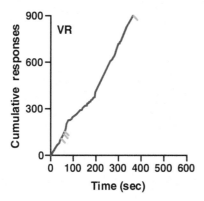

Figure 11.6 A cumulative record depicting a pigeon's stable key pecking on a VR 360 schedule of reinforcement.

Source: Data from Ferster, C. B., & Skinner, B. F. (1957). Schedules of reinforcement. New York: Appleton-Century-Crofts.

each time. Second, note that there is little to no pause in responding right after the reinforcer. Instead, the pigeon immediately begins working for the next reinforcer after it eats the last one. Post-reinforcement pauses can occur under VR schedules, but they are always shorter than under a comparable FR schedule. Third, the VR response rate is higher than the FR rate that was shown in Figure 11.4. This high-rate pattern of responding, with only occasional pauses under a VR schedule, has proven replicable in many labs and with many species, including humans (Kelleher, 1958; Orlando et al., 1958; Viemeister et al., 1964).

The Behavioral Economics of Ratio Schedules

As previously mentioned, a ratio schedule of requirement can be thought of as the *price* of the reinforcer. For example, under an FR 20 schedule, the price of the reinforcer is 20 responses. Price is an intuitive way to think about ratio schedules – an FR 2 offers the reinforcer at a lower price than an FR 20, which in turn is a lower price than an FR 200. This relation between ratio schedules and economic prices has allowed behavior analysts to branch into behavioral economics and, interestingly, many of the laws of economics derived from studying human behavior have proven just as applicable to animal behavior (Kagel et al., 1995).

One example of this universality of behavioral-economic outcomes is shown in Figure 11.7. Here we can see what happens to behavior when the price of the reinforcer is changed. That is, as the FR requirement is increased from left to right along the x-axis of each graph, the price of the reinforcer increases. Regardless of the species, as prices increase so does the amount the individual works to obtain the reinforcer. However, there is a limit on this. At some point, the price increase will prove to be too much. After that, efforts to acquire the reinforcer will decline.

To get a more intuitive understanding of these data, imagine what would happen to our gasoline-purchasing behavior if the price of gas changed. If gas was super cheap, say $0.10 a gallon, we would spend very little on gas in any given month – just like the subjects in Figure 11.7 responded very little to obtain their reinforcers at low prices. Later, when the price of gas goes up, we can use the data in Figure 11.7 to predict two things. First, moderate price increases will cause us to spend more on gas each month. No doubt we will be upset by these

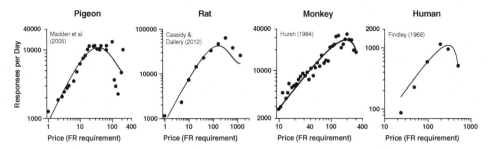

Figure 11.7 As the price of the reinforcer is increased, pigeons, rats, monkeys, and humans increase the amount that they work. This allows them to mostly (but not entirely) defend their daily consumption of the reinforcer (consumption data not shown). However, as prices continue to rise, spending eventually declines, regardless of the species or the reinforcer (food for nonhumans, cigarette puffs for humans).

Sources: Cassidy, R. N., & Dallery, J. (2012). Effects of economy type and nicotine on the essential value of food. *Journal of the Experimental Analysis of Behavior, 97*(2), 183–202. https://doi.org/10.1901/jeab.2012.97-183; Findley, J. D. (1966). Programmed environments for the experimental analysis of human behavior. In W. K. Honig (Ed.), Operant behavior: Areas of research and application (pp. 827–848). Englewood Cliffs, NJ: Prentice-Hall.; Hursh, S. R. (1984). Behavioral economics. *Journal of the Experimental Analysis of Behavior, 42*(3), 435–452.; Madden, G. J., Dake, J. M., Mauel, E. C., & Rowe, R. R. (2005). Labor supply and consumption of food in a closed economy under a range of fixed- And random-ratio schedules: Tests of unit price. *Journal of the Experimental Analysis of Behavior, 83*(2). https://doi.org/10.1901/jeab.2005.32-04

higher prices, but we'll pay them because, hey, we've got to get to work. Second, we can predict that very large price increases will cause us to eventually reduce our spending on gasoline. If the price of gas skyrocketed to $100 a gallon, most of us would have to leave our cars parked on the street while we take public transportation, walk, or maybe even hitchhike (Reed et al., 2014). These outcomes are predictable given the uniformity of behavior under ratio schedules of reinforcement (Cassidy & Dallery, 2012; Findley, 1966; Hursh, 1984; Madden et al., 2005). To paraphrase B. F. Skinner (1956): *Pigeon, rat, monkey, human – which is which? It doesn't matter once you have allowed for differences in the way they earn their reinforcers. What remains is astonishingly similar.*

The Underappreciated VR Schedule

Although the price of gas fluctuates a little over the course of a year, the current price is predictable – it's posted on the sign out front. In this way, the gas station posts the FR value for all to see. Want a gallon of our gas? Give us $3.45 of your labor (at your job) in exchange.

Now, for a bit of fun. Imagine that the posted price was switched to a VR schedule. Now the *average price* is $3.45 per gallon, but the price of any one gallon is unpredictable. Sometimes a gallon costs $0.01 and sometimes $10. As you pump the gas, a

Source: itsallgood, Adobe Stock Photo

digital display indicates how much the just-pumped gallon cost. Yes! We just got one for $0.05. Ugh, that one cost $5.34. Oooh, another winner at $0.35 a gallon. Pumping gas would certainly be more fun at this VR station, but would you buy your gas here? VR or FR? Which would you prefer?

Several experiments have posed this FR vs. VR question to nonhuman animals and their answer is clear – as the price of the reinforcer increases (i.e., more work is required to get the reinforcer), subjects strongly prefer the VR schedule (Ahearn et al., 1992; Fantino, 1967; Field et al., 1996; Kacelnik & Bateson, 1996; Lagorio & Winger, 2014; Repp & Deitz, 1975). This finding is illustrated in Figure 11.8. When these four pigeons could choose between an FR 3 and a VR 3 (the data point furthest to the left), they did not prefer one over the other – their choices were 50–50. But as the work requirements on the FR and VR schedules increased, all four pigeons came to strongly prefer the VR schedule.

Humans have rarely been given this choice, but it appears that they also prefer VR schedules (Repp & Deitz, 1975), particularly at high-ratio requirements (Meyer et al., 2011) and when they have the opportunity to occasionally "win" the reinforcer after a single response (Mullane et al., 2017). Indeed, the reason VR schedules are preferred is closely linked to these occasional "wins" that are arranged on the VR, but never on the FR. That is, those few times when the individual obtains a reinforcer after very little effort, like a slot machine player who wins on the very first play. If these occasional wins don't occur under the VR schedule (but the ratio value remains the same), preference for

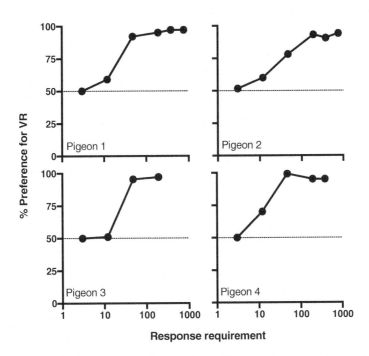

Figure 11.8 Individual pigeon's preference for a VR over an otherwise equivalent FR schedule of food reinforcement. FR and VR schedule values (response requirements) are shown on the logarithmic x-axis.

Source: Madden, G. J., & Hartman, E. C. (2006). A steady-state test of the demand curve analysis of relative reinforcer efficacy. *Experimental and Clinical Psychopharmacology, 14*, 79–86. doi:10.1037/1064-1297.14.1.79

the VR vanishes (Field et al., 1996; Mullane et al., 2017). The allure of gambling, of course, is the "win" – a big reward obtained after very little work. Casinos understand VR schedules and they use them to keep players spending because the very next wager could be a winner.

Here's a wild idea – if humans, like nonhuman animals, have a strong preference for VR over FR schedules, then perhaps we could encourage more eco-friendly behavior by using VR schedules. For example, instead of taking $0.10 off our grocery bill because we remembered to bring in our reusable bags (a meaningless consequence that probably has no reinforcer efficacy), why not put this environmentally conscious behavior on a VR schedule? Specifically, if we check out with our reusable bags, then there is a 1 in 100 chance that we will win $10 in cash – a VR 100. When someone in the store wins the cash prize, a celebration occurs, so everyone can see that winning happens all the time. A very similar technique is used in the casinos. This simple, cost-neutral change in the schedule of reinforcement may encourage more green behavior (plus it would make checking out a lot more exciting).

Another reason VR schedules might be advantageous is that, when prices are high, VR schedules can maintain more behavior than an FR schedule (De Luca & Holborn, 1990, 1992; Ferster & Skinner, 1957; Kacelnik & Bateson, 1996; Madden et al., 2005; Rider, 1983; Zeiler, 1979). This is illustrated in Figure 11.9. When pigeons worked for their daily meals under a VR 768 (a high ratio-requirement), their peak response rates were twice as high as under an FR 768 (Madden et al., 2005). The price was the same – 768 responses per food reinforcer – but the occasional VR "win" kept the pigeons responding where the FR did not; Ferster and Skinner (1957) reported very similar outcomes. Likewise, in a human study, VR schedules maintained higher peak levels of exercising in obese children than did FR schedules (De Luca & Holborn, 1990, 1992). Indeed, under the VR schedules, obese children gradually came to exercise at rates comparable to nonobese children; something not achieved under FR schedules.

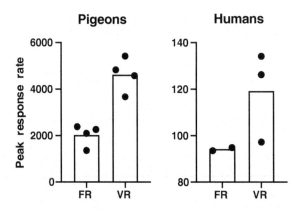

Figure 11.9 The maximum rate of key pecking (pigeons) or stationary bike exercising (human children's rotations per minute) under FR and VR schedules of reinforcement. Dots correspond to individual subjects and bars to the average of the group.

Source: Based on Madden, G. J., Dake, J. M., Mauel, E. C., & Rowe, R. R. (2005). Labor supply and consumption of food in a closed economy under a range of fixed- And random-ratio schedules: Tests of unit price. *Journal of the Experimental Analysis of Behavior*, *83*(2). https://doi.org/10.1901/jeab.2005.32-04; De Luca, R. V, & Holborn, S. W. (1992). Effects of a variable ratio reinforcement schedule with changing criteria on exercise in obese and nonobese boys. *Journal of Applied Behavior Analysis*, *25*, 671–679.; De Luca, R. V., & Holborn, S. W. (1990). Effects of fixed-interval and fixed-ratio schedules of token reinforcement on exercise with obese and nonobese boys. *The Psychological Record*, *40*(1), 67–82. https://doi.org/10.1007/bf03399572

So, if we prefer VR schedules over FR, and we are more productive under VR schedules than FR, then *why aren't VR schedules used more often*? Video game programmers understand VR schedules and they build unpredictability and surprise "wins" into their games, to enhance player engagement (Burke, 2014). But in our daily lives, the VR schedule is a rarity. Why is this such an underappreciated schedule of reinforcement? Perhaps we fear that VR schedules are a "gateway" to pathological gambling. But if that were true, we would have widespread prohibitions on all games of chance – no more Yahtzee for you! A more likely answer is that nobody outside the game-design and behavior-analytic world knows about the potential of the VR schedule. Your parents don't know about the VR, nor do your managers or teachers. But now you know about it. What will you do with this knowledge? How can you creatively use VR schedules to positively influence behavior?

Reading Quiz 1

1. When the reinforcer is provided after every response, the contingency is described as _____ (continuous or intermittent) reinforcement.
2. When the reinforcer is only provided after some responses, or only after a response is made after some time has passed, the contingency is described as _____ (continuous or intermittent) reinforcement.
3. A _____ of reinforcement precisely specifies the nature of the contingent relation between a response and its reinforcer.
4. A _____ schedule of reinforcement specifies the number of responses that must be made in order for the reinforcer to be delivered.
5. In a ratio schedule of reinforcement, the term "ratio" refers to the ratio of responses to _____.
6. A _____-ratio schedule is operating when the number of responses required per reinforcer is the same every time.
7. In a _____-ratio schedule, the number of responses required per reinforcer is not the same every time.
8. A graph that shows responding as it unfolds over of time is known as a _____ _____.
9. Under a _____-ratio schedule, nonhumans animals will respond with a _____ and _____ pattern.
10. In this FR pattern, the "break" refers to a post-reinforcement _____ and the "run" refers to a _____ rate of responding.
11. Under a _____-ratio schedule, the usual response pattern is a high rate of responding with infrequent pausing.
12. As response requirements (or prices) increase, subjects prefer _____-ratio schedules over _____-ratio schedules.
13. When reinforcers are probabilistic, as they are when we roll the dice, play the odds, or gamble, our behavior is operating under a _____ schedule of reinforcement.
14. All else being equal, _____-ratio schedules maintain higher peak response rates than _____-ratio schedules.

Interval Schedules of Reinforcement

Now we will transition away from response-based ratio schedules of reinforcement and begin discussing the other category of reinforcement schedules studied by Ferster and Skinner (1957) – the interval schedules. An **interval schedule of reinforcement** *specifies the amount of time that must elapse before a single response will produce the reinforcer.* For example, an interval schedule might specify this contingency: *IF 30 seconds pass and then a response is made → THEN the reinforcer is provided.* If 30 seconds have not yet elapsed, then responding

Source: Steven/Adobe Stock Photo; 045/startupstockphotos.com

(no matter how much or how rapid) produces nothing. Interval schedules are time-based schedules – sometimes we just have to wait.

The two most important types of interval schedules are the fixed-interval and the variable-interval schedules of reinforcement. We turn to those next.

Fixed-Interval Schedules

A **fixed-interval (FI) schedule** *specifies a constant time interval that must elapse before a single response will produce the reinforcer.* For example, under an FI 60-second schedule, the first response after 60 seconds is reinforced. Figure 11.10 shows the operation of an FI 60-s schedule of reinforcement. As the 60 seconds timer is ticking away, responses are occasionally made; however, they are never reinforced – they are wasted responses because they do not make the reinforcer come any sooner. Instead, when 60 seconds pass (red dotted lines), the very first response is reinforced. If we changed to an FI 4-minute schedule, the first response made after 4 minutes elapsed would be the one that was reinforced. Any responses made before 4 minutes would be wasted.

There are not many real-world examples of FI schedules, so the reader may wonder why we study them. The answer is that they can tell us about an individual's perception of the passage of time. Time perception can impact our everyday behavior. For example, if we per-

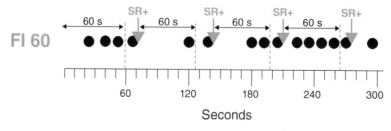

Figure 11.10 A visual representation of an FI 60-s schedule of reinforcement.

ceive that time is passing very slowly, then we may be less patient when asked to wait – "what's taking so long!". The FI schedule allows us to observe a behavior influenced by time perception. As noted by Ferster and Skinner (1957), if an individual had perfect time perception, they would not waste their efforts by responding prior to the passage of an FI 60-s timer. Instead, they would wait for 60 seconds and then make a single response. Adult humans are capable of this highly efficient response pattern (Weiner, 1969), but nonhuman animals and preverbal infants (who cannot count) are not.

We will have more to say about the response patterns maintained under FI schedules in a moment. But first, Table 11.3 provides some simple examples of FI schedules. Practice identifying the type of schedule and/or the interval length by filling in the spaces. The answers appear at the end of the chapter.

Table 11.3 Examples of FI schedules. The blank spaces offer an opportunity for you to identify the <u>type of schedule</u> and/or <u>interval duration</u>.

1. A rat earns 1 food pellet for pressing a lever after every 90 seconds elapses. (FI _____)
2. A manager times her employee-supervision task to occur once ever 3 hours. When she arrives on the factory floor, she praises the first safe behavior that she observes one of her employees doing. (___ ____)
3. Every 6 hours, the video game restocks the player's coin bank. To see if the bank has been restocked, the player must go into the game app. If the player opens the app sooner than 6 hours, the effort is wasted – the bank has not been restocked and the player cannot play. (_____ _____)
4. The #4 bus leaves the station every 15 minutes. Janus arrives at the station and sees the #4 bus leaving without him. He sits down and reads, occasionally looking up to see if the bus is coming while he waits. (_____ _____)
5. Tammy likes to listen to the New York Times *The Daily* podcast, which is dropped at 5 AM every day. Although Tammy does not know what time the podcast is dropped, she knows that it happens early in the morning every day. Tammy does not check her podcast app in the afternoon or in the evening, she only checks in the morning. (____ _____)

Figure 11.11 shows the **typical FI response pattern of nonhuman subjects** – *a post-reinforcement pause gives way to an accelerating response rate that terminates with a reinforcer.* This curved pattern of an accelerating response rate is referred to as a "scallop" because it resembles the curved shell of a sea scallop.

If the post-reinforcement pause lasted exactly 120 seconds (the FI value in Figure 11.11), then the pigeon would not waste a single response – the pigeon would make one well-timed response, and it would be reinforced every time. However, the nonverbal pigeon is incapable of such precise timing. It cannot silently count, "one one-thousand, two one-thousand," and so on. Instead, it waits until the time since the last reinforcer is perceived as resembling prior intervals that have separated reinforcer deliveries. As the waiting time is perceived as increasingly similar to these prior intervals, the pigeon's response rate increases. In this way, scalloped response patterns inform us of the pigeon's perception of time.

Ferster and Skinner (1957) found that rats and pigeons had scalloped response patterns under FI schedules. Similarly, human preverbal infants have scalloped FI performances, but as they age and acquire language (and the ability to count) their response patterns shift toward those of adult humans – either very efficiently responding once after the FI timer elapses or not pausing at all after each reinforcer (Bentall et al., 1985). Why adult humans

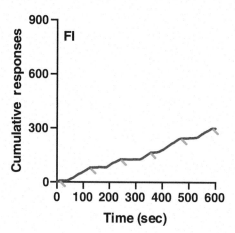

Figure 11.11 A cumulative record showing a typical response pattern for a pigeon responding under an FI 120-s schedule of reinforcement.
Source: Data from Ferster, C. B., & Skinner, B. F. (1957). Schedules of reinforcement. New York: Appleton-Century-Crofts.

sometimes respond at a high rate on FI schedules is unclear at this time. Perhaps they perceive that the experimenter wants them to keep responding and not take a break, or perhaps they never notice that regular time intervals separate the delivery of each reinforcer. Whatever the reason, it is clear that verbal humans behave differently than nonhuman animals under FI schedules of reinforcement (Hyten & Madden, 1993; Poppen, 1982).

Variable-Interval Schedules

The other type of interval schedule of reinforcement is the variable-interval schedule. Under a **variable-interval (VI) schedule**, *the amount of time that must elapse before the first response is reinforced is not the same every time.* With a VI schedule, the numerical value of the schedule specifies the *average* interval of time that separates reinforcer availabilities. For example, under a VI 60-second schedule, the timer that controls reinforcer availability will be set to a different value each time, with the average of all the VI values equal to 60 seconds. This is shown in Figure 11.12. The first VI value is 30 seconds, and the first response after that time elapses is reinforced. Subsequently, reinforcers become available after 70 seconds, 55 seconds, and then

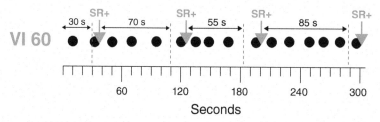

Figure 11.12 A visual representation of a VI 60-s schedule of reinforcement.

85 seconds. The average of all these intervals is 60 seconds ([30 + 70 + 55 + 85]/4 = VI 60 seconds). Because of the irregular intervals, under a VI schedule it is impossible to predict exactly when the next reinforcer will be available.

Where FI schedules are rare in our daily lives, VI schedules are more much common. Consider social-media reinforcers. They become available after the passage of time and it's impossible to exactly predict when the next interesting event (a great meme, a retweet, a new follower, or the "liking" of one of our posts) will become available inside the app. In this way, posts that reinforce our social-media checking behavior are available on a VI schedule. The unpredictability of

Source: Laura Stanley/Getty Images

these reinforcer availabilities makes us feel like we are missing out on something good, if only we could check in and see. Many of us check social media too often, doing so even when we are not supposed to – when with a friend who needs us, in a class that requires our attention, or while driving. Alas, we are all beholden to the power of the VI schedule to maintain our constant attention.

Those who enjoy hunting and fishing should know that their love of these sports is also a product of the VI schedule of reinforcement. Bagging the deer or catching the fish are the reinforcers that maintain the behavior of the hunter/fisher as they vigilantly search for game or angle for a fish. Increasing the rate of these behaviors will not produce reinforcers any faster; if deer or fish are not present, hunting/fishing behaviors will not be reinforced. Instead, one must wait for the game to arrive and one cannot predict exactly when that will happen. As a result, like the social-media maven who fears missing out, the hunter does not want to leave the field lest they miss out on a trophy buck. We are *all* beholden to the power of the VI schedule.

Table 11.4 provides more examples of VI schedules. Use the spaces to identify the type of schedule and/or the average time requirement. The answers appear at the end of the chapter.

Table 11.4 Examples of VI schedules. The blank spaces offer an opportunity for you to identify the <u>type of schedule</u> and/or the <u>average interval duration</u>.

1. A pigeon earns grain for pecking a light after an average of 50 seconds. (VI ____)
2. Manuel is watching the night sky for falling stars. If he watches the sky constantly, he sees one, on average, about every 9 minutes. (____ ____)
3. The teacher tells her students that when the bell chimes, if everyone is in their seat studying quietly, the class will get a 10-minute break outside. She sets the timer for a different duration each time, but the average time to the bell's chime is 25 minutes. (____ ____)
4. Aaliyah frequently glances at the email window on her desktop. When she sees that a new email has arrived, she switches to that window and reads it. On Monday morning, new emails arrived after 1 minute, 19 minutes, 13 minutes, and 23 minutes. (____ ____)
5. The writing student checks online to see if his professor has graded his essay yet. Nothing yet. On average, the professor takes two weeks to grade the essays and release them online; sometimes less time, sometimes more. (____ ____)

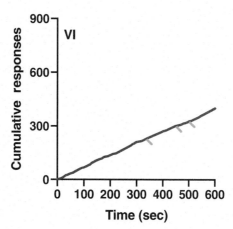

Figure 11.13 A cumulative record showing a typical response pattern for a pigeon responding under a VI 120-s schedule of reinforcement.
Source: Data from Ferster, C. B., & Skinner, B. F. (1957). Schedules of reinforcement. New York: Appleton-Century-Crofts.

Figure 11.13 shows the **typical pattern of responding under a VI schedule** – *a steady, moderate response rate with little to no post-reinforcement pause.* There are four things to note about the VI response record. First the line is not as steep as we saw with the VR schedule (Figure 11.6). Again, responding faster will not produce the reinforcer any sooner on an interval schedule, so why waste the effort? But because the pigeon cannot predict exactly when the reinforcer will become available, it pecks at a steady, moderate rate, so as to obtain the reinforcer soon after the VI timer elapses. Second, the response rate is fairly constant – no scalloping occurs under this schedule. Third, the response rate maintained by the VI 120-s schedule is higher than was maintained by the FI 120-s schedule in Figure 11.11. Again, under the VI, pecking is sometimes reinforced a few seconds after the last reinforcer, but these early responses are never reinforced under an FI schedule (so they don't happen). Thus, the VI schedule reinforces continuous, moderate-rate responding. Finally, notice that the delivery of reinforcers occurs at irregular intervals – 120-s is the *average* time between reinforcers, not the exact time between them.

Putting it All Together

Figure 11.14 provides a side-by-side comparison of idealized cumulative records under the four reinforcement schedules. Note how the response rates are higher under the ratio schedules of reinforcement than the interval schedules. Faster responding produces reinforcers more quickly under a ratio schedule but not an interval schedule.

Note also that post-reinforcement pausing occurs under the FR and FI schedules. The variable schedules (VR and VI) maintain steadier response rates.

Finally, note how the VR schedule maintains the highest response rate of them all. Other than in the gambling and video-gaming industries, it truly is the underappreciated of the schedules of reinforcement.

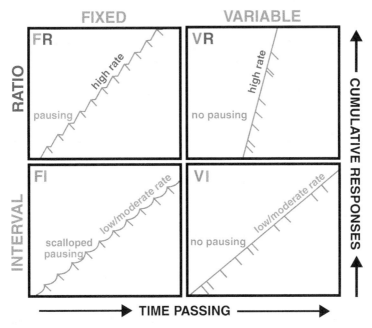

Figure 11.14 Idealized cumulative records for the four simple schedules of reinforcement.

Reading Quiz 2

1. In a(n) _____ schedule of reinforcement, the first response emitted after the timer elapses is reinforced.
2. Under a(n) _____ schedule of reinforcement, the faster one responds, the faster the reinforcer will be obtained. However, this is not true under _____-schedules. Under the latter, all responses made before the timer elapses are wasted – they will never be reinforced.
3. There are two kinds of interval schedules: the _____-interval schedule and the _____-interval schedule.
4. Under a _____-interval schedule, the amount of time that must elapse before the first response is reinforced is not the same every time.
5. When nonhuman animals and preverbal humans respond on a _____-interval schedule, the response pattern is described as "scalloped."
6. Under a _____-interval schedule, pausing is infrequent; instead a steady, moderate response rate is maintained.
7. In an interval schedule, a single _____ produces the reinforcer after the FI or VI elapses.
8. The FI schedule is primarily used to study an individual's perception of the passage of _____.
9. Under a _____-_____ schedule, it is impossible to predict exactly *when* the next reinforcer will become available.

10. Suppose an FI 1-minute schedule is in place. After 10 minutes of no responding, the organism finally emits a single response. How many reinforcers will be delivered?
11. Suppose an FI 1-minute schedule is in place. In the first 50 seconds, the individual makes 152 responses. How many reinforcers will be delivered?
12. Higher response rates are maintained by variable-_____ schedules than variable-_____ schedules.

Why Study Schedules of Reinforcement?

We have devoted a lot of space in this chapter to describing pigeons pecking response keys and rats pressing levers. What does any of this have to do with positively influencing human behavior? When we understand how ratio and interval schedules maintain behavior, we can use that knowledge to accurately predict and positively influence important human actions.

Consider the opioid crisis, heroin-use disorder, and the death toll it has imposed in our time. For generations, lawmakers and presidents have approached this problem by trying to stop drugs at the border. If successful, the street price of heroin would increase and, the politicians predict, drug use will decline.

However, this approach can have unintended side effects that are predictable from an understanding of ratio schedules of reinforcement. This is illustrated in Figure 11.15. The red dot shows a heroin-user's spending on heroin when it costs $7.50 a bag (one hit) and the black curve summarizes spending at a wider range of heroin prices (Jacobs & Bickel, 1999). Because the curve is nearly identical to that of the pigeons, rats, monkeys, and human cigarette smokers in Figure 11.7, we can predict what would happen if the street price of heroin increases.

If the border crackdown was highly effective, and the price of heroin tripled, our law-enforcement efforts would be "rewarded" with an *increase* in user's spending on heroin (green data point). At a population level, some of that increased spending will come from criminal activities, so our well-meaning "cops at the border" policy will have the unintended side effect of *increasing crime*; not to mention the *Breaking Bad* scenario in which law-abiding citizens get into the drug trade because of the flood of new money in the heroin market (Hursh, 1991).

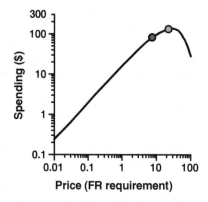

Figure 11.15 Heroin-dependent individuals' prospective spending on heroin when available at a range of street prices.

Source: Jacobs, E. A., & Bickel, W. K. (1999). Modeling drug consumption in the clinic using simulation procedures: Demand for heroin and cigarettes in opioid-dependent outpatients. *Experimental and Clinical Psychopharmacology*, 7(4), 412–426. https://doi.org/10.1037/1064-1297.7.4.412

And it's not just in law enforcement that knowledge of contingencies is important. Unintended side effects of complex contingencies of reinforcement have, according to its CEO, Jack Dorsey, been the rule at Twitter. The creators of Twitter, Dorsey suggests, were naïve about the effects of the complex contingencies they were programming on "likes," "followers," "retweets," "retweets with comments," and so on. What seemed in the early days like an empowering platform connecting the world gradually became an environment in which emotion-eliciting posts filled with misinformation and conspiracies were differentially reinforced; thoughtful discourse was extinguished.

Source: JD Lasica/Flickr/Creative Commons Attribution license

"If we were to do all of this over again …" Dorsey said in 2020, "I wish we would have understood and hired a game theorist [behavioral scientist] to understand the ramifications of the tiny decisions that we make" (Jackson & Ibekwe, 2020). Accurately predicting behavior under complex contingencies of reinforcement is a core goal in behavior analysis and Twitter's experience helps us understand why – predicting unintended side effects allows us to avoid those effects. To their credit, Dorsey and Twitter have taken behavioral research more seriously in recent years. They are working to improve their platform, so it reinforces more nuanced, prosocial communications. We applaud these efforts, as they will be important if we are to undertake meaningful dialogues to solve those crises, like opioid-use disorders and global heating, that have at their core disordered contingencies of reinforcement that maintain maladaptive human behavior. Extra Box 1 explores the use of complex contingencies of reinforcement in the treatment of substance-use disorders. The outcomes are impressive.

EXTRA BOX 1:   CONTINGENCY MANAGEMENT

Consider a maladaptive behavior that you wish you could give up. Maybe it's scrolling too long through Instagram, binge watching a series for the third time, or playing video games when you should be doing something else, something that could make you feel better about yourself. Think of the behavior that you most wish you could stop doing. Can you quit? Maybe for a while, but how long until you relapse? A day? A week? An hour?

Now imagine that your government begins an ad-campaign saying, "Just say no to Netflix." Helpful? About as helpful as Nike's "Just do it" was in getting us all off the couch and into the gym. These campaigns masquerade as behavior-change strategies designed to impact, for example, the obesity epidemic. But they are really just designed to sell shoes, athletic clothing, or politicians. They are not effective in positively influencing behavior.

When it is time to change behavior, to really change it, we draw upon behavior-analytic principles (Roediger, 2004). Paramount among those principles are complex schedules of reinforcement, the building blocks of which are the ratio and interval schedules covered in this chapter. An example of behavior analysts using complex contingencies to address maladaptive human behavior is *contingency management of substance-use*. Here, complex contingencies of reinforcement are arranged to promote drug abstinence among individuals whose lives have been negatively impacted by illicit drugs (Higgins & Silverman, 1999). Considerable research has revealed that contingency management is among the most successful approaches to

Source: https://pixabay.com/photos/drugs-cocaine-user-addiction-908533/

reducing substance-use disorders, including heroin dependence (Benishek et al., 2014; Prendergast et al., 2006).

One approach to contingency management of substance-use employs a VR schedule of reinforcement (Petry & Martin, 2002; Petry et al., 2000). Rather than a pigeon pecking a key at a high rate, getting the occasional "win" as in Figure 11.6, drug abstinence is occasionally reinforced when an abstinent patient draws a lucky slip of paper out of a fishbowl and wins a prize. This unpredictable response-based schedule of reinforcement incentivized continuous abstinence because (a) draws from the fishbowl were contingent upon drug-free urine samples, (b) more abstinence yields more reinforcement, and (c) as is true of all VR schedules, the very next instance of abstinence *always* has a chance of earning the big prize. This VR approach to contingency management reduces cocaine and heroin use significantly more than the other widely used treatment approaches, and these better outcomes are sustained over time (Petry & Martin, 2002). Indeed, the VR approach was so successful, the US Veterans Administration adopted it in their treatment of service-people struggling with substance abuse (Petry et al., 2014).

When it is time to get serious about changing behavior, catchy slogans will not do. What's needed is a scientific approach – an approach informed by decades of research on complex contingencies of reinforcement.

Schedule Thinning

When learning a new behavior, it is important to receive reinforcement each time a correct response is made. Continuous reinforcement is critical in these early learning periods because correct responses are infrequent relative to incorrect responses. For example, imagine learning to play the bagpipes; we know, this requires some imagination. If we are just starting out and our instructor reinforces correct technique on an FR 60 schedule, we may never learn to execute clear notes – giving up before ever making the 60th correct response. Thus, continuous reinforcement is important at the beginning, when acquiring new behaviors.

However, it is often impractical to reinforce correct responses each time they occur, particularly when the performance improves and they occur at a high rate. Indeed, when we are playing well, we don't want the bagpipe teacher to yell "Yes! Yes! Good one laddie!" each time we correctly play a note. And, if asked to do this, the teacher would complain that it takes too much time and energy. Therefore, after a new skill has been acquired, it is important to transition from continuous to intermittent reinforcement.

How best to make this transition, ensuring that the newly acquired behavior is maintained, can be a challenge. Consider a clinical situation in which a child with autism engages in destructive behavior – self-injury, aggression, and so on. If a functional analysis of behavior reveals that these problem behaviors are maintained by attentional-reinforcers, then, as discussed in Chapter 7, an effective intervention will be *differential reinforcement* – we will teach the child to

Source: sharonang, Pixabay

ask for attention (reinforcing each appropriate request) *and* we will extinguish problem behaviors when they occur. This *functional-communication training* approach is effective (Tiger et al., 2008) but a challenge is faced when requests occur so often that they cannot be practically reinforced every time. Although we would like to transition from continuous to intermittent reinforcement, we must be careful to reinforce often enough to ensure destructive behavior does not resume (Hagopian et al., 2011).

The solution is **schedule thinning**, a *procedure for gradually reducing the rate of reinforcement, while maintaining the desired behavior*. By thinning the schedule of reinforcement, we can ensure that the adaptive behavior can be maintained outside the clinic, where it will not be reinforced every time (LeBlanc et al., 2002).

Schedule thinning can be accomplished in several ways. The correct method depends on the desired outcome. If we want the behavior to occur frequently, but it is impractical to reinforce every response, then we can increase the ratio requirement from FR 1 (continuous reinforcement) to FR 2. If the behavior is maintained and problem behavior is infrequent, further increases can be implemented (FR 3, etc.; Piazza et al., 1996).

But sometimes the goal is not to have more of the desired behavior, but to have it occur at a reasonable rate. This is the case in our clinical example – we want appropriate requests for attention to occur occasionally, not constantly. One approach is to shift from FR 1 to a very brief FI schedule, and then gradually increase its duration as long as destructive behavior remains low (e.g., FI 2-s, FI 4-s, etc.). This was the approach taken by Hanley et al. (2001). Although destructive behavior was infrequent, thinning the FI schedule did not reduce appropriate requests for attention to a reasonable rate. Much better outcomes were obtained by visually signaling when appropriate requests would be reinforced (when a white card was saliently displayed) and when these requests would not be reinforced (when a red card was displayed). Schedule thinning occurred by presenting the red card (operant extinction) for longer and longer intervals of time. The positive effects of this procedure have been replicated by other clinicians (Sidener et al., 2006).

Although these methods of schedule thinning have yielded some successes, there remains much to be learned. A common difficulty is that as the schedule is thinned, the individual fails to obtain the reinforcer, which, of course, means the adaptive behavior is undergoing extinction. When that happens, many of the secondary effects of extinction can occur: unwanted emotional behavior, variations on the adaptive behavior (e.g., yelling the request), and resurgence of destructive behavior (Briggs et al., 2018). If these behaviors are inadvertently reinforced, destructive behavior can be very difficult to treat (St. Peter Pipkin et al., 2010). Therefore, it is important that schedule thinning be done with great care by an appropriately trained behavior analyst.

Scheduling Reinforcers to Enhance Human Performance and Happiness

By now it should be apparent that reinforcement schedules have broad applicability. By carefully arranging complex reinforcement contingencies, behavior analysts can enhance human performance and, when skillfully used, enhance human happiness. These successes occur in academic, play, and wellness behaviors. We highlight a few of these applications here.

In schools, teachers face a range of classroom challenges that can have detrimental effects on students and the learning environment of their peers (Hulac

Source: CDC/Unsplash.com

et al., 2016). Fortunately, educators have successfully used schedules of reinforcement to improve the performance of students of all ages (Lee & Belfiore, 1997) and from diverse backgrounds (Dunlap & Kern, 1996). Interval and ratio schedules have been used to reduce undesirable behavior, increase appropriate behavior, and help children learn valuable academic skills. For example, when teachers used a VI schedule to quietly praise academic engagement, fourth graders spent more time vigilantly working on their assignments in class (Henderson et al., 1986; Martens et al., 1992). Teachers have also used ratio schedules to improve student behavior when completing academic tasks (Duhon et al., 2004). Thus, schedules of reinforcement have practical applications in schools and have been used to improve learning outcomes.

At play, it has long been known that reinforcing skillful performances improves player performance in sports such as golf (Fogel et al., 2010), football (Stokes et al., 2010), and yoga (Ennett et al., 2019). But schedules of reinforcement have also been used to increase and then maintain exercising behaviors in non-athletes. In these efforts to address the obesity crisis, behavior analysts have successfully used FR, VR, FI, and VI schedules to increase physical activity and then to thin the frequency of reinforcement, so exercising can shift from an incentivized behavior to a daily habit (Andrade et al., 2014; Cohen et al., 2002; Finkelstein et al., 2008; Kuhl et al., 2015; Mitchell et al., 2019; Petry et al., 2013). Such schedule-influenced changes in behavior have improved patients' weight, blood pressure, and fitness (e.g., Petry et al., 2013).

Wellness apps use schedules of reinforcement too. Artem Petakov, President and co-founder of Noom®, recently described how his team combined artificial intelligence with behavioral psychology (i.e., the principles of behavior analysis) to develop their behavior-change and weight-loss product (Nelson & Houlihan, 2020). Noom® uses positive reinforcement and shaping to gradually increase daily activity and control food consumption. Coaches within the app arrange variable schedules of reinforcement, though exactly how it works is unknown. The behavioral technology used is proprietary information, known only to the company's behavioral design engineers. In sum, schedules of reinforcement have practical utility when it comes to improving academic, play, and wellness behaviors.

Reading Quiz 3

1. After a new skill has been acquired, it is important to transition from continuous to intermittent reinforcement. To do this, behavior analysts use a technique known as schedule
_____.

2. Early in training the desired behavior was maintained with continuous reinforcement (FR 1). Then, the ratio schedule was thinned. Name one of the many possible FR values that could be used to thin the schedule.

Summary

A schedule of reinforcement describes how the response-reinforcer contingency works and can range from the very simple (continuous reinforcement and operant extinction) to the very complex (e.g., VR schedules). This chapter described ratio (response-based) and interval (time-based) schedules of reinforcement. Under a ratio schedule, reinforcers are provided after a specific number of responses are emitted. That number can be the same every time – FR schedules – or it can vary around an average value – VR schedules. Under the time-based interval schedules, the first response made after the interval elapses is reinforced. The interval can be the same every time – FI schedules – or it can vary around an average value – VI schedules.

These schedules of reinforcement produce predictable and distinct patterns of responding. All else being equal, ratio schedules produce higher rates of responding than interval schedules, and VR schedules produce the highest rates of them all. Under FI schedules, nonhuman animals and preverbal humans pause after the reinforcer is obtained, and thereafter begin responding as the time that the reinforcer will be available gets closer. In this way, they reveal their ability to time the interval. As humans acquire language, however, this pattern of behavior changes, in part because they learn to count to themselves, thereby improving the accuracy of their timing.

The practicality of schedules of reinforcement has been demonstrated in many published experiments, but the potential of these complex contingencies of reinforcement remains largely untapped. Although complex contingencies have been arranged to decrease drug-taking, increase exercise, and thin the rate of reinforcement of adaptive behaviors, these contingencies are not widely understood or used outside of experiments conducted by behavioral scientists. Unfamiliarity with complex contingencies has led to problems at Twitter and, undoubtedly, other organizations, public and private. When skillfully used by behavior analysts, complex contingencies have improved academic, play, and wellness behaviors. There is much work left to be done. The many behaviors that underlie the existential crises of our time await the next generation of behavior analysts to show us new and clever ways to arrange complex contingencies. Are you up for the challenge?

Answers to Reading Quiz Questions and Questions Posed in Tables 11.1–11.4

Table 11.1

1. 5
2. 20
3. FR 100
4. FR 20
5. FR 2
6. FR 2

Table 11.2

1. 4
2. VR 9
3. VR 100
4. VR 75
5. VR 3
6. VR 12,000

Reading Quiz 1

1. continuous
2. intermittent
3. schedule
4. ratio
5. reinforcers
6. fixed
7. variable
8. cumulative record
9. fixed; break; run
10. pause; high-constant (*high*, *constant*, or *steady* are also acceptable answers)
11. variable
12. variable; fixed
13. variable-ratio (VR)
14. variable; fixed

Table 11.3

1. 90-s
2. FI 3-h

3. FI 6-h
4. FI 15-min
5. FI 24-h

Table 11.4

1. 50-s
2. VI 9-min
3. VI 25-min
4. VI 14-min
5. VI 2-weeks

Reading Quiz 2

1. interval
2. ratio; interval
3. fixed; variable OR variable; fixed
4. variable
5. fixed
6. variable
7. response
8. time
9. variable-interval
10. 1
11. 0; all 152 responses are wasted. However, the first response made after 1-minute elapses will be reinforced.
12. ratio; interval

Reading Quiz 3

1. thinning
2. FR 2 or higher

Notes

1. Punishment also can be arranged according to a wide variety of complex contingencies. However, for the purposes of this introductory text, we will confine our discussion to complex contingencies of *reinforcement*.
2. Technically speaking, when reinforcers are probabilistic, the operative schedule of reinforcement is a *random-ratio* schedule. But because this is an introductory textbook, we will not make a distinction between random-ratio and the very similarly operating variable-ratio schedule.

References

Ahearn, W., Hineline, P. N., & David, F. G. (1992). Relative preferences for various bivalued ratio schedules. *Animal Learning & Behavior, 20*(4), 407–415.

Andrade, L. F., Barry, D., Litt, M. D., & Petry, N. M. (2014). Maintaining high activity levels in sedentary adults with a reinforcement-thinning schedule. *Journal of Applied Behavior Analysis, 47*(3), 523–536. https://doi.org/10.1002/jaba.147

Azrin, N. H. (1961). Time-out from positive reinforcement. *Science, 133*, 382–383.

Benishek, L. A., Dugosh, K. L., Kirby, K. C., Matejkowski, J., Clements, N. T., Seymour, B. L., & Festinger, D. S. (2014). Prize-based contingency management for the treatment of substance abusers: A meta-analysis. *Addiction, 109*(9), 1426–1436. https://doi.org/10.1111/add.12589

Bentall, R. P., Lowe, C. F., & Beasty, A. (1985). The role of verbal behavior in human learning: II Developmental differences. *Journal of the Experimental Analysis of Behavior, 43*(2), 165–181. https://doi.org/10.1901/jeab.1985.43-165

Briggs, A. M., Fisher, W. W., Greer, B. D., & Kimball, R. T. (2018). Prevalence of resurgence of destructive behavior when thinning reinforcement schedules during functional communication training. *Journal of Applied Behavior Analysis, 51*(3), 620–633. https://doi.org/10.1002/jaba.472

Burke, B. (2014). *Gamify: How gamification motivates people to do extraordinary things.* New York: Bibliomotion.

Cassidy, R. N., & Dallery, J. (2012). Effects of economy type and nicotine on the essential value of food. *Journal of the Experimental Analysis of Behavior, 97*(2), 183–202. https://doi.org/10.1901/jeab.2012.97-183

Castillo, M. I., Clark, D. R., Schaller, E. A., Donaldson, J. M., DeLeon, I. G., & Kahng, S. (2018). Descriptive assessment of problem behavior during transitions of children with intellectual and developmental disabilities. *Journal of Applied Behavior Analysis, 51*(1), 99–117. https://doi.org/10.1002/jaba.430

Cohen, S. L., Chelland, S., Ball, K. T., & LeMura, L. M. (2002). Effects of fixed ratio schedules of reinforcement on exercise by college students. *Perceptual and Motor Skills, 94*(3 PART 2), 1177–1186. https://doi.org/10.2466/pms.2002.94.3c.1177

Corry, J. (2019, December 18). Agent's take: Performance bonus projections for 25 key players, including Aaron Rodgers, Jason Witten and more. Retrieved from https://www.cbssports.com/nfl/news/agents-take-performance-bonus-projections-for-25-key-players-including-aaron-rodgers-jason-witten-and-more

De Luca, R. V., & Holborn, S. W. (1990). Effects of fixed-interval and fixed-ratio schedules of token reinforcement on exercise with obese and nonobese boys. *The Psychological Record, 40*(1), 67–82. https://doi.org/10.1007/bf03399572

De Luca, R. V., & Holborn, S. W. (1992). Effects of a variable ratio reinforcement schedule with changing criteria on exercise in obese and nonobese boys. *Journal of Applied Behavior Analysis, 25*, 671–679. https://doi.org/10.1901/jaba.1992.25-671

Duhon, G. J., Noell, G. H., Witt, J. C., Freeland, J. T., Dufrene, B. A., & Gilbertson, D. N. (2004). Identifying academic skill and performance deficits: The experimental analysis of brief assessments of academic skills. *School Psychology Review, 33*(3), 429–443. https://doi.org/10.1080/02796015.2004.12086260

Dunlap, G., & Kern, L. (1996). Modifying instructional activities to promote desirable behavior: A conceptual and practical framework. *School Psychology Quarterly, 11*(4), 297–312. https://doi.org/10.1037/h0088936

Elliott, J. P., McTaggart Cowan, I., & Holling, C. S. (1977). Prey capture by the African lion. *Canadian Journal of Zoology, 55*, 1811–1828. https://doi.org/10.1139/z77-235

Ennett, T. M., Zonneveld, K. L. M., Thomson, K. M., Vause, T., & Ditor, D. (2020). Comparison of two TAGteach error-correction procedures to teach beginner yoga poses to adults. *Journal of Applied Behavior Analysis, 53*(1), 222–236. jaba.550. https://doi.org/10.1002/jaba.550

Fantino, E. (1967). Preference for mixed- versus fixed-ratio schedules. *Journal of the Experimental Analysis of Behavior, 10*, 35–43. https://doi.org/10.1901/jeab.1967.10-35

Ferster, C. B., & Skinner, B. F. (1957). *Schedules of reinforcement.* New York: Appleton-Century-Crofts.

Field, D. P., Tonneau, F., Ahearn, W., & Hineline, P. N. (1996). Preference between variable-ratio and fixed-ratio schedules: Local and extended relations. *Journal of the Experimental Analysis of Behavior, 66*(3), 283–295. https://doi.org/10.1901/jeab.1996.66-283

Findley, J. D. (1966). Programmed environments for the experimental analysis of human behavior. In W. K. Honig (Ed.), *Operant behavior: Areas of research and application* (pp. 827–848). Englewood Cliffs, NJ: Prentice-Hall.

Finkelstein, E. A., Brown, D. S., Brown, D. R., & Buchner, D. M. (2008). A randomized study of financial incentives to increase physical activity among sedentary older adults. *Preventive Medicine, 47*(2), 182–187. https://doi.org/10.1016/j.ypmed.2008.05.002

Fogel, V. A., Weil, T. M., & Burris, H. (2010). Evaluating the efficacy of TAGteach as a training strategy for teaching a golf swing. *Journal of Behavioral Health and Medicine, 1*(1), 25–41. https://doi.org/10.1037/h0100539

Galizio, M. (1979). Contingency-shaped and rule-governed behavior: Instructional control of human loss avoidance. *Journal of the Experimental Analysis of Behavior, 31*(1), 53–70. https://doi.org/10.1901/jeab.1979.31-53

Gentry, W. D. (1968). Fixed-ratio schedule-induced aggression. *Journal of the Experimental Analysis of Behavior, 11*(6), 813–817. https://doi.org/10.1901/jeab.1968.11-813

Hagopian, L. P., Boelter, E. W., & Jarmolowicz, D. P. (2011). Reinforcement schedule thinning following functional communication training: Review and recommendations. *Behavior Analysis in Practice, 4*(1), 4–16. https://doi.org/10.1007/bf03391770

Hanley, G. P., Iwata, B. A., & Thompson, R. H. (2001). Reinforcement schedule thinning following treatment with functional communication training. *Journal of Applied Behavior Analysis, 34*(1), 17–38. https://doi.org/10.1901/jaba.2001.34-17

Henderson, H. S., Jenson, W. R., & Erken, N. F. (1986). Using variable-interval schedules to improve on-task behavior in the classroom. *Education and Treatment of Children, 9*(3), 250–263. https://www.jstor.org/stable/42898977

Higgins, S. T., & Silverman, K. (1999). *Motivating behavior change among illicit-drug abusers: Research on contingency management interventions.* Washington DC: American Psychological Association.

Hulac, D., Benson, N., Nesmith, M. C., & Wollersheim Shervey, S. (2016). Using variable interval reinforcement schedules to support students in the classroom: An introduction with illustrative examples. *Journal of Educational Research and Practice, 6*(1), 90–96. https://doi.org/10.5590/jerap.2016.06.1.06

Hursh, S. R. (1984). Behavioral economics. *Journal of the Experimental Analysis of Behavior, 42*(3), 435–452. https://doi.org/10.1901/jeab.1984.42-435

Hursh, S. R. (1991). Behavioral economics of drug self-administration and drug abuse policy. *Journal of the Experimental Analysis of Behavior, 56*(2), 377–393. https://doi.org/10.1901/jeab.1991.56-377

Huston, J. P., & Desisto, M. J. (1971). Interspecies aggression during fixed-ratio hypothalamic self-stimulation in rats. *Physiology and Behavior, 7*(3), 353–357. https://doi.org/10.1016/0031-9384(71)90313-1

Hyten, C., & Madden, G. J. (1993). The scallop in human fixed-interval research: A review of problems with data description. *The Psychological Record, 43*, 471–500. Retrieved from https://search.proquest.com/openview/a772670cf60f57fb83381d7dbb85b663/1?pq-origsite=gscholar&cbl=1817765

Jackson, L., & Ibekwe, D. (2020). Jack Dorsey on Twitter's mistakes. The New York Times. Retrieved from https://www.nytimes.com/2020/08/07/podcasts/the-daily/Jack-dorsey-twitter-trump.html

Jacobs, E. A., & Bickel, W. K. (1999). Modeling drug consumption in the clinic using simulation procedures: Demand for heroin and cigarettes in opioid-dependent outpatients. *Experimental and Clinical Psychopharmacology, 7*(4), 412–426. https://doi.org/10.1037/1064-1297.7.4.412

Jessel, J., Hanley, G. P., & Ghaemmaghami, M. (2016a). A translational evaluation of transitions. *Journal of Applied Behavior Analysis, 49*(2), 359–376. https://doi.org/10.1002/jaba.283

Jessel, J., Hanley, G. P., & Ghaemmaghami, M. (2016b). Interview-informed synthesized contingency analyses: Thirty replications and reanalysis. *Journal of Applied Behavior Analysis*, *49*(3), 576–595. https://doi.org/10.1002/jaba.316

Kacelnik, A., & Bateson, M. (1996). Risky theories - The effects of variance of foraging decisions. *American Zoologist*, *36*(4), 402–434. https://doi.org/10.1093/icb/36.4.402

Kagel, J. H., Battalio, R. C., & Green, L. (1995). *Economic choice theory*. Cambridge, UK: Cambridge University Press.

Kelleher, R. T. (1958). Stimulus-producing responses in chimpanzee. *Journal of the Experimental Analysis of Behavior*, *1*(1), 87–102. https://doi.org/10.1901/jeab.1958.1-87

Kuhl, S., Rudrud, E. H., Witts, B. N., & Schulze, K. A. (2015). Classroom-based interdependent group contingencies increase children's physical activity. *Journal of Applied Behavior Analysis*, *48*(3), 602–612. https://doi.org/10.1002/jaba.219

Lagorio, C. H., & Winger, G. (2014). Random-ratio schedules produce greater demand for i.v. drug administration than fixed-ratio schedules in rhesus monkeys. *Psychopharmacology*, *231*(15), 2981–2988. https://doi.org/10.1007/s00213-014-3477-6

LeBlanc, L. A., Hagopian, L. P., Maglieri, K. A., & Poling, A. (2002). Decreasing the intensity of reinforcement-based interventions for reducing behavior: Conceptual issues and a proposed model for clinical practice. *The Behavior Analyst Today*, *3*(3), 289–300. https://doi.org/10.1037/h0099991

Lee, D. L., & Belfiore, P. J. (1997). Enhancing classroom performance: A review of reinforcement schedules. *Journal of Behavioral Education*, *7*(2), 205–217. https://doi.org/10.1023/A:1022893125346

Lee, J. J. (2013, July 23). *Long-held myth about cheetahs busted*. https://doi.org/10.1098/rsbl.2013.0472

Madden, G. J., Dake, J. M., Mauel, E. C., & Rowe, R. R. (2005). Labor supply and consumption of food in a closed economy under a range of fixed- and random-ratio schedules: Tests of unit price. *Journal of the Experimental Analysis of Behavior*, *83*(2), 99–118. https://doi.org/10.1901/jeab.2005.32-04

Madden, G. J., & Hartman, E. C. (2006). A steady-state test of the demand curve analysis of relative reinforcer efficacy. *Experimental and Clinical Psychopharmacology*, *14*, 79–86. doi:10.1037/1064-1297.14.1.79

Madden, G. J., & Perone, M. (1999). Human sensitivity to concurrent schedules of reinforcement: Effects of observing schedule-correlated stimuli. *Journal of the Experimental Analysis of Behavior*, *71*(3), 303–318. https://doi.org/10.1901/jeab.1999.71-303

Martens, B. K., Lochner, D. G., & Kelly, S. Q. (1992). The effects of variable-interval reinforcement on academic engagement: A demonstration of matching theory. *Journal of Applied Behavior Analysis*, *25*(1), 143–151. https://doi.org/10.1901/jaba.1992.25-143

Meyer, S. F., Schley, D. R., & Fantino, E. (2011). The role of context in risky choice. *Behavioural Processes*, *87*(1), 100–105. https://doi.org/10.1016/j.beproc.2011.01.010

Mitchell, M. S., Orstad, S. L., Biswas, A., Oh, P. I., Jay, M., Pakosh, M. T., & Faulkner, G. (2019, May 15). Financial incentives for physical activity in adults: Systematic review and meta-analysis. *British Journal of Sports Medicine*. BMJ Publishing Group. https://doi.org/10.1136/bjsports-2019-100633

Mullane, M. P., Martens, B. K., Baxter, E. L., & Steeg, D. V. (2017). Children's preference for mixed-versus fixed-ratio schedules of reinforcement: A translational study of risky choice. *Journal of the Experimental Analysis of Behavior*, *107*(1), 161–175. https://doi.org/10.1002/jeab.234

Nelson, K., & Houlihan, T. (2020, April 4). Artem Petkov: The biggest competitor is the couch. [Audio Podcast]. Retrieved from https://www.podbean.com/media/share/pb-ja7ep-d9a908?utm_campaign=w_share_ep&utm_medium=dlink&utm_source=w_share

Orlando, R., & Bijou, S. W. (1960). Single and multiple schedules of reinforcement in developmentally retarded children. *Journal of the Experimental Analysis of Behavior*, *3*(4), 339–348. https://doi.org/10.1901/jeab.1960.3-339

Petry, N. M., Andrade, L. F., Barry, D., & Byrne, S. (2013). A Randomized study of reinforcing ambulatory exercise in older adults. *Psychology and Aging*, *28*(4), 1164–1173. https://doi.org/10.1037/a0032563

Petry, N. M., DePhilippis, D., Rash, C. J., Drapkin, M., & McKay, J. R. (2014). Nationwide dissemination of contingency management: The veterans administration initiative. *The American Journal on Addictions*, *23*(3), 205–210. https://doi.org/10.1111/j.1521-0391.2014.12092.x

Petry, N. M., & Martin, B. (2002). Low-cost contingency management for treating cocaine- and opioid-abusing methadone patients. *Journal of Consulting and Clinical Psychology*, *70*(2), 398–405. https://doi.org/10.1037/0022-006X.70.2.398

Petry, N. M., Martin, B., Cooney, J. L., & Kranzler, H. R. (2000). Give them prizes, and they will come: Contingency management for treatment of alcohol dependence. *Journal of Consulting and Clinical Psychology*, *68*(2), 250–257. https://doi.org/10.1037/0022-006X.68.2.250

Piazza, C. C., Moes, D. R., & Fisher, W. W. (1996). Differential reinforcement of alternative behavior and demand fading in the treatment of escape-maintained destructive behavior. *Journal of Applied Behavior Analysis*, *29*(4), 569–572. https://doi.org/10.1901/jaba.1996.29-569

Pink, D. H. (2018). *When*. New York: Riverhead Books.

Poppen, R. (1982). The fixed-interval scallop in human affairs. *The Behavior Analyst*, *5*(2), 127–136. https://doi.org/10.1007/BF03392381

Prendergast, M., Podus, D., Finney, J., Greenwell, L., & Roll, J. (2006). Contingency management for treatment of substance use disorders: A meta-analysis. *Addiction*, *101*(11), 1546–1560. https://doi.org/10.1111/j.1360-0443.2006.01581.x

Reed, D. D., Kaplan, B. A., Roma, P. G., & Hursh, S. R. (2014). Inter-method reliability of progression sizes in a hypothetical purchase task: Implications for empirical public policy. *Psychological Record*, *64*(4), 671–679. https://doi.org/10.1007/s40732-014-0076-1

Repp, A. C., & Deitz, S. M. (1975). Comparison of fixed ratio and variable ratio token production schedules with human subjects. *The Psychological Record*, *25*(1), 131–137. https://doi.org/10.1007/BF03394296

Rider, D. P. (1983). Preference for mixed versus constant delays of reinforcement: Effect of probability of the short, mixed delay. *Journal of the Experimental Analysis of Behavior*, *39*(2), 257–266. https://doi.org/10.1901/jeab.1983.39-257

Roediger, H. L. (2004). What happened to behaviorism. *Association for Psychological Science Observer*, *17*(3). Retrieved from https://www.psychologicalscience.org/observer/what-happened-to-behaviorism

Schaller, G. B. (1967). The deer and the tiger. Chicago and London: University of Chicago Press.

Schlinger, H. D., Derenne, A., & Baron, A. (2008). What 50 years of research tell us about pausing under ratio schedules of reinforcement. *The Behavior Analyst*, *31*(1), 39–60. https://doi.org/10.1007/BF03392160

Sidener, T. M., Shabani, D. B., Carr, J. E., & Roland, J. P. (2006). An evaluation of strategies to maintain mands at practical levels. *Research in Developmental Disabilities*, *27*, 632–644. doi:10.1016/j.ridd.2005.08.002

Skinner, B. F. (1956). A case history in scientific method. *American Psychologist1*, *11*, 221–233. https://doi.org/10.1037/h0047662

St. Peter Pipkin, C., Vollmer, T. R., & Sloman, K. N. (2010). Effects of treatment integrity failures during differential reinforcement of alternative behavior: A translational model. *Journal of Applied Behavior Analysis*, *43*(1), 47–70. https://doi.org/10.1901/jaba.2010.43-47

Stokes, J. V., Luiselli, J. K., & Reed, D. D. (2010). A behavioral intervention for teaching tackling skills to high school football athletes. *Journal of Applied Behavior Analysis*, *43*(3), 509–512. https://doi.org/10.1901/jaba.2010.43-509

Tiger, J. H., Hanley, G. P., & Bruzek, J. (2008). Functional communication training: A review and practical guide. *Behavior Analysis in Practice*, *1*(1), 16–23. https://doi.org/10.1007/bf03391716

Viemeister, N. F., Pierce, J., & Tyler, D. W. (1964). Bar press behavior reinforced by pup retrieval. *Proceedings of the Iowa Academy of Science*, *71*(1), 429–432.

Weiner, H. (1969). Controlling human fixed-interval performance. *Journal of the Experimental Analysis of Behavior*, *12*(3), 349–373. https://doi.org/10.1901/jeab.1969.12-349

Williams, D. C., Saunders, K. J., & Perone, M. (2011). Extended pausing by humans on multiple fixed-ratio schedules with varied reinforcer magnitude and response requirements. *Journal of the Experimental Analysis of Behavior, 95*(2), 203–220. https://doi.org/10.1901/jeab.2011.95-203

Zeiler, M. D. (1979). Output dynamics. In M. D. Zeiler & P. Harzem (Eds.), *Advances in analysis of behaviour: Reinforcement and the organization of behaviour* (pp. 79–115). Chichester, England: Wiley.

Antecedent Stimulus Control

12

It is quiet in class. Everyone is concentrating on the exam. You are too. Suddenly, you hear the cellphone in your pocket begin to loudly play its Harry Potter ringtone. In a semi-panicked state, you fumble into your pocket and silence the phone.

We have all experienced something like this or seen others experience it. Isn't it interesting how a stimulus event like this can instantaneously change our behavior? The ringtone was the stimulus event (we heard it) and then our behavior changed dramatically – we went from

Source: U.S. Air Force ROTC

concentrating on an exam to desperately trying to press a button. This sequence of a stimulus event followed by a change in our behavior happens all the time. The walk sign is lit (stimulus event) and then we walk through the intersection (behavior). Our roommate comes home (stimulus event) and then we say, "I'm so glad you're here. You won't believe what happened to me today while I was taking my exam …" (behavior).

Earlier in this book we indicated that operant behavior is influenced by antecedent and consequent events. Since then, we have spent most of our time talking about consequences – reinforcers and punishers. This chapter focuses on antecedent stimulus events and how they can come to control behavior because of their relation with consequences. An **antecedent stimulus**, you will recall, is *an observable stimulus that is present before the behavior occurs.*

An Introduction to Behavior Analysis, First Edition. Gregory J. Madden, Derek D. Reed, and Florence D. DiGennaro Reed.
© 2021 John Wiley & Sons Ltd. Published 2021 by John Wiley & Sons Ltd.

The ringtone was present just before we sprang into action, trying to silence its embarrassing sound. Likewise, the arrival of our roommate is an antecedent stimulus. The roommate arrived just before we began speaking about our recent embarrassment.

Any stimulus that precedes behavior is an antecedent stimulus. But in behavior analysis, we are really only interested in those that have a behavioral function. Said another way, we only care about those stimuli that influence behavior. This functional focus is consistent with the two goals of our science. If we want to *accurately predict behavior*, then it would be nice to know which antecedent stimuli increase and which decrease behavior. Such antecedent stimuli are *functional variables* that may be used by behavior analysts to positively influence behavior. But this is all very abstract. Let's get into the specifics. Let's dive into what we know about functional antecedent stimuli that control behavior. We will begin by talking about some antecedents that you already learned about way back in Chapter 4.

Phylogenetic and Pavlovian Stimulus Control

You will recall that some of our behaviors are phylogenetic reflexes elicited by antecedent stimuli. That is, an unconditioned stimulus (US) elicits the unconditioned response (UR). The object placed in an infant's hand is an antecedent US that elicits the palmar grasp reflex (UR). A loss of support to the infant's body (US) elicits the Moro reflex (arms out, palms forward, fingers at the ready, should there be something to grasp onto; UR). These unlearned reflexes help infants stay alive, but only if they do them at the right time. An infant that made Moro-reflex responses at random times would be ill equipped to survive. Natural selection has prepared our species to react reflexively to important antecedent stimuli, like a loss of support.

The other functional antecedent stimulus that you already learned about is the Pavlovian conditioned stimulus (CS). After the individual learns that the CS signals a delay reduction to the US ("The US is coming! The US is coming!"), this antecedent stimulus will evoke a conditioned response (CR). For example, the smell of chocolate chip cookies baking in the oven signals a delay reduction to a warm, chewy, chocolatey cookie ("The cookies are coming! The cookies are coming!"). Therefore, the smell of those Toll House treats (the CS) not only whets our appetite, it wets our mouth with saliva (the CR). But you already knew all of that. Let's move on and spend the rest of the chapter talking about antecedent stimuli that influence operant behavior.

Discriminated Operant Behavior

Returning to an earlier example, walking through a busy intersection is operant behavior. It is not phylogenetically elicited by the walk sign, nor do we begin walking because we have learned that the sign signals a delay reduction to some unspecified US. Instead, walking is operant behavior because it is influenced by an antecedent stimulus (the walk sign) *and* it is influenced by consequences; two of them actually: (1) we get to the other side of the intersection and (2) we avoid being hit by a car.

To understand why antecedent stimuli influence operant behavior, answer this question: Is walking through an intersection *always* reinforced with these two consequences? If you are having a hard time seeing the point of such a question, imagine an intersection in New York City with hundreds of cars passing through. If, upon arrival, you immediately walk into the intersection, will the consequences be (1) getting to the other side and (2) avoiding being hit by a car? No. Walking into the intersection as soon as you arrive is a good way to get yelled at, honked at, and possibly killed. Therefore, it is very important that our street-crossing be **discriminated operant behavior**; that is, *operant behavior that is*

Source: metschers/Pixabay

systematically influenced by antecedent stimuli. When a walk sign is lit, pedestrians will walk through the busy intersection – their discriminated operant street-crossing behavior is systematically influenced by this antecedent stimulus.

Our everyday operant behaviors are so tightly controlled by antecedent stimuli that we rarely notice the control. To illustrate, imagine for a moment that we have a magic wand that has only one spell – it *de-stimulizes*. When we cast the de-stimulizing spell, the recipient will, for 24 hours, engage in their usual behaviors, but none of them will be controlled by antecedent stimuli. Sounds like fun, and our friend Mario asks to be de-stimulized. We cast the spell and, poof, Mario's behavior is no longer controlled by functional antecedent stimuli. Now, normally Mario kisses his romantic partner when they arrive (a functional antecedent stimulus), but after the spell is cast, he begins kissing the air in front of him. Kissing is a perfectly normal behavior, but it is not being controlled by the usual antecedent stimulus – the arrival of Mario's romantic partner.

At first, Mario's air-kissing is hilarious, but then things take a turn for the worse. Mario begins to disrobe, in our living room! This is perfectly normal behavior (before taking a shower); it's just that it's happening without regard to antecedent stimulus control. Nothing we say deters Mario from taking all his clothes off because, well, he's been de-stimulized!

Next, Mario walks into the street naked, is nearly hit by a car, and then begins talking to no one while making motions as though he is eating his breakfast cereal – all perfectly normal behaviors, none of them being controlled by antecedent stimuli. A few minutes later, the police arrive, wrap a blanket around poor Mario, and take him to the psychiatric hospital for evaluation. As this thought experiment illustrates, if our operant behavior is not under tight antecedent stimulus control, within just a few minutes it would be identified as "highly unusual," "dangerous," perhaps even "psychotic." Discriminated operant behavior is the norm (Davison & Nevin, 1999).

Now that we have established how important antecedent stimulus control of operant behavior is, let's discuss the varieties of the functional antecedent stimuli that exert this control. Unlike a US that elicits a UR without any prior learning, the functions of antecedent stimuli that control operant behavior have to be learned. Specifically, we need to learn which antecedent stimuli are present when a response has been (and has not been) reinforced. Similarly, we need to learn which antecedent stimuli are present when a response has been (and has not been) punished. The next sections discuss each of these functional antecedent stimuli that control operant behavior.

The Discriminative Stimulus (S^D)

A **discriminative stimulus (S^D)** is *an antecedent stimulus that can evoke a specific operant response because the individual has learned that when the S^D is present, that response will be reinforced* (Michael, 1980). Before he was de-stimulized, the sight of Mario's romantic partner approaching functioned as an S^D (pronounced, "*ess-dee*")–it evoked his kissing behavior because Mario's past experiences had taught him that when this S^D is present, kissing his romantic partner will be reinforced. That is, they will return Mario's affections. When this S^D is absent, air-kissing is not reinforced.

Some of the earliest laboratory research on the S^D was conducted by Skinner (1933, 1938). In one experiment, a rat was placed in an operant chamber equipped with a lever and a small light. When the light was turned on, pressing the lever produced a reinforcer (a food pellet). When the light was turned off, pressing never produced a pellet. By interacting with these antecedents (light on/off) and consequences (food/no-food), the rat learned to respond when the light was turned on and to not respond when the light was off – *discriminated operant behavior*.

Figure 12.1 shows how Skinner's experiment is replicated every Halloween, with human children instead of rats. As any experienced trick-or-treater will tell you, knocking on the doors of houses with the lights on and Halloween decorations in the front yard will be reinforced with candy. Conversely, knocking on the door of a house with the lights off and no decorations is almost never reinforced. Like Skinner's rats, first-time trick-or-treaters quickly learn that *IF they knock at a well-lit, decorated house* → *THEN they will get some candy* and *IF they knock at a dark, undecorated house* → *THEN they will get no candy*. The product of this learning – *discriminated operant behavior* – is shown in the inset graph in Figure 12.1. By the end of the first hour of candy-foraging, our first-time trick-or-treaters

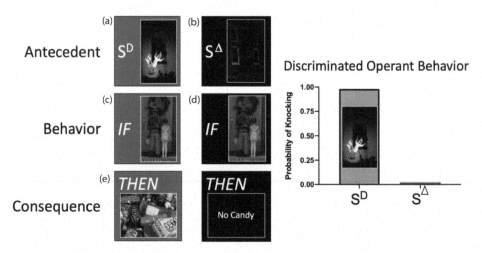

Figure 12.1 Common antecedents, behaviors, and consequences on Halloween night. By attending to the lights in and around the houses, the children learn that their behavior will be reinforced with candy when the house is decorated, or all the lights are on. By contrast, the same behavior is almost never reinforced when all the lights are out. The inset graph shows how the children's door-knocking behavior will become discriminated. That is, the behavior will be highly probable when the S^D is present and highly improbable when the S^Δ is observed.

will almost always knock on the doors of well-lit, decorated houses, and almost never knock on the doors of dark, undecorated houses. When operant behavior is discriminated in this way, we can classify the antecedent stimulus that increases behavior as an S^D.

Here's a final example for those readers who don't love rats or never went trick-or-treating. Imagine that we are on an early morning drive in a new city and we want a cup of coffee. We see a coffee shop up ahead and wonder if it is open. The likelihood of our stopping, getting out of the car, and walking to the coffee-shop door (the operant response) will be greatly increased by an OPEN sign in the window. The sign is an antecedent stimulus that functions as an S^D. We long ago learned that when an OPEN sign is lit, parking the car and going in will be reinforced. The S^D increases our stopping behavior, relative to when we cannot see an illuminated OPEN sign. Coffee shop owners intuitively understand discriminated operant behavior, so they use OPEN signs to clearly signal when coffee-buying behaviors will be reinforced.

The S^Δ

The second functional antecedent stimulus that controls operant behavior is the S^Δ (pronounced "ess-delta"). An **S^Δ** is *an antecedent stimulus that decreases a specific operant response because the individual has learned that when the S^Δ is present, that response will not be reinforced (extinction)*. In Figure 12.1, the S^Δ was the dark house. The antecedent S^Δ decreases behavior relative to the S^D. The trick-or-treater's behavior is *discriminated*. Their precious candy-collecting time will not be wasted on S^Δ houses.

Because we have not been *de-stimulized*, S^D and S^Δ stimuli are constantly controlling our behavior. For example, specific facial expressions function as S^Ds, whereas others function as S^Δs. Imagine you are at a party and a person you are attracted to is giving you some S^D facial expressions. You know what we are talking about; those flirtatious looks that people make, in your experience, when they are highly likely to reinforce your social behaviors (talking, flirting, etc.). Stimulus discrimination occurs if you are more likely to approach someone giving you an S^D facial expression than someone giving you an S^Δ look (extreme disinterest). Not only would a de-stimulized person not be controlled by these facial expressions, but they would also spend most of their evening talking to a barstool.

The S^{Dp}

The antecedent stimulus control of operant behavior also extends to punishment. Consider a late-night drive home that is interrupted by a red traffic light. We stop at the intersection, and wait … and wait … and wait. We are about the run the light when we see a police vehicle parked across the street. Where just a moment ago we were poised to break the law, the sight of the police car (an antecedent stimulus) decreases the probability of a criminal act. We long ago learned that violating traffic laws in front of the police will be punished with a costly ticket (consequence).

In this example, the sight of the police vehicle functions as an **S^{Dp}** – *an antecedent stimulus that decreases a specific operant response because the individual has learned that when the S^{Dp} is present, that response will be punished* (O'Donnell, 2001). You can think of the S^{Dp} as a warning stimulus or – to use the language of Chapter 10 – *the watchful eye of the punisher*. As long as the warning stimulus (S^{Dp}) is present, the response is suppressed. When the S^{Dp} is removed (the police cruiser drives away), the punishable behavior increases in probability.

The response-suppressing effects of the S^{Dp} have been demonstrated many times in the lab. For example, in an experiment conducted by Honig (1966), pigeons were taught to peck a white response key by arranging a variable-interval (VI) 20-second schedule of food reinforcement (S^D = white). When a black line was projected onto the key, pecking it occasionally produced a brief electric shock (S^{Dp} = black line). During each session, these contingencies periodically alternated back and forth, always accompanied by the S^D or the S^{Dp}. Figure 12.2 shows the discriminated operant behavior of the four pigeons that participated in Honig's experiment. Like our red-light running behavior, the pigeons' pecking was tightly

Source: Josh Hild/Unsplash

controlled by the S^D and the S^{Dp}. On average, the pigeons pecked about once per second when the S^D was on, and they virtually never pecked during the S^{Dp}. The S^{Dp} decreased the operant response.

Outside the lab, another everyday example of an S^{Dp} is a bee that lands on our arm. When we see this antecedent stimulus, it decreases the probability that we will attempt to pick up the bee. We have long ago learned that touching a bee is a good way to get stung, a consequence that punishes this behavior. The outcome of this learning is that now, when we see a bee land on our arm, we will do nothing (decreased behavior) until the bee flies off (the S^{Dp} is removed). The arrival of the bee is a warning stimulus – an S^{Dp} – which decreases insect-touching behaviors.

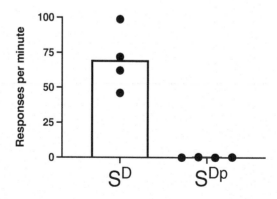

Figure 12.2 Filled circles show individual pigeon's rates of pecking a white key, which functioned as an S^D; that is, pecking was reinforced when the key was white. Rates of pecking fell to zero during the S^{Dp}, as that stimulus was correlated with the punishment of key-pecking.

Source: Honig, W. K. (1966). The role of discrimination training in the generalization gradient of punishment. *Journal of the Experimental Analysis of Behavior*, 9(4), 377–384. https://doi.org/10.1901/jeab.1966.9-377

The Three-term Contingency

As individuals interact with reinforcement contingencies in an environment filled with antecedent stimuli, they learn that specific operant behaviors (e.g., grasping, drawing the hand to mouth, and tilting the wrist) are only reinforced in the presence of an S^D (a full glass of water) and are never reinforced in the presence of an S^Δ (an empty glass). Discriminated operant behavior occurs in context – the context of S^Ds and S^Δs. If we were all de-stimulized, operant behavior would occur independent of its context and, as we saw with poor Mario, that would be disastrous. Not simply because we would periodically walk into the street naked, but also because our operant behavior would largely fail to acquire reinforcers. When we want a drink of water, we would engage in the grasping-drawing-tilting behavior thousands of times before we happened to do it while a glass of water was between our thumb and fingers. Stimulus control of operant behavior is critical to the survival of the individual.

We refer to *the functional relation between antecedent, behavior, and consequence* as the **three-term contingency** (Skinner, 1938); this is sometimes referred to as the A-B-C contingency. This adds a third term (the antecedent stimulus) to the two-term (*IF response →
THEN consequence*) contingency that we have discussed in previous chapters. The three-term contingencies discussed so far may be represented as follows:

	Antecedent		Behavior			Consequence
IF	S^D	AND	Response →	THEN		Reinforcer
IF	S^Δ	AND	Response →	THEN		No Consequence
IF	S^{Dp}	AND	Response →	THEN		Punisher

As noted by Skinner (1972), when individuals interact with consequences in the presence of an S^D, S^Δ, or S^{Dp}, the development of discriminated operant behavior is "practically inevitable." Consistent with that observation, well-controlled laboratory experiments have demonstrated that nonhuman animals (Colwill & Rescorla, 1990) and humans (Gámez & Rosas, 2007) explicitly learn the relation between all three terms in the three-term contingency.

Reading Quiz 1

1. A(n) _____ stimulus is an observable stimulus that is present before the behavior occurs.
2. A(n) _____ is an observable stimulus change that happens after behavior occurs.
3. The antecedent stimulus that controls (elicits) phylogenetic behavior is the _____ stimulus.
4. After Pavlovian learning is complete, the antecedent stimulus that controls (evokes) the conditioned response is the _____ stimulus.
5. Operant behavior that is systematically influenced (controlled) by antecedent stimuli is referred to as _____ operant behavior.
6. A(n) _____ is an antecedent stimulus that decreases a specific operant response because the individual has learned that when that stimulus is present, that response is likely to be punished.

7. A(n) _____ is an antecedent stimulus that evokes a specific operant response because the individual has learned that when this stimulus is present, that response is likely to be reinforced.

8. A(n) _____ is an antecedent stimulus that decreases a specific operant response because the individual has learned that when this stimulus is present, that response will not be reinforced (extinction).

9. The relation between antecedent, behavior, and consequence is referred to as the _____-_____ contingency.

In each of the items here, we have identified an antecedent, the behavior, and a consequence (the three-term contingency). Your job is to decide if the antecedent is an S^D, S^Δ, or S^{Dp}. In doing so, please assume that any consequence that sounds like it might be a reinforcer is a reinforcer and any consequence that sounds like it might be a punisher is a punisher. Remember that the answers appear at the end of the chapter.

Antecedent	Behavior	Consequence
10. CLOSED sign in window	Stopping at the coffee shop	Shop door does not open
This antecedent is an _____.		
11. The car is shifted out of Park and into Drive	Driver presses accelerator pedal	Car moves forward
This antecedent is an _____.		
12. Shop owner is watching	Customer momentarily refrains from, but then steals the pearl necklace	Shop owner calls the police, who arrest the customer
This antecedent is an _____.		
13. Soda machine appears operational	Swipe credit card, push button	Soda is dispensed
This antecedent is an _____.		
14. Soda machine is dark and unplugged	Swipe credit card, push button	Soda is not dispensed
This antecedent is an _____.		
15. Cellphone text notification	Unlock phone, open texting app	See a funny new text
This antecedent is an _____.		
16. Making it to the front of the line	"I'll have a latte please"	A delicious latte
This antecedent is an _____.		
17. The class bully arrives	Josh talks less than normal	The bully criticizes Josh when he speaks
This antecedent is an _____.		
18. A red line through "Chalupa" on the menu	"I'll have the chalupa please"	"I'm sorry, we've sold out of the chalupa"
This antecedent is an _____.		

Antecedent	Behavior	Consequence
19. Traffic light turns red	Step on the brake pedal	Stop and avoid accident
This antecedent is an _____.		
20. The Snooze button appears during an alarm on the phone	Press the Snooze button	Annoying alarm ends
This antecedent is an _____.		
21. Clock indicates you snoozed through your exam	Go to class ready to take exam	Another class is in the room
This antecedent is an _____.		
22. Word in bold and italicized definition in this book	Make and study the flashcard	Better grade on exam
This antecedent is an _____.		

Discriminative Stimuli and Establishing Operations

An S^D is a functional antecedent stimulus – it precedes behavior and it evokes a specific operant behavior (the one that has been reinforced when that stimulus is present). However, if the behavior is not habitual, the S^D will evoke this response *only* if the consequence currently functions as a reinforcer. To illustrate, consider that a restaurant is an S^D for food-purchasing behaviors *only* when a meal functions as a reinforcer. If we just finished eating lunch, the restaurant S^D will not evoke food-purchasing behavior. Instead, we will not even notice the restaurant's existence. By contrast, if we are famished, we will notice the S^D and may stop in for a meal.

In Chapter 9 we discussed how an establishing operation (EO), like food-deprivation, has two effects: (1) it temporarily increases the efficacy of a reinforcer and (2) it increases operant behaviors that produce that reinforcer. Not eating for 6 hours is an EO because it increases the efficacy of food as a reinforcer *and* it increases the probability that we will buy and consume food. To do this, we will look for an S^D – a stimulus that signals our food-seeking behaviors will be reinforced. If we did not look for S^Ds when hungry, we would be just as likely to order food in a nail salon as in a restaurant. Such de-stimulized people would go hungry.

One more example may help to make the point about the relation between EOs and S^Ds. Imagine that we ordered a taco at a fast-food restaurant. When the bag of food is handed to us through the drive-thru window, we notice there is no salsa. This functions as an EO that temporarily increases the reinforcing efficacy of a packet of salsa and initiates our search for an S^D; a stimulus that signals our salsa-requesting behavior will be reinforced. So, where, in our past experience, will our salsa-requesting behavior be reinforced? In a nearby park? At a gas station? Under the hood of our car? Obviously not. The EO will initiate our search for an employee of the restaurant – the S^D. When we see one, we will wave and, when they open the window, politely request a packet of salsa. When an EO increases the efficacy of a reinforcer, we begin looking for S^Ds that signal the availability of that reinforcer.

Discrimination Training

On the one hand, the development of discriminated operant behavior in the laboratory is "inevitable" (Skinner, 1972). On the other hand, in the real world, making the right response at the right time is far from inevitable. There are many human behaviors that require meticulously accurate discriminations; errors can be disastrous. Consider the behavior of a baggage screener at the airport. Their job is to briefly look at scanned images of the contents of our bags and quickly decide if the bag contains a banned item such as a gun, a knife, or an explosive. At the same time, they must not burden passengers by incorrectly flagging a bag that needs no further screening. Missing a dangerous item could have catastrophic outcomes; too many false alarms and the screener could lose their job. Clearly, this job requires finely discriminated operant behavior. Training these screeners will involve *discrimination training.*

Discrimination training is *a procedure in which an operant response is reinforced in the presence of an S^D and extinguished in the presence of an S^Δ.* This was the procedure used by Skinner (1933, 1938) – in the presence of the S^D (light on) lever pressing was reinforced. In the presence of the S^Δ (light off), the same response was never reinforced. Discrimination training is also used on Halloween night. When knocking on the door is reinforced in the presence of the S^D and extinguished in the presence of the S^Δ, these stimuli acquire behavioral function. They control when the response will be emitted and when it will be withheld.

Applied to training airport baggage screeners, the goal is to ensure that the scanned image of a knife functions as an S^D for flagging the bag for further screening. At the same time, it is important that scanned images of pencils, toothbrushes, and tweezers are passed over for further screening. Discrimination training will involve (1) presenting scanned images of knives and reinforcing their detection and (2) presenting scanned images of pencils, tweezers, and other long narrow objects (S^Δs) and withholding reinforcement if the item is erroneously flagged. When the image of a knife reliably evokes the flagging response, and no other image does, then the response is under tight stimulus control – it occurs when the S^D is present and not when an S^Δ is displayed.

Effective Methods of Discrimination Training

Considerable research efforts have been expended to discover the most effective and efficient methods of conducting discrimination training. The real-world utility of this is obvious. For example, efficient methods of establishing discriminated operant behavior are useful in helping children learn to read (see Extra Box 1). Likewise, if employee safety requires that they quickly learn to read hazmat signs (S^Ds) so that they will strictly follow a safety protocol (response) and avoid serious injury (negative reinforcer), then the technology of discrimination training can literally save lives.

Of course, discrimination training will be more effective if its defining properties are strictly adhered to: (1) the response is reinforced in the presence of the S^D, and (2) it is not reinforced in the presence of the S^Δ:

$$IF \quad S^D \quad AND \quad Response \rightarrow THEN \quad Reinforcer$$
$$IF \quad S^\Delta \quad AND \quad Response \rightarrow THEN \quad No \quad Reinforcer$$

There are two further points to be made here. First, if conditions change and the response is no longer reinforced in the presence of the S^D, the function of that stimulus will gradually change – it will function as an S^Δ and will no longer evoke the response. Thus, it is important that the contingencies be strictly adhered to in the presence of the S^D (reinforcement) and the S^Δ (extinction). Second, discrimination training arranges *both* the S^D and S^Δ contingencies because experience with both produces better learning that experience with the S^D alone (Dinsmoor, 1995b, 1995a; Honig et al., 1959). Alternating randomly between the S^D and the S^Δ is also a good idea, as it ensures the learner is attending to the antecedent stimuli rather than the sequence in which they are presented.

Therefore, if we want to quickly teach baggage screeners to flag knife-containing luggage for further screening, then the best strategy is to randomly alternate between images that contain a knife (S^D) and other images of long-narrow objects that are not knives (S^Δs). That is, it is just as important to know when *not* to flag a piece of luggage for further screening as it is to learn to positively identify knives. Indeed, some evidence suggests that having more experience with the S^Δ than the S^D produces faster learning and more accurate discriminations (Andrzejewski et al., 2007; Sherman et al., 1964).

That said, there is undoubtedly an upper limit on the relative number of S^Δ images. If the S^D is extraordinarily rare, the learner's attention will wane in a sea of S^Δs. In US airports, for example, knives, guns, and explosives in carry-on luggage are extraordinarily rare and, perhaps as a result, the baggage screeners fail to detect these items more often than they flag them for further screening (Frank, 2009; Levenson & Rose, 2019). Finding the optimal ratio of S^D and S^Δ images in discrimination training and the long-term maintenance of discriminated operant behavior is an important area for future research (Hogan et al., 2009).

Using Discrimination Training to Positively Influence Behavior

Effective discrimination training was critical in the landmine-detection project conducted in Tanzania by APOPO (the Dutch acronym for *Anti-Personnel Landmines Detection Product Development*). APOPO taught African pouched rats to detect landmines buried in the dirt (Poling et al., 2011a). Prior to this project, these rats were considered vermin, a nuisance. After the project, they were viewed as lifesavers.

According to UNICEF, over 110 million landmines remain buried in 64 countries worldwide. Scores of innocent people and large animals (e.g., tigers, elephants) have been injured or killed when they strayed from well-worn paths and stepped on a mine. These countries can experience food shortages because uncleared fields

Source: Gooutside/Wikipedia

cannot be farmed, and parents live with the fear that their child will be the next victim of these underground killers.

Enter APOPO. Equipped with their knowledge of behavior-analytic principles, this group used discrimination training to teach the African pouched rats to sniff out landmines, which can then be disarmed by their human handlers. Relative to other mine-clearing methods, African pouched rats are inexpensive, they have a great sense of smell, and they are too light to explode the mines they step on.

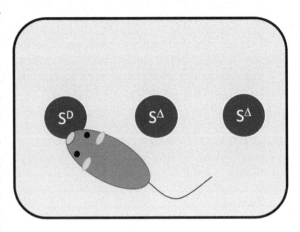

Training begins in a cage with three holes in the floor. Below the holes are small pots containing dirt that either contains TNT (the S^D) or contains just dirt (the S^Δ). When the rat lingers over the S^D hole, a clicker is used to present a conditioned reinforcer, followed by a bit of tasty food. Between response opportunities, the location of the S^D is randomly assigned. Rats soon learn to detect the smell of TNT, discriminating it from ordinary dirt. The rat earns an initial training certification when its operant behavior is highly discriminated – it only lingers over soil containing TNT.

Next, the rats are trained in a small area in which perforated steel balls have been buried, some of which contain TNT. When the rats dig at the ground above these balls (S^D), they earn a click and a treat. Digging anywhere else (S^Δ) is extinguished. Eventually, after the rats earn more training certifications, they make their way to the field, where their handlers will systematically walk them through an area, disposing of the landmines these highly trained rats detect.

By 2019, these rats had cleared mines in Angola, Cambodia, Mozambique, Tanzania, and Zimbabwe. Mark Shukuru, originally from Tanzania, and now the head rat-trainer for the Cambodia project, described its success, "Everyone was surprised, even me … We have never missed anything with the rats. We're doing good."

And now the challenge for you, the reader. What good is yet to be done with discrimination training? Could rats and other animals with excellent olfactory sensitivity help us to

Source: Gooutside/Wikipedia

quickly and inexpensively identify individuals with a contagious disease (like COVID-19); yes, they can (Jendrny et al., 2020; Poling et al., 2011b; Stead Sellers, 2020; Weetjens et al., 2009). Could pigeons learn to screen baggage at the airports; maybe so (Herrnstein et al., 1976). If you have an idea, share it with your instructor. Perhaps you too could do good, save lives, and positively influence behavior.

EXTRA BOX 1: DIRECT INSTRUCTION OF READING SKILLS

There are many approaches to teaching children to read. One approach is to show the child a whole word, like JUST and teach them to say "just." The child may learn to read 10 new words in an afternoon, but mistakes will be frequent; for example, saying "just" when the word is actually JEST. A different approach is to teach more fundamental discriminated operant responses. Instead of teaching 10 whole words in an afternoon, the child will instead learn the sounds of 10 individual letters. For example, when the child sees the letter C (S^D), saying "kuh" will be reinforced. Saying "kuh" when other letters are shown will be extinguished (S^Δ). When, at the end of the discrimination-training session, the child is able to make 10 different phonetic sounds under the tight stimulus control of 10 different letters, they will have the fundamental skills necessary to begin sounding-out hundreds of three-letter words, like "cat" (Watkins & Slocum, 2004).

This use of discrimination training to establish fundamental skills that will form the foundation of higher-order thinking is the strategy employed in Direct Instruction (DI). The DI approach uses empirically supported behavior-analytic principles to design a curriculum that (a) moves systematically from the fundamental to the complex, (b) ensures that every child is actively responding and learning from their successes and mistakes, and (c) tailors the curriculum to individual learning. The development of DI materials involves careful design and repeated testing to ensure student success.

In the late 1960s, the US government conducted a massive study to identify the reading curriculum that produced the best results in impoverished communities across the country. Of the 20 curricula tested, only DI produced positive outcomes on all outcome measures (Kennedy, 1978). Despite these results, most school districts did not adopt the DI curriculum, often preferring a curriculum that had far worse learning outcomes.

In the years that followed, the DI curriculum was improved and expanded to math, language, spelling, and so on. More than 300 published studies have since evaluated the efficacy of DI and the nearly 3,000 outcomes are impressive. Children who attend DI schools demonstrate gains in academic achievement that a recent literature review described as "large" and "huge" (Stockard et al., 2018). These outcomes have been consistent over 50 years and do not depend on grade, race ethnicity, household income, or student at-risk status. Children who attend DI schools for more years have better outcomes than those with limited access.

Despite all of these data, DI is still not widely used in US schools. Why not is hard to say. One reason may be that parents and administrators embrace "student-led" and "inquiry-based" forms of education – they sound great in the abstract (who doesn't want their child to be inquisitive and "self-motivated"?). Another reason may be that the active-learning style of DI doesn't appeal to teachers, parents, and administrators who prefer quiet classrooms. DI schools are noisy because everyone is actively responding and learning – no one raises their hand to answer a question. Others fear that DI involves rote memorization, which DI is explicitly designed not to do; hence, the better scores when testing for higher-order cognitive processes. So, it's a mystery why DI is not more popular. Perhaps one day you will be the parent who successfully lobbies to bring DI, and better learning outcomes, to your child's school.

Source: kali9/Getty Images

Generalization

If a young reader has learned to say "just" when she sees the written word JUST, it will not surprise us when she mistakenly says "just" when the written word on the page is actually JEST. These two written words closely resemble each other, differing by just a single letter. We might say that the verbal response "just" has *generalized* to a new stimulus that very closely resembles the S^D. That is, **generalization** occurs *when a novel stimulus resembling the S^D evokes the response, despite that response never having been reinforced in the presence of that novel stimulus*. Saying "just" has never been reinforced in the presence of JEST (the novel stimulus), but this verbal response occurs because JEST so closely resembles JUST (the S^D).

This sort of generalization was first demonstrated in the laboratory by Guttman and Kalish (1956). They trained pigeons to peck a yellow response key by reinforcing those pecks on a VI schedule. As is typical of VI schedules, the birds pecked the yellow key at a constant rate. Next, during a test session in which no reinforcers were ever delivered, the key was lit with 11 different colors, presented individually in a random order. As you can see in Figure 12.3, the pigeons pecked at the highest rate during the portion of this test when the key was yellow (S^D). When the key was lit with a novel color, responding decreased, and the amount of that decrease was an orderly function of the amount of the color change. As the key color looked less and less like the S^D, the pigeons pecked it less and less.

The approximately bell-shaped response curve in Figure 12.3 is called a **generalization gradient**; that is, *a graph depicting increases in responding as the novel antecedent stimulus more closely resembles the S^D*. The bell-like shape of the generalization gradient has been replicated in laboratory settings many times, in many stimulus modalities (visual, auditory, etc.), and in many species, including humans (Fox et al., 2013; Galizio, 1985; Jenkins & Harrison, 1960; Podlesnik & Miranda-Dukoski, 2015). Outside the lab, a common experience of generalization is the "phantom vibration." A vibrating cellphone functions as a tactile S^D, which leads us to check our phone. But sometimes we have a tactile sensation that is not exactly like the S^D, but we check it anyways. When we find no new text, push, or news notification, we can attribute this hallucination to *generalization* – the tactile stimulus that we sensed was similar to the vibration produced by our phones.

It is sometimes the case that generalization is problematic. For example, in Figure 12.4 we use our pigeons' generalization gradient to illustrate why a beginning human reader might incorrectly say "just" when she sees a written word that closely resembles JUST. The written words seen by the child are shown on the x-axis, and the probability of reading it as "just" is shown on the y-axis. Consistent with the bell shape of the generalization gradient, when the child sees a word like JEST, which looks a lot like the S^D (JUST), the vocal response *generalizes* to this novel stimulus. The probability of incorrectly reading the word increases as the word more closely resembles the S^D and decreases as the word looks less and less like JUST.

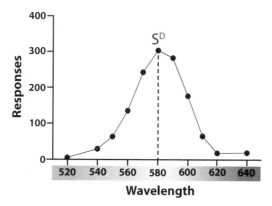

Figure 12.3 The average number of responses made by pigeons at a variety of wavelengths of visible light (nanometers). The discriminative stimulus at which pigeons were trained to peck the key was 580 nm. Based on data reported by Guttman and Kalish (1956).

Source: Guttman, N., & Kalish, H. I. (1956). Discriminability and stimulus generalization. *Journal of Experimental Psychology, 51*(1), 79–88. https://doi.org/10.1037/h0046219

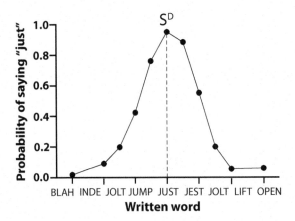

Figure 12.4 The generalization gradient from Figure 12.3 is used to illustrate how, after a child has learned to say "just" when she sees the written word JUST, other words that physically resemble JUST might evoke this verbal operant response.

Using Discrimination Training to Improve Stimulus Control

If a child is forever misreading words because of their resemblance to other words, that child will never become a fluent reader. She will find reading frustrating (the sentences make no sense), she will not read books at home, and she will struggle in school. As noted in Extra Box 1, the alternative to teaching children to read whole words is to teach them the sounds that individual letters make. Once they have mastered this skill, we can teach them to sound-out letter combinations that form simple words. When this is accomplished, the child has the fundamental skills needed to read thousands of simple words (Watkins & Slocum, 2004).

For example, our budding reader may first be taught to say "kuh" when she sees the letter K. That is, we will reinforce saying "kuh" when K is the antecedent stimulus, and we will extinguish "kuh" when it occurs at other times. This discrimination training session will alter the function of K, such that it becomes an S^D that evokes the vocal response "kuh."

The left panel of Figure 12.5 illustrates the generalization gradient we might expect after a brief lesson in which she is shown the letter K and "kuh" is reinforced. The child is very likely to say "kuh" each time she sees the letter K (the S^D), but she will also say "kuh" when she sees letters that look like K. Consistent with the bell-shape of the generalization gradient, those letters that look more like K will evoke more "kuh" responses than letters that less resemble K. The right panel in the figure shows improved stimulus control – the letter K is the only antecedent stimulus that evokes the "kuh" response. The response is nearly perfectly discriminated, and that is what we need if the child is to learn to read.

To get our young reader's performance to transition from the left to the right panel of Figure 12.5, we will use discrimination training. As noted earlier, discrimination training works better when the S^D is presented at random times, intermixed with S^Δ stimuli. This can be accomplished with 11 flash cards, shuffled periodically, each showing one of the letters

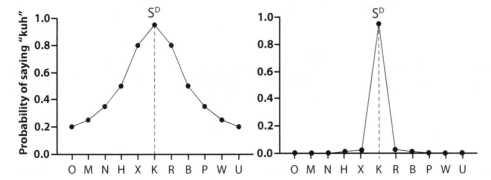

Figure 12.5 The left panel shows a hypothetical generalization gradient that might be obtained after a single session in which a child is taught to say "kuh" when shown the letter K (the S^D). After that training, other letters, particularly those that resemble K, will also evoke the "kuh" response. The right panel shows what the generalization gradient of an adult reader might look like. For this individual, only the S^D evokes the verbal response "kuh".

along the x-axis of Figure 12.5. When K is shown and our reader says "kuh" the response will be reinforced ("very good!"). When any of the other letters are shown, "kuh" will be extinguished. On these S^Δ trials, the correct response is no response. We are teaching the child that K is an S^D for "kuh" and all of the other letters that more or less resemble a K are S^Δs for this verbal response. After a brief discrimination training lesson, the child's generalization gradient will "tighten up" as she begins to emit the "kuh" sound when she sees the K, and not when she sees any of the other letters. When she has mastered this, then she is ready to add another discriminated operant to her repertoire; perhaps learning to say "tuh" when she sees the letter T.

As this example illustrates, it is often important for behavior to be under tight stimulus control. The same is true of our African pouched rats. The smell of TNT (S^D) must powerfully evoke digging behaviors and all other smells must not. If the rats repeatedly dig in places where there are no landmines (a "false positive"), the rats will prove useless. Ditto for airport baggage screeners. The technology of discrimination training greatly aids in establishing and maintaining tight stimulus control (Edwards et al., 2015).

At other times, however, tight stimulus control is maladaptive. That is, we would like behavior acquired in the presence of the S^D to generalize to other stimulus situations. For example, if a client makes excellent weekly progress in the behavior therapist's office (S^D), we would like to see the newly acquired skills generalize to life outside the office, in daily living. The next section discusses strategies to promote such generalization and the maintenance of behavior over time.

Promoting Generalization and Maintenance

As this chapter has made clear, when an operant behavior is reinforced in the presence of an S^D, that stimulus (and others that closely resemble it) will evoke that response. When an applied behavior analyst or behavior therapist helps their client to acquire a new, adaptive behavior, they will face the challenge of getting the client's behavior to generalize beyond the therapy setting, where it must be maintained over time if the intervention is to be successful.

An illustrative example occurs in parenting classes. New parents, or parents of at-risk children, enroll in these courses to acquire behavior-analytic skills (reinforcement, extinction, punishment, etc.) that will help them to raise well-adjusted, emotionally well-regulated children (Eyberg et al., 2008). Parents acquire these skills in a classroom setting in which they learn behavioral principles and role-play appropriate parenting behaviors with feedback from the instructor. The utility of this training, however, entirely depends on generalization and maintenance over time. If parents only use these skills in the classroom when the instructor is watching and not at home as their children grow up, then the parent-training sessions would be a waste of time and a lost opportunity. Thus, a technology for promoting the generalization and maintenance of adaptive behavior is critical (Dass et al., 2018). Stokes and Osnes (1989) outlined several tactics for promoting such generalization and maintenance. Three of their most important tactics are described next.

TACTIC 1: TEACH BEHAVIORS THAT WILL CONTACT NATURAL CONTINGENCIES OF REINFORCEMENT.

When a new response is acquired in a therapeutic setting, artificial (therapist provided), reinforcers will be arranged. For example, instructors of parent-training classes will reinforce correct parenting behaviors when they occur during role-playing sessions. For obvious reasons, these artificial reinforcers will not be provided when the parent implements one of their good-parenting skills at home. Therefore, if the skill is to be consistently used at home, it needs to contact a natural contingency of reinforcement. Said less technically, the skill will have to work. If it does, the behavior acquired in a classroom setting will generalize to the home (and beyond) and will be maintained over time.

To facilitate contact with these natural contingencies of reinforcement, parent-training instructors will promote generalization by giving parents homework assignments. These assignments ask parents to implement their newly acquired skills at home *and* collect direct-observation data, so they will see when their skills were effective and when they need further refinement in class. Such assignments put parents in contact with the natural contingencies operating at home. By teaching behaviors that will contact natural contingencies of reinforcement, applied behavior analysts are ensuring that the skills they teach are skills that will serve the client well in daily life (Kohler & Greenwood, 1986; Neely et al., 2016).

TACTIC 2: TRAIN DIVERSELY.

Rather than teaching a skill in one setting, with one teacher, and with one reinforcer, generalization can be promoted by training in multiple settings, with multiple teachers and with a variety of reinforcers. Each time the skills training moves to a new setting, new instructor, and so on, an opportunity for generalization is presented and, if it occurs and is reinforced, the individual may learn that the skill is applicable to many settings, not just the S^D setting in which it was acquired.

TACTIC 3: ARRANGE ANTECEDENT STIMULI THAT WILL CUE GENERALIZATION.

There are a variety of ways to arrange antecedents that will cue generalization. One strategy is to take a salient stimulus from the setting to which the behavior needs to generalize and incorporate it into training. For example, a parent might be encouraged to bring their child (a salient stimulus from the home setting) to the next parent-training session. During that session, role-playing of appropriate parenting skills may be practiced while the child is present. Thereafter, the child may function as an S^D, evoking good-parenting responses at home, where it counts. Another strategy in this vein is to arrange reminders to emit the good-parenting response. For example, the parent may set an alarm to go off at random times, twice per day. At each alarm, the parent will stop what they are doing and look for an opportunity to demonstrate a good-parenting skill, such as noticing something their child is doing that can be positively reinforced – "I like the way you two are cooperating. Thank you."

These three tactics for promoting generalization will also help to maintain the newly acquired adaptive behavior over time. The behaviors that we emit every day of our lives are those that are consistently reinforced by natural contingencies operating in our environments. These natural contingencies are so reliable that our behavior can become habitual. As you may recall from Chapter 9, habitual behavior occurs under tight antecedent stimulus control, even when we have no real motivation to engage in the behavior. If a parent habitually deploys behavior-analytic skills in a compassionate way, that parent is likely to raise children who will do good in the world themselves. Therefore, applied behavior analysts will be tactical in promoting generalization of adaptive skills that are so compatible with the natural contingencies of reinforcement that those skills become habitual.

Reading Quiz 2

1. _____ _____ is a procedure in which an operant response is reinforced in the presence of an S^D and extinguished in the presence of an S^Δ.
2. Discrimination training will be more effective if we teach the individual to make the response in the presence of the S^D and to not make the response in the presence of the _____.
3. In a brilliant demonstration of the effective use of _____ _____, APOPO has trained African pouched rats to detect landmines buried in the dirt.
4. When APOPO teaches the rats to detect landmines, they reinforce digging in the dirt when TNT is present and extinguish digging when it occurs in landmine-free dirt. This training changes the function of the smell of TNT. Where previously the rats would largely ignore it, now it functions as a(n) _____ that reliably evokes the digging response.
5. _____ occurs when a novel stimulus resembling the S^D evokes the response, despite that response never having been reinforced in the presence of that novel stimulus.
6. A(n) _____ _____ is a graph depicting increases in responding as the novel antecedent stimulus more closely resembles the S^D.
7. Generalization gradients are typically _____-shaped.
8. When it is important to make fine discriminations, _____ _____ may be used to bring the behavior under tighter control of S^D and S^Δ stimuli.
9. When it is important that a behavior acquired in a therapeutic setting (S^D) also occurs in novel settings, behavior analysts will use tactics designed to promote _____.

10. One of those generalization-promoting tactics is to teach the individual to engage in behaviors that will contact the _____ contingencies of reinforcement.

11. A second generalization-promoting tactic is to train _____. That is, teach the skill in multiple settings, with multiple teachers, and with a variety of reinforcers.

12. The third generalization-promoting tactic is to arrange antecedent stimuli that will _____ (or remind) the individual to use their newly acquired skill in the novel setting.

For the remaining items, indicate if the bold term is an S^D or an EO.

13. A student hasn't had anything to drink for hours. The student starts looking for **a drinking fountain**, eventually finds one, and then fills their water bottle.

14. A student **hasn't had anything to drink for hours**. The student starts looking for a drinking fountain, eventually finds one, and then fills their water bottle.

15. You are sitting at home and **you feel cold**. You look around the room and see a blanket on the couch. You grab the blanket and put it over your body. Within a few moments, you feel warmer.

16. You are sitting at home and you feel cold. You look around the room and see **a blanket on the couch**. You grab the blanket and put it over your body. Within a few moments, you feel warmer.

Stimulus-Response Chains

Thus far, we have discussed S^Ds that evoke reinforced behaviors. For example, a push-notification on our phone evokes a phone-checking behavior because, in our past experience, these notifications signal that checking our phone will be reinforced. What's lost in this summary is that a behavior like phone-checking is composed of a sequence of responses that must be executed in a precise order. When the phone presents the S^D, this *initiates* our reaching for the phone. This response has a consequence – the tactile feel of the phone in our hand. This consequences undoubtedly functions as a reinforcer:

IF push-notification (S^D) AND reach for phone → THEN phone in hand

But the push notification's interesting news story has not yet been accessed. To see the story, two more responses are needed, and they need to be made in the right order:

IF phone in hand (S^D) AND unlock phone → THEN news icon visible

followed by …

IF news icon visible (S^D) AND tap icon → THEN news story presented

Note how the consequence of reaching for the phone (having the phone in hand) functions as a reinforcing consequence for that response *and* as an S^D for the next response in the chain. This dual S^D/reinforcer functioning happens a second time when the consequence of unlocking the phone (the news icon is visible on the face of the phone) functions both as a reinforcer *and* as an S^D for the next response – tapping the icon. This *fixed sequence of operant responses, each evoked by a response-produced S^D*, is referred to as a **stimulus-response chain**.

Stimulus-response chains are common in daily life (tying our shoes, making macaroni and cheese, mowing the grass). Even a seemingly simple behavior like buying a soda from a machine involves a fixed sequence of responses starting with:

IF soda machine visible (S^D) AND approach machine → THEN machine accessible

Thereafter, the consequence of each response in the stimulus-response chain functions as an S^D, evoking the next link (response) in the chain.

IF machine accessible (S^D) AND swipe credit card → THEN "Make Selection" icon lit

IF "Make Selection" icon lit (S^D) AND press button → THEN soda delivered

These common, everyday stimulus-response chains were acquired many years ago and most of us cannot recall how we learned them. Perhaps someone told us how to do them; perhaps we imitated the behavior of someone else. Whatever their origin, the correct execution of stimulus-response chains is an important part of daily living.

Teaching Stimulus-Response Chains

Individuals with significant development disabilities and early language delays can struggle to acquire new stimulus-response chains. They often cannot understand instructions or imitate the behavior of others. Acquiring a stimulus-response chain such as using the toilet, making popcorn, or accessing a favorite game on a tablet can greatly enrich their life and that of their parents. Therefore, a behavioral technology for teaching stimulus-response chains represents one more opportunity to positively influence behavior.

Consider the case of Emily, a 4-year old diagnosed with autism spectrum disorder. At baseline, she spoke no more than one word at a time, frequently made throat clearing sounds, and often dropped to the floor while crying and screaming. The behavior analysts who worked with Emily sought to teach her how to use a tablet computer to verbally ask for something she wanted, like an Elmo phone (King et al., 2014). To accomplish this, they first conducted a **task analysis**; that is, they provided *a precise specification of the sequence of antecedents, responses, and consequences that comprise a stimulus-response chain.* For Emily, one of her stimulus-response chains was

1. *IF see tablet elsewhere (S^D) AND walk to and pick up tablet → THEN tablet in hand*
2. *IF tablet in hand (S^D) AND search for Elmo icon → THEN find Elmo icon*
3. *IF see Elmo icon (S^D) AND touch Elmo icon → THEN tablet says "Elmo phone" and Emily is given the Elmo phone to play with*

Thus, Emily had to learn three behaviors, emit them in a precise sequence, and do so under tight antecedent stimulus control. This would be simple to teach to a typically developing 4-year old, but Emily's developmental disability made this a challenge.

To teach this stimulus-response chain, the behavior analysts used a training technique known as *backward chaining*. When using **backward chaining**, *the final link in the stimulus-response chain is taught first and, once that link is mastered, additional links are added in reverse order.* **Forward chaining** can also be done; it involves *teaching the links in the stimulus-response chain in the order they will need to be emitted.* Both techniques are effective (Slocum & Tiger, 2011).

In Emily's case, backward chaining involved first teaching her to touch the Elmo icon on the tablet computer – the last response in the chain. When that response was under stimulus control, the preceding response in the chain – searching for the Elmo icon on a screen containing several reward-depicting icons – was taught. Note how the consequence of Emily's screen-searching behavior produced the S^D (the Elmo icon) that then evoked the final response in the chain (touching the icon to earn some play time with the Elmo phone).

Eventually Emily mastered the entire chain and, in so doing, acquired a bit more independence. Now when she wanted to play with her favorite toy, she could grab her tablet and tell her parents exactly what she wanted. Prior to acquiring this stimulus-response chain, Emily must have experienced frustration with her inability to communicate her desires; frustration that could lead to disruptive behavior.

Prompting and Fading

When working with children who have limited verbal and nonverbal skills, showing them an Elmo icon will not automatically evoke an icon-touching response. If we are to establish the Elmo button as an S^D that evokes this response, then we will need the response to occur *and* to be reinforced. When Emily did not spontaneously press the Elmo button, King et al. (2014) used a procedure known as *prompting and fading*. A **prompt** is *an antecedent stimulus that facilitates or guides the desired response when it is not happening under appropriate discriminative-stimulus control.*

A variety of prompts are possible; we will mention three: *physical, stimulus,* and *modeling* prompts. For Emily, a *physical prompt* was used – her finger was gently guided to the Elmo icon. When she pressed it, Emily was allowed to play with the Elmo phone. Later, when Emily wanted to play with the Elmo phone again, the physical prompt was withheld for a few seconds, to allow her to press the icon independently. If that did not happen, then the behavior analyst offered the minimum amount of physical prompting needed, always giving Emily the opportunity to finish the response herself. The *gradual removal of a prompt as the response is increasingly emitted under discriminative-stimulus control* is called **fading**.

A second prompting strategy is to arrange a *stimulus prompt* that provides a "hint" at the desired response. An example is provided in Figure 12.6. Here the Elmo icon on the tablet computer is much larger than the other icons and is framed in red to make it stand out. As Emily correctly presses the Elmo icon, we can fade out this stimulus prompt by removing the red frame and gradually reducing the size of the icon, making sure that Emily's responding remains accurate throughout. Some evidence suggests that these stimulus prompts are more effective than physical (response-guiding) prompts (Cengher et al., 2018).

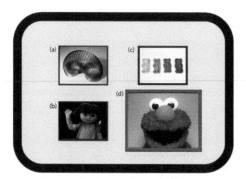

Figure 12.6 An example of how a stimulus prompt may be used to provide a hint about which is the correct response. As the child is successful in pressing the Elmo icon and obtaining reinforcers, the stimulus prompt will be gradually faded out, allowing behavior to be controlled by the unprompted S^D (the regularly sized/colored Elmo icon).

The third type of prompt that behavior analysts have explored is the *modeling prompt*. That is, the therapist clearly demonstrates how to make the desired response while the client watches. Video modeling has proven to be an effective way to prompt the desired response under S^D control (Bellini & Akullian, 2007; Shipley-Benamou et al., 2002). For example, Emily could watch a video of another child touching the Elmo icon and then getting to play with the Elmo phone. Prompting the desired behavior and gradually fading the prompt as the learner gains independence is an effective strategy in establishing antecedent stimulus control of adaptive behaviors (Cengher et al., 2018).

Extra Box 2 extends this chapter's concepts and analyses to consciousness. What is it? Who is conscious? How can we tell?

EXTRA BOX 2:   CONSCIOUSNESS

What is it like to be a bat? This is the question posed by the philosopher Thomas Nagel in his 1974 essay on consciousness. To Nagel, the study of consciousness is possible only if we can agree on what consciousness is. He turned to bats to shine light on the topic. For Nagel, "an organism has conscious mental states if and only if there this something that it is like to *be* that organism – something it is like *for* the organism." Is a bat conscious? Is there anything that it is like to *be* a bat; anything *for* the bat? This is a bit of a mind-bender, but this definition of consciousness points to awareness of *interoceptive stimuli*, that is, our private, inner, subjective experiences. Is a bat consciously aware of interoceptive stimuli or is it simply a well-oiled insect-catching machine?

Although Nagel (1974) argued there was no way to know if a bat was conscious, most consciousness researchers disagree (Blackmore, 2005). It is possible, in theory, to test for the bare minimum of consciousness by arranging special contingencies of reinforcement to alter the function of an interoceptive stimulus and to make that private, inner stimulus an S^D. Parents arrange these contingencies all the time, for example, when they teach their child to say "tummy ache" under the discriminative-stimulus control of an interoceptive stimulus – the sensation of pain in the mid-section:

IF pain in the mid-section (S^D) AND child says, "tummy ache" THEN parental care

Because the parent cannot feel the child's pain, they look for indirect evidence of that inter- oceptive stimulus – the child is crying and holding her belly (Skinner, 1945, 1957). Once acquired, if the child's verbal response "tummy ache" generalizes to an antecedent knock on the head, the parent will not reinforce it:

IF pain in the head (S^Δ) AND "tummy ache" THEN "no honey, you have a head-ache"

This discrimination-training approach comes natural to parents who need their children to accurately report on other private stimuli such as hunger, thirst, symptoms of an illness, and so on. Such discrimination training "tightens" interoceptive stimulus control and might be said to expand the child's consciousness (Blanshard & Skinner, 1967). That is, they become more aware of and attuned to their private, interoceptive stimuli.

But what of bats, rats, and other nonhuman animals? Are they conscious? We cannot say for sure. We know that several nonhuman species are *capable* of discriminating at least one internal, private stimulus – that produced by drugs – but these demonstrations happen in the lab, not in the wild. In these drug-discrimination studies, pressing a lever after a morphine injection (which produces an interoceptive S^D we might describe as "feeling high") is reinforced with food. On other days, the injection is saline (S^Δ) and pressing the "I feel high" lever is not reinforced. When the animal accurately presses on test days (when no reinforcers are provided), we may infer that its behavior is under interoceptive S^D and S^Δ control (Maguire et al., 2013).

So, on the one hand, nonhuman animals are *capable* of discriminating their internal, subjective states. But, on the other hand, in the wild we assume that no such discrimination-training contingencies exist. To the best of our knowledge, bats are not hanging about asking each other about a tummy ache. Thus, nonhuman consciousness of interoceptive stimuli seems unlikely, but the question remains unanswered.

An anecdotal piece of evidence about consciousness in the absence of discrimination-training contingencies comes from the case of Helen Keller. Keller, who lost her hearing and sight at 19 months, learned to communicate only at age 6, when Anne Sullivan arrived and used a form of discrimination training to teach her to communicate through tactile stimulation in the palms of her hands. Years later, Keller (1908) reflected on her days before that discrimination training began:

> *Before my teacher came to me, I did not know that I am. I lived in a world that was no-world … I never contracted my forehead in the act of thinking. I never viewed anything beforehand or chose it … never in a start of the body or a heart-beat did I feel that I loved or cared for anything. My inner life, then, was a blank without past, present, or future, without hope or anticipation, without wonder or joy or faith.*

Keller's reflections on consciousness (or the lack thereof) must be treated with caution. They come decades after her self-described emergence into consciousness. Nonetheless, these reflections raise the possibility that without contingencies of reinforcement that make interoceptive stimuli functional (S^D and S^Δ), we would not attend to those stimuli; we would not be conscious of our own inner lives.

Want to get a sense of the emergence of consciousness? Play the yellow car game with a friend. You both have to find one yellow car per day, take a picture of it, and text it to the other player. To earn a point, the yellow car needs to be a different one each day:

IF new yellow car (S^D) AND you text it to friend → THEN you have scored a point.

Now, for the duration of time you play the game, notice how your attention is drawn to yellow cars. Where previously you had *no conscious awareness* of yellow cars, now you see them everywhere. Now they have a behavioral function. Your consciousness of yellow cars is expanded when they function as an S^D. A similar expansion of consciousness may occur when interoceptive stimuli come to function as S^Ds and S^Δs, through discrimination training.

So, is there anything that it is like to be a bat? Perhaps not. Not unless contingencies of reinforcement are arranged that make interoceptive stimuli important (functional), something to take notice of because, like a yellow car, those stimuli acquire S^D or S^Δ properties. Perhaps it is contingencies that turn the lights of consciousness on. Perhaps.

Reading Quiz 3

1 A(n) _____-_____ _____ is a fixed sequence of operant responses, each evoked by a response-produced S^D.

2 When behavior analysts develop a precise specification of the sequence of antecedents, responses, and consequences that comprise a stimulus-response chain, they are writing a _____ _____.

3 After the task analysis is written, the behavior analyst must decide the order in which to teach each response in the stimulus-response chain. If we begin by training the first response in the chain, and teach the remaining responses in the order they will be emitted, we are using the _____ chaining technique.

4 If instead, we first train the individual to make the final link in the chain, and then add more links in reverse order, we are using the _____ chaining technique.

5 When working with individuals with developmental disabilities, it is often the case that the desired response does not occur when it should – when the S^D is presented. To facilitate the acquisition of the desired response, it is often useful to provide a _____. That is, a stimulus that facilitates or guides the desired response when it is not happening under appropriate stimulus control.

6 When prompts are used, it is important to gradually remove them as the individual is increasingly able to independently make the response under discriminative stimulus control. This gradual removing of prompts is called _____.

7 Behavior analysts commonly use three kinds of prompts: _____, _____, and _____ prompts.

Summary

In this chapter we remind the reader of two antecedent stimuli that influence human and nonhuman behavior – the US, which elicits reflexive responding (UR), and the CS, which evokes responses because of prior Pavlovian learning. To this, we have added the discriminative stimulus (S^D), which evokes operant behavior; the S^Δ, which decreases reinforcer-seeking behaviors because none have been acquired in its presence; and the S^{Dp}, which suppresses behavior because our past experience tells us punishment is likely. These stimuli, because of their relation to important consequences, influence our behavior every moment of the day. If we were momentarily "de-stimulized," it would be obvious to everyone else – our behavior would not fit its surroundings and our survival would soon be in peril.

This chapter also introduced the reader to generalization gradients and the default tendency for operant behavior to generalize to stimuli that physically resemble the S^D. When generalization is a problem, discrimination training will "tighten" stimulus control by simultaneously teaching the individual that a single response will be reinforced in the presence of the S^D but not in the presence of the S^Δ. Tight stimulus control is necessary for many important human behaviors; for example, when reading the words on this page, when understanding warning symbols, and when screening baggage at the airport. For other behaviors, like social and healthy living skills, generalization is adaptive. When this is so, the behavior analyst will take steps to promote generalization; for example, teaching skills that are a good fit with the natural contingencies of reinforcement.

What should be clear by this point in the book is that many functional variables that influence behavior have been discovered, replicated, and employed in the service of improving the lives of others, such as a child who wishes to express her desire to play with an Elmo phone, but does not have the words (see stimulus-response chains). What should be clear is how antecedent events can motivate our actions (EOs), elicit our actions (US), evoke our actions (CS and S^Ds), decrease our actions (S^Δ), and suppress our actions (S^P). These discoveries underlie the assumptions of behavior analysts that were explored in Chapter 1 – behavior is determined by knowable, functional variables, and the scientific method is a valid approach to discovering those variables. The work is ongoing and the next two chapters explore two frontiers of that work – choice and clinical behavior analysis.

Answers to Reading Quiz Questions

Reading Quiz 1

1. antecedent
2. consequence
3. unconditioned (US)
4. conditioned (CS)
5. discriminated
6. S^P
7. discriminative stimulus (S^D)
8. S^Δ
9. three-term
10. S^Δ: We have long ago learned that trying to open a door with a CLOSED sign in the window is rarely reinforced (with entry into the business). The CLOSED sign decreases the probability that we will try the door.
11. S^D: Seeing that the car is in Drive increases the probability that we will press the gas pedal.
12. S^{Dp}: The watchful eye of the store owner decreased stealing for a few minutes, but when the necklace was stolen, this behavior was punished.
13. S^D: Assuming we want a soda, a lit soda machine increases the probability that we will use it to obtain the desired reinforcer.
14. S^Δ: Assuming we want a soda, a dark soda machine decreases the probability that we will use it because that response is unlikely to be reinforced.
15. S^D: A text notification increases texting behaviors because we have learned that the notification means these behaviors will be reinforced (by seeing a new text).
16. S^D: We place our order when we make it to the front of the line because we have learned that this position is the only one where our latte-ordering behavior will be reinforced.
17. S^{Dp}: The arrival of the bully decreases the amount that Josh speaks because Josh has learned that the bully is likely to criticize (punish) whatever he says.
18. S^Δ: A line through our menu selection decreases the probability we will order it. We have previously learned that ordering it will not get us the chalupa that we want (extinction).
19. S^D: We may not like red lights, but they do control our behavior. They increase the probability that we will step on the brakes because doing so keeps us safe (negative reinforcement of the avoidance variety).

20. S^D: The Snooze button is presented on our phones when the alarm is going off. The annoying alarm motivates us (EO) to turn the sound off, but how? Should we press our pillow, the nightstand, or something else? We have long ago learned that pressing the Snooze button produces a negative reinforcer – it terminates the alarm (for the moment).
21. S^Δ: When a clock tells us that it's too late to take the exam, we don't bother going to the exam hall, as doing so would not be reinforced.
22. S^D: If you are doing well in this class, then there is a good chance that the words in bold and italicized definitions have functioned as S^Ds. The have increased the probability of making a flash card and studying it.

Reading Quiz 2

1. discrimination training
2. S^Δ
3. discrimination training
4. S^D
5. Generalization
6. generalization gradient
7. bell
8. discrimination training
9. generalization
10. natural
11. diversely
12. cue
13. S^D
14 EO
15. EO
16. S^D

Reading Quiz 3

1. stimulus-response chain
2. task analysis
3. forward
4. backward
5. prompt
6. fading
7. physical, stimulus, modeling

References

Andrzejewski, M. E., Ryals, C. D., Higgins, S., Sulkowski, J., Doney, J., Kelley, A. E., & Bersh, P. J. (2007). Is extinction the hallmark of operant discrimination?: Reinforcement and SΔ effects. *Behavioural Processes*, *74*(1), 49–63. https://doi.org/10.1016/j.beproc.2006.09.010

Bellini, S., & Akullian, J. (2007). A meta-analysis of video modeling and video self-modeling interventions for children and adolescents with autism spectrum disorder. *Exceptional Children, 73*(3), 264–287. https://doi.org/10.1177/001440290707300301

Blackmore, S. (2005). *Consciousness: A very short introduction.* Oxford and New York: Oxford University Press.

Blanshard, B., & Skinner, B. F. (1967). The problem of consciousness - A debate. *Philosophy and Phenomenological Research, 27*(3), 317–337. https://doi.org/10.2307/2106060

Cengher, M., Budd, A., Farrell, N., & Fienup, D. M. (2018, April 1). A review of prompt-fading procedures: Implications for effective and efficient skill acquisition. *Journal of Developmental and Physical Disabilities, 30*, 155–173. https://doi.org/10.1007/s10882-017-9575-8

Colwill, R. M., & Rescorla, R. A. (1990). Evidence for the hierarchical structure of instrumental learning. *Animal Learning & Behavior, 18*(1), 71–82. https://doi.org/10.3758/BF03205241

Dass, T. K., Kisamore, A. N., Vladescu, J. C., Reeve, K. F., Reeve, S. A., & Taylor-Santa, C. (2018). Teaching children with autism spectrum disorder to tact olfactory stimuli. *Journal of Applied Behavior Analysis, 51*(3), 538–552. https://doi.org/10.1002/jaba.470

Davison, M., & Nevin, J. A. (1999). Stimuli, reinforcers, and behavior: An integration. *Journal of the Experimental Analysis of Behavior, 71*(3), 439–482. https://doi.org/10.1901/jeab.1999.71-439

Dinsmoor, J. A. (1995a). Stimulus control: Part I. *The Behavior Analyst, 18*(1), 51–68.

Dinsmoor, J. A. (1995b). Stimulus control: Part II. *The Behavior Analyst, 18*(2), 253–269.

Edwards, T. L., Cox, C., Weetjens, B., Tewelde, T., & Poling, A. (2015). Giant African pouched rats (*Cricetomys gambianus*) that work on tilled soil accurately detect land mines. *Journal of Applied Behavior Analysis, 48*(3), 696–700. https://doi.org/10.1002/jaba.214

Eyberg, S. M., Nelson, M. M., & Boggs, S. R. (2008). Evidence-based psychosocial treatments for children and adolescents with disruptive behavior. *Journal of Clinical Child & Adolescent Psychology, 37*(1), 215–237. https://doi.org/10.1080/15374410701820117

Fox, A. T., Smethells, J. R., & Reilly, M. P. (2013). Flash rate discrimination in rats: Rate bisection and generalization peak shift. *Journal of the Experimental Analysis of Behavior, 100*(2), 211–221. https://doi.org/10.1002/jeab.36

Frank, T. (2009). *Unsafe skies? TSA missed 6 of 10 "bombs".* https://abcnews.go.com/US/story?id=3746204&page=1

Galizio, M. (1985). Human peak shift: Analysis of the effects of three-stimulus discrimination training. *Learning and Motivation, 16*(4), 478–494. https://doi.org/10.1016/0023-9690(85)90028-1

Gámez, A. M., & Rosas, J. M. (2007). Associations in human instrumental conditioning. *Learning and Motivation, 38*(3), 242–261. https://doi.org/10.1016/j.lmot.2006.11.001

Guttman, N., & Kalish, H. I. (1956). Discriminability and stimulus generalization. *Journal of Experimental Psychology, 51*(1), 79–88. https://doi.org/10.1037/h0046219

Herrnstein, R. J., Loveland, D. H., & Cable, C. (1976). Natural concepts in pigeons. *Journal of Experimental Psychology: Animal Behavior Processes, 2*(4), 285–302. https://doi.org/10.1037/0097-7403.2.4.285

Hogan, L. C., Bell, M., & Olson, R. (2009). A preliminary investigation of the reinforcement function of signal detection stimulated baggage screening: Further support for the vigilance reinforcement hypothesis. *Journal of Organizational Behavior Management, 29*, 6–18. https://doi.org/10.1080/01608060802660116

Honig, W. K. (1966). The role of discrimination training in the generalization gradient of punishment. *Journal of the Experimental Analysis of Behavior, 9*(4), 377–384. https://doi.org/10.1901/jeab.1966.9-377

Honig, W. K., Thomas, D. R., & Guttman, N. (1959). Differential effects of continuous extinction and discrimination training on the generalization gradient. *Journal of Experimental Psychology, 58*(2), 145–152. https://doi.org/10.1037/h0048484

Jendrny, P., Schulz, C., Twele, F., Meller, S., Von Köckritz-Blickwede, M., Osterhaus, A. D. M. E., … Volk, H. A. (2020). Scent dog identification of samples from COVID-19 patients - A pilot study. *BMC Infectious Diseases, 20*(1), 536. https://doi.org/10.1186/s12879-020-05281-3

Jenkins, H. M., & Harrison, R. H. (1960). Effect of discrimination training on auditory generalization. *Journal of Experimental Psychology*, *59*(4), 246–253. https://doi.org/10.1037/h0041661

Keller, H. (1908). *The world I live in*. New York: The Century Co.

Kennedy, M. M. (1978). Findings from the Follow Through planned variation study. *Educational Researcher*, *7*(6), 3–11. https://doi.org/10.3102/0013189X007006003

King, M. L., Takeguchi, K., Barry, S. E., Rehfeldt, R. A., Boyer, V. E., & Mathews, T. L. (2014). Evaluation of the iPad in the acquisition of requesting skills for children with autism spectrum disorder. *Research in Autism Spectrum Disorders*, *8*(9), 1107–1120. https://doi.org/10.1016/j.rasd.2014.05.011

Kohler, F. W., & Greenwood, C. R. (1986). Toward a technology of generalization: The identification of natural contingencies of reinforcement. *The Behavior Analyst*, *9*(1), 19–26. https://doi.org/10.1007/bf03391926

Levenson, E., & Rose, S. (2019). Delta passenger who carried firearm through TSA screening returned from Japan to US on the same day.

Maguire, D. R., Yang, W., & France, C. P. (2013). Interactions between μ-opioid receptor agonists and cannabinoid receptor agonists in rhesus monkeys: Antinociception, drug discrimination, and drug self-administration. *Journal of Pharmacology and Experimental Therapeutics*, *345*(3), 354–362. https://doi.org/10.1124/jpet.113.204099

Michael, J. (1980). The Discriminative Stimulus or SD. *The Behavior Analyst*, *3*(1), 47–49. https://doi.org/10.1007/BF03392378

Nagel, T. (1974). What is it like to be a bat? *Philisophical Review*, *83*, 435–450. https://doi.org/10.2307/2183914

Neely, L. C., Ganz, J. B., Davis, J. L., Boles, M. B., Hong, E. R., Ninci, J., & Gilliland, W. D. (2016). Generalization and maintenance of functional living skills for individuals with autism spectrum disorder: A review and meta-analysis. *Review Journal of Autism and Developmental Disorders*, *3*(1), 37–47. https://doi.org/10.1007/s40489-015-0064-7

O'Donnell, J. (2001). The discriminative stimulus for punishment or SDp. *The Behavior Analyst*, *24*, 261–262. https://doi.org/10.1007/BF03392036

Podlesnik, C. A., & Miranda-Dukoski, L. (2015). Stimulus generalization and operant context renewal. *Behavioural Processes*, *119*, 93–98. https://doi.org/10.1016/j.beproc.2015.07.015

Poling, A., Weetjens, B., Cox, C., Beyene, N. W., Bach, H., & Sully, A. (2011a). Using trained pouched rats to detect land mines: Another victory for operant conditioning. *Journal of Applied Behavior Analysis*, *44*(2), 351–355. https://doi.org/10.1901/jaba.2011.44-351

Poling, A., Weetjens, B., Cox, C., Beyene, N., Durgin, A., & Mahoney, A. (2011b). Tuberculosis detection by giant African pouched rats. *Behavior Analyst*, *34*(1), 47–54. https://doi.org/10.1007/BF03392234

Sherman, J. G., Hegge, F. W., & Pierrel, R. (1964). Discrimination formation as related to the amount of s-delta training. *Psychonomic Science*, *1*(2), 43–44. https://doi.org/10.3758/BF03342780

Shipley-Benamou, R., Lutzker, J. R., & Taubman, M. (2002). Teaching daily living skills to children with autism through instructional video modeling. *Journal of Positive Behavior Interventions*, *4*(3), 166–177. https://doi.org/10.1177/10983007020040030501

Skinner, B. F. (1933). The rate of establishment of a discrimination. *The Journal of General Psychology, 9*, 302–348. https://doi.org/10.1080/00221309.1933.9920939

Skinner, B. F. (1938). *The behavior of organisms: An experimental analysis*. Oxford, England: Appleton-Century.

Skinner, B. F. (1945). The operational analysis of psychological terms. *Psychology Review*, *52*(5), 270–277. https://doi.org/10.1037/h0062535

Skinner, B. F. (1957). *Verbal behavior*. New York: Appleton-Century-Crofts.

Skinner, B. F. (1972). *Cumulative record: A selection of papers* (3rd ed.). New York: Appleton-Century-Crofts.

Slocum, S. K., & Tiger, J. H. (2011). An assessment of the efficacy of and child preference for forward and backward chaining. *Journal of Applied Behavior Analysis*, *44*(4), 793–805. https://doi.org/10.1901/jaba.2011.44-793

Stead Sellers, F. (2020, August 18). Can dogs detect the novel coronavirus? The nose knows. *The Washington Post.* https://www.washingtonpost.com/science/2020/08/18/dogs-sniff-coronavirus-detection/?arc404=true

Stockard, J., Wood, T. W., Coughlin, C., & Rasplica Khoury, C. (2018). The effectiveness of direct instruction curricula: A meta-analysis of a half century of research. *Review of Educational Research, 88*(4), 479–507. https://doi.org/10.3102/0034654317751919

Stokes, T. F., & Osnes, P. G. (1989). An operant pursuit of generalization. *Behavior Therapy, 20*(3), 337–355. https://doi.org/10.1016/S0005-7894(89)80054-1

Watkins, C. L., & Slocum, T. A. (2004). The components of direct instruction. In N. E. Marchand-Martella & T. A. Slocum M. R. C. (Eds.), *Introduction to direct instruction* (pp. 28–65). Boston, MA: Allyn & Bacon.

Weetjens, B. J., Mgode, G. F., Machang'u, R. S., Kazwala, R., Mfinanga, G., Lwilla, F., … Verhagen, R. (2009). African pouched rats for the detection of pulmonary tuberculosis in sputum samples. *The International Journal of Tuberculosis and Lung Disease, 13*(6), 737–743.

Choice

13

Decision-making (i.e., making choices) is one of the most significant and complicated things we do every day. Shall I get out of bed or snooze the alarm? How much shampoo should I use: a little or a lot? Should I walk, take the bus, or drive? Shall I stick with my healthy eating plan or splurge on junk food with friends? Do I scroll further through my social-media feed, or do I study instead? Should I study in the library or the coffee shop where I know I will be distracted by music and nearby conversations? Do I succumb to peer pressure and have another drink/smoke?

Our *verbal* answers to these questions – "Yes, I'll get out of bed when my alarm goes off " – may be different than our *behavioral* answers. What we verbally decide to do and our actual choices (pressing the snooze button eight times before getting out of bed) may be very different. The choices we actually make, by behaving one way or the other, are much more important than what we say we will do. Our New Year's resolutions will not improve our lives; only by repeatedly choosing to adhere to them can we improve our health, well-being, and the health of the environment.

What does behavior analysis have to say about choice? Can behavioral scientists accurately predict the choices people make? Have they identified functional variables that can be used to positively influence these decisions? Spoiler alert: We can predict some choices, but we are a long way from being able to predict all of them. Once again, this is where readers of this book are important. If you *choose* a career in the behavioral sciences, you could make discoveries that help to improve the accuracy of our predictions and, importantly, improve the efficacy of interventions designed to positively influence human decision-making. So, let's get started.

An Introduction to Behavior Analysis, First Edition. Gregory J. Madden, Derek D. Reed, and Florence D. DiGennaro Reed.
© 2021 John Wiley & Sons Ltd. Published 2021 by John Wiley & Sons Ltd.

What Is Choice?

When a judge considers what punishment is appropriate to a crime, an important question is whether the individual who committed the crime *chose* to do it. If the criminal action was an involuntary response (e.g., an elicited startle-reflex caused harm to another person), then the judge would dismiss the case. For punishment to be imposed, the individual needs to have chosen to commit the crime.

Source: WavebreakmediaMicro, Adobe Stock Photo

Choice may be defined as *voluntary behavior occurring in a context in which alternative behaviors are possible.* Two parts of this definition are noteworthy. First, choice is *voluntary* behavior, which is to say choice is not a phylogenetically determined reflex response or a Pavlovian response evoked by a conditioned stimulus (see Chapter 4). We don't choose when to begin digesting a meal, whether to salivate, vomit, or startle; these are involuntary reflexes either elicited by unconditioned stimuli or evoked by conditioned stimuli. Readers should not equate "voluntary behavior" with "willed behavior," that is, a behavior that we *feel* like we initiate. Instead, by "voluntary" all we mean is *nonreflexive*.

Second, choice *occurs in a context is which alternative behaviors are possible*. After putting your money into the vending machine, several alternative behaviors are possible – you could press one button to get a bag of chips, another button to select a sleeve of cookies, and another button still to obtain the healthier granola bar. Similarly, when considering which colleges to apply to, deliberations occur in a choice context – one in which alternative behaviors are possible.

When you think about it, almost all of our voluntary actions are choices. When walking, consider that we could be running, crawling, or balancing on one leg while sipping tea. Alternative behaviors are almost always possible. You began reading this chapter in a choice context – alternative behaviors were possible. Indeed, alternative behaviors are possible right now. You can always stop reading and engage in literally thousands of other behaviors at any time. But here you are reading. Why? While there are many theories of choice in the psychological and social sciences, we will begin by focusing on four simple variables that strongly influence choice. These variables will be familiar to you, as we discussed them in previous chapters.

Four Variables Affecting Choice

Imagine there are two identical buttons in front of you. You can choose to press either one and you are free to switch between them any time you like. Furthermore, if you don't want to press either button, preferring instead to stand on one leg while sipping tea, you can do that too. Before you press the buttons, we will assume you have no preference between them – one is as good as the other. However, if the consequences of pressing the buttons are different, a preference will develop. The next four sections describe variables that will strongly influence choice. Indeed, when these variables alone are at work, they tend to produce *exclusive choice* for one alternative over the other.

Reinforcement vs. No Consequence

In Figure 13.1, when you press the right button (B_R) nothing happens, ever. When you press the left button (B_L), your press is immediately accompanied by a "beep" and a display on a computer screen that says "25 cents have been added to your earnings," which we will assume functions as a reinforcer. You press the left button 24 more times and more money is added to your account each time. Score!

So, which of these buttons would you choose to press going forward? Obviously, you will exclusively press the button that produced the reinforcer (B_L). The reason is clear – pressing the left button is reinforced and pressing the other one is not.

Every species of nonhuman animal tested so far prefers reinforcement over non-reinforcement. For example, in an experiment conducted by Rybarczyk et al. (2001), cows preferred to press the left lever (B_L) because it was followed by a food reinforcer. They chose not to press the right lever (B_R) after learning that it never provided a reinforcer. In sum, *individuals choose reinforcement over no consequence.*

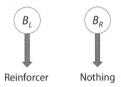

Figure 13.1 Two buttons are available. Pressing the right one (B_R) gets you nothing. Pressing the left one (B_L) produces a monetary reinforcer. When such differential reinforcement contingencies are arranged, the reinforced alternative is consistently chosen (preferred).

Reinforcer Size/Quality

The second variable that strongly influences choice is the size or the quality of the reinforcer. Given a choice between a small ($0.05) and a large ($5.00) reinforcer, all else being equal, the larger one will be chosen exclusively (see Figure 13.2). To be sure that this outcome was influenced by the difference in reinforcer size ($0.05 vs. $5.00) and not a preference for the button on the right, we could switch the contingencies so the smaller reinforcer is assigned to the right button (B_R) and the $5 reinforcer to the left (B_L). When behavior shifts toward B_L, we would conclude that reinforcer size strongly influences choice.

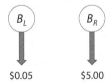

Figure 13.2 Now pressing the left button adds 5 cents to your account, whereas pressing the right one produces a $5 deposit. Not surprisingly, the alternative producing a larger reinforcer will be strongly preferred.

Because reinforcer *quality* has the same effect as reinforcer size, we can use choice to answer the question, which reinforcer is qualitatively better? For example, animal-welfare advocates can give farm animals choices between different living arrangements. Such behavioral research has shown that cows prefer quiet settings over noisy ones, a plant-based over a meat-based diet, and that chickens prefer smaller cages than humans might expect (Foster et al., 1996; Lagadic & Faure, 1988). If you are an animal lover, you should know that this work is underappreciated and represents an important area for future growth in behavior analysis (see Abramson & Kieson, 2016 for a discussion of this potential). But for now, just remember that *individuals choose larger (higher-quality) reinforcers over smaller (lower-quality) reinforcers.*

Effort

The third variable that produces exclusive choice is effort. When people and other animals are given a choice between working hard to get a reinforcer and working less hard to get the same reinforcer, they exclusively choose the less effortful option. Figure 13.3 shows an experiment conducted by Herrnstein and Loveland (1975). Under these conditions, pigeons exclusively chose less work (fixed ratio [FR] 1) over more work (FR 10) in pursuit of the same reinforcer.

Translating this to your everyday life, if you need an elective course in plant science and you hear that one section is taught by an instructor who assigns a lot of busy work (B_R) and another section is taught by a professor who doesn't assign any homework (B_L), all else being equal, you will choose to enroll in the course taught by professor B_L. The reason why is that both professors offer the same reinforcer (elective credits in plant science) but one requires less effort than the other. Why waste your effort?

Similarly, many consumers exclusively buy products online because of the reduced effort in ordering. For example, Amazon's "dash buttons" allow you to order products like laundry detergent by pressing the button, conveniently located in the laundry room, once. What could be easier? Compare this with making a shopping list, driving to the store, finding the laundry detergent, and then hauling it home. Simply put, all else being equal, *individuals choose low-effort reinforcers over high-effort reinforcers.*

Source: Alexander Klink/ Wikipedia/CC BY 4.0

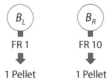

Figure 13.3 Pecking the left key once is reinforced with a food pellet (FR 1). By contrast, to get a pellet on the right key, the pigeon must peck 10 times (FR 10).

Reinforcer Delay

The final variable that produces exclusive choice is reinforcer delay; that is, how long you have to wait for the reinforcer after having made your choice. For example, if two online retailers offer the headphones you want for $50, but one of them ($B_L$) can ship them twice as quickly as the other one (B_R), then you will choose B_L because of the difference in reinforcer delay (see Figure 13.4). Once again, many consumers exclusively buy online products from Amazon.com because they ship them to customers faster than other retailers.

Delays to reinforcers strongly influence our daily decision-making. Consider that many iPhone users spent large sums of money on a new phone in 2017 when Apple slowed the processing speed of their older phones. Customers on Reddit accused Apple of using behavioral technology (reinforcer delays) to induce customers to buy a new iPhone. Apple denied the charge and offered to fix the cause of the spontaneous shut-downs (older batteries) at a reduced price.

Figure 13.4 If you choose online retailer B_L, you will receive your headphones tomorrow. If you choose B_R, you will have to wait 2 days before they arrive.

Summary

This section has considered four variables that, all else being equal, will generate exclusive choice. When we say "all else being equal," we mean that the only difference between the two alternatives is that one, for example, produces the reinforcer faster than the other. If there are no other differences, then an exclusive choice will develop for the alternative that yields (1) a reinforcer (vs. one that does not), (2) a bigger/better reinforcer, (3) the same reinforcer less effortfully, and (4) the same reinforcer sooner.

The remainder of this chapter will focus on *nonexclusive choices*. That is, situations in which we prefer B_L, but we don't choose it all the time; sometimes we choose B_R. For example, an angler may prefer to fish in lake B_L but will sometimes fish in lake B_R. Similarly, a shopper may prefer clothing store B_L, but will sometimes shop in B_R (to see if they have any bargains). In both of these situations, the consequences of choice are less certain than discussed earlier and, as a result, choice is nonexclusive; that is, we prefer one lake/store but search for reinforcers in both.

Another form of nonexclusive choice is variously described as impulsivity, self-control, or delay of gratification. Sometimes we make choices that we describe as "impulsive" and then regret the decision. For example, we order a high-calorie dessert after eating a full meal, and after enjoying the immediate benefits of this choice, we regret our decision and berate ourselves for our lack of "self-control" or "willpower." Appealing to reifications like "impulsivity" and "willpower" reveals how little we understand the choices we make. As you will see later, nonexclusive choices between, for example, dieting and breaking from the diet, are predictable (one of the goals of behavior analysis). More importantly, some progress has been made in iden-

Source: auricadina75/Pixabay

tifying functional variables that can be used to positively influence choice. As always, we hope readers of this book will further this progress and will help to reduce impulsive choices such as problem drug use, uncontrolled eating, and pathological gambling.

Reading Quiz 1

1. Choice is defined as _____ behavior occurring in a context in which _____ behaviors are possible.
2. Choice is strongly influenced by four variables. On the lines below, list those four variables.

_____

_____

_____

_____

The Rich Uncle Joe Experiment

Before we continue, we would like you to answer a few questions that we will revisit later in this chapter. It will not take you long to answer these questions. Answering them will give you greater insights about your own choices and the variables that affect them. If you are ready, grab a pen and read on.

Imagine that a trusted member of your family, your rich Uncle Joe, says he is going to give every member of your immediate family $1,000 in cash in 5 years. Until that time, the money will be in a safety deposit box, where it will earn no interest. At the end of 5 years, Uncle Joe's lawyer will give you the cash.

Next imagine that a friend of the family, Camille, says that she would like to purchase one of Uncle Joe's $1,000 gifts. Camille will pay in cash right now and, in 5 years, Uncle Joe's lawyer will give her the $1,000 gift that she purchases. Because everyone in the family is at least a little interested in selling their gift to Camille, she suggests everyone privately write down their selling price. Camille will buy the gift from the family member who writes down the lowest price. Please write your answer here.

*"I will sell Uncle Joe's gift ($1,000 in **5 years**) if you give me $_____ in cash right now."*

Now erase that scenario from your mind. This time, imagine that your rich Uncle Joe is going to put your $1,000 gift into his safety deposit box for just 1 month. After that, Uncle Joe will give you the cash. Now what is <u>the smallest amount</u> of cash that you would sell this for?

*"I will sell Uncle Joe's gift ($1,000 in **1 month**) if you give me $_____ in cash right now."*

If you are paying attention and answering honestly, the amount you just wrote down will be more than the amount you sold the gift for when it was delayed by 5 years.

We will do this two more times and then be done. This time, imagine that Uncle Joe is going to put the money into his safety deposit box for 1 year. Now what is <u>the smallest amount</u> of cash that you would sell the gift for?

*"I will sell Uncle Joe's gift ($1,000 in **1 year**) if you give me $_____ in cash right now."*

And finally, imagine that Uncle Joe's gift will sit in the safety deposit box for 25 years. Uncle Joe's law firm has instructions to give you the money in 25 years, should Uncle Joe die before the time elapses. Now what is <u>the smallest amount</u> of cash that you would sell the gift for?

*"I will sell Uncle Joe's gift ($1,000 in **25 years**) if you give me $_____ in cash right now."*

Choosing between Uncertain Outcomes

Later in the chapter we will return to the choices you just made, but for now consider the choice you make when leaving home and deciding where to go shopping for clothes. There are many options, but for simplicity we will confine our choices to two stores: Moxx or Rass. Which one will you choose? You cannot be certain which store will have that great bargain you are looking for, so you will have to decide based on your past experiences. That is, you will have to decide which one has had more bargains in the past.

In the 1960s, Richard Herrnstein conducted some of the first operant learning experiments on choice. He studied choices made by rats and pigeons. As animals are uninterested in shopping for clothes, Herrnstein arranged food as the reinforcer. Rather than building two little grocery stores that the subjects could shop in, he arranged two response keys (pigeons) or two levers (rats) on the wall of the chamber; by pecking or pressing them they could occasionally obtain these reinforcers.

The individual animals participating in these experiments were free to do whatever they chose, whenever they wanted. They could peck one key for a while and then the other, they could choose to press one lever exclusively, or they could do something else, such as walk around, groom themselves, or take a nap.

In one experiment with pigeons, Herrnstein (1961) programmed a variable-interval (VI) 90-second schedule of reinforcement to control the availability of reinforcers on the left key (B_L), whereas pecks on the right key (B_R) were never reinforced. Note that the consequence of pecking B_L is uncertain. Sure, pecking this key will be reinforced once, on average, every 90 seconds, but it is impossible to be certain *which* peck will be reinforced. Despite this uncertainty, the pigeons spent all of their time pecking the left key (another example of *preference for reinforcement over no consequence*).

Herrnstein's Matching Equation

Herrnstein (1961) developed a simple equation that predicted how pigeons chose to allocate their behavior between pecking the left (B_L) and right keys (B_R). He hypothesized that these choices would be influenced by the reinforcers obtained on the left (R_L) and the right (R_R) keys:

$$\textit{Herrnstein's matching equation:} \quad \frac{B_L}{B_L + B_R} = \frac{R_L}{R_L + R_R}$$

Before we plug any numbers into Herrnstein's equation, note that behavior (pecking B_L or B_R) appears on the left side of the equation and reinforcers (R_L and R_R) appear on the right. The equals sign in the middle is important. The equals sign indicates that the proportion of B_L responses should match (or be equal to) the proportion of reinforcers obtained on the left (R_L). If you are more familiar with percentages than proportions, then Herrnstein's equation says the percentage of responses allocated to B_L should match (or be equal to) the percentage of reinforcers obtained on the left (R_L). To convert proportions to percentages, we simply multiply the proportion by 100.

Let's plug some very simple numbers into the equation. In Herrnstein's (1961) experiment, the VI 90-second schedule arranged reinforcers to occur at a rate of 40 per hour (i.e., 1 reinforcer, on average, every minute and a half), whereas extinction arranged none. Thus,

$$R_L = 40 \quad R_R = 0$$

Simple enough. Next, we plug these rates of reinforcement into the matching equation:

$$\frac{B_L}{B_L + B_R} = \frac{40 \textit{ per hour}}{40 \textit{ per hour} + 0 \textit{ per hour}} \rightarrow \frac{B_L}{B_L + B_R} = \frac{40}{40} \rightarrow \frac{B_L}{B_L + B_R} = \frac{1}{1}$$

By multiplying the right side of the equation by 100, we obtain the percentage of reinforcers available on the left:

$$\frac{B_L}{B_L + B_R} = \frac{1}{1} \times 100 \rightarrow \frac{B_L}{B_L + B_R} = 100\% \textit{ of the reinforcers are on the left key}$$

If the right side of the equation is 100%, then Herrnstein's equation predicts that the percentage of responses allocated to the left key should match this number; that is, 100% of the responses should be made on B_L (exclusive choice). Figure 13.5 shows this prediction graphically. On the x-axis is the percentage of reinforcers obtained on the left, and on the y-axis is the percentage of left-key pecks. The lone data point on the graph shows that when 100% of the reinforcers were arranged on the left, the pigeons should choose to allocate 100% of their pecks to that key. The pigeons conformed to this prediction, allocating over 99% of their behavior to B_L.

MORE UNCERTAINTY

In the next part of Herrnstein's experiment, uncertainty was increased by programming a VI schedule on both keys. A VI 3-minute schedule was arranged on the left key ($R_L = 20$ reinforcers per hour) and a different VI 3-minute schedule was arranged on the right ($R_R = 20$ reinforcers per hour too). In many ways, this resembles the reinforcement schedules operating when you choose between shopping at two comparable stores like Moxx and Rass. Reinforcers

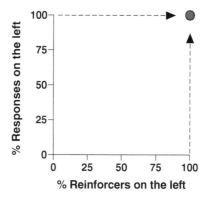

Figure 13.5 When 100% of the reinforcers were obtained on the left key (R_L), pigeons allocated 100% of their behavior to that key (B_L).

Source: Herrnstein, R. J. (1961). Relative and absolute strength of response as a function of reinforcement. *Journal of the Experimental Analysis of Behavior, 4(3), 267–272.* https://doi.org/10.1901/jeab.1961.4-267

(bargain buys) are found intermittently; we cannot predict when the next one will be found, but our experience tells us that they are found about equally often at the two stores ($R_{Moxx} = R_{Rass}$). If, in all other ways, the stores are the same (same distance from your apartment, same quality of clothes, etc.), then you should visit both stores equally often.

This is what Herrnstein's equation predicts when a VI 3-minute schedule is programmed on the left and right keys:

$$\frac{B_L}{B_L + B_R} = \frac{20\ per\ hour}{20\ per\ hour + 20\ per\ hour} \rightarrow \frac{B_L}{B_L + B_R} = \frac{20}{40} \rightarrow \frac{B_L}{B_L + B_R} = \frac{1}{2} \times 100 = 50\%$$

If 50% of the reinforcers are obtained by pecking the left key, then choice should match this percentage: half of the pecks should be directed toward that key. As shown in Figure 13.6, the pigeons behaved in accord with this prediction, allocating an average of 53% of their responses to B_L. To make it easier for you to see deviations from predictions of the matching equation, we added a blue line to the figure. The matching equation predicts all of the data points should fall along this blue line.

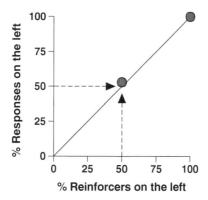

Figure 13.6 When half of the reinforcers were obtained on the left key (R_L), pigeons allocated about half of their behavior to that key (B_L).

Source: Herrnstein, R. J. (1961). Relative and absolute strength of response as a function of reinforcement. *Journal of the Experimental Analysis of Behavior, 4(3), 267–272.* https://doi.org/10.1901/jeab.1961.4-267

In another phase, Herrnstein's equation was tested by assigning a VI 9-minute schedule on the left key (R_L = 6.7 reinforcers per hour) and a VI 1.8-minute schedule on the right key (R_R = 33.3

reinforcers per hour). Now, reinforcers are obtained more often on the right key, the key the pigeons previously dispreferred. Plugging these reinforcement rates into the matching equation,

$$\frac{B_L}{B_L + B_R} = \frac{6.7}{6.7 + 33.3} \rightarrow \frac{B_L}{B_L + B_R} = \frac{6.7}{40} \rightarrow \frac{B_L}{B_L + B_R} = 0.1675 \times 100 = 16.75\%$$

we can see that about 17% of the reinforcers are obtained by pecking the left key. Therefore, the matching equation predicts the pigeons will choose to allocate 17% of their behavior to the left key (and the other 83% to the right key). As shown in Figure 13.7, in Herrnstein's experiment this prediction was pretty accurate.

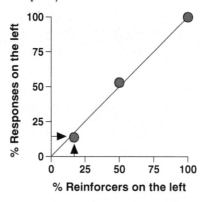

Figure 13.7 When 17% of the reinforcers were obtained on the left key, pigeons allocated about 14% of their behavior to that key.
Source: Herrnstein, R. J. (1961). Relative and absolute strength of response as a function of frequency of reinforcement. *Journal of the Experimental Analysis of Behavior, 4(3), 267–272.* https://doi.org/10.1901/jeab.1961.4-267

Translating this to shopping, if we rarely find bargains at Rass but usually find them at Moxx, then Herrnstein's matching equation predicts we should spend most, but not all of our time shopping at Moxx. Makes sense, but imagine that our local Rass store gets a new acquisitions manager and now shopping there is reinforced twice as often as it is at Moxx. The matching equation predicts that we will switch our allegiance and spend two-thirds of our time shopping at Rass. As shown in Figure 13.8, when Herrnstein tested this prediction, his pigeons did exactly this. The additional green data points in the figure show choice data from other conditions in which Herrnstein tested the predictions of the matching equation. As you can see, the predictions were quite accurate.

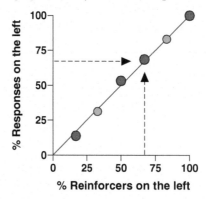

Figure 13.8 When two-thirds of the reinforcers were obtained on the left key (R_L), pigeons allocated just two-thirds of their behavior to that key (B_L).
Source: Herrnstein, R. J. (1961). Relative and absolute strength of response as a function of frequency of reinforcement. *Journal of the Experimental Analysis of Behavior, 4(3), 267–272.* https://doi.org/10.1901/jeab.1961.4-267

RESEARCH SUPPORT FOR HERRNSTEIN'S EQUATION

Herrnstein's matching equation has been studied in rats, pigeons, chickens, coyotes, cows, and monkeys; it does a good job of predicting how behavior will be allocated when the outcomes of choice are uncertain (Dallery & Soto, 2013; Davison & McCarthy, 1988). If you take more advanced coursework in behavior analysis, you will learn that Herrnstein's matching equation does not always make perfect predictions. For example, cows tend to deviate from predictions of the matching equation more than the pigeons in Figure 13.8 (Matthews & Temple, 1979). In these more advanced classes, you will consider exceptions to the matching equation and will study theories proposed to account for these exceptions.

What about humans? Can the matching equation be used to predict actual choices made by humans? Early research supported the predictions of the matching equation: humans chose to allocate more of their behavior toward the richer of two VI schedules of reinforcement (e.g. Bradshaw et al., 1976, 1979). However, a series of important experiments conducted by Horne and Lowe (1993) revealed several problems with these early studies. For example, subtle cues informed participants about the frequency of reinforcers. When these cues were removed, very few participants behaved in accord with the matching equation (Horne & Lowe, 1993).

More recent research suggests humans conform to the predictions of the matching equation, but only when participants are paying attention. Much of the early research on human choice and the matching equation arranged button-pressing tasks resembling those used with rats and pigeons. While these tasks engage nonhuman attention, humans find them boring and mostly press the buttons without paying attention to the consequences of their behavior. Madden and Perone (1999) explored the role of participant attention by changing the task from one in which choices could be made without paying much attention, to one that was more engaging. As expected, when human attention was elsewhere, choice did not closely conform to the predictions of the matching equation. However, as shown in Figure 13.9, the matching equation accurately predicted human choice when participants paid attention to the engaging task. Other experiments have reported comparable findings

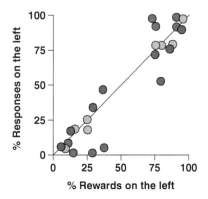

Figure 13.9 When human participants are given a choice task that holds their attention in a way comparable to nonhuman attention, the matching equation accurately predicts their choice. The different colored symbols represent the behavior of the three adult participants.
Source: Madden, G. J., & Perone, M. (1999). Human sensitivity to concurrent schedules of reinforcement: Effects of observing schedule-correlated stimuli. Journal of the Experimental Analysis of Behavior, 71(3), 303–318. https://doi.org/10.1901/je

with tasks that effectively engage human attention (Baum, 1975; Buskist & Miller, 1981; Critchfield et al., 2003; Magoon & Critchfield, 2008; Schroeder & Holland, 1969). We have prepared a reading quiz to give you practice calculating and graphing the predictions of Herrnstein's matching equation. For readers who wonder why all of these graphs and calculations matter, we invite you to read Extra Box 1. The matching equation makes strong, empirically supported predictions about what controls human decision-making and, as such, has important things to say about how to solve existential threats that have at their core disordered human choice.

Reading Quiz 2

1. In Herrnstein's matching equation, B_L and B_R refer to _____ allocated to the left and right choice alternatives, respectively.
2. In Herrnstein's matching equation, R_L and R_R refer to the rates of _____ programmed on the left and right alternatives, respectively.
3. The matching equation makes predictions about _____ by specifying how behavior will be allocated between the alternative sources of reinforcement.

   A good way to become more familiar with the predictions of the matching equation is to plug numbers into the equation and graph the results. For questions 4–10, use the graph provided below.

4. A variable-interval (VI) 20-second schedule arranges reinforcers at a rate of 3 per minute. If a VI 20-second schedule is programmed on the left lever in an operant chamber for rats, R_L=_____ reinforcers per minute.
5. If a VI 60-second schedule is arranged on the right lever, R_R=_____ reinforcers per minute.
6. Given the values in questions 4 and 5, the matching equation predicts the rat will prefer the _____ lever.
7. Using the values from items 4 and 5, what is the proportion of reinforcers obtained on the left lever? $\dfrac{R_L}{R_L + R_R} =$ _____
8. Find the place on the x-axis corresponding to the reinforcement proportion just calculated. Next, to predict how the rat will allocate its behavior between the left and right levers, move up from the x-axis to the diagonal line on the graph. Draw a data point there. Can you see how the matching equation predicts the proportion of behavior (y-axis) will match the proportion of reinforcers (x-axis)?

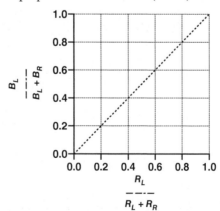

9. What percentage of the rat's responses does the matching equation predict will be allocated to the left lever? To calculate this, simply multiply the proportion from item 7 by 100. _____

10. Here is how the rat actually allocated its behavior: B_L=80 responses per minute; B_R=40 responses per minute. Using these values,

calculate the proportion of responses made on the left lever: $\dfrac{B_L}{B_L + B_R}$ _____

11. To graph this, starting from 0.75 at the x-axis, move your pen up until you reach the proportion that you just calculated. Add a different symbol to show the obtained response allocation of this rat.

If your calculations are correct and you drew the data correctly, then the obtained data point should be a little below the predicted data point. If you did not get this, check your answers against those in the answer key at the end of the chapter. For questions 12–17, use the graph shown here.

12. This time we will graph some real data collected with one human participant.[1] First, calculate the $\dfrac{R_L}{R_L + R_R}$ quotients for Conditions A through D:

	Obtained SR+ Rate		
Condition	R_L	R_R	Proportion Left
A	4/minute	29/minute	_____
B	10/minute	23/minute	_____
C	16/minute	17/minute	_____
D	2/minute	1/minute	_____

13. Now use the participant's response rates to calculate the $\dfrac{B_L}{B_L + B_R}$ quotients:

	Response Rate		
Condition	B_L	B_R	Proportion Left
A	5/minute	39/minute	_____
B	7/minute	15/minute	_____
C	9/minute	10/minute	_____
D	13/minute	4.7/minute	_____

14. Using the reinforcement (x-axis) and response proportions (y-axis), plot a data point on the graph corresponding to Condition A.

15. Using the reinforcement (x-axis) and response proportions, plot a second data point on the graph corresponding to Condition B.

16. Using the reinforcement and response proportions, plot third data point on the graph corresponding to Condition C.

17. And finally, plot a fourth data point corresponding to the data collected in Condition D.

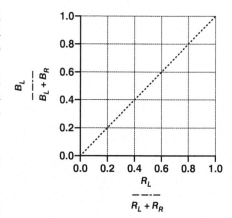

As you can see from your graph, the predictions of the matching equation were not perfect, but they were very close; accurately predicting which alternative source of reinforcement would be preferred, and about how much it would be preferred by. In sum, a considerable amount of evidence supports Herrnstein's matching equation in a wide variety of species, including humans. Because of this empirical support, Herrnstein's equation is often referred to as the matching law.

EXTRA BOX 1:   THE MATCHING LAW, TERRORISM, AND WHITE NATIONALISM

Some of the most difficult to understand choices are those that we find reprehensible. For example, violent terrorist acts that take the lives of innocents are difficult for us to comprehend. What could possess someone to do something so evil? Likewise, why would anyone join a neo-Nazi group and march through the streets of Charlottesville while chanting, "Jews will not replace us!" If we could predict and influence such choices, we could reduce violence and hate.

In her documentary films *Jihad* and *White Right: Meeting the Enemy*, the groundbreaking filmmaker, Deeyah Kahn explores

Source: Fuuse Films/Wikipedia/CC BY-SA 4.0

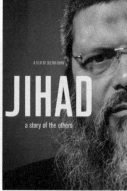

Source: Fuuse Films/Wikipedia/CC BY-SA 3.0

the variables that lead young men to make these choices. In *Jihad*, Kahn interviews young Muslim men who leave their homes in the West to join Jihadi movements in the Middle East. In most cases, these men are struggling to succeed in the West. They are failing to establish friendships and romantic relationships; they are not meeting the expectations of their parents or their culture. Most of their interactions with Westerners left them feeling ashamed and humiliated. In a word, they perceived themselves as failures.

Then came their first interactions with a Jihadi recruiter. While no one in the West was giving them any positive reinforcement, the recruiter spent hours online interacting with them, telling them how important they were, describing how they could be part of a life-changing movement, and how, if they died in the movement, they would be handsomely rewarded in the afterlife.

The matching law makes clear predictions about the choices these young men are susceptible to making. First, we define B_{West} as the behavior of interacting with people in the Western world, and R_{West} as the reinforcers obtained in these pursuits. If B_{West} is rarely reinforced (i.e., R_{West} approaches zero), then the matching law predicts interacting with the Jihadi recruiter (B_{Jihad}) will occur if this behavior is richly reinforced with the kind of attention the Jihadi recruiters regularly provide (R_{Jihad}):

$$\frac{B_{Jihad}}{B_{Jihad} + B_{West}} = \frac{R_{Jihad}}{R_{Jihad} + R_{West}}$$

These recruiters not only richly reinforce these online interactions, they shape increasingly hardline opinions when the recruits begin to mimic the recruiter's radical ideas. In extreme cases, among those young men who are the most alienated (i.e., the least likely to obtain social reinforcers from anyone in the West), they leave their homes and join the extremist movement. Consistent with this analysis, Deeyah Khan reported that these young men are not drawn to the movement by religion; they are more loyal to their recruiters than to their religion. These recruits are escaping alienation (i.e., a low value of R_{West}) in favor of a rich source of social reinforcement (R_{Jihad}).

In her movie *White Right: Meeting the Enemy*, Khan found that a similar profile of young white men were drawn to the neo-Nazi movement. Those without friends, gainful employment, or supportive families were drawn to the reinforcers obtained by joining the gang of "brothers" who agree with one another, march with one another, and make headlines with one another.

Not only does the matching law predict these outcomes, it tells us how to prevent them. According to the matching law, the answer is to identify those who are failing in life and offer them assistance, friendship, and a source of reinforcement for engaging in socially appropriate behavior. In other words, increase the value of R_{West}.

Could this work? In her films, Kahn documents several cases of white nationalists and Jihadis who come to reject their radical beliefs when they begin interacting with those they hate. When they are befriended by these professed enemies. When they are accepted, even in the face of their hateful speech. Likewise, organizations that work with incarcerated white nationalists (e.g., Life After Hate) report that such underserved kindness from others can play an important role in turning these individuals away from hate. Of course, case studies fall short of experimental, scientific evidence, but these conversions from hate to love are predicted by the matching law. They suggest we should approach our enemies and shape their behavior with love, not revile them from afar.

Substitutes

In Herrnstein's experiments and the hundreds of choice experiments that have replicated his findings, the animals and humans chose between two identical reinforcers. For rats, the choice was between food reinforcers earned by pressing the B_L lever and the same food reinforcers available for pressing the B_R lever; similarly, for humans it was a choice between money and money.

However, most of the choices we make in our daily lives are between different reinforcers. For example, at snack time we might choose between having a slice of chocolate cake or chips and salsa. Can the matching law be used to predict and influence these choices as well?

The answer is, "it depends"; it depends on whether the two reinforcers *substitute* for each other. Before we dive into the "it depends" answer, let's explain what we mean by *substitute*. When we say two reinforcers substitute for one another, it helps to think of ingredients in a recipe. If we are out of coriander, we might Google "What substitutes for coriander." The answer will be a spice that has a similar taste (equal parts cumin and oregano). If we cannot easily obtain one reinforcer (coriander), the reinforcer that will take its place (a cumin/oregano mix) is a substitute.

The more technical definition of a **substitute reinforcer** is *a reinforcer that is increasingly consumed when access to another reinforcer is constrained*. For example, if the price of coffee increases substantially, our access to this reinforcer is constrained – we can't afford to drink as much coffee as we normally do. When coffee prices spike, we will substitute other caffeinated drinks like tea, caffeine shots, and energy drinks. Likewise, if your partner moves to another city, your access to intimate reinforcers is greatly constrained. Substitute reinforcers might include social reinforcers from friends, intimate reinforcers from a new partner, or drug reinforcers from a bottle.

Now back to the "it depends" answer. The matching law can be used to predict and influence choice if the two different reinforcers substitute for one another. For example, clothes stocked by Moxx and Rass substitute for one another – if Rass raises their prices, we buy more clothes at Moxx – so the matching law applies. However, if the two reinforcers do not substitute for one another, then no, the matching law does not apply. For example, clothes and hamburgers do not substitute for one another. If the price of clothes goes up, you will not begin wearing hamburgers. The study of substitute reinforcers has revealed some important findings in the area of substance use disorders. This topic is explored further in Extra Box 2.

EXTRA BOX 2: WHAT SUBSTITUTES FOR DRUG REINFORCERS?

If you grew up in the US in the last 40 years, there is a good chance you were taught that drugs are the ultimate reinforcers; they are so powerful that they have no substitutes. If you start using drugs, you were told, no other reinforcer will be able to compete and your life will be ruined. Is this true? No, not really.

In his 2015 TedMed talk, Columbia University neuroscientist, Dr. Carl Hart, discusses the research that started the myth of drugs as the ultimate reinforcers. In these studies, rats were placed in an operant chamber where they could press a lever to self-administer a drug reinforcer, such as cocaine. Most of the rats pressed the lever and consumed high doses of drugs on a daily basis. When this finding was translated to humans, policy-makers concluded that drugs were the ultimate reinforcers; that a "war on drugs" was necessary, as were mandatory minimum jail sentences for those found in possession of drugs. What policy makers didn't realize was that these experiments were conducted in impoverished environments – the researchers made only one reinforcer available and it was a drug reinforcer.

Dr. Carl Hart
Columbia University

Source: Eileen Barroso/
Wikipedia/CC BY 2.0

Meanwhile, other researchers were collecting data that challenged the policy-makers' conclusions. Researchers like Dr. Bruce Alexander wondered if drugs would lose their "ultimate reinforcer" status if the environment was not impoverished; that is, if other reinforcers were available that might compete with (substitute for) drugs. To find out, Dr. Alexander and his colleagues (Hadaway et al., 1979) raised one group of rats in an impoverished environment (living alone in a cage with nothing to do); these rats used a lot of morphine when given the opportunity. The other group of rats was raised in an environment in which there were opportunities to engage in behaviors that produced natural reinforcers – they could play with each other, they could climb on objects, and they could build nests. These animals raised in the "rat park" consumed far less morphine than their isolated counterparts. Was this because of alternative reinforcers, or was it because the rats living alone were stressed out?

To find out, Dr. Marilyn Carroll housed monkeys in cages and periodically gave them the opportunity to press a lever to self-administer a drug (phencyclidine or "angel dust"). In one phase of the experiment, only one lever was inserted into the cage – take it or leave it. In another condition, two levers were inserted and the monkeys could choose between phencyclidine or a few sips of a sweet drink. The results were clear – monkeys took drugs less often when given a choice between drugs or soda pop (Carroll, 1985; Carroll et al., 1989). Yes, soda pop substituted for angel dust.

The finding that substitute reinforcers can dramatically decrease drug use has been replicated many times, with many drugs (Comer et al., 1994), with many different substitutes (Cosgrove et al., 2002; Venniro et al., 2018), and in other species (Anderson et al., 2002; Carroll et al., 1991) including humans (Hart et al., 2000, 2005). Importantly, this finding is consistent with the predictions of the matching law (Anderson et al., 2002). If the rate of reinforcement for non-drug-taking activities is very low (e.g., $R_{NonDrug}$=1 reinforcer per week), and the rate of reinforcement for taking drugs is twice as high (R_{Drug}=2 reinforcers per week), then the matching law predicts that, all else being equal, 67% of the individual's time should be spent in drug-related activities (B_{Drug}):

$$\frac{B_{Drug}}{B_{Drug} + B_{NonDrug}} = \frac{R_{Drug}}{R_{Drug} + R_{NonDrug}}$$

$$\frac{B_{Drug}}{B_{Drug} + B_{NonDrug}} = \frac{2}{2+1}$$

$$\frac{B_{Drug}}{B_{Drug} + B_{NonDrug}} = \frac{2}{3} \rightarrow 0.67 \times 100 = 67\%$$

In Dr. Carl Hart's TedMed talk, he discusses the implications of this behavioral research on public policy. Drug use is not a moral failing, he argues, it is the result of a lack of substitute reinforcers. To prevent drug use, Dr. Hart suggests, we must increase the value of $R_{NonDrug}$. That is, if an individual can obtain contingent reinforcers for engaging in non-drug-taking activities, that individual will be much less likely to develop a substance-use disorder.

Perhaps the most effective of these non-drug-taking activities is work. Being gainfully employed substantially reduces one's risk of substance abuse. When economic prospects are dim, as they are in the areas of the United States where the opioid crisis has killed thousands, the risk of problem drug use is increased. Showing compassion by increasing $R_{NonDrug}$ isn't a political stance; it is a scientific stance.

Using the Matching Law to Positively Influence Behavior

It should be clear by now that Herrnstein's matching equation may be used to accurately *predict* choices between substitute reinforcers available in uncertain environments. What about the other goal of behavior analysis? Can the matching equation identify functional variables that may be used to positively influence behavior? If you read Extra Boxes 1 and 2, then you will know the answer is "yes." This section explicitly identifies those functional variables and specifies how to positively influence choice.

In the matching equation, the functional variables appear on the right side of the equals sign, that is, R_1 and R_2. By changing these variables, we can increase socially desirable behavior and decrease undesirable behavior.

Let B_1 serve as the frequency of socially desirable behavior. Given Herrnstein's equation, there are **two ways to increase the proportion of behavior allocated to B_1**. *The first technique is to increase R_1.* That is, ensure that the socially desirable behavior is reinforced more often. This advice is entirely consistent with everything presented in the book thus far – if we want to see more of B_1, reinforce it more often. The top portion of Table 13.1 provides an example of this prediction.

Table 13.1 Two techniques for increasing a desirable behavior (B_1).

Technique 1. Increase R_1:

Phase	R_1	R_2	%B_1	%B_2
Baseline	10/minute	10/minute	50%	50%
Increase R_1	30/minute	10/minute	75%	25%

Technique 2. Decrease R_2:

Phase	R_1	R_2	%B_1	%B_2
Baseline	10/minute	10/minute	50%	50%
Decrease R_2	10/minute	3.3/minute	75%	25%

Herrnstein's matching equation: $$\frac{B_1}{B_1 + B_2} = \frac{R_1}{R_1 + R_2}$$

The second technique for increasing B_1 is to decrease R_2. Said another way, if we want to increase socially desirable behavior, get rid of other substitute reinforcers. If we reduce R_2 to zero, then we will have arranged a differential reinforcement procedure. That is, B_1 will be reinforced, but B_2 will not. The matching equation predicts differential reinforcement, if perfectly implemented, will yield exclusive choice for B_1, the reinforced behavior. But short of reducing R_2 to zero, the matching equation predicts a nonexclusive shift toward B_1, the socially desirable behavior. This is demonstrated in the lower portion of Table 13.1.

The matching equation also prescribes **two techniques for decreasing an undesired behavior (B_2).** *The first technique is to decrease R_2.* As shown in the upper part of Table 13.2, when we decreased R_2 from 10 reinforcers per minute to 2, the percentage of behavior allocated to B_2, the undesired behavior, decreased from 50% to 17%. *The second technique for decreasing an undesired behavior (B_2) is to increase R_1.* This prediction is shown in the lower

Table 13.2 Two techniques for decreasing an undesirable behavior (B_2).

Technique 1. Decrease R_2:

Phase	R_1	R_2	$\%B_1$	$\%B_2$
Baseline	10/minute	10/minute	50%	50%
Decrease R_2	10/minute	2/minute	83%	17%

Technique 2. Increase R_1:

Phase	R_1	R_2	$\%B_1$	$\%B_2$
Baseline	10/minute	10/minute	50%	50%
Increase R_1	50/minute	10/minute	83%	17%

Herrnstein's matching equation: $\dfrac{B_2}{B_2 + B_1} = \dfrac{R_2}{R_2 + R_1}$

portion of Table 13.2. When the rate of reinforcers on R_1 is increased (from 10/minute to 50/minute), the percentage of behavior allocated to inappropriate B_2 behaviors decreases from 50% to 17%.

In sum, Herrnstein's matching equation makes practical predictions about how to positively influence behavior. An advantage it has over other theories of choice is its quantitative precision. That is, it makes precise predictions that are falsifiable; the mark of a good theory in any science.

The Matching Law and Attention

The world in which we live is filled with thousands, if not millions, of stimuli, yet we attend to very few of them. For example, when is the last time that you chose to attend to the space on the ceiling in the corner opposite from you right now. Have you ever looked at that spot?

Why do you instead spend so much time attending to books, your computer, and your phone? In the 1980s, no one spent 4 hours a day looking at their phones. What changed?

If you have understood this chapter so far, you should be able to propose a falsifiable hypothesis about the allocation of your attention. The hypothesis forwarded by the matching law is that more attention will be allocated to stimuli predictive of higher rates of reinforcement (like your phone today), less attention will be allocated to stimuli

Source: Alexas_Fotos, Pixabay

predictive of lower rates of reinforcement (like phones in the 1980s), and no attention will be allocated to stimuli predictive of no reinforcers (like that spot on the ceiling).

The evidence for this matching law hypothesis of attention comes from several laboratory studies. Rats, pigeons, and humans reliably attend to stimuli signaling higher rates of reinforcement than they attend to stimuli signaling lower rates, or no reinforcement, exactly as the matching law predicts (Della Libera & Chelazzi, 2006, 2009; Shahan & Podlesnik, 2008; for review see Shahan, 2013). Your everyday experience is consistent with these findings. Your attention is easily drawn to the sound of your name across a noisy room because this auditory stimulus has reliably signaled a momentary increase in the probability of a reinforcer. For example, when a friend calls your name, attending to them might provide an opportunity to watch a funny video, hear a juicy bit of gossip, or get invited to a party. Similarly, your attention is readily drawn to a $20 bill blowing across campus, but not at all drawn to a candy wrapper rolling in the wind.

The matching law's account of human attention may also help to explain why humans choose to allocate more of their news-gathering activities to biased sources, either progressive or conservative. These news outlets provide a higher rate of reinforcement; that is, they more frequently publish stories their audiences find reinforcing. For example, individuals who describe themselves as progressive choose to allocate more of their attention to newspapers and cable news channels that frequently publish stories and editorials consistent with their world view (e.g., MSNBC), and less attention to news outlets that frequently publish news appealing to a conservative audience (e.g., Breitbart, Fox News). Those with the opposite world view allocate their attention in the opposite direction, where *they* find the higher rate of reinforcement.

If you let Google or Facebook choose what news you read, then you should know that their artificial intelligence algorithms have learned what you find reinforcing, and, to keep your attention directed at their platform, they feed you a steady diet of news stories predicted to be reinforcing (Zuboff, 2019). The downside of this is that different individuals have different sets of "facts," leading to the shared belief that the other tribe is "nuts."

Summary

As you can see, the predictions of the matching law have been subjected to a large number of empirical tests involving a wide variety of choices and species. The preponderance of the evidence is supportive of the matching law. More advanced courses in behavior analysis will outline even further the quantitative predictions of the matching law, but these are beyond the scope of this text. The next section explores one of these predictions without going into any further quantitative details. As you will see, the matching law helps us to understand some of the maladaptive and irrational choices that we all make every day.

Reading Quiz 3

1. The matching equation makes accurate predictions about choice when the two alternatives arrange reinforcers that _____ for one another.

$$\text{Herrnstein's matching equation: } \frac{B_1}{B_1 + B_2} = \frac{R_1}{R_1 + R_2}$$

2. According to Herrnstein's matching equation, there are two ways to increase B_1. One way is to increase _____. The other way is to decrease _____.
3. The matching equation also predicts how to decrease B_2. One way is to decrease _____. The other way is to increase _____.
4. This one will be a *little* more difficult. According to Herrnstein's matching equation, there are two ways to increase B_2. One way is to increase _____. The other way is to decrease _____.
5. If you got the last one right, this one will be easy. According to Herrnstein's matching equation, there are two ways to decrease B_1. One way is to increase _____. The other way is to decrease _____.
6. Where we choose to direct our _____ also appears to be predicted by Herrnstein's matching equation.

Impulsivity and Self-Control

In our everyday language, we often refer to people as "impulsive" or "self-controlled." Sometimes these words are used as descriptions of behavior ("I bought the dress on impulse"), and sometimes as explanations of behavior ("You know why she bought that dress – because she's so impulsive"). In the latter case, the cause of impulsive (or self-controlled) behavior is hypothesized to be inside the person. That is, we see an individual make several impulsive choices and then speculate that the cause of those choices is "impulsivity" or a lack of "willpower." Conversely, if we see someone resist a temptation, we point to "self-control" as the cause. As we have previously discussed, such explanations are circular (see Chapter 9). The only evidence for an internal "impulsivity" or "self-control" is the external pattern of choices made. When the only evidence for the cause (impulsivity) is the effect (impulsive choice), the explanation is circular.

A more scientific approach to understanding impulsive and self-control choice begins by specifying behavioral definitions (what is an impulsive choice), and then looking for functional variables that systematically influence these choices. We will use these definitions:

Impulsive choice *Choosing the smaller-sooner reward and foregoing the larger-later reward.*

Self-control choice   *Choosing the larger-later reward and foregoing the smaller-sooner reward.*

Let's apply these definitions to some everyday impulsive choices. How about the choice between eating junk food (impulsive choice) and eating healthy food (self-control choice)? To put some meat on this example, imagine going to Taco Bell for lunch and eating a beef quesarito, cheesy fiesta potatoes, and a medium Mountain Dew. This meal gives you the immediate enjoyment that only a beef quesarito can provide. However, by choosing to eat this, you are consuming almost all the calories you are allowed under your diet. Because you already had a mocha frappuccino for breakfast and you do not plan to skip dinner, you have chosen to forego your long-term weight loss goal.

Is eating this meal an impulsive choice? Most of us would intuitively say yes, but does it meet the behavioral definition of an impulsive choice – is junk food a smaller-sooner reward that requires you to forego a larger-later reward? Relative to the long-term benefits of sticking to your diet (weight loss, improved health, reduced risk of disease, higher self-esteem, etc.), that beef quesarito is a pretty small reward. Is it *sooner*? Yes, the benefits of eating the quesarito meal are experienced right now. The benefits of sticking to your diet will not be felt for months. Therefore, eating junk food is impulsive – you are choosing the smaller-sooner reward and foregoing the larger-later reward. Conversely, choosing to stick to the diet is a self-control choice because you are preferring the larger-later reward and foregoing the smaller-sooner one.

Before we provide more examples of impulsive and self-control choices, note that when we make an impulsive choice (like eating an unhealthy snack) we feel a strong sense of wanting. However, almost immediately after eating, we regret our decision. This is quite common with impulsive choices and we will have more to say about this later, in the section on "Preference Reversals." But for now, Table 13.3 provides more examples of impulsive and self-control choices. See if you would feel tempted by these impulsive choices, only to later regret having made them.

Predicting Impulsive Choice

The first task for a behavioral science is, as always, to accurately predict behavior; in the present case, predicting impulsive choice. At the opening of this chapter, we discussed four variables affecting choice. You may have noticed that two of those variables – reinforcer size/quality and reinforcer delay – are relevant to impulsive and self-control choices. These two variables are pulling behavior in opposite directions. A larger-later reward is attractive because of its larger reinforcer size/quality, but it is a less effective reinforcer because it is delayed. The smaller-sooner reward has immediacy going for it, but it is a less effective reinforcer because of its small size or lower quality. These two functional variables pull behavior in opposite directions – we want more, but we also want it now.

If the delayed benefits of adhering to our diet could be obtained right after refusing dessert ("No cake for me please." Poof! You lose 1 pound of unwanted fat), no one would ever eat dessert again. Unfortunately, these health benefits are delayed and, therefore, much of their value is lost on us.

This reduction in the subjective value of a delayed reinforcer is illustrated in Figure 13.10. Instead of showing the value of delayed health outcomes, we show the subjective value of the

Answers appear at the end of the chapter.

Table 13.3 Fill in the blank by indicating if this is an impulsive or a self-control choice.

Choice	Reward(s)	Reward amount	Delivered when?	Impulsive or self-control
Smoke a cigarette	Get a nicotine rush	Smaller	Sooner	_____
Abstain from smoking	Avoid lung cancer, heart disease, etc. Less coughing and shortness of breath	Larger	Later	_____
Study for tomorrow's exam	Better grade on the anatomy exam, instructor praise, etc.	Larger	_____	_____
Watch TV	Episode of Grey's Anatomy	Smaller	_____	_____
Have another drink	Small increase in intoxication	_____	Sooner	_____
Refuse the next drink	Avoid hangover and reputation loss among friends	_____	Later	_____
Get out of bed on time	Arrive to work on time and avoid being yelled at	_____	_____	_____
Press the snooze button	A little more low-quality sleep	_____	Sooner	_____
Succumb to peer pressure	Peer pressure ends and praise begins	_____	_____	_____
Behave in accord with your values	All the benefits of living a values-consistent life	_____	Later	_____
Cheat on your partner	Enjoyable sexual experience	_____	_____	_____
Choose to be faithful	Maintain a healthy relationship, avoid lasting feelings of guilt	_____	_____	_____
Choose not to lie in a tanning bed	Healthier skin when older (fewer wrinkles, less skin cancer, etc.)	_____	_____	_____
Laying in a tanning bed	Get an attractive tan	_____	_____	_____

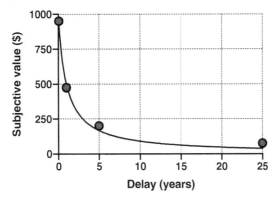

Figure 13.10 The subjective value of a $1,000 reward that will be provided only after the delay indicated on the x-axis. Humans and other animals discount delayed rewards according to a hyperbolic function.

delayed monetary reward that Rich Uncle Joe promised us earlier in the chapter. The red data points in the figure plot how someone might subjectively value a $1,000 gift promised 1 month, 1 year, 5 years, and 25 years in the future. How did you subjectively value these delayed gifts (the subjective values are those amounts that you wrote in each blank of the Rich Uncle Joe survey)? Go back to the survey and add your own subjective values to Figure 13.10. If you said that you would sell the $1,000 in 5 years for $300 in cash right now (and not a penny less), then you should add a data point at $300 on the y-axis and 5 years on the x-axis.

The first thing to note about the data in Figure 13.10 is that the subjective value of a reinforcer does not decline linearly (i.e., according to a straight line). Instead, the line is curved in a way that reflects the fact that, for our hypothetical decision-maker whose data are shown, reinforcers lose most of their value at short delays (≤ 5 years in Figure 13.10). Another way to say this is that the value of the reinforcer was *discounted* steeply in this range of delays. At delays longer than 5 years, the curve declines less steeply. In this range, waiting longer has less impact on the discounting of the delayed gift.

The shape of this ***delay discounting curve*** is called a *hyperbola*. Importantly, this hyperbolic shape is predicted by a version of the matching law whose quantitative details we will not explore – you've had enough math for one day.[2] This predicted hyperbolic discounting of delayed reinforcers has been evaluated and confirmed in many experiments. Rats, pigeons, monkeys, and humans all hyperbolically discount the value of delay events (Bickel & Marsch, 2001; Green et al., 2007; Laibson, 1997; Logue, 1988; Madden et al., 1999; Mazur, 1987; Rachlin et al., 1991).

Now that we know delayed reinforcers are discounted hyperbolically, we can predict when impulsive choices will be made. Figure 13.11 shows another hyperbolic discounting curve but this time the x-axis is reversed to show time passing from left to right. If you are the stick-figure decision-maker in the figure, you must choose between a smaller-sooner reward (SSR; the short green bar) and a larger-later reward (LLR; the tall red bar).

Because the smaller-sooner reward is available right now (e.g., that slice of cake), it maintains its full value, which is given by the height of the green bar. By contrast, the subjective value of the larger-later reward (the health benefits of eating a healthy diet) is discounted because this consequence is delayed. The hyperbolic discounting curve sweeping down from the red bar shows the discounted value at a wide range of delays.

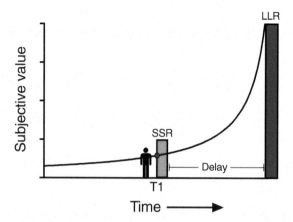

Figure 13.11 The stick-figure decision-maker at T1 faces a choice between a smaller-sooner reward (SSR) that may be obtained immediately, and a larger-later reward (LLR) that is delayed. Because the LLR is delayed, it is discounted in value according to a hyperbolic discounting function. The small red data point at T1 shows the discounted value of the LLR. Because that value is below that of the SSR, the impulsive choice is made.

At T1, where the stick-figure decision-maker is making its choice, the discounted value of the larger-later reward is shown as a red dot. The red dot is lower than the height of the green bar; therefore, the value of the smaller-sooner reward is greater than the subjective value of the larger-later reward. Said another way, the smaller-sooner reward feels like it is worth more than the discounted value of the larger-later reward. Because choice favors the reward with the higher subjective value, our stick-figure decision-maker makes the impulsive choice; that is, they choose the smaller-sooner reward and forego the larger-later reward.

Predicting Preference Reversals

Figure 13.12 illustrates a unique prediction of hyperbolic discounting – that there are predictable times when, from one moment to the next, we will change our minds about what is important in life. In the graph from the preceding section (Figure 13.11), when dessert was immediately available, our decision-maker preferred cake (SSR) over the delayed benefits of dieting (LLR). But in Figure 13.12, neither reward is immediately available at T2, where the stick-figure decision-maker contemplates its options. From this location in time, *both rewards* are hyperbolically discounted in value and, importantly, these subjective values have changed places. Now the subjective value of the LLR (red dot) is greater than the discounted value of the SSR (green dot). At T2 the decision-maker can clearly see the benefits of dieting and resolves to stick with it. Unfortunately, when an immediately available dessert is encountered again, moving the decision-maker from T2 to T1 (in Figure 13.11), a "change of mind" will occur. The subjective values reverse positions again, dessert is consumed, and self-loathing ensues. Our stick-figure decision-maker notes its lack of "willpower" and resolves to buy a self-help book (*How to _Stick_ to Your Decisions*).

Preference reversals have been extensively studied by behavioral scientists interested in human and nonhuman behavior; they predictably occur when the decision-making is

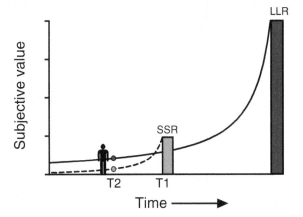

Figure 13.12 In this illustration, at T2 neither the SSR nor the LLR is immediately available. From the vantage point of our decision-maker, the subjective (or discounted) values of the two rewards have reversed relative to where they were at T1 (Figure 13.11). Now the subjective value of the LLR is greater than that of the SSR. This predicts the LLR will be preferred at T2, even though it was rejected at T1.

moved, in time, from T1 to T2 (or vice versa; Ainslie & Herrnstein, 1981; Green et al., 1994; Kirby & Herrnstein, 1995).

One reason for the interest in preference reversals is that "changing your mind" from a self-control choice to an impulsive choice is maladaptive. Another reason is that it seems so irrational, and yet we all do it. For example, most of us set the alarm with good intentions to get up, but when the alarm goes off we snooze it at least once. This is a preference reversal. The night before (at T2 in Figure 13.12), the subjective value of getting up early (the red dot at T2) was higher (more valuable) than the discounted value of a little more sleep tomorrow morning (the green dot at T2). However, while sleeping, the decision-maker moves from T2 to T1. When the alarm goes off at T1, extra sleep is an immediate reinforcer and it is more valuable than the discounted value of the delayed benefits of getting up on time.

A very similar preference reversal occurs when individuals with a substance-use disorder commit to outpatient therapy with the best of intentions to quit (Bickel et al., 1998). These choices are often made at T2, in the therapist's office when drugs are not immediately available. Here the subjective value of the delay benefits of drug abstinence (the red dot at T2) is subjectively greater than the discounted value of drugs (the green dot at T2). A few days later when drugs *are* available immediately (T1), the individual finds that they cannot resist the immediate temptation of drug use. The subjective values of these choice outcomes have reversed, as has the decision to abstain from drugs.

Influencing Impulsive Choice

Steeply discounting the value of future consequences (solid curve in Figure 13.13) can lead to impulsive choices. When the subjective value of the smaller-sooner reward (height of the green bar) exceeds that of the larger-later reward (red dot at T1), the impulsive choice is made. By contrast, when delayed rewards are discounted more shallowly (dashed curve), the

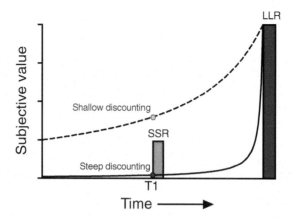

Figure 13.13 Steeper discounting of delayed rewards reflects a strong preference for the SSR at T1. At that point in time, the subjective value of the LLR (red dot) is far below the value of the SSR. By contrast, at T1, the shallow discounting curve keeps the subjective value of the LLR higher than the SSR. This reflects a strong preference for the LLR. Steeper delay discounting curves are correlated with addictions.

subjective value of the larger-later reward (blue dot at T1) exceeds that of the smaller-sooner reward, and the self-control choice is made. If, in Figure 13.10, your own Rich Uncle Joe discounting curve was steeper than ours, there is a good chance that you are young and not wealthy; younger and less well-off individuals tend to have steeper discounting curves (Reimers et al., 2009).

Consistent with the analysis shown in Figure 13.13, a substantial amount of evidence suggests steeply discounting the future is correlated with substance-use disorders such as cigarette smoking and the misuse of alcohol, cocaine, methamphetamine, heroin and other opiates (Bickel et al., 1999; Heil et al., 2006; Madden et al., 1997). Likewise, steeply discounting delayed consequences is correlated with relapsing during drug-abuse treatment (Coughlin et al., 2020; Harvanko et al., 2019; MacKillop & Kahler, 2009). Similarly, pathological gambling and behaviors that risk significant health losses are correlated with steep delay discounting (Dixon et al., 2003; Herrmann et al., 2015; Kräplin et al., 2014; Odum et al., 2000).

Perhaps you remember from Chapter 2 that *correlation does not imply causation*. No experiments have established that steeply discounting the value of future consequences plays a causal role in addictions. However, there are some findings that are suggestive. For example, studies that have assessed delay discounting in human adolescents have reported that steep delay discounting precedes and predicts early drug use (Audrain-McGovern et al., 2009) and similar findings have been reported in rats (Perry et al., 2008). Such findings suggest reducing delay discounting early in life might improve decision-making and lessen human suffering. The following sections describe two methods for reducing impulsive choice. One method – using a commitment strategy – works by engineering the environment to improve the choices we make. The second method – delay-exposure training – works through learning.

COMMITMENT STRATEGIES

If we are more likely to choose the larger-later reward at T2 (Figure 13.12), when neither reward is immediately available, then an effective strategy for improving self-control is to make choices in advance, before we are tempted by an immediate reward. For example, making a healthy lunch right after finishing breakfast is a commitment strategy for eating a healthy lunch. After eating breakfast, we are full and, therefore, are not tempted by a beef quesarito. However, we know we will be tempted at lunch time, so it would be wise to use a commitment strategy now. By packing a healthy lunch, we commit to our diet, and the larger-later rewards it entails. Of course, we will be tempted to change our mind at T1, when lunch time approaches, but having the packed lunch can help in resisting the temptation to head to Taco Bell.

Rachlin and Green (1972) first studied commitment strategies in pigeons. In their experiment, pigeons chose between pecking the orange and red keys at T2 as shown in Figure 13.14. At this point in time, no food reinforcers were immediately available, so hyperbolic discounting suggests the larger-later reward will be preferred. If the red key was pecked, a delay occurred until T1, at which time the pigeon chose between one unit of food now (smaller-sooner reward of pecking the green key) and three units of food after a delay (larger-later reward). Given these options, if the pigeons found themselves at T1, they nearly always made the impulsive choice. But note what happens when the pigeons chose the orange key at T2. Instead of waiting for another choice at T1, they were given no choice at all. By choosing the orange key, the pigeon *committed* itself to making the self-control choice at T1. Consistent with hyperbolic discounting of delayed reinforcers, Rachlin and Green's (1972) pigeons frequently committed themselves to this course of self-control.

The Nobel prize-winning behavioral economist, Richard Thaler, used a similar commitment strategy to help employees save money for retirement (Thaler & Benartzi, 2004). New employees are reluctant to sign up for a retirement savings program, in part, because money put into savings is money not used to purchase smaller-sooner rewards. Thaler's insight was to commit to saving money at T2, when the money to be saved is not immediately available. This was accomplished in the *Save More Tomorrow* program by asking employees to commit some of their *next* pay raise, which would not be experienced for many months, to retirement savings. At T2, with no immediate temptations present, the number of employees who signed up for retirement savings more than tripled. Although employees were free to reverse their decision at T1, when the pay raise was provided, very few took the time to do so. The program has been widely adopted in business and is estimated to have generated at least $7.4 billion in new retirement savings (Benartzi & Thaler, 2013). This is a wonderful example of how behavioral science can positively influence human behavior.

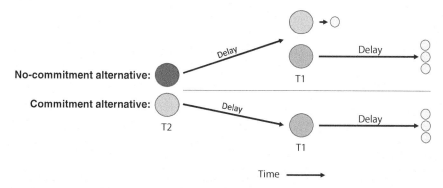

Figure 13.14 Schematic representation of the choices given to pigeons in the Rachlin and Green (1972) experiment. See text for details.

DELAY-EXPOSURE TRAINING

The second method for reducing delay discounting and impulsive choice takes a different approach. Instead of arranging an environment in which impulsive choice is less likely to occur, delay-exposure training teaches the individual by giving them a lot of experience with delayed reinforcers. The logic is simple – if we are used to waiting (we do it all the time) – then waiting for a larger-later reward is nothing out of the ordinary; why not choose the larger-later reward? By contrast, if we are used to getting what we want when we want it, then delays are unusual, aversive, and may signal that we are not going to get what we want.

Delay-exposure training has been studied in several different species and several methodologies have been employed. For example, Mazur and Logue (1978) exposed pigeons to delayed reinforcers for several months and found that this experience produced long-lasting reductions in impulsive choice. Similar findings have been reported in laboratory studies with rats and humans (Binder et al., 2000; Eisenberger & Adornetto, 1986; Stein et al., 2015). A form of delay-exposure training has been used in preschools to improve self-control choice and reduce the problem behaviors that can occur when preschoolers don't get what they want when they want it (Luczynski & Fahmie, 2017).

Reading Quiz 4

1. If we choose the smaller-sooner over the larger-later reward, we have made the _____ choice.
2. If we choose the larger-later over the smaller-sooner reward, we have made the _____ choice.
3. When rewards are delayed, they lose some of their value. This devaluation of delayed rewards is called delay _____.
4. The shape of the delay-discounting function is _____.
5. When the subjective (discounted) value of the larger-later reward exceeds the value of the smaller-sooner reward, the individual will make a(n) _____ choice.
6. There is a robust correlation between _____ (steep/shallow) delay discounting and substance-use disorders.
7. It is easier to make a self-control choice when the smaller-sooner reward is not _____ available.
8. When using the _____ strategy, the individual chooses the larger-later reward well before they encounter the temptations of an immediately available smaller-sooner reward. Importantly, this strategy requires that the decision-maker "lock in" their choice, so they do not change their mind later on, when the immediate temptation is encountered.

Summary

This chapter defined choice as a voluntary behavior occurring in a context in which alternative behaviors are possible. We reviewed four variables that tend to produce exclusive choice for one alternative over another. That is, we strongly prefer to obtain a reinforcer instead of nothing, to get a larger over a smaller reinforcer, to work less for the same reinforcer, and to receive reinforcers sooner rather than later. Choice is less exclusive when the outcomes of choice are uncertain. This describes the hunter-gatherer environment in which human behavior evolved. Whether hunting game or foraging for berries, our ancestors learned where food was more likely to be found, but there were no guarantees. In this uncertain environment, their behavior probably conformed to Herrnstein's matching equation, which holds that choice is influenced by relative rates of reinforcement. In modern times, the matching law can help us understand choices that are otherwise difficult to explain: terrorism, substance-use disorder, and white nationalism. In each case, the matching law suggests reducing these behaviors may be achieved by arranging alternative reinforcers that will substitute for the problematic reinforcer. These reinforcers will be more competitive for human behavior if they are more meaningful (and more immediate) than those reinforcers currently maintaining behaviors destructive to self and others.

The chapter also explored the impulsive choices we all make but later regret. These preferences for a smaller-sooner over a larger-later reward can have a negative impact on our lives. We sleep longer than we planned, lapse from our diet, and may even cheat on our partner because the benefits of doing so are immediate and the benefits of doing otherwise are delayed and, therefore, discounted in value. Many studies conducted in many species have established that delayed rewards are discounted in value and that the shape of the delay-discounting function is a hyperbola. Hyperbolic discounting can explain why we repeatedly change our minds – preferring the larger-later reward most of the time, and defecting on these good intentions when the smaller-sooner reward may be obtained immediately. While steeply discounting the value of delayed rewards is correlated with substance-use disorders and other health-impacting behaviors, there are methods for reducing impulsive choice. One method is the commitment strategy – choosing the larger-later reward well in advance, when the smaller-sooner reward is not immediately available. To the extent that this commitment cannot be reversed, this greatly increases self-control choices. The other method, delay-exposure training, provides the individual lots of experience with delayed reinforcers. Delay-exposure training seeks to change the individual's learning history, thereby producing large and lasting reductions in impulsive choice.

Answers to Reading Quiz Questions and Questions Posed in Table 13.3

Reading Quiz 1

1. voluntary; alternative
2. reinforcement (vs. no consequence); reinforcer size/quality; effort; reinforcer delay

Reading Quiz 2

1. behavior (responses)
2. reinforcement
3. choice

4. 3
5. 1
6. Left
7. 0.75
8. Your graph should look like this:

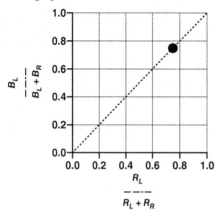

9. 75%
10. 0.667
11. Your graph should look like this:

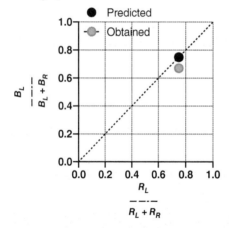

12.

	Obtained SR+ Rate		
Condition	R_L	R_R	**Proportion Left**
A	4/minute	29/minute	**0.12**
B	10/minute	23/minute	**0.30**
C	16/minute	17/minute	**0.48**
D	2/minute	1/minute	**0.67**

13.

	Response Rate		
Condition	B_L	B_R	Proportion Left
A	5/minute	39/minute	0.11
B	7/minute	15/minute	0.32
C	9/minute	10/minute	0.47
D	13/minute	4.7/minute	0.73

14. Condition A:

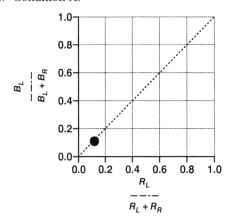

15. Condition B:

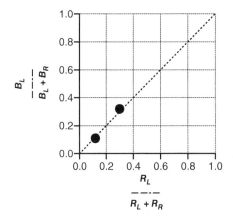

16. Condition C:

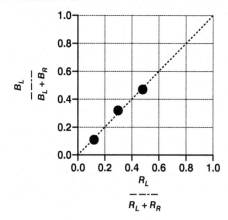

17. Condition D:

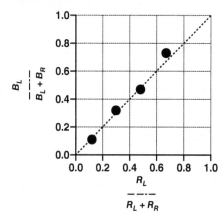

Table 13.3

Smoke a cigarette:	Impulsive
Abstain from smoking:	Self-control
Study for tomorrow's exam:	Later; self-control
Watch TV:	Sooner; impulsive
Have another drink:	Smaller; impulsive
Refuse the next drink:	Larger; self-control
Get out of bed on time:	Larger-later; self-control
Press the snooze button:	Smaller; impulsive
Succumb to peer pressure:	Smaller-sooner; impulsive

Behave in accord with your values:	Larger; self-control
Cheat on your partner:	Smaller-sooner; impulsive
Choose to be faithful:	Larger-later; self-control
Choose not to lie in a tanning bed:	Larger-later; self-control
Laying in a tanning bed:	Smaller-sooner; impulsive

Reading Quiz 3

1. substitute
2. R_1; R_2
3. R_2; R_1
4. R_2; R_1
5. R_2; R_1
6. attention

Reading Quiz 4

1. impulsive
2. self-control
3. discounting
4. hyperbolic
5. self-control
6. steep
7. immediately
8. commitment

Notes

1. Participant "Doug" in Baum (1975).
2. For readers who want to learn more about this expanded version of the matching law, a good summary is provided by Grace and Hucks (2013).

References

Abramson, C. I., & Kieson, E. (2016). Conditioning methods for animals in agriculture: A review. *Ciência Animal Brasileira*, *17*(3), 359–375. https://doi.org/10.1590/1089-6891v17i341981

Ainslie, G., & Herrnstein, R. J. (1981). Preference reversal and delayed reinforcement. *Animal Learning & Behavior*, *9*(4), 476–482. https://doi.org/10.3758/BF03209777

Anderson, K. G., Velkey, A. J., & Woolverton, W. L. (2002). The generalized matching law as a predictor of choice between cocaine and food in rhesus monkeys. *Psychopharmacology*, *163*(3–4), 319–326. https://doi.org/10.1007/s00213-002-1012-7

Audrain-McGovern, J., Rodriguez, D., Epstein, L. H., Cuevas, J., Rodgers, K., & Wileyto, E. P. (2009). Does delay discounting play an etiological role in smoking or is it a consequence of smoking? *Drug and Alcohol Dependence*, *103*(3), 99–106. https://doi.org/10.1016/J.DRUGALCDEP.2008.12.019

Baum, W. M. (1975). Time allocation in human vigilance. *Journal of the Experimental Analysis of Behavior*, *23*(1), 45–53. https://doi.org/10.1901/jeab.1975.23-45

Benartzi, S., & Thaler, R. H. (2013). Behavioral economics and the retirement savings crisis. *Science*, *339*, 1152–1153. https://doi.org/10.1126/science.1231320

Bickel, W. K., Madden, G. J., & Petry, N. M. (1998). The price of change: The behavioral economics of drug dependence. *Behavior Therapy*, *29*(4). https://doi.org/10.1016/S0005-7894(98)80050-6

Bickel, W. K., & Marsch, L. A. (2001). Toward a behavioral economic understanding of drug dependence: Delay discounting processes. *Addiction*, *96*(1), 73–86. https://doi.org/10.1046/j.1360-0443.2001.961736.x

Bickel, W. K., Odum, A. L., & Madden, G. J. (1999). Impulsivity and cigarette smoking: Delay discounting in current, never, and ex-smokers. *Psychopharmacology*, *146*(4), 447–454. https://doi.org/10.1007/PL00005490

Binder, L. M., Dixon, M. R., & Ghezzi, P. M. (2000). A procedure to teach self-control to children with attention deficit hyperactivity disorder. *Journal of Applied Behavior Analysis*, *33*(2), 233-237. https://doi.org/10.1901/jaba.2000.33-233

Bradshaw, C. M., Szabadi, E., & Bevan, P. (1976). Behavior of humans in variable-interval schedules of reinforcement. *Journal of the Experimental Analysis of Behavior*, *26*(2), 135–141. https://doi.org/10.1901/jeab.1976.26-135

Bradshaw, C. M., Szabadi, E., Bevan, P., & Ruddle, H. V. (1979). The effect of signaled reinforcement availability on concurrent performances in humans. *Journal of the Experimental Analysis of Behavior*, *32*(1), 65–74. https://doi.org/10.1901/jeab.1979.32-65

Buskist, W. F., & Miller, H. L. (1981). Concurrent operant performance in humans: Matching when food is the reinforcer. *The Psychological Record*, *31*(1), 95–100. https://doi.org/10.1007/BF03394723

Carroll, M. E. (1985). Concurrent phencyclidine and saccharin access: Presentation of an alternative reinforcer reduces drug intake. *Journal of the Experimental Analysis of Behavior*, *43*(1), 131–144. https://doi.org/10.1901/jeab.1985.43-131

Carroll, M. E., Carmona, G. G., & May, S. A. (1991). Modifying drug-reinforced behavior by altering the economic conditions of the drug and a nondrug reinforcer. *Journal of the Experimental Analysis of Behavior*, *56*(2), 361–376. https://doi.org/10.1901/jeab.1991.56-361

Carroll, M. E., Lac, S. T., & Nygaard, S. L. (1989). A concurrently available nondrug reinforcer prevents the acquisition or decreases the maintenance of cocaine-reinforced behavior. *Psychopharmacology*, *97*(1), 23–29. https://doi.org/10.1007/BF00443407

Comer, S. D., Hunt, V. R., & Carroll, M. E. (1994). Effects of concurrent saccharin availability and buprenorphine pretreatment on demand for smoked cocaine base in rhesus monkeys. *Psychopharmacology*, *115*(1–2), 15–23. https://doi.org/10.1007/BF02244746

Cosgrove, K. P., Hunter, R. G., & Carroll, M. E. (2002). Wheel-running attenuates intravenous cocaine self-administration in rats: Sex differences. *Pharmacology Biochemistry and Behavior*, *73*(3), 663–671. https://doi.org/10.1016/S0091-3057(02)00853-5

Coughlin, L. N., Tegge, A. N., Sheffer, C. E., & Bickel, W. K. (2020). A machine-learning approach to predicting smoking cessation treatment outcomes. *Nicotine & Tobacco Research*, *22*(3), 415–22. https://doi.org/10.1093/ntr/nty259

Critchfield, T. S., Paletz, E. M., MacAleese, K. R., & Newland, M. C. (2003). Punishment in human choice: Direct or competitive suppression? *Journal of the Experimental Analysis of Behavior*, *80*(1), 1–27. https://doi.org/10.1901/jeab.2003.80-1

Dallery, J. L., & Soto, P. (2013). Quantitative description of environment–behavior relations. In G. J. Madden, W. V. Dube, T. D. Hackenberg, G. P. Hanley, & K. A. Lattal (Eds.), *APA handbook of behavior analysis* (pp. 219–249). Washington, DC: American Psychological Association.

Davison, M., & McCarthy, D. (1988). *The matching law: A research review*. Hillsdale, NJ: Erlbaum.

Della Libera, C., & Chelazzi, L. (2006). Visual selective attention and the effects of monetary rewards. *Psychological Science, 17*(3), 222–227. https://doi.org/10.1111/j.1467-9280.2006.01689.x

Della Libera, C., & Chelazzi, L. (2009). Learning to attend and to ignore is a matter of gains and losses. *Psychological Science, 20*(6), 778–784. https://doi.org/10.1111/j.1467-9280.2009.02360.x

Dixon, M. R., Marley, J., & Jacobs, E. A. (2003). Delay discounting by pathological gamblers. *Journal of Applied Behavior Analysis, 36*(4), 449–458. https://doi.org/10.1901/jaba.2003.36-449

Eisenberger, R., & Adornetto, M. (1986). Generalized self-control of delay and effort. *Journal of Personality and Social Psychology, 51*(5), 1020–1031. https://doi.org/10.1037/0022-3514.51.5.1020

Foster, T. M., Temple, W., Robertson, B., Nair, V., & Poling, A. (1996). Concurrent-schedule performance in dairy cows: Persistent undermatching. *Journal of the Experimental Analysis of Behavior, 65*(1), 57–80. https://doi.org/10.1901/jeab.1996.65-57

Grace, R. C., & Hucks, A. D. (2013). The allocation of operant behavior. In G. J. Madden, W. V. Dube, T. D. Hackenberg, G. P. Hanley, & K. A. Lattal (Eds.), *APA handbook of behavior analysis, Vol. 1: Methods and principles* (pp. 307–337). Washington, DC: American Psychological Association. https://doi.org/10.1037/13937-014

Green, L., Fristoe, N., & Myerson, J. (1994). Temporal discounting and preference reversals in choice between delayed outcomes. *Psychonomic Bulletin & Review, 1*(3), 383–389. https://doi.org/10.3758/BF03213979

Green, L., Myerson, J., Shah, A. K., Estle, S. J., & Holt, D. D. (2007). Do adjusting-amount and adjusting-delay procedures produce equivalent estimates of subjective value in pigeons? *Journal of the Experimental Analysis of Behavior, 87*(3), 337–347. https://doi.org/10.1901/jeab.2007.37-06

Hadaway, P. F., Alexander, B. K., Coambs, R. B., & Beyerstein, B. (1979). The effect of housing and gender on preference for morphine-sucrose solutions in rats. *Psychopharmacology, 66*(1), 87–91. https://doi.org/10.1007/BF00431995

Hart, C. L., Haney, M., Foltin, R. W., & Fischman, M. W. (2000). Alternative reinforcers differentially modify cocaine self-administration by humans. *Behavioural Pharmacology, 11*(1), 87–91. https://doi.org/10.1097/00008877-200002000-00010

Hart, C. L., Haney, M., Vosburg, S. K., Comer, S. D., & Foltin, R. W. (2005). Reinforcing effects of oral Δ9-THC in male marijuana smokers in a laboratory choice procedure. *Psychopharmacology, 181*(2), 237–243. https://doi.org/10.1007/s00213-005-2234-2

Harvanko, A. M., Strickland, J. C., Slone, S. A., Shelton, B. J., & Reynolds, B. A. (2019). Dimensions of impulsive behavior: Predicting contingency management treatment outcomes for adolescent smokers. *Addictive Behaviors, 90*, 334–340. https://doi.org/10.1016/J.ADDBEH.2018.11.031

Heil, S. H., Johnson, M. W., Higgins, S. T., & Bickel, W. K. (2006). Delay discounting in currently using and currently abstinent cocaine-dependent outpatients and non-drug-using matched controls. *Addictive Behaviors, 31*(7), 1290–1294. https://doi.org/10.1016/J.ADDBEH.2005.09.005

Herrmann, E. S., Johnson, P. S., & Johnson, M. W. (2015). Examining delay discounting of condom-protected sex among men who have sex with men using crowdsourcing technology. *AIDS and Behavior, 19*(9), 1655–1665. https://doi.org/10.1007/s10461-015-1107-x

Herrnstein, R. J. (1961). Relative and absolute strength of response as a function of frequency of reinforcement. *Journal of the Experimental Analysis of Behavior, 4*(3), 267–272. https://doi.org/10.1901/jeab.1961.4-267

Herrnstein, R. J. & Loveland, D. H. (1975). Maximizing and matching on concurrent ratio schedules. *Journal of the Experimental Analysis of Behavior, 24*(1), 107–116. https://doi.org/10.1901/jeab.1975.24-107

Horne, P. J., & Lowe, C. F. (1993). Determinants of human performance on concurrent schedules. *Journal of the Experimental Analysis of Behavior, 59*(1), 29–60. https://doi.org/10.1901/jeab.1993.59-29

Kirby, K. N., & Herrnstein, R. J. (1995). Preference reversals due to myopic discounting of delayed reward. *Psychological Science*, 6(2), 83–89. https://doi.org/10.1111/j.1467-9280.1995.tb00311.x

Kräplin, A., Dshemuchadse, M., Behrendt, S., Scherbaum, S., Goschke, T., & Bühringer, G. (2014). Dysfunctional decision-making in pathological gambling: Pattern specificity and the role of impulsivity. *Psychiatry Research*, 215(3), 675–682. https://doi.org/10.1016/J.PSYCHRES.2013.12.041

Lagadic, H., & Faure, J. M. (1988). Operant conditioning and use of space by caged laying hens. *Behavioural Processes*, 16, 43–56. https://doi.org/10.1016/0376-6357(88)90016-2

Laibson, D. (1997). Golden eggs and hyperbolic discounting. *The Quarterly Journal of Economics*, 112(2), 443–478. https://doi.org/10.1162/003355397555253

Logue, A. W. (1988). Research on self-control: An integrating framework. *Behavioral and Brain Sciences*, 11(4), 665–679. https://doi.org/10.1017/S0140525X00053978

Luczynski, K. C., & Fahmie, T. A. (2017). Preschool life skills: Toward teaching prosocial skills and preventing aggression in young children. In P. Sturmey (Ed.), *The Wiley handbook of violence and aggression* (pp. 1–12). Hoboken, NJ: John Wiley & Sons Ltd. https://doi.org/10.1002/9781119057574.whbva059

MacKillop, J., & Kahler, C. W. (2009). Delayed reward discounting predicts treatment response for heavy drinkers receiving smoking cessation treatment. *Drug and Alcohol Dependence*, 104(3), 197–203. https://doi.org/10.1016/J.DRUGALCDEP.2009.04.020

Madden, G. J., Bickel, W. K., & Jacobs, E. A. (1999). Discounting of delayed rewards in opioid-dependent outpatients: Exponential or hyperbolic discounting functions? *Experimental and Clinical Psychopharmacology*, 7(3), 284–293. https://doi.org/10.1037/1064-1297.7.3.284

Madden, G. J., & Perone, M. (1999). Human sensitivity to concurrent schedules of reinforcement: Effects of observing schedule-correlated stimuli. *Journal of the Experimental Analysis of Behavior*, 71(3), 303–318. https://doi.org/10.1901/jeab.1999.71-303

Madden, G. J., Petry, N. M., Badger, G. J., & Bickel, W. K. (1997). Impulsive and self-control choices in opioid-dependent patients and non-drug-using control participants: Drug and monetary rewards. *Experimental and Clinical Psychopharmacology*, 5(3), 256–262. https://doi.org/10.1037/1064-1297.5.3.256

Magoon, M. A., & Critchfield, T. S. (2008). Concurrent schedules of positive and negative reinforcement: Differential-impact and differential-outcomes hypotheses. *Journal of the Experimental Analysis of Behavior*, 90(1), 1–22. https://doi.org/10.1901/jeab.2008.90-1

Matthews, L. R., & Temple, W. (1979). Concurrent schedule assessment of food preference in cows. *Journal of the Experimental Analysis of Behavior*, 32(2), 245–254. https://doi.org/10.1901/jeab.1979.32-245

Mazur, J. E. (1987). An adjusting procedure for studying delayed reinforcement. In M. L. Commons, J. E. Mazur, J. A. Nevin, & H. Rachlin (Eds.), *Quantitative analysis of behavior: The effect of delay and of intervening events on reinforcement value* (pp. 55–73). Hillsdale, NJ: Lawrence Erlbaum Associates.

Mazur, J. E., & Logue, A. W. (1978). Choice in a "self-control" paradigm: Effects of a fading procedure. *Journal of the Experimental Analysis of Behavior*, 30(1), 11–17. https://doi.org/10.1901/jeab.1978.30-11

Odum, A. L., Madden, G. J., Badger, G. J., & Bickel, W. K. (2000). Needle sharing in opioid-dependent outpatients: Psychological processes underlying risk. *Drug and Alcohol Dependence*, 60(3), 259–266. https://doi.org/10.1016/S0376-8716(00)00111-3

Perry, J. L., Nelson, S. E., & Carroll, M. E. (2008). Impulsive choice as a predictor of acquisition of IV cocaine self-administration and reinstatement of cocaine-seeking behavior in male and female rats. *Experimental and Clinical Psychopharmacology*, 16(2), 165–177. https://doi.org/10.1037/1064-1297.16.2.165

Rachlin, H., & Green, L. (1972). Commitment, choice and self-control. *Journal of the Experimental Analysis of Behavior*, 17(1), 15–22. https://doi.org/10.1901/jeab.1972.17-15

Rachlin, H., Raineri, A., & Cross, D. (1991). Subjective probability and delay. *Journal of the Experimental Analysis of Behavior*, 55(2), 233–244. https://doi.org/10.1901/jeab.1991.55-233

Reimers, S., Maylor, E. A., Stewart, N., & Chater, N. (2009). Associations between a one-shot delay discounting measure and age, income, education and real-world impulsive behavior. *Personality and Individual Differences, 47*(8), 973–978. https://doi.org/10.1016/J.PAID.2009.07.026

Rybarczyk, P., Koba, Y., Rushen, J., Tanida, H., & de Passillé, A. M. (2001). Can cows discriminate people by their faces? *Applied Animal Behaviour Science, 74*(3), 175–189. https://doi.org/10.1016/S0168-1591(01)00162-9

Schroeder, S. R., & Holland, J. G. (1969). Reinforcement of eye movement with concurrent schedules. *Journal of the Experimental Analysis of Behavior, 12*(6), 897–903. https://doi.org/10.1901/jeab.1969.12-897

Shahan, T. A. (2013). Attention and conditioned reinforcement. In G. J. Madden, W. V. Dube, T. D. Hackenberg, G. P. Hanley, & K. A. Lattal (Eds.), *APA handbook of behavior analysis*, Vol. 1. Methods and principles (pp. 387–410). Washington, DC: American Psychological Association.

Shahan, T. A., & Podlesnik, C. A. (2008). Quantitative analyses of observing and attending. *Behavioural Processes, 78*(2), 145–157. https://doi.org/10.1016/J.BEPROC.2008.01.012

Stein, J. S., Renda, C. R., Hinnenkamp, J. E., & Madden, G. J. (2015). Impulsive choice, alcohol consumption, and pre-exposure to delayed rewards: II. Potential mechanisms. *Journal of the Experimental Analysis of Behavior, 103*(1), 33–49. https://doi.org/10.1002/jeab.116

Thaler, R. H., & Benartzi, S. (2004). Save more tomorrow™: Using behavioral economics to increase employee saving. *Journal of Political Economy, 112*(S1), S164–S187. https://doi.org/10.1086/380085

Venniro, M., Zhang, M., Caprioli, D., Hoots, J. K., Golden, S. A., Heins, C., … Shaham, Y. (2018). Volitional social interaction prevents drug addiction in rat models. *Nature Neuroscience, 21*(11), 1520–1529. https://doi.org/10.1038/s41593-018-0246-6

Zuboff, S. (2019). *The age of surveillance capitalism: The fight for a human future at the new frontier of power*. PublicAffairs.

Verbal Behavior, Rule-Following, and Clinical Behavior Analysis

14

Humans are one of the few species on the planet who learn and teach a complex language to their offspring and peers. Our linguistic capacity exceeds that of any other species (Snowdon, 1990). This chapter outlines a behavior-analytic account of verbal behavior – talking, listening, reading, and so on. This account has led to teaching methods that have proven useful in helping children with autism and other developmental disabilities to acquire language. Needless to say, these successes have made a huge difference in the lives of these individuals and their parents.

Among language-able humans, an important category of verbal activity involves rules – creating rules, following rules, breaking the rules, and so on. Parents typically provide and enforce rules (no screen-time after 8:00 pm; be nice to grandma; don't drink milk out of the carton). That is, they verbally specify expected and forbidden behaviors and arrange consequences when the rules are followed or violated. Likewise, countries, cultures, and social groups provide verbally specified rules, norms, expectations, and laws. Those following/violating these rules will, likewise, experience the consequences. We also create our own rules, maxims, and personal codes of ethics. These verbally specified rules often make explicit contingencies of reinforcement ("You catch more bees with honey than vinegar") and punishment ("If you speed through 7th street, you'll get a ticket"). This chapter introduces two categories of rule-following. These are important in understanding human compliance with social norms and with authority figures.

Finally, this chapter discusses an activity that we all do, every day, during most of our waking hours – we talk to ourselves. This self-talk *is behavior* (an individual living organism's activity, public or private, which may be influenced by external or internal stimulation). What we say to ourselves may be influenced by external stimulation ("When will this light

An Introduction to Behavior Analysis, First Edition. Gregory J. Madden, Derek D. Reed, and Florence D. DiGennaro Reed.
© 2021 John Wiley & Sons Ltd. Published 2021 by John Wiley & Sons Ltd.

turn green!") and internal stimulation ("My stomach hurts; why did I order the diablo wings?"). Our internal dialogue is such a constant presence that most of us regard the voice in our head as *me*. For some, that voice is persistently positive ("I am so dope"), but for others the voice is chronically negative ("I am ugly, stupid, and unlovable"). Our self-talk may voice rules that work well in the short run ("I don't want to feel anxious so I'm not going to the party") but not in the long run ("I have no friends").

When the verbal content of cognition has a significant negative impact on daily living, many seek the help of a psychologist or behavior therapist. Many of the behavior-analytic principles covered in this book have helped people who seek such therapy, and we have covered many of them already (e.g., *graduated exposure therapy* and *contingency management of substance-use disorder*). This chapter focuses on new principles that clinical behavior analysts use to improve the lives of those who seek their help. These principles were derived from the study of human language, so let's start the chapter there.

Behavioral Approaches to Language

When you were young, you learned to communicate with others who spoke the same language, be that English, Portuguese, or sign language. Later, when you went to school, you learned about the parts of speech (nouns, verbs, etc.), syntax, and grammar (we know, it was horrible). But before you ever entered a classroom, you had a *functional* understanding of language. By *functional*, we mean that you were already able to "use your words" to obtain reinforcers and avoid punishers. You could ask for something you wanted ("Can I have a drink of water?"). You could imitate the words of others ("Daddy said 'bite me.'"). You could use your words to help others ("Watch out for that rock; it hurt my foot."). You could lie to avoid getting grounded ("No, I didn't do it.").

B. F. Skinner (1957) recognized the importance of language, and provided a functional approach to understanding it. Where his contemporaries catalogued language by its *structure*, Skinner provided a taxonomy of *functions*; that is, verbal behaviors (talking, writing, signing, etc.) that are operant activities, influenced by different kinds of antecedent stimuli, and different kinds of consequences. A thorough summary of Skinner's theory of verbal behavior is beyond the scope of this chapter. However, his taxonomy has helped behavior analysts to identify and remediate language deficiencies in children with autism and other developmental disabilities (Sundberg & Sundberg, 2011). For that reason, we provide a brief introduction to Skinner's functional taxonomy.

Skinner's Functional Taxonomy of Speaker Behavior

Skinner's account of verbal behavior focused on the behavior of the speaker; that is, the individual who is talking, writing, signing, and so on. Four of his categories of verbal operants are defined and described here. These categories have generated the most research and have proven most useful in helping children with autism acquire language skills (DeSouza et al., 2017).

ECHOIC

An **echoic** is *a verbal operant in which the response resembles the verbal antecedent stimulus and is maintained with a variety of socially mediated reinforcers.* Said less for-

Antecedent   Behavior   Consequence

mally, when the speaker makes an echoic response, they approximately or exactly repeat what someone else just said – they *echo* someone else's response. New parents spend a lot of time teaching their infants echoics such as "mama" and "dada." Mom, for example, says "mama" clearly for the baby, exaggerating her lip movements and doing so in a way that holds the baby's attention. When the echoic finally occurs, it is showered with social reinforcers.

Learning to make a vocal response that closely resembles a verbal antecedent stimulus is useful when teaching children with severe language deficits to speak. A child who has acquired the echoic operant will listen to the verbal stimulus ("cow"), attempt to say the same thing ("caa"), and will receive reinforcers from the teacher ("Yes! That's it! That is so good!"). Shaping may be used to improve the form of the response, moving from "caa" to "caw" to "cow." Mastering the echoic (i.e., repeating all verbal antecedent stimuli when asked to do so) is a foundational skill in learning to say new words. The next step is learning to say them under the right stimulus conditions.

MAND

An infant may first learn to say "water" as an echoic, but will later emit this verbal operant to get a drink. In doing so, the function of the verbal response "water" has changed – it is influenced by different antecedent stimuli and

Antecedent   Behavior   Consequence

different consequences. A **mand** is *a verbal operant occasioned by an establishing operation and maintained by the verbally specified reinforcer.* Less technically, manding is asking for something that will satisfy a current need – water, a turn with a toy, or attention. "Mand" derives from the word "de*mand*." The mand places a de*mand* on the listener – go get me a drink of water.

Manding benefits the speaker (Skinner, 1957). When faced with a difficult task (estab-lishing operation), we often mand "help," as this produces the reinforcer that meets our cur-rent need – assistance. Typically developing children acquire mands very early in the process of language learning, asking for food, water, toys, hugs, and a host of other momentarily effective reinforcers. Mands acquired by children with severe language deficits allow them to get the reinforcers they want, when they want them.

TACT

Saying "water" has a different function still when it is a tact. A **tact** is *a verbal operant occasioned by a nonverbal stimulus and maintained by a variety of social reinforcers.* When "water" is a

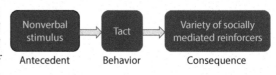

Antecedent   Behavior   Consequence

tact, it is said in the presence of water (a glass of water, a waterfall, a raindrop landing on the skin). When parents hear their toddler tact "water" in the presence of any of these water-related stimuli, they reinforce this behavior – "Yes, that is water! You're so smart." They do not reinforce saying "water" in the presence of other stimuli such as a toy, a chair, or a plate.

Note how "water" is a tact when occasioned by con*tact* with the nonverbal stimulus (the sight, taste, or feel of water) and a mand when initiated by an establishing operation (thirst). When tacting, one describes the environment to others ("Look, a falling star!") and the others (the listeners) reinforce this verbal behavior in a variety of ways ("Whoa, that was amazing!"). When we tact we share our experiences with others, often to their benefit. Tacts such as "The new Marvel movie is great!" or "Watch out!" benefit the listener who may otherwise miss these opportunities to experience positive and negative reinforcers.

Teaching a child with a language deficit to tact also benefits that child. If the child can accurately tact, they become more helpful to those around them, their parents, their siblings, their future friends. Our friends and loved ones are people who help us out. Teaching a child to tact teaches them to help others in one specific way – by drawing the attention of others to important things in their environment – water, falling stars, good movies. When a child learns to tact, they learn a behavior that helps them to be a friend.

INTRAVERBAL

An **intraverbal** is *a verbal response occasioned by a verbal discriminative stimulus, but the form of the response does not resemble that stimulus; intraverbals are main-*

| Antecedent | Behavior | Consequence |

tained *by a variety of social reinforcers.* In everyday language, intraverbals allow us to meaningfully interact with other verbal humans. For example, when asked "How are you?" (a verbal S^D), we respond with the intraverbal: "I'm doing well; how about you?" This everyday intraverbal is socially reinforced by the listener when they say, "I'm good too; thanks for asking." Intraverbals are the operants that make for meaningful conversations. For example, when we hear our friend say, "I think my boyfriend is cheating on me" (verbal S^D), our intraverbal response – "You deserve better" – is reinforced when our friend replies, "Thanks; that means a lot to me." As these examples make clear, intraverbals are important behaviors in our social interactions.

Intraverbals are also important in education. Your responses on exams are controlled by the questions. For example, if an item on an upcoming exam asks, "What is an intraverbal," this functions as a verbal S^D that increases the probability of providing a specific intraverbal response, a correct response that will be socially reinforced with points on the exam. Thus, not only is the intraverbal important in a child's social development, but it is also important in their ability to participate in an educational setting (Carr & Firth, 2005; Goldsmith et al., 2007; Sundberg & Michael, 2001). For these reasons, behavior analysts will teach children with autism important intraverbals such as answering questions and how to respond appropriately in a conversation (Charlop-Christy & Kelso, 2003; Sherer et al., 2001).

Training Verbal Operants

Typically developing children acquire echoics, mands, tacts, and intraverbals with seeming ease. These verbal operants are useful in acquiring new words (echoics), in recruiting the aid of others (mands), in helping others (tacts), and in interacting socially (intraverbals). Among children with autism and other developmental disabilities, these verbal operants may be limited in number and usage. This not only prevents them from successfully integrating into society, but it also impairs their ability to acquire the reinforcers available to language-able individuals. For example, an inability to address an establishing operation by manding evokes feelings of frustration in the child and their parents who are helpless to address the unspecified need. The child's frustration can take the form of problem behaviors, such as aggression or self-injury; these could be avoided if only the child could mand (Greer et al., 2016).

Source: Jose Luis Pelaez Inc./Getty Images

Behavior analysts have developed successful techniques for training verbal operants to children with autism and other developmental disabilities. There are too many of these techniques to list here, so we note just four of the most commonly used techniques, all of which will be familiar to you. Readers wanting more are referred to one of the many excellent review articles on this topic (DeSouza et al., 2017; Heath et al., 2015; Lorah et al., 2015; Sundberg & Sundberg, 2011).

The first of the commonly used techniques in teaching verbal operants is *contact with the antecedent stimulus*. Because verbal operants are influenced by antecedent stimuli, it is important that the individual observe those stimuli (Kisamore et al., 2013). For example, if a child does not hear the verbal stimulus "mama," an echoic response (saying "mama") is impossible. Likewise, if the individual does not see the cow in the field, tacting "cow" cannot happen.

The second technique is *prompting and fading* the correct verbal response (Leaf et al., 2016; Thomas et al., 2010). That is, when the antecedent stimulus does not evoke the correct response, it is prompted; "Are you hungry?" prompts the child to observe internal stimuli then tacted as "hungry." When the verbal response is later influenced by the stimulus alone ("I feel hungry mommy"), prompts are faded out.

The third technique is *shaping* (Newman et al., 2009). That is, when an approximation of the correct verbal response is emitted ("hungwy"), it is reinforced. Later, the individual will be asked for a closer approximation to obtain the reinforcer.

The final technique is to *arrange an effective reinforcer* (Hartman & Klatt, 2005), like lunch for a "hungwy" child. Readers are referred to Chapter 9 for a review of how to identify and arrange effective reinforcers.

Reading Quiz 1

For questions 1–8, indicate if the verbal response, given in bold, is an example of an echoic, a mand, a tact, or an intraverbal. For all items we will assume that the consequence functions as a reinforcer.

1. Jango is flying in to Paris for the first time. He looks out the window and sees the Eiffel Tower. He excitedly says to the person sitting next to him, **"Look, it's the Eiffel Tower!"** The person next to him looks out the window and nods, saying, "It's so beautiful."

2. Marina says, **"Take the picture of me in front of the fountain!"** Her Instragram boyfriend complies.
3. Bobby is a little bit thirsty when he sees his father walk into the living room with an ice-cold beer. Bobby says, **"Daddy, can I have a sip of your beer?"** Bobby's father gives him a sip.
4. Gregory asks his nephew, "How old are you?" His nephew replies, **"I'm free."** Gregory replies, "You're three? I thought you were four or five. You are such a smart child."
5. The psychiatrist is conducting an evaluation of a new patient. She holds up a Rorschach ink-blot card and says, **"Tell me what you see."** The patient says, "I see an elephant. Here are its ears, its mouth, its trunk." The psychiatrist nods knowingly.
6. Mom says, "Simon says, say 'moose.'" Jason replies **"moose."** Jason remains in the game.
7. The new employee extends his hand toward Carla and says, "Hello, nice to meet you." Although he looks like Carla's ex-boyfriend, she replies, **"It's nice to meet you as well."** The new employee smiles and Carla avoids being criticized for her rudeness (had she not replied politely).
8. Simone has an office with a window and sees that it is snowing outside. She loves the snow and walks to the interior of the building, where her coworkers do not have access to a window. She says, **"It's snowing! It's snowing!"** Her coworkers respond positively to this news, though not as positively as Simone.
9. When teaching children with language deficits to acquire new verbal operants, four techniques have proven useful. The first is that the individual needs to come into contact with the _____ _____. For example, if the individual is unaware that mom just said, "Simon says, say 'moose,'" it will be impossible to make the correct echoic response.
10. The second useful technique when teaching verbal operants is _____ and _____. When the verbal response is not happening when it should, this can really help. Once the verbal response happens, it can be reinforced.
11. The third useful technique when teaching verbal operants is _____. That is, reinforce the verbal response even if its form is not perfect. Over time, the teacher can reinforce successively closer approximations of the desired verbal response.
12. The fourth useful technique when teaching verbal operants is to arrange an effective _____. This is critical because these consequences are necessary for the acquisition, shaping, and maintenance of verbal behaviors.

The Behavior of the Listener

Skinner's functional approach to human language focused on the behavior of the speaker. Less emphasis was placed on how listeners understand what people are saying, writing, or signing. Discoveries made in the late twentieth century rekindled behavior analysts' interest in the behavior of the listener (Sidman & Cresson, 1973; Sidman & Tailby, 1982) and refined the meaning of "verbal behavior."

To have insights on this topic, we invite you to recall how you learned to understand the word "cow." Of course, you cannot remember this early learning, but enough research has been done that we can make some educated guesses. Even before your first words, your parents said "cow" while you looked at a picture book containing many barnyard animals, one of which was a cow. They pointed to the cow and said "cow," and later asked you to "Show me the cow." If you pointed to the correct animal, they were elated and, as shown in the left panel of Figure 14.1, provided social reinforcers ("That is a cow, you are so smart!").

Not to demean your accomplishment, but we could teach your dog something similar. If you don't believe us, check out the YouTube video called *Dog Understands 1022 Words*. There you will see how a dog named "Chaser" learned to "show me the cow" by finding a stuffed cow among a pile of toys. Although this is amazing, we would not consider Chaser's behavior *verbal*. We will point out the missing ingredient in a moment, but first notice what your parents did after they taught you to point to the cow (something we would never do with Chaser the dog); your parents showed you the picture of the cow and said, "What is this?" When you did not say "cow," they trained it first as an echoic ("Say *cow*") and then as an intraverbal tact. That is, you learned to say "cow" only when the picture of the cow was presented (tact) *and* when someone asked "What is this?" (intraverbal). When you correctly said "cow," your parents went out of their minds with joy, showered you with reinforcers, and asked you to repeat this display of genius for every visitor.

The second of these explicitly trained behaviors is illustrated in the center panel of Figure 14.1 – saying "cow" when asked to say what you see. The right panel shows the end-product of this training: symmetric relational responding. **Symmetric relational responding** is defined as *the behavior of relating two arbitrary stimuli as, in many ways, the same*. That is, when you heard someone say "cow" you related that auditory stimulus as, in many ways, the same as a picture of cow (right-pointing arrow in the right panel of Figure 14.1). When you saw a picture of a cow, you related that visual stimulus as, in many ways, the same as the sound "cow" (left-pointing arrow in the right panel of Figure 14.1). Chaser the dog could relate "cow" as the same as a stuffed cow in a pile of

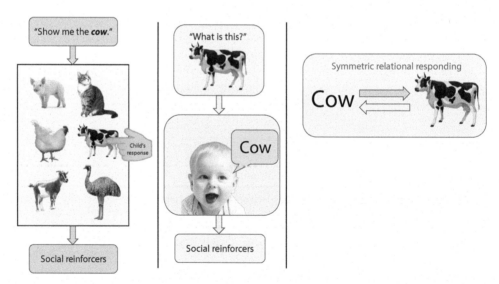

Figure 14.1 Parents typically teach their children the two relating behaviors shown at left. When they hear "cow," pointing to a cow is reinforced. When asked what a cow is, saying "cow" is reinforced. In this way, children learn to relate these stimuli symmetrically.

Source: cleanpng.com

toys (i.e., he could find the cow toy), but he could not say "cow," so there was no way for him to show us if he could relate the stuffed cow as the same as the word "cow." Symmetric relational responding is the key ingredient in verbal behavior. When these two stimuli are related symmetrically, the child is responding verbally; the child understands what "cow" means.

It is important to note a key term in the definition of symmetric relational responding – that word is "arbitrary." By this, we mean that neither the auditory stimulus "cow" nor the spoken word "cow" physically resembles a cow. "Cow" does not sound like a cow mooing, eating, or anything else that cows do. There is nothing about "cow" that suggests it should be related symmetrically with a cow. The relation between these stimuli is completely *arbitrary*, such that a cow could just as easily be related symmetrically with "vaca" (which it is, in Spanish speaking communities). Because "cow" and a cow do not in any way resemble each other, the principle of *generalization* (Chapter 12) cannot help us understand why a child relates "cow" with a cow. This symmetric relating of arbitrary stimuli is something unique to human speakers and listeners.

Of course, as a child, you didn't just learn about "cows," you also learned about "pigs," "hens," "goats," and other farm animals; not to mention learning to symmetrically relate "mama" with your mother, "dada" with your father, "breakfast" with that food they fed you in the morning, and "music" with pleasant sounds that allowed you to do the diaper dance. *Teaching an individual to symmetrically relate arbitrary stimuli, over and over again, with multiple examples*, like those shown in Figure 14.2, is referred to as **multiple-exemplar training**.

Figure 14.2 Parents explicitly teach their children to symmetrically relate many objects in their environment to words. That is, they teach them to orient toward the object when they hear the word *and* to say the words, when asked to identify the object. Eventually, children learn that if one relation is taught ("emu" → picture of emu) the symmetric version of that relation (picture of emu → "emu") will be reinforced too. That is, they master symmetric relational responding.
Source: cleanpng.com

If you have children one day, you can informally watch your own behavior as you conduct multiple-exemplar training, teaching your child to symmetrically relate verbal stimuli with their referents. "Show me the pig…(child points to pig)…that is a pig!" "What is this…can you say pig?" You will teach this hundreds, if not thousands, of times until, one day, after your child acquires a new unidirectional relational response ("show me the emu) → point to the picture of the emu) the symmetric relational response will occur with no further training. That is, your child, "all by herself," points to the emu and says "emu" (see the green dashed arrow at the bottom of Figure 14.2). The young speaker, through prior training experiences (multiple-exemplar training), has learned that, when it comes to verbal behavior, symmetric relational responding is always reinforced (Barnes-Holmes et al., 2004; Greer et al., 2007; Luciano et al., 2007; Petursdottir & Carr, 2007).

Nonverbal organisms, like Chaser the dog, are normally not taught to symmetrically relate stimuli in this way. Obviously, they cannot articulate a word like "emu." But if they were allowed to point at symbols instead of speaking, could they learn to relate stimuli symmetrically? A considerable amount of research has explored this question and the results thus far show that pigeons and sea lions can learn to do this, but only if they are given specialized training that they normally do not receive (Galizio & Bruce, 2018; Lionello-DeNolf, 2009). Other species such as rats, monkeys, baboons, and chimpanzees have thus far failed these tests of symmetric relational responding. (Lionello-DeNolf, 2009; Sidman et al., 1982). Perhaps one day researchers will arrange better training that will allow these species to pass a test of symmetric relational responding (Urcuioli, 2008). But one thing is for sure, animals in the wild do not learn to relate arbitrary stimuli symmetrically; they are not verbal.

EXPANDING THE VERBAL REPERTOIRE

The horizontal beige arrow in the top panel of Figure 14.3 illustrates prior training in which a child was explicitly taught to point to a horse when they hear "horse." That is, "horse" is the antecedent stimulus (e.g., "show me the horse") and the child points to a horse, standing in a field. The dashed green arrow pointing in the opposite direction shows the emergent (untrained) symmetric relational response. That is, because of prior multiple-exemplar training (Figure 14.2) the child spontaneously (without additional training) is able to say "horse" while looking at it.

In the same panel of Figure 14.3, the vertical beige arrow shows that the child was subsequently taught to say "horse" when they hear "colt" (e.g., the parent asks, "What is a colt?" and the child replies "A horse."). Once again, the dashed green arrow pointing in the opposite direction reveals the emergent (untrained) symmetric relational response; saying "colt" when they hear "horse."

Notice that in the upper panel the child has not been taught to relate "colt" and a horse as in any way the same. That is, the child was never asked to "show me the colt" nor to say "colt" while looking at a horse. The blue and orange dashed arrows in the lower panel of Figure 14.3 show these two untrained relating responses. If the child correctly says "colt" when they see a horse in the field (blue arrow) and points to the horse in the field when they hear "colt" (orange arrow), then we might say the child understands what "colt" means. Figure 14.3 makes explicit the relational responding that understanding is composed of.

Behavior analysts refer to this understanding as **stimulus equivalence**. *After explicitly teaching a unidirectional relation between three or more arbitrary stimuli (e.g., "horse" → real horse, "colt" → "horse"), symmetric relational responding is demonstrated between all stimuli (real horse → "horse", "horse" → "colt", real horse → "colt", "colt" → real horse). That is, the individual relates all of the stimuli, in many ways, as equivalent to one another.*[1]

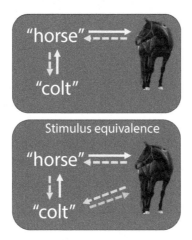

Figure 14.3 The upper panel shows two symmetric relational responses very similar to those in Figures 14.1 and 14.2. The lower panel shows two other relating behaviors (blue and orange dashed arrows) that emerge in language-able humans without explicit training. The combination of all of these relations is referred to as *stimulus equivalence*.

Source: cleanpng.com

Not surprisingly, only humans have demonstrated stimulus equivalence; not pigeons, not sea lions, not even a colt. In human infants, the ability to demonstrate stimulus equivalence is correlated with the acquisition of language (Peláez et al., 2000). That is, children with greater language proficiency do better on tests of stimulus equivalence. In short, human language and the ability to understand words is fundamentally about relational responding, that is, relating arbitrary stimuli as, in many ways, equivalent to one another.

Verbal Behavior and Emotions

When listening to an engaging podcast filled with tense moments, inviting love stories, or compelling descriptions of the unfairness of others, we experience emotions as if we were in direct contact with these events. Objectively we realize we are just driving and listening to words, but our emotions of fear, tenderness, or anger reveal something else is going on; something not experienced by the family dog, riding along with its head out the window. Our emotional responses to verbal stimuli are such a common experience that we rarely realize how uniquely human it is or wonder why it occurs. As you have probably guessed, the answer has something to do with verbal behavior and stimulus equivalence.

The **psychological function of verbal stimuli** refers to *the emotion-evoking function of verbal stimuli, despite those stimuli having never acquired Pavlovian conditioned-stimulus (CS) function*. Figure 14.4 will walk us through this definition using an example from Chapter 4. You may recall from that chapter a young girl, Annora, who had a negative experience with a dog and subsequently experienced a debilitating fear of all dogs. The dog that originally attacked her acquired a Pavlovian CS function. That is, the sight of the dog signaled a delay reduction to the unconditioned stimulus (US) event – a vicious attack. Because of Pavlovian learning, the mere sight of the dog (the CS alone) evoked Annora's fear (the conditioned response, CR); see the top panel of Figure 14.4.

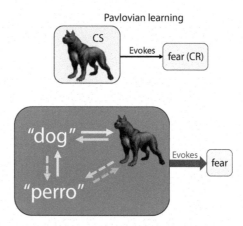

Pavlovian learning

Figure 14.4 For Annora, the sight of a dog evoked a fear response because of prior Pavlovian learning. Because Annora is a verbal human, she demonstrates all of the relational responses shown in the gray panel (*stimulus equivalence*). Because Annora relates the verbal stimuli "dog" and "perro" as equivalent with an actual dog, these words evoke a fear response similar to that evoked by an actual dog.

Source: cleanpng.com

Because Annora had previously learned to relate the auditory stimulus "dog" symmetrically with actual dogs, this verbal stimulus readily evoked a fear response. For example, when her older brother tormented her by yelling "dog!", Annora displayed fear despite no dog being present. When Annora learned that "perro" means "dog" in Spanish (vertical arrows in Figure 14.4), this auditory stimulus was readily added to form a three-member stimulus equivalence class composed of "dog," "perro," and actual dogs. Because the three stimuli are treated, in many ways, as equivalent to one another, when her brother yelled "perro!", Annora displayed a fear response, despite "perro" never having signaled a delay-reduction to a canine attack (Dougher et al., 1994).

As you might predict, when Annora's fear response was extinguished through Pavlovian extinction-based therapy (see Chapter 4 for details), the verbal stimuli related as equivalent with dogs also lost their ability to evoke Annora's fear response. Bad news for her tormenting brother, but good news for Annora, who, to this day, has no lingering fear of actual dogs, "dogs," or "perros."

Reading Quiz 2

1. The characteristic of verbal behavior that makes it verbal is _____ relational responding. For example, the auditory stimulus "book" is related, in many ways, as the same as a book.

2. It appears that the way in which we learn to relate verbal stimuli symmetrically is through _____ _____ training. That is, we are trained with many, many examples of how symmetrically relating verbal stimuli (e.g., "book") with its referent (a book) is always reinforced. With enough training with new examples, it appears that humans begin symmetrically relating novel verbal stimuli, without explicit training with the novel stimuli.

3. When an individual can relate three or more stimuli in all of the trained and untrained ways illustrated in Figure 14.3, they have demonstrated stimulus _____. They behave as though all of the stimuli are, in many ways, the same.
4. The only species to unequivocally demonstrate stimulus equivalence is the _____ species.
5. Stimulus equivalence emerges developmentally as children acquire _____.
6. A verbal stimulus, like "dog" has a _____ function if it evokes an emotional response, despite that verbal stimulus never having acquired a Pavlovian CS function.

Rules and Rule-Governed Behavior

Now that we have a basic understanding of the learning and relational responding that underlies human language, let us explore one of the key advantages conferred to those who have mastered verbal behavior. Humans, because of language, have a massive advantage over other, nonverbal species – they don't have to learn things in a trial-and-error fashion. Instead, they can learn from others who tell them what to do.

You might recall Thorndike's cat from Chapter 5, who was tasked with escaping from a puzzle box. The cat no doubt made hundreds of futile attempts before stumbling upon the correct response that opened the door. By contrast, were any of us placed in the puzzle box, the simple verbal instruction "pull the string" would readily lead to the response that opens the door. Likewise, a larger set of instructions can guide us through the assembly of a FJÄLLBO (shelving unit) purchased at Ikea. Without these instructions, we may never correctly assemble the unit.

Behavior acquired and maintained by interacting with the contingencies of reinforcement alone is called **contingency-shaped behavior** (Skinner, 1966). The behavior of Thorndike's cat was contingency shaped; it was acquired and maintained by interacting with the contingency of reinforcement (*IF string-pull → THEN escape from the box*).

Some human behaviors are contingency shaped. For example, you learned to walk through a contingency-shaping process. Much like the cat in the puzzle box, you made hundreds of futile attempts to stand and walk before you eventually took your first successful step. Even if your parents said things like "take a step, take a step," such instructions were useless in specifying the motor movements needed to maintain balance. By interacting with the contingencies of punishment (falling to the floor when the behavior failed) and reinforcement (maintaining balance), gravitational contingencies shaped your first steps. Even today, our walking is contingency shaped. We cannot verbally specify all of the small muscular adjustments necessary to maintain balance while walking. The best we can do is to provide a gross description of what we can see, "Well, you put one foot in front of the other…"

By contrast, **rule-governed behavior** describes *behavior influenced by a verbal description of the operative three-term contingency (antecedent-behavior-consequence*; Peláez & Moreno, 1999; Skinner, 1966). For example, the instructions provided with the FJÄLLBO describe antecedents ("When you have completed Step 12 …"), behaviors ("… attach the shelf labeled D"), and consequences ("With the completion of this step, your FJÄLLBO is ready for use"). Following these instructions is reinforced with a useful shelving unit, a consequence the user may otherwise have never achieved.

Why Follow the Rules?

Among humans, rule-governed behavior is quite common. When your mother told you to "Put your dirty dishes in the dishwasher…now!", you complied with this command (or "mand" to use the taxonomy introduced earlier). When our mapping app tells us to turn left on 18th street, we follow this instruction too. These examples point to two reasons for following rules, both rooted in reinforcement. We will differentiate two kinds of rule-governed behaviors – *pliance* and *tracking* – based on the kinds of reinforcers that maintain these behaviors.

PLIANCE

The first category of rule-governed behavior occurs because of socially mediated positive and negative reinforcers. For example, if you followed your mother's instruction by loading the dishwasher, your rule-following contacted a negative reinforcer of the avoidance variety (SR_A-); that is, you avoided her wrath. Alternatively, if you had a kind mother, then her socially mediated consequence was a positive reinforcer ("Thank you dear; you're such a help to me"). *Rule-governed behavior occurring because of socially mediated positive or negative reinforcers* is called **pliance** (as in com*pliance*; Hayes et al., 1989).

Pliance is common in everyday life. When children are given an instruction by parents, teachers, baby-sitters, and so on, there are often socially mediated reinforcing consequences for following those rules. For example, the baby-sitter may reinforce pliance by reading an extra bedtime story. Likewise, there are socially mediated consequences for complying with societal rules such as "Stand respectfully when the national anthem is played." Complying with this rule allows us to avoid a glaring look, a "tisk tisk" from someone nearby, or a reputational loss (SR_A-). As evidence that these socially mediated negative reinforcers play a role in our pliance, consider that we never stand respectfully when the national anthem is played on TV (e.g., during the Olympics or before watching a baseball game) because the probability of a socially mediated consequence is zero.

You may be familiar with the Stanley Milgram experiments on obedience. The studies were conducted at Yale University in the 1960s to better understand the atrocities of World War II. Specifically, how could German soldiers obey Nazi officers' orders to exterminate millions of predominantly Jewish concentration camp detainees? Milgrim wanted to know if Americans would similarly comply with the instructions of an authority figure (labeled E, for "experimenter," in the inset picture) to administer a series of increasingly painful electric shocks to another human being (labeled A, for "actor"). Of course, the shocks were not real, but the actor receiving them behaved as though they were painful and dangerous ("Let me out of here! My heart is bothering me!").

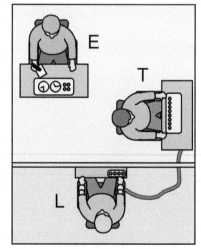

Source: Fred the Oyster, https://commons.wikimedia.org/wiki/File:Milgram_experiment_v2.svg#/media/File:Milgram_experiment_v2.svg, CC BY-SA 4.0

The results of the study were alarming: 100% of the subjects (S in the picture) pressed all of the sequentially arranged buttons on their panel until they reached the one labeled "300 volts" (which is a shock that can kill). Worse still, 65% of the subjects complied with all instructions provided by the authority figure, delivering the highest shock possible – 450 volts (Milgram, 1963). A contemporary derivation of the Milgram experiment is Derren Brown's Netflix special, *The Push*. A cleverly engineered series of instructions and gradually intensifying negative consequences for failing to comply produce an extreme form of pliance – following instructions to push someone off a building. Brown's results were similar to Milgram's; most participants reluctantly complied with the instruction to push the actor to his "death."

The obedience of Milgram and Brown's participants could be described as *pliance* if they followed these instructions because they anticipated socially mediated positive and negative reinforcers for instruction-following. In Milgram's experiment, unmistakable stimuli gave the experimenter his authority (an individual wearing a lab coat and speaking authoritatively in an office at an Ivy League university). The close proximity of the authority figure appears also to have functioned as an S^D signaling that important negative consequences could be avoided by following orders; much like the negative reinforcement contingencies employed by Nazi officers. Supporting this hypothesis, Milgram found that pliance dropped substantially when the S^D was removed, when the experimenter provided instructions by telephone. But when the experimenter entered the room to provide the same instructions in person, pliance immediately increased with this reintroduction of the S^D (Milgram, 1965).

To summarize, pliance is common because we are surrounded by people who positively and negatively reinforce rule-following. Like other operant behaviors, pliance is more likely to occur in the presence of S^Ds that signal a high probability of socially mediated reinforcement. Thus, we comply with our boss' instructions, but are less likely to follow the same instruction given by a low-status employee who cannot give us a raise or terminate our employment. We are least likely to follow instructions in S^Δ situations – pliance is improbable when an internet ad instructs us, "Don't delay! Order your vita-juicer today." Because the ad cannot deliver a socially mediated reinforcer, pliance does not occur. If you do order the vita-juicer, it is because your instruction-following is an instance of *tracking*, which is maintained by a different category of reinforcers.

TRACKING

The second category of rule-following occurs because doing so allows us to access reinforcers that would otherwise be difficult to obtain. For example, if we open the box containing the 59 parts needed to assemble our new FJÄLLBO, but no assembly instructions are found, our chances of success are very low. Likewise, trying to find 3436 West Sierra St. in a new city would be next to impossible without instructions provided by a navigation app, a resident of the city, or our friend who lives at that address. Without instructions, we would drive for hours in a trial-and-error fashion before eventually finding the street or giving up.

Tracking may be defined as *rule-following occurring because the instructions appear to correctly describe operant contingencies (reinforcement, extinction, or punishment) that operate in the world* (Hayes et al., 1989). The words and diagrams in the FJÄLLBO instructions appear to correctly describe how to build the shelving unit. Thus, we follow the instructions to obtain the positive reinforcer (a fully assembled FJÄLLBO). Similarly, broken down on the side of the road we access a YouTube video instructing us how to change a flat tire. Tracking follows because it appears that following the steps described will lead to the specified reinforcer – a changed tire. We track the instructions provided by our mapping app because doing so is reinforced, not by the app, but by the natural contingencies operating in the world – we arrive at our destination.

It is important to note that one cannot discriminate between pliance and tracking based on the topography of rule-following. These categories are based on *function*, not on *form*. That is, a *functional relation* exists between pliance and pliance-contingent socially mediated positive and negative reinforcers. Likewise, a *functional relation* exists between tracking and operant contingencies that naturally operate in the world.

Persistently Following Incorrect Rules

In 1998, Dr. Andrew Wakefield and his colleagues published a paper in the prestigious British medical journal, the *Lancet*. The authors claimed that the measles, mumps, and rubella (MMR) vaccine caused autism in children. Wakefield's research methods broke many of the rules of good experimental design that were outlined in Chapter 2. For example, their data were correlational (correlation does not imply causation) and were based in part on parents' self-reports (subject to human biases and recall errors). Later reporting revealed that Wakefield altered the medical records of every single child in the study published in the *Lancet* (he faked his data). A hearing convened by the British government's General Medical Council concluded in 2010 that Wakefield was a fraud, and 10 of his coauthors on the *Lancet* paper agreed. In the same year, after many scientifically valid studies revealed no connection between the MMR vaccine and autism, the *Lancet* retracted Wakefield's article. However, these decisions were too late in coming. By 2008, hundreds of thousands of parents had adopted the rule, "*IF you vaccinate your child →* THEN *the child will develop autism.*"

Source: Fibonacci Blue/Flickr/CC BY 2.0

These anti-vax parents are adamant in their adherence to this rule. From their perspective, they are tracking. That is, they are following the "don't vaccinate" rule because it appears to correctly describe a contingent relation between refusing vaccinations (behavior) and the avoidance of autism (SR_A-). This is a sad example of how humans will sometimes persistently follow incorrect rules. Sad because this rule-following has led to an historic increase in MMR and no decrease whatsoever in the prevalence of autism (Centers for Disease Control and Prevention, 2018).

Laboratory research on rule-following suggests that humans will often follow rules that do not accurately describe the reinforcement contingencies in operation. For example, Hayes et al. (1986) arranged alternating contingencies of point-delivery that were expected to maintain a high rate of responding when a fixed-ratio (FR) schedule was in operation, and a low rate when a differential reinforcement of low rate (DRL) schedule was in effect. One group of participants was given minimal instructions and they gradually learned to press the button quickly when the FR was in effect (orange light on) and to press more slowly when the DRL was active (red light on). However, when a different group of participants was instructed that the best way to earn points was to press slowly regardless of which light was on, they rigidly follow these instructions, earning fewer points when the FR schedule was in effect.

Hayes et al. (1986) reasoned that following the "press slowly" rule was not an instance of tracking – the rule did not accurately describe how to effectively earn points. Instead, following the instruction was an instance of *pliance*; participants followed the instructions because they came from an authority figure – the experimenter – and authority figures can deliver socially mediated consequences for compliance and noncompliance (as in the Milgram experiment).

As a thought experiment, imagine what would happen if the "press slowly" instruction was provided by an agent who had no authority; that is, they could never deliver a reinforcing consequence for following their rule. For example, while playing a video game that sometimes requires fast button-pressing and sometimes slow button-pressing, an in-game character, we'll call him Jasper, appears on the screen and tells you to "press slowly." We know that

Jasper's advice is worthless, so we will not engage in tracking. But will we engage in pliance? It depends. If Jasper has the ability to handsomely reinforce our rule-following, then we will do what he says (pliance). However, if Jasper is powerless, pliance is unlikely to occur (see Cerutti, 1994 for data consistent with the outcomes of this thought experiment).

The more reinforcers and punishers an authority figure controls, the more pliance will occur. This can help us understand the behavior of anti-vax parents who live in the Hasidic

Source: Dennis Jarvis/Flickr/CC BY-SA 2.0

Jewish neighborhoods in Brooklyn, New York. This tightly knit, tradition-bound community strictly adheres to religious rules regarding diet, prayer, and dress. So when a prominent rabbi instructed the community to refuse vaccinations (Belluz, 2019), their pliance is understandable. Similarly, parents who identify strongly with a social group committed to anti-vax practices may refuse vaccines because doing so is positively reinforced with credit, praise, and so on from the group and negatively reinforced by avoiding criticism as a "sellout" (pliance).

Are We Hopelessly Compliant?

The results of the Milgram experiments and Derren Brown's Netflix special are a little depressing. Although their findings make us wonder if humans are hopelessly compliant, this is the wrong question to ask. A better question is, *what conditions increase and decrease pliance?* Such a question is consistent with the second goal of behavior analysis – to identify functional variables that can influence behavior.

We have already identified one functional variable that increases and decreases pliance – if the individual or group giving the instruction controls powerful reinforcers, pliance is likely to occur; if they do not, pliance is less likely. Another pliance-decreasing variable is punishment. Specifically, when pliance produces an easily discriminated, highly negative consequence, pliance decreases (Cerutti, 1991; Galizio, 1979). For example, if a coach instructs a player to cheat and the compliant athlete is disqualified from the competition (an easily discriminated negative consequence of pliance), complying with the coach's unethical instructions is unlikely to happen again.

A similar outcome occurred among the Hasidic Jews of Brooklyn. As a measles epidemic spread through this small community (an easily detectable, highly negative consequence), parents began rejecting the rules provided by their rabbi. Because the negative consequences of following anti-vax rules are more difficult to see in other communities (where most children are vaccinated and rates of MMR are low), anti-vax pliance continues.

To summarize, rules, instructions, and norms are useful. When they accurately describe operant contingencies operating in the world (*IF you smoke cigarettes → THEN you are likely to die of cancer*), they can literally save our lives. When we follow these adaptive rules, we are *tracking*. Other instances of rule-following – *pliance* – occur because of social consequences (*IF you sit in that chair, young man → THEN you will be in trouble*). In daily life, tracking contingencies are sometimes pitted against pliance contingencies. That is, tracking pulls our behavior in one direction (*IF I vaccinate my child → THEN we will avoid measles, mumps, and rubella*) and pliance pulls in the opposite direction (*IF I vaccinate my child → THEN my close community of anti-vaxxers will shun me*). What we choose to do often depends on the choice-influencing variables discussed in Chapter 13 – reinforcer immediacy, frequency, size, and so on.

The Dark Side of Tracking

When Skinner (1969) discussed the many advantages of rules and rule-following, he also discussed their dark side. When given an accurate set of instructions, a code of conduct, or a rule of the road (to name a few), tracking ensues, reinforcers are earned, and punishers avoided. However, there is a price to be paid for this efficiency – rules can suppress variability, and this leaves behavior unprepared for the inevitable changes in contingencies of reinforcement and punishment. To take an extreme example, the behavior of a robotic arm that welds parts together on an auto assembly line strictly fol-

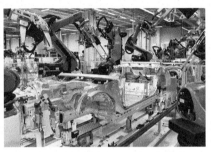

Source: BMW Werk Leipzig/Wikipedia/CC BY-SA 2.0

lows the rules of its programming: detect object entering welding zone, move left, weld, move right, repeat. This produces amazing safety and efficiency until the contingencies change, when an employee accidentally enters the welding zone, and the arm behaves as instructed.

Human behavior, established by a simple rule like "press slowly," can produce lockstep tracking that, like the robotic arm, lacks the variability that prepares it for a contingency change (Hayes et al., 1986; Matthews et al., 1977). Outside the lab, an assembly-line worker may have been given the rule, "Hard work is always rewarded" and tracked the rule in a lockstep fashion for years. While this resulted in regular paychecks and occasional promotions, the employee may have been more successful if a different rule were followed: "Work hard when the boss is around; the rest of the time take it easy." The latter adaptively conserves energy and may reduce injuries on the job.

The dark side of tracking is that this form of rule-following constrains behavioral variability. Why explore an alternative behavior if rule-following is working? Recognizing this dark side of tracking, innovators encourage us to "Question everything" (Euripides), "Live dangerously … Send your ships into uncharted seas!" (Friedrich Nietzche), or "Don't let your mind set limits that are not really there" (Zadie Smith).

As discussed in Chapter 5, artificial intelligence arrives at more effective solutions by sending its ships into uncharted seas, occasionally trying something new, and carefully evaluating if the outcome is superior. So, here's a maxim to live by, "If a rule is working, mostly follow it; but periodically try something different and carefully note the consequences. If that something else works better, do that more often." Not

Zadie Smith (1975 - present)

Source: David Shankbone/ Wikipedia/CC BY 3.0

as catchy as Apple's "Think different," but its specificity is inspired by behavioral and computer science.

1. Behavior acquired and maintained by interacting with the contingencies of reinforcement alone is called _____-_____ behavior.

2. _____-_____ behavior describes behavior influenced by a verbal description of the operative three-term contingency (antecedent–behavior–consequence).

For questions 3–6, indicate if the behavior given in bold is rule-governed or contingency-shaped.

3. The student was unable to study at her usual time, in the evening. So, she **studied in the morning**, before she went to work. After studying in the morning, she found that she remembered the course materials better than when she studied at night. As a result, she earned better test scores and was better able to use what she was learning in her daily life. Going forward, the student chooses to do her studying in the morning, before she goes to work.

4. Stenny thinks the stop sign at the corner of 7th and Main streets is stupid. No one is ever there, so stopping seems unnecessary and it slows him down. Nonetheless, **Stenny stops** every time he comes to the corner of 7th and Main streets.

5. When he was young, Steve was told to chew his food 40 times before swallowing. He followed this rule throughout his life, despite never experiencing any negative consequences when he occasionally chewed less, nor any positive consequences for **chewing 40 times**.

6. Marge is a waitress at the diner. On Friday a man comes in for a cup of coffee. She provides him good service, filling his cup whenever it nears empty. He leaves her a sizable tip. On Saturday the man returns and orders a full breakfast. **Marge goes out of her way to provide the man with excellent service**. Once again, he leaves her a big tip. The man returns a year later and Marge, once again, is rewarded for the excellent service she provides him.

7. _____ is defined as rule-following occurring because the instructions appear to correctly describe operant contingencies operating in the world.

8. Rule-governed behavior occurring because of socially mediated consequences (positive or negative reinforcers) is called _____.

For questions 9–13, indicate if the rule-following behavior given in bold is an instance of pliance or tracking.

9. A man sits in Angel's section of the diner. As she is approaching him, Marge stops by and says, "Give that man really good service; he's a good tipper." **Angel provides good service** and receives a large tip in return.

10. Lynn's toilet is overflowing and she needs to turn the water off *now!* She reaches down to the water supply knob and remembers her dad's rule, "Righty tighty, left loosey." **She turns the knob to the right** and the water stops flowing out of the toilet and onto the floor.

11. "If you know what's good for you, you will clean your room right now." **The child begins cleaning the room.**

12. The shift supervisor says, "Whoever sells the most deserts tonight wins a $50 gift certificate." **The waitstaff works hard to sell deserts to their customers.**

13. In April, Atticus told his father that the Lady Gaga episode was the worst episode of the Simpsons. In June, his father is channel surfing and the Lady Gaga episode of the Simpsons comes on. **Atticus' father changes the channel.**

14. Pliance is more likely to occur when the individual who provided the rule has the authority to deliver _____ for rule following (compliance) and _____ for rule-breaking (noncompliance).

15. The *dark side of tracking* is that rules suppress behavioral _____. This can leave us without a solution when the operant contingencies change. It also makes it less likely that we will discover new, more efficient, and effective ways to behave.

Breaking the Rules in Clinical Psychology

Some of the behavior analysts who studied rule-governed behavior in the late twentieth century were clinical psychologists who were also conducting talk therapy with clients experiencing depression, anxiety, obsessive-compulsive disorder, and so on. These researchers recognized the parallels between the maladaptive rule-following observed in the lab and the problems experienced in daily life by their clients (e.g., Zettle & Hayes, 1982). Specifically, clients appeared to be rigidly following a set of maladaptive rules; rules that they regarded as absolutely correct and never to be strayed from. For example, a rule like "*IF I attend the party → THEN others will notice how awkward/ugly/stupid I am*" is maladaptive because, when followed, it is unfalsifiable. That is, if the client stays home, they will never know that a good time might have been had at the party. Such *maladaptive tracking* can greatly constrict healthy living.

Maladaptive pliance is also an issue in therapy. Individuals seeking the assistance of a therapist often rigidly follow rules because they place a high value on social positive reinforcers (praise, credit, etc.) and social negative reinforcers (the avoidance of blame, criticism, etc.). This social reinforcement contingency can undermine progress in therapy if, for example, the client follows the therapist's advice not because it leads to effective action (tracking) but because it pleases the therapist (pliance; Hayes et al., 1989). When therapy ends and social reinforcers are no longer provided by the therapist for adhering to the rules of therapy, it should be no surprise when pliance undergoes extinction and the benefits of therapy are lost.

ESB Professional/Shutterstock.com

Recognizing these pitfalls of rule-following, these clinical researchers sought a new approach to conducting talk therapy; one informed by behavioral research (Hayes et al., 1999, 2004, 2009). To understand what was new about this therapy, it helps to know something about most other forms of psychotherapy, which are grounded in the commonly held intuition that thoughts are important – they play a causal role in human behavior (Beck, 2005). This "thoughts are important" hypothesis accords well with the client's belief that changing their thoughts is a prerequisite to valued behaviors such as behaving confidently, responsibly, and compassionately toward others. With this mutually agreed upon hypothesis, the traditional psychotherapist's job is to search for maladaptive thoughts, as though they revealed a "computer virus" in the brain. When the virus is detected in the thoughts voiced by the client, the therapist installs a "software patch," of sorts, by challenging the maladaptive thoughts and replacing them with more rational modes of thinking. This is intuitively appealing – if thoughts cause behavior, then "installing" better thoughts should change behavior.

But, like all behavior analysts Hayes et al. (1999, 2009) recognized the fallacy of this "thoughts cause behavior" hypothesis. Their new approach, called *Acceptance and Commitment Therapy* or ACT (pronounced "act"), was designed to therapeutically undermine the client's rules about the causal nature of thoughts. For example, the client might argue that their depressive thoughts *caused* them to stay home instead of attending the party. Is this true? Chapter 1 discussed the fallacy of arguing that one behavior (a depressive thought) causes a second behavior (staying home). The fallacy is revealed by asking, "And what caused the depressive thought; a third behavior? And what caused the third behavior, a fourth behavior?" Causal variables are to be found elsewhere, and this book has summarized a myriad of functional variables that influence behavior.

In talk therapy, the ACT therapist might undermine the "thoughts cause behavior" rule by asking the client to walk around the room while repeating the thought, "I can't walk." As the client realizes it is possible to have this thought *and* behave in a way that contradicts it, the "thoughts cause behavior" hypothesis is held a little less firmly. The ACT therapist uses many such techniques to undermine the belief that thoughts are important and must be controlled in order to behave in accord with one's values (Levin et al., 2012).

A second tactic used by ACT therapists is to point out why the client's "I must control my thoughts" rule is both impossible and leads to suffering. This tactic was inspired by the *verbal behavior* research summarized earlier in this chapter. In particular, the finding that what makes verbal behavior *verbal* is symmetric relational responding. When the client has the thought "*IF I have depressive thoughts and feelings → THEN I cannot behave in accord with my values,*" they are presenting to themselves a verbal stimulus ("depressive thoughts and feelings") that is related symmetrically with, you guessed it, actual depressive thoughts and feelings. And when, at other times, actual depressive feelings arise, you will not be surprised to learn that depressive thoughts follow (Wenzlaff et al., 1991). Thus, rules about controlling thoughts and feelings serve only to prompt into existence that which the client is trying so desperately to suppress.

This process may be experienced firsthand when we tell you, "Whatever you do, don't think of a white bear. No, really, your life depends on it – don't think of a white bear." When you read or hear this, what do you inevitably do? Because you long ago learned that "white bear" should be related symmetrically with images of white bears (see Figure 14.5), you cannot help but think of a white bear (Wegner & Schneider, 2003).

Consistent with this inability to suppress unwanted thoughts and feelings, clients who try to control these private events suffer more than those who adopt a different coping strategy

Figure 14.5 Verbal behavior involves symmetric relational responding between the verbal stimulus (e.g., "white bear") and other stimuli (like polar bears). When asked to not think of a white bear, we automatically respond symmetrically and think of a white bear (Wegner & Schneider, 2003). Thus, the advice/rule – "Don't think those problematic thoughts; think these thoughts instead" – may serve to increase the probability of thinking those problematic thoughts.

Source: pixabay.com

(Degenova et al., 1994; Hayes et al., 2006; Masedo & Esteve, 2007). Consider the panic-disorder client who feels a twinge of anxiety and tries to suppress this by thinking "I must not have a panic attack." Because the verbal stimulus "panic" is related symmetrically with feelings of anxiety, the privately stated rule serves only to induce more anxiety and perhaps a full-blown panic attack. For the same reason, the rule, "Just say no to drugs and alcohol," is a failing strategy for promoting drug abstinence. The implication for ACT therapy is that the path to behavior change does not involve trying to control thoughts and feelings. Indeed, from an ACT perspective, attempting such control *is the problem*, not the solution (Hayes & Wilson, 1994). These concepts are explored in Extra Box 1.

EXTRA BOX 1: IF THOUGHTS ARE IMPORTANT, PREPARE TO SUFFER

While language allows our species to stand on the shoulders of giants and improve living conditions in ways unimaginable to our ancestors, it appears to come with some unwanted baggage. Humans are the only species on the planet who, when blessed with ample food, shelter, freedom from disease, and a partner that loves them, can nonetheless feel anxious, depressed, unloved, unworthy, and, in some cases, suicidal (Hayes et al., 1999, 2009). While it is tempting to blame our hectic lifestyles, social media, or income inequality, unwarranted human suffering is far older than these social ills. Suicide is ancient; its prevalence led the Greeks to debate it and the Bible to admonish against it. More than 2,400 ago, the Buddha's teachings on psychological suffering resonated with his fellow iron-age people: "it is only suffering that I describe, and the cessation of suffering."[2]

More recently, Mark Twain is said to have quipped, "I am an old man and have known a great many troubles, but most of them never happened." This points to something older than social media and income inequality, something as old as human language. Where other species experience negative emotions only when aversive events are occurring, humans experience these emotions before, during, and after the aversive event. Indeed, as Twain notes, most of the thoughts that occasion negative emotions are thoughts about things that will never occur – we call this "worrying".

We might know that worrying makes us miserable, but we feel powerless to stop it. When we master symmetric relational responding, we experience thoughts of the past and future as, in many ways, equivalent to the things thought about. Figure 14.4 illustrated how overt verbal stimuli can evoke negative emotions, and it appears the same principle applies to private verbal stimuli – self-talk (see inset diagram; Hayes et al., 1999, 2009; Skinner, 1953, 1969). Thus, the recollection of past events, or imagined future events, puts language-able humans in a position to experience psychological suffering like no other species on earth – congratulations.

Source: Sheryl Griffin/Getty Images; cleanpng.com

Evaluating if language is responsible for human psychological suffering is difficult. Parents are understandably unwilling to have their children randomly assigned to a control group who never acquires language, despite the possibility that they might suffer less. Instead, we must look for "natural experiments" in which circumstances conspire to turn OFF verbal behavior. Such was the case for Dr. Jill Bolte Taylor, who experienced a massive stroke on the left side of her brain – the side involved in verbal behavior. What she was left with was the right hemisphere, which focuses on stimuli happening right now, not what has happened before, and not what one imagines will happen in the future. In a 2008 TED talk, Dr. Bolte Taylor describes how she gradually, over the course of a few hours, lost all ability to engage in verbal behavior; her self-talk went completely silent; her ability to read, write, or understand the verbal behavior of others was entirely lost. And what was her experience? Years later, after acquiring the verbal behavior necessary to describe the experience, she described it as peaceful, euphoric, liberating; hardly the stuff of human psychological suffering.

Learning to skillfully live with this gift of verbal behavior, particularly private verbal behavior – cognition – is the goal of ACT therapy. The overarching goal is to adopt a more flexible approach to thinking. Thoughts are not going away, so learning to *have them*, instead of *them having you*, is a skill worth mastering. The following sections continue to provide a brief overview of some of the techniques used by ACT therapists to help their clients "think different" about thoughts. Of course, space does not permit a complete description of ACT. If the approach described here is of interest, and developing a flexible approach to cognition sounds like a skill worth acquiring, there are several practical workbooks available for use outside of formalized therapy sessions. A few of these books are listed in the "Further Readings" section at the end of this chapter.

The "Acceptance" in Acceptance and Commitment Therapy

Clients seeking the help of a behavior therapist often have developed avoidance rules that guide their behavior. For example, the rule – "*IF I don't talk to people I am attracted to→ THEN I will avoid feelings of anxiety and rejection*" – specifies a strategy for avoiding unwanted thoughts and feelings. But the rule requires that the client close off a rather large part of the world. Thus, the price paid for safety from unwanted thoughts and feelings is a narrowing of the places one might go, the people one might interact with, and the behaviors one might attempt.

Because attempts to suppress unwanted thoughts and feelings paradoxically increase these feelings (the white bear problem), ACT therapists embrace the opposite approach – *acceptance*. Instead of trying to push thoughts away and avoid situations in which they might arise, **acceptance** means *approaching the thought, so as to examine it flexibly, with a sense of curiosity*. The ACT therapist promotes such acceptance with exercises designed to undermine our default tendency to take thoughts literally. For example, the ACT therapist might encourage the client to repeat an unwanted thought over and over again ("I am worthless, I am worthless, …"). After doing this for a few minutes, the words lose their literal meaning and become closer to what they really are – odd sounds emanating from their mouth. Sounds that one can occasionally choose, when it would be adaptive to do so, to *not* symmetrically relate with worthlessness.

A complementary approach is to practice observing thoughts as each one arises. The client is encouraged to sit quietly with eyes closed and, when feeling relaxed, direct their attention to discrete thoughts as they arise. Let's assume that the next thought is "I am worthless." When this verbal stimulus is observed, the client has a choice – they can take the thought literally (symmetric relational responding between "worthless" and actual worthlessness) or they can do something else, something more flexible. For example, the client might calmly note "I am having the thought that I am worthless." From this perspective, the thought is a bit of behavior not unlike noticing that their right hand is scratching an itch. Both may be calmly observed and, from this perspective, a range of flexible responses are available. With the thought, the client might be encouraged to imagine placing it on a leaf and watching it float down a stream. Alternatively, the thought might be inspected more closely. It is a big thought or a small thought? Where is the thought? What color is the thought? The goal of such exercises is not to reduce the frequency of unwanted thoughts, but to acquire new behaviors that allow the client to *have a thought* instead of the *thought having the client*. Such flexible, nonliteral behaviors can help clients to have a thought while continuing to behave in a values-driven way.

The "Commitment" in Acceptance and Commitment Therapy

Accepting thoughts as they arise is an important skill to master if one is to live in accord with one's values. For example, if one of our values is "making lasting relationships," then behaving in a committed way to this value means meeting new people, even when thoughts of emotional insecurities arise. Helping clients identify their personal values is an important component of ACT. Accepting thoughts and recognizing that they are not incompatible with behaving in accord with one's values are complementary skills acquired in ACT.

Values are defined in ACT as *client-selected qualities of behavior that may be continuously emitted without reaching an end-goal*. Therefore, "finding a mate" is not a value (it is an end-goal) but "making lasting relationships" is. Articulating a set of values and behaving in accord with them may enhance the reinforcing efficacy of consequences we were already interested in. If, for example, *making lasting relationships* is a newly articulated value, then introducing one's self to a stranger at a party produces a consequence (the person interacts with us) that may function as a more effective positive reinforcer than before. This enhanced reinforcing value may be important in tipping the scale of choice toward behaving in a values-consistent direction, instead of an experiential-avoidance direction.

Importantly, the ACT therapist lets the client's values, not the therapist's, direct therapy. Again, if the client's behavior is following the therapist's advice mostly to earn the approval of the therapist – pliance – it is unlikely that the client's adaptive behavior will continue after therapy concludes (and approval from the therapist is no longer available). The client needs to pursue their own values. Successful values-driven actions will produce the reinforcers best suited to maintaining the client's adaptive behavior.

Does ACT Work?

Empirical evaluations of ACT have often taken a bottom-up approach, testing the component parts of ACT to find out which ones work, which can be improved and which should be discarded as a waste of the client's time. These studies have revealed the efficacy of *acceptance* exercises in persisting with a therapeutic task even though it produces distressing thoughts and feelings (Villatte et al., 2016; Vowles et al., 2007). Likewise, responding flexibly to thoughts (as thoughts) reduces emotional reactions to negative thoughts about one's self (Masuda et al., 2009, 2010), and values-based components of ACT increase self-reported engagement in values-consistent behavior and quality of life (Villatte et al., 2016).

Larger studies have evaluated multicomponent versions of ACT, as it is typically implemented by therapists outside of a research setting. These efficacy experiments use the group experimental designs described in Chapter 3. That is, treatment-seeking individuals are randomly assigned to an ACT group and others are assigned to a control group. The control group might receive a different type of psychotherapy or no therapy at all. Overall, substantial evidence reveals ACT is effective in treating anxiety and depression (Hacker et al., 2016) and other mental- and physical-health deficits, such as chronic pain (A-Tjak et al., 2015). ACT appears to work at least as well as other evidence-based psychotherapies (Hacker et al., 2016) with some studies suggesting ACT is modestly more effective (Lee et al., 2015; Ruiz, 2012). In sum, over 300 published studies have established the efficacy of ACT.

Further Reading

If you are interested in learning more about ACT and applying it in your daily life, we recommend these books:

- *Get Out of Your Mind and Into Your Life: The New Acceptance and Commitment Therapy* by Steven C. Hayes.
- *The Mindfulness and Acceptance Workbook for Anxiety: A Guide to Breaking Free from Anxiety, Phobias, and Worry Using Acceptance and Commitment Therapy* by John P. Forsyth and Georg H. Eifert.
- *The Mindfulness and Acceptance Workbook for Depression: Using Acceptance and Commitment Therapy to Move through Depression and Create a Life Worth Living* by Kirk D. Strosahl, Patricia J. Robinson, and Steven C. Hayes.

Reading Quiz 4

1. A common belief among those suffering from anxiety and depression is that _____ cause behavior. The ACT therapist will seek to undermine this rule that impairs healthy living and leads to human suffering.
2. Most psychologists approach therapy with the same belief as the client – that _____ cause behavior and, therefore, we must find and replace problematic cognition.
3. The _____ _____ problem refers to our inability to suppress thinking of things that are verbally named. This symmetric relational responding, a behavior we acquired

decades ago, can backfire if our thoughts are filled with verbal stimuli such as "sad," "anxious," or "unlovable."

4. ACT therapy is different than other approaches to psychotherapy. There is no attempt to replace bad thoughts with good thoughts. Instead, the therapist helps the client realize that unwanted _____ are not incompatible with behaving in a values-driven way.

5. The "A" in ACT stands for _____. This is the opposite of rejecting unwanted thoughts. It means approaching these thoughts, examining them flexibly, with a sense of curiosity.

6. ACT therapists help clients to identify their own personal _____; that is, qualities of behavior that may be continuously emitted without reaching an end-goal

7. The "C" in ACT stands for _____. The ACT therapist helps the client identify ways in which they can walk a value-driven path, even when experiencing unwanted thoughts.

Summary

Behavior analysts have long recognized the importance of verbal behavior, whether it is spoken, signed, read, or merely thought. Skinner (1957) outlined a functional taxonomy of verbal operants, each occasioned by a different type of stimulus, and maintained by a different type of reinforcer. Later researchers observed that humans acquire verbal behavior at a young age, when they learn to symmetrically relate verbal and nonverbal stimuli, like "ball" and a toy ball, as, in many ways, the same. They acquire this relating behavior through multiple-exemplar training.

With verbal behavior comes the ability to understand and follow rules. Two categories of rule-following are pliance and tracking; each is maintained by a different category of operant consequences. Pliance is maintained by social reinforcers and punishers for complying with the rule. Tracking occurs because it allows the rule-follower to obtain positive reinforcers and avoid aversive events (negative reinforcers).

Pliance is most likely to occur when the rule is provided by an authority figure, as in the Milgram experiment. This tendency toward pliance speaks to the importance of recognizing power differentials. Authority figures must be careful to avoid taking advantage of the less powerful, who are more likely to follow their rules, instructions, and demands, even when it is not in their best interest to do so.

Our unique verbal abilities give our species behavioral adaptations impossible in other species. But verbal behavior also comes with unwanted baggage – a tendency toward psychological suffering. Our verbal thoughts can occasion unwanted feelings, and maladaptive rules may hamper our ability to live a valuable life. ACT is a behavioral approach to psychotherapy. It can help clients learn new ways to interact with their thoughts. One that is less literal, freeing us to focus on what is important – behaving in accord with our values.

Reading Quiz 1

1. Tact: The verbal response is occasioned by the sight of the Eiffel Tower. The tact is socially reinforced by the passenger's appreciative reply.
2. Mand: This verbal response is occasioned by a establishing operation – Marina wants a picture of herself so she can post it on Instagram. The reinforcer that maintains this mand (the boyfriend takes the picture) was specified by the verbal response.
3. Mand: Asking for something is often a mand. Bobby does not demand a sip of the beer, but his request is occasioned by a establishing operation – whatever made him thirsty. The reinforcer – the sip of beer – was specified by Bobby's request.
4. Intraverbal: The nephew's verbal response was occasioned by the verbal S^D – "How old are you?" The response, "I'm free," does not resemble this verbal S^D. The intraverbal appears to be maintained by Gregory's reply.
5. Mand: The verbal response is occasioned by an establishing operation – to conduct the psychiatric evaluation, she needs the patient to respond to the Rorschach card. The reinforcer that maintains the psychiatrist's mand is the patient's verbal response.
6. Echoic: The form of Jason's verbal response closely resembles mom's "moose." Remaining in the game is a socially mediated reinforcer.
7. Intraverbal: The polite reply was occasioned by a verbal S^D and was reinforced with both a social positive reinforcer (the smile) and a social negative reinforcer (avoiding being criticized for her rudeness, had she not been polite).

   If you answered *echoic*, this too is a defensible answer. The form of Carla's verbal response partially resembles that of the new employee. Because the resemblance is only partial, the better answer is *intraverbal*.

8. Tact: The verbal response is occasioned by the sight of the snow. The tact is socially reinforced by her coworkers' positive responses.
9. antecedent stimulus
10. prompting; fading
11. shaping
12. reinforcer

Reading Quiz 2

1. symmetric
2. multiple exemplar
3. equivalence
4. human
5. language
6. psychological

Reading Quiz 3

1. contingency-shaped
2. Rule-governed
3. Contingency-shaped: It seems she discovered this adaptive behavior on her own, without anyone providing her with a verbal rule. It was reinforced when she better remembered the materials and earned better test scores.
4. Rule-governed: Stenny is following the rule posted on the stop sign. Because the rule is not well suited to the operative contingencies of reinforcement and punishment, we can be sure that his behavior is not contingency-shaped.
5. Rule-governed: The verbal rule was followed, but not because of any reinforcement or punishment contingencies.
6. Contingency-shaped: No rules are described.
7. tracking
8. pliance
9. Tracking – Angel followed the rule, not because of any consequences that Marge would deliver, but because Marge's rule appeared to correctly describe a continency of reinforcement – *IF you provide good service, THEN you will get a good tip*.
10. Tracking – Lynn's father was not there to provide any consequences for rule following. Instead, she follows the rule because it correctly describes a reinforcement contingency – *IF the knob is turned right, THEN the water supply will be shut off*.
11. Pliance – Cleaning the room is an example of rule-following that occurs because of a socially mediated consequence: avoidance of an unspecified consequence.
12. Pliance – Desert selling occurs because of a socially mediated consequence: the promise of a gift certificate.
13. Tracking – The father changes the channel, not because Atticus is present to deliver a consequence, but because Atticus' rule appears to correctly describe an operant contingency – *IF you watch the Lady Gaga episode of the Simpsons, THEN you will be disappointed (extinction)*.
14. reinforcers; punishers
15. variability

Reading Quiz 4

1. thoughts
2. thoughts
3. white bear
4. thoughts
5. acceptance
6. values
7. commitment

Notes

1. Behavior analysts use a more formal definition of *stimulus equivalence* than is provided here. There are technical names for all of the different relational responses illustrated by dashed arrows in Figure 14.3. These technical names and definitions are, however, beyond the scope of this text.
2. From the Sutta Nipata, first written 2,400 years ago and based on the memorized chants of Buddhist nuns and monks.

References

A-Tjak, J. G. L., Davis, M. L., Morina, N., Powers, M. B., Smits, J. A. J., & Emmelkamp, P. M. G. (2015). A meta-analysis of the efficacy of acceptance and commitment therapy for clinically relevant mental and physical health problems. *Psychotherapy and Psychosomatics*, *84*(1), 30–36. https://doi.org/10.1159/000365764

Barnes-Holmes, Y., Barnes-Holmes, D., Smeets, P. M., Strand, P., & Friman, P. (2004). Establishing relational responding in accordance with more-than and less-than as generalized operant behavior in young children. *International Journal of Psychology and Psychological Therapy*, *4*, 531–558. Retrieved from http://mural.maynoothuniversity.ie/403

Beck, A. T. (2005). The current state of cognitive therapy. *Archives of General Psychiatry*, *62*(9), 953. https://doi.org/10.1001/archpsyc.62.9.953

Belluz, J. (2019, April 10). New York's Orthodox Jewish community is battling measles outbreaks. Vaccine deniers are to blame. *Vox*. https://www.vox.com/science-and-health/2018/11/9/18068036/measles-new-york-orthodox-jewish-community-vaccines

Carr, J. E., & Firth, A. M. (2005). The verbal behavior approach to early and intensive behavioral intervention for autism: A call for additional empirical support. *Journal of Early and Intensive Behavior Intervention*, *2*(1), 18–27. https://doi.org/10.1037/h0100297

Centers for Disease Control and Prevention. (2018). *Data & statistics on autism spectrum disorder*. Retrieved from https://www.cdc.gov/ncbddd/autism/data.html

Cerutti, D. T. (1991). Discriminative versus reinforcing properties of schedules as determinants of schedules as determinants of schedule insensitivity in humans. *The Psychological Record*, *41*(1), 51–67. https://link.springer.com/article/10.1007/BF03395093

Cerutti, D. T. (1994). Compliance with instructions: Effects of randomness in scheduling and monitoring. *The Psychological Record*, *44*, 259–269. https://doi.org/10.1007/BF03395133

Charlop-Christy, M. H., & Kelso, S. E. (2003). Teaching children with autism conversational speech using a cue card/written script program. *Education & Treatment of Children*, *26*(2), 108–127. https://www.jstor.org/stable/42899741

Degenova, M. K., Patton, D. M., Jurich, J. A., & MacDermid, S. M. (1994). Ways of coping among HIV-infected individuals. *The Journal of Social Psychology*, *134*(5), 655–663. https://doi.org/10.1080/00224545.1994.9922996

DeSouza, A. A., Akers, J. S., & Fisher, W. W. (2017). Empirical application of Skinner's verbal behavior to interventions for children with autism: A review. *The Analysis of Verbal Behavior*, *33*(2), 229–259. https://doi.org/10.1007/s40616-017-0093-7

Dougher, M. J., Augustson, E., Markham, M. R., Greenway, D. E., & Wulfert, E. (1994). The transfer of respondent eliciting and extinction functions through stimulus equivalence classes. *Journal of the Experimental Analysis of Behavior*, *62*(3), 331–351. https://doi.org/10.1901/jeab.1994.62-331

Forsyth, J. P., & Eifert, G. H. (2016). *The mindfulness and acceptance workbook for anxiety: A guide to breaking free from anxiety, phobias, and worry using acceptance and commitment therapy* (2nd ed.). Oakland, CA: New Harbinger

Galizio, M. (1979). Contingency-shaped and rule-governed behavior: Instructional control of human loss avoidance. *Journal of the Experimental Analysis of Behavior, 31*(1), 53–70. https://doi.org/10.1901/jeab.1979.31-53

Galizio, M., & Bruce, K. E. (2018). Abstraction, multiple exemplar training and the search for derived stimulus relations in animals. *Perspectives on Behavior Science, 41,* 45–67. https://doi.org/10.1007/s40614-017-0112-y

Goldsmith, T. R., LeBlanc, L. A., & Sautter, R. A. (2007). Teaching intraverbal behavior to children with autism. *Research in Autism Spectrum Disorders, 1*(1), 1–13. https://doi.org/10.1016/j.rasd.2006.07.001

Greer, B. D., Fisher, W. W., Saini, V., Owen, T. M., & Jones, J. K. (2016). Functional communication training during reinforcement schedule thinning: An analysis of 25 applications. *Journal of Applied Behavior Analysis, 49*(1), 105–121. https://doi.org/10.1002/jaba.265

Greer, D. R., Stolfi, L., & Pistoljevic, N. (2007). Emergence of naming in preschoolers: A comparison of multiple and single exemplar instruction. *European Journal of Behavior Analysis, 8*(2), 109–131. https://doi.org/10.1080/15021149.2007.11434278

Hacker, T., Stone, P., & MacBeth, A. (2016). Acceptance and commitment therapy – Do we know enough? Cumulative and sequential meta-analyses of randomized controlled trials. *Journal of Affective Disorders, 190*, 551–565. https://doi.org/10.1016/J.JAD.2015.10.053

Hartman, E. C., & Klatt, K. P. (2005). The effects of deprivation, presession exposure, and preferences on teaching manding to children with autism. *The Analysis of Verbal Behavior, 21*(1), 135–144. https://doi.org/10.1007/BF03393015

Hayes, S. C. (2005). *Get out of your mind and into your life*. Oakland, CA: New Harbinger.

Hayes, S. C., Brownstein, A. J., Zettle, R. D., Rosenfarb, I., & Korn, Z. (1986). Rule-governed behavior and sensitivity to changing consequences of responding. *Journal of the Experimental Analysis of Behavior, 45*(3), 237–256. https://doi.org/10.1901/jeab.1986.45-237

Hayes, S. C., Strosahl, K. D., & Wilson, K. G. (1999). *Acceptance and commitment therapy: An experiential approach to behavior change*. New York: The Guilford Press.

Hayes, S. C., Strosahl, K. D., & Wilson, K. G. (2009). *Acceptance and commitment Therapy* (2nd ed.). Washington, DC: American Psychological Association.

Hayes, S. C., Zettle, R. D., & Rosenfarb, I. (1989). Rule-following. In S. C. Hayes (Ed.), *Rule-governed behavior: Cognition, contingencies, and instructional control* (pp. 191–220). New York: Plenum.

Hayes, S. C., Luoma, J. B., Bond, F. W., Masuda, A., & Lillis, J. (2006). Acceptance and commitment therapy: Model, processes and outcomes. *Behaviour Research and Therapy, 44*(1), 1–25. https://doi.org/10.1016/J.BRAT.2005.06.006

Hayes, S. C., Strosahl, K. D., Bunting, K., Twohig, M., & Wilson, K. G. (2004). What is acceptance and commitment therapy? In *A practical guide to acceptance and commitment therapy* (pp. 3–29). Boston, MA: Springer US. https://doi.org/10.1007/978-0-387-23369-7_1

Hayes, S. C., & Wilson, K. G. (1994). Acceptance and commitment therapy: Altering the verbal support for experiential avoidance. *The Behavior Analyst, 17*, 289–303. https://www.ncbi.nlm.nih.gov/pmc/articles/PMC2733476/pdf/behavan00024-0090.pdf

Heath, A. K., Ganz, J. B., Parker, R., Burke, M., & Ninci, J. (2015). A meta-analytic review of functional communication training across mode of communication, age, and disability. *Review Journal of Autism and Developmental Disorders, 2*(2), 155–166. https://doi.org/10.1007/s40489-014-0044-3

Kisamore, A. N., Karsten, A. M., Mann, C. C., & Conde, K. A. (2013). Effects of a differential observing response on intraverbal performance of preschool children: A preliminary investigation. *The Analysis of Verbal Behavior, 29*(1), 101–108. https://doi.org/10.1007/BF03393127

Leaf, J. B., Townley-Cochran, D., Mitchell, E., Milne, C., Alcalay, A., Leaf, J., … Oppenheim-Leaf, M. L. (2016). Evaluation of multiple-alternative prompts during tact training. *Journal of Applied Behavior Analysis, 49*(2), 399–404. https://doi.org/10.1002/jaba.289

Lee, E. B., An, W., Levin, M. E., & Twohig, M. P. (2015). An initial meta-analysis of acceptance and commitment therapy for treating substance use disorders. *Drug and Alcohol Dependence, 155*, 1–7. https://doi.org/10.1016/J.DRUGALCDEP.2015.08.004

Levin, M. E., Hayes, S. C., & Vilardaga, R. (2012). Acceptance and commitment therapy: Applying an iterative translational research strategy in behavior analysis. In G. J. Madden (Ed.), *APA handbook of behavior analysis: Vol. 2. translating principles into practice* (pp. 455–479). Washington, DC: American Psychological Association. Retrieved from https://www.researchgate.net/publication/232805285

Lionello-DeNolf, K. M. (2009). The search for symmetry: 25 years in review. *Learning & Behavior*, *37*(2), 188–203. https://doi.org/10.3758/LB.37.2.188

Lorah, E. R., Parnell, A., Whitby, P. S., & Hantula, D. (2015). A systematic review of tablet computers and portable media players as speech generating devices for individuals with autism spectrum disorder. *Journal of Autism and Developmental Disorders*, *45*(12), 3792–3804. https://doi.org/10.1007/s10803 014 2314 4

Luciano, C., Becerra, I., & Valverde, M. (2007). The role of multiple-exemplar training and naming in establishing derived equivalence in an infant. *Journal of the Experimental Analysis of Behavior*, *87*(3), 349–365. https://doi.org/10.1901/jeab.2007.08-06

Masedo, A. I., & Esteve, M. R. (2007). Effects of suppression, acceptance and spontaneous coping on pain tolerance, pain intensity and distress. *Behaviour Research and Therapy*, *45*(2), 199–209. https://doi.org/10.1016/J.BRAT.2006.02.006

Masuda, A., Hayes, S. C., Twohig, M. P., Drossel, C., Lillis, J., & Washio, Y. (2009). A parametric study of cognitive defusion and the believability and discomfort of negative self-relevant thoughts. *Behavior Modification*, *33*(2), 250–262. https://doi.org/10.1177/0145445508326259

Masuda, A., Twohig, M. P., Stormo, A. R., Feinstein, A. B., Chou, Y., & Wendell, J. W. (2010). The effects of cognitive defusion and thought distraction on emotional discomfort and believability of negative self-referential thoughts. *Journal of Behavior Therapy and Experimental Psychiatry*, *41*(1), 11–17. https://doi.org/10.1016/J.JBTEP.2009.08.006

Matthews, B. A., Shimoff, E., Catania, A. C., & Sagvolden, T. (1977). Uninstructed human responding: Sensitivity to ratio and interval contingencies. *Journal of the Experimental Analysis of Behavior*, *27*(3), 453–467. doi:10.1901/jeab.1977.27-453

Milgram, S. (1963). Behavioral study of obedience. *Journal of Abnormal and Social Psychology*, *67*, 371–378. https://doi.org/10.1037/h0040525

Milgram, S. (1965). Some conditions of obedience and disobedience to authority. *Human Relations*, *18*(1), 57–76.

Newman, B., Reinecke, D., & Ramos, M. (2009). Is a reasonable attempt reasonable? Shaping versus reinforcing verbal attempts of preschoolers with autism. *The Analysis of Verbal Behavior*, *25*, 67–72. Retrieved from https://link.springer.com/content/pdf/10.1007/BF03393070.pdf

Peláez, M., Gewirtz, J. L., Sanchez, A., & Mahabir, N. M. (2000). Exploring stimulus equivalence formation in infants. *Behavioral Development Bulletin*, *9*(1), 20–25. https://doi.org/10.1037/h0100534

Peláez, M., & Moreno, R. (1999). Four dimensions of rules and their correspondence to rule-governed behavior: A taxonomy. *Behavioral Development Bulletin*, *8*(1), 21–27. https://doi.org/10.1037/h0100528

Petursdottir, A. I., & Carr, J. E. (2007). A review of recommendations for sequencing receptive and expressive language instruction. *Journal of Applied Behavior Analysis*, *44*(4), 859–879. https://doi.org/10.1901/jaba.2011.44-859

Ruiz, F. J. (2012). Acceptance and commitment therapy versus traditional cognitive behavioral therapy. *International Journal of Psychology and Psychological Therapy*, *12*(3), 333–357. Retrieved from https://dialnet.unirioja.es/servlet/articulo?codigo=4019738

Sherer, M., Pierce, K. L., Paredes, S., Kisacky, K. L., Ingersoll, B., & Schreibman, L. (2001). Enhancing conversation skills in children with autism via video technology. *Behavior Modification*, *25*(1), 140–158. https://doi.org/10.1177/0145445501251008

Sidman, M., & Cresson, O. (1973). Reading and crossmodal transfer of stimulus equivalences in severe retardation. *American Journal of Mental Deficiency*, *77*(5), 515–523.

Sidman, M., & Tailby, W. (1982). Conditional discrimination vs. matching to sample: An expansion of the testing paradigm. *Journal of the Experimental Analysis of Behavior*, *37*, 5–22.

Sidman, M., Rauzin, R., Lazar, R., Cunningham, S., Tailby, W., & Carrigan, P. (1982). A search for symmetry in the conditional discriminations of rhesus monkeys, baboons, and children. *Journal of the Experimental Analysis of Behavior, 37*(1), 23–44. https://doi.org/10.1901/jeab.1982.37-23

Skinner, B. F. (1953). *Science and human behavior.* New York: Macmillan.

Skinner, B. F. (1957). *Verbal behavior.* New York: Appleton-Century-Crofts. Retrieved from https://books.google.com/books?hl=en&lr=&id=_SXaamdgVS4C&oi=fnd&pg=PA1&dq=skinner+verbal+behavior+1957&ots=FzzV7wZTqo&sig=5hw__s7bh5H2QjZRUbQX7upNqCk

Skinner, B. F. (1966). An operant analysis of problem solving. In B. Kleinmuntz (Ed.), *Problem solving: Research, method, and theory.* (pp. 225–257) New York: Wiley.

Skinner, B. F. (1969). *Contingencies of reinforcement: A theoretical analysis.* New York: Appleton-Century-Crofts.

Snowdon, C. T. (1990). Language capacities of nonhuman animals. *Yearbook of Physical Anthropology, 33*, 215–243.

Strosahl, K. D., Robinson, P. J., & Hayes, S. C. (2017). *The mindfulness and acceptance workbook for depression: Using acceptance and commitment therapy to move through depression and create a life worth living* (2nd ed.). Oakland, CA: New Harbinger.

Sundberg, M. L., & Michael, J. (2001). The benefits of Skinner's analysis of verbal behavior for children with autism. *Behavior Modification, 25*(5), 698–724. https://doi.org/10.1177/0145445501255003

Sundberg, M. L., & Sundberg, C. A. (2011). Intraverbal behavior and verbal conditional discriminations in typically developing children and children with autism. *The Analysis of Verbal Behavior, 27*(1), 23–44. https://doi.org/10.1007/BF03393090

Thomas, B. R., Lafasakis, M., & Sturmey, P. (2010). The effects of prompting, fading, and differential reinforcement on vocal mands in non-verbal preschool children with autism spectrum disorders. *Behavioral Interventions, 25*(2), 157–168. https://doi.org/10.1002/bin.300

Urcuioli, P. J. (2008). Associative symmetry, antisymmetry, and a theory of pigeons' equivalence-class formation. *Journal of the Experimental Analysis of Behavior, 90*(3), 257–282. https://doi.org/10.1901/jeab.2008.90-257

Villatte, J. L., Vilardaga, R., Villatte, M., Plumb Vilardaga, J. C., Atkins, D. C., & Hayes, S. C. (2016). Acceptance and commitment therapy modules: Differential impact on treatment processes and outcomes. *Behaviour Research and Therapy, 77*, 52–61. https://doi.org/10.1016/J.BRAT.2015.12.001

Vowles, K. E., McNeil, D. W., Gross, R. T., McDaniel, M. L., Mouse, A., Bates, M., … McCall, C. (2007). Effects of pain acceptance and pain control strategies on physical impairment in individuals with chronic low back pain. *Behavior Therapy, 38*(4), 412–425. https://doi.org/10.1016/J.BETH.2007.02.001

Wegner, D. M., & Schneider, D. J. (2003). The white bear story. *Psychological Inquiry, 14*(3), 326–329. https://doi.org/10.1080/1047840X.2003.9682900

Wenzlaff, R. M., Wegner, D. M., & Klein, S. B. (1991). The role of thought suppression in the bonding of thought and mood. *Journal of Personality and Social Psychology, 60*(4), 500–508. https://doi.org/10.1037/0022-3514.60.4.500

Zettle, R. D., & Hayes, S. C. (1982). Rule-governed behavior: A potential theoretical framework for cognitive-behavior therapy. In P. C. Kendall (Ed.), *Advances in cognitive-behavioral research and therapy* (pp. 73–118). New York: Academic Press.

APPENDIX

Foundational Knowledge Accompanying the BACB Fifth Edition Task List

Here, you will find the list of principles and concepts identified by the Behavior Analysis Certification Board (BACB) as *Foundations*. The chapter in which each principle/concept is discussed is listed here. Because this is an introductory textbook, not all items on the BACB's list are covered; see "NA" topics below.

A. PHILOSOPHICAL UNDERPINNINGS

A-1	Identify the goals of behavior analysis	Chapter 1
A-2	Philosophical assumptions underlying the science of behavior analysis	Chapter 1
A-3	Describe and explain behavior from the perspective of radical behaviorism	Chapters 1 and 9
A-4	Distinguish among behaviorism, the experimental analysis of behavior, applied behavior analysis, and professional practice guided by the science of behavior analysis	Chapter 1
A-5	Describe and define the dimensions of applied behavior analysis (Baer et al., 1968)	Chapters 1–3

B. CONCEPTS AND PRINCIPLES

B-1	Define and provide examples of behavior, response, and response class	Chapters 1 and 5
B-2	Define and provide examples of stimulus and stimulus class	Chapters 4, 5, and 12
B-3	Define and provide examples of respondent [Pavlovian] and operant conditioning	Chapters 4 and 5
B-4	Define and provide examples of positive- and negative-reinforcement contingencies	Chapters 5 and 6
B-5	Define and provide examples of schedules of reinforcement	Chapter 11
B-6	Define and provide examples of positive- and negative-punishment contingencies	Chapter 10
B-7	Define and provide examples of automatic and socially mediated contingencies	Chapter 7
B-8	Define and provide examples of unconditioned [primary], conditioned, and generalized reinforcers and punishers	Chapters 8 and 10

An Introduction to Behavior Analysis, First Edition. Gregory J. Madden, Derek D. Reed, and Florence D. DiGennaro Reed.
© 2021 John Wiley & Sons Ltd. Published 2021 by John Wiley & Sons Ltd.

C. MEASUREMENT, DATA DISPLAY, AND INTERPRETATION

D. EXPERIMENTAL DESIGN

GLOSSARY

A-B-A design. See *reversal design*.

Abolishing operation (AO). An environmental and/or biological event that (1) temporarily decreases the value of a specific reinforcer and (2) decreases the probability of behaviors yielding that reinforcer.

Acceptance. Within ACT therapy, acceptance means approaching the thought, so as to examine it flexibly, with a sense of curiosity.

Alternating-treatments design. In this single-subject design, the independent variable(s) is turned ON and OFF rapidly to evaluate if this systematically and repeatedly changes behavior.

Antecedent stimulus. An observable stimulus that is present before the behavior occurs.

Automatic reinforcer. A consequence that is directly produced by the response – it is not provided by someone else – and that increases the behavior above a no-reinforcer baseline.

Avoidance behavior. Negatively reinforced operant behavior that prevents an aversive stimulus from happening.

Backup reinforcer. The reinforcer provided after the conditioned reinforcer signals the delay reduction to its delivery.

Backward chaining. A method of teaching an individual to emit a stimulus-response chain. The final link in the stimulus-response chain is taught first, and once that link is mastered, additional links are added in reverse order.

Behavior. An individual living organism's activity, public or private, which may be influenced by external or internal stimulation.

Behavior analysis. A natural science that seeks to (1) accurately predict behavior and (2) identify functional variables that can be used to positively influence behavior. This science assumes that (1) behavior is determined by knowable environmental and biological variables and (2) the scientific method is a valid way to identify those determinants.

Behavioral definition. A precise specification of the target behavior, allowing observers to reliably identify instances and non-instances.

Between-individuals replication. When a between-individuals replication is conducted, the experiment is repeated with additional subjects and the same result is obtained.

Breakpoint. The maximum amount of behavior the reinforcer will maintain. Reinforcers with higher breakpoints are more effective than those with lower breakpoints.

Chain. See *stimulus-response chain*.

Chaining. See *forward chaining* and *backward chaining*.

Choice. Voluntary behavior occurring in a context in which alternative behaviors are possible.

Comparison design. This single-subject design arranges two phases – a baseline phase (independent variable OFF) and an experimental phase (independent variable ON). This design cannot rule out confounds.

Conditioned punisher. A contingent consequence that signals a delay reduction to a backup punisher.

Conditioned reinforcers. Those consequences that function as reinforcers only after Pavlovian learning occurs – the individual must learn that the conditioned reinforcer signals a delay reduction to a backup reinforcer.

Confound. Variables that are influencing behavior within an experiment, but are not controlled by the researcher. Variables confounded with the independent variable may be responsible for a behavior change that would otherwise be attributed to the independent variable.

Consequence. An observable stimulus change that happens after behavior occurs.

Contingency. See *response–consequence contingency*.

Contingency-shaped behavior. Behavior acquired and maintained by interacting with the contingencies of reinforcement alone.

Continuous reinforcement. Every instance of the response is reinforced.

Correlation. A positive correlation exists when two variables have a tendency to happen together. For example, in children, there is a positive correlation between height and weight – taller children tend to weigh more than shorter children. Just because two variables are correlated does not mean that a causal relation exists between them.

Cumulative record. A graphical display of responding as it unfolds over time.

Delay discounting. The devaluation (or discounting) of the value of a reinforcer because it is delayed.

Dependent variable. The dependent variable in a behavior-analytic experiment is the objectively measured target behavior.

Differential reinforcement. A procedure in which a previously reinforced behavior is placed on extinction while a second behavior is reinforced.

Differential reinforcement of alternative behavior (DRA). A differential reinforcement procedure in which the problem behavior is extinguished while a different (alternative) response is reinforced.

Differential reinforcement of high-rate behavior (DRH). A differential reinforcement procedure in which responding at a rate below a specified threshold is extinguished and responding at a rate above that threshold is reinforced.

Differential reinforcement of incompatible behavior (DRI). A differential reinforcement procedure in which the problem behavior is extinguished while a different response – one that cannot be emitted while engaged in the problem behavior – is reinforced.

Differential reinforcement of low-rate behavior (DRL). A differential reinforcement procedure in which responding at a rate above a specified threshold is extinguished and responding at a rate below that threshold is reinforced.

Differential reinforcement of other behavior (DRO). A differential reinforcement procedure in which the problem behavior is extinguished and abstaining from this behavior for a specified interval of time is reinforced.

Differential reinforcement of variability. A differential reinforcement procedure in which repetition is extinguished and novel responding is reinforced.

Direct observation. When behavior is directly observed, the behavior is recorded as the behavior occurs, or a lasting product of the behavior is recorded at a later time.

Discriminated operant behavior. Operant behavior that is systematically influenced by antecedent stimuli.

Discriminative stimulus (S^D). An antecedent stimulus that can evoke a specific operant response because the individual has learned that when the S^D is present, that response will be reinforced.

Discrimination training. A procedure in which an operant response is reinforced in the presence of an S^D and extinguished in the presence of an S^Δ.

Duration. A dimension of behavior – the interval of time between the start and the end of the behavior.

Duration recording. A direct-observation method used when measuring the latency or duration of a target behavior.

Echoic. A verbal operant in which the response resembles the verbal antecedent stimulus and is maintained by a variety of socially mediated reinforcers.

Elicit. When a specific stimulus occasions a specific reflex response, we say that the stimulus *elicits* the response.

Environmental events. All of the things you experience through your senses (tastes, smells, sights, sounds, tactile sensations).

Escape behavior. Negatively reinforced operant behavior that terminates an aversive stimulus.

Escape extinction. Responding that meets the negative reinforcement contingency no longer removes or reduces the aversive event. As a result, responding falls to baseline (no-reinforcer) levels.

Establishing operation (EO). An environmental and/or biological event that (1) temporarily increases the value of a specific reinforcer and (2) increases the probability of behaviors yielding that reinforcer.

Event recording. Each instance of behavior is recorded at the moment it occurs.

Evoke. When a specific stimulus increases the probability of a specific ontogenetic response (i.e., a response acquired during the lifetime of the individual), we say that the stimulus *evokes* the response.

Experiment. In behavior analysis, experiments evaluate falsifiable hypotheses. They do this by manipulating an independent variable to see if this reliably produces a systematic change in behavior.

Extinction (operant). See *operant extinction*.

Extinction (Pavlovian). See *Pavlovian extinction*.

Extinction burst. Temporary increase in the rate, magnitude, or duration of the previously reinforced response.

Extinction-induced emotional behavior. A temporary increase in negative emotions following a transition from positive reinforcement to operant extinction.

Extinction-induced resurgence. When one operant behavior is extinguished, other behaviors that were previously reinforced are emitted again.

Extinction-induced variability. An increase in the variety of operant response topographies following extinction.

Extrinsic reinforcers. A psychological (not a behavior-analytic) concept. An extrinsic reinforcer is a reinforcer that is not automatically obtained by engaging in the behavior. Instead, these reinforcers are artificially arranged.

Fading. The gradual removal of a prompt as the response is increasingly emitted under discriminative-stimulus control.

Fixed-interval (FI) schedule. Specifies a constant time interval that must elapse before a single response will produce the reinforcer.

Fixed-interval schedule – typical response pattern of nonhuman subjects. A post-reinforcement pause gives way to an accelerating response rate that terminates with a reinforcer.

Fixed-ratio (FR) schedule. The number of responses required per reinforcer is the same every time.

Fixed-ratio schedule – typical response pattern. A post-reinforcement pause followed by a high-constant rate of responding that ends with a reinforcer.

Flow. A state in which one feels immersed in a rewarding activity, and in which we lose track of time and self.

Forward chaining. A method of teaching an individual to emit a stimulus-response chain. It involves teaching the links in the stimulus-response chain in the order they will need to be emitted.

Frequency. A dimension of behavior – the response count divided by time (response rate) or opportunity to respond.

Functional analysis of behavior. Scientific method used to (1) determine if a problem behavior is an operant and (2) identify the reinforcer that maintains that operant.

Functional communication training (FCT). A differential reinforcement procedure in which the problem behavior is extinguished while an adaptive verbal response is reinforced.

Functional variable. A variable that, if changed, will reliably and systematically influence behavior.

Generalization (operant). When a novel stimulus resembling the S^D evokes the response, despite that response never having been reinforced in the presence of that novel stimulus.

Generalization (Pavlovian). When a novel stimulus resembling the CS evokes the response, despite no prior experience with the novel stimulus signaling a delay reduction to the US.

Generalization gradient. A graph depicting increases in responding as the novel antecedent stimulus more closely resembles the S^D.

Generalized conditioned reinforcer. A conditioned reinforcer that signals a delay reduction to more than one backup reinforcer.

Graduated exposure therapy. A Pavlovian extinction-based therapy in which the client suffering from a phobia is gradually exposed to successively stronger approximations of the conditioned stimulus (CS). Before each new CS is presented, steps are taken to reduce/eliminate a fear evoked by the prior CS approximation.

Group experimental designs. These designs evaluate if the behavior of a treatment group (independent variable ON) is statistically significantly different from that of a control group (independent variable OFF). If so, then the difference is attributed to the independent variable.

Habit. An operant behavior that (1) is evoked by antecedent stimuli and (2) persists despite the imposition of an abolishing operation (AO).

Habituation. Gradual reduction in responding following repeated presentations of the eliciting stimulus.

Impulsive choice. Choosing the smaller-sooner reward and foregoing the larger-later reward.

Independent variable. A publicly observable change, controlled by the experimenter, which is anticipated to influence behavior in a specific way.

Instrumental behavior. A synonym of *operant behavior*.

Intermittent reinforcement. The response is sometimes but not always reinforced.

Interobserver agreement (IOA). The extent to which two independent observers' data are the same after having directly observed the same behavior at the same time.

Internal validity. When an experiment provides clear evidence that a functional relation exists between the independent variable and behavior change, that experiment has internal validity.

Interval recording. A category of direct-observation methods. See *partial-interval recording* and *whole-interval recording*.

Interval schedule of reinforcement. Specifies the amount of time that must elapse before a single response will produce the reinforcer.

Intraverbal. A verbal response occasioned by a verbal discriminative stimulus, but the form of the response does not resemble that stimulus; intraverbals are maintained by a variety of social reinforcers.

Intrinsic motivation. A psychological (not a behavior-analytic) concept describing the natural drive to engage in a behavior because it fosters a sense of competence.

Latency. A dimension of behavior – the interval of time between the opportunity to respond and the response itself.

Level. The prevalence of the behavior during the stable portion of a phase/condition.

Loss aversion. The tendency for loss prevention (SR_A-) to influence behavior more than presentation of the same stimulus (SR+).

Magnitude. A dimension of behavior – the force or intensity of a behavior.

Mand. A verbal operant occasioned by a motivating operation and maintained by the verbally specified reinforcer.

Marking. When a conditioned reinforcer immediately follows the response, this helps the individual learn which response produced the backup reinforcer.

Matching law/equation. An equation developed by Richard Herrnstein to predict how individuals will allocate their behavior between choice alternatives.

Mentalistic explanations of behavior. These "explanations" put the cause of behavior in the individual's vaguely defined "mind." See Chapter 9 for a summary of why behavior analysts reject mentalistic explanations of behavior.

Motivating operation (MO). An environmental and/or biological event that (1) temporarily alters the value of a specific reinforcer and (2) increases/decreases the probability of behaviors that yield that reinforcer.

Multielement design. See *alternating-treatments design*.

Multiple-baseline design. A single-subject design that evaluates the functional relation between an independent variable and behavior by conducting a series of time-staggered A-B comparisons either across behaviors, across situations, or across individuals.

Multiple-exemplar training. Teaching an individual to symmetrically relate arbitrary stimuli, over and over again, with multiple examples.

Negative punishment. The contingent removal, reduction, or prevention of a reinforcer, the effect of which decreases the future probability of the behavior below its no-punishment level.

Negative reinforcement. See *negative reinforcement – avoidance* and *negative reinforcement – escape*.

Negative reinforcement – avoidance (SR_A-). A consequent prevention of a stimulus change, the effect of which is to increase operant behavior above its no-reinforcer baseline level.

Negative reinforcement – escape (SR$_E$-). A consequent removal or reduction of a stimulus, the effect of which is to increase operant behavior above its no-reinforcer baseline level.

Neutral stimulus. A stimulus that has no behavioral function. For example, it neither elicits nor evokes the response of interest.

Noncontingent consequence. A consequence occurring after the response, but not because the response caused it to occur.

Operant behavior. A generic class of responses influenced by antecedents, with each response in the class producing the same consequence.

Operant extinction. Responding that meets the reinforcement contingency no longer produces the reinforcer and, as a result, falls to baseline (no-reinforcer) levels.

Outcome recording. Recording the distinct, observable, lasting product(s) of behavior, instead of the behavior itself.

Partial-interval recording. A direct-observation method used to estimate how frequently behavior occurs. Observers record whether the behavior occurs during any portion of each in a series of contiguous intervals.

Partial reinforcement extinction effect (PREE). Direct relation between prior reinforcement rate and how quickly behavior undergoes extinction. If the behavior has been frequently reinforced, it will undergo extinction quickly. Infrequently reinforced behavior will take longer to extinguish.

Pavlovian extinction. The procedure of repeatedly presenting the conditioned stimulus (CS) without the unconditioned stimulus (US), the effect of which is a reduction or elimination of the CS's ability to evoke the conditioned response (CR).

Pavlovian generalization. Conditioned responding to a novel stimulus that resembles the conditioned response (CS).

Phylogenetically important event. A stimulus event important in the survival of the individual.

Phylogenetically selected behaviors. Behaviors that increased our evolutionary ancestors' chances of survival; these behaviors are genetically passed from parent to progeny.

Pliance. Rule-governed behavior occurring because of socially mediated positive or negative reinforcers.

Positive punishment. The contingent presentation of a consequence that decreases the future probability of the behavior below its no-punishment level.

Positive reinforcement. The presentation of a consequence, the effect of which is to increase operant behavior above its no-reinforcer baseline level.

Preference assessment. See *stimulus preference assessment.*

Preference hierarchy. List of stimuli (potential reinforcers) rank ordered from most to least preferred.

Premack principle. Access to a high-probability behavior will function as a reinforcer when made contingent upon a low-probability behavior.

Primary punisher. A contingent consequence that functions as a punisher because, in the evolutionary past of the species, this consequence decreased the chances of survival.

Primary reinforcer. A consequence that functions as a reinforcer because it is important in preserving the life of the individual or the continuation of the species.

Prompt. An antecedent stimulus that facilitates or guides the desired response when it is not happening under appropriate discriminative-stimulus control.

Psychological function of verbal stimuli. The emotion-evoking function of verbal stimuli, despite those stimuli having never acquired Pavlovian conditioned-stimulus (CS) function.

Punishment. The process or procedure whereby a punisher decreases the future probability of an operant response.

Punisher. A contingent consequence that decreases the future probability of behavior below its pre-punishment level.

Ratio schedule of reinforcement. Specifies the number of responses that must be made in order for the reinforcer to be delivered.

Reactivity. Behavior changes because the individual is aware that they are being watched.

Reinforcement. The process or procedure by which a reinforcer increases operant behavior above its baseline level.

Reinforcer. A consequence that increases operant behavior above its baseline level.

Reinforcer quality. The subjective value of a reinforcer, which can vary from one individual to the next.

Reinforcer survey. A structured interview or written survey that asks the individual to identify preferred incentives that might be used as reinforcers.

Response. A single instance of behavior.

Response-cost punishers. Negative punishers that involve the removal or reduction of a reinforcer.

Response–consequence contingency. Describes the causal (IF → THEN) relation between an operant behavior and its consequence.

Response topography. The physical movement or form of the response.

Reversal design. A single-subject experimental design in which the individual's behavior is evaluated in repeatedly alternating baseline and experimental phases.

Rewards. Beneficial consequences that we *think* will function as reinforcers, but we don't know yet if they will.

Rule-governed behavior. Behavior influenced by a verbal description of the operative three-term contingency (antecedent–behavior–consequence).

Schedule of reinforcement. Precisely specifies the nature of the contingent relation between a response and a reinforcer.

Schedule thinning. A procedure for gradually reducing the rate of reinforcement, while maintaining the desired behavior.

S^D. See *discriminative stimulus*.

S^{Dp}. An antecedent stimulus that decreases a specific operant response because the individual has learned that when the S^{Dp} is present, that response will be punished.

S^{Δ}. An antecedent stimulus that decreases a specific operant response because the individual has learned that when the S^{Δ} is present, that response will not be reinforced (extinction).

Secondary reinforcer. See *conditioned reinforcers*.

Self-control choice. Choosing the larger-later reward and foregoing the smaller-sooner reward.

Self-report. A way of measuring behavior in which individuals are asked to report on the occurrence of the behavior of interest. One must be careful about the accuracy of these reports.

Shaping. Differential reinforcement of successive approximations to a terminal behavior.

Single-subject experimental designs. Sometimes called "single-case" experiments, these designs expose individuals to baseline (independent variable OFF) *and* experimental (independent variable ON) phases to determine if the independent variable systematically and reliably changes behavior.

Spontaneous recovery. An increase in conditioned responding following the passage of time since Pavlovian extinction.

Social validity of a behavioral definition. The consumer of the intervention, or an expert in the field, indicates that the behavioral definition accurately reflects the behavior of interest.

Social validity of an intervention effect. Is the relevant stakeholder satisfied with the improvement in behavior? If so, then the intervention has produced a socially valid effect.

Spontaneous recovery of operant behavior. Temporary resumption of operant responding following time away from the extinction setting.

Stable. Behavior is stable when, over repeated observations, there is little "bounce" and no systematic trend.

Stimuli. The plural of "stimulus."

Stimulus. Something that you can see, hear, smell, taste, or feel.

Stimulus equivalence. After explicitly teaching a unidirectional relation between three or more arbitrary stimuli (A → B, C → A), symmetric relational responding is demonstrated between all stimuli (B → A, A → C, B → C, C → B). That is, the individual relates all of the stimuli, in many ways, as equivalent to one another.

Stimulus preference assessment. A technique in which individuals choose between two or more concurrently available items. The preferred item is likely to be an effective reinforcer. The stimulus preference assessment yields a rank-ordered list of preferred stimuli – the *preference hierarchy*.

Stimulus-response chain. A fixed sequence of operant responses, each evoked by a response-produced S^D.

Substitute reinforcer. A reinforcer that is increasingly consumed when access to another reinforcer is constrained. For example, if the price of coffee increases (constraining our access to this commodity), we may substitute another caffeinated beverage.

Symmetric relational responding. The behavior of relating two arbitrary stimuli as, in many ways, the same.

Superstitious behavior. Occurs when the individual behaves as though a response–consequence contingency exists when, in fact, the relation between response and consequence is noncontingent.

Tact. A verbal operant occasioned by a nonverbal stimulus and maintained by a variety of social reinforcers.

Task analysis. A precise specification of the sequence of antecedents, responses, and consequences that comprise a stimulus-response chain.

Taste-aversion learning. An instance of Pavlovian learning in which the taste of a food or drink acquires conditioned stimulus function because it preceded illness, vomiting, and so on. As a result of this learning, the individual acquires an aversion to the taste, smell, and possibly even the sight of the food or drink.

Teleology. Explaining things by pointing to their future purpose, instead of their past and present causes.

Three-term contingency. The functional relation between antecedent, behavior, and consequence.

Time-out from positive reinforcement. A signaled response-contingent suspension of a positive-reinforcement contingency, the effect of which decreases the future probability of problem behavior.

Topography. See *response topography*.

Tracking. Rule-following occurring because the instructions appear to correctly describe operant contingencies (reinforcement, extinction, or punishment) that operate in the world.

Trend. A systematic change in behavior over time.

Two-term contingency. See *response–consequence contingency*.

Unconditioned reinforcer. See *primary reinforcer*.

Values. Within ACT therapy, values are defined as client-selected qualities of behavior that may be continuously emitted without reaching an end-goal (e.g., behaving with sincerity or with compassion).

Variable-interval (VI) schedule. The amount of time that must elapse before the first response is reinforced is not the same every time.

Variable-interval schedule – typical response pattern. A steady, moderate response rate with little to no post-reinforcement pause.

Variable-ratio (VR) schedule. The number of responses required per reinforcer is not the same every time.

Variable-ratio schedule – typical response pattern. A high-rate of responding with little or no post-reinforcement pause.

Visual analysis. One approach to answering the question, *did behavior change when the independent variable was changed?* In the visual analysis, the researcher looks at a graph of time-series single-subject behavior to evaluate if a convincing change occurred when the independent variable was introduced/removed.

Within-individuals replications. In an experiment, the independent variable is manipulated more than once and it produces the same effect on the individual's behavior each time.

Whole-interval recording. A direct-observation method used to estimate how frequently behavior occurs. Observers record whether the behavior occurs throughout each in a series of contiguous intervals.

AUTHOR INDEX

Note: Page numbers with n indicate end notes.

SUBJECT INDEX

Note: Page numbers with f indicate figures; page numbers with t indicate tables; page numbers with n indicate end notes.

An Introduction to Behavior Analysis, First Edition. Gregory J. Madden, Derek D. Reed, and Florence D. DiGennaro Reed.
© 2021 John Wiley & Sons Ltd. Published 2021 by John Wiley & Sons Ltd.